Contemporary Business Communication

Louis E. Boone
Ernest G. Cleverdon Chair of Business and Management
University of South Alabama

David L. Kurtz
R.A. and Vivian Young Chair of Business Administration
University of Arkansas

Judy R. Block
President, JRB Communications, Inc.

Edward Kilgour
AT&T Canada LDS

Lauralee Kilgour
Northern Alberta Institute of Technology

Prentice Hall Canada Career & Technology
Scarborough, Ontario

This book is dedicated to Ben for maintaining the balance and joy in our lives.
Lauralee and Ed

Canadian Cataloguing in Publication Data

Main entry under title:

Contemporary business communication

Canadian ed.
Accompanied by CD-ROM.
Includes bibliographical references and index.
ISBN 0-13-089032-4

1. Business communication. 2. Business writing. I. Boone, Louis E.

HF5718.C68 2000   651.7   C00-930207-7

Prentice-Hall, Inc., Upper Saddle River, New Jersey
Prentice-Hall International (UK) Limited, London
Prentice-Hall of Australia, Pty. Limited, Sydney
Prentice-Hall Hispanoamericana, S.A., Mexico City
Prentice-Hall of India Private Limited, New Delhi
Prentice-Hall of Japan, Inc., Tokyo
Simon & Schuster Southeast Asia Private Limited, Singapore
Editora Prentice-Hall do Brasil, Ltda., Rio de Janeiro

ISBN 0-13-089032-4

Vice-President, Editorial Director: Laura Pearson
Acquisitions Editor: Nicole Lukach
Signing Representative: Nicole Lukach
Marketing Manager: Sophia Fortier
Developmental Editor: Dawn du Quesnay
Editorial Assistant: Susan Ratkaj
Copy Editor: Karen Alliston
Production Editor: Melanie M. Meharchand
Production Coordinator: Kathrine Pummell
Permissions: Susan Wallace-Cox
Cover Design: Julia M. Hall
Cover Image: Stock Illustration Source/Nikolai Punin
Page Layout: Nelson Gonzalez

Original edition published by Prentice-Hall Inc., Upper Saddle River, New Jersey
Copyright © 1997, 1994

1 2 3 4 5 RRD 03 02 01 00

Printed and bound in the United States of America.

The opinions expressed herein represent those of the author only and do not
necessarily represent the opinions or policies of AT&T Canada LDS Company.

Visit the Prentice Hall Canada Web site! Send us your comments, browse our
catalogues, and more. **www.phcanada.com** Or reach us through e-mail at
phabinfo_pubcanada@prenhall.com

Brief Contents

Contents

Preface

As we count down the remaining days of the twentieth century, we are gratified that our efforts to provide textbook value to our students and colleagues have been successful.

In writing and editing the manuscript for the first Canadian edition of *Contemporary Business Communication*, we kept in mind the words of Morris Wolfe, Canadian radio and television critic: "If there were an International Need to Communicate Award, Canada would win every year. Our huge land mass, small population, and proximity to the United States have created in us an obsession with keeping in touch with one another."

Like Morris Wolfe, we believe that clear communication is the basis for business success. As a result, a fundamental objective of *Contemporary Business Communication* is to link effective written and oral communication with the ability to find and keep a challenging, personally satisfying job in today's competitive business world. To achieve this objective, *Contemporary Business Communication* focuses on effective writing and oral communication skills. From opening vignettes to end-of-chapter exercises, every chapter emphasizes the key communication skills necessary for business success.

The first Canadian edition of *Contemporary Business Communication* brings a *business* focus to business communication. Examples and applications from actual companies add relevance to learning. Students are introduced to critical business communication concepts and see their applications in real-world situations. Here are some highlights of the first Canadian edition:

▼ Selected **end-of-chapter technology exercises** help students build the skills they need to navigate and do research on the Internet.

▼ **"Building Your Business Notebook"** exercises at the end of selected chapters require students to review, analyze, and revise documents and visual aids. These exercises spotlight the steady progress that students make toward becoming accomplished business writers.

▼ Dozens of **real-world examples** demonstrate the application of business communication concepts. In addition, we include **interviews with business communication professionals** such as Bill Catucci, President and CEO of AT&T Canada Long Distance Services Company, and John Reber, the Manager of Public Relations for Air Canada.

▼ End-of-chapter **Applied Communication Techniques (ACT)** are related to Appendix II, Basics of Grammar and Usage, in order to strengthen the student's writing techniques.

▼ **Internet-focused discussion of technology** from a user's point of view assists the student in understanding the myriad of communication tools available in the twenty-first century.

▼ **Weblinks** at the end of each chapter point students to interesting web sites relevant to the chapter.

▼ Discussion of the unique **Canadian multicultural environment** is essential to the Canadian student experience of diversity in our business environment.

▼ Extensive use of **Canadian sources** helps students to identify with their own environment.

▼ **Job search tools** in the form of information on and examples of electronically scanned résumés, tips on using the Internet to find a job, checklists to clarify the job search process, and behavioural descriptive interview questions are included to help strengthen students' job-search skills.

▼ The importance of **team communication** is emphasized throughout the text.

▼ **Thoroughly Canadian context,** provided in interviews, vignettes, supporting case studies, and examples, increases the book's relevance to Canadian students.

▼ **Extremely current information** anticipates the role of communication in the future. State-of-the-art concepts in both technology and the job search put this book on the leading edge.

▼ **Concise writing** provides a sharp focus on key business communication concepts and applications for today's business student.

The result is the first Canadian edition of *Contemporary Business Communication*—a text that, in the words of an Olympic high jumper, "raises the bar" of quality expectations for a successful business communication text.

Focus on Effective Written, Oral, and Employment Communication

The backbone of this text is the written, oral, and employment communication skills:

▼ *Contemporary Business Communication* helps build—and cement—the writing skills necessary for communication success through quality-tested documents, in-text examples that compare and contrast effective and ineffective writing, practical writing tips features, end-of-chapter document-writing exercises and cases, and text discussion.

▼ Through excerpts from speeches, planning outlines, and speaking notes; and meeting agendas and meeting logs, *Contemporary Business Communication* reinforces effective oral communication in public speaking and oral presentations as well as in collaborative, small-group settings.

▼ Students can learn the information and skills they need to find their first job from step-by-step personal and job-market analyses, sample scanner and human-friendly résumés and cover letters, employment interview strategies, and contemporary job-search tools, all of which are examined in *Contemporary Business Communication*.

Focus on State-of-the-Art Communication Technologies

The dramatic changes in the world of business communication require a text that can prepare students for these changes. We begin with Chapter 2, Mastering Communication Technology, the most complete—and useful—communication technology chapter in any introductory-level business communication text. Chapter 2 demystifies the otherwise complicated world of telecommunications by focusing on practical understanding rather than technical detail. It permits the student to appreciate the "big picture" of technology integration and anticipates communication principles as we go forward into the twenty-first century.

Technology coverage is not confined to a single chapter; it is infused throughout the text. For example, Chapter 11, Planning and Researching Business Reports and Proposals, includes extensive coverage of online research. Chapter 17, Targeting Your Career: Résumés and Cover Letters, includes a discussion on conducting an online job search. We also describe how to cite online research resources in Appendix I and explain the basics of Internet research in Appendix III.

Finally, the Weblinks feature at the end of each chapter lists a series of relevant websites as an additional student resource. The list below shows the many references to electronic media and the Internet in *Contemporary Business Communication*.

Ch. 1: Communicating in an Organization

Ch. 2: Mastering Communication Technology
Perpetual Motion Executives, p.37
Written Communication and Technology, pp. 41–46
Oral Communication and Technology, pp. 46–48
Collaborative Communication: Log On and Let the Discussion Begin, p. 48
The Internet, pp. 51–57
A Question of Ethics: Is Your E-Mail Private?, p. 52
Practical Tips: Using Voice Mail Effectively, p. 56
Portable Communication Technologies, pp. 57–59
Telecommuting, pp. 59–62
Interview: Back to Basics with Technology, pp. 60–61
Building Your Technology Skills—observing how business sites communicate with their customers (4 sites listed), pp. 66–67

End-of-Chapter Exercises That Develop Writing and Technology Skills

In our writing we attempt to implement the ancient Chinese philosophy: "I hear and I forget. I see and I remember. I do and I understand." Our explanation-and-example approach is reflected in three new types of exercise. First, we have included a **Building Your Business Notebook** feature in each writing chapter and in the visual aids chapter. These exercises ask students to review, organize, edit, and revise documents and visual aids, applying the writing concepts learned in the chapter. Second, we have included technology exercises called **Building Your Technology Skills** at the end of 16 chapters, beginning with Chapter 2, the technology chapter. These exercises ask students to write e-mail, navigate the Internet, conduct online research, and much more.

Third, we have included **Applied Communication Techniques (ACT)** at the end of each chapter. These exercises focus on the effective use of words and grammar.

Focus on Collaborative Communication and Communication Ethics

A collaborative communication feature appears regularly throughout the text. Among the topics covered in this feature are:

- ▼ Building a Team
- ▼ Log On and Let the Discussion Begin
- ▼ A Group Exercise in Cultural Coping
- ▼ Brainstorming in a Group
- ▼ Oh No! I'm Being Interviewed by the Whole Team

The topic of collaboration is also part of many chapter features. In Chapter 16, the opening vignette discusses how the Saskatchewan Roughriders used team communication to help them with their 1997 Grey Cup Challenge. In Chapter 17, Beverley McLachlan discusses her collaboration with clients in order to determine their career goals.

A communication ethics feature also appears regularly in the text. Among the topics covered are:

- ▼ Plagiarism: The World's Dumbest Crime
- ▼ Is Your E-Mail Private?
- ▼ Is the Employer Discriminating Against You?
- ▼ Job References, Ethics, and the Law
- ▼ Persuasive Evidence Equals Ethical Evidence

Critical-thinking questions follow each collaborative communication and ethics feature, and encourage students to analyze and solve problems.

Focus on Workplace Diversity

With the twenty-first century rapidly approaching, the first Canadian edition of *Contemporary Business Communication* recognizes and incorporates, throughout the text, the reality of workplace diversity. Chapter 3 investigates communication across international boundaries and within our own culture. This chapter takes a skills approach to teach students how to adapt to communication differences, covering such topics as the differences dividing people in high- and low-context cultures. It also examines how gender, ethnicity, age, and physical abilities and disabilities affect business communication in our society.

Focus on Skill-Building for Future Success

Today's students are pragmatic. They want to know that their classroom experience will help them obtain a job and succeed in the world of work. *Contemporary Business Communication* offers students the chance to develop or strengthen valuable business skills needed to compete effectively in the twenty-first century. In its report, *A Decade of Private Sector Restructuring: Lessons for Educators*, the Conference Board of Canada identifies the ability to communicate as being particularly critical to corporate survival. Organizations seek competent, literate employees who can strengthen the bottom line through time savings, increased output, lower costs, and improvements in the quality of work. We have analyzed the skills that make people more employable and successful in the workplace. Not surprisingly, employers focus on the need to teach students the same core skills: focused problem-solving and analytical thinking skills; personal qualities, including integrity and achievement drive; and interpersonal skills, such as teamwork, negotiation, and customer focus.

Here is how *Contemporary Business Communication* helps teach students these competencies:

- ▼ *Focused Problem-Solving and Analytical Thinking Skills*: This work highlights the importance of creative, focused problem solving; the ability to make connections between various issues; and vision. Text features on collaborative communication and ethics enhance these thinking skills through critical-thinking questions that appear at the end of each feature. The cross references within each chapter highlight and refer students to related concepts in other chapters. The end-of-chapter cases; application problems; and the Building exercises, such as Building Your Business Notebook and Building Your Technology Skills, require students to analyze and apply concepts from many chapters to creatively solve problems.

▼ *Exhibiting Personal Qualities*: Employers want "stewards of quality standards" who have integrity and sociability, understand others' needs, and strive to achieve. We recognize that no book can teach innate qualities. However, *Contemporary Business Communication* can help students improve their ability to maintain high personal standards in the workplace.

First, in Chapter 1 and ethics features that appear throughout the text, we expose students to ethical issues they may face on the job. Second, collaborative communication and diversity issues are emphasized throughout the text, chapter features, and end-of-chapter exercises and cases. This emphasis sensitizes students to others' perspectives and teaches them to work with others to accomplish goals. Third, *Contemporary Business Communication* provides ample opportunity for students to achieve—and measure their achievement—through numerous pedagogical features. For instance, periodic Progress Checks in each chapter help students assess whether they have mastered the basic concepts. Chapter summaries, review questions, and application exercises reinforce the basic concepts. The cases and the end-of-chapter document review, research, technology, and teamwork skills exercises require students to apply the concepts.

▼ *Exhibiting interpersonal skills*: *Contemporary Business Communication* makes team communication one of its central themes. Collabo-

ration is introduced in Chapter 1 and is discussed further in Chapter 11, in the context of writing effective business reports and proposals. The collaborative theme is highlighted in regularly appearing text features and is discussed in many chapter interviews. The topic of negotiation is examined in Chapter 16, Oral Communication in Groups; and cultural diversity is covered in Chapter 3, Communication Challenges in a Diverse World. After its introduction in Chapter 1, Communicating in an Organization, customer service becomes an underlying message in the discussion of effective business writing and speaking.

Interviews with Business Communicators _____

The skills focus of *Contemporary Business Communication* is also emphasized in the eighteen interviews included in the text. In each chapter a business or communication professional shares concrete communication guidelines to help students improve their written, oral, and employment communication skills. The interview subjects and their topics are:

▼ Chapter 1. President and CEO of AT&T Canada Long Distance Services, Bill Catucci, on communicating in a business organization

▼ Chapter 2. Technology consultant Teresa Lindsey on communication technologies

▼ Chapter 3. First Nations Chief Eugene Poitras, President and CEO of File Hills Telecommunications Corporation, on multicultural communication

▼ Chapter 4. Professor and author Lynn Quitman Troyka on planning business communication

▼ Chapter 5. Chief Information Officer for the Government of Alberta, George Samoil, on organizing, composing, and designing business documents

▼ Chapter 6. Edmonton television host Balan Mathews on revising and editing business documents

- ▼ Chapter 7. Writing consultant and author Mary A. De Vries on writing direct requests
- ▼ Chapter 8. Manager of Public Relations for Air Canada, John Reber, on writing good-news, goodwill, and informative messages
- ▼ Chapter 9. Warden of the Edmonton Institution of Correctional Services Canada, Jack Linklater, on bad-news and negative messages
- ▼ Chapter 10. New Brunswick call centre consultant and trainer, Guylaine Demers, on persuasive messages
- ▼ Chapter 11. Manager of the Baffin Business Development in Iqaluit, Nunavat, Matthew Spence, on planning and researching business reports and proposals
- ▼ Chapter 12. Author and consultant Gene Zelazny on using visual aids in business reports and proposals
- ▼ Chapter 13. RCMP officer and trainer, Corporal Dan MacLean, on organizing and writing reports
- ▼ Chapter 14. Labrador business owner Hilda Broomfield Letemplier on organizing and writing proposals
- ▼ Chapter 15. President of Yukon College, Sally Ross, on delivering speeches and oral presentations
- ▼ Chapter 16. Lead pilot of the Canadian Snowbirds, Major Darryl Shyiak, on oral communications in groups
- ▼ Chapter 17. Founder of the Career Center on America Online, James C. Gonyea, on electronic career and employment-guidance services
- ▼ Chapter 18. International private banker G. Frederick Reinhardt III on interviewing for an overseas job

Supplements for the Instructor

Contemporary Business Communication is a comprehensive teaching/learning package. Although the text is the most critical element in the package, it is only one part. Following are the additional teaching materials that support our text.

INSTRUCTOR'S RESOURCE MANUAL (ISBN# 0-13-081517-9)

The Instructor's Manual includes the following instructional materials for every chapter:

- ▼ Annotated Chapter Objectives
- ▼ Key Terms
- ▼ Lecture Outlines
- ▼ Guest Lectures
- ▼ Answers to:
  Review and Discussion Questions
  *Application Exercises
  *Case Questions and Applications
  *Building Your Business Notebook
  *Building Your Technology Skills
  *Building Your Teamwork Skills
  *Building Your Research Skills

Lecture notes for the transparencies are included in the Instructor's Manual in a separate section.

To support the Communications Briefings video series, a video guide that includes synopses of each video and suggested discussion questions is included.

TEST ITEM FILE (ISBN# 0-13-081516-0)

The Test Item File contains approximately 1000 questions: multiple choice, short answer, and true/false.

PRENTICE HALL ALLYN AND BACON CUSTOM TEST (WINDOWS VERSION ISBN# 0-13-081536-6; MAC VERSION ISBN# 0-13-082798-3)

Based on the best-selling, state-of-the-art test generation software program developed by Engineering Software Associates (ESA), *Prentice Hall Custom Test*'s user-friendly test creation and powerful algorithmic program can generate an unlimited number of versions of tailor-made tests quickly, easily, and accurately. The program allows you to administer each exam traditionally or online, evaluate and track students' results, and analyze the success of the exam—all with a click of the mouse.

VIDEO SERIES FROM COMMUNICATION BRIEFINGS

The feedback from users and reviewers of our text confirms that our video materials add value to the classroom experience because they link directly to major text concepts. The outstanding video series that accompanies *Contemporary Business Communication* is a set of eight videos from Communication Briefings, a firm renowned for its content and production quality. The video set is available at no cost to teachers using *Contemporary Business Communication*, first Canadian edition. To order the videos, simply call 1-800-388-8433. Included in the video series are the following:

- ▼ Building Cooperation: How Everyone Can Win at Work (NEW)
- ▼ How to See Opportunity in a Changing Workplace (NEW)
- ▼ How to Tap Employee Idea-Power (NEW)
- ▼ Resolving Conflicts: Strategies for a Winning Team (NEW)
- ▼ Listen and Win: How to Keep Customers Coming Back (NEW)
- ▼ Make the Phone Work for You
- ▼ Make Presentations Work for You
- ▼ Better Business Grammar

Supplements for the Student

CONTEMPORARY BUSINESS COMMUNICATION BASICS: A USAGE AND GRAMMAR WORKBOOK
(ISBN# 0-13-080825-3)

Written by Ken Horsman of Algonquin College, this workbook contains additional explanations and exercises on points of grammar and usage discussed in the text. It is an excellent resource for honing business communicatons skills.

COMPANION WEBSITE
(ISBN# 0-13-081669-8)

A new way to deliver educational content, this exciting supplement offers customized online resources, an interactive online study guide with immediate feedback, and access to a vast array of reference materials.

Acknowledgments

A number of people have made significant contributions to the first Canadian edition of *Contemporary Business Communication*. Their insights, advice, and

suggestions helped us to make this a more valuable and user-friendly book. We are extremely grateful to these contributors for their invaluable assistance and advice throughout the work. *Contemporary Business Communication* benefited greatly from the efforts of a number of dedicated business communication professionals who served as consultants and manuscript reviewers. Thanks are also due to the 18 communication professionals who agreed to be interviewed for the text. We would especially like to thank the following:

Heather Armstrong, Cantel AT&T, Toronto, Ontario

Vanessa Arnold, University of Mississippi

Carole Barnum, Southern College of Technology

Diane Barth, Indiana University

Tabitha Beaton, Smart Technologies Inc., Calgary, Alberta

Susan Becker, Illinois Central College

Carl Bridges, Ohio State University

Hilda Broomfield Letemplier, Pressure Pipe Steel Fabrication, Ltd., Goose Bay, Labrador

Ken Brown, Royal Bank of Canada, Calgary, Alberta

William Buchholz, Bentley College

Dwight Bullard, Middle Tennessee State University

Gloria L. Campbell, Wartburg College

Bill Catucci, AT&T Canada LDS, Toronto, Ontario

Jack Cole, University of Akron

Alice Coleman, AT&T Canada LDS, Toronto, Ontario

James Conley, Eastern Michigan University

Guylaine Demers, AT&T Canada LDS, Edmundston, New Brunswick

Donna Doucette, Nortel, Calgary, Alberta

Sharon Elliott, Motorola, Mississauga, Ontario

Bob Fagan, Canadian Human Rights Commission, Edmonton, Alberta

Marissa Fleming, Georgian College

John Flemming, New Hampshire College

Alan Ford, Saskatchewan Roughriders, Regina, Saskatchewan

David H. Gigley, Ohio University-Chillicothe

Georgia Hale, Arkansas State University

Garth Hanson, Brigham Young University

Debbie Hasley, Bluefield State College

Sean Hawkins, BCTel, Kelowna, British Columbia

Elizabeth Hunt, E. Hunt and Associates, Toronto, Ontario

Geraldine Hynes, University of Missouri-St. Louis

Thomas Inman, Southwest Missouri State University

Marcia James, University of Wisconsin-Whitewater

Jessie Kempter, International Business Machines, New York

Benjamin Kilgour, Management Support and Services, St. Albert, Alberta

Paul Killorin, Portland Community College

Leo Knappen, Bombardier, Dorval, Quebec

Gary Kohut, University of North Carolina-Charlotte

Suzanne Lambert, Broward Community College

Gerald Lemay, Internet Institute, Ottawa

Mary Leslie, Grossmont Community College

Shirley Lewis, Merit Industries, Charlottetown, Prince Edward Island

Stephen Lewis, Middle Tennessee State University

Jack Linklater, Edmonton Institution, Edmonton, Alberta

Terry Long, Ohio State University-Newark

Aime Mallory, Northern Illusions, Yellowknife, Northwest Territories

John Martell, Western Michigan University

Jeanette Martin, University of Mississippi

Rachel Mather, Adelphi University

Balan Mathews, CFRN Television, Edmonton, Alberta

Kenneth Mayer, Cleveland State University

Beverley McLachlan, LNI Group Inc., Vancouver, British Columbia

Dan McLean, RCMP Regina, Saskatchewan

Bill McPherson, Indiana University of Pennsylvania

Thomas Lee Means, Louisiana Technical College

Lisa Michaud, AT&T Canada LDS, Edmundston, New Brunswick

Rita Mignacca, SUNY Brockport

Thomas M. Miles, West Virginia University

David Moorcroft, Royal Bank of Canada, Toronto, Ontario

Wayne Moore, Indiana University of Pennsylvania

Glena Morse, Georgia College

Brian Napier, EPCOR, Edmonton, Alberta

Alexa North, Georgia State University

C. Glenn Pearce, Virginia Commonwealth University

Binford Peoples, Memphis State University

Devon Perry, Brigham Young University

Captain Mike Perry, 431 Air Demonstration Squadron, Snowbirds, Moose Jaw, Saskatchewan

Doris Phillips, University of Mississippi

Chief Eugene Poitras, Balcarres, Saskatchewan

Merton E. Powell, Ferris State University

John Reber, Air Canada, Dorval, Quebec

Patricia Rice, Finger Lakes Community College

Elizabeth Robertson, Tennessee State University

Marion Ross, Georgian College

Sally Ross, Yukon College, Whitehorse, Yukon

Ilona Ryder, Grant MacEwan Community College

Tim Saben, Portland Community College

George Samoil, Government of Alberta, Edmonton, Alberta

Carole Sequin, National Archives of Canada, Ottawa, Ontario

Stephen Shirring, Butler County Community College

Herb Smith, Southern College of Technology

Mathew Spence, Baffin Business Development Center, Nunavut

Frankie Sprague, Palm Beach Community College

Jacqueline Stowe, McMurry University

Roberta M. Supnick, Western Michigan University

Tracy A. Thompson, University of Washington, Tacoma

Eric Tillman, Toronto Argonauts, Toronto, Ontario

Vincent Trofi, Providence College

Mary L. Tucker, Nicholls State University

Hilda Turner, Arkansas Technical University

Gayle Uchida, Resumix, Sunnyvale, California

Edward Wachter, Jr., Point Park College

John L. Waltman, Eastern Michigan University

Stan Wayne, Southwest Missouri State College

Judy West, University of Tennessee-Chattanooga

Larry Whitney, Water Planning and Development, Winnipeg, Manitoba

Jerry L. Wood, Northern Montana College

Barry Woodcock, Tennessee Technological University

Dan Wunsch, Northern Illinois University

Donald K. Zann, University of Wisconsin-Whitewater

We would also like to thank the many professionals at Prentice Hall Canada who made the first Canadian edition of *Contemporary Business Communication* possible.

Your Internet companion to the most exciting, state-of-the-art educational tools on the Web!

T he Prentice Hall Canada Companion Website is easy to navigate and is organized to correspond to the chapters in this textbook. The Companion Website is comprised of four distinct, functional features:

1) **Customized Online Resources**

2) **Online Study Guide**

3) **Reference Material**

4) **Communication**

Explore the four areas in this Companion Website. Students and distance learners will discover resources for indepth study, research and communication, empowering them in their quest for greater knowledge and maximizing their potential for success in the course.

A NEW WAY TO DELIVER EDUCATIONAL CONTENT

1) Customized Online Resources

Our Companion Websites provide instructors and students with a range of options to access, view, and exchange content.

- **Syllabus Builder** provides *instructors* with the option to create online classes and construct an online syllabus linked to specific modules in the Companion Website.

- **Mailing lists** enable *instructors* and *students* to receive customized promotional literature.

- **Preferences** enable *students* to customize the sending of results to various recipients, and also to customize how the material is sent, e.g., as html, text, or as an attachment.

- **Help** includes an evaluation of the user's system and a tune-up area that makes updating browsers and plug-ins easier. This new feature will enhance the user's experience with Companion Websites.

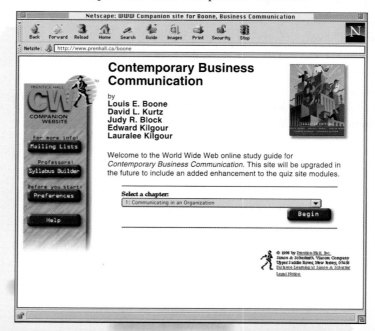

www.prenticehall.ca/boone

2) Online Study Guide

Interactive Study Guide modules form the core of the student learning experience in the Companion Website. These modules are categorized according to their functionality:

- True-False
- Multiple Choice
- Essay questions

The True-False and Multiple Choice modules provide students with the ability to send answers to our grader and receive instant feedback on their progress through our Results Reporter. Coaching comments and references back to the textbook ensure that students take advantage of all resources available to enhance their learning experience.

3) Reference Material

Reference material broadens text coverage with up-to-date resources for learning. **Web Destinations** provides a directory of Web sites relevant to the subject matter in each chapter. **NetNews (Internet Newsgroups)** are a fundamental source of information about a discipline, containing a wealth of brief, opinionated postings. **NetSearch** simplifies key term search using Internet search engines.

4) Communication

Companion Websites contain the communication tools necessary to deliver courses in a **Distance Learning** environment. **Message Board** allows users to post messages and check back periodically for responses. **Live Chat** allows users to discuss course topics in real time, and enables professors to host online classes.

Communication facilities of Companion Websites provide a key element for distributed learning environments. There are two types of communication facilities currently in use in Companion Websites:

- **Message Board** – this module takes advantage of browser technology providing the users of each Companion Website with a national newsgroup to post and reply to relevant course topics.

- **Live Chat** – enables instructor-led group activities in real time. Using our chat client, instructors can display Website content while students participate in the discussion.

Note: CW '99 content will vary slightly from site to site depending on discipline requirements.

The Companion Websites can be found at:

www.prenticehall.ca/boone

PRENTICE HALL CANADA

1870 Birchmount Road
Scarborough, Ontario M1P 2J7

To order:
Call: 1-800-567-3800
Fax: 1-800-263-7733

For samples:
Call: 1-800-850-5813
Fax: (416) 299-2539
E-mail: phabinfo_pubcanada@prenhall.com

Chapter

1

Communicating in an Organization

Chapter Objectives

After studying this chapter, you should be able to:

1. Discuss how effective business communication is linked to personal career success.

2. Describe the communication process and identify communication barriers.

3. Explain the importance of nonverbal communication.

4. Outline the stages of listening and the ways of becoming an effective listener.

5. Explain the importance of effective internal and external communication.

6. Describe the nature of formal and informal communication channels.

7. Identify the role of collaborative communication in business organizations.

8. Outline the three communication challenges that influence the ways in which businesspeople communicate.

If there were an International Need to Communicate Award, Canada would win every year. Our huge land mass, small population, and proximity to the United States have created in us an obsession with keeping in touch with one another.

Morris Wolfe
Canadian radio and television critic

Refining the Art of Communication During a Hostile Takeover

It probably was no coincidence that IBM Chairman Louis V. Gerstner Jr. chose June 5, 1995, as the day IBM would launch a hostile takeover bid for Lotus Development Corporation, the Massachusetts-based software developer. June 5 was the anniversary of D-Day—the day the Allies left England to land on the Normandy beaches in an assault that brought about the end of World War II. If everything went according to plan, this June 5 would be the day IBM began to challenge Microsoft Corporation as the undisputed leader of personal computer software.

What IBM wanted most from Lotus was Notes, the enormously powerful and successful program that allows users to exchange documents via personal computers and to collaborate on documents within and between companies and across the world. Notes would give IBM the software it needed to compete with Microsoft in network operating systems. Although Gerstner wanted Lotus badly enough to pay a premium price—$3.5 billion—he realized that money alone would not ensure success. How IBM communicated during the negotiations—with decision makers at Lotus, with Lotus employees, and with industry leaders—could make or break the deal.

D-Day itself was not planned with greater precision. Around April 1—more than two months before the takeover bid—ten key staff members at IBM began studying how Notes and other Lotus products would mesh with the software IBM already licensed. The group presented its findings to key executives, including Gerstner, who gave the go-ahead to prepare for the bid. Although senior IBM executives had tried talking with Lotus Chairman Jim P. Manzi about an acquisition, the talks had gone nowhere. Now impatient, Gerstner moved ahead with a more aggressive plan. A hostile bid seemed IBM's best choice.

The plan had considerable risk. IBM worried that key Lotus employees would leave the company when they heard news of IBM's hostile takeover. If negotiations turned ugly, IBM faced the possibility of losing the very software designers it wanted to keep, including Raymond Ozzie, the developer of Notes.

Allaying the fears of Lotus employees was not easy, as it is illegal to communicate directly with employees of a target company involved in a takeover bid. So, working with its public relations firm, IBM posted critical messages about the bid on the Internet. These messages told Lotus employees, customers, and business suppliers alike that IBM would continue to develop Notes as an "open" product that was compatible with all computer operating systems, not just those sold by IBM.

The days between May 12 and June 5 were not easy. Rumours spread that Lotus was negotiating with another potential partner. Although the news left Gerstner and his team nervous that their bid would be too late, they had no choice but to wait. For a deal this size, they needed the formal approval of IBM's board of directors, and the board meeting was not scheduled until May 31.

Gerstner moved rapidly after receiving the board's approval. Between June 2 and June 4, the team rehearsed what would occur on the morning of June 5. Gerstner even subjected himself to a mock press conference, conducted by members of his public relations staff. The fast-paced and extremely tough questions were designed to put him to the test; if Gerstner could handle these questions, he could handle anything from industry analysts and the business press.

At around 8:30 A.M. on June 5, Gerstner placed a call to Manzi, then set his staff in motion: Calls were made to the stock exchanges where IBM and Lotus are traded. Gerstner himself called the chief executive officers of Hewlett-Packard and

AT&T, companies involved in partnerships with Lotus. Then stock analysts were informed, via "blast fax," that Gerstner would hold a conference call for them at 11:00 A.M.; 259 analysts participated. A 1:30 P.M. press conference was announced via press release. An announcement of the takeover bid, a letter outlining the bid from Gerstner to Manzi, letters from Gerstner to IBM employees, and edited transcripts of Gerstner's news conferences were then posted on IBM's Internet home page.

Although the takeover attempt might have lasted for months, it took less than a week to get Manzi's agreement and the blessings of the IBM board of directors. Part of the reason for its swift conclusion was IBM's attention to precise written and oral communication. Without effective communication involving formal and informal communication channels; high-technology messages sent through the Internet, faxes, and conference calls; teamwork involving intensive research, written reports, and oral presentations; a public relations assault that focused on different audiences both inside and outside of Lotus; as well as letters, phone calls, and face-to-face meetings with key participants, the deal would not have turned into a textbook case. ▼

Sources: Judith H. Dobrzynski, "The Art of the Hostile Deal," New York Times, 22 June 1995, D1, D28; William J. Cook, "Software Struggle," U.S. News & World Report (June 19, 1995): 46.

Chapter Overview --

No matter what kind of organization you work for—whether a large corporation like IBM, an individually owned bakery, or a nonprofit organization such as a public school—effective communication is essential to your success. **Communication,** the meaningful exchange of information through messages between one person or group to another, is a composite of everything we do and say. **Business communication**—the communication required of an organization in both its internal and external environments—is complex and varied.

In this chapter we will examine how business communication skills can enhance your personal career success. We will also investigate the communication process, including barriers to communication and listening skills. As you will see later in the chapter, the communication process takes place with different audiences and through formal and informal channels that often involve collaborative communication. As we enter the twenty-first century, Canada's export-based economy demands that we communicate more efficiently and effectively than ever before. Advancements in technology, globalization, and organizational restructuring are not only driving the way we do business, but also the way we communicate with other Canadians and the rest of the world.

Today, innovations in information technologies enable us to utilize a myriad of tools to communicate more effectively. International business markets and remote sources of information encourage us to apply our communication tools and skills across borders and time zones. Similarly, organizational communication is under reform; along with corporate restructuring for the new millennium, employees are becoming empowered to make a greater contribution to corporate goals. Their team-based contribution anticipates participation, self-direction, and more open lines of communication.

As the environment for communication becomes increasingly complex, so do the communication challenges faced by all business communicators.

Business Communication and Personal Career Success —————————————————

In a recent survey of recruiters from companies with more than 50 000 employees, communication skills were cited as the single most important criterion in choosing managers. These skills include the ability to make effective written and oral presentations and the ability to work with others. Although these so-called soft skills do not involve sophisticated, theoretical knowledge, companies are convinced that they hold the key to job success.[1] Table 1-1 lists the specific communication competencies that are required of business graduates in several fields.

Despite the growing importance of communication skills, many people still come to the workplace unable to compete. In a recent survey, 65 percent of human resources executives said that employee writing skills need improvement, 62 percent cited difficulties in interpersonal communication skills, and 59 percent cited poor customer service skills.[2]

As competitive pressures increase, people who come to the workplace unprepared to write and speak effectively are being either turned away or dismissed. For example, when the National Association of Manufacturers surveyed 4000 companies, it found that one out of three regularly turn away job candidates because of poor writing and reading skills. For every dismissal based on a failure to do work properly, there were two dismissals due to personality and communication problems.[3]

To become a proficient communicator, it is important to understand the communication process. We will turn to that process next.

Progress Check

1. Why is it important to develop effective communication skills?
2. As jobs become more complex in the twenty-first century, do you think employers will consider communication skills more or less important than they are today?

The Communication Process and Its Barriers —————————————————

Communication is influenced by the interplay among the sender and the receiver of a message and the message itself. Communication context affects message reception. Effective communication also involves feedback from an audience—the individual or group to whom the message is sent.

Table 1-1 Jobs Requiring Communication Skills

Job Title	Communication Skills Required
Product manager	Develop and communicate product objectives and strategies
Training manager	Prepare training materials, reports; outstanding verbal and written communication skills
Market research analyst	Prepare questionnaires, analyze and validate study results, and prepare reports of the analyses
Regulatory affairs manager	Prepare government regulatory submissions and analyze new regulatory proposals in accordance with government and company policies
Human resources analyst	Assist in drafting all group insurance documents, including insurance policies, service contracts, private health care, and employee booklets

Source: Adapted from Vanessa Dean Arnold, "The Communication Competencies Listed in Job Descriptions," *The Bulletin of the Association for Business Communication* (June 1992): 15–17.

Effective business communication is audience-centred. **Audience** here refers to receivers of verbal, nonverbal, and written messages. A message can be successful only when both the sender and the receiver—the audience—perceive it in the same way. Consideration of your audience is the key ingredient in all successful oral and written communication.

Six elements that make up the communication process—sender, message, channel, receiver, feedback, and context—are illustrated in Figure 1-1. Here you see that while the message flows from sender to receiver, feedback from the receiver gives the sender the opportunity to adjust the message. All communication takes place through a specific channel and in a broad situational and cultural context.

Communication barriers are the problems that arise at every stage of the communication process and have the potential to create misunderstanding and confusion. Such problems may not only hinder communication but can actually alter meaning. For example, a writer may unintentionally send a message that seems hostile because it was written too quickly and thus sounds abrupt. An unprepared speaker may sound unintelligent. We may allow our emotions to take over or come to an exchange intellectually unprepared. As a business communicator, your goal is to minimize the frequency and seriousness of communication barriers.

> *We are talking at each other instead of to each other. That is not communication; it is monologue.*
>
> James D. Robinson III
> Former CEO, American Express

Elements of the Communication Process

We will look next at each element of the communication process—sender, message, channel, receiver, feedback, and context—and the communication barriers that affect each element. Each element is so closely tied to all others that they often interrelate. We refer to these elements as *stages* because we want to emphasize that communication is a *process*.

SENDER

Participants in the communication process who communicate messages to an audience are called **senders.** Their messages are influenced by **sender credibility**—the extent to which the sender is perceived to be credible, trustworthy, or authoritative. In other words, your personal reputation and the organization's reputation affect the way audiences react to what they read or hear. Purolator Canada, a Mississauga, Ontario, courier company, realized the importance of sender credibility; it withdrew its corporate sponsorship after Ben Johnson tested positive for illegal anabolic steroids and lost his 1988 Olympic gold medal for sprinting.[4]

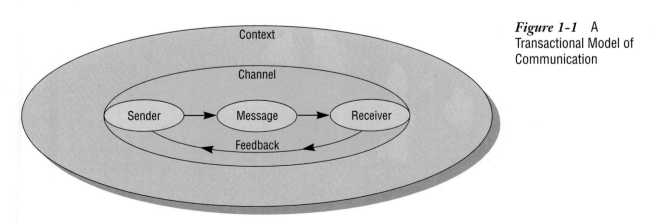

Figure 1-1 A Transactional Model of Communication

In business communication, credibility is closely linked to the sender's knowledge of the material, the audience, and the context in which the message is communicated. It is also linked to position and title, which communicate whether the sender has the authority to send the message and whether communication is taking place between the right people. Says Diane Sanchez, president and CEO of Miller, Heiman, Inc., a West Coast sales-management consulting firm, "Generals like to talk to generals, lieutenants to lieutenants."[5]

BARRIERS TO SENDING EFFECTIVE MESSAGES Many problems may arise at this stage of the communication process, including poor preparation or flawed personal communication styles.

Failure to Know Your Material or Audience A failure to know your material can lead to a poor, disorganized, or halting presentation. The result may be an unfocused, unclear message that reduces credibility. Typically, your audience will respond to lack of preparation by "tuning out" your message—people simply stop reading or listening—or by dismissing what you say. In either case, the impact of the message is minimized, if indeed not lost.

A failure to know your audience can create still other barriers to communication. An audience will not be receptive to your message if it is too long, too difficult or dull, or uses unexplained jargon. In short, a message that does not focus on audience concerns decreases the chances of getting your point across.

Communication also fails when the sender lacks audience empathy. **Empathy** is the ability to experience the world from another person's perspective. It is an essential element in effective communication because it allows you to set aside your own opinions as you reach for common ground with your audience. Empathetic communicators may be able to anticipate how people will respond to their messages and, as a result, can prepare messages more effectively.

Personal Style Personal style can enhance or obstruct communication. An abrasive personality, for example, typically makes feedback difficult and an openness to change impossible. It can also create communication tension—when people do not like the way a speaker addresses them, attention often wanes. An abrasive style is often expressed in an abrupt, dismissive, angry, or condescending tone. Consider the differences between the following versions of a manager's communication to an employee:

The best communicators understand that the relationship between speaker and audience often determines message success. According to psychologist Beatrice Harris, speakers miss an important communication opportunity "when they focus exclusively on the content of the message at the expense of what they want to happen on a relationship level." What clues do you have that this speaker may be trying to build a positive relationship with his listeners?

| Version 1 | "Evan, print 500 copies of the new advertising brochure right away." |
| Version 2 | "Evan, our new brochure has information about next month's promotion. To generate interest about the promotion, could you please send copies of the brochure to our established customers?" |

While Version 1 issues orders, Version 2 explains. Such differences in tone can have an important influence on audience response.

An abrasive personality is as evident in writing as it is in conversation. A condescending, angry, or negative tone comes through clearly on paper. Indeed, because written messages give the audience the opportunity to reread what has been said, they can create even bigger problems than spoken messages.

Making a Poor First Impression   First impressions count in business as well as in personal affairs. Capitalize on the power of first impressions by trying to anticipate negative reactions. Dress appropriately, shake hands firmly, speak well, and be organized. Before sending written messages, reread every letter, memo, and report from the perspective of the person who will receive it. Analyzing your audience can help eliminate unfortunate mistakes.

MESSAGE

A **message** is the written, oral, or nonverbal communication that the sender transmits to an audience. Your words and tone, your method of organization, the soundness of your argument and its emotional impact, what you choose to communicate and what you choose to leave out, and your style of presentation are part of every message.

Messages have both intellectual and emotional components. Through the use of reason and evidence, we seek to inform or convince. Through the use of emotional or motivational appeals, we seek to arouse feelings, change minds, and encourage action.

BARRIERS TO EFFECTIVE MESSAGES   Not surprisingly, messages that are poorly focused and organized, use inappropriate language and tone, or contain technical errors create communication problems. Spoken language that contains slang or that is punctuated by too many "you knows," "ums," or "ehs" reduces the impact of the message. Similarly, sloppy or poorly formatted letters, memos, and reports make communication difficult to understand. Part II, Writing Basics, examines effective written messages, while Part V, Forms of Oral Communication, focuses on public speaking, meetings, and other forms of oral communication.

CHANNEL

Every message is transmitted through a **channel**—the medium through which the message sender and the message receiver communicate. Means of verbal communication include face-to-face discussions, and the telephone. Generally, written messages are transmitted in one of three forms: letter, memo, or report. However, as we will see in Chapter 2, technology has spawned a host of new communication channels, such as the Internet, video conferences, and electronic mail.

CHANNEL BARRIERS   According to communication theorists, **noise** is anything that interferes with message transmission by distorting the message or otherwise changing its meaning. Physical noise may take the form of environmental sounds (such as a wailing siren) that prevent one person from hearing another. In written communication, "physical" noise might be a poorly printed page or smudged paper. Other forms of noise that interfere with listening will be explored later in this chapter.

RECEIVER

Receivers are the audience to whom messages are directed. As a rule, receivers enter every communication transaction with a preconceived set of ideas and feelings that influence how they respond. The most successful communicators take these needs into account and use them as the starting point in their effort to inform or persuade.

All audiences react to messages with the basic, self-centred question, "How will this help me?" A customer, for example, wants your letter to resolve his or her credit problem. A supervisor expects your report to contain recommendations for a new project. To a large extent, these needs determine audience interest and response.

RECEIVER BARRIERS   When your audience does not have the skill or interest to listen to or read a message, communication is compromised. Without an ability to understand and accept new ideas, a willingness to find interest in seemingly uninteresting messages, and a commitment to pay attention and overcome first impressions, your audience may turn away from the message before its value becomes clear.

An audience may have trouble paying attention when more than one message is competing for its attention. Conflicting messages reduce the attention that a receiver can give any single message, so no message may be given its fair due. Finally, because communication is a process, both receivers and senders must make positive impressions. If communicators believe that the audience is not responding to the message, they may simply stop trying. For example, if a manager repeatedly tells sales representatives to focus on dealer relations but continues to receive numerous dealer complaints, the manager may decide to fire the salespeople responsible for the problem rather than repeat the message for the entire salesforce.

FEEDBACK

Feedback consists of messages—verbal and nonverbal—that convey a reaction to the communicator's message. Based on feedback, a sender may either alter the presentation of the message or cancel it entirely. In verbal communication, feedback is often immediate. Listeners tell the sender how they feel whenever they interrupt, frown, yawn, smile, or applaud. In contrast, feedback on written materials is delayed. The sender must wait for either written or oral response before deciding what to say next and how to say it.

Feedback often allows an audience to clarify messages. Through pointed fact-finding questions, for instance, receivers can ensure that their understanding of a message is correct. A message like the following typically benefits from this sort of questioning:[6]

Message:	"As a result of company downsizing, all employees are expected to increase their productivity."
Fact-finding question:	"Does this mean that we are expected to shorten our lunch hour and take less vacation time?"

BARRIERS TO FEEDBACK   An atmosphere that discourages discussion may make it impossible for employees to provide feedback on what they read or hear. Companies in financial trouble often discourage criticism. According to business consultant Orry Shackney, these companies may put "preventive measures" in place to discourage dissension. "Someone will be called in," he explains, "and told, 'You've had a lot of negative things to say; you're getting a reputation as a negative person. You don't want to be seen that way.' "[7] The predictable then happens: Fearing for their jobs, many people in these organizations stop offering feedback—even on serious problems.

CONTEXT

The communication **context** refers to the situation in which communication takes place and to every factor affecting its transmission. This context may include anything in the immediate environment or broader culture. The firm's operating environment, for example, may have an immediate effect on communication—a request for an activity report in the midst of a corporate merger will be treated differently from the same request made under more normal circumstances. Other immediate factors might include any of the following:

- ▼ the purpose of the message (such as a supervisor's request for a proposal);
- ▼ co-workers' attitudes toward one another;
- ▼ the number of people communicating the message (the communication dynamics of a large group meeting will differ from those of a small group meeting); or
- ▼ the amount of information competing for the receiver's attention (a manager with three pressing projects may respond differently to a memo than a manager without time pressure).

The broader cultural context involves the corporate culture, community and national cultures, and the international cultures that now constitute both the marketplace for many Canadian products and the workplace for many Canadian citizens. **Corporate culture** refers to the patterns, traditions, and values that make one organization distinctly different from another.[8] Cultural differences within an organization may be expressed in different working styles and schedules that influence the unwritten rules of communication. Some cultures encourage decision making by consensus, often a time-consuming process, whereas other cultures encourage leaders to make quick decisions.

CONTEXTUAL BARRIERS   One of the most serious contextual barriers to communication is **information overload**—the demands made on receivers by an ever-expanding number of messages. Today, businesspeople must read letters, memos, reports and proposals, professional journals, newspapers, magazines, and books. Too much information and too little time leaves many with the sinking feeling that none of their messages has received the attention it deserves.

Failing to understand how cultural differences affect communication styles can also lead to serious misunderstandings. Chapter 3 will examine how to overcome cultural barriers so that you can communicate effectively with diverse groups in this country and abroad.

> ### Progress Check
>
> 1. Name the six elements of the communication process.
> 2. Identify barriers for each element of the communication process.
> 3. What is feedback, and when does it occur?

How Messages Are Sent

Messages in the communication process actively convey meaning both through written and spoken words and through nonverbal language. Although the primary focus of this book is verbal messages, nonverbal language can sometimes be more powerful than words. We will examine the nature of nonverbal language and its function in business communication next.

NONVERBAL COMMUNICATION

In oral communication we actively send messages to one another both with and without words. **Nonverbal communication** is communication that takes place through nonverbal cues; through such forms of *nonvocal* communication as gestures, eye contact, facial expressions, clothing, and personal space; and through the form of nonverbal vocal communication known as *paralanguage*. One value of such nonverbal messages is the power to reveal feelings. Nonverbal communication delivers meaning through a **subtext** of nonverbal cues.[9] Research attests to the power of subtext. In one study, for example, 93 percent of a message's emotional impact came from nonverbal signals such as hand motions.[10]

NONVERBAL CUES   Nonverbal cues have several functions. For one thing, they can *repeat* verbal messages. For example, a factory worker telling a supervisor that he or she cannot understand how a new machine works may punctuate the plea with open palms held at chest level—a common sign of helplessness. Nonverbal cues can also *substitute* for verbal messages. In our culture, shaking your head up and down while saying nothing is an accepted way of saying yes. Nonverbal clues can *regulate*, or *control*, verbal interaction. Changing vocal tones in normal conversation, for instance, may provide other people with cues for when to speak and when to listen. Finally, nonverbal cues may *contradict* verbal messages. Listening to an executive ramble on at a meeting, participants may feign interest while looking around the room or turning their bodies away from the speaker.

Even when we make a conscious effort to say nothing, nonverbal language may continue to send messages. For example, fiddling with papers or doodling during a meeting may be signs of boredom, whereas folding your arms across your chest may communicate defensiveness. The fact that everyone "leaks" nonverbal cues means that an ever-changing source of uncensored data is always present, just waiting to be noticed and interpreted correctly. As we have already indicated, nonverbal cues are especially powerful in communicating a wide range of feelings and attitudes. A discrepancy between a person's tone of voice and gestures may even signal that a lie is being told.

Nonverbal cues are also easily misinterpreted, and conventional wisdom about the meaning of such cues is often questionable. For example, realizing that these cues are often culturally biased, officials responsible for upgrading the Washington-Moscow hot line decided not to use video and voice communication, relying instead on written messages. In a crisis, reasoned the experts, "we wouldn't want to leave room for mistaken interpretations or impressions that might be drawn from facial expressions or voice patterns."[11]

NONVOCAL COMMUNICATION   Nonverbal cues fall into two broad categories. **Nonvocal communication** refers to gestures, eye contact, facial expressions, posture, clothing, and the use of space; **nonverbal vocal communication** refers to tone of voice and such voice qualities as loudness and pitch.

Gestures   Gestures can both complement and contradict other forms of communication. For example, when one person tells another to turn "left" while pointing right, the gesture contradicts the spoken words. If a person says to turn right and also points right, the gesture complements the words.

The gestures that you see in everyday business communication include a wide range of hand and arm movements. When examined in context, they may have specific meanings:

▼ Baton-like pointing movements of the hands and arms punctuate words and may communicate control.

▼ Finger wagging and arms crossed over the chest may be signs of disagreement.

- ▼ A hand or finger covering the mouth may indicate that the speaker is holding something back or is too embarrassed or reluctant to speak.
- ▼ Hands on the hips with thumbs back communicates toughness and a reluctance to back down.
- ▼ Counting off on fingers may be a sign of clear thinking and logic.

Although gestures can be used deliberately to communicate honesty, self-confidence, straightforwardness, and control, most are used unconsciously.

Eye Contact When people look directly into each other's eyes, they make eye contact. Eyes can send messages as well as receive information. Indeed, eye contact can be the most powerful form of nonverbal communication. In business, as in personal relationships, eye contact sends different messages. Purposefully looking at someone is a signal of recognition. Direct eye contact tells a job applicant that you are interested in learning more. Purposefully looking away from someone may be a sign of arrogance or anger.

The length of time that eye contact is held has a message of its own. Eye contact with a stranger is instantaneous. More than a glance makes both parties uncomfortable. Maintaining eye contact with a person of the opposite sex for too long can mean sexual interest—an inappropriate business message. Extended eye contact between men who do not know each other may be perceived as an implicit threat. By contrast, it is acceptable in public speaking to hold eye contact with audience members as a sign of involvement and engagement.

Eye contact is the most difficult of all facial expressions to fake. Even subtle changes in contact and expression have the power to show strong feelings if interpreted correctly.

Facial Expressions Closely linked to eye contact, facial expressions—movements of the face that reflect attitudes and emotions—are often difficult to read. With the vast number of possible expressions, the speed at which they change, and the ability of most people to "mask" messages they do not want to send, all but the most obvious expressions may be misinterpreted. Psychologists have identified six emotions that are expressed facially in all parts of the world: happiness, sadness, anger, disgust, surprise, and fear.

Posture Posture—the position of your body as you sit or stand—can communicate strong nonverbal cues. For example:

- ▼ Turning your body away from a speaker may be a sign of noninvolvement.
- ▼ Letting your head drop, leaning back, and supporting your head with your hand expresses boredom.
- ▼ Adopting an "open" sitting posture, with your head and body to one side and legs uncrossed, often communicates agreement.
- ▼ Walking rapidly with your hands moving freely at your sides may communicate confidence and goal orientation.

Research has shown that *status* also affects body posture. When employees talk with supervisors, for example, their posture is often tense. The supervisor, on the other hand, may lean back in his or her chair in a relaxed pose.[12]

Clothing In the business world, clothes act as a signal about your willingness to conform to organizational standards. Being neither overdressed nor underdressed, that is, "looking the part" and expressing it with personal flair, shows your acceptance of organizational rules. Consultants believe that your wardrobe should say nothing about you except that you are part of the group. This, some believe, suggests competence and stability.

In most business offices, conservative clothing is the norm—a suit, shirt, and tie for men and a suit or dress for women. Usually, the more conservative the industry—banking, for instance—the more sober the dress. However, in many companies, such as AT&T Canada LDS, strict dress codes have given way to a more relaxed look. This company embraced a new dress code that allowed employees to ditch their constricting ties and pinched feet for the comfort of sports shirts and sensible heels. Many other organizations have introduced casual days, where employees have the luxury of wearing casual attire to work at least once a week.

Personal Space   The physical distance between people who are engaged in communication is known as **personal space.** Customary usage of this space indicates a great deal about social relationships. As you can see from Table 1-2, most business conversations between members of our culture take place in a *social zone* that places individuals between one and four metres apart. Anything closer generally indicates an intimacy that is inappropriate for business. Note especially the differences in the relationships between verbal and nonverbal cues as the zone widens from *personal* to *public*.

It is important to remember that spatial relationships can be manipulated to one person's advantage. A supervisor who wants to intimidate an employee may stand in the employee's personal zone while speaking. Similarly, a crafty salesperson may position him- or herself deliberately close to a prospect.

The arrangement of space in an office can also be used either to ease communication or to increase control over it. For example, a desk that is positioned so as to keep visitors at a distance acts as an emotional as well as a physical barrier. In a less intimidating arrangement, the visitor's chair is placed at the side of the desk, reducing the distance between people as they talk and thus eliminating the feeling that the person behind the desk is somehow "in charge" of the conversation.

PARALANGUAGE   Nonverbal vocal messages are known as **paralanguage.** Depending on their tone, emphasis, speed, pitch, volume, use of pauses, and fillers such as "um" and "you know," messages can be communicated with a wide variety of effects. In fact, emphasis and intonation often hold the key to meaning. For example, when you say "I'm very nervous about this deal," you deliver a different message than when you say "I'm *very* nervous about this deal" or "I'm very nervous about *this* deal."

Table 1-2   Zones of Social Interaction

Zone	Size	Description
Intimate	0 to 1/3 metre	For family and close friends. Touching, whispering, and comforting are common.
Personal	1/3 to 1 metre	For talking with friends or close colleagues. Limited touching, speech becomes louder; eye contact becomes important.
Social	1 to 4 metres	Most business conversations occur in this zone. Communication becomes more formal. Touching is rare. Visual cues are important, and voices are louder than in the personal zone.
Public	4 metres or more	For formal business exchanges, such as a speech to a large group. Voices must be loud or amplified, and it is impossible to see detailed facial expressions.

Source: Peter March, ed., *Eye to Eye: How People Interact* (Topsfield, Mass.: Salem House, 1988), 42.

Research has shown that paralanguage can communicate language even more strongly than the content of words and that when vocal qualities actually contradict words, the paralanguage will have more impact.[13] For example, shouting at a supplier while claiming that you are not angry at him or her for missing an important deadline lacks credibility: your paralanguage contradicts the content of your verbal message by communicating the intensity of your anger.

THE DIFFICULTY IN READING NONVERBAL COMMUNICATION Despite the potential impact of nonverbal communication, studies have found that our ability to read and interpret nonverbal cues is limited. According to social psychologist Robert Gifford, "people read much into nonverbal cues that just isn't there, while missing much that is."[14] For example, while obvious traits such as gregariousness are relatively easy to read, more subtle traits are often misjudged. When Gifford showed videotapes of job applicants to 18 experienced corporate recruiters, the recruiters were able to judge obvious social skills but were poor judges of motivation, a key element of job success. The recruiters believed, for instance, that highly motivated candidates smiled, gestured, and talked more than candidates with low motivation. Other studies reveal additional problems in interpreting nonverbal cues:

▼ Although it is commonly believed that dominant people make greater eye contact than submissive people, the opposite is true.

▼ People who have little eye contact or people whose arms remain folded and whose hands and legs move very little while talking are not as "cold" and "quarrelsome" as is commonly thought.

▼ "Shifty" eyes are not necessarily a clue to lying because liars have as much direct eye contact as do people telling the truth. A more accurate measure of lying are *inconsistent* nonverbal cues—for example, differences between tone of voice and gestures.

Progress Check

1. How often do we communicate nonverbally?
2. Name the two categories of nonverbal cues.

Learning to use these cues to communicate messages can be as important to business success as the ability to write and speak effectively. Although nonverbal cues are more subtle than these other forms of communication, they often have greater impact.

How Messages are Received

Reading and listening are complements to writing and speaking. The communication process would be incomplete without readers and listeners acting as message receivers.

READING
Effective reading requires the ability to focus attention on a topic, even in the midst of distractions. It requires the ability to analyze and evaluate information and respond in an appropriate manner. It also requires *introspection*. The best readers understand that responses to written material are tied to what they know and feel about the material and the writers.

Businesspeople are being asked to read, absorb, and analyze more and more written materials, many of which are technical and complex. But according to recent statistics, only 58 percent of the nation's approximately 24 million adults possess the literacy skills needed to cope with everyday reading requirements. This is cause for concern, since it may limit the ability of Canada's firms to compete well in a global market.[15]

Many companies employ workers who lack basic reading skills. The result is estimated to cost billions of dollars each year in business productivity losses, errors, and accidents attributed to poor literacy. Companies are often reluctant to hire recent graduates and people without experience and look instead for workers with a proven track record, a positive attitude, and strong communication skills.[16]

The ability to read, analyze, and absorb written information is critical to business success. By the year 2000, for example, only one in four jobs will fall into "low-skilled" categories like maintenance worker and supermarket bagger. The others will require not only well-developed reading skills but also an ability to research, organize, and prepare written materials. In fact, many firms report having to interview up to eight job applicants before they find one who is acceptable.

LISTENING

Listening is the act of sensing, interpreting, evaluating, and reacting to what is said. Listening may be the most used, but least taught communication skill. As a result, many of us often do not "see" because we lack the skill to "observe." Not surprisingly, then, successful business leaders stress the importance of listening in effective communication.

THE IMPORTANCE OF LISTENING SKILLS   In business, effective listening can mean the difference between maintaining a customer's goodwill or losing it forever, between working effectively with a fellow employee or making no headway, between keeping your job because you do what your supervisor wants or being fired because of poor performance. Despite the importance of listening, however, most people are poor listeners. According to Lyman K. Steil, a pioneer in listening research, although listening is the first communication skill we learn and the one we use most often, it is also the skill to which we pay least attention.[17]

Perhaps listening is undervalued as a communication tool because it seems to come so easily. In reality, listening well is harder than we think. For example, although the average person talks at about 150 words per minute, the brain can actually handle about 400 words per minute—an overcapacity that can lead to inattention, misinterpretation, and boredom.[18] Table 1-3 lists ten common reasons for not listening. One reason—"I want to talk first"—can prevent effective listening

You can see a lot by observing.

Yogi Berra
New York Yankee catcher

Despite the importance of listening, most people are poor listeners.

Table 1-3 Common Reasons for Not Listening

What You Say to Yourself . . .

I want to talk first.

I'm thinking about what I'm going to say.

I'm not interested in the subject.

That's too hard to understand.

I don't like you.

I don't like the way you talk.

I'm too upset, or worried, about other things.

I don't want to believe what I know you're about to tell me.

I'd rather give my attention to people or activities around me.

I'd rather daydream or doodle.

Source: Donald Walton, *Are You Communicating?* (New York: McGraw-Hill, 1989), 27.

is because, instead of listening to the comments of others, all you think about is making your own points. Your internal focus may prevent you from appreciating the contributions of others.

In addition, research has shown that the information we *hear* often fails to coincide with the information we *comprehend*. According to listening researcher Ralph G. Nichols, immediately after listening we are likely to remember only half of what was said to us. Several days later, we may at best recall only a quarter of the content—and often nothing at all.[19]

STAGES OF LISTENING The listening process is made up of four progressive stages: sensation, interpretation, evaluation, and reaction. These stages are shown in Figure 1-2.[20]

Sensation On its most basic level, listening involves **sensation**—the physiological process by which the ears hear sound waves and transmit them to the brain. Sensation is affected by the loudness and clarity of the speaker's voice, as well as background noise or other sensations. For instance, the din of competing sounds, such as a factory blast furnace, may impede how well a message is heard. Perfume-filled rooms and overheated buildings, hunger, work pressures, and personal problems are also sensations that may hinder the listening process.

Interpretation The second listening stage involves **interpretation**—attributing meaning to a message. For example, when Herman Moore, a manufacturing manager

Figure 1-2 Four Stages of Listening

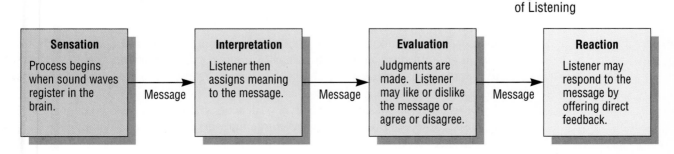

at Reynolds Metals Co. aluminum-rolling plant, attends afternoon staff meetings, he listens to plant employees discussing problems in verbal shorthand: "Change the two-J's. . . . No. 5 is down . . . I can't run it at 45 percent . . . we've got to hit that 80 million . . . we're running out of time here!"[21] Although outsiders would be baffled by these "coded" messages, Moore's business experience allows him to interpret them as part of a listening process.

Preconceived notions, a point of view that differs from the speaker's, a lack of knowledge, and the inability to deal with message complexity can all be intellectual barriers to listening. Similarly, when speakers or their messages evoke negative emotional responses, listening becomes harder. For example, a supervisor who is angry with a worker for losing an important letter may be less willing to listen to the employee's ideas about an unrelated project.

Evaluation   **Evaluation** involves the decision to accept or reject, like or dislike, agree or disagree with a message. Part of this process involves deciding whether a new message is consistent with your personal values. When you are exposed to information that contradicts your value system, that information may place you in a state of conflict, or mental stress, known as **cognitive dissonance.**[22] In order to reduce this discomfort, you may reject the new idea, sometimes simply because it is different. Effective listening involves an understanding of this tendency to reject most messages that contradict your own value system.

Reaction   As a stage of listening, **reaction** refers to the response generated by a message—a response that may take the form of direct feedback. Wilt Wagner, a Reynolds vice president and Herman Moore's boss, explains Moore's reaction style as that of "a new breed. When he disagrees with me," Wagner admits, "I'm going to hear about it."[23] This type of direct response minimizes misunderstanding, whereas responses that do not include feedback may perpetuate communication problems.

FORMS OF LISTENING   Different types of listening are as common in business as they are in personal communication. Consider the following two types:

- ▼ In **polite listening,** a kind of mechanical listening characterized by inattention, listeners really want the speaker to stop talking so that they can begin. Because polite listeners often rehearse their own lines instead of paying attention, polite listening usually accomplishes little. Job applicants are often guilty of this behaviour. Instead of actively listening to the job recruiter's message, they are planning what to say next. Conversations based on polite listening rarely move people from their original points of view.
- ▼ **Active listening** requires both sincere involvement with the information and empathy with the speaker's situation. Active listening means that the hearer concentrates on the speaker's message. In business, active listening is the basis for effective communication and is considered one of the most powerful communication tools.

BECOMING AN EFFECTIVE LISTENER   You can improve your listening skills in both formal and informal business situations by applying the following principles. Many of the same principles can also be used to improve reading.

Learn the Art—and Wisdom—of Silence   Silence gives someone else the opportunity to speak. However, even experienced communicators feel the overwhelming need to

INTERVIEW Teamwork and AT&T Canada's Corporate Fabric

William V. Catucci, President and CEO, AT&T Canada Long Distance Services Company

As the President and Chief Executive Officer of AT&T Canada Long Distance Services Company in Toronto, Bill Catucci is no stranger to the challenges of communicating with his more than 2800 employees in 35 locations across Canada.

A product of an early classical liberal-arts education, Catucci believes in the power of the message. Inspired by the writing of Roman orator and statesman Cicero (106–43 BC), he demonstrates the belief that the key to successful communication is preparedness and presentation. He quotes from Cicero, "No matter who your audience, present yourself in the most favourable light when speaking."

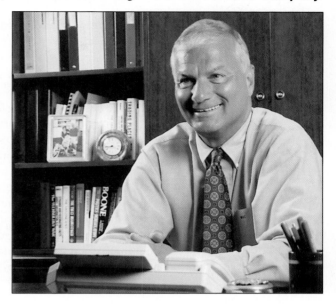

Question: How would you characterize your communication style, and why is it successful?

Answer: I would like to believe that my style of communication is both open and honest, but not at the expense of accuracy and forethought. I believe my communication style is successful, in part, because it appeals to the value and the integrity of most of the people whom I address.

Question: What communication skills are most important to business success?

Answer: Articulation, and the ability to deliver clear and precise messages. I often write my own speeches, or else I modify those from the public relations office in order to reflect my own style or to deliver something explicit. It is important to present complex issues clearly and simply in order that your audience may understand and relate to your message. Without such clarity, most people tend to tune out.

Question: What are the greatest challenges that influence the ways in which businesspeople communicate?

Answer: In my business, the greatest challenge is to be able to productively communicate with specialists from a broad range of disciplines. This complex, highly technical environment in which we live and work cultivates many complex and esoteric points of view. The challenge is to interpret those diverse perspectives and channel them into meaningful and productive effort.

Question: How effective is collaborative communication in business organizations?

Answer: Collaborative communication is an essential function of any progressive business, for without it there can be no collaborative effort, or teamwork. Teamwork is part of AT&T's corporate fabric, and is essential to our success in the marketplace. I think of it as a jazz band, where each musician plays an instrument in his or her own accomplished way—improvising and enhancing on the basic theme and making perfectly good individual music. The net result of such musical collaboration is great jazz!

Question: What conscious change in communication style occurs when businesspeople interact with both internal and external customers?

Answer: There should be no change in communication style when dealing with internal or external customers. Both groups deserve your respect and a consistent message that reflects your business practices and honest relationship.

Source: Interview with William Catucci.

fill the void of silence. As a result, after only a slight pause, they are likely to begin speaking again.

Be Aware of "Emotional Filters"　Ask yourself whether you have strong opinions about the subject of the message or the person to whom you are listening. Emotional reactions to words, people, or situations can cloud your thinking.

Be Slow to Judge　If your tendency is to interrupt and argue when you disagree with what you hear, you may lose the opportunity to learn and, perhaps, to change your opinions. Everyone has preconceived views. Effective listeners are aware of their prejudices and refrain from judging alternative ideas too quickly.

Turn Lack of Interest into Avid Interest　If you let your mind wander during a meeting, you may miss an opportunity to discover and apply helpful ideas. Assume, for example, that you are head of maintenance for Canadian Pacific Hotels, a nationwide hotel chain. When the chain announces that dissatisfied customers will receive full, unconditional refunds, you might wonder why you were asked to attend meetings to discuss this new competitive strategy.[24] Instead of becoming an inactive listener, however, you think further about the impact of the new campaign on your job. Before long, you probably will have many job-related questions: Should hotel maintenance be improved? Should changes in maintenance be geared to customer complaints or to an internal monitoring system? Are staff changes necessary? Such enlightened self-interest can mean the difference between effective and ineffective listening.

> My greatest strength as a consultant is to be ignorant and ask a few questions.
>
> Peter F. Drucker
> Business philosopher and management consultant

Ask Questions to Focus Your Listening　"The only dumb question is the question not asked." This maxim is as true in business as it is in personal communication. When you do not understand a concept, word, or phrase, be direct and ask, "What does that mean?" In the end, these interruptions are time-savers, not time-wasters. Listening patiently without understanding accomplishes little. When you are finished asking questions, use clarifying statements to make sure that your understanding is correct. By restating the message, you reassure yourself and the message sender that the communication transaction was successful.

Focus on What Is Important　It is estimated that only one in four people listening to a formal speech actually grasps the speaker's main idea.[25] In normal business conversation you can make listening easier by asking pointed questions, taking clear notes, being sensitive to repetition, and recognizing language that highlights key concepts. For example, if a co-worker's memo repeats her concern over a deadline three times, the repetition should emphasize the seriousness of the message. Similarly, if she uses phrases like "I want to emphasize . . ." or "Let me stress . . .", she is also focusing attention on a specific point.

Be an Active Listener　To avoid becoming an inattentive listener, focus your "extra" listening time—the time available to you because listening is faster than speaking—on the speaker's message: Try to anticipate what will be said next, review and summarize the points already made, evaluate and question the presentation, and listen between the lines (remember that changes in volume, tone, and body language can be more important than words). Active concentration is the key to effective listening.[26] Finally, bear in mind that active listening may involve note taking.

Progress Check

1. Why are effective listening skills vital to your success in business?
2. Everyone talks about how important listening is, but few people seem to be good at it. Why?
3. In your view, what makes someone a "good listener"?

Effective listening is especially important when dealing with customers. Customers want to know that you are open to their ideas and that you will provide fast feedback—concrete proof of the intensity of listening. Feedback may take the form of a letter summarizing the actions you plan to take as a result of a meeting.

The communication process takes place in the context of a business organization, which has multiple audiences.

The Audiences of Business Organizations

To be successful, a business must communicate effectively with two main audiences: the company's **internal audience,** which consists of its employees and owners; and its **external audience,** which includes the general public, customers, vendors and other businesses, and government officials. For example, while company newsletters illustrate communication with internal audiences, general press releases target external audiences. In discussing both audiences, our focus will be on *formal* communication channels approved by the management of the organization. Later in the chapter, we will look at differences between formal and informal communication channels.

COMMUNICATING WITHIN
AN ORGANIZATION

Effective communication among employees is crucial to the success of all organizations. **Internal communication** involves communicating back and forth *within* the organization through such written and oral channels as memos, reports, proposals, meetings, oral presentations, speeches, and person-to-person and telephone conversations. Internal communication takes place among co-workers as well as between supervisors and supervisees. Internal communication promotes problem detection and solutions. It also fosters decision making and policy setting. AT&T Canada LDS, a Toronto-based telecommunications facility provider, is committed to improving its internal communication systems. Functional groups of employees meet to discuss solutions to problems that are identified in their ongoing quality program.

When organizational communication breaks down, a strike may occur. This was the case with Canada Post in 1997.

As a result of open communication and teamwork, telephone service provisioning improved from 15 days to 8 days. Order-processing capability also improved, tripling the revenue processed with no change in the number of staff.[27]

Using a variety of methods—including face-to-face conversation, formal meetings, speeches, phone calls, electronic mail, and questionnaires—companies link success and profitability to effective internal communication.

An effective internal communication system is especially important in organizations of great size and complexity. Management authors Thomas J. Peters and Robert H. Waterman Jr. point out that while the employee head count may increase arithmetically, demands on communications increase geometrically. As a result, many firms try to simplify their communication networks. Procter & Gamble, for example, now insists that memos be no longer than one page.[28]

Poor communication can frustrate small organizations as well as large ones. Each year, thousands of partnerships and small businesses break up because of communication problems. Although many breakups are unavoidable, others can be prevented through frequent meetings, teamwork, constructive feedback, open discussions, and written agreements.[29]

COMMUNICATING OUTSIDE AN ORGANIZATION

A company's external communication is as important as its internal communication. **External communication** refers to communication with an organization's major audiences—the general public, customers, vendors and other businesses, and government officials. Through external communication, organizations establish themselves in the marketplace and work to keep their operations functioning.

Companies communicate with the public in an attempt to influence consumer decisions. Advertising, for example, creates an organizational image, provides information, and differentiates your products from similar products that are also available.

Firms communicate with customers through such activities as sales presentations, order fulfillment, and handling complaints. Customer communication may take the form of face-to-face conversations, telephone calls, meetings, letters, written proposals, and oral presentations. **Customer service**—the act of ensuring that customers feel valued and that their needs are met—is the foundation of effective business. Always consider yourself a company spokesperson and every letter and conversation a messenger of goodwill. (We will discuss the principles of writing goodwill messages in Chapter 8.)

Businesses communicate with other firms through letters, written proposals and reports, oral presentations, meetings, telephone calls, and informal conversations. One company, for example, may purchase goods or services from another in order to produce its own products or to sell another company's products in its retail stores. Each interaction is an opportunity to cement a business relationship or in some way promote your firm's best interests.

Business-to-government communication takes on a very different form. Both business sales contracts, and requests from the government for information or proposals, are of public domain and are available under the Freedom of Information and Privacy Protection Act (FOIPP). Federal and provincial governments have stringent communication requirements due to the public nature of their external business as well as their public responsibilities.

Formal and Informal Communication Channels_____

Within the context of an organization's internal and external communication networks are formal and informal communication channels that define the manner in which messages are sent. **Communication channels** are pathways of communication. Formal channels include letters, reports, memos, proposals, speeches, and oral presentations. Informal channels include the office grapevine.

Formal and informal channels operate both within and outside the organization. Whereas a memo is usually considered a formal internal message, a conversation around the water cooler is normally regarded as an informal internal message. Similarly, a press release is a formal way to communicate with outsiders; a casual phone conversation to a friend at another company is part of the informal external grapevine.

FORMAL CHANNELS

The **formal communication channel** includes communication that is sanctioned by management—for instance, when a regional sales manager reports directly to a vice president of sales and marketing. Formal communication channels follow a company's organizational structure. Often, this structure is laid out in an organization chart—a blueprint for the organization that indicates formal lines of communication. Figure 1-3 illustrates one model for a formal communication network.

COMMUNICATION FLOWS   The direction taken by communication within the formal channel is known as the **communication flow.** Communication can flow downward, upward, or horizontally. As Figure 1-4 shows, the type of message to be delivered is linked to the communication flow. Information, for example, generally flows upward while directives are generally sent downward.

Downward Communication   A message that flows from a supervisor to a supervisee is known as **downward communication.** The importance of this communication

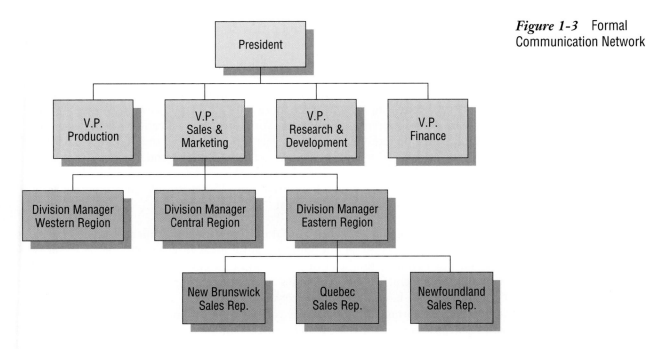

Figure 1-3 Formal Communication Network

Figure 1-4 Message Types and the Communication Flow

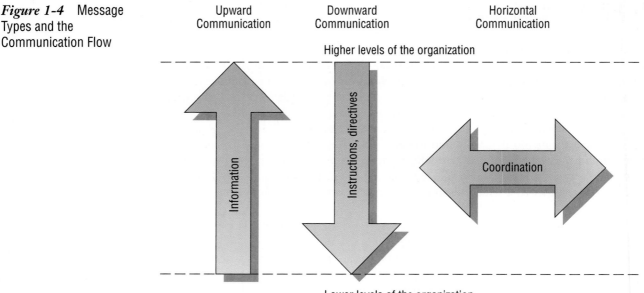

flow cannot be underestimated. Most employees consider immediate supervisors to be their primary formal sources of information.[30]

Downward communication can be written or oral. For example, a manager's memo delegating responsibilities on a new project is a written document, as is an employee-orientation handbook. Oral presentations also communicate messages to supervisees through downward flow. For example, a regional sales manager may hold a meeting to inform the salesforce of new travel and entertainment rules.

Downward communication sometimes becomes flawed as it passes from one organizational level to the next. This situation may result from a number of factors, ranging from lack of clarity on the part of the sender to distortion as the message is transmitted due to poor listening or reading habits among receivers.

Upward Communication   Communication that flows from a supervisee to a supervisor is known as **upward communication.** This flow is essential to organizational success. However, an increasing number of top executives now realize that they are insulated from the workforce by various levels of management. Middle managers may filter information and present a distorted picture to top-level management.

Upward communication is often more difficult than downward communication because of *status* differences. People initiating the communication have a lesser status than the people receiving it and may fear repercussions if they say or write something perceived to be inappropriate. As a result, workers communicate with their supervisors far less frequently than their supervisors communicate with them. One study of managers, for example, found that only 15 percent of total communication time involved messages directed upward.[31]

Horizontal Communication   In **horizontal communication** (sometimes called **lateral communication**), people at the same organizational level communicate with one another. For example, the head of production in a clothing manufacturer may talk with the design chief about difficulties in manufacturing a suit within budget. As companies grow larger and more complex, horizontal communication becomes increasingly important. In an insurance company, for instance, the head of the underwriting department must work closely with counterparts in claims and sales.

Because horizontal communication involves people at the same organizational level, interactions are generally friendlier and less formal than those in other communication flows. However, problems can result when people perceive that they are competing for the same limited company resources.[32]

Horizontal communication is crucial to teams' success. When Ford Motor Company decided to redesign the Mustang, the first step was to gather a team of about 400 people from every department, including engineering, interior design, purchasing, manufacturing, marketing, and finance. The group, which came to be known as Team Mustang, worked together under one roof, enabling team members to be in constant touch as development progressed. Teamwork, and the improved communication that was part of it, helped Ford cut 25 percent from the normal product development time cycle and reduce development costs by 20 percent.[33]

Communication Flow Outside the Organization   The formal flow of communication to outsiders is often handled by the public relations department. **Public relations** is the communication that an organization conducts with its various publics, including, among others, stockholders and the general public. The broad goal of public relations is to build the organization's prestige and reputation. Written communication often takes the form of formal press releases—documents that send company announcements to the various media, including newspapers, magazines, television, and radio. Press conferences are meetings in which the message is communicated orally.

INFORMAL CHANNELS

Communication patterns that are independent of the formal channels approved by management are called **informal communication channels.** These channels may be more efficient than formal channels, but often operate independently of management control. As the following examples show, informal communication channels can be both internal and external:

▼ While exercising in the local fitness centre, the marketing vice president mentions to the controller that a new advertising campaign is being considered.

▼ During a weekly tennis match with a friend in a client company, a sales representative hears about a business opportunity.

▼ A rumour spreads that a popular food product manufactured by the company is contaminated by pesticides.

INFORMAL INTERNAL COMMUNICATION   Instead of learning about policy and personnel changes and new projects from supervisors and official company documents, employees sometimes gain information through unofficial, independent sources. These informal, internal communication channels are known as **grapevines.** According to one survey, although they much prefer formal information sources, employees frequently cite the grapevine as their most frequent source of information. The graph in Figure 1-5 details the results of this survey, itemizing the information sources cited most often by participants.

Keith Davis, a human relations expert who has studied informal communication patterns for more than 30 years, has characterized the grapevine according to its accuracy, speed, base of operations, confidentiality, and its ties to formal communication:

▼ *Accuracy.* Grapevines pass on accurate information between 75 percent and 95 percent of the time. However, even though the failure rate is relatively low, small inaccuracies can garble an entire message.

Figure 1-5 Actual and
Preferred Sources of
Employee Information

Employees were asked:
From which source do you
now get the most useful
information about your
company? From which
source *would you prefer* to
get this information?
Source: 1991 Hay Research for
Management Database.

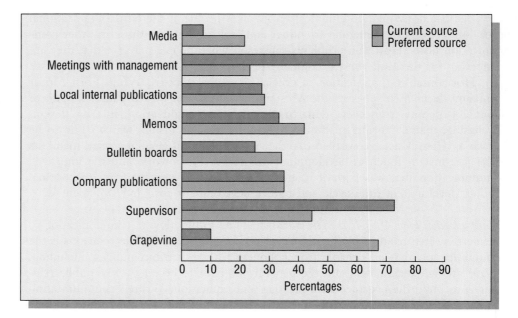

▼ *Speed.* Communication travels through the grapevine at an extremely fast pace. While a message sent through formal channels may take days to reach its audience, messages sent through the grapevine can travel in hours.

▼ *Base of operations.* Grapevine communication occurs primarily during working hours and at the workplace.

▼ *Confidentiality.* Contrary to popular belief, confidential information is often protected as it passes through the grapevine.

▼ *Ties to formal communication.* The grapevine supplements formal communication. The two systems operate jointly.[34]

Not surprisingly, managers who believe that the grapevine undermines their control feel threatened by it. However, instead of attempting to destroy the grapevine (which may be impossible), many managers work with it to provide accurate information. Realizing the danger of unanswered rumours, managers may deal with them through memos, meetings, and other formal communication channels. They may also place someone in the grapevine who can provide them with accurate information.

INFORMAL EXTERNAL COMMUNICATION   Informal grapevines also operate outside the firm and have the ability to affect business. Rumours that spread through the general public can be particularly troublesome. According to Frederick Koenig, a social psychologist who consults with organizations victimized by rumours, companies must use the four steps outlined in Table 1-4 to put rumours to rest.

Table 1-5 summarizes the distinct communication channels examined in this section. Each is characterized by its formality or informality and by its focus inside or outside the organization.

As you will see next, collaboration is a factor in many communication interactions. It has become more important as businesses' use of work teams grows.

Table 1-4   How to Fight a Rumour

Step 1: Be Alert

On first hearing a rumour, track the location and wording. Stay alert for further reports. If you hear ten or more, try to ask people who repeat it where they heard about it. Businesses targeted by rumours, for example, can request distributors, salesmen, and others in contact with the public to check with competitors to see if they share the problem.

Step 2: Evaluate the Rumour

See how damaging it is; for instance, a company can check whether it is slowing sales. Monitor whether it is damaging the morale of those who are its target. Try to determine how many people who hear the rumour believe it to be true.

Step 3: Plan a Counterattack

Assemble all facts about the forms of the rumour and where it has spread. Focus the counterattack in regions where it is most heavily concentrated. If it is local, treat it locally.

Step 4: Launch the Counterattack

Refute the rumour point by point, with solid evidence, backed by experts. Don't deny any more than is alleged in the rumour. Point out that the rumour is both untrue and unjust and that it is unfair to spread lies.

Source: Reprinted with permission from Daniel Goldman, "Anatomy of a Rumor: It Flies on Fear," *New York Times,* 4 June 1991, C5.

Table 1-5   Communication Channels and Message Types

Channel	Type of Business Message
Formal, internal	Memos, reports, meetings, written proposals, oral presentations, agendas, meeting minutes
Formal, external	Letters, written proposals, oral presentations, speeches, press releases, press conferences
Informal, internal	Rumours spread through the grapevine
Informal, external	Rumours spread through the grapevine

Collaborative Communication

Collaborative communication involves two or more people who join together in a team to accomplish one or more of the following functions: planning, organizing, composing, editing, finalizing, delivering oral and written presentations, and taking part in face-to-face and telephone meetings. Major business projects involving written documents and oral presentations are routinely handled by teams of people working together to achieve a specific business goal. A **team** is a small group of people with complementary skills who have been brought together to accomplish a specific purpose and who hold themselves accountable for the team's success or failure. Collaboration can take place at any stage of the work and involves efforts to increase productivity, quality, and profits. Teams cannot succeed without maintaining effective communication.

COLLABORATIVE COMMUNICATION

Building a Team

When senior executives in 340 companies were asked to identify the most important problems facing their organizations, they pointed to customer service, cost reduction, and product quality. They also cited teamwork as a solution to these problems. Teams—and the collaborative communication necessary to make them work—are now integral parts of small, mid-size, and large companies throughout the country. For example:

▼ Davis and Henderson, an Ontario-based data-imaging and cheque-printing company, uses small functional teams to identify issues and opportunities for improvement in their manufacturing process.

▼ Motorola's success in producing small, lightweight, high-quality cellular phones with only a few hundred parts was the result of a team effort.

▼ Taking the concept of recycling one step further, Xerox Canada Inc. is recycling and re-manufacturing office equipment. Manufacturing teams at Xerox process tonnes of used office equipment, preventing it from ending up on the scrap heap. They help conserve resources and save the company millions of dollars in material.

All these teams are involved in the task of improving a process or product—an effort that requires meetings, research, and the drafting and finalization of documents and oral presentations. If group members always remain focused on their goal, most of these tasks will be completed quickly and efficiently. However, intrapersonal and interpersonal issues often stand in the way of effective collaboration. As a result, the first step in building goal-directed communication is understanding what these issues are. They fall into three categories:

▼ *Personal identity within the team.* Team members worry about how they will fit into the team. Will they be an insider or outsider? What influence will they have on group decisions? Will other group members treat their ideas with respect?

▼ *Relationships among team members.* Will group members like and respect each other? Will they be able to work together to achieve team goals? How will people from different departments and with different ranks act toward one another? Will group members have an informal, casual business relationship or will interactions be formal and structured?

▼ *Team identity within the organization.* When team members come together on a project, they do not stop identifying with their own departments or divisions. As a result, they may wonder whether their loyalty to the team conflicts with their loyalty to their departments and whether their responsibility to the team will conflict with their non-team duties.

By starting with the understanding that personal issues and relationships can either enhance or impede collaboration, you will increase your chance—and your group's chance—of success.

Questions for Critical Thinking

1. As a team member, you will be dealing with personal issues that may impede communication. List five methods to resolve conflict within yourself about your participation on the team and five ways to resolve conflicts with other team members.

2. Do you believe that personal issues can be resolved completely at the start of a team project, or must team members pay constant attention to these issues throughout the project? Explain your answer.

3. Why are upward and downward communication patterns likely to cause more problems than horizontal communication in a team setting?

4. What is the relationship between effective collaboration communication skills and personal career success?

Sources: Mark A. Frohman, "Do Teams . . . But Do Them Right," *Industry Week* (April 3, 1995): 21–24; Nancy K. Austin, "Making Teamwork Work," *Working Woman* (January 1993): 28–30; Jon R. Katzenback and Douglas K. Smith, *The Wisdom of Teams* (New York: HarperBusiness, 1993), 15; Peter R. Scholtes, *The Team Handbook: How to Use Teams to Improve Quality* (Madison, Wisc.: Joiner Associates, 1988), 4-1–4-4.

A study revealed that nine out of ten businesspeople have had experience with collaborative communication. Other research suggests that collaboration is in fact the standard in the writing of formal reports and proposals.[35] The word *collaboration* inspires immediate real-life associations of two or more people working together; for example, data-imaging leaders Davis and Henderson of Ontario, and the Toronto Argonauts football club.

Collaborative communication has many benefits. For example, when a long and complex report must be written in a very short time, it may be impossible for a single individual to complete it on schedule. Dealing with a team also makes available a wider range of expertise. A sales proposal for some state-of-the-art equipment, for instance, might include sales personnel, sales management, product developers, and production personnel. Collaboration is also important when a document or oral presentation must reflect a consensus among key decision makers. Having everyone contribute means that everyone assumes "ownership" of writing decisions along the way.

Many business executives believe that teams engaged in collaborative communication are the wave of the future. Teams are used extensively in such companies as Xerox Canada, BCTel, and Nortel. As you will see in the Collaborative Communication features that appear throughout this text, companies face a continuing challenge to help workers communicate effectively as they engage in team projects. Collaborative communication as it applies to planning and researching business reports and proposals is also explored in Chapter 11.

Communication Challenges within the Organization

No matter what type of business, the complexities of business communication will continue to grow during the last years of the twentieth century because of three distinct challenges:

1. the challenge of *ethical communication;*
2. the challenge of communicating in a *global and diverse marketplace and workforce;* and
3. the challenge of *communication technology.*

THE ETHICAL CHALLENGE

Ethics is the standards of conduct and moral judgment accepted by society. Although ethics are first and foremost standards for the individual, they also apply to businesses as institutions and to businesspeople as responsible agents. The ethics of business communication focuses on applying values to determine what is good and bad or right and wrong, and raises questions about who is—or is not—harmed by specific business actions. Ethical considerations confront companies and individuals in numerous communication situations, including the following:

▼ *Ethics influences what a candidate tells a prospective employer and the questions that the employer asks the candidate in return.* For example, some job candidates exaggerate their qualifications and experiences on résumés and in job interviews.

▼ *Ethics influences the information that a company reveals about goods and services and the information that it holds back.* For example, what responsibility does a hair dryer manufacturer have to inform consumers about the possible link between the use of this appliance and health issues relating to electromagnetic fields?

▼ *Ethics influences how companies handle consumer complaints.* For example, after an automaker has received numerous customer complaints about cracking windshields, does the company begin a recall program or does it wait until the government forces action?

First there is the law. It must be obeyed. But the law is the minimum. You must act ethically.

IBM employee guidelines

- ▼ *Ethics influences the use of confidential information.* When information is communicated in confidence, ethical judgments determine the extent to which it is protected or revealed. A lapse in confidentiality can have serious business repercussions. For example, when confidential information is leaked prior to a public announcement, it can influence a company's stock price.
- ▼ *Ethics influences respect for individual privacy.* Lack of respect for individual privacy is an abuse of business ethics. For example, if nurses in the company medical department reveal details of a worker's medical history, they have invaded the employee's privacy. In most cases, such details cannot be revealed without employee consent—even if a supervisor requests them.
- ▼ *Ethics influences how people respond to business pressures.* What happens, for example, if a project manager falsifies shipping dates on internal reports because of pressure from his or her boss to meet an earlier deadline? The environment that creates this pressure comes from management—as does the potential solution. If a job takes four weeks of full-time labour, asking for it in two weeks may encourage unethical behaviour.

Excessive pressure also influences the way in which employees are informed about bad news. Fearing reprisals, Texas Instruments used to wait until the last minute before telling employees about layoffs. After rethinking the ethics of this policy, managers now tell workers about future restructuring plans up to a year in advance in order to give them the opportunity to make career plans.[36]

IMPROVING THE ENVIRONMENT FOR ETHICAL COMMUNICATION   It is not just rhetoric to say that ethical communication is "good business." According to one university study, corporations that have paid dividends for 100 years or more tend to be companies that place a high priority on ethics. In addition, a Deloitte Touche survey of corporate leaders, business school administrators, and politicians found that 63 percent of the respondents believed businesses with high ethical standards to be stronger than those with relaxed standards.[37]

An ethics checklist like the one in Table 1-6 will help you evaluate the moral integrity of your business communication practices. As you can see, business communication ethics affects message purpose, research and selection of material, development of ideas, and use of language.

THE GLOBAL CHALLENGE

No longer a market unto itself, Canada is becoming part of an expanding global economy. This shift to a global marketplace is reflected in sales and sales goals. For example, Digital Equipment Canada, which exports 49 percent of its $1.2 billion sales, has a global mandate: it sells personal computers in North and South America, point-of-sale terminals globally, and network servers globally except in Europe.[38]

The Canadian business environment is also becoming increasingly diverse. In its Immigration Plan of 1994, the Canadian government introduced new selection criteria that will focus on applicants' language, education, work experience, and *adaptability to a changing labour market.* According to Citizenship and Immigration Canada, by the year 2000 more than half of all migrants to Canada may be economic immigrants.[39] A challenge related to increasing diversity is to develop new communication patterns that will enable men, women, and people from different cultural backgrounds to understand each other and work together. In addition, with customers becoming increasingly diverse, businesspeople must learn new communication skills in order to maintain the same or a greater level of business activity. Diversity will be examined in more detail in Chapter 3.

Table 1-6   A Checklist for Ethical Communication

	Yes	No
Message Purpose		
If I accomplish my purpose, will it be in the best interest of my audience?	❏	❏
Am I targeting a small group who will benefit at the expense of a larger group?	❏	❏
Do hidden agendas affect my purpose?	❏	❏
Research Methods		
Did I conduct thorough research or cut corners because of pressure to complete the assignment?	❏	❏
Did I use recent, reliable, and unbiased sources?	❏	❏
Selection of Source Materials		
Did I choose sources that accurately represent the information available on my topic?	❏	❏
Did I reveal relevant information in documents and conversation or hold key details back to protect my interests?	❏	❏
Did I protect confidential information or ask permission before revealing confidential sources?	❏	❏
Development of Ideas		
Have I used sound logic and reasoning?	❏	❏
Did I rely too heavily on emotional appeals?	❏	❏
Have I avoided exaggerating or otherwise distorting information?	❏	❏
Language Usage		
Have I avoided jargon that would confuse my audience?	❏	❏
Are my references concrete and specific instead of ambiguous and abstract, since ambiguities and abstractions will also confuse the audience?	❏	❏

Source: Based on Judi Brownell and Michael Fitzgerald, "Teaching Ethics in Business Communication: The Effective/Ethical Balancing Scale," *The Bulletin of the Association for Business Communication* (September 1992): 18.

THE TECHNOLOGY CHALLENGE

Communication technology—including such office necessities as word processors, fax machines, electronic mail, voice mail, and video conferences—has changed the ways in which businesspeople communicate. Communication today is immediate, allowing people from different locations to communicate as if they were in the same office. The challenge of technology is knowing how to use it effectively in both written and oral communication and understanding how new technologies influence the messages that people are asked to send.

> **Progress Check**
>
> 1. Identify three forces influencing today's business environment.
> 2. Describe standards for ethical communication.
> 3. Why are changes in technology and the increasing globalization and diversity of business considered business communication challenges?

What's Ahead

Increasingly, the fundamentals of business communication include mastering the various forms of communication technology. Chapter 2 will explore communication technologies as they apply in a business setting.

$\blacksquare$ TUDENT RESOURCE CENTRE

Summary of Chapter Objectives

1. *Discuss how effective business communication is linked to personal career success.*

   Managers are increasingly identifying the ability to communicate, both in writing and through effective speech, as the single most important criterion in choosing employees. People who do not have effective communication skills are being either turned away or dismissed when the nature of their problems becomes obvious.

2. *Describe the communication process and identify communication barriers.*

   The communication process consists of six elements: sender, message, channel, receiver, feedback, and context. Senders—speakers or writers—communicate messages to receivers who take in the information, interpret and evaluate it, and provide feedback. Messages are transmitted through different channels—for example, face-to-face verbal communication, and written letters and memos. Message transmission is influenced by the communication context, which includes environmental and cultural forces.

   Communication barriers arise during the communication process and may create misunderstanding and confusion. Communication barriers are created by senders who fail to know their material or audience, have ineffective personal styles, or make poor first impressions. The message itself can block communication by being poorly organized or by using inappropriate language and tone. In its various forms, noise can obstruct the communication channel. Receivers who have poor listening or reading skills, lack empathy for the sender's message, or have various messages competing for their attention can also create communication barriers.

3. *Explain the value of nonverbal communication.*

   Nonverbal communication—which includes gestures, eye contact, facial expressions, posture, clothing, personal space, and nonverbal vocal qualities—often adds meaning to the message. Nonverbal cues may complement, substitute for, emphasize, or contradict verbal messages. Although

nonverbal cues are especially powerful in communicating emotions, they are often misread.

4. *Outline the stages of listening and the ways of becoming an effective listener.*

   In the first stage of listening, sensation, the ears pick up sound waves and transmit them to the brain. In the second stage, interpretation, listeners attribute meaning to the message. In the third stage, evaluation, they make judgments about the message. The final stage, reaction, involves listener response—perhaps in the form of direct feedback.

   Effective listeners are active listeners who become involved with both the information and the speaker. Effective listening requires a conscious effort to be silent when others speak, an awareness of preconceived notions, keeping an open mind, involvement with the information, a focus on what is important, and a willingness to ask questions and seek feedback.

5. *Explain the importance of effective internal and external communication.*

   Through a system of internal communication, messages are communicated up and down the organizational hierarchy and horizontally among co-workers. Through an effective internal communication system, policies are established and disseminated, business decisions are made, and problems are analyzed and solved. Internal communication tools include memos, reports, meetings, oral presentations, speeches, and face-to-face and telephone conversations.

   External communication involves messages sent outside the organization. The chief audiences for this communication are the general public, customers, suppliers and other businesses, and government officials. To be successful, external communication must be sensitive to the specific needs and requirements of each audience.

6. *Describe the nature of formal and informal communication channels.*

   Formal communication consists of the written and oral messages that are sanctioned by company management. Formal communication inside the business can flow downward, from supervisor to supervisee; upward, from supervisee to supervisor; or horizontally, between colleagues. Formal communication outside the organization may take the form of press releases and press conferences.

Informal communication is not approved by management. Informal internal communication is characterized by the grapevine, which is uncontrolled by senior management and whose communication links are often random. Informal grapevines also exist outside the company and may spread rumours about the business.

7. *Identify the role of collaborative communication in business organizations.*

In collaborative communication, two or more people work together in teams to accomplish a business goal that involves written or oral communication. Collaborative communication is beneficial because, through teamwork, projects can be completed at a faster pace than projects done individually, and the team brings together people with different skills and expertise.

8. *Outline the three communication challenges that influence the ways in which businesspeople communicate.*

The challenge of ethical communication requires individuals to communicate according to the standards of conduct and moral judgment accepted by society. The challenge of communicating in a global, diverse marketplace and workforce is tied to the role of Canada as a global trading partner and to the changing demographic patterns of the Canadian workforce. Finally, the challenge of communication technology is linked to the need to adapt to the technologies that are changing the way business is conducted.

Review and Discussion Questions

1. Explain how business communication can help you succeed personally. Cite specific examples. *(Ch. Obj. 1)*

2. Explain the elements of the communication process and how they interrelate. *(Ch. Obj. 2)*

3. Discuss possible communication barriers that can affect each of the following: *(Ch Obj. 2)*
   (a) the sender   (b) the message
   (c) the channel   (d) the receiver
   (e) feedback   (f) the context

4. What is nonverbal communication? What function(s) does it serve? *(Ch. Obj. 3)*

5. What is listening? Explain how you can become a more effective listener. *(Ch. Obj. 4)*

6. What is the difference between internal and external communication? Why are both types of communication important? *(Ch. Obj. 5)*

7. Distinguish between formal and informal communication channels. *(Ch. Obj. 6)*

8. What is the grapevine? Summarize its benefits and drawbacks for an organization. *(Ch. Obj. 6)*

9. What is meant by "collaborative communication"? Why is it important to business organizations? *(Ch. Obj. 7)*

10. Describe three major challenges faced by contemporary business communicators. *(Ch. Obj. 8)*

Application Exercises

1. A friend in another town asks why you're taking a business communications class. Write a letter explaining why it's important to develop good communication skills. *(Ch. Obj. 1)*

2. Think of a recent conversation that you didn't find satisfactory. Now, draw a diagram illustrating the elements of the communication process. Identify each of the six elements and communication barriers involved in this conversation. Analyze this particular communication transaction. How did the barriers affect your feelings about the process? *(Ch. Obj. 2)*

3. During his state visit to the United States in the fall of 1997, Chinese President Jiang Zemin agreed to establish a *hot line* between Beijing and Washington, DC. This act of diplomacy reflected the cold-war communication link established between Moscow and Washington some 20 years earlier.

   Considering the broad range of communication technology available to us today, would you now recommend an alternate form of communication link to the one chosen by the officials on page 10? Write a memo summarizing your recommendation. *(Ch. Obj. 2)*

4. Pay attention to your preconceived ideas and feelings while communicating with people for several days. What preconceptions do you have when starting a conversation with your best friend? With an instructor? With someone you don't know well? Do these preconceptions differ, and if so, how? When might your preconceptions act as communication barriers? Write a paragraph describing what you observe. *(Ch. Obj. 2, 4)*

5. Next time you're with a group of people, observe their nonverbal communication. How large is each person's personal space? Notice their gestures, eye contact, expressions, and postures. Can you tell which members of the group already know each other and which don't? If so, how? Write a summary of your observations. *(Ch. Obj. 3)*

6. Chapter 1 notes that many of us are poor at interpreting nonverbal cues. Why? *(Ch. Obj. 3)*

7. Your friend Joe is getting ready to interview for his dream job. Understandably, he has some questions. What advice would you give Joe about how he can use listening skills to learn more and make a good impression? *(Ch. Obj. 1, 4)*

8. Pair off with a partner (preferably someone whom you don't know well). One of you should speak for about two minutes on a topic while the partner simply listens. (The topic is up to you—perhaps something that you read this morning, or a favourite hobby.) After you've finished, your partner should paraphrase what you've just said, being careful not to make judgments or express opinions. Analyze the interchange. Were you able to communicate effectively? Did your partner listen well? Now it's your partner's turn: he or she gets to talk for two minutes on any topic while you listen and then paraphrase. Again, check your communication skills. What did you learn from this exercise? *(Ch. Obj. 2, 4)*

9. The CEO of your company, knowing that you're studying business communication, asks you to suggest improvements in the firm's internal and external communications. Write a memo in which you recommend several changes that you feel would help your employer be more effective. Be sure to explain why good communication is good for business. *(Ch. Obj. 5)*

10. As a student, you are a customer of your school. Describe how the school communicates with its customers. What types of oral and written communication does it use? What channels does it use? Do you feel that these forms of communication are effective in "selling" you on the school? How might the school improve its external communication system? Explain your answer. *(Ch. Obj. 5, 6)*

11. Think of an important event that took place at your job or school (maybe someone was hired or lost a job, maybe a new procedure was introduced, an office opened or a plant closed). Write a brief description comparing the information that you received on that occasion from both formal and informal communication channels. Were the informal channels accurate? Were they faster than official channels? Did they convey more or less information than "approved" channels? Which did you trust more, and why? *(Ch. Obj. 6)*

12. Team up with three or four classmates and write a report on the current competitive status of a firm the group selects. Be sure various majors or fields of study are represented in your group. What did you learn from this exercise in collaborative communication? *(Ch. Obj. 1, 7)*

13. Think for a moment of communication technologies with which you're familiar—perhaps CD-ROM, electronic mail, fax machines, or answering machines with enhanced capabilities. What about "old" technologies such as telephones, television, and radio? How have these technologies changed the nature of your communication skills and practices? (For instance, how would you compare writing a paper by hand with writing it on a computer? Writing a letter to a friend versus talking to that friend on the phone?) Write a brief essay in which you discuss the impact of these technologies on communication between people. *(Ch. Obj. 8)*

14. Many companies have adopted official policies regarding business ethics. Go to a library and read about the policies of three different companies. Take notes and then write a brief paper (one to two pages) that describes each firm's policy and ethics program. How does each company define ethical behaviour? What procedures has it established to allow employees to report wrongdoing? Which program sounds best to you? Explain your answer. *(Ch. Obj. 8)*

15. Does a company really have a responsibility to behave ethically? Some management theorists believe that a corporation's real responsibility is to its

shareholders—that it owes its owners a profit. Others feel that a business has a certain amount of responsibility to society in general—that it owes it to society to behave ethically. What do you think? Write a brief essay stating your opinion and explaining why you feel the way you do. *(Ch. Obj. 8)*

ACT: Applied Communication Techniques

Applied Communication Techniques (ACT) exercises work to build your basic grammar skills. Begin by referring to the Nouns section of Appendix II, then correct the grammar, spelling, and usage errors in the following sentences. Check your answers in Appendix V.

1. The Mayor of Saskatoon congradulated the olympic medalists upon their return from Nagano, Japan.
2. In the open office concept, employees' deskes are often found grouped together and separated only by moveable divideres.
3. The wifes of the canadian bobsled team were jubilent when their husbands earned the gold medal.
4. At the calgary zoo, children enjoyed watching the games played by the monkeyes.
5. On our adventure through the yukon, we saw three mooses and nine deer.
6. My two brother-in-laws are enterpreneurs working out of Chatham, Ontario.
7. Aurora college trained five students teacher in Dr. Waterton's Physics class.
8. The result of ten years of work was tracked in piles on her desk.
9. The childrens' faces expressed surprise as the hologram figure appeared and began to speech.
10. Earl Jones' daughter was successfull in achieveing a place on the Canadian womens speed skating team.

Building Your Research Skills

Business communication textbooks (like this one) say that communication is an important business skill. Are they correct? Let's find out.

Go to the library and find two examples of business situations in which communication—or the lack of it—played a role. (Possible sources might include the *Financial Post, Globe and Mail, Maclean's*, or your local newspaper. The communication could be either written or oral, good news or bad.) Write a short report summarizing each situation and the role that communication played. Was the communication effective or ineffective? Did the challenges of technology, globalization or diversity, or ethics affect the communication? Could the people involved have communicated better? If so, what would you recommend?

Your instructor may wish to have you present your report to the class.

Building Your Teamwork Skills

Examine the Corporate Case "Can This Partnership Be Saved?" at the end of this chapter. Then divide into groups of four. Two students in each group will take the part of Cap Pannell, while the other two will take the role of Arthur Eisenberg. Each "Cap" pair will prepare an explanation of why Cap acted the way he did, present his views on what went wrong in the business, and suggest what should be done about it. Meanwhile, each "Arthur" pair will do the same from Eisenberg's viewpoint. Finally, the two pairs will present their respective point. sides and discuss their options. (Remember to practise active listening!)

When all four of you have agreed on what Cap and Arthur should do, have one person from your group present your decision to the class. (Note: If there's an odd number of students in the class, one group could consist of three students, with the third serving as moderator. The moderator could practise active listening and offer clarifying statements to help Cap and Arthur state their positions.)

The Communication Process
http://spider.hcob.wmich.edu/bis/faculty/bowman/comproc.html

Five Styles of Communication
http://www.wuacc.edu/services/zzcwwctr/diction-5styles.txt

International Association of Business Communicators
http://www.iabc.com

Business & Organizational Writing
http://www.wuacc.edu/services/zzcwwctr/businessorg_menue.html

CASE STUDIES

CORPORATE CASE:

Ethyl Canada Opens Second Front on MMT

In the fall of 1997, a U.S. manufacturer of a gasoline additive initiated a second challenge to the federal law that effectively banned its use in Canada.

Earlier that year, as the Canadian Parliament was passing the Fuel Additives Act, Ethyl Corporation, based in Richmond, VA, filed a $350 million damage claim alleging that the new law breached Canada's obligations under the North American Free Trade Agreement (NAFTA).

Its Canadian subsidiary, Mississauga-based Ethyl Canada Inc., then launched a second and constitutional action in the Ontario Courts General Division that may have quashed the legislation as an invasion of provincial rights.

The fundamental law that went into force in June of 1997 bans the import for commercial purposes or interprovincial trade in methylcyclopentadienyl manganese tricarbonyl (MMT), a substance that boosts gasoline octane levels. Ethyl Corp. is the lone North American manufacturer of MMT.

In the NAFTA action, the parent organization contended that legislation would force Ethyl Canada Inc. to close its mixing plant near Sarnia, Ontario, which employs 40 people.

The constitutional action involved a claim that the law invades the province's sole jurisdiction over property rights. Ottawa's position was that the law, passed for health and environmental reasons, is a valid exercise of federal jurisdiction over trade and commerce.

Questions and Applications

1. If you were the recipient of the second charge, what would your reaction have been? What response, if any, would you have made?

2. Relate this case to the discussion of external communication audiences in Chapter 1. What conclusion do you reach?

3. How do you think cultural diversity challenged the communication process between U.S.-based Ethyl Corp. and the Ontario Courts?

4. Discuss Ethyl Corporation's claim in an ethical and ecological context.

Source: Adapted from Tom Claridge, "Ethyl Canada opens second front on MMT," The Globe and Mail, (October 27, 1997): B4

CORPORATE CASE:

Can This Partnership Be Saved?

Sad but true: poor communication can destroy a booming business. Let's look at one real-life example.

Arthur Eisenberg and Cap Pannell seemed to have the perfect partnership. Quiet Cap concentrated on design; outgoing Arthur won clients over. With Pannell's wife, Carol St. George, as head copywriter, they created a successful design firm called Eisenberg/Pannell/St. George. Sales began to soar;

revenues rose 50 percent in two years, pushing the $2-million mark; a national magazine praised their work.

Behind the scenes, however, resentment was building between Arthur and Cap. One problem: the two partners had never really discussed what each wanted from their business venture. How much profit did each of them want? What did they expect from each other? Workaholic Arthur admits that "this company is my life. I do not have anything else." Cap, on the other hand, had a wife and a new baby—and other priorities besides working constantly. When Cap refused to work all night long or to take business trips at a moment's notice, Arthur resented what he saw as a lack of commitment to the company. Arthur was furious when Cap and Carol brought baby Ben to work (even though, says Cap, they'd agreed that "we could have the baby at the office with us, with a nanny").

Did Arthur communicate his growing anger? Certainly—but not to Cap or Carol. Instead, he complained to other employees. Meanwhile, Cap and Carol resented Arthur's resentment and talked about it to each other—but not to Arthur. Recalls Cap, "We were coming home every day and saying, 'Gee, I can't believe he did that today.'" Adds Carol: "Early on, Arthur made noises about how difficult it was to have a married couple there. But I don't think it registered with us. That was kind of dumb on our part."

The crisis occurred when Cap and Carol returned from vacation. Three days later, Arthur asked them into his office and broke the news: "I'd like to discontinue the relationship." Stunned, Cap replied, "If you don't want me around, I don't want to be around." Cap and Carol left the office in silence and collected their belongings. "It was humiliating," remembers Cap. "We had to pack everything we had ourselves. Everybody was watching us, all the employees. He didn't offer us anything. I can't bring myself to think we were treated right." "As far as I'm concerned," charges Carol, "we were used and then discarded."

Cap and Arthur haven't spoken to each other since their partnership floundered. Cap, still bitter, says, "The business always did well. I don't even know the real reason we split up. I really cannot forgive him right now in my heart." For his part, Arthur insists, "If Cap and I were at a party, we'd shake hands and talk about old times. . . . I think Cap was as unhappy as I was. He probably wanted out of the situation, too . . . I wish I knew what he felt."[38]

Questions and Applications

1. Discuss the communication barriers that plagued Cap and Arthur's partnership.

2. Carol admits that Arthur's "noises" about the difficulty of working with a married couple hadn't "registered" with them. Why not?

3. Arthur says he wishes that he knew how Cap felt. What could Arthur have done?

4. As an employee at Eisenberg/Pannell/St. George, you're familiar with the tensions between Cap and Arthur. Arthur has asked you to write a report for the firm's advisory board explaining why Cap and Carol left. Write this report, keeping in mind that many of the board's members are longtime friends of Cap, Arthur, and Carol.

5. When asked why their partnership broke up, Arthur answers, "My problem is that I didn't research my partner enough." Cap says, "I guess I didn't realize that Arthur was just an opportunist." What do you think about their answers? Write a paragraph explaining why you think their business ended. What steps could they have taken, if any, to save it?

2

Mastering
Communication Technology

Chapter Objectives

After studying this chapter, you should be able to:

1. List the benefits of communication technology.
2. Identify the six communication functions performed by computers.
3. Explain the benefits of writing with word processing software.
4. Outline the ways in which computers are used as telecommunication tools.
5. Explain how computer, telecommunication, and database technology come together to form the Internet.
6. Identify the features, advantages, and disadvantages of voice mail.
7. Describe how to conduct electronic meetings via teleconferences and video conferences.
8. Explain how wireless telephones, pagers, and portable computers affect business travel.
9. Describe telecommuting and how to overcome its pitfalls.

I do not fear computers. I fear the lack of them.

Isaac Asimov
Science fiction writer

Perpetual Motion Executives

They are called perpetual motion executives— or PMXs—and we all know who they are. They are the most efficient businesspeople among us because they know how to stay in touch all the time. Their skills are especially obvious during long flights. After checking their wristwatch pager for messages, they use an in-flight telephone to make business calls that can't wait until the end of the flight. Then, with their palmtop computers or personal digital assistants (PDAs), they draft and edit letters, memoranda, reports, and proposals. Again using an in-flight telephone, the most urgent of these are sent via fax or electronic mail (e-mail) to the recipients for immediate action.

Brian Napier is a PMX. As past Chairman and CEO of the Canadian Business Telecommunications Alliance, a Canadian telecommunications association, Napier relies on technology to effectively communicate within and across time zones with clients, suppliers, employees, and business associates. The majority of his communication is by e-mail. Napier, originally from the Northwest Territories, sends and receives about 80 e-mail messages a day, more than double the 30 or so voice-mail messages he receives in the same period. "A temporary inconvenience!" says Napier, lamenting the current inability of the PDA to accommodate voice mail. Computer manufacturers are already addressing this shortcoming.

Napier carries a virtual office on his belt. While claiming not to use state-of-the-art equipment, with his wireless telephone on one side, PDA on the other, and hands at the ready, he resembles the modern-day business equivalent of the gunfighters of old. These current-day six-shooters, along with a pocket modem, form Napier's communications lifeline, giving him the flexibility to conduct business anytime and almost anywhere. "I regularly check my e-mail between 6 A.M. and 10 P.M.," he says, remarking that he is more easily reached by e-mail than in person due to his mobility.

"Of course, mobility has a price—it's the cost of operation. My decision to use technology takes into account the expected outcome of my daily activities. Sometimes it's better to access my e-mail after regular hours via the Internet than to access during prime time. It is this usage and personal cost that dissuades potential adapters of technology."

"In all cases, I know my mannerisms change while I'm on the move—I'm much more impersonal and business-focused than when I'm in the office." Napier further states, "The greatest PMX impact is definitely not the application of technology, but rather the corporate expectations and subsequent societal shifts the technology creates."

PMXs use technology to communicate anywhere and anytime. Successful PMXs use technology to create a corporate competitive advantage through effective communication. Technology is the telecommunicator; the person is the communicator. PMXs know and respect the difference. ▼

Source: Interview with Brian Napier.

Chapter Overview _____

Brian Napier is a master at staying in touch, and the same equipment and services that allow him easy access are available to most businesspeople. As technology becomes an increasingly more acceptable part of our day-to-day lives, we often take for granted the efficiencies and benefits that modern telecommunication networks and computers offer our business environment. Today, documents created on a single office computer may be edited, stored, copied, or distributed around the office, the company, or the world in minutes. The mountains of paper documents characteristic of previous business generations are giving way to electronic documents.

Computers equipped with infrared interfaces can exchange documents without being physically connected. Those with **fax modems** can transmit documents directly to a fax machine or another computer equipped with a fax modem. Computers linked to wireless telephones can download information while in remote locations, and those with a **personal digital assistant** (PDA) interface can copy schedule, address, calendar, and other vital information to the removable PDA.

Technology is also changing business practice. Pagers and voice-mail systems, electronic assistants, personal communication service (PCS) phones, teleconferencing, and video conferencing make it possible to keep in touch at any time of the day or night from anywhere in the world. These technologies also give businesspeople the freedom to leave the office without fear of missing an important call or meeting, and permit international business to continue regardless of time or national boundaries.

This chapter examines how technology is transforming traditional business communication. We will introduce the concept of telematics—the integration of computer, telecommunication, and information technologies. We will discuss the links between written and oral communication and communication technology, and we will also examine telecommuting, which allows businesspeople to work from home or a variety of other non-office locations. We begin by placing the broad range of communication technology into perspective.

Communication Technology _____

Communication technology has revolutionized the workplace by permitting businesspeople to exchange messages and information faster and more efficiently than ever before. It has provided us with both private and public networks. In the same way, communication technology has dramatically influenced today's marketplace. For instance, hundreds of millions of messages—many of them travelling around the world—are sent and received via telephone, electronic mail, and voice mail by just one company—Eastman Kodak. Bruce Hoeffel, executive director of international human resources at 3M, sums up the impact of new technologies on global communication: "The speed of communications that we have today has greatly aided the ability of the manager to perform global work without working 24 hours a day."[1]

In his summary, Bruce Hoeffel refers to the Public Switched Telephone Network (PSTN), the international telephone network with which we are all familiar. He also refers to a computer network for his electronic mail, and a combination of telephone network and computer technology to support Eastman Kodak's voice-mail system. Indeed, complex communication technology is at the heart of corporate Canada as we enter the twenty-first century.

Most common in organizations today is the **Intranet**, a corporate-based network of computers, often configured as local-area networks, which permit employees in an organization to communicate freely with each other through a simplified but specific address scheme. Intranet users can communicate with users outside of their organization by expanding their address to include the Intranet form from which they are working. In this way, people on dissimilar Intranets can communicate with each other, expanding the reach of their communication to a broader, more global communications network known as the **Internet**. In a recent survey,[2] there were approximately 4800 such Intranets in Canada alone, and this number was growing exponentially.

In each case the telecommunication network represents the media, computers represent communication tools, and the user is the communicator. Figure 2–1 represents a corporate network in which voice, computer, and multi-media communication technology is used. This conceptual view of the technology used between a company's headquarters, remote offices, branch offices, and home illustrates the basic networks that would be in place to support a medium-sized corporation. Note the satellite, mobile, and local-area network applications as typical use of communication technology.

SO, WHAT ARE THE BENEFITS?

Communication technology enables us to create, organize, and distribute information more efficiently and cost effectively. For example:

▼ Personal computers (PCs), when loaded with word processing software, allow business writers to create documents, insert and delete material, and move blocks of text from one point to another with a couple of key strokes or clicks of the mouse button. Document revisions are easily made to produce a clean, finished copy that can be distributed to other PCs within the network.

▼ Network computers (NCs) are low-cost devices designed specifically for use on the Internet. All necessary operating software is downloaded to the NC. It is a compact device, with no permanent memory capability, that manipulates video, audio, graphical, and text applications found on the Internet.

The newest computer can merely compound, at speed, the oldest problem in the relations between human beings, and in the end, the communicator will be confronted with the old problem of what to say and how to say it.

Edward R. Murrow

Telematics is a term used to denote the integration of telecommunication and computer technologies. It is the technical means to communicate and transfer data by intelligent devices. The productivity of telematic applications is evident in these examples:

▼ Electronic mail and fax machines reduce delivery time to a bare minimum. Instead of writing a letter and waiting for the mail to deliver it—a process that may take days—messages delivered via computer-based technologies are immediate. Responses can be obtained without considering conventional-mail delivery wait time.

▼ Teleconferences and video conferences allow interactive meetings without the expense or inconvenience of business travel.

▼ International investors are drawn to the speed and convenience of online trading. Stock market traders are able to buy and sell corporate stock directly from investment banks, saving valuable time and potential profits.

As you study this chapter, keep in mind that for all its advantages, there are times when the use of communication technology may be the wrong choice. Video conferences, faxes, and electronic mail are often no substitute for face-to-face communication, which establishes trust and personal ties. When a major manufacturing problem arose in Japan, for example, Xerox executive Brian Stern flew there to

Figure 2-1 Conceptual view of a medium-sized organization's network technology.

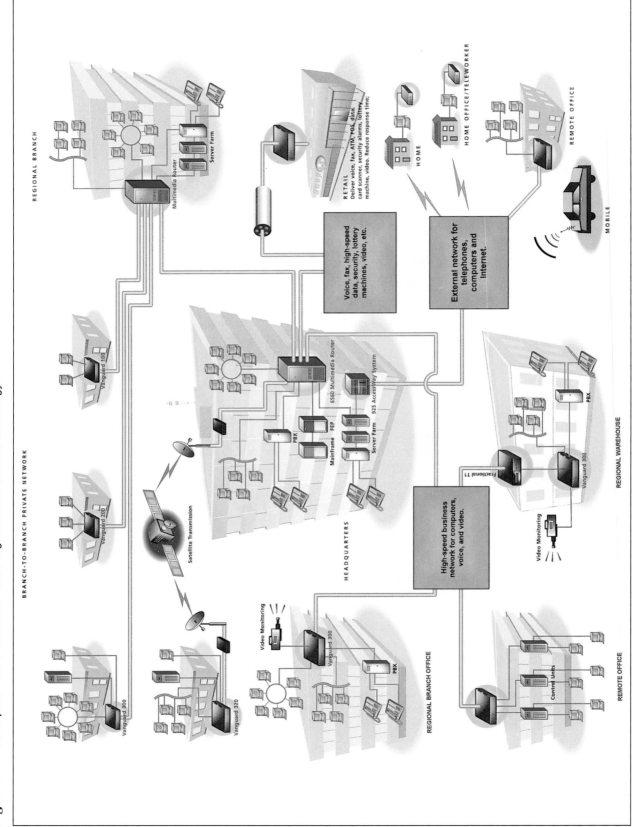

resolve it in person—even though he could have held a video conference from his office. Stern believes that when the stakes are high, personal contact is critical.

Written Communication and Technology

Personal computers and the proliferation of business support software have transformed business writing. Word processing, local computer networking, and database management have made creating and revising documents much faster and simpler. Scanners, high-speed printers, and photocopiers have also become essential equipment in today's creative environment. Table 2–1 describes the use of these devices.

COMPUTERS AS A WRITING TOOL

In 1978, Apple Corporation introduced the first commercially available PC.[3] IBM followed quickly, hoping to sell perhaps 250 000 machines over the life of the product. Needless to say, IBM's estimate was off the mark. Between 1990 and 1992, more than 32 million PCs were manufactured in the United States, 26 million in Western Europe, almost 7 million in Japan, and 3 million in Canada. Today, 41 percent of Canadian homes have PCs, and 58 percent of our population use one at work.[4]

There is a world market for about five computers.

Thomas J. Watson
Founder, IBM

If you own a PC, you are aware of what it can do. You can type letters, maintain your personal budget, play games, and listen to music from the compact disc (CD-ROM). You are now able to watch a CD-ROM-based movie from the same CD-ROM player.

Table 2-1 Communication Technologies for Business Writers

Technology	Use
Word processing software	Develop, draft, revise, proofread, and format written documents
Electronic mail	Send and receive messages via computer networks
Electronic bulletin board	Share information with other bulletin board users
Online database	Access excellent sources of current business research
Internet	Connect to the world's largest network for business and personal communications and information
Database management software	Store data in computer files for easy access when needed to create business documents such as mailing lists, letters, and presentations
Office suite	Combine word processing, database management, presentation graphics, communications, and spreadsheet software into an integrated package
Computer printer	Produce printed hard copies of words and images from a computer
Photocopier	Duplicate single and multiple copies of original material
Facsimile machine	Transmit original materials instantly over telephone lines
Scanner	Transform printed material into digitalized data that the computer can read, store, retrieve, and manipulate as instructed
All-in-one office	Combine several functions, such as printing, faxing, copying, and scanning, into a single office machine

Today's business professionals employ a dazzling array of communication tools to perform their jobs and serve their customers. Flettene Parks Neal, a creative director for an advertising agency, and Thaddeus E. Russell, a finance expert, use their Apple portable computers to store everything and anything—from ideas for new campaigns, lists of freelancers, client financial profiles, and payroll records to letters to Mom and the budget for the Christmas party.

In today's business world PCs have five primary functions, all of which involve the preparation and presentation of information: they store, retrieve, edit, display, and prepare information for printing. A sixth function, that of transmitting information, is possible when the PC is configured and connected to a network.

STORING INFORMATION   Computers act like giant filing cabinets by internally storing letters, budgets, games, and other information in internal files. These files are kept on internal media such as disks, tapes, or CD-ROMs. The most obvious advantage of storing data in a computer rather than on paper is that it takes up very little space. Some electronic media are more space-efficient than others. For example, a conventional 3.5 inch diskette may hold up to 400 full pages of text, whereas a standard CD-ROM can potentially hold as many as 213 000 full pages of text.

RETRIEVING INFORMATION   Because users can store related information in separate locations, usually called *directories*, it can be retrieved easily and quickly. Just a few appropriate keystrokes or clicks of the computer mouse will retrieve the required information.

EDITING INFORMATION   Once information is retrieved, it appears on the computer screen. It can then be revised by rearranging, adding, or deleting material, changing the format, and so on. For example, you may decide that the last paragraph of a sales report is better suited to your introduction, or that you should include more current sales figures. Correcting and reformatting your document is an easy task on a computer.

DISPLAYING INFORMATION   A computer's ability to display information in different ways can be helpful both in analyzing and presenting the information to an audience. For example, a presentation-graphics program allows you to create bar charts, pie charts, line charts, or other types of graphs to illustrate your sales figures.

PRINTING INFORMATION   Print characteristics depend on both the software you use and your printer's ability to carry out those software instructions. Computer instructions tell the printer to produce *hard copy*, a computer printout with any number of different features. For example, you can instruct the computer to use boldface or italics, to print in colour, or to print multiple copies.

TRANSMITTING INFORMATION   A sixth and vitally important function of a PC is the ability to transmit, or communicate information to another computer. This function turns the document-producing computer into a communication tool. With the addition of a network connection (often a modem), the physical connection to a network, and the appropriate communication software, information produced on the otherwise stand-alone computer can be communicated to others in the network. Information can be transmitted through *telecommunication networks*—the media by which information is converted to electrical impulses and transmitted through ordinary telephone or high-speed data lines to another computer that converts it into usable information. Computers and telecommunication networks are the basis for Internet communication, electronic mail, electronic bulletin boards, and online databases.[5]

WORD PROCESSING SOFTWARE— THE WRITER'S DREAM

IBM coined the term *word processor* in 1964 to refer to a software program that transforms a computer into a sophisticated electronic typewriter. While the earliest word processors were machines dedicated to printing letters and numbers, today's **word processing software** is also used for creating documents, data management, and graphical enhancements. It is used extensively in multi-functional computer systems in the home and throughout industry.

Word processing software serves a number of indispensable functions for business writers. Those functions include taking notes and organizing, drafting and developing, revising and editing, proofreading, and formatting all sorts of business documents.[6]

Figure 2-2   Today's Printers Provide Quality Colour Reproduction

Today's user-friendly presentation-graphics software allows businesspeople to create attractive and informative visual aids. In addition to generating colourful charts, today's presentation-graphics packages offer such additional features as three-dimensional or animated charts. The Sony Multiscan monitor shown here will display geometrically straight lines on a 40-inch screen and is compatible with virtually any input.

TAKING NOTES   Rather than relying on handwritten notes that can be easily lost, it is often more efficient to take notes on a computer as you gather research material for proposals or reports. New information and ideas, as well as any needed changes, can be easily and quickly entered anywhere in the document at any time.

ORGANIZING DOCUMENTS   Once information has been gathered and stored in your computer, it can be easily arranged by either moving or copying notes from one point to another. Because most word processing software automatically numbers pages, footnotes, and endnotes, rearranging information does not involve the task of renumbering as changes are made. The ability to easily reorganize your material is not only helpful in the creation of documents but invaluable in the later stages of document development, when changes are often necessary.

DRAFTING AND DEVELOPMENT   As a document-drafting tool, word processing software provides enormous flexibility. For example, you can start to write at any point in your document—the beginning, middle, or end—and insert surrounding material later. Because computer software accommodates additions, deletions, and reorganization of text, your introduction can be entered after the rest of the document is complete.

High-quality graphics are especially important in business reports and proposals. They can be added during the drafting process. **Presentation-graphics software**, which is often bundled together with word processing software, can create sophisticated charts and other graphics from data already stored in the computer. Graphics software also allows the transfer of colour images to blank acetates via a computer printer. During an oral presentation, an overhead projector can then display the acetate on a larger screen.

REVISING AND EDITING   Revising and editing documents can be fast and painless if you use your word processing software's editing capabilities. For example, using the search-and-replace feature, you can have your computer search for all occurrences of specific text and automatically replace that text with other material. Or the computer can pause and ask you to decide whether to make the replacement.

In a document on international bank loans, for instance, you can use the search-and-replace feature to change *underdeveloped countries* to *emerging nations* every time the term appears. However, be aware that the replacement term can have more than one meaning. Instructing the computer to replace the term *Indian* with the term *First Nations* may result in the sort of inadvertent error illustrated in these two sentences:

Sentence 1:   We look forward to a long *Indian* summer this year.
Sentence 2:   We look forward to a long *First Nations* summer this year.

Word processing software is also capable of producing foreign letters, accent marks, mathematical expressions, and graphical symbols. This capability is especially useful in a bilingual nation such as Canada, where accents are required on some characters in French.

PROOFREADING   Most word processing programs include a spell-check feature that finds and corrects spelling mistakes and is available in multiple languages. Spell checkers compare words used in your document against a built-in dictionary. Questionable entries are highlighted for correction. Most word processing packages also include a grammar checker and a thesaurus.

FORMATTING   Document formatting features are simplified with word processing software. These features include:

- ▼ pre-designed document templates
- ▼ margins and borders
- ▼ indents
- ▼ headers, footnotes, and endnotes
- ▼ type styles
- ▼ page numbers

Specific instructions for applying these features are a function of the particular word processing software that you use. You are well advised to review the reference manual when using unfamiliar software.

QUALITY WORK   The following suggestions will help improve the quality and speed of writing on a computer equipped with word processing software:

> *A computer does not substitute for judgment any more than a pencil substitutes for literacy. But writing without a pencil is no particular advantage.*
>
> Robert McNamara
> Executive and Statesman

- ▼ During the drafting stage, practise "free writing," a process in which you type thoughts as they occur. Do not stop to correct spelling or grammar, make stylistic changes, or reorganize ideas.
- ▼ Consider printing a paper copy of the document and making revisions on it. Incorporate final changes on the computer.
- ▼ Make adequate revisions, but limit fine-tuning. Spending too much time finding the right word or phrase is counterproductive.
- ▼ Use the search command to locate and eliminate overused or wordy phrases such as *the fact that* and *there are*.
- ▼ Proofread your document twice—once on the computer screen and once on paper. Often, mistakes you miss on the screen will be obvious on your printout.

▼ Learn to merge information from two or more files. For example, merging a form letter with a database of names and addresses produces personalized letters for everyone on the list.

▼ Use consistent type styles for headings. For example, you may decide to use boldface each time a client's firm is mentioned.

Progress Check

1. Describe the five primary functions of a stand-alone computer.

2. List the conditions under which the stand-alone computer becomes a powerful communications tool.

3. How has word processing software affected business productivity? Explain your answer by referring to the specific functions of word processing software.

4. How can using word processing software help improve business writing?

Consider using the document templates that are part of your word processing software. A *template* is a blueprint or pattern for all documents that fit into a certain category—such as an agenda, award, calendar, fax cover sheet, letter, memo, newsletter, and résumé. Templates format the document by using preset margins and creating customized styles for such elements as the title page, table of contents, part openers, headings, and index. For example, a business letter template uses preset margins and line spaces for the date, the recipient's name and address, the salutation, the signature line, and so on.

The template also allows you to print the letter on business letterhead or plain paper, and adjust the text accordingly. The *Wizard*, shown in Figure 2-3, is the Microsoft word processing software's step-by-step help in creating these documents.

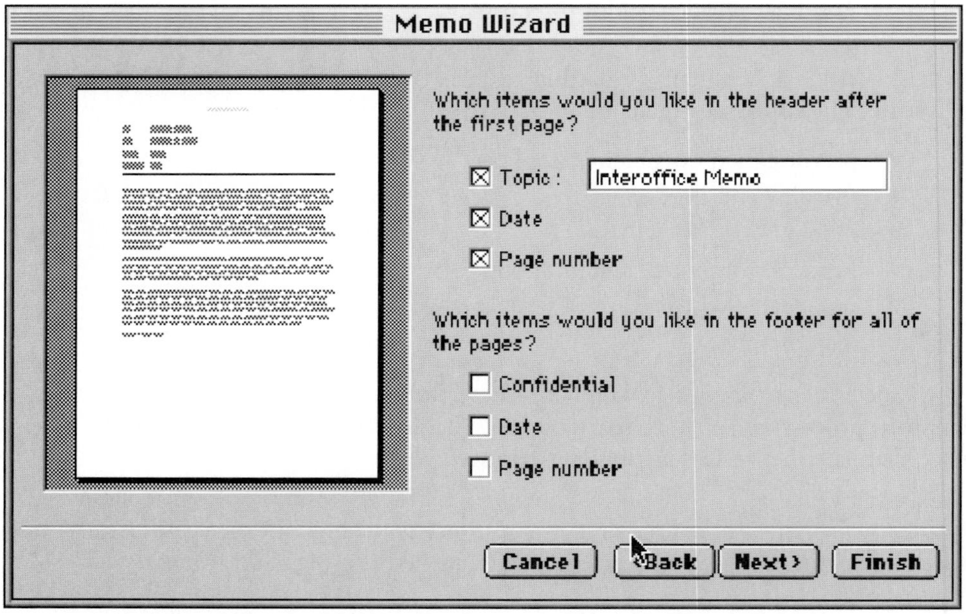

Figure 2-3 Using Microsoft's Wizard to Format an Office Memo

Oral Communication and Technology

While technology is transforming the way in which words are written, transmitted, and presented, it is having a similar impact on oral communications. *Voice mail* and *electronic meetings* offer businesspeople new tools for conducting more productive conversations and meetings.

VOICE MAIL

Voice mail is quickly replacing the answering machine as a device for handling telephone messages. Voice mail is a computer-based system that processes both incoming and outgoing telephone calls. Special computer chips and software convert the human voice into a digital recording that can be stored on the computer's magnetic disks. The recording can then be retrieved at any time for playback. In 1991 only 16 000 companies used a combination of telephone operators and voice-mail systems to handle telephone calls. By 1993 that number had climbed to 40 000 systems.[7] Today voice mail is a common method of messaging. Depending on the system, it can help in the following ways:

▼ Messages can be sent regardless of time zones or work schedules.

▼ Businesspeople can leave recorded messages for anyone who has an access code. For example, if you are out of the office and want to inform a business client when a meeting is scheduled, you can give the client your code and leave a voice-mail message.

▼ Voice mail allows messages to be recorded and saved in a mailbox. A voice-mail system can also forward messages to another location and/or to other office members.

▼ Voice-mail messages can be sent to a number of people simultaneously.

▼ Voice mail can also serve as an automated telephone operator by answering calls with a standard recording.[8]

THE PROS AND CONS   The most obvious advantage of voice mail is that it ensures that no telephone calls are missed. When Crawford Cragun, a bank officer, was temporarily unemployed, he purchased a voice-mail system that would answer all telephone calls when his line was busy. In this case, voice mail saved him from missing calls from prospective employers. Says Cragun, "I'll never use my answering machine again."[9]

Voice mail also handles messages quickly and efficiently and, if used correctly, may eliminate the annoying practice of telephone tag—two people exchanging call after call because each is missing the other in turn. A caller can leave a detailed message that the receiver can listen to later.

However, voice mail has some disadvantages. Callers forced to listen to long messages can find the system annoying. Voice mail also delivers the implicit message that the caller's time is less valuable than the recipient's. Responding to customer complaints, Ed Winguth, owner of Winguth, Donahue & Co., an executive search firm, scrapped his company's voice-mail system after only two years. "At first clients said it was terrific that we were in the twenty-first century," said Winguth. "But soon customers started saying it was too cold and annoying. Our repeat customers really got annoyed."[10]

Because voice mail can now be delivered as a public telephone network service, carriers such as AT&T Canada LDS and Stentor can make available many sophisticated features. For example, voice mail can help employers deal with diversity in the workforce—AT&T Canada LDS will provide voice mail services in several different languages. A company's voice-mail language of choice will provide workers and customers access to the company's voice mail without encountering a language barrier.

While voice mail lacks the richness of direct communication, there are some fundamental practices that should be considered to improve voice mail interactions:

▼ Consider stating and changing the date of your greeting message on a daily basis. This provides the caller with information that you are, in fact, in touch with your voice mail system.

▼ Record an appropriate announcement on your greeting message when

The computer revolution is the most advertised revolution in world history. Yet one of the funny things about it is that we probably still underestimate its impact.

Herman Kahn
American futurist

leaving for vacation or other extended periods of time when you will not be checking your voice mail for incoming messages.

▼ When leaving messages for others, state your name and phone number clearly and at a pace slow enough for transcription.

▼ State your message clearly and succinctly.

▼ Specify the action you wish to occur.

▼ Indicate when you will be available to receive a return call.

▼ Consider your tone of voice and impression that you are leaving with your message.

▼ Avoid leaving lengthy messages.[11]

ELECTRONIC ASSISTANT

The one-number, voice-activated **electronic assistant** that manages telephone communication can be accessed from any telephone. It is a telematic application that manages personal daily telephone traffic, voice mail, and conference calls. Not unlike a real administrative assistant, the electronic assistant can screen and route calls, as well as arrange future appointments and file messages by caller.

COLLABORATIVE COMMUNICATION

Log On and Let the Discussion Begin

Collaborative communication is becoming an increasingly popular technique in business, so it is not surprising that computer software that aids collaborative work is now available. Conferencing software, also known as groupware, allows you to exchange information and ideas without having to attend face-to-face meetings, video conferences, or conference calls. Using groupware products such as Lotus Notes, Collabra Share, OpenMind, TeamTalk, and TeamWare Forum, several people can collaborate over a period of days, weeks, or even months while the software builds a file and organizes messages.

The online conference begins when you post a message that requires a response. The software collects the responses, as well as any other comments participants make. The software then arranges messages by topic within a conference. Participants are free to comment on the general topic, answer a particular message, or start a new line of discussion. They can also attach document files to their responses so that the entire group can collaborate on the document and reach a consensus on changes. Lotus Notes, for example, allows documents to be distributed, discussed, revised, and finalized based on the input of a few or hundreds of conference participants.

Office-based participants are connected to the software via a local area network. Those outside the office are connected via modem. The system's portability transforms conferencing software into an effective information centre. For example, a sales manager about to visit a company for the first time can use a groupware product like Lotus Notes to access important infor-

mation, including marketing and sales reports and messages from co-workers. Messages can be sorted by author, date, or a key word. If another message is added, Lotus Notes will automatically route it to other participants.

The downside of conferencing software is that team members lose the spontaneity often found in face-to-face meetings, and not all members may be proficient at using groupware. But benefits can outweigh losses. People who are reluctant to speak up at a meeting may feel free to communicate online. And the software's role as an information centre will help harness, organize, and distribute the collective knowledge of team members, making for a more effective team effort.

Questions for Critical Thinking

1. What role does conferencing software play in computerized meetings?

2. As you saw in the opening vignette of Chapter 1, IBM believed so much in the future of Lotus Notes that it bought Lotus. How do you react to this acquisition, considering what you now know about conferencing software?

3. Describe a business situation in which conferencing software would help you to become a more effective team member.

Sources: Jerry Michalski, "Taking Notes: Why Lotus Is So Hot," *Newsweek* (June 19, 1995): 50; Glenn Rifkin, "A Skeptic's Guide to Groupware," *Forbes ASAP* (June 5, 1995): 76–91; and Jiri Weiss, "No More Meetings?" *PC World* (May 1995).

ELECTRONIC MEETINGS

Many companies use electronic meetings, including teleconferences and video conferences, to reduce travel costs and losses in productivity that result from time spent away from the office. Both types of meetings require special communication skills.

Depending on the situation, teleconferences and video conferences can be as or more effective than face-to-face meetings because they force people to be prepared. Realizing that every minute costs money, participants are motivated to be organized. However, electronic meetings are less valuable during brainstorming or creative sessions that require personal interaction.

TELECONFERENCES   When software manufacturer Computer Associates International announced its $1.7-billion acquisition of Legent Corp. in 1995, the stock market initially reacted by dropping the price of Computer Associates' stock by $2 per share. Within 45 minutes of the announcement, Computer Associates' President Sanjay Kumar began a teleconference with 300 institutional investors and analysts explaining the benefits of the merger. By the time the call ended 1 hour and 15 minutes later, the stock price had risen $5 per share. Ironically, although Kumar is the head of one of the largest technology companies in the world, he was forced to make this critical conference call from a telephone booth on the side of a major New York highway where he was stuck in traffic on the way to the office.[12]

Teleconferences, also known as **conference calls**, are telecommunication-based meetings that use ordinary telephone lines to bring together three or more people at various locations. Services offered by such commercial carriers as AT&T Canada LDS and your regional Stentor company can connect dozens of people to the same call. Teleconferences can involve local, national, or international calls.

To communicate successfully during a teleconference, always remember that you are part of a meeting involving many people. Here are some specific teleconferencing suggestions:

▼ If you are a single participant at your location during a teleconference, use a lightweight headset consisting of earphones and a built-in microphone.

A teleconference is a fast, cost-effective means of convening geographically dispersed people. In a matter of seconds, a conference call can bring together three or three thousand people anytime, anyplace.

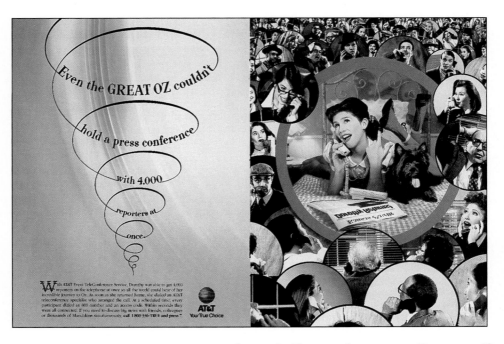

The headset allows you to move around the room with both hands free as you take notes or search through documents. It also averts fatigue during more lengthy teleconferences.

▼ Identify yourself when speaking and direct your questions or comments to people by name.

▼ Remember that comments not specifically directed to an individual will be perceived as intended for the entire group.

▼ Speak naturally as you would during any telephone call but pause for others to comment.

VIDEO CONFERENCES   **Video conferences** are an important tool in collaborative communication. For example, since 1994, Queen's University, Ontario, has successfully conducted a two-year Executive MBA program for students across Canada via national video conference.[13] Video conferencing is a telematics application that allows participants in scattered geographic locations to see and hear one another on television monitors by way of images transmitted over telephone or data lines. A typical company can reduce employee travel costs between 20 and 50 percent as a result of video conferencing.[14] Because video conferences can connect people in many different locations, participants need special skills to communicate efficiently. The following practical guidelines will help you improve communication during video conferences. Here are several to consider:

▼ If your company offers a training session, take advantage of it. Familiarize yourself with the video conference room and its technology before your first meeting.

▼ Video conferences transmitted over telephone lines have slight sound delays and images that may appear choppy. Participants must be careful listeners because these delays can make the communication more difficult.

▼ Introduce yourself and your group at the start of a meeting and identify who you are addressing throughout the conference. Remember that

although the meeting may include many participants in various locations, the monitor displays only one location at a time.

▼ Be more deliberate or restrained in your gestures. Sudden arm and hand movements, for example, may seem exaggerated when transmitted.

▼ Be aware of body language, just as you would be in a face-to-face meeting. Body language that might go unnoticed in a face-to-face meeting is magnified in a video conference.

▼ Learn to speak directly to the camera, as if it were a person.

▼ Because the same microphone that carries your voice will also pick up sounds that you may not want amplified, avoid such distractions as tapping your fingers on the table or laughing too loudly.

▼ Prepare and rehearse answers to questions that you anticipate from other participants.

▼ Prepare visual aids using large print sizes, with individual letters no smaller than half a centimetre in height, and bold, simple drawings that contain only the essentials.

▼ Consider your appearance, including clothing, grooming, cosmetics, poise, and physical position.

Table 2-2 summarizes the various communication technologies for business speakers and identifies their primary use.

Progress Check

1 Distinguish between e-mail and voice mail. What are some guidelines for the effective use of voice mail?

2. How are teleconferences used in business, and what communication guidelines help improve their effectiveness?

3. Describe how video conferences operate and how participants can use them effectively.

Table 2-2 Communication Technologies for Business Speakers

Technology	Use
Voice mail	Handle incoming and outgoing phone calls; receive, record, and send telephone messages
Teleconference	Conduct business conferences by telephone with three or more people
Video conference	Conduct electronic meetings by transmitting pictures and voices of two or more people in different locations

The Internet

The most popular method of communicating through technology is the Internet. The Internet is a global communications network that enables people and businesses to exchange information through a PC. The Internet's phenomenal growth is in stark contrast to its humble beginnings, when more than 30 years ago government authorities in the United States were studying the hypothetical problem of how to communicate successfully after a nuclear war. The issue stemmed from the fact that any central communication exchange would be an obvious and immediate target for the enemy.

WHERE DID IT COME FROM? The Rand Corporation proposal of 1964 suggested that a network should be developed with no central communications exchange. Furthermore, the proposal stated that it should be "designed from the beginning to operate in tatters."

The concept was simple: the network would be of robust design, and all of its switches and computers (*nodes*) would be of equal status. Each node would have its own authority to originate, pass, and receive data. The route that the data took to

A QUESTION OF ETHICS

Is Your E-Mail Private?

Privacy has become a major concern among those who rely on computerized systems to conduct business communications. Consider these two scenarios:

▼ After reading his firm's newly released financial report, a manager told a co-worker that he thought the report was phony. He communicated this message through the company's e-mail system. When his boss read the message, he fired the manager, citing company disloyalty.

▼ Even though an employee was given a textbook-perfect letter of dismissal, she believed that she was the victim of discrimination. Her case was proven when her lawyer uncovered earlier e-mail messages from the company president to the head of human resources. The messages—which read "Dump the bitch"—had been deleted from the computer screen, but were still in the computer's memory.

Weren't these e-mail messages private? The law is unclear. While there are laws to protect messages sent over outside agency networks such as the government, police, and commercial ISP facilities, the law does not protect messages sent through a company's internal communication system. As David Greschler, an expert on computer networks and privacy, points out, "A company can say, 'We own everything you write.' " That gives employers the right to look at your electronic mail.

Companies like Federal Express and AT&T advise employees that the company reserves the right to monitor electronic messages. According to critics, however, this approach may satisfy lawyers, but not those concerned with ethics. "While companies have been successful in the courts in winning the battle to monitor internal e-mail messages—both incoming and outgoing—there are arguments being made by lawyers based on the expectation of privacy," says Constantine Karbaliotis, a Toronto lawyer and consultant specializing in computer- and Internet-related issues. While the legal question is in review, the real question may be whether or not such monitoring is ethical. If the company has not clearly stated its intent to monitor employees' e-mail, then there may be a conflict.

Questions for Critical Thinking

1. In your opinion, is it ethical for an employer to read employees' e-mail? When you join a business organization, do you give up certain privacy rights?

2. Employers who inspect e-mail may also want to listen to voice-mail messages. Do you feel this is ethical?

3. Does informing employees that others may read their e-mail eliminate ethical concerns?

4. What would you do if you discovered that an unauthorized co-worker read your private e-mail messages?

Sources: Patrice Duggan Samuels, "Who's Reading Your E-Mail? Maybe the Boss," *New York Times,* 12 May 1996, F11; Lesley Alderman, "Safeguard Your Secrets from Your Nosey Boss," *Money* (December 1994): 31–34; Barbara Kantrowitz, "Who Holds the Key to the E-Mailbox?" *Newsweek* (December 20, 1993): 108; Robert A. Mamis, "Ensuring E-Mail Privacy," *Inc.* (July 1994): 100; and Robert A. Mamis, "The Perils of E-Mail," *Inc.* (August 1993): 38; Elizabeth Hunt, "The Downside of E-Mail: User Beware," *CGA Magazine* (May, 1997): 21.

get to the final destination was unimportant. If some nodes were busy or out of order, the data would simply take another route.[15]

Today, many business computers are linked via *local area networks* (LANs) and *wide area networks* (WANs). These networks can connect a few computers in one office or thousands of computers located in several countries throughout the world. LANs and WANs encourage communication between workers, making it easy for them to share data and ideas. For example, Dow Chemical of Fort Saskatchewan, Alberta, created a computer network to connect its other plants in Sarnia, Ontario; Midland, Michigan; and Brussels, Belgium. Since they started using the network regularly, both production development time and travel expenses have been reduced dramatically.

LANs, WANs, AND WIRE   The popularized Internet is a collection of independent computer LANs and WANs interconnected by a telecommunications network.

The network employs **routers**, which are devices that route information from one network to another. Routers allow independent networks to function as a large **virtual network** so that users of any one network can reach users of any other.

A 1996 survey conducted by Nordicity[16] revealed that 23 percent of Canadians access the Internet. While this number represents only 7 million Canadians, it also represents only 15 percent of worldwide Internet users; current estimates suggest that there are 50 million users on the Internet. Of those, 86 percent *sign on* from North America, 10 percent from Europe, and 4 percent from Asia.[17]

While there are many private commercial networks, the Internet is the largest collection of networks in the world. Some examples of Canadian networks that are attached to the Internet are:

▼ ACJNet (http://www.acjnet.org) This acronym stands for Access to Canadian Justice Network. This network provides Canadian justice and legal information and services, including legislation, publications, and discussion forums.

▼ Rock Radio Network (http://www.rockradionetwork.com) This network is an interactive service that provides the Rock Report, Rockline, and information on many more rock shows.

▼ Canadian History on the Web (http://www.interchange.ubc.ca) This is a network of sources of Canadian history, from historical documents and archives to museums.

▼ Newsworld On Line (http://www.newsworld.cbc.ca) This network provides text and video clips from the Canadian news network.

Unlike traditional voice or data networks, there is no charge for the long-distance component of the Internet. However, Internet providers will charge users a fee for local connection to the Internet, and charges may apply for access to some databases.

FUNCTIONS OF THE INTERNET

So, what can you do with the Internet? Five basic functions will allow you to optimize it:

▼ transferring data files
▼ joining discussion groups
▼ performing remote computing
▼ researching topics of interest
▼ sending and receiving electronic mail

DATA FILE TRANSFERS   DFT allows Internet users to access remote computers and retrieve data or text. Many computers connected to the Internet can access public data files anonymously and copy them free of charge.

DISCUSSION GROUPS, or news groups, are collections of users who exchange news and debate issues of interest. There are many thousands of news groups on the Internet, each for the purpose of discussing a unique topic.

REMOTE COMPUTING is one of the original concepts of the Internet that is still alive: remote computing can still be achieved by those programmers and scientists who need the power of remote computers, or by those who need to tap into large databases.

RESEARCH collective Internet functions allow students and business professionals alike to research topics of interest. Clearly, the Internet supplements more familiar resources such as books and periodicals.

ELECTRONIC MAIL

E-mail (electronic mail) is a computerized mail service that enables users to transmit messages and documents over networks from one computer to another. In many companies, employees are connected to their own Intranet, or private e-mail system. Those companies that subscribe to the Internet provide their employees with unique e-mail addresses to which both internal and external Internet users can communicate.

EXPONENTIAL GROWTH   E-mail has become the backbone of many business communication systems. In a recent study of office workers' preferences, researchers found that in most situations, e-mail is favoured over paper-based letters and memos. Workers also preferred e-mail to paper-based requests for information, document drafting, and for coordinating activities.[18]

Largely as a result of increased access, the number of people sending e-mail messages grew 50 percent in 1994 to 60 million.[19] The Electronic Messaging Association predicts that by the year 2000, there will be 108 million e-mail users exchanging 7 trillion messages a year.[20] However, the unregulated exponential growth requires caution; it suggests that organizations need to implement guidelines.

E-MAIL RISKS   Elizabeth Hunt, the Managing Director of Elizabeth Hunt & Associates, a business communications firm in Toronto, asks, "Has our ability to communicate kept up with the rate of technology?" In her research, Hunt discovered that while the Internet is becoming more popular, most companies have a surprising lack of concern about e-mail risks. Unacceptable and inconsistent e-mail practices can develop into problems that range from system overload to public relations and legal issues. Unless the organization has a policy in place, users may not know they are using the e-mail incorrectly. Unintentional e-mail problems include overuse of messages, inappropriate length of messages, failure to credit the original author, impulsive or inappropriate use, poor communication, and a misunderstanding of the single-dimension aspect of e-mail.[21] Table 2–3 provides examples and recommended solutions to various e-mail issues.

RETAIN THE MEANING AND GET IT READ   Hunt suggests that while the printed word has long been governed by widely accepted rules of etiquette, the guidelines for using e-mail are still evolving. Her advice for retaining the meaning of the message, and ensuring that it will be read, is listed here:

- ▼ Learn to use appropriately all the e-mail features.
- ▼ Clearly identify the subject so that the reader can determine if the message is important. Be similarly clear and precise in your message.
- ▼ Avoid using bold, italics, and fancy lettering, as they may be misinterpreted by the reader as denoting urgency when none is intended.
- ▼ Avoid using special formatting. Special formatting commands in e-mail word processing programs are not universal and may be garbled during transmission to readers who do not have identical programs.
- ▼ Since you would not send a printed document with spelling or grammatical errors, don't send an e-mail with these mistakes either.
- ▼ Temper the speed and efficiency of e-mail by carefully proofreading every document for accuracy, tone, and content.

Table 2-3   Guide to an E-Mail Policy

Issue	Example	Solution or Advice
Privacy	A credit-card number or personal information sent over the Internet	Do not send any information that you would not put on a postcard.
Security	A confidential password given to an unauthorized or temporary employee	No system is totally secure, but administer it with vigilance and retain tight control of access privilege .
Legal issues	An agreement made over the Internet	Legal enforcement of online agreements has not yet been tested in Canada. This is a particularly important issue when inter-provincial or international agreements are considered. Do not attempt to make binding agreements through Internet e-mail.
Copyright	Copying and forwarding company-owned material	Be aware of copyright and ownership issues. Add a copyright symbol to all corporate material intended for Internet posting.
Forgery	Revising a document and forwarding it under the original sender's name	Select a *read only* status for critical documents and retain a time-stamped record of original documents.
Gossip and rumours	A libelous message is broadcast over the corporate e-mail network	Alert users to the fact that e-mail messages are admissible as libel evidence.
Chain letters	An e-mail warning of the consequences of not passing a message on to other e-mail users	Establish a strict policy that outlines what type of e-mail is permissible.
Harassment	The distribution of offensive jokes or disparaging remarks	Establish a code of e-mail conduct that identifies unwarranted remarks and other potentially harassing practices.
Language	A casual and conversational form of e-mail communication leads to poor and unfiltered correspondence	Educate e-mail users in the style and form of acceptable correspondence. Practise the avoidance of hasty responses.
Corporate representation	The use of company e-mail to conduct private communication	Require the author to include a disclaimer stating that the views expressed in the e-mail are those of the author and not necessarily those of the company's.

Adapted from *CGA Magazine:* Hunt, E., "The Downside to E-Mail: User Beware." May, 1997, 20-24.

▼ Don't forward confidential mail to others without obtaining permission.
▼ Avoid sending highly emotional, sensitive, or controversial information.
▼ Do not burden the receivers with unnecessary information. Use a more conventional method of communication for long, complex documents.

Implementing suggestions like these will be easier if you remind yourself that a person—not just a computer—is on the receiving end of your electronic message.

ELECTRONIC BULLETIN BOARDS   Much like their cork-board predecessors, **electronic bulletin boards** are public message centres that appear on computer networks. While e-mail is intended for one recipient, electronic bulletin board messages are intended for anyone and everyone with access to the network. The Internet has a collection of electronic bulletin boards, known as the *Usenet*, which are organized by subject categories. Electronic bulletin boards are also an integral part of such commercial networks as CompuServe, Prodigy, America Online, and Delphi.

You can gain access to the Internet through a direct connection or through an *Internet Service Provider* (ISP) such as Netcom, or your local cable or telephone service provider. Commercial communication services such as CompuServe and America Online will provide Internet services as well as such subsidiary services such as news pages, search engines, and management software. Once you have access, *search engines* and *navigators* can be used to research the wealth of information stored on the Internet. These search engines are further discussed in Appendix III.

TELEMATIC APPLICATIONS

Telebanking, teleshopping, teleconferencing, video conferencing, and electronic commerce are but a few examples of telematic developments that influence both public and private business environments. Through computer, telecommunication, and database advancements, industry has developed intelligent applications that integrate and take advantage of these powerful technologies.

OTHER TECHNOLOGIES

PERIPHERAL TECHNOLOGY   Computer printers, photocopiers, fax machines, and scanners can duplicate original documents. Printers and photocopiers have been familiar fixtures in business offices for many years. Although fax machines began appearing in offices only within the past decade, almost all businesses use them. Scanners, the newest technology, are quickly growing in popularity. So are all-in-one office products that perform printer, photocopier, fax machine, and scanner functions within a single unit.

DATABASES   Many organizations create custom **databases**—sets of logically related computer files that can be accessed for different purposes. For example, a database may contain the names, addresses, telephone numbers, and purchasing activity of all past and current customers. The data can be output as lists, reports, personalized letters, or mailing labels. A report of last month's sales for each salesperson in a specific geographic region can be retrieved almost immediately from a database.

Many Web sites offer **online databases**—commercially owned information sources that a user can subscribe to through a PC. As you will see in Chapter 11, online databases can be invaluable sources of business research. For example, you can obtain economic and business information through Dow Jones News-Retrieval, Nexis, and CompuServe.

Although using an online database can be expensive (fees for many services are based on connection time), many firms subscribe because they feel that the available information is an essential business tool. Information can be accessed faster and more efficiently than through conventional means—making employees more productive. Generally, online database computer searches are also more extensive than conventional compilations of information.

PRACTICAL TIPS

Using Voice Mail Effectively

The following practices have helped many companies establish policies for voice-mail systems. Through these practices, companies should ask the fundamental question, "Do our customers *really* need to use voice mail in order to contact us?"

▼ Consider your audience before deciding whether or not to use voice mail. Ask yourself whether your callers would be uncomfortable speaking to a computer (many people are), and keep in mind that people who use rotary phones will be excluded, as voice-mail technology requires Touch-Tone service.

▼ Keep messages short and to the point. Remember that callers will hear the same message every time they call. It is also important to minimize the menu of choices. For example, most systems allow callers to choose an option at any time without being forced to listen to the entire menu before making a selection.

▼ Consider having a receptionist as the first point of contact, who may then pass the caller to an employee's voice mailbox.

INTEGRATED OFFICE SUITES   Computers use five primary categories of business software: word processing, databases, presentation graphics, communications, and spreadsheets. Although each category started as a stand-alone software product, packaged and sold separately, in the business world they are usually used in an integrated fashion. For example, a manager could use a section from a word processing document in a presentation slide. A spreadsheet software program allows a worker to manipulate numerical information to determine how changes affect outcomes, such as how financial changes affect profits or sales, and then produce a report.

Recognizing that users want their computers and software to imitate actual business styles, major software developers have introduced *integrated office suites*, which bundle together all the primary business software. For example, Microsoft's Office Professional contains Word (word processing), Excel (spreadsheet), PowerPoint (presentation graphics), Mail (communications), and Access (database management).

Progress Check

1. List several communication guidelines that apply when using electronic mail.
2. What are electronic bulletin boards and how might they function in business?
3. Describe the functions of online databases and the Internet.

Portable Communication Technologies

Despite the convenience of electronic meetings, business travel is often essential. Fortunately, technology can help improve communication for business travellers and telecommuters. No longer are travellers forced to be out of touch for long periods of time. Rather, they can be connected anytime and nearly anyplace through such devices as wireless telephones, pagers, and portable computers. An example of how pervasive these personal communication services are is Boeing's new 292-passenger aircraft—the 777—that offers a workstation with full communication capabilities, including ports for portable computers and built-in wireless telephones.[22]

WIRELESS TELEPHONES AND PAGERS

If you don't already have a wireless telephone, chances are you've seen someone using one. In ten short years, the number of North Americans with wireless (previously known as cellular) telephone service grew from only 2200 people to more than 18 million. Examples of the propagation is evidenced by the many rental cars that are now equipped with wireless telephones. One luxury car company, British Leyland, builds the Jaguar XJ8 with a wireless telephone as standard equipment. Wireless telephones have also become common on scheduled airlines as a personal service to travellers.[23]

CELLULAR PHONES   When wireless telephones were launched in Canada in 1985, they used analogue transmission, which allowed a person to carry a portable telephone and make and receive calls within a certain service area known as a cell site—hence the old term of **cell**, or **cellular phone**.

DIGITAL PHONES   In 1992, Rogers Cantel Inc. became the first company in Canada to launch digital transmission for wireless calls. This early digital service enabled channels to carry more traffic, and enhanced both the capabilities and security of the call.

PCS PHONES   **Personal Communication Services**, or PCS, combines all of the benefits that wireless communication has to offer through an extraordinary suite of enhanced features and services designed to increase the users' productivity and efficiency, such as:

Portable wireless telephones enable users to remain productive when out of the office.

▼ Calling Line Identification and Visual Call Waiting, which enable users to manage incoming calls by showing the number of the caller before they answer the call;

▼ Voice mail, which ensures that users never miss a call;

▼ PCS messaging, which enables users to receive numeric and text messages right on the display screen of the PCS telephone;

▼ E-mail messaging, which provides a dedicated e-mail address for the PCS phone to enable text messages to be sent directly to the display screen from any e-mail service with an Internet access.

Industry analysts predict that the 14 percent of Canadians who currently use these services will grow to 40 percent by the year 2005.[24]

Wireless telephones so enhance productivity today that Stuart F. Crump Jr., a columnist for *Mobile Office* magazine, recommends that wireless telephone users even take advantage of travel time to return the bulk of their telephone messages and save only the most important messages for the office. He also suggests that users should "quit waiting around the office at the end of the day for the important telephone call. Forward it to your car telephone and head for home. Shift that waiting time to commuting time." Because the cost of wireless calls remains relatively high, Crump also recommends encouraging brevity by telling the call recipient that the call is being made on a wireless telephone.[25]

PAGERS   To keep in contact while away from your office, give people your pager number. **Pagers** are small, battery-powered devices that signal telephone messages and allow you to stay in touch with your office and clients while on the road at far less cost than wireless telephones.

Instead of the traditional (and sometimes annoying) beeps, many pagers signal by means of vibrations or tiny blinking lights. Some models allow callers to enter the telephone numbers where they can be reached. The caller's number is instantly transmitted to your pager's display screen. *Alphanumeric pagers*, better known as *voice pagers*, allow callers to leave short messages, such as "Trip cancelled," "Kelly says yes," or "Call Tom. 555-1234." Some systems combine paging and voice mail to connect callers to your voice mailbox and alert you when the message is complete. Businesspeople often carry both wireless telephones and pagers to take advantage of lower combined operating costs. When your pager signals a call from a specific telephone number, you can thus decide whether to call back immediately from your wireless telephone or wait to use a regular telephone.[26]

PORTABLE COMPUTERS

Just about anything you can do with a desktop system can now be done with lightweight **portable computers**, powered either by rechargeable batteries or connected to a power outlet with special AC adapters. Portables can be used while waiting in airline terminals, riding in cars or trains, working in hotel rooms, or sitting on your patio at home.

PORTABLE COMPUTERS   Portables come in many different shapes and sizes, with most falling into one of the following categories:

- ▼ *notebooks*, which usually weigh between 2.3 and 3.5 kilograms
- ▼ *sub-notebooks*, which weigh from 1.5 to 1.8 kilograms
- ▼ *palmtops*, weighing about 0.5 kilograms
- ▼ *personal digital assistants (PDAs)*, weighing about 0.45 kilograms

A computer isn't smart enough to make a mistake. Computers are dumb. Fast and efficient and dumb. No computer ever had an idea.

IBM advertisement

This technology, when connected to portable printers, makes it possible to produce finished products while away from the office. Geoff Poli, sales director of Reed Exhibition Companies, spends two to three weeks a month travelling and always takes his portable computer with him. Having access to a computer has helped Poli avoid potentially serious business problems. He recalls, "I was going to be presenting to a small group using my portable [computer] … As I was sitting in the client's lobby, I decided to take one last look. I found a few typos in the text, so I quickly fixed them and stored the new pages into the presentation before the client came to get me for the meeting."[27]

PERSONAL DIGITAL ASSISTANTS offer maximum portability but have limited memory. While they have been used primarily as schedulers and telephone/address books in the past,[28] users of PDAs now enjoy enhanced services such as the ability to connect and communicate with the Internet, interpret cursive writing made on the PDA screen, and many other powerful features. A summary of portable communication technologies can be found in Table 2–4.

Telecommuting

WORKERS WHO TRAVEL   Some 9.1 million North Americans are **telecommuters**—workers who travel to and from their jobs by way of such communications technology as e-mail, voice mail, teleconferencing, answering machines, and telephone call-forwarding.[29] As telematic applications become more sophisticated, more companies are turning to telecommuting as a viable working arrangement. For example, by allowing employees with disabilities to work at home, telecommuting

Table 2-4   Portable Communication Technologies

Technology	Description
Cellular telephone	An analogue wireless telephone used within cell-site range
Digital telephone	A digital wireless telephone with calling-line features and many more secure channels
PCS telephone	Personal Communication System—a wireless digital telephone that provides all calling-line features, voice mail, paging, and an e-mail gateway to the Internet
Pager	A small battery-powered device that signals telephone messages
Notebook computer	Weighing between 2.3 and 3.4 kilograms; used for all the same functions as a desktop computer
Palmtop computer	Weighing about half a kilogram; has a reduced memory and application capability but performs many of the functions of a desktop computer
Personal Digital Assistant	Able to fit into shirt pocket, the battery-powered PDA has limited memory and no moving parts but can run scaled-down desktop applications and maintain schedulers and telephone books downloaded from a desktop computer; also has Internet e-mail capabilities

 NTERVIEW   Back to Basics with Technology

Teresa Lindsey, Office Automation Consultant

In nearly every corporation, entry-level businesspeople are expected to know how to use computers to create, revise, and design documents, research information, and go online. With technology changing every day, being comfortable with these tasks is no small accomplishment. Teresa Lindsey, an office automation consultant and a "personal trainer" in microcomputer hardware and software, recognizes the challenge of mastering communication technologies as she advises individual executives and such corporate clients as Major League Baseball and "Big Six" certified public accounting firms. Although technology is Lindsey's business, she believes that becoming a skillful technician cannot mask deficiencies in clear writing, speaking, and thinking.

Question: What communication technology skills are absolutely essential for an entry-level business career?

Answer: Companies expect new employees to be familiar with basic word processing software such as Microsoft Word and WordPerfect. Windows-based packages are user-friendly and have similar interfaces, so once you learn one package, you'll be able to learn others fairly easily. The ability to navigate online services is also important, since more and more research is being conducted via the Internet and such online services as CompuServe and America Online.

Question: Can businesspeople starting their first job expect technical help from their companies and co-workers?

Answer: Depending on their size, many organizations have training sessions to help people get acclimated to different software packages. Large companies also have "help desks" to deal with software and hardware problems. On a person-

helps companies comply with the Employment Equity Act, a federal law that requires businesses to accommodate the disabled.

VIRTUAL OFFICE The development of *virtual offices*—offices located wherever employees happen to be—have added to the number of employees who work outside the confines of an office building. Portable computers, wireless telephones, portable printers, fax machines, and pagers make any space a virtual office—your home, car, or a customer's office. By 1995, AT&T had 35 000 telecommuters and 12 000 workers in virtual offices. These employees represent nearly 20 percent of the AT&T workforce.[30]

OVERCOMING PROBLEMS Despite the advantages of telecommuting for both workers and companies, personal communications and long-term career success may suffer when people spend too much time out of the office. Personnel consultant James E. Challenger explains:

Man is still the most extraordinary computer of all.

John F. Kennedy
35th President of the United States

"Far from the centre of power, telecommuters can't greet the boss personally each morning or converse casually over coffee during a co-worker's birthday celebration. Personal relationships and personal growth also can't occur when all communication is electronic. This keeps telecommuters stalled at their present level, and professionals working at the office are more likely to win promotions."[31]

---

to-person level, people seem to love to help with technical questions. I've seen workers demonstrate document prototypes to less experienced colleagues. The "expert" takes the beginner through the ropes of retrieving the prototype from the word processing software and filling in the blanks.

Question: What should a businessperson know about the Internet?

Answer: First, that it is changing. The Internet of today is not the Internet of tomorrow. When I say tomorrow, I literally mean that radical changes are taking place every 24 hours. In the past several years the Internet has evolved from an electronic medium for educators and scientists into a commercial entity for online business.

Businesspeople also have to realize that the Internet requires the right hardware. Just as you wouldn't get on a freeway with a bicycle, you shouldn't try to access the Internet with a computer or modem that is too slow for the environment. Without the right equipment, the Internet will lead to endless frustration because of the time you have to wait for a response.

Question: Would you dare to make any projections about the changes in communication technology that will take place over the next five years?

Answer: Just one. I predict an explosion in the category of software known as groupware. With more and more companies dismantling the physical boundaries that define traditional office space and embracing the concept of the virtual office, people in one city are working with people in other cities on complex documents and projects. Groupware lets these teams collaborate without being in the same room.

Question: If you were to give students one piece of advice about communication technologies, what would that advice be?

Answer: To remember that technologies are a complement to, not a replacement for, basic communication skills. Technologies cannot replace effective writing, speaking, and analysis. They are tools that augment your ability to think and create.

Source: Interview with Teresa Lindsey.

To overcome career anxieties and feelings of isolation, telecommuters must develop strategies to make themselves more visible. The following suggestions will help telecommuters participate more fully in office-based operations:

▼ Attend meetings and special functions whenever possible. Meetings give you a high profile in front of a large group of people.

▼ Submit reports personally rather than through e-mail. If you've been working on a major project for a month, don't use the computer to transmit it.

▼ Put yourself on an electronic mailing list for office memos. Even the most routine memos allow you to stay in touch with changes in the company.

▼ Become part of your firm's voice-mail system to avoid missing business calls.

▼ Use the telephone to stay in touch by calling the office once or twice a day.[32]

Telecommuters should also keep their home and office work separate. Home is home and work is work, and even though you work at home, try to maintain that distinction by creating a separate work space, setting definite work hours, and eliminating interruptions.[33]

Progress Check

1. How are wireless telephones, pagers, and portable computers changing the nature of business communication?
2. What is the relationship between virtual offices and portable business communication technologies?
3. Do you think you would enjoy telecommuting to a job? Explain your answer.

What's Ahead

In Chapter 3 we move from discussion of communication technologies to person-to-person communication in the context of a diverse global marketplace. Specifically, we will examine the challenges of communicating with diverse co-workers and customers in a world marketplace.

STUDENT RESOURCE CENTRE

Summary of Chapter Objectives

1. *List the benefits of communication technology.*

Communication technology has dramatically improved the speed and efficiency of sending and receiving messages. It has also fostered access to the global marketplace. Efficiency is improved by the contributions of computer technology, data management, word processing, and telecommunications.

2. *Identify the six communication functions performed by computers.*

Computers facilitate communication by storing information on magnetic disks and other electronic media rather than on paper. Information is easily retrieved from the computer's memory and projected on the computer screen to be analyzed and edited. Because the computer can display information in different forms, various types of analysis and presentation are possible. Hard copies with different visual features are produced on the computer printer. Finally, when configured correctly, a computer's telecommunications capability enables users to transmit and receive messages among computers in the same network.

3. *Explain the benefits of writing with word processing software.*

Writing with word processing software helps with note taking, document organization, drafting and development, revising and editing, proofreading, and formatting. Using word processing software requires learning a series of simple commands and using them appropriately.

4. *Outline the ways in which computers are used as telecommunications tools.*

Computers operate as telecommunications tools in three primary ways. They send and receive e-mail messages directed to specific individuals. They display public electronic bulletin board messages, and they transmit online databases that contain valuable sources of business information. Computers connected to the Internet offer users access to a wide range of communication and research services.

5. *Explain how computer, telecommunication, and database technology come together to provide the Internet.*

Individuals and company users of personal computers are connected via local area and wide area networks (LANs and WANs), enabling them to communicate and share information (data). When these networks are further connected through the Public Switched Telephone Network, a global community of users can communicate and share information. The network through which the global community communicates is known as the Internet.

6. *Identify the features, advantages, and disadvantages of voice mail.*

Voice mail is a telecommunications-based voice-processing computer system that handles incoming and outgoing telephone calls. Using voice mail, you can record messages for specific individuals or groups, and save messages in your private voice mailbox. The voice-processing computer system can also function as an automated attendant. Although it often eliminates the game of telephone tag, voice mail tends to depersonalize telephone conversations, and so special consideration is necessary to use voice mail effectively.

7. *Describe how to conduct electronic meetings via teleconferences and video conferences.*

Teleconferences, or conference calls, bring together three or more people at different locations by means of ordinary telephone lines. Video conferences allow participants in scattered geographic locations to see and hear one another on television monitors. Although electronic meetings share similarities with both ordinary telephone calls and face-to-face meetings, they require special communication skills.

8. *Explain how wireless telephones, pagers, and portable computers affect business travel.*

Wireless telephones, pagers, and portable computers enable business travellers to stay in constant touch with their offices. Using these technologies, businesspeople can send and receive e-mail, voice mail, and faxes, and can use word processing and database software.

9. *Describe telecommuting and how to overcome its pitfalls.*

Telecommuters work out of their homes or from satellite offices and communicate with headquarters via such sophisticated technologies as e-mail, voice mail, and teleconferencing. Although telecommuting generally improves productivity, it tends to place telecommuters outside of the communication mainstream. To overcome this problem, telecommuters should attend scheduled office meetings, present completed assignments personally rather than electronically, and stay in close touch with managers and co-workers by phone.

Review and Discussion Questions

1. What advantages does communication technology offer to business? *(Ch. Obj. 1)*

2. Name the major communication functions that computers serve in business. *(Ch. Obj. 2)*

3. Describe the benefits to be gained from writing with word processing software. *(Ch. Obj. 2)*

4. Describe how businesses and individuals can use computers as a telecommunication tool. *(Ch. Obj. 4)*

5. Explain the concept of connecting LANs and WANs together to build the global Internet service. *(Ch. Obj. 5)*

6. What is voice mail? Explain its advantages and disadvantages. *(Ch. Obj. 6)*

7. Distinguish between teleconferences and video conferences. What are their advantages and disadvantages? *(Ch. Obj. 7)*

8. How have communication technologies such as wireless telephones, pagers, and portable computers changed business travel? *(Ch. Obj. 8)*

9. What is telecommuting? Why is it a growing trend in business? *(Ch. Obj. 9)*

10. Which communication technologies make telecommuting possible? *(Ch. Obj. 1,9)*

Application Exercises

1. For the next week, keep a written list of the types of communication technology that you use. Try to imagine what you would have done if that technology had not been available. How would it have changed the nature of your communication? Would you have communicated differently? Would you have been able to communicate at all? *(Ch. Obj. 1)*

2. Thanks to its international marketing and overseas sales of athletic clothing, CanukSport, which began with two employees, now employs 26. Like many growing companies, CanukSport is discovering that growth makes it harder for staff members to communicate with each other. Due to space limitations, for example, CanukSport employees occupy three separate floors of one downtown building. Also, many employees travel abroad for weeks at a time on business trips. You've noticed that employees who travel are forced to spend valuable time reading their mail and catching up on the latest developments when they return to the office. You've also observed that employees in one department don't always know what those in other departments are doing. You suggest to Jim Mason, CanukSport's founder and CEO, that the firm needs to install an e-mail system. Jim is skeptical. "I've never even touched a computer," he says, "and I've gotten along just fine. Besides, look at how much the software costs!" Nonetheless, Jim respects your opinion. He asks you to write a proposal outlining the advantages and disadvantages of electronic mail and describing how CanukSport would use an e-mail system. Write this proposal. *(Ch. Obj. 4)*

3. John, an account executive at CanukSport, is angry with Lauren, another account executive. Apparently, Lauren called on one of John's clients and gave him information that differed from what John had told the client previously. John found out what happened only because the client happened to mention it to him during a telephone call. Seething, John immediately called Lauren's office, only to find that she has gone on a two-week business trip. Lauren's secretary does not know if Lauren knew that the client in question was John's customer.

John is still furious, however, so he logs onto the e-mail system and types the following message:

LAUREN—WHAT DO YOU THINK YOU'RE DOING???!!!
APPARENTLY YOU'RE TRYING TO STEAL MY CUSTOMERS AND MAKE ME LOOK BAD. WELL, IT'S NOT GOING TO WORK! I'VE TOLD THIS GUY THAT HE'S STILL MY CUSTOMER, NO MATTER WHAT YOU TOLD HIM. DON'T EVER GO BEHIND MY BACK AGAIN!!!
JOHN

John sends this message to Lauren's mailbox for her to see the next time she checks her mail. For good measure, he also sends the memo to all other CanukSport employees, including Lauren's boss.

Is John using e-mail appropriately? Explain your answer. How would you suggest he communicate with Lauren about this situation? *(Ch. Obj. 4)*

4. CanukSport decides to upgrade its telephone lines to allow for teleconferencing. At the same time, it adds video conference equipment to its largest meeting room. You suggest to CEO Jim Mason that CanukSport's staff might need some training in how to conduct effective teleconferences and video conferences.

"Why?" asks Jim. "Isn't it just like talking on the telephone?" You take a deep breath and decide that you'd better write a memo to all employees that summarizes instructions and guidelines for making the best use of the new teleconferencing equipment. Write this memo. *(Ch. Obj. 7)*

5. You've been assigned to an important new project at your company, and things are going well. Now your boss has asked you to make a 20-minute presentation to the board of directors in which you will explain the importance of this project to the company, summarize the progress so far, and describe what still needs to be done. Because the project is fairly technical, you will have to make sure that your

points get across even to board members who don't understand the technical details. You want to give a great presentation to impress the board.

Describe how you could use the various technologies discussed in this chapter to prepare and present an effective presentation. *(Ch. Obj. 1–8)*

6. Recently, Northern Beecham's pharmaceutical division handed out portable computers and portable printers to all of its 1800 salespeople. Managers estimate that each salesperson now averages 1.5 more sales calls per week. Explain this result. Relate Northern Beecham's experience to the discussion in this chapter. *(Ch. Obj. 1, 8)*

7. Communication technologies have many positive uses. Take computerized pharmaceutical databases, for example. A nationwide database allows prescriptions to be filled quickly, day or night, even if you're not in your hometown. Many people, however, feel that these technologies can also have negative effects, such as a potential invasion of privacy.

Write a one-page essay discussing the ethical questions raised by communication technologies. Describe the ways in which computers and communication technologies might affect privacy. Do you feel that the potential risks are worth the advantages? Explain your answer. *(Ch. Obj. 1–8)*

8. At last you are going to fulfill a lifelong dream: starting your own business. A local bank is offering small business loans to help entrepreneurs purchase communication equipment needed to run their companies. The bank's corporate loan officer has agreed to meet with you to discuss a possible loan. She asks you to bring to the meeting a written business proposal summarizing the equipment you would like to buy, how your company would use these various technologies, and why they would help you to operate your business more effectively and efficiently.

Think about how you would use the technologies discussed in this chapter to start, manage, and market your company—not to mention providing your good or service, billing customers, and managing your cash flow. Then write the proposal. *(Ch. Obj. 1–8)*

9. Three employees at CanukSport have asked the company to let them telecommute to their jobs from home. Angela, who heads up the human resources department, is intrigued by the idea but doesn't know much about it. She knows, however, that you're taking a business communications course in which you have discussed this trend, so she pays you a visit. "Is this telecommuting a good idea?" she asks. "I'm afraid we might lose touch with these employees and not know what they're really working on. What are the pros and cons of telecommuting for an employer?"

What would your answer be? How can an employer stay informed about telecommuters' performance? *(Ch. Obj. 9)*

10. Based on your recommendations, CanukSport gives these employees the go-ahead to telecommute. The employees come to you for advice about what communication technologies they should have in their home offices. What would you advise? *(Ch. Obj. 1, 9)*

11. Interview a businessperson about how his or her organization uses the various technologies discussed in this chapter. Which technologies does the company use? Which seem most useful? Which employees have access to these tools? For instance, if the firm uses electronic mail, do all of its employees belong to the e-mail system? How did the firm decide which workers to include? Does the company use any of these tools to communicate internationally? What advantages and disadvantages does this person see in using communication technology? How have these technologies changed business procedures? Take notes during the interview and write a report summarizing what you learn. *(Ch. Obj. 1–8)*

12. For each of the following business situations, describe what type(s) of communication technology, if any, you would recommend as the most effective. Explain your recommendations. *(Ch. Obj. 1–8)*

(a) A company president wants to thank every one of her 1072 employees for their hard work after the company winds up its most profitable year ever.

(b) The company's president wants to send every employee instructions explaining the new and rather complicated procedures for accessing the company's customer database.

(c) A marketing manager wants to discuss an important sale with a possible new client in Japan.

(d) The vice president for human resources decides to hold a meeting that includes all eight of the company's vice presidents, who are geographically dispersed in North America, Asia, and Europe. The purpose of the meeting is to discuss plans for a new company-wide training program on cultural diversity.

ACT: Applied Communication Techniques

Begin by referring to the sections up to and including Pronouns in Appendix II, then correct the grammar, spelling, and usage errors in the following sentences. Check your answers in Appendix V.

1. An employee of west edmonton mall wants their parking stall located outside the nearest entrance to their job location.
2. Although Ross and Karrie both used Burton snowboards, he used a different length.
3. Every figure skater and spead skater have suffered bruises from falling on the ice.
4. Every member of the sales team expressed his opinion regarding the quotas.
5. Stephan and me attended every meeting held for the volunteers in the Special Olympics.
6. The award for the volunteers whom made the greatest contribution was given to Stephan and I.
7. The hockey coach asked Wayne and I to travel to victoria to work with a Junior team.
8. At the 1998 Olympics, the winner of the mens' figure skating was me.
9. The committee must review it's policy regarding foriegn languages.
10. The athletes who's performances were successful were rewarded with Olympic metals.

Building Your Research Skills

Selecting and buying the right computer can be a difficult—but very important—decision, both for businesses and for individuals. This is true for the other communications tools discussed in this chapter as well. Suppose that your employer put you in charge of purchasing new technology tools. How would you decide what to buy? Let's find out.

Your instructor will divide the class into teams, each of which will research a particular type of communication technology discussed in this chapter, such as PCs, PDAs, word processing software, database software, fax machines, wireless telephones, office suite software, computer printers, and photocopiers. Each group will identify the most popular brands in its technology category and compare prices. Other factors to research include reliability, repair history, strengths and weaknesses, and common uses in business. Something else to find out: If the equipment malfunctioned or you couldn't understand the instructions, who would you call for help? Take notes and be prepared to discuss your findings with the other members of your team.

Building Your Teamwork Skills

Meet with your team members from the previous exercise and discuss what you learned about your particular communication technology. Working as a group, draft a report that summarizes what to look for in purchasing this equipment. What are the advantages and disadvantages of the major brands? Which brand(s) would you recommend and why? Appoint a spokesperson to present your report to the class.

Building Your Technology Skills

The Internet is revolutionizing business communication. One way to understand the Internet's business potential is to visit business Web sites and analyze how firms are promoting their goods and services and communicating with customers.

Visit two of the following sites. Observe how the sites communicate with their customers and other visitors.

AT&T Canada http://www.attcanada.com
Canadian Airlines http://www.cdnair.ca

Tilley Endurables http://www.tilley.com
Bombardier, Inc. http://bombardier.com

Write a one-to-two page paper in which you discuss the sites you visited. Include in your discussion the following:

▼ How does each company use the Internet to communicate with customers? What services does each site offer? Why would a customer want to visit the site? Does it foster a relationship?

▼ How does each company use the new media? Is the media more or less effective than traditional communication methods? Is each site informative, easy to use, and persuasive? Would customers want to visit the site again? Why or why not?

Weblinks Internet Resources for this Chapter

Word Processing
http://www.newcastle.edu.au/department/ar/
architecture/study-areas/PS-Computing/LUP220/
LUP220P1.html

Intranets
http://ireland.iol.ie/.ie/.ie3/beyond.htm

Voice Mail
http://www.123sortit.com/BO/mail/
voice-mail.html

Computer Conferencing
http://www.soi.city.ac.uk/homes/ec567/
comco.html

Monitoring Employees' Electronic Communications
http://aftab.com/privacy.htm

A Guide to Telecommuting
http://www.pacbell.com/products/business/
general/telecommuting/tcguide/tc-1.html

CASE STUDIES

CORPORATE CASE:

Checkfree Corp. and Libby Perszyk Kathman: E-Mail Communication Is Crucial to the 21st Century

Checkfree Corp. trains its customer service reps in both phone and e-mail etiquette, and with good reason. Two-thirds of the department's calls come by e-mail.

The company provides an electronic bill-payment service. That so many people prefer e-mail speaks to the changing face of customer service.

Checkfree's customers asked for and got a direct e-mail connection to the company. Without having to log on to a commercial service, customers can ask why a cheque was posted a day early—and receive a reply within 24 hours.

Similarly, a package-design firm was nudged into the digital age by a major client. "Procter & Gamble stressed the advantages of e-mail," says Nancy Goodfellow, an account executive at Libby Perszyk Kathman. Her Microsoft Mail address list includes a score of managers at P&G's Oil of Olay and Folgers brands. "I send e-mail to my clients at least 30 times a day," she says.

That e-mail connection was crucial when the Folgers staff recently requested a quick turnaround on uncontracted work. "There was no funding for it," she explains. The account exec quickly e-mailed her proposed budget to P&G, and within 24 hours the client had approved it.[34]

Questions and Applications

1. How has e-mail affected the communication process at Checkfree Corp. and at Libby Perszyk Kathman?

2. What communication challenges, if any, do you think Checkfree Corp. and Libby Perszyk Kathman will face due to their e-mail technology?

CORPORATE CASE:
Résumé Technology

Have you ever applied for a job, only to be told, "Thanks, we'll keep your résumé on file"? Most likely, you assumed that the only file your résumé would ever see was a wastebasket sitting next to someone's desk.

While this situation is no doubt frustrating for you, the job candidate, it may also be frustrating for the company to which you have applied. Many firms receive tens of thousands of résumés every year, and keeping track of the paper deluge can be a nightmare.

Technology comes to the rescue! Recently, Johnson & Johnson installed a new computer system that scans résumés and stores the information in an electronic database called a résumé bank. Now Johnson & Johnson's recruiters can search the database for applicants who fit specific job guidelines. LouAnn Miller, director of professional recruiting at Prudential Insurance Co., is also sold on this approach. "If everyone was in résumé banks," she is convinced, "it would make things so much easier." Computers are also moving into other aspects of job hunting. If you apply for a job with Nortel in Calgary, you might never meet with a human interviewer; you'll fill out an application directly on a computer screen.

Promising though these developments may be, job application and résumé tracking technologies still leave something to be desired. The devices that "scan" résumés into the computer, for example, often have trouble with coloured paper. Fancy details such as unusual typefaces and underlining can also confuse them.

However, perhaps the biggest advantage posed by technology is the promise of fair treatment for all applicants. "You can easily keep race and gender information," explains Edward Gagen, a recruiting manager at Johnson & Johnson, "and companies can use such data to maintain culturally diverse workforces." Individual companies are also using the Internet to match job seekers with jobs. Web sites sponsored by companies as well as government agencies, recruiters, and non-profit organizations include résumé-retrieval databases. These Web sites also post jobs and offer career counselling and tips on effective résumé writing. In addition, as you will see in Chapter 17, online services, such as CompuServe, enable job seekers to distribute their résumés to companies and employment agencies located anywhere in the world.

The availability of these high-technology career services places the burden on job seekers to know where to look on the Internet and how to manoeuvre electronically when they get there. A good place to start is The Monsterboard job search site on the World Wide Web. The Monsterboard is an international job search service with more than 50 000 positions posted. Many Canadian organizations post opportunities on The Monsterboard.[35]

Questions and Applications

1. How are computerized technologies changing the job application process?

2. What are the advantages and disadvantages of this trend for job applicants?

3. What are the advantages and disadvantages of these technologies from an employer's perspective?

4. Using these technologies removes some of the "human" element from hiring; it also makes the hiring process more objective. Do you feel this trend is positive or negative? Explain your answer.

Communication Challenges in a Diverse World

Chapter Objectives

After studying this chapter, you should be able to:

1. Explain how culture, ethnocentrism, and language differences affect communication.

2. Contrast the communication differences between low-context and high-context cultures.

3. List the key elements in successful written and oral communication across national boundaries.

4. Identify the major demographic changes that are transforming the Canadian workplace and marketplace.

5. Explain the differences between communication styles of men and women and describe how to deal with sexual harassment.

6. Describe the special communication needs of older people and persons with disabilities.

7. Explain the nature and importance of diversity training.

Interdependence recreates the world in the image of a global village.

Marshall McLuhan
Canadian communication theorist

Communicating within the Walls of a Canadian Prison

Communication between incarcerated people is not something that most of us are familiar with; however, the lines of communication that exist behind our Canadian prison walls represent those belonging to another Canadian minority. "On an average day, in 1993–94, some 32 803 inmates were in custody."[1]

A prison, especially a maximum security institute where many of the inmates are serving lengthy sentences, acts as a community. It has structure, laws and policies, management citizens, living and dining quarters, and locations of work and recreation. And like any community, it has a communication system that networks its constituents.

Effective communication between staff members is especially important since the staff may be exposed to extremes of violence, depression, and disruption that require the support of staff, peers, or specialists such as an institute psychologist, chaplain, or warden. Jack Linklater, warden of the Edmonton Institution, a maximum security prison for male offenders, states that one of the keys to successful prison management is building a team with excellent leadership and effective communication skills.

What we consider to be trivial events become major ones to inmates who face years, perhaps even life, in the same institution. Therefore, Linklater has adopted a mediation plan where two inmates and one staff member have been trained to communicate with, and mediate between, angry inmates. This type of communication serves to defuse potentially explosive situations.

Central to the successful communication of the Edmonton Institution is the Inmate Committee. Where Inmate Committees exist, most prison administrators turn to them for advice and counsel on all matters. Administrators believe this is an important mechanism for ensuring that they are communicating with all the inmates in the prison population. In fact, administrators rely upon the Inmate Committee to determine if the prison is in a stable state.

The need to communicate effectively with inmate populations is a critical factor in successful prison administration. Therefore, it is essential that the members of the Inmate Committee are relatively free of coercion by the inmate hierarchy. To ensure this, Warden Linklater has set strict criteria for inmates who wish to be elected by their peers to represent their unit on the Committee. Elected inmates must be following their correctional plan; they must be employed full time within the prison; they must be participating in programs related to the correction plan;

and they must be willing to volunteer and meet during non-employment, non-program time. In this way, Warden Linklater is attempting to discourage influential inmates from contaminating the election process.

Meetings between the Inmate Committee and the administrators of the Edmonton Institution occur on a frequent and regular basis. Mr. Linklater asserts that these lines of communication will be effective only if the Inmate Committee is a group of well-motivated volunteers, and if the administrators are responsive, listen well, and take action.[2] ▼

Source: Canada Year Book (Statistics Canada, 1997), p. 476; Jack Linklater, "Six Keys to Successful Prison Management," May 30, 1997.

Chapter Overview _____

As you can see in the opening vignette, despite the most challenging circumstances Jack Linklater and his team have developed an effective communication system that bridges the cultural gap within this obscure, but nonetheless significant, Canadian minority. Cultural gaps occur when we communicate with diverse groups at home, at work, and in the global marketplace. Realizing that different patterns exist between and within societies is the first step in overcoming the barriers to effective communication.

In this chapter we will examine the differences in race and ethnicity as well as differences in gender, age, and physical ability that often create strong communication barriers. Cultural differences can produce distinctly different communication patterns. As we analyze these patterns, keep in mind that we are describing *general* communication patterns. Individual differences play a large part in any communication interaction, as does the degree to which an individual has been assimilated into mainstream culture.

We begin our discussion by examining business communication in the context of the global marketplace. Since Canada's mid-sized open economy depends on the import and export of goods and services, the expanding global marketplace has become increasingly important to Canadian businesses and workers.[3]

The Global Business Environment _____

In today's business environment a large number of Canadians travel internationally, work outside Canada, or work in Canada for foreign-owned companies. In this ever-growing global marketplace, businesspeople must learn to communicate effectively, despite differences in language and culture.

Increasingly, Canadian companies are conducting business with international customers, suppliers, distributors, and so on. Our exports accounted for more than 40 percent of the country's gross domestic product in 1997 and continue to grow at a faster rate than virtually any other major nation; Canada's exports have doubled since 1989. Supported by the federal government, Prime Minister Jean Chrétien has led no fewer than five TeamCanada business delegations abroad in the five years of his office.[4] For businesspeople who travel internationally the ability to bridge cultural differences in written and oral communication is crucial.

Although headquartered in Canada, companies like Nortel, Bombardier, and ATCO are considered multinational corporations—firms that conduct significant business activities outside their home countries and that view the world as their marketplace. It is estimated that more than 2 million North Americans, many of whom work for multinational organizations or other foreign-based businesses, reside in foreign countries. Bombardier, of Montreal, employs 41 000 people, 20 000 of whom work in Canada. According to some estimates, only 20 percent of transplanted workers do well, while 40 percent to 60 percent either return home before completing their assignments or perform poorly.

Many foreign-based multinationals have active operations in North America. Working for one of these companies typically requires learning to communicate within the context of the culture that foreign managers bring with them. As more foreign industry moves into Canada, Canadian workers will be confronted more and more with foreign cultures.

Canadians working outside Canada will succeed in the global environment if they can adapt effectively to the culture and communication styles of their host country. Similarly, Canadians working for a multinational doing business in Canada will benefit if they adapt successfully to the culture of the parent company.

Culture and Communication

The shared customs, beliefs, and social structures of human society make up its **culture.** Many components of culture—languages, rules, myths, family patterns, and political systems—determine the way people communicate.

Canadian citizens, like other national groups, communicate according to distinct cultural patterns that often do not coincide with the cultural patterns of other groups. Such patterns frequently inspire generalizations about a culture. Canadians, for example, are considered to be more deliberate and careful, with a less dynamic and aggressive business style, than our U.S. counterparts. We are also viewed as being sensitive to the economic impact of the United States, and to being portrayed as Mounties and lumberjacks in a frigid French outpost.[5] These generalizations, and others like them, can be the root of stereotypes and prejudice.

Yet despite these perceived differences between Canadians and Americans, we can encounter similar communication difficulty when doing business abroad. For example, our concept of time influences such communication strategies as word choice. According to communication consultant Sana Reynolds:

> We like the feeling of adrenaline that communicating with verbs gives us. However, our style often offends cultures that use lengthy sentence lines. We're too brusque. We get to the point too quickly. . . . The Koran [the sacred book of Islam] states that Arabs should not do business with anyone until they know their business partner's father, his father's father, and his father's father's father. When we expect to conclude an agreement quickly solely on the basis of whether or not it is beneficial, we are perceived as rushing things along.[6]

Two common barriers to successful cross-cultural communication are ethnocentrism and language differences.

ETHNOCENTRISM

Successful global communication requires an awareness of the dangers of ethnocentrism and an effort to avoid them. **Ethnocentrism** is the tendency to judge other cultures by the standards of one's own. Ethnocentric communication often results from an insistence on using one's own business values with little or no awareness of their differences from the values of other cultures.

Harry C. Triandis, an authority on cross-cultural communication patterns, provides the example in Figure 3-1 of an American and a Greek talking at cross-purposes because of a basic failure to understand each other's cultural patterns. As you read it, keep in mind that Greeks perceive supervisors as more authoritarian than do Americans. What is said by a boss—in this case, the American—is what a subordinate (the Greek) believes must be done. What the parties *say* appears on the left side of the diagram; what they are *thinking* appears on the right. Communication success or failure will be determined by the content that appears in the right-hand column. Neither the American's nor the Greek's response is "right" or "wrong." Differences exist that must be acknowledged, accepted, and understood in order to communicate effectively.

ACCOMMODATION   In order to counter ethnocentric tendencies, you must adapt. Although you naturally start with a certain sensitivity toward your own culture, you must be willing to accommodate communication differences that exist in other cultures. You must realize, for example, that it is considered inappropriate in Egypt to

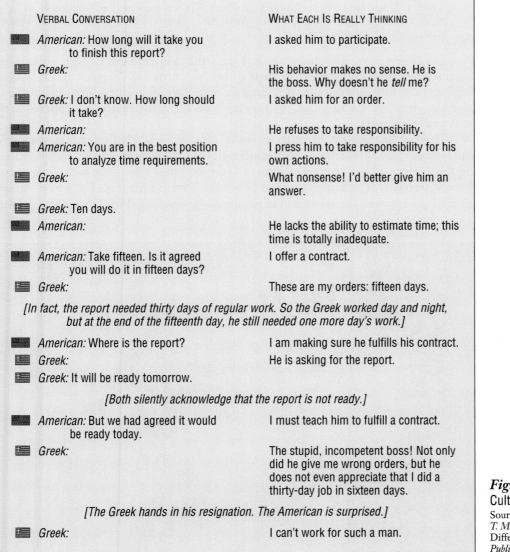

VERBAL CONVERSATION	WHAT EACH IS REALLY THINKING
American: How long will it take you to finish this report?	I asked him to participate.
Greek:	His behavior makes no sense. He is the boss. Why doesn't he *tell* me?
Greek: I don't know. How long should it take?	I asked him for an order.
American:	He refuses to take responsibility.
American: You are in the best position to analyze time requirements.	I press him to take responsibility for his own actions.
Greek:	What nonsense! I'd better give him an answer.
Greek: Ten days.	
American:	He lacks the ability to estimate time; this time is totally inadequate.
American: Take fifteen. Is it agreed you will do it in fifteen days?	I offer a contract.
Greek:	These are my orders: fifteen days.

[In fact, the report needed thirty days of regular work. So the Greek worked day and night, but at the end of the fifteenth day, he still needed one more day's work.]

American: Where is the report?	I am making sure he fulfills his contract.
Greek:	He is asking for the report.
Greek: It will be ready tomorrow.	

[Both silently acknowledge that the report is not ready.]

American: But we had agreed it would be ready today.	I must teach him to fulfill a contract.
Greek:	The stupid, incompetent boss! Not only did he give me wrong orders, but he does not even appreciate that I did a thirty-day job in sixteen days.

[The Greek hands in his resignation. The American is surprised.]

Greek:	I can't work for such a man.

Figure 3-1 Cross-Cultural Communications
Source: *Philip R. Harris and Robert T. Moran*, Managing Cultural Differences, *3rd ed. (Houston: Gulf Publishing Co., 1991), 271.*

use first names unless invited to do so, or to address someone without including a rank or title. Similarly, in Hong Kong, aggressive communication is considered inappropriate—the Chinese are reserved and modest in conducting business. In Brazil, events—not hours and minutes—define time. When you meet with a Brazilian client, it is a mistake to launch immediately into business decisions.[7] Successful communication accommodates the customs, behaviours, and discussion topics of your foreign audience.[8]

LANGUAGE LIMITATIONS

Even though English is generally considered the international language of business, it is nevertheless a mistake to assume that every foreign businessperson either knows English or can understand North American usage. In fact, only about half of the 800 million people who speak English learned it as their first language, and those who speak English as a second language are much more limited than native speakers.[9] Moreover, in some Arabic-speaking countries, including Tunisia and Lebanon, French—not English—is considered the language of international trade. Here is one example of the English you may encounter in non–English-speaking countries:

> From a Tokyo car rental company's brochure: "When passenger of foot heave in sight, tootle the horn. Trumpet him melodiously at first, but if he still obstacles your passage then tootle him with vigor."[10]

Canadians must also learn to deal with the nonstandard English spoken by international business contacts in such diverse countries as Nigeria, India, Singapore, and the Philippines. Although English is the official business language in these countries, it is not the language of everyday speech and, therefore, is peppered with nonstandard phrases.

Lack of *language fluency* often makes it difficult for foreign managers, company representatives, and executives to compete globally. Language fluency means learning the correct way to speak and write a language other than your own. Language-fluency problems are likely to increase as foreign governments take the lead in insisting that government contracts and negotiations be conducted in the language of the

The need to communicate in different languages to people around the globe led communications giant AT&T to offer interpretation services to its customers. AT&T Language Line Services provides interpreters for 140 languages 24 hours a day.

contract-granting country. This is already the case in such nations as Belgium, Spain, and Thailand.[11]

A recent study by Dunhill Personnel Systems revealed that only one out of four managers surveyed is fluent in a foreign language. Japanese and German, considered important languages for the twenty-first century, are spoken by few. And only one in sixteen managers considered foreign-language skills a must for his or her career.[12]

Language limitations are dividing the Internet, which is dominated by the use of English. Since the vast majority of the world's population does not speak English, millions of computer users have no Internet access. Ultimately, this may encourage non–English-speaking people to learn English because it is the common language of the computer world. It has already encouraged software manufacturers to develop translation software with the power to automatically translate an e-mail message sent in English into French before it is deposited into the recipient's electronic mailbox.[13]

Progress Check

1. What communication problems confront Canadians who work abroad?
2. Give some examples of patterns of thought and behaviour that characterize "Canadian culture." How might some of these patterns create communication barriers for foreign businesspeople?
3. Why is language fluency an important part of business communication? Besides taking language courses in college or university, what can you do to improve your fluency in a foreign language?

Low-Context versus High-Context Cultures

Although the process of bridging the cultural communication gap begins with language, it does not end there. The process also requires that you understand the cultural context in which communication takes place.

Edward T. Hall, an anthropologist and authority on cross-cultural communication, divides cultures into two basic types: low-context and high-context. Communication in **low-context cultures** depends on explicit written and verbal messages. Germany, Switzerland, the Scandinavian countries, the United States, and Canada are considered low-context cultures. By contrast, communication in **high-context cultures** depends not only on the message itself but also on everything that surrounds the explicit message, including nonverbal language. China, Korea, Japan, and the Arab countries are considered high-context cultures. Figure 3-2 places 11 world cultures on Hall's continuum.

ADDING CONTEXT TO INTERNATIONAL COMMUNICATION

Communication context directly influences communication style. In low-context cultures, for example, written agreements and messages determine business deals. In high-context cultures, written correspondence and agreements are often far less important than interpersonal relationships, personal status and titles, and the social environment in which the deal takes place. Several factors affect communication in low- and high-context cultures: personal relationships, timing, level of formality, and body language.

PERSONAL RELATIONSHIPS   In high-context cultures, trust often precedes business. Trust is usually built on personal relationships established over time. While North

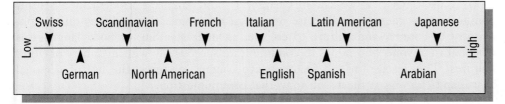

Figure 3-2 High- and Low-Context Cultures

Americans, for example, may try to cement a business relationship by getting straight to the point, members of high-context cultures frequently engage in a kind of courting behaviour before business begins. In such countries as Guatemala, Japan, and Saudi Arabia, experienced businesspeople build relationships by engaging in small talk about such topics as their countries, families, and business associates. They allot time for relaxed dinners or lunches in which business is not discussed. Only when personal relationships are cemented does business begin. Thus, to be successful in high-context cultures, Canadians must learn to approach partners and clients gradually until personal relationships are established.

In high-context communication, personal relationships are based on information about you and your company. Therefore, before the start of a meeting or presentation, send an annual report or other documents describing your company's products and history. Enclose a résumé or letter describing your personal background. When beginning a business relationship by mail, it is even more important to introduce yourself through such documents. In many cases, an introduction is necessary. In Korea and other high-context countries, a proper intermediary will open doors that would otherwise be closed if you worked alone.

TIMING   While promptness characterizes business culture in Canada, inattention to time characterizes many high-context cultures. For example, while a Canadian may consider it an insult to be kept waiting, a Latin American or Arab businessperson may feel no such pressure.

LEVEL OF FORMALITY   High-context cultures generally demand formality and proper etiquette in both personal and written communication. Unless the culture requires otherwise, you should address foreign business associates by their surnames and use titles and formal forms of address.

Formality is such an entrenched part of the business culture in Mexico that when a non-Mexican manager attempted to show his democratic spirit, his colleagues objected. The manager heard through the business grapevine that supervisors and subordinates alike considered him a boor because of his clothing (jeans and rumpled sports shirts) and his insistence that business be done on a first-name basis. "His behaviour ran counter to the prevailing Mexican view that formality in manners and dress, and keeping one's distance, are appropriate behaviours in the workplace," explains Mariah E. de Forest, an international management consultant.[14]

In most countries, proper etiquette requires that meetings begin with a formal handshake. Indeed, in Europe and South America, people shake hands at every encounter, even if they have met, spoken, and shaken hands earlier in the day. In Japan and other Asian countries, people bow when they meet. In many cultures, handshakes less firm than those exchanged by Canadians are the accepted norm.

Generally, the exchange of business cards is an important exercise in formal behaviour. In Japan and other Asian countries, business cards are given to almost everyone you meet. They are presented in a formal way, using both hands, handled with care, and read slowly and carefully. Turning the card over and writing on the back would also be considered offensive.

BODY LANGUAGE   As we saw in Chapter 1, body language in virtually all forms communicates messages. Because nonverbal communication patterns differ from country to country and culture to culture, an understanding of body language is essential to anyone who hopes to communicate successfully with members of other cultures. This discussion will focus on eye contact, gestures, the use of personal space, and clothing as means of nonverbal communication.

→ *Cross Reference*
Nonverbal communication was discussed in Chapter 1, pages 9–13.

Eye Contact   Prolonged direct eye contact suggests an intimacy with which few Canadian businesspeople are comfortable. Yet extended eye contact is common in many high-context cultures. Arabs, for example, believe that the eyes are the windows to the soul and that staring is permissible to discover what is in the other person's heart. From the Arab point of view, avoiding direct eye contact can thus communicate impoliteness, insincerity, and, at its extreme, dishonesty. Americans, on the other hand, may view Arab eye-contact behaviour as intrusive and even threatening.

A different pattern exists in Japan, where children are taught never to look directly at someone who has superior status—a teacher, for example. This pattern persists into adulthood, with Japanese workers lowering their eyes, as a sign of respect, when speaking with supervisors.

Gestures   Far from being universal, gestures have very different meanings in different cultures. Here are just a few examples of these differences:

▼ In Hong Kong, winking or beckoning with one's index finger is considered rude.

▼ In Brazil, the Canadian sign for "okay"—thumb and index finger touching to form a circle—is considered vulgar. In France, the same sign means zero; in Japan, it refers to money.

▼ In Australia, flashing a "V" sign with the back of your hand is an obscene gesture rather than a signal of victory.

The frequency of gestures also differs from culture to culture. While the French and Italians use many more gestures than do Canadians, the Japanese use far fewer. Figure 3-3 demonstrates how the meaning of certain gestures varies in different parts of Europe.

Progress Check

1. Why is it so important to understand the difference between the communication patterns of high-context and low-context cultures?

2. Describe some basic differences in the communication patterns that you would use to do business with someone from Japan as compared with someone from Denmark.

3. Why do you think Canadians have so much trouble adapting to high-context business cultures?

Figure 3-3   Gestures in Europe: Regional Differences Prevail

Although Western Europe may be moving toward economic unity, its tapestry of cultures remains diverse. Gestures, for example, continue to reflect centuries of cultural differences. As in Canada, the thumb-and-index circle means "okay" in most of Europe; in Germany, it's an indelicate reference to the receiver's anatomy. In most of Great Britain—England and Scotland—the finger tapping the nose means, "You and I are in on the secret"; in nearby Wales, however, it means, "You're very nosy." If you tap your temple just about anywhere in Western Europe, you're suggesting that someone is "crazy"; in Holland, you'll be congratulating someone for being clever.

Personal Space   Concepts of the appropriate personal space for conducting business differ markedly from country to country. For example, Latin Americans insist on conducting business in what North Americans consider "intimate" and "personal" zones. Workers who feel uncomfortable with this behaviour often back away and may be perceived as cold and unfriendly. To protect themselves from such a personal "threat," experienced North Americans use desks or tables to separate themselves from their Latin American counterparts. "The result," explains Edward T. Hall, "is that the Latin American may even climb over the obstacles until he has achieved a distance at which he can comfortably talk."[15]

Arabs follow a pattern similar to that of Latin Americans. Because Arabs consider smelling another person a sign of involvement, they sometimes stand so close to others that they can smell and be smelled. For Arabs, reports Hall, to smell another person "is not only nice, but desirable, for to deny him your breath is to act ashamed."[16] The Arab pattern is difficult for Canadians, who normally conduct business in an environment that considers breathing in another's face to be impolite. Ironically, in an effort to be polite, the Canadian may unknowingly communicate shame to his or her Arab associate. Not surprisingly, failing to understand differences like these can lead to serious miscommunication.

Clothing   One of the biggest mistakes that a businessperson can make in a foreign country is to advertise citizenship through inappropriate clothing. A Calgarian wearing flashy boots and a ten-gallon hat or a Floridian sporting white shoes and an open shirt is out of place in Asia, where businessmen dress in traditional suits and businesswomen in tailored dresses. When travelling to Japan, wear socks without holes. Custom requires that people remove their shoes when entering restaurants and homes.

Table 3-1 summarizes the major differences in low-context and high-context cultures.

Table 3-1   Comparing High- and Low-Context Cultures

	Low-Context Cultures	High-Context Cultures
Personal Relationships	Relatively unimportant compared to the details of the deal.	Very important because business is built on personal trust.
Time	Business is conducted according to the clock; punctuality is valued.	Events rather than the clock determine schedules.
Formality	A certain level of formality is expected, including handshakes and identification by title and company.	A high degree of formality is required during personal meetings and in correspondence.
Body Language		
▼ *Eye Contact*	Minimal direct eye contact.	Arabs: extended direct eye contact. Japanese: avert eyes from superiors as a sign of respect.
▼ *Gestures*	Meanings vary throughout the world.	Meanings vary throughout the world.
▼ *Personal Space*	North Americans conduct business within the social zone, standing or sitting one to four metres apart.	Arabs and Latins conduct business within the intimate zone, standing or sitting between 145 and 120 centimetres apart.
▼ *Clothing*	Suits are expected attire for both men and women.	In general, the same customs apply.

Guidelines for Successful Cross-Cultural Communication _____

The cultural differences that we have examined so far have a direct impact on all forms of communication. We will explore this impact next as we suggest practical guidelines for both writing and speaking in cross-cultural contexts.

IMPROVING WRITTEN COMMUNICATION

The following guidelines for effective written communication will help you adapt your writing to the needs of foreign audiences. They focus on language usage, stylistic preferences, and handling foreign correspondence.[17]

LANGUAGE USAGE   Start with the assumption that most non–English-speakers who have studied English possess a basic vocabulary of about 3000 English words. It is important to rely on these words—which are the most common words in English—to communicate your thoughts. The following guidelines will help you to communicate through basic English:

1. When you have a choice, eliminate infrequently used words. Write *dishonesty* rather than *duplicity; send* rather than *disseminate; uncommon* rather than *esoteric.*

2. Avoid using slang or phrases whose meaning is obvious only in Canada. For those unfamiliar with Bob and Doug McKenzie, reference to "take off, eh!" will be lost. Similarly, avoid using allusions to sports. References to "scoring a touchdown" or "stepping up to the plate" will be confusing.

3. Choose specific-action rather than general-action verbs. For example, refer to "*purchasing* new equipment," rather than "*getting* new equipment." The verb *get* makes the action ambiguous. The reader is not sure whether you are going to borrow the equipment, lease it, or buy it.

4. Use correct grammar and punctuation. Be especially sensitive to sentence fragments, run-on sentences, and subject-verb agreement.

5. Eliminate redundant, unnecessary words—they will only obscure meaning.

LEARNING TO DIRECT FOREIGN CORRESPONDENCE   Foreign correspondence is addressed differently from correspondence in Canada. The examples in Figure 3-4 illustrate the correct format for addressing envelopes to foreign businesspeople in England and Japan. In the letter itself, there are differences in the treatment of job titles and names; there are also differences in the ways you should handle the foreign correspondence that you receive.

Job Titles   It is essential to use correct job titles in all addresses and to use these titles in correspondence. Do not use first names in a letter unless you are specifically invited to do so. In addition, learn the appropriate use of respectful titles. In Mexico, for example, refer to professionals by profession and name: *Architecto (architect) Hernandez* or *Licenciado (lawyer) Valdez.* Do not, however, assume that titles have the same meaning in different countries. For example, the designation *deputy* in England is equivalent to the Americans' vice president, while managing director refers to the chief executive officer of a corporation.

First and Last Names   A potential problem in communicating with Asians of Chinese descent is the correct use of given names and surnames. The Chinese surname is placed first and the given name last. To illustrate, assume that you are about to write to Song Wei. His name is not Mr. Wei—that is tantamount to calling someone

Don't overlook the importance of worldwide thinking. A company that keeps its eye on Tom, Dick, and Harry is going to miss Pierre, Hans, and Yoshio.

Al Ries
Chairman, Trout & Ries Inc.
advertising agency

Figure 3-4 Envelopes Addressed to Foreign Correspondents

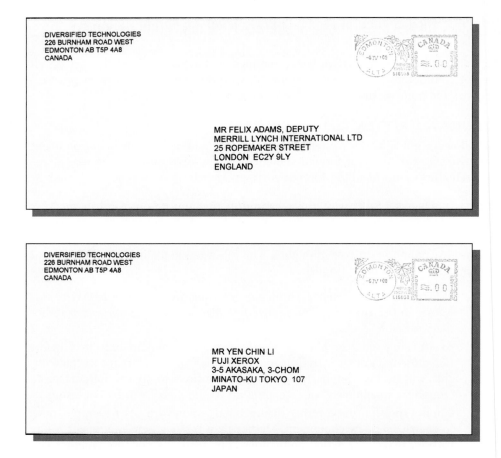

DIVERSIFIED TECHNOLOGIES
226 BURNHAM ROAD WEST
EDMONTON AB T5P 4A8
CANADA

MR FELIX ADAMS, DEPUTY
MERRILL LYNCH INTERNATIONAL LTD
25 ROPEMAKER STREET
LONDON EC2Y 9LY
ENGLAND

DIVERSIFIED TECHNOLOGIES
226 BURNHAM ROAD WEST
EDMONTON AB T5P 4A8
CANADA

MR YEN CHIN LI
FUJI XEROX
3-5 AKASAKA, 3-CHOM
MINATO-KU TOKYO 107
JAPAN

Mr. Billy. Because the Chinese surname is placed first, this individual should be addressed as Mr. Song. Many Asians assist their Western counterparts by underlining their last name on business cards or in written correspondence.

If you speak three or more languages, you're multilingual. If you speak two languages, you're bilingual. If you speak one language, you're American.

Anonymous

Receiving Foreign Correspondence   Foreign business correspondence appearance and mail service may differ from Canadian correspondence. For example, letters may be handwritten because of a shortage of computers or even typewriters. Because Germans prefer to de-emphasize personal contributions to their company, German workers may sign letters on company letterhead but their names may not be typed below the signatures. Naturally, this practice makes responding difficult when the signature is illegible. Response reliability also differs due to poor mail service. In India, for example, if you receive no response after a period of time, assume the letter is lost and send it again.

IMPROVING ORAL COMMUNICATION

Your audience's cultural background influences what you say and how you say it. Although effective oral communication is important in ordinary conversation and in business meetings, we will focus on improving your communication skills in oral presentations.[18]

ORAL PRESENTATIONS   Successful oral presentations allow for differences in formality, tempo, and audience behaviour. The guidelines below will help you understand these three critical differences:

Formality   As you will see in Chapter 15, the Canadian business culture considers the best oral presentation style to be informal, but informative. That is, effective speakers deliver presentations in a natural, conversational style. Presenters often interact with the audience through visual aids, writing comments and instructions on chalkboards, flip charts, and overhead transparencies as they speak. However, this presentation style may be considered unacceptable in countries where more formal, rehearsed presentation styles are required. In countries as diverse as Germany and Japan, the Canadian approach may be interpreted as a lack of preparation—even an insult. When we write on visual aids, for instance, we risk sending the message that we did not take the time to complete our work in advance.

In high-context cultures, formality also requires that the individuals involved in the presentation be similar in rank and age to their audience members. Despite his or her competence, a presentation delivered by a 30-year-old to a group of senior Japanese executives is considered inappropriate and bad business practice.

Tempo   As a rule, deliver your presentation in a foreign host country at a slower pace than you would in Canada. In high-context cultures, always allow an extended period at the beginning for the exchange of greetings and other forms of socializing. In general, prove your personal integrity first, communicate your company's reputation next, and then present your proposal or product.

When you are delivering a presentation in English to an audience that speaks English as a second language, slow down during the question-and-answer period. Rushing someone who is trying to search for a precise English word is considered disrespectful.

Expect interruptions in such high-context cultures as Saudi Arabia, Japan, and Latin America, where presentations are normally delivered in small segments, each followed by a question-and-answer period. Because such interruptions digress from the topic and allow people time to relax before returning to business, they are considered social as well as information-gathering activities.

Audience Behaviour   In Canada, we are used to certain behaviour on the part of listeners who may ask questions or communicate nonverbally. In contrast, when Japanese disagree with a speaker's comments, they may begin talking among themselves. You can defuse the situation by turning immediately to another subject. Find out later what caused the problem and, if possible, develop an alternative strategy.

As we learned earlier, Asians frequently avoid direct eye contact. Instead of looking directly at the speaker, Chinese, Malaysian, and Japanese listeners often stare at the floor. This behaviour shows respect rather than inattention.

Conducting business in the global marketplace requires sensitivity to other cultures' communication styles. Keep in mind, however, that no discussion in a book can give you the in-depth information needed to actually conduct business abroad. Perhaps the best information is gained firsthand; perhaps the most desirable quality is the willingness to accept differences among cultures, societies, and individuals. Most universities sponsor student organizations for different ethnic groups, and the foreign-language faculty at your school may be able to assist you with information about conducting business in foreign countries. After you enter the workforce, you may be able to enroll in a company-sponsored workshop on multicultural communication.

> ## Progress Check
>
> 1. Describe how you should adapt your use of English in written and oral communication when dealing with business associates who speak English as a second language.
> 2. How can you help an interpreter or translator effectively communicate your message?
> 3. When writing or speaking to businesspeople from a high-context culture, describe the importance of formality.

COLLABORATIVE COMMUNICATION

A Group Exercise in Cultural Coping

To teach businesspeople to deal effectively with foreign cultures, many experts recommend small-group communication exercises that highlight cultural differences. One exercise used by Fons Trompenaars, a Dutch leader of workshops on multicultural management, involves a game in which one group tries to teach another, culturally dissimilar group how to build paper towers. In Trompenaars' experiment, four Swedish participants are designated "international experts" in building paper towers. The rest play natives of a make-believe village called Derdia.

The experts are sent out of the room to learn how to make the towers and prepare to pass that skill on to Derdia. Meanwhile, Mr. Trompenaars initiates the Swedes into the strange customs of Derdia.

Derdians' greetings involve kissing one another on the shoulder. Holding out a hand to someone means "Please go away." If they disagree, Derdians say "Yes!" and nod their heads vigorously. What's more, Derdian women have a taboo against using paper or scissors in the presence of men, while men would never use a pencil or a ruler in front of women. . . .

Soon, two "experts" are allowed back into the room for a brief study of Derdian culture. The Derdians flock to the experts and gleefully kiss them on their shoulders. The experts turn red. They seem lost already.

"Would you please sit?" asks Hans Olav Friberg, a young expert who, back home in Sweden, works for a company that makes flooring.

"Yesss!" the Derdians say in chorus. But they don't sit down.

"Who is in charge here?" Mr. Friberg inquires. "Yesss!" the Derdians reply.

Mr. Friberg leaves the room to confer with his fellow experts. "They didn't understand us," he tells them. But fellow expert Hakan Kalmermo is not about to be deterred by strange habits. He is taking charge. As he briskly practices making a paper tower, Mr. Kalmermo says firmly to the other experts: "The target is to have them produce one tower."

The four experts carry paper and other supplies to the adjoining room, now known as Derdia. They begin to explain the process to the Derdians very slowly, as if speaking to small children.

When one of the Derdians shows he understands the workings of a pair of scissors, Mr. Kalmermo exclaims, "Good boy!"

Although Mr. Kalmermo works hard at making himself clear, the Derdian customs and taboos obstruct progress. The men won't use rulers as long as women are around but don't explain this behavior to the experts. The answer to every question seems to be "Yesss!" At the end of 30 minutes, no tower has been completed.

The game is over; now comes the self-criticism. "They treated us like idiots," protests one of the Derdians.

The lessons are clear, but Mr. Trompenaars drives them home: If you don't figure out the basics of a foreign culture, you won't get much accomplished. And if your biases lead you to think of foreign ways as childish, the foreigners may well respond by acting childish.

Questions for Critical Thinking

1. Hakan Kalmermo, the take-charge member of the expert team, believed that if his team had an additional hour, it could have taught the Derdians to build 15 towers. Do you agree with him? Explain your answer.

2. Does collaboration make it easier or harder to work through the complexities of a different culture?

3. Craft a similar group exercise. In a group of eight to ten, select a leader to develop customs for a culture and choose a simple task that "experts" must teach to natives of the culture. Divide the remaining group members into teams of experts and natives. While the group leader explains the customs to the natives, the experts, in a separate area, should master the task. When the natives know the customs, the experts may spend 25 minutes trying to teach the natives the task. Discuss your experiences after the exercise is over. What did you learn that will help you communicate with cultural competency?

Source: Bob Hagerty, "Learning to Turn the Other Shoulder," *Wall Street Journal*, 14 June 1993, B1, B6.

Cultural Diversity within Canada

Successful communication involves recognizing and accepting the great diversity among people everywhere. Although people may be grouped together in classifications based on such factors as gender, age, race, or employment, tremendous diversity exists among the members of each group.

To understand cultural diversity at home, we might begin by appending the concept of Canada as a "patchwork quilt" with an imperative for the twenty-first century: Do unto others as others would want done unto them.[19] Many of the 288 000 Canadians who are considered **culturally Deaf,**[20] who use American Sign Language (ASL), understood this imperative when they, with other ASL users, decided to change the the sign used for *Japanese*, which was made by moving the little finger next to the eye. Recognizing that this sign referred to slanted eyes, a potentially uncomplimentary stereotype, they adopted the sign that Japanese deaf people use to describe themselves. As shown in Figure 3-5, they press the thumb and index fingers of both hands together and pull them apart to represent the geographic area of Japan.[21]

Figure 3-6 identifies each element of the cultural diversity pie, but it is important to recognize the extent to which the slices overlap each other. For instance, although some classification systems refer to racial/ethnic groups, a *racial* group is, technically speaking, a subgroup of an *ethnic* group. The broader term *ethnic group* encompasses such characteristics as race, religion, national origin, and culture.

Learning to communicate successfully in a diverse marketplace involves an awareness of how prejudices and stereotypes affect communication. It means understanding *racial/ethnic diversity* and *gender differences* in communication styles. It means recognizing that diversity extends to the *elderly* and the *physically challenged*. Finally, it means defining what diversity means to each of us and adapting preconceptions to improve our communication skills. We will begin with a closer look at the changing face of the Canadian population.

THE DEMOGRAPHY OF CHANGE

Until recently, the communication barriers that now characterize our diverse Canadian culture were given relatively little attention. Because most managerial positions in Canada were traditionally held by white males, communication patterns were typically based on the behaviour and requirements of that group. However, the demographics of today's workforce and business customers are changing radically, and trends reveal that even more change lies ahead. These population trends are analyzed by the social science of **demography,** the statistical study of population size, density, and geographic distribution.

Increasingly, women and minorities are entering the Canadian workforce and bringing their own style of communication with them. At the Interchange of

> *The company that gets out in front of managing diversity, in my opinion, will have a competitive edge.*
>
> David Kearns
> CEO, Xerox Corporation

> *Change is the law of life. And those who look only to the past or present are certain to miss the future.*
>
> John F. Kennedy
> 35th President of the United States

THE SIGN FOR JAPAN OR A JAPANESE PERSON

The old way

The new way

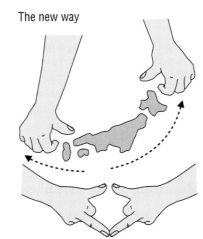

Figure 3-5 Sign Language Evolves to Reflect Heightened Sensitivity
Source: *Frederic Jondreau, American Sign Language Institute. Megan Jaegermon/*The New York Times. *Found in Jennifer Senior, "Language of the Deaf Evolves to Reflect New Sensibilities,"* The New York Times, *January 3, 1994, p. A1.*

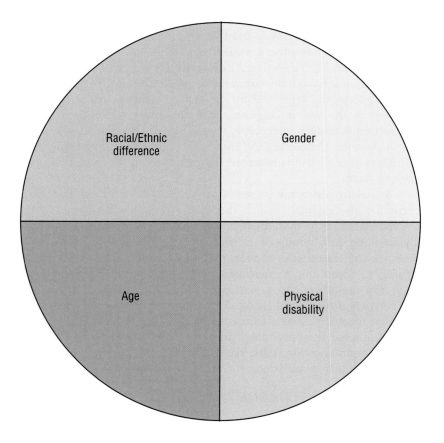

Figure 3-6 The Major
Elements of Diversity

Canadian Studies conference in Prince Albert, Saskatchewan, delegates heard Michelle Falardeau-Ramsey describe Canada's ethnic, cultural, and religious diversity. She reported that today women constitute 45 percent of our workforce; 12 percent are visible minorities, and 4 percent are First Nations, Inuit, or Métis.[22]

Just as the workforce has changed, so has consumer demography. On July 1, 1995, Canada's population reached 29 606 100—nearly 30 million people. In the year preceding that count, more than 217 000 new arrivals settled in Canada from some 200 different countries. Only about one-fifth of those came from Europe and the United States, and almost half came from Asia.[23] Others came from the Caribbean, South and Central America, Africa, and countries as diverse as Bhutan, Tibet, and Reunion. With projections that our population will reach about 32 million by the year 2001,[24] this new immigrant consumer group is increasingly being viewed as a major force in the Canadian marketplace. The Royal Bank of Canada, for example, provides ATM signage, marketing literature, and banking facilities in Chinese wherever the ethnic business so demands; French and English voice mail and automated attendants are commonplace; and some nationally broadcast television shows are produced in one or more of the 100 languages that are alive and well in Canada.[25]

When we couple these statistics with the approximately 16 percent of Canadians who speak both French and English—our two official languages—and the richness of our Aboriginal population (almost 1.6 percent), it is evident that the Canadian culture is a mixture of many cultures, not a homogeneous or static entity.

A WORD ABOUT RACIAL AND ETHNIC IDENTITY   Although it may sometimes be implied in this discussion that such groups as Anglo-Canadians are monolithic in nature—that is, rigidly unified in identity and purpose—it is erroneous to base judgments on such an assumption. Strong cultural variation exists between those who trace their roots back hundreds of years in this country, like the Cree, French or English, and first- or second-generation Ukrainians, Germans, or persons from other European countries. The same is true for Spanish Canadians, Portuguese Canadians, and Chinese, Japanese, and other Asian Canadians.

In this discussion, it is prudent to distinguish between racial and ethnic identity. By **racial identity** we mean an identity given to a category of people who share similar physical characteristics; **ethnic identity** refers to a range of shared characteristics including values, communication patterns, and behaviours. It is important to remember, however, that racial and ethnic diversity are not mutually exclusive. It is possible, for example, that a Ukrainian who has lived in Quebec may have communication patterns similar to those of French Canadians—and quite different from those of other Ukrainians.

Progress Check

1. How is the Canadian workforce expected to change by 2001?
2. Distinguish between racial identity and ethnic identity.

Stereotypes and Prejudices

Stereotypes are responsible for a great deal of the miscommunication that occurs among diverse groups of people. **Stereotypes** are distorting generalizations based on the distinguishing characteristics of particular groups. Such characteristics may range from gender, race, and physical appearance to occupation and place of residence. The stereotyped group need not be a minority. Just as there are stereotypes of Ukrainians, French, Asians, older people, and the physically challenged, stereotypes also exist for so-called WASPs—White Anglo-Saxon Protestants, both male and female. Although each group may possess real differences in values, attitudes, and behaviours that distinguish it from other groups, these differences become stereotypes when they are simplified and distorted—that is, when they are used to ignore facts about individual group members that do not conform to generalizations about the group.

The less secure a man is, the more likely he is to have extreme prejudice.

Clint Eastwood
Actor

Stereotypes lead to faulty thinking about groups and their members, and faulty thinking may lead, in turn, to tendencies in behaviour. Prejudice is one form of such behaviour. Prejudice, then, is a combination of belief and behaviour that results from the preconceived judgments that we sometimes make about other groups of people.

CONFIRMATION BIAS

Table 3-2 identifies many of the stereotypes found in our contemporary culture. Once we form stereotypes, we are more likely to find specific examples that reinforce our beliefs and attitudes. This process is known as *confirmation bias*. Stereotypes like these are so pervasive that they were noted in a report of the Federal Glass Ceiling Commission. For example, according to the report, male executives perceived women as "not tough enough" and Asians as "more equipped for technical than people-oriented work."[26]

Stereotypes are based on an *ethnocentric* view of the world. As we saw earlier in the chapter, the meaning that one group attaches to the communication style of another is often based on meanings derived from the culture of the judging group. This is just one important way in which stereotypes lead to miscommunication and poor judgment. An Anglo male manager, for example, may decide not to promote an Asian to a managerial position because of the Asian's

Progress Check

1. What is the relationship between stereotypes and prejudices?
2. What is confirmation bias and how does it relate to an ethnocentric view of the world?

Table 3-2 Contemporary Cultural Stereotypes

French Canadians	Anglo Canadians
Passionate	Arrogant
Emotional	Insensitive
Don't want to speak English	Abusers of power
Volatile	Oppressors

Asians	African Americans
Intelligent and industrious	Good athletes
Clannish	Undisciplined
Arrogant	Not academically strong
Good technicians; poor managers	Violent and criminal

Women	Men
Intuitive; nonanalytical	Insensitive
Poor in math	Macho
Emotional	Treat women like objects
Not committed to career	Unemotional
Poor leaders	Threatened by women in power

Elderly	Physically Challenged
Intolerant of change	Physical impairment generalized to mental impairment
Prone to illness	Need constant care
Hard to teach new ways	Expect others to drop everything to help them
Unmotivated	
Hard of hearing	
Set in their ways	

Source: Adapted and Canadianized from Marilyn Loden and Judy B. Rosener, *Workforce 2000: Managing Employee Diversity as a Vital Resource* (Homewood, Ill.: Business One Irwin, 1991), 65–67.

> *I traveled a good deal all over the world, and I got along pretty good in all those foreign countries, for I have a theory that it's their country and they got a right to run it like they want to.*
>
> Will Rogers
> Actor and humorist

modesty, unwillingness to speak during meetings, and unwillingness to make eye contact. The Anglo manager may believe that the Asian lacks leadership skills, while the Asian, steeped in a culture that marks aggressive behaviour as inappropriate, is doing what, for him, is culturally correct.

Gender and Communication

Men and women often send and receive information from such contrasting vantage points that their conversations are akin to cross-cultural communication. These gender differences affect communication as strongly in the workplace as they do at home. We will examine one of the more extreme consequences of a breakdown in interactions between male and female colleagues: sexual harassment.

GENDER DIFFERENCES IN COMMUNICATION STYLES

Facing an important business decision, a female manager is likely to consult with her colleagues to hear their ideas. In many ways, the discussion is as important as the decision itself because it shows evidence of involvement, connection, and communication. Faced with a similar decision, a male colleague might tend to take matters into his own hands and act accordingly. If he can make the decision himself, he may feel that there is no need for conversation. In such a case, a woman trying to get input from a male colleague by asking "What do you think?" might find that her colleague views her questions as a signal that she wants him to decide the issue.

In this illustration, the source of potential conflict is a difference in gender communication styles. According to Deborah Tannen, a professor of linguistics and an expert on gender differences in communication, the conflict here could result from a very common task encountered in business interactions: asking for information and offering help. Men and women also differ in the way they interpret the purpose of conversation—a distinction that Tannen calls report-talk (male) versus rapport-talk (female). Tannen also believes that patterns of speech follow two different styles—powerful and powerless—and that there are distinct differences in body language.[27] In addition, many gender-related stylistic differences may relate to what Tannen calls "conversational rituals"—the automatic ways we speak that influence how we are perceived by others, including colleagues and supervisors.

As we explore the nature of gender differences in communication, keep in mind that there is no one best conversation style for all situations. The more you recognize different conversation styles, the more you can adapt to overcome communication conflicts.

ASKING FOR INFORMATION AND OFFERING HELP   Although asking for information and help is a common business activity, the act of asking is frequently interpreted differently by men and women. A male listener may interpret a woman's request for help as a signal that she is saying, "I am weaker and less knowledgeable than you," which implies a status difference that many men find uncomfortable. Conversely, a male listener may perceive a woman's offer to help as a message that the speaker believes she has higher status and competence: "I know the information and am, therefore, more competent than you."

Many women tend to avoid asking men for help because when they ask they are made to feel incompetent. However, when women themselves are faced with requests for help, they tend to provide as much information as possible as clearly as possible. Unlike men, their goal often is to create connections, and to do so, they try to minimize the perception of a difference in knowledge or expertise.

REPORT-TALK VERSUS RAPPORT-TALK   Regardless of the medium of the interchange, women generally seek to establish relationships whereas men are more likely to focus on information: the difference that Tannen describes as "report-talk" versus "rapport-talk." Because men tend to view conversation as a mechanism to negotiate status, they also see the interchange as an opportunity to exhibit their knowledge and skill—that is, to report to others. Consequently, men often take centre stage and monopolize conversation.

Women, in contrast, may focus on similarities and connections as they seek to build rapport—that is, sympathetic relationships. Instead of emphasizing the status difference that comes with displaying knowledge and expertise, they tend to place less emphasis on these differences in an attempt to develop rapport.

The tendency to take centre stage even in private conversation also tends to make many men more comfortable than women in delivering public speeches. These

Whether women are better than men I cannot say—but I can say they are certainly no worse.

Golda Meir
Former prime minister of Israel

Eugene Poitras, Chief of the Peepeekisis First Nations People

For Chief Eugene Poitras, Chief of the Peepeekisis First Nations people of File Hills, Saskatchewan, skillful communication supports his diverse responsibilities as cultural leader, councillor, and CEO and President of the File Hills Telecommunication Company. He also represents First Nations people on the provincial boards of Health and Education.

As a regional cultural leader, Chief Poitras is accountable to over 1800 First Nations people as they consensually develop and govern the First Nations Constitution and organizational policies that flow from this constitution. As CEO and President, he is at the helm of a significant telecommunications organization committed to delivering technological benefits to First Nations people of Canada.

Chief Poitras' approach to communication is derived from his ancestry, wherein parents and elders taught respect, trust, and honesty among people of all nations. His style serves him well, both within and outside his community.

Question: What kind of communication differences do you encounter when conducting business outside of your culture?

Answer: One observable difference is our approach to cross-cultural communication. To the First Nations people, the bottom line is not the most important factor behind our business communication; we tend to be more reserved and less aggressive than other cultures. These differences are most apparent when communication includes business negotiations. We depend more upon attentive listening, reading between the lines, and nonverbal communication.

Question: What advice about communication would you give to anyone wishing to conduct multicultural business?

Answer: Lessons can be learned from observing other cultures in their own environment. For example, when the Japanese first determine they will do business in a foreign country, they send emissaries ahead of time to learn the nuances of that foreign culture. It is most important that you learn who you are doing business with, so

men simply use the mechanism of report-talk to establish their expertise in a public setting. When faced with public audiences, many women may experience self-doubt, in part because they are not used to putting themselves on display. Claiming attention by publicizing expertise and credibility is not the way these women prefer to communicate.

Interestingly, the report-talk versus rapport-talk roles of men and women are often reversed when communicating via computer. While women tend to focus on the machine's utility—the job it will do for them—many men are more comfortable with the technology and with communicating in cyberspace. As a result, many men are better able to have "extended conversations" on their computers than in face-to-face or telephone meetings.[28]

POWERFUL VERSUS POWERLESS LANGUAGE   By the very nature of their language

Question: Why is it important to understand cultural differences?

Answer: Clearly understanding cultural differences helps to develop a comfort zone where a meaningful exchange of ideas can take place. A successful exchange establishes a partnership that is based on trust and friendship. I believe that business relationships, as well as personal retionships, should be lasting.

Question: How is the communication style of your culture unique?

Answer: First Nations people have a strong history of oral communication, which includes stories and legends that have linked the past with the present and future. Therefore, our culture is guided by verbal communication. Of course, we conduct written communication but we place a great deal of importance on verbal communication that is honest.

Question: Why is your communication style successful?

Answer: I believe my communication style is successful because I have inherited the wisdom of my forefathers; a wisdom that is both innate and spiritual. For example, our forefathers have taught us to listen and carefully observe the universe. I am able to translate this insight into successful communication with others.

that you can make them feel comfortable and thereby avoid distancing yourself from them.

Question: Does your culture maintain conversational rituals?

Answer: Rituals of communication within our community are always based upon dignity and respect. For example, when addressing an elder, we never speak first; rather, it is the privilege of the elder to initiate the conversation.

Question: In your culture, do you have any form of a collaborative communication process? If so, how does it work?

Answer: Within our collective system we have many people with talents and strengths. We rely upon them for their expertise in resolving issues of all types. It is a similar concept to cross-functional teams, where meetings include people who contribute on the basis of their various competencies. A prime example of collaborative communication are band meetings, where all members may attend and share information.

Question: If you were to give communication students one piece of advice, what would that advice be?

Answer: My advice is to always be very clear on the message you want to communicate, and to create an environment where the receiver interprets the message accurately.

Source: Interview with Chief Eugene Poitras.

choices, men and women communicate differently. For example, many women tend to build relationships through indirect, overly "polite" language choices. Whereas men tend to ask directly for what they need ("Please get this memo back to me before lunch"), women often use an indirect approach that may be perceived as powerless ("I have a deadline to meet and don't know how I can do it and get the memo out, too. Can you help me by finishing this memo before lunch?"). According to Tannen, rather than actual powerlessness, indirect language may reflect women's preferences for making connections.

DIFFERENCES IN BODY LANGUAGE   Body language also reflects gender differences. Tannen notes that whereas many women attempt to establish intimacy by sitting close to one another and establishing eye contact, men are more likely to sit at angles and rarely look at one another directly. Indeed, our culture has given men reasons to avert their gazes. One man looking directly at another may be interpreted as a show of hostility—a nonverbal threat. The exchange of direct looks between men and women can also be interpreted as having sexual overtones that are certainly inappropriate for business.

CONVERSATIONAL RITUALS   Men and women are socialized to say things that may have little to do with the literal meaning of words. For example, when we ask, "How are you?" upon meeting a business associate, we are not really asking for a list of the person's aches and pains. Rather, we are simply following a greeting ritual. Two conversational rituals that are often used differently by men and women involve apologies and helping others save face.

Women tend to apologize more often than men—even when they did nothing wrong. The apology serves as a ritual mechanism to restore balance to a conversation. Thus, notes Tannen, " 'I'm sorry' can be an expression of understanding—and caring—about the other person's feelings rather than an acceptance of blame. This ritual often works against women who are perceived as so lacking in confidence that they think everything is their fault."

Women also tend to use conversational rituals to help the person with whom they are dealing "save face." For example, a woman might defuse a tense situation in which a male colleague failed to provide the detailed information she needed on a new computer system by saying, "I'm a little confused." This ritual can work well if the woman's male colleague understands what she is doing and takes responsibility for his failing. But, says Tannen, "ritually claiming confusion can make [women] look confused to someone who doesn't recognize it as a ritual."

SEXUAL HARASSMENT   The overwhelming majority of victims of sexual harassment are women. For example, four female employees recently reached a $2.2 million settlement with the Chevron Corp. as a result of the actions of male employees who sent them offensive e-mail messages and pornography, and the company inaction after managers were informed of the problem. However, victims can also be men. A male employee at a Los Angeles hot-tub manufacturer won a $1 million court decision because of the daily sexual harassment he endured from the company's female chief financial officer.[29]

Sexual harassment, more than a breakdown in communication, consists of behaviours ranging from blatant physical contact to subtle, sexually oriented hints, suggestions, and comments that contribute to a hostile working environment. Under the Canada Labour Code, sexual harrassment in the workplace is defined as any conduct, comment, gesture, or contact of a sexual nature that is likely to cause offence or humiliation to any employee or that might, on reasonable grounds, be perceived by that employee as placing a sexual condition on employment or on any opportunity for training or promotion. The Canadian Human Rights Act prohibits sexual harassment in the workplace.[30] The standard for judgment, then, is whether a reasonable person would perceive sexual conditions on employment, or is offended or humiliated by certain actions.

Sexual harassment charges are based on one or more of the following forms of behaviour: improper physical conduct, unwelcome sexual advances, coercion, favouritism, and visual and indirect harassment. In many cases, however, both men and women remain confused about what is acceptable communication and what is not. Sexual harassment will disappear only through awareness, education, and mutual respect. Table 3–3 illustrates how harassment differs from acceptable conversation.[31]

Progress Check

1. List some of the major differences in the ways men and women communicate.
2. What is sexual harassment, and how can good channels of organizational communication help both individuals and businesses discourage its occurrence?

Table 3-3   Differences between Harassment and Acceptable Conversation

Acceptable	Harassment
"You look very nice today."	"You have a great body."
A handshake, a pat on the shoulder, or casual eye contact	Patting or touching private body parts or staring lewdly
Asking a co-worker for a date but not insisting or pestering	Repeatedly asking a co-worker for a date and refusing to take no for an answer

DEALING WITH HARASSMENT   Psychologists have found that people use a range of behaviours to deal with sexual harassment. As Table 3-4 shows, while some of these responses focus on confronting the harasser and seeking help, others not only do little to correct the problem but can actually damage the victim's self-esteem. The most adaptive responses for the harassment victim and the business organization involve clear channels of communication.

Table 3-4   Strategies for Dealing with Sexual Harassment

Strategies	Example
Internally Focused Strategies	
Detachment	Minimizing the situation, treating it as a joke or deciding that it is not really important
Denial	Pretending that nothing is happening; trying not to notice, hoping it will stop; trying to forget about it
Relabelling	Offering excuses for the harasser or interpreting the behaviour as flattering
Illusory Control	Attributing harassment to one's own behaviour or attire
Endurance	Suffering in silence, either through fear of retaliation, blame, or embarrassment or in the belief that no one will help
Externally Focused Stratregies	
Avoidance	Quitting a job; dropping a class; finding transportation alternatives; moving
Assertion/Confrontation	Confronting the harasser, making it clear that the behaviour is unwelcome
Institutional Help	Asking for help; reporting the incident
Social Support	Seeking support and acknowledgment of the reality of the occurrence
Appeasement	Attempting to placate the harasser

Source: Table based on comments made by Dr. Louise Fitzgerald and reported in Daniel Goldman, "Sexual Harassment: It's about Power, Not Lust," *New York Times*, 22 October 1991, C12.

Seniors, Juniors, and Persons with Disabilities _____

Just as racial, ethnic, and gender differences affect communication, so do differences that result from age and physical ability. In examining the role of seniors, the young, and persons with disabilities, as both workers and consumers, we will see that many of our habits in communicating with them result as much from our preconceptions as from reality.

MATURITY AND DIVERSITY

Canada's population continues to age. According to Statistics Canada, between 1996 and the year 2000, some 1.3 million Canadians will turn 60 years of age, another 1.2 million will turn 65, and 350 000 will celebrate their 85th birthday. Further, one-third of our current population is entering middle age, and the oldest will be turning 65 shortly after the year 2010. This growing percentage of aging population may have a profound effect on domestic and international corporations.[32]

How we perceive the disabled influences the opportunities they have at work. When we view persons with disabilities in terms of their skills and talents—rather than their physical limitations—we encourage the acceptance of individual differences. ITT Hartford also sees a connection among perception, productivity, and medical cost containment.

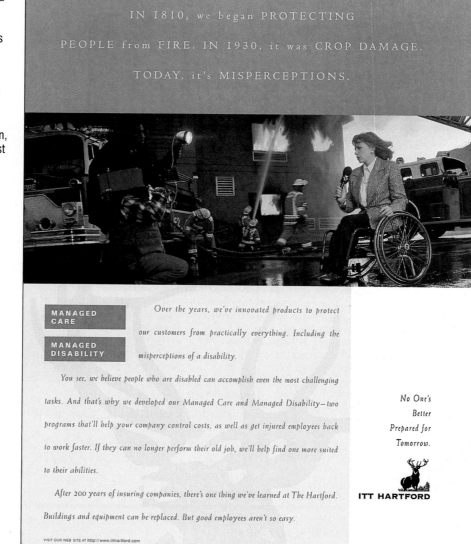

COMMUNICATING WITH SENIORS   Stereotypes influence communication across generational lines. A number of common communication fallacies can be avoided. One widely held stereotype is that age necessarily entails physical impairment. For example, many people shout at older people, assuming that they cannot hear as well as younger people. Often, this is not the case.

A second tendency is talking down to older people. Never assume that age has impaired a person's ability to understand concepts. Indeed, the older person's under-standing may be greater than that of the speaker. Similarly, supervisors and fellow workers should not be patronizing. Rather, they should assume that if an older person needs help, he or she will ask for it.

Managers and colleagues should also avoid equating reluctance to change with inability to change. Although older workers may have performed a task a certain way for years, they are just as likely as younger workers to change if given adequate reasons.

Finally, many older people are more "formal" than younger people in their business interactions. When writing to any customer—and especially to an older one—it is a good idea to refer to the person by his or her last name unless you are asked specifically to use the recipient's first name. For example, "Dear Mr. Abbot" would be more appropriate than "Dear Joe."

COMMUNICATING WITH YOUNGER PEOPLE   Today, young people prepare for such contemporary jobs as computer technicians, software developers, and personal trainers at fitness clubs, all of which barely existed 30 years ago.[33]

Along with these occupations the new generation has developed alternative communication styles. For example, it is often assumed that the staccato dialogue and minimal vocabulary of many younger people is the result of a lack of classical learning. While that may be so, the proliferation of computers, computer-based training, telecommunications, and audio-visual stimuli/response technology they use has encouraged this generation to dispense with more elaborate discourse. In its place we find a generation with excellent hand-eye coordination, a stunning familiarity with technology, and an uninhibited sense of innovation and application.

Empirical skills such as these are most desirable in the new global marketplace and may represent an invaluable resource in reducing the retraining requirements of so many less adaptable mature workers.

DISABILITY AND DIVERSITY

Passage of the Employment Equity Act in 1986 marked the outcome of the Royal Commission's Report on Equality in Employment two years earlier. It laid the groundwork for federal employment equity legislation and programs that addressed obstacles to true equity of opportunity faced by women, aboriginal peoples, members of visible minorities, and persons with disabilities. The tabling of new Employment Equity legislation in Parliament promises to amend the Act in view of a fundamental premise of the democratic market economy, where everyone should be judged solely on their merits, without regard to irrelevant factors like skin colour or gender.[34]

PERSONS WITH DISABILITIES AS COLLEAGUES   According to Mel Graham, of the Council of Canadians with Disabilities, approximately 14 percent of the Canadian population is considered to have some form of disability and, generally speaking, people with disabilities have the most difficulty overcoming job barriers. Although their representation in the workforce subject to the Act improved from 1.6 percent in 1987 to 2.6 percent in 1993, it remained well below the 6.5 percent availability estimate.[35] Notwithstanding one goal of the Act, which is to provide reasonable

Operations research analyst June Rooks exemplifies the capabilities of persons with disabilities. The military scientist is also an effective spokesperson for Saturn automobiles.

accommodation for the physically challenged, commercial Canada has not embraced the concept of providing true equity for this capable but marginalized community. In 1997, only 14 organizations (representing 270 000 employees) entered voluntary review agreements to set specific goals for improving the representation of target groups in the workplace and to established an action plan for removing barriers to fair hiring and promotion. Typically, the plan then lists such measures as:

▼ recruitment activities aimed at reaching qualified individuals from designated groups
▼ consultation with organizations representing them
▼ removal of unnecessary job requirements
▼ accommodation of special needs
▼ training to promote greater respect for diversity throughout the institution
▼ regularly reporting to the Commission on the progress achieved.[36]

Many other organizations have already made changes to implement the Act. One can occasionally find braille menus in restaurants, ramped access to public buildings, enlarged stalls in public washrooms, wider and more convenient parking stalls, and special lift mechanisms on some public transporation vehicles, such as The Red Arrow, an express bus service between Edmonton and Calgary. Major organizations such as Bell Canada, CN Rail, VIA Rail, the Royal Bank of Canada, and Marine Atlantic are among the Canadian organizations leading efforts to benefit from the economic and intellectual contribution that persons with disabilities may make.

COMMUNICATING WITH THE PHYSICALLY CHALLENGED   No law, of course, can legislate away entrenched communication patterns that commonly put persons with disabilities at a disadvantage. In the workplace, these changes generally come about only through the concerted personal efforts of every employee. Management, however, can help improve communication by providing flexibility whenever possible. For example, when Henry Chi, who is deaf, started his food-industry career with Gainers in Edmonton, his managers had to find a way to get his attention. "When they want to call me," reports Chi, "they just blink the lights on and off. Sometimes the boss sends someone to get me." According to Chi, some co-workers have learned rudimentary sign language and many often simply write things down. Notes can also be sent through e-mail.

Communication assistance sometimes comes in the form of the latest technology. The Kurzweil Personal Reader, manufactured by Xerox, uses computer technology to read printed words to visually impaired people at a rate of up to 350 words per minute. In addition, voice-operated computer systems allow employees disabled by repetitive strain injuries to use a computer even though they cannot operate a

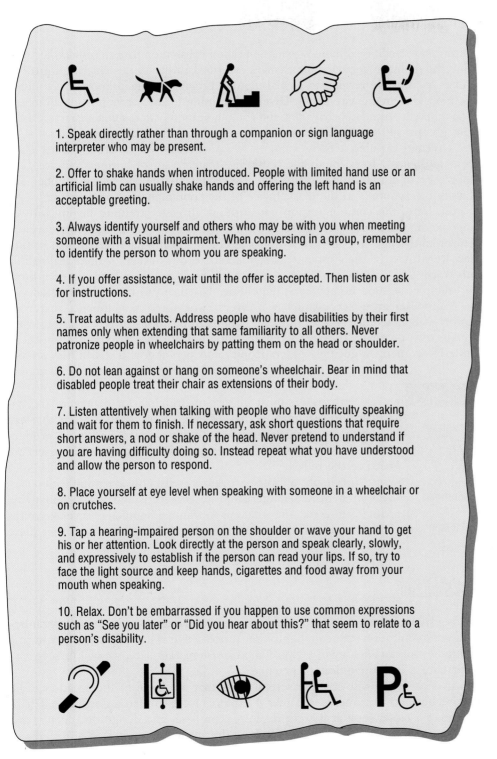

1. Speak directly rather than through a companion or sign language interpreter who may be present.

2. Offer to shake hands when introduced. People with limited hand use or an artificial limb can usually shake hands and offering the left hand is an acceptable greeting.

3. Always identify yourself and others who may be with you when meeting someone with a visual impairment. When conversing in a group, remember to identify the person to whom you are speaking.

4. If you offer assistance, wait until the offer is accepted. Then listen or ask for instructions.

5. Treat adults as adults. Address people who have disabilities by their first names only when extending that same familiarity to all others. Never patronize people in wheelchairs by patting them on the head or shoulder.

6. Do not lean against or hang on someone's wheelchair. Bear in mind that disabled people treat their chair as extensions of their body.

7. Listen attentively when talking with people who have difficulty speaking and wait for them to finish. If necessary, ask short questions that require short answers, a nod or shake of the head. Never pretend to understand if you are having difficulty doing so. Instead repeat what you have understood and allow the person to respond.

8. Place yourself at eye level when speaking with someone in a wheelchair or on crutches.

9. Tap a hearing-impaired person on the shoulder or wave your hand to get his or her attention. Look directly at the person and speak clearly, slowly, and expressively to establish if the person can read your lips. If so, try to face the light source and keep hands, cigarettes and food away from your mouth when speaking.

10. Relax. Don't be embarrassed if you happen to use common expressions such as "See you later" or "Did you hear about this?" that seem to relate to a person's disability.

Figure 3-7 Ten Commandments for Disability Etiquette

Source: *National Center for Access Unlimited, Boston, MA.*

keyboard. Catalogue outfitter L.L. Bean equips some of its disabled employees with DragonDictate Classic software, which converts the spoken word into text.[37]

Basic advice for communicating with any person with disabilities is summarized in Figure 3-7. These ten commandments are useful for any person who interacts with physically challenged friends, colleagues, or the general public.

Diversity Training

Realizing that traditional business communication is based on patterns established long before the dramatic demographic changes described earlier in this chapter, a growing number of firms are turning to formal training programs to help improve communication in a changing environment. **Diversity training** focuses on improving awareness of the different attitudes, behaviours, and communication patterns that characterize different groups, and aids in developing skills to deal with these differing patterns.

Diversity training benefits white male managers as well as other groups, all of whom must learn to adapt to the prevailing mainstream of business culture. The importance of this training is also directly related to the increasing number and diversity of customers in the marketplace of the contemporary company.

Bridging the communication gap through diversity training begins with an understanding that it is cross-cultural communication, requiring the same development of knowledge and positive attitudes as communicating across national boundaries. Regardless of their intent, managers and fellow workers should realize that both words and actions can have negative effects on other individuals or groups. For example, because humour is often culture-based, it can be misinterpreted.

Communicating successfully in a diverse workforce is as much a matter of comfort as competence. For example, if Anglos in positions of power are uncomfortable with diversity, they are likely to communicate that discomfort to others. Similarly, women, minorities, older people, and persons with disabilities should realize that the need to "fit into" an organization can be as important as hard work.

Perhaps the most important principle for managers and co-workers to recognize is that differences are assets—assets that can make the organization stronger, more creative, and more productive.[38] It is the duty of the organization to ensure that its assets are used to the fullest.

Inevitably, a diverse workforce with poor communication creates high turnover, increased absenteeism, and low productivity. Moreover, companies that fail to train and empower diverse groups will lose the problem-solving and creative perspectives that these groups bring with them.

Progress Check

1. What have you learned from this chapter that will help you communicate more effectively with older and younger employees and customers?
2. What are some steps you can take to facilitate communication with persons with disabilities?
3. How does diversity training help improve communication?

What's Ahead

Having explored the fundamentals of business communication in terms of organizational communication, the communication process, and the challenges of mastering communication technology in a global and diverse marketplace, we will turn next to the first steps in communication practice.

In Part II we will examine several tasks that are basic to the creation of all effective business documents. Chapter 4 explores ways to plan a document; Chapter 5 takes a closer look at how to organize, compose, and design documents; and Chapter 6 deals with how to edit and revise documents.

STUDENT RESOURCE CENTRE

Summary of Chapter Objectives

1. **Explain how culture, ethnocentrism, and language differences affect communication.**

   Culture determines the way people communicate. Canadians communicate according to distinct cultural patterns that may or may not coincide with the patterns followed by other national groups. Ethnocentrism refers to the judgment of other cultures by the standards of one's own. Without some degree of accommodation, ethnocentrism will make effective communication impossible.

   Canadian businesspeople working in non–English-speaking countries often encounter disadvantages when they do not speak the language. Nuances are lost as translations move thoughts from one language to another. When communicating with foreign businesspeople who speak English, Canadians should use simple, clear language and avoid slang or figures of speech.

2. **Contrast the communication differences between low-context and high-context cultures.**

   In low-context cultures, communication depends on explicit written and verbal messages. In high-context cultures, communication is linked not only to explicit messages but also to the context of the communication and to nonverbal language. Personal relationships, timing, level of formality, etiquette, and body language have different meanings in low- and high-context cultures. Understanding these differences affects communication success.

3. **List the key elements in successful written and oral communication across national boundaries.**

   Effective written communication depends on the use of translators when necessary, proper language usage, adaptation to communication styles, and sensitivity to cultural preferences. You must also learn the correct format for directing foreign correspondence.

   Oral communication follows many of the same guidelines as written communication. Language must be simple, direct, and jargon-free. During oral presentations and meetings, formality, tempo, and audience behaviour differ in high- and low-context cultures. When language barriers exist, interpreters can bridge the communication gap.

4. **Identify the major demographic changes that are transforming the Canadian workforce and marketplace.**

   An increasing number of women, older workers, and minorities are transforming the workforce. By the year 2010, one-third of the current population will be turning 65 years of age, and it is conceivable that the Anglo-Canadian male worker will become a minority.

5. **Explain the differences between communication styles of men and women and describe how to deal with sexual harassment.**

   While men tend to speak a language of status and independence, women tend to focus on connection and intimacy. This fundamental difference expresses itself in the way men and women ask for information or offer help, in the way they relate to one another through report-talk versus rapport-talk, in differences in nonverbal communication, and in the use of conversational rituals.

   Sexual harassment consists of behaviours that range from blatant grabbing and touching to subtle, sexually oriented hints, suggestions, and comments that create a hostile working environment.

6. **Describe the special communication needs of older people and persons with disabilities.**

   The passage of federal legislation and the aging of the population combine to ensure that older people and people with disabilities will have a place of increased importance in the workforce. The elderly and people with disabilities are also important business customers. Because many workers are younger and are likely to have no physical disability, miscommunication can occur. The communication differences that separate people with disabilties and older people from others can be as profound as those between men and women and between racial and ethnic groups.

7. **Explain the nature and importance of diversity training.**

   Diversity training focuses on improving awareness of the attitudes, behaviours, and communication patterns that characterize women, minorities, older workers, and people with disabilities. It is also

Review and Discussion Questions

1. What do we mean by the word culture? Explain how cultural backgrounds can influence communication styles. *(Ch. Obj. 1)*

2. Describe several key differences between Canadian business communication practices and those of other countries. *(Ch. Obj. 1)*

3. Distinguish between low-context and high-context cultures. Summarize key factors that affect communication in low- and high-context cultures. *(Ch. Obj. 2)*

4. Create a table that compares the preferences of low- and high-context cultures regarding personal relationships and body language. *(Ch. Obj. 2, 3)*

5. Describe steps that Canadian businesspeople can take to adapt their writing, communications, and presentations to a high-context culture and a low-context culture. *(Ch. Obj. 2, 3)*

6. Summarize key demographic trends in the Canadian workforce. Assuming that these trends will continue, estimate the percentage of Canadians over 60 by the year 2001. Explain your answer. *(Ch. Obj. 4)*

7. Explain how the Canadian workforce will benefit from changes in demography in the next ten years. *(Ch. Obj. 4)*

8. Describe some key differences between typical communication styles of women and men. *(Ch. Obj. 5)*

9. What is sexual harassment? Why is it so difficult to define precisely? *(Ch. Obj. 5)*

10. Why is diversity training important? What can businesses do to bring together diverse groups in the workplace? *(Ch. Obj. 7)*

Application Exercises

1. Jim Mason runs CanukSport, a small firm that manufactures athletic clothing decorated with the logos of Canadian sports teams. He has been reading a lot lately about how the world is turning into a "global village," and figures that there must be a market for his products outside Canada. As an experienced entrepreneur who's not afraid to take risks, Mason has decided to add exporting to his company's activities. He feels ready to take on this new challenge because he just finished two semesters of Spanish at a local community college. "One year of Spanish should be enough to get by," reasons Mason. "After all, Spanish is a pretty easy language. Besides, everybody down there knows English." What advice would you give Jim Mason? *(Ch. Obj. 1)*

2. Your advice so impresses Jim Mason that he asks you to write a letter in English to the firm's first Latin American prospect, a Bolivian business owner. Your letter will be the firm's first contact with this customer. Keep in mind that although your Bolivian correspondent reads English, it is not his first language. *(Ch. Obj. 1, 2, 3)*

3. After several letters have been exchanged, the Bolivian prospect invites Jim Mason down for a visit.

Mason asks you to go along. During the flight to La Paz, he asks you for pointers about the best way to approach his prospective business deal. What would you tell him? *(Ch. Obj. 1, 2, 3)*

4. Unfortunately, a shipment of CanukSport shirts meant for Basel, Switzerland, mistakenly arrived in Brussels. Jim Mason is so upset that he sits down and writes a personal note of apology to Walther Zimmer, the Swiss distributor. Because you know Mason, you offer to look at the letter before it is sent. Here's the letter:

> Dear Walther:
> I feel really low about this whole business. Apparently, we dropped the ball and sent the stuff to the wrong town. I just don't know how it happened. Of course, Brussels does sound a little like Basel, but still, we goofed. We're sending another shipment and it should arrive momentarily. Sorry about the mix-up, but you're a cool dude, and I know you won't have a cow. Keep in touch.
> Sincerely,
> Jim

Would you suggest any changes to this letter? If so, rewrite it. *(Ch. Obj. 1, 3)*

5. The *Globe and Mail* has asked you to write a short article entitled "Communicating in a Global Mar-

ketplace." Choose a country that was discussed in this chapter and write an article summarizing the ways in which the nation's customs affect its business practices. Does this country have a high- or low-context culture? How do its business practices differ from those in Canada? What advice would you offer a Canadian planning a business trip to that country? *(Ch. Obj. 1, 2, 3)*

6. Several exporters in Mexico were impressed by your *Globe and Mail* article. They have asked you to give a presentation in English at their professional association's annual meeting in Mexico City. The topic they have requested is "Effective Business Communication in Canada." You know that these businesspeople are eager to increase their Canadian business and are looking to you for practical tips on how Canadian businesspeople communicate. Write a draft of your speech. *(Ch. Obj. 1, 3, 4)*

7. Marta Schultz was sent to Tokyo to represent her company in important business negotiations with a new customer. You see her after she returns and eagerly ask how the trip went. "Terrible!" she says. "I've never been so frustrated in my life. When I handed Mr. Yakamoto my business card, he spent the next five minutes scrutinizing it. I felt like he wasn't listening to me at all because he never looked at me. I kept trying to establish eye contact, but he just kept his eyes lowered." Marta's assistant, Bob, chimes in, "Yeah, it was really strange. They kept asking me the questions even though I told them that Marta is my boss." The worst thing, Marta continues, is that she couldn't tell whether they liked her presentation. "I kept asking them to agree to our terms, but they kept avoiding the issue. Finally, I had to leave because I had an appointment to keep with a supplier." What advice would you give Marta? *(Ch. Obj. 1, 3, 5)*

8. Jim Mason, the CEO of athletic clothing maker CanukSport, has decided to explore new markets inside Canada, starting with Asians. Borrowing a Japanese-English dictionary from the library, he translates the company name into Japanese, has it printed on company stationery, and asks you to spearhead a direct-mail campaign targeting Asians in Canada. Do you agree with Jim's approach? Explain your answer. *(Ch. Obj. 1, 4)*

9. During the next week, listen carefully to conversations around you. See if you can find examples of "male" and "female" communication patterns as discussed in this chapter. Notice examples of report-talk/rapport-talk; asking for information/offering help; and powerful/powerless language. Record your observations and explain how these conversations exemplify male and female communication patterns. *(Ch. Obj. 5)*

10. What do you think are the advantages and disadvantages of typical male patterns and typical female patterns of communication? Which approach might be more effective in today's workplace? Explain your answer. *(Ch. Obj. 5, 7)*

11. Interview a businessperson in your community about how his or her company meets the special needs of older and disabled customers and staff. What does the company do to make its physical facilities accessible? How does it meet the special communication needs of physically challenged people? Do you have any recommendations for how this company might improve its services to these people? Take notes during your interview; then write a report and turn it in to your instructor. *(Ch. Obj. 6)*

12. The chamber of commerce in your community has asked you to give a speech on "Diversity as a Business Strategy for the 21st Century." Local businesspeople are interested in hearing your opinions on why diversity is an important issue. They'd like to know what makes a good diversity-training program and how such a program can affect their profitability. Write a one-page summary of your speech. *(Ch. Obj. 7)*

ACT: Applied Communication Techniques

Begin by referring to the sections up to and including Verbs in Appendix II, then correct the grammar, spelling, and usage errors in the following sentences. Check your answers in Appendix V.

1. I wish he was able to communicate in french.

2. Neither Yoshi nor Pierre are clear what the english speaker meant by the expression "break a leg."

3. Never assume that age impaired a person's ability

to understood concepts.

4. Every culture in Canada have added value to this countries great diversity.

5. Each of the foreign students are requesting an extention of their time in Saskatchewen.

6. Gender differences affects communication in the workplace just as it does at home.

7. The physicaly challenged student, along with his

wife and daughter, travel to Kelowna every summer.

8. The overwelming majority of victims of sexual harasment is women.

9. Stereotypes is responsible for a great deal of miscomunication that occurrs amoung diverse groups of people.

10. The number of immigrents to Canada are increasing.

Buiding Your Research Skills

Jim Mason is so thrilled with the success of CanukSport's overseas marketing that he decides to expand into other nations. Imagine that your communications class is the entire marketing department at CanukSport and that Mason has asked all of you to help develop international marketing plans. Your instructor will act as Mason's chief operating officer and will divide the class into small teams, each of which will target a particular nation, such as Saudi Arabia, China, Nigeria, England, Hungary, Mexico, Australia, and the United States.

Each team should research the customs and traditions of its designated country. Think about how these factors might influence the country's cultural and communication patterns. Take notes on what you read so that you can report back to the group.

Building Your Teamwork Skills

Reassemble into the groups that you formed for the exercise in Building Your Research Skills. Team members should discuss what they learned from their research and then develop a set of communication guidelines appropriate for the country that the group targeted and researched. Can you think of any marketing ideas that might work for this nation? Are there any marketing ideas that work for Canadian consumers but should definitely be avoided in foreign marketing? Create a written report summarizing your team's conclusions. A team spokesperson can then present this report to the class.

Building Your Technology Skills

You have just been asked to develop a diversity-training program for your company that focuses on First Nations, French-Canadian, and Italian-Canadian cultures. You decide to learn more about these cultures by conducting research on the Internet. Visit the following Web sites to begin your research.

First Nations of Canada:
http://indy4.fdl.cc.mn.us/~isk/canada.html
French Canadians:
http://frenchcaculture.miningco.com/mbiopage.htm
Italian Canadians:
http://www.shoc.com/SHOC_Treatment/SHOC_ing/multi/itindex.html

Use two Internet search engines to further your knowledge. Refer to Appendix III for information on these search engines.

Yahoo Canada   http://www.yahoo.ca
AltaVista Canada   http://www.altavistacanada.com

When you have finished researching, write a two-page paper that includes:

▼ Cultural information that might influence communication with First Nations, French Canadians, and Italian Canadians.

▼ An analysis of how the communication styles of these cultures differ from each other.

Weblinks Internet Resources for this Chapter

Cross Cultural Communications for Business and Industry
http://www.bena.com/ewinters/xculture.html

Nonverbal Communications Around the World
http://www.worldculture.com/gestures.htm

Avoiding Gender Bias
http://condor.stcloud.msus.edu/~scogdill/339/polcor.html

Diversity Training
http://www.corcommunications.com/cc2.html

CASE STUDIES

DIVERSITY CASE:

News American-Style Doesn't Work

India is a huge economy undergoing considerable growth. CNN, a U.S. cable news channel, cracked the Indian market by teaming up with Doordarshan, the government-owned network. However, CNN's 1995 launch was flawed by communication problems.

Network teaser footage featured cattle blocking traffic in Bombay. Since cattle are considered sacred by Hindus, this footage offended many in India's population. CNN Vice President Peter Vessey responded to the network's critics by announcing that the teaser was really an analogy that pointed up the "bullishness" of the Indian economy. Vessey's remarks did little to quiet critics who suggested that CNN was not presenting the correct image of modern India.

As if the Bombay cow footage weren't enough, a CNN weather map showed the disputed province of Kashmir as part of Pakistan, not India. Another wave of protest hit the U.S. network. One opposition party leader, L. K. Advani, said the CNN-Doordarshan deal was a "sellout of the nation's interests." Advani went on to characterize the weather map flap as an "ominous pointer of the shape of things to come."[39]

Questions and Applications

1. What could CNN have done to avoid these communication mistakes?

2. Assume CNN Vice President Vessey asked your advice about how to improve the situation. What advice would you give him?

3. Now suppose that CNN decides to start up business in Pakistan. What advice would you give Vessey about entering that market? Examine the possibility that Indian citizens can gain access to the CNN channel in Pakistan.

CORPORATE CASE:

When in Japan, Do as the Japanese Do

In the past, doing business in Japan was a difficult, complicated, and often unsuccessful venture. In addition to different languages, social customs, and histories, the United States is a low-context culture; Japanese culture is high-context. In recent years, however, several U.S. companies have overcome the many economic and cultural barriers facing foreigners in Japan.

DSP Group Inc. is one such company. The California-based semiconductor manufacturer generates nearly half its profits from sales in Japan. That's why the firm's chief executive officer moved with his family to Tokyo and lived there for more than a year, cultivating Japanese customers and suppliers. The Tokyo office consists of six desks wedged into a tiny building, but DSP executives see it as a good start in "fitting in." Says one, "To compete in the consumer electronics market, we have to be here."

DSP management has also learned to take care of the details. Japanese consumers are discriminating buyers, and small imperfections—small, that is, by American standards—are large for Asian customers. Japanese customers pay close attention to the quality of work put into products, and notice such things as shoddy soldering or welding. Even a slight imperfection can kill a sale if a Japanese consumer questions whether all the products are made poorly. Sloppy packaging signals careless manufacturing to Japanese consumers, so DSP devotes extra care to packaging.

Finally, DSP managers and other foreign businesspeople who want to make money in Japan must learn to watch their image. Firms that sell items through catalogues have found it prudent to remove some low-priced products from Japanese catalogues even though the same items are big sellers in other countries. Why? Japanese consumers tend to judge products according to product lines and overall performance of their manufacturers. If some catalogue items seem cheap, Japanese consumers may very well question the quality of all the merchandise in the catalogue.[40]

Questions and Applications

1. Discuss some key cultural differences between the United States and Japan.

2. Explain how these cultural differences can affect business communication patterns.

3. What can U.S. firms learn about doing business in Japan from reading this case?

Chapter

4

Planning Business Documents

I skate to where the puck is going to be, not to where it has been.

"

Wayne Gretzky
Canadian-born NHL player

Chapter Objectives

After studying this chapter, you should be able to:

1. Identify the stages in the writing process.
2. Describe why the Internet is considered the greatest research tool of contemporary times.
3. Explain the general purpose, specific purpose, and core idea objectives of a business document.
4. Define and identify primary and secondary audiences for business documents.
5. Identify and briefly explain alternative audience-analysis techniques.
6. Describe the role of research in document planning.
7. Explain the prewriting techniques of brainstorming, mindmapping, freewriting, and asking journalists' questions.

allmark Writers Say It for Us

Congratulations, sympathy, humor, encouragement, in love, out of love, looking for love . . . it isn't always easy to find the right words to say. That is where Hallmark Cards comes in. The people who write these verses must be creative. They have to say a hundred things in a hundred different ways. Over the years, the creativity of Hallmark cards has been apparent, but what is often overlooked is the planning and effort that determine which cards are produced.

Each card's message must be unique and yet appeal to a massive audience— some 8 million Hallmark cards are bought every day. The planning process often begins when an editor holds a brainstorming meeting with writers, searching for ideas. Together they create "Need Lists" that contain orders for Hallmark's creative staff of writers: need new jokes about hospitals—not nurses or food; need lines of encouragement for marital problems, alcoholism, or drug abuse.

Five years ago, senior editor Susan Giffen identified a need for recovery cards for substance abusers, their families, and friends. "During lunch, a friend of mine told me that her husband was an alcoholic, that he was trying to deal with it, and that this was an awful time for them. I went back to the office thinking, 'Gee, I wish there was an appropriate card—just something supportive.' "

Giffen and her staff conducted extensive research, attended conventions of Adult Children of Alcoholics, and talked with professionals about recovery and being in a co-dependency relationship with someone recovering from substance abuse. They also learned the etiquette of the Alcoholics Anonymous 12-step program.

Once the market was identified and evaluated, the next step was assigning the task to the writers and artists. The writers engaged in *freewriting*—a creative activity that encourages the free expression of ideas and words without worrying about criticism or censorship. The cards hit the shelf under the broad heading, *Just for Today: Cards of Support and Encouragement.* They covered a variety of needs from apologies ("I regret the pain I've caused you . . .") to pep talks ("Sometimes it may seem that therapy is slow going . . .") to humor ("Recovery Man, able to leap 12 steps in a single bound!"). Giffen was not surprised to learn that they achieved immediate sales success.

All 700 writers work to create cards that express ideas and emotions shared by almost everyone at one time or another. To aid writers' efforts, Hallmark has a farmhouse not far from their headquarters where writers meet to relax, lower their guards, and begin freewriting. During a typical workshop afternoon, six to ten writers sit around a table freewriting, where the only commodities that count are good ideas and a catchy way of saying them. One group member may be having a dry spell that day; another may create lush verses.

Hallmark writers face the enormous challenge of being creative all the time. For instance, the writers for Shoebox Greetings, Hallmark's alternate humor line, must come up with about 150 new ideas a day—ideas that are often the result of research, brainstorming, and freewriting sessions that permit writers to unleash their creativity. ▼

Source: Gerri Hershey, "Happy [   ] Day to You," *New York Times Magazine,* 2 July 1995, 20–27, 43–45.

Chapter Overview _____

At Hallmark, writers are nurtured as is the writing process. Management understands the importance of planning tools, such as brainstorming, freewriting, and research.

This chapter explains the importance of the planning process in effective business communication. We begin by showing how planning fits into the entire writing process—a process involving research, organization, composition and design, and revision. We then divide the planning process itself into three major steps: defining a document's objectives, defining its audience, and implementing the plan. Finally, we survey a variety of prewriting strategies—including those used at Hallmark—to gather and organize ideas.

Stages in the Writing Process _____

Successful writing results from knowing how to structure ideas on paper. To structure ideas well, writers must move through the writing process, which we will describe briefly in the sections that follow. Figure 4-1 shows the six stages in the writing process: planning, research, organization, composition, design, and revision.

PLANNING

In business writing, **planning** is the process of setting document objectives, analyzing audience needs and responses, and developing a course of action to accomplish the objectives. Effective planning takes time at the start of a project, but overall it saves time because it helps writers to focus on their goals.

Figure 4-1 The Writing Process

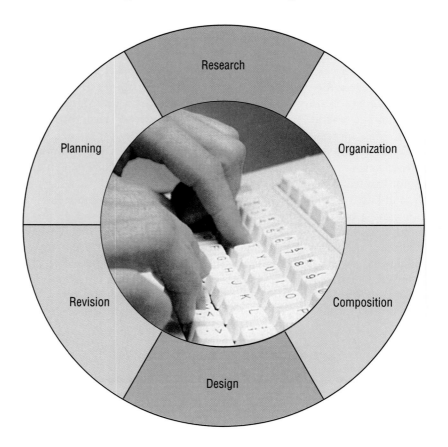

RESEARCH

For Hallmark's Susan Giffen, researching her idea to produce a recovery line of cards not only verified how much market potential the product had, it produced ideas about how to develop the cards. An important part of the planning process is **research**—the systematic investigation of a subject in order to discover facts, opinions, or beliefs. The amount of research needed for a written assignment depends on the nature of the document and the information available about the subject. While minimal research is usually needed for simple memos or letters, longer, more complex documents may require extensive fact-finding.

No doubt, the Internet has become the greatest research tool of contemporary times. According to Internet experts Jim Carroll and Rick Broadhead, "We are seeing an explosion in a number of massive search systems designed to help you find information about a particular topic, person, or organization on the Internet."[1] Without actually visiting the local library and wading through paper indexes, books, journals, and files, an immense amount of information can be had right at your fingertips. The Internet is fast, easy, convenient, and very effective! Along with these benefits, however, Internet research does present some disadvantages. If you consider that the Internet is a medium for anyone to publish anything at any time, the dangers are obvious.

> **→ Cross Reference**
> We discuss Internet research in greater detail in Appendix III of this book.

ORGANIZATION

Based on their communication objectives, audience requirements, and format limitations, writers make crucial decisions about **organization.** These decisions determine the order in which they present their ideas, the logical connections that exist among these ideas, and the approach they take to present the ideas. (Chapter 6 identifies various approaches to written documents and explains how each can reflect different purposes.)

> *When you come to a fork in the road, take it.*
>
> Yogi Berra
> Longtime New York Yankee catcher

COMPOSITION AND DESIGN

The process of **composition** involves following your organizational writing plan to produce a rough draft. As writers compose, they make decisions about such matters as tone, style, and level of formality. At Hallmark composition begins during the writing workshops, where writers and artists both praise and criticize each other's ideas. At this stage writers usually begin developing an effective design for their document.

Many of Hallmark's card designs reflect the message of the card. Boldface letters are often used for humorous messages, while an ornate script might be used for a wedding announcement. **Design** is the process of placing information on a page so that it is easily read. Various design elements help clarify organization, including headings, underlining, and bulleted lists.

REVISION

The final stage in the writing process is **revision**—specific steps that transform a rough draft into a finished document. These steps include:

- ▼ ensuring the most appropriate words, style, and tone are used to communicate your message;
- ▼ checking for clarity and conciseness and removing all jargon;
- ▼ eliminating all punctuation, grammatical, and spelling errors;
- ▼ focusing on coherence through the use of effective transitions; and
- ▼ checking for factual errors.

Learning to use feedback to improve the quality and professionalism of your work is also a crucial step in the writing process. We now turn in more detail to the concept of planning.

Strategic and Tactical Planning

Business decision making typically involves two forms of planning. **Strategic planning** is the process by which managers determine the major objectives of an organization and choose courses of action to achieve those objectives. **Tactical planning** is the process by which objectives are translated into specific, achievable plans. Honda's decision to construct automobile assembly plants in Ontario and Ohio to build cars for the Canadian and American market was part of Honda's strategic plan. Its advertising campaign, which sought to convince the Canadian and American car buyer that Honda is a regional automobile, was part of its tactical plan.

Strategic planning can guide business writers as they identify the purpose of a document, define its objectives, analyze its audience, and choose a course of action. Tactical planning for business writing begins with organizing, composing and designing business documents, and concludes with editing and revising.

Progress Check

1. Define planning in the context of business writing.
2. List the stages in the writing process.
3. Distinguish between strategic planning and tactical planning as they apply to business writing.

Although the planning process, like the writing process, may be examined as a series of distinct steps that naturally follow one another, the steps are actually interactive and overlapping. For example, brainstorming and audience analysis may be conducted before, during, or after research. Throughout the planning process, then, experienced business writers move back and forth from one stage to another. In this sense, each of the three stages summarized in Table 4-1 should be considered an ongoing activity.

Table 4-1   Stages in the Planning Process

Stage	Purpose
Define objectives	Provide clear and specific direction for your writing effort
Define audience	Identify audience needs, knowledge, and interests
Implement plan	Research the core idea and revise it, if necessary, based on research findings; gather ideas through prewriting strategies; and select the most effective written communication

Defining Your Document Objectives

To be effective, objectives should focus on what the message says and the best way to communicate that message to a specific audience. Defining objectives, the most critical step in the planning process, helps limit the scope of the topic. When you decide what information to include and exclude, you address the needs of your audience most effectively. Objectives serve four primary functions:

▼ They provide a sense of direction as you gather information, analyze your audience, and begin to compose.

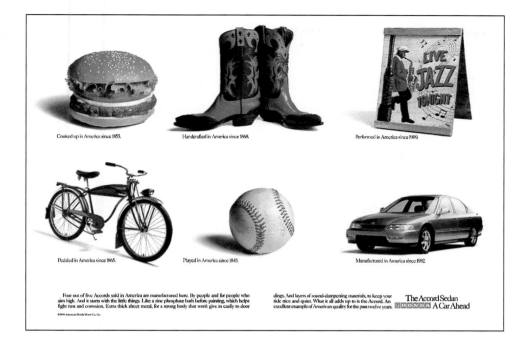

Cooked up in America since 1855.

Handcrafted in America since 1868.

Performed in America since 1909.

Pedaled in America since 1865.

Played in America since 1845.

Manufactured in America since 1982.

Four out of five Accords sold in America are manufactured here. By people and for people who aim high. And it starts with the little things. Like a zinc phosphate bath before painting, which helps fight rust and corrosion. Extra thick sheet metal, for a strong body that won't give in easily to door dings. And layers of sound-dampening materials, to keep your ride nice and quiet. What it all adds up to is the Accord. An excellent example of American quality for the past twelve years. HONDA A Car Ahead

The Accord Sedan

© 1994 American Honda Motor Co., Inc.

This message combines the image of a Honda Accord with a number of symbols typically associated with Canadian and American lifestyles. Honda Canada and American Honda Motor Company use this approach in their efforts to persuade the car-buying public that the automobile they typically think of as Japanese is manufactured at home.

▼ They focus your efforts. With limited time available for any task, effective time management is crucial.

▼ They guide writing decisions. Stating objectives helps you choose the best way to organize material, the right words, the most effective tone and format, and when and how to send a document.

▼ They help you evaluate your progress as you write. Objectives provide the standard against which you can measure your work.

There is nothing so useless as doing efficiently that which should not be done at all.

Peter Drucker
Business philosopher and author

Objectives work best when they are clear in the writer's mind and are incorporated clearly in a document. Defining a document's objectives involves defining its general purpose, specific purpose, and core idea.

DEFINE YOUR GENERAL PURPOSE

Although you may have several reasons for business writing—such as trying to create a good impression—a document's **general purpose** is its main objective. The three most common general purposes of written communication are to *inform*, to *persuade*, and to *initiate action*.

Much of business writing is informative. Examples include status reports on current projects, memos to schedule meetings, and letters to customers regarding delayed orders or merchandise credits. The primary purpose of the letter in Figure 4-2 is to communicate information.

Persuasive writing tries to convince the reader of the validity of your message. Persuasive documents include proposals for new procedures, letters of recommendation, and sales brochures. Figure 4-3 is an example of a persuasive document.

Many letters ask the reader to act or respond in a certain way. Examples include sales letters, requests for information, and job-application letters. Although *action-oriented* letters can also inform or persuade, their main purpose is to produce responses that have concrete results. Figure 4-4 is an action-oriented letter that also informs.

July 23, 2000

Ms. Alice Letemplier
1700 Boat Street
Kelowna, BC V1X 4R3

Dear Ms. Letemplier:

Your request for a credit card at Miranda's Department Store is now being processed. You can expect to hear from us before August 5.

As a credit card customer, you will be informed of private storewide sales and will also receive special discounts. In fact, the discounts begin today. By spending five minutes completing the enclosed new-customer questionnaire, you will receive a free gift, compliments of Miranda's.

Much more is coming. When you receive your credit card, look for news of Miranda's fall fashion parade.

Sincerely,

Susan Amery

Susan Amery
Manager, New Accounts

Enclosure

Figure 4-2 Writing to Inform

DEFINE YOUR SPECIFIC PURPOSE AND CORE IDEA

Think of the **specific purpose** of a document as a brief summary of your reason for writing the message. Your specific purpose may be thought of as a note to yourself.[2] Here, for example, is a summary of a specific purpose:

> . . . to inform all new Canadian Prairie Harvest employees that they will receive a sample of every small appliance the company manufactures.

Developed from the specific purpose summary, the **core idea** (sometimes called the *thesis statement*) is the central message in the document. Ideally, it can be stated in a single sentence. For example, you could use the previous specific purpose summary to create this core idea for your document statement:

> As a new employee, you should be aware that Canadian Prairie Harvest will give you, free of charge, a sample of every Canadian Prairie Harvest product as our way of building goodwill and increasing your product knowledge.

Knowledge is a process of piling up facts; wisdom lies in their simplification.

Martin H. Fisher
Author and educator

```
MEMORANDUM




          To:        Annette Billings
                     Training Manager

          From:      Carlos Sanchez
                     Director of Computer Training

          Date:      September 3, 2000

          Subject:   Training Temporary Employees

          I recommend that we test all temporary workers
          registered with our agency for knowledge of the
          Windows 98 operating system and initiate a training
          program for those unfamiliar with the system.  This
          recommendation stems from the following trends:

          •   Windows 98 has become our clients' standard
              operating system.  As a result, clients will
              require temporary employees who can use that
              system.

          •   Our competitors, including Olsten Staffing
              Services, Renfrew Temporary Services, and Kelly
              Services, include computer training as a standard
              part of upgrading for their temporary clients.

          I will call you next week to discuss a training plan.
```

Burlington *Temporary Staffing Service*

www.burlington.com
2512 Ironwood Street, Mississauga, ON L5N 3R9
(905) 555-1234 (phone)   (905) 555-4321 (fax)
csanchez@berlington.com (email)

Figure 4-3 Writing to Persuade

In long reports and proposals, the core idea often appears as a *purpose statement* that informs readers why they received your document. The purpose statement can be as simple as the following sentences in a cover memo.

> Attached are the regional crime reports for the six largest budget motels. This data should help clarify the issues you raised last week.

Sometimes more detail is necessary to tell your reader what to expect:

> Many law enforcement agencies report increased burglaries, rapes, and homicides at low-priced motels. However, according to law officers, crime at higher-priced hotels, such as ours, has not increased. This report examines the relationship between crime and the price of lodging, crime prevention measures, and ways to market the value of safety to business travellers who now use budget lodging.

Taken together, your specific purpose and core idea can show you whether your document is trying to accomplish too much. For example, the following summary of specific purpose fails to limit the scope of the memo:

IMAGE ADVERTISING INC.

www.image.com

11 Ridge Road, Whitehorse, Yukon Territory Y1A 3L1
Phone (867) 555-2345 • Fax (867) 555-5432
E-mail: image@yukon.com

Transmitted Via Fax: (867) 555-9090

November 11, 2000

Mr. Devon Mack
Tech Electronics Inc.
164 Centre Street
Yellowknife, NT X1A 5X5

Dear Devon:

As you know, Keith Brightsky of the *Toronto Star* plans to write an article on Tech Electronics' new advertising campaign. He has agreed to conduct an interview for the story at our Whitehorse office at 10:00 a.m. on Tuesday, November 30. This story will appear on Friday, December 3 in the *Toronto Star* and may also be picked up by the *Ottawa Citizen*.

Because the interview must focus on Tech Electronics, and not on Image Advertising, it is vital that either you or another Tech Electronics representative of your choice attend. Our Image Advertising representative, Richard Cardinal, will be on hand to assist with any information you may require.

To ensure that the interview goes smoothly, please let me know by November 18 who the Tech Electronics representative will be. Thanks for your cooperation, Devon.

Regards,

Michael Cooper

Michael Cooper
Creative Director

Figure 4-4   Writing to Initiate Action

To inform all new Canadian Prairie Harvest employees of the free company products they will receive and to describe our employee-based system for improving productivity.

Progress Check

1. Why is defining a document's objectives considered the most critical step in the planning process?
2. Define and differentiate a document's general purpose, specific purpose, and core idea. Give an example of each.

Combining two important purposes into one document weakens the impact of both messages and guarantees that neither will get the attention it deserves.

After you write your specific purpose summary and core idea statement, include the core idea in your first draft. If the core idea does not communicate to your audience or the research does not support your point, you should revise your specific purpose and core idea statements.

Five Symptoms of Poor Writing

Five common problems result in poor writing. Fortunately, each problem has a solution.

1. *Unclear thinking and planning.* Without a plan, writing often lacks direction. Ideas are lost as the audience struggles to follow your train of thought. Effective planning, however, leads to clear organization. One widely used and highly effective method for planning a document is arranging information in outline form. Because information is presented to the audience in a step-by-step fashion, you achieve clarity.

2. *Failing to write with your audience in mind.* Failure to analyze your audience can result in writing at a level too high or too low for your readers. Your writing may also fail to address readers' interests and needs. An audience-centered approach tells readers what they want to know in a way that is useful to them. Some familiar examples of writer-centered rather than audience-centered documents are computer manuals, Revenue Canada tax forms, and insurance policies.

3. *Writing to impress rather than communicate.* Nothing impresses readers more than clear, simple communication. Flowery language, jargon, and long, complex sentences hinder communication and ignore readers' needs. If, for example, you provide information on a new design for a product label, avoid describing the print as reflecting a "contemporary style." Instead, state that "the print is large and can be read easily when placed beside competing product lines on retail store shelves."

4. *Designing documents poorly.* Because of information overload, businesspeople are often too busy to wade through details to get to the point. To help readers grasp your points quickly, plan and revise document design as you plan and revise its content. Use headings, bulleted lists, indented paragraphs, and plenty of white space.

5. *Failing to revise and edit.* Few documents are right the first time. They need fine-tuning and sometimes major revision. A document review may alert you that a minor point has been emphasized more than a major one. This overemphasis could detract from the document's purpose. For example, although a document's purpose might pertain to the company as a whole, it is easy to let facts that directly affect your department become a major focus.

Source: Adapted from Sherry Sweetnam, *The Executive Memo: A Guide to Persuasive Business Communications* (New York: John Wiley & Sons, 1986), 9–11.

Who's My Audience?

Although clearly stating your objectives typically answers many questions, it can raise others. For example:

To do two things at once is to do neither.

Publilius Syrus
Writer of mimes

▼ Are my objectives relevant to my audience?

▼ Is my message too trivial? Too technical? Too detailed?

▼ Will my document stand alone or must it be reviewed with other documents?

▼ Is my document intended for one or more than one audience?

These and other questions can only be answered through careful **audience analysis**—an examination of the needs and knowledge of readers in order to improve communication effectiveness. Audience analysis is crucial in written and oral business communication.

Consider, for example, the following informal sales presentation that hinges on a certain confusion about customers and audiences:

A fisherman went into a sporting goods store to buy a lure. Happy to oblige, the salesclerk showed him a wide array of coloured feathers, plastic insects, and other clever gadgets designed to attract the fish. Confused by the array and not sure whether any would really work, the fisherman inquired, "Do fish really like this sort of thing?" Without hesitating, the clerk responded, "I don't sell to fish."[3]

The moral of the story is clear: If your persuasive message has the specific purpose of selling fishing lures, the people who fish—not the fish—are your primary audience. However, the story's ramifications may be more complex. Successful communication depends on the ability to identify the *primary* and *secondary audiences* who will receive your document. In this section, we will define these audiences and offer a model for understanding audience motivation.

PRIMARY AND SECONDARY AUDIENCES

Business documents often have more than one audience. Readers of corporate annual reports, for example, include employees, stockholders, customers, suppliers, government officials, the media, and the general public.[4] Readers with whom you must communicate to achieve your purpose are the **primary audience.** Decision makers and opinion leaders are examples of primary audience members. For instance, if you write a letter requesting a new fax machine for your department, your primary audience would be those who must approve your request.

Although formal letters typically are addressed to the primary reader, this is not always true with internal memos and reports. For example, a company's director of market research might ask a research analyst for a status report on the impact of a new advertising campaign. The director explains that the vice president for corporate advertising requested the report to help evaluate the campaign's costs and benefits. Although the analyst sends the report to the market research director, the primary audience is the vice president for corporate advertising.

Other audiences, known as **secondary audiences,** are readers who may be asked to comment on a document's content or those who use the information but are not directly affected by the communication. After reviewing the report, for example, the vice president for corporate advertising may send a copy to the developers who created the campaign to keep them informed of the evaluation.

Once you have identified your audiences, you should consider their requirements and draft your communication to fit their needs.

In 1995 Microsoft Corporation introduced Windows 95, one of the most highly publicized software innovations of the decade. This message introducing Microsoft Office for Windows 95 was aimed at a primary audience comprising the millions of potential Windows 95 purchasers seeking to integrate their existing software programs with the new system.

WHAT DOES MY AUDIENCE NEED?

The following suggestions will help focus your document on audience concerns. These suggestions make it clear that your audience's response to your message is as important as the message itself.[5]

CONSIDER THE READERS' KNOWLEDGE   When you consider your readers' knowledge of a subject, think about their background, their knowledge of your company, other documents they have read, and other people with whom they have spoken. Assume, for example, that a superior who interviewed and reviewed a consultant's report on alternative office space asked you to study the report and make recommendations. You need not repeat the consultant's suggestions in detail. The manager wants your opinion of the consultant's advice, not a rehashing of a report she has already read or conversations she has already had. Similarly, if you produce a document as part of a collaborative effort, plan the document with the team's total contribution in mind. Avoid placing the reader in the position of reading the same information in multiple places.

CONSIDER THE READERS' QUESTIONS   Many readers want to know why they should read a document. Put yourself in the readers' shoes by phrasing your summary of specific purpose as a question that readers might ask. For example, if your specific purpose for a memo is to persuade the company's art director to print a new brochure in colour rather than black and white, you might phrase your summary of purpose as the question, "Why should I print the new brochures in colour?" Then be sure your document answers the question completely and clearly. If it doesn't, your communication will confuse or frustrate your audience.

LEARN TO INTERPRET REQUESTS   Similarly, if you are writing in response to a request, turn the request into a question that must be answered in your written response. For example, if a superior asks for a memo on the distribution problem at the Saskatoon plant, he is really asking what steps can be taken to solve the problem at the Saskatoon plant. In answering your own rephrased question, you provide a more satisfactory reply to the request.

CONSIDER THE READERS' POSITION   Ask yourself whether you are writing to a supervisor, subordinate, or a co-worker. According to communication consultant John Fielden, when communicating to superiors, an argumentative or insulting tone is likely to cause trouble. Similarly, when writing to a subordinate, an overbearing or insulting tone will limit a manager's effectiveness.[6]

CONSIDER THE READERS' BIASES AND INTERESTS   Suppose you suggest a new menu item to the managers of a pizza restaurant chain—dessert pizzas. You might decide to focus on the appeal of these dishes to new restaurant customers. In this case, your memo could begin, "Expanding our menu by offering a Very Cherry Pizza and a Perfect Peach Pizza will attract customers looking for a new pizza experience."

However, if one of the managers is most concerned about ensuring the success of two new outlets, the memo might begin: "Approximately 10 000 teenagers live within a three-kilometre radius of the two new restaurants in Surrey and Port Moody, British Columbia."

You should also remember that readers are less likely to read overly long or overly detailed documents. Write with the readers' information needs in mind, and keep written messages short, simple, and as easy to read as possible.

MEASURE YOUR LEVEL OF FORMALITY   Make the document's level of formality complement the style preferred by your reader. For example, a client who has done business with your company for 20 years might prefer a message that acknowledges a business rather than a personal relationship. In that case, you could use the company's name rather than *I* or *we*. For example, "International Life Insurance Company stands behind every policy it writes." However, the following opening would be acceptable in an informal letter: "As an agent for International Life, I want to personally assure you that the company stands behind every policy."

GUARD AGAINST FALSE ASSUMPTIONS Never forget that assumptions can result in miscommunication. Review the following common assumptions:

▼ *Gender.* Assuming that someone is a man or a woman based on an ambiguous first name; assuming certain stereotyped roles and responsibilities

▼ *Age.* Assuming knowledge and attitudes tied to certain age groups

▼ *Education.* Assuming that everyone reached the same position through the same educational route

▼ *Income.* Assuming that income has little effect on people's responses to goods and services

▼ *Occupation.* Assuming that people with similar titles in different organizations perform the same function or have the same income and authority level

▼ *Knowledge.* Assuming that everyone reads a document with the same level of knowledge about the subject

▼ *Attitudes.* Assuming that everyone shares the same feelings about an idea, a person, or a product

Progress Check

1. Define and compare primary and secondary audiences.
2. Why is visualizing your audience important before you begin writing?

MAKE SURE YOU MAKE SENSE Finally, ask yourself whether your document makes sense. The writer of the following letter from a tax service never applied the simple test of common sense. The letter was addressed to a dead man instead of to the widow who had filed her late husband's tax return.

> We are processing your gift tax return, Form 709 . . . and find we need more information. Please provide your date of death. . . . We apologize for any inconvenience we may have caused you, and thank you for your cooperation.[7]

Implementing a Writing Plan

There is no point in doing well, that which you should not be doing at all.

Thomas K. Connellan
Performance Research Assoc., Inc.

Having satisfied yourself that you have sufficient knowledge about your audience, you are ready for step three of the planning process: developing specific methods for *implementing* a writing plan. These methods involve:

1. testing your core idea against your research;
2. revising, if necessary, to reflect new information or points of view; and
3. defining and redefining the specific ideas that will make up the body of your document.

RESEARCHING THE CORE IDEA

Research involves gathering both primary and secondary information that either supports your position or forces revisions. **Primary sources** contain new information, such as statistics and other data. Primary sources might include Census Canada data, survey data, or interviews that you conduct yourself. **Secondary sources** are compilations of the ideas of others. For example, a *Maclean's* magazine article on a study of injury rates for airbag-equipped cars is a secondary source. The primary source is the original study. As you will see in Chapter 11, it is important to evaluate all your research sources in terms of accuracy and usefulness.

USING YOUR RESEARCH TO REEVALUATE YOUR CORE IDEA

Before implementing your writing plan, test your core idea against your research findings. The following example demonstrates how to make such an "accuracy check." Assume that you are a marketing analyst working for a major credit card company and believe that a vast untapped market of credit card customers exists among students enrolled in the nation's colleges and universities. You decide to write a memo to your manager, suggesting that the company begin an aggressive marketing program directed toward this group. Your preliminary core idea states:

> Canada's almost one million full-time college and university students are prime candidates for an aggressive credit card marketing program, and I recommend that we begin such a program at once in order to tap the potential of this market.

In addition to stating your point of view, your core idea should define the scope of your research. Primary research in this case might mean surveying the spending habits of college students who are currently credit card users. Secondary sources might include articles on college student credit card use found on the Internet, and a bimonthly trade newsletter that recently ran a series of articles on the student market. Perhaps you will also find a comprehensive review on the subject in a major newspaper such as the *Vancouver Province, Calgary Herald, Ottawa Citizen, Financial Post, Globe and Mail*, or the *Montreal Gazette*.

Assume that your research not only confirms your suspicion that college and university students represent a large untapped market of potential credit card users but also reveals that these individuals can be considered the market of the future. After all, the average non-student cardholder already owns seven cards. However, you also uncover a small but disturbing trend: a high rate of nonpayment among cardholders who are full-time students. This discovery causes you to revise your core idea, which now reads:

> Canada's almost one million full-time college and university students are prime candidates for an aggressive credit card marketing program, and I recommend that we begin such a program at once, using such prescreening measures as detailed credit histories, income requirements, and parental signatures to eliminate obvious credit risks.[8]

Your research changed the focus of your core idea by emphasizing the need for applicant screening and stringent credit requirements.

USING PREWRITING STRATEGIES

Developing the specifics of a document is part of the planning phase. It is also crucial in the organizing process and sets the stage for a formal outline. It is during idea development that certain prewriting strategies are employed. **Prewriting strategies** are techniques for gathering and organizing ideas that involve such processes as brainstorming, mindmapping, freewriting, and asking journalists' questions. The goal is to begin putting your plan on paper.

BRAINSTORMING   Getting your thoughts on paper is the first real challenge a writer faces. **Brainstorming** is a planning technique in which you list ideas as they come to mind. Because it is difficult to be both creative and judgmental at the same time, no evaluation of ideas occurs until after the brainstorming session. Quantity is desired at this stage, and a freewheeling method is encouraged—indeed, the stranger the idea, the better.[9]

To convince current and potential clients of the importance of retirement planning, New York Life advertisers used secondary data sources in a highly creative manner. By contrasting the relatively short life expectancies of many animals with the average 72-year life span of the typical North American male, the message emphasizes the core idea of the need to begin planning for the years following retirement.

Brainstorming is an unstructured writing tool that involves two distinct steps. First, the writer must create an uncensored list of words, phrases, and sentences that express topic-related points. Assume, for example, that you work for Puma, the athletic-shoe manufacturer, and have been assigned the task of analyzing the high end of the running shoe market for the last five to ten years. After conducting research—but before writing—you decide to brainstorm. As you write, you do not organize ideas, for example, by priority. Rather, you simply write them down as they occur to you. You come up with the following list:

▼ Nike Air is market leader
▼ $5.5 billion running shoe market
▼ what's hot today is gone tomorrow
▼ fickle teenage market
▼ Reebok Pump is dated
▼ Reebok targeted adults but kids bought
▼ unhappy customers
▼ Reebok's answer: Double Pump
▼ customers wary of high-tech hype
▼ gimmicks are in
▼ too many offerings is confusing
▼ Puma's new Disc System advantages
▼ problems competing with Reebok/Nike
▼ small ad budget compared to Reebok/Nike
▼ problems with pump

After all your ideas are written down, the second step is to organize them into patterns. In this step, you group your list into five categories:

1. Nature of the Industry

COLLABORATIVE COMMUNICATION

Brainstorming in a Group

The late Jim Henson, world-renowned creator of the Muppets, valued the ideas of everyone who worked for him. Puppeteers, writers, and producers worked alongside Henson to create Kermit the Frog, Miss Piggy, Fozzie Bear, and others. According to Brian Henson, now the CEO of Jim Henson Productions, the show worked because his father valued a diversity of ideas. "He wanted people who were wildly and eccentrically different from himself," recalls Brian. "He loved seeing what they could do and how they would surprise him. That philosophy created an incredible and diverse pool of company talent."

At Henson Productions and other companies, this collaborative talent is tapped during brainstorming sessions that unleash group creativity. In its free-form approach, brainstorming encourages excitement and involvement and often results in new and different ways to solve problems. The following general sequence demonstrates just one way to conduct a brainstorming session:

▼ *The topic to be brainstormed is introduced, often by asking "why," "how," and "what" questions.* For example, "How can our marketing brochures increase awareness of our products in the 18-to-35 age group?" or "How can we streamline book production costs to offset increasing paper costs?"

▼ *Everyone is given time to think about the question.* How much time depends on the question's complexity and on the information group members already have. Participants may need only a few minutes to think about familiar topics.

▼ *Group members then call out ideas. No critique, praise, or other comments are allowed.* Ideas are written on a flipchart.

▼ *With the brainstorming session over, the group then discusses the merit of each idea.*

Throughout the session, participants should avoid censoring their own ideas by labelling them silly or stupid. Similarly, group members should not pass judgment on the ideas of others. Negative comments or grimaces can kill a brainstorming session faster than no air conditioning on a hot summer day. The goal should be intellectual synergy—the piggybacking of one idea on top of another to produce results that no single member could have thought of alone.

Questions for Critical Thinking

1. Why is the lack of censorship so important in brainstorming sessions?

2. How can brainstorming help produce consensus—the acceptance and support of an idea by the entire group?

3. Why is it important to withhold discussion until all ideas are presented and written down?

4. List three ways that collaborative brainstorming skills can help you in your career.

Sources: Brian Henson, "Setting the Stage," *Inc.* (June 1994): 23–24; Peter R. Scholtes, *The Team Handbook: How to Use Teams to Improve Quality* (Madison, Wisc.: Joiner Associates), 2-38–2-40.

---

      gimmicks are in
      $5.5 billion running shoe market
      what's hot today is gone tomorrow

2. Market
      fickle teenage market
      Reebok targeted adults but kids bought shoes

3. Competition
      Nike Air is market leader
      Reebok Pump dated
      problems with pump
      unhappy customers
      Reebok's answer: Double Pump

4. Future Trends
      customers wary of high-tech hype
      too many offerings are confusing

5. Where Puma Stands
   Puma's new Disc System running shoe advantages
   problems competing with Reebok/Nike
   limited ad budget compared to Reebok/Nike[10]

MINDMAPPING   A closely related prewriting technique, **mindmapping** (or **clustering**) is a visual technique for grouping information into categories. This technique's nontraditional format allows many writers to associate ideas more easily and more freely.

Figure 4-5 is designed to apply the information gathered in our athletic-shoe market report to the following general guidelines for effective mindmapping. Like brainstorming, mindmapping is a technique for practising the association of ideas; don't worry if your organization appears to be random. There are four simple steps in mindmapping:

1. Draw a circle in the centre of an unlined piece of paper.
2. In the circle, write your document's topic.
3. Draw lines from the centre circle to outer circles, each of which is a subdivision of your main topic.
4. Include in each subdivision all related topics; each topic is circled.

Figure 4-5 Applying the Technique of Mindmapping

INTERVIEW Planning — A Personal Process

Lynn Quitman Troyka, Writing Authority

As a professor with a specialty in writing and as author of the *Simon & Schuster Handbook for Writers,* Lynn Quitman Troyka has helped thousands of students discover the link between effective planning and effective writing. We asked Troyka about the nature of the planning process and, more specifically, how individual writers can learn and practise the planning techniques that work best for them.

Question: How should writers begin to plan?

Answer: They can start by experimenting with different planning techniques. While some writers use mindmapping, freewriting, and other devices with great success, others have a hard time putting these techniques to good use. Instead, they discover what they want to say by talking with associates or friends. Or they plan as they write. In the end, there is no right way or wrong way to plan—only individual approaches to an extremely personal process.

Question: Is the nature of the process affected by what is being planned?

Answer: Different tasks require different types of planning. While I might freewrite a short business memo, I probably couldn't use this technique to plan a research report.

Question: Are there different levels of planning?

Answer: There are two kinds of planning—one relating to content, the other to presentation. Planning what you want to accomplish in terms of specific goals is the first part of the process. Superimposed on that is a plan of presentation—for example, what points you want to make first. Do you start with a compliment and then tell the reader what has to be done or vice versa? Decisions like this determine the way material is organized.

Question: Do all writers focus on the content of the message and the audience at the same time?

Answer: People learn in different ways, think in different ways, and conceptualize how they want to put thoughts on paper in different ways. While it's helpful for some people to think about the audience at the start, others have to focus on the message before the audience. If they mix the two, they may worry about what the reader will think and be unable to write. Although they ultimately revise the document with the audience in mind, they make these adjustments after they've written the message.

Question: If you were to give business writers one piece of advice about planning, what would that advice be?

Answer: When a document is complete, take a few minutes and reflect on what you did during the planning stages that made it turn out well or poorly. Use your insights the next time you plan. As always with writing, be your own monitor—and judge—before anyone else sees your work.

Source: Interview with Lynn Quitman Troyka.

Budget planners at Pacific Bell have used mindmapping in group sessions in which employees are asked to suspend traditional ways of thinking in order to focus on priorities.[11] Figure 4-5 shows how you might mindmap your athletic-shoe report.

FREEWRITING **Freewriting** is an unstructured writing process that allows you to express your thoughts without worrying about spelling, grammatical mistakes, or

# BUSINESS WRITING IN ACTION

This special feature will help you see how the concepts discussed in each chapter in Part II apply to a real-world business writing assignment. All aspects of document planning will be covered in these assignments. The features in Chapters 5 and 6 build on what you learn here.

THE ASSIGNMENT: PLANNING A BUSINESS MEMO TO ALL COMPANY EMPLOYEES

As marketing manager of the Cadillac division of General Motors, you have been assigned to write a memo to all department employees. The memo's purpose is to inform employees of the changes that are occurring at Cadillac in order to reestablish Cadillac's position as a leader in the luxury-car market.

THE METHOD: COMPLETE THE FOLLOWING THREE STEPS

Step 1: Set Memo Objectives

General Purpose: To inform.

Specific Purpose: To inform marketing department employees in the Cadillac division of General Motors of problems attracting consumers under age 40 and what marketing steps the company is taking to attract these buyers, especially women.

Core Idea: The average age of Cadillac buyers is 63; the Cadillac division is trying to attract younger consumers, including women, to the first new model in a decade.

Step 2: Analyze the Audience

Audience Identification: Employees in Cadillac's marketing department

Identification Method: Question and Answer

Question: How much does the audience know about my subject?

Answer: Marketing department employees know a great deal about Cadillac's declining market share, but they have not yet been introduced to the new model, called the Catera.

Question: Are my readers likely to be interested in what I have to say?

Answer: Yes. Cadillac's struggle against such luxury foreign imports as the Lexus, Mercedes Benz, and BMW affects the survival of the division.

Question: What kind of response can I expect from the audience?

Answer: The goal is to inform marketing department employees of the changes and encourage them to think about and plan for the marketing challenges that lie ahead.

Audience Motivation: To satisfy safety and security needs relating to freedom from financial worry. It is in everyone's financial best interest to maintain the financial viability of the division.

Step 3: Implement the Plan

Conduct Research: Analyze marketing data.

1. Gather data that reflect Cadillac's position in the luxury-car market.
2. Analyze marketing demographics, including the age and sex of average buyers.
3. Analyze what women want in a luxury car and the specific steps Cadillac can take to attract female buyers to the Catera.

Reevaluate the Core Idea Based on Research Findings: No change in core idea

Write Down Ideas: Use mindmapping

Select the Best Form of Written Communication: Memo sent through interoffice and e-mail

organizational problems. As in brainstorming and mindmapping, the primary goal of this stream-of-consciousness process is to begin putting your ideas on paper. The following section of our athletic-shoe market report reflects the typical result of a freewriting exercise, including the absence of complete sentences and the omission of such words as *the* and *in:*

> I want to talk about industry—and competition. Young kids wearing running shoes look for something new. Reebok started it all with the Pump. But the Pump is old hat. Also problems that turned customers off. "Several of my customers brought the Pump back because soles fell off or because of flat-tire feeling in arch area," reported Byron Mundee, Assistant Manager, Avanti Shoes in Fredericton, New Brunswick. Consequently, the Pump lost its status symbol. Even though kids want something new, they've also overdosed on too much high-tech hype. Too many offerings, too much confusion.

As you can see, quotations and other research can be roughly woven into freewriting to help focus thinking. Again, note that the writer is not concerned about complete sentences at this point.

ASKING JOURNALISTS' QUESTIONS   It is difficult to say where or when the six questions *Who? What? When? Where? Why?* and *How?* were first grouped together on paper. They are referred to as journalists' questions because journalists use them as guidelines to focus their thinking in preparing stories. Because answering these six questions helps to analyze information from different perspectives, they can also be used to plan business documents. They can, for example, be applied as starting points for analyzing our athletic-shoe market report:

Who?	Who buys our high-end running shoes? Who is the market leader?
What?	What is the nature of the industry today? What do customers want? What advantage does Puma's Disc System hold over the competition?
When?	When should Puma introduce its new running shoe line?
Where?	Where is the market still growing?
Why?	Why is the market so fickle? Why are customers wary of high-tech hype?
How?	How can Puma take advantage of market weakness? How can Puma compete with Nike and Reebok? How can we maximize our advertising budget?

In particular, journalists' questions can focus your writing on what is known and what is *not* known—both of which are critical in the planning stage.

THINKING CRITICALLY ABOUT YOUR DOCUMENT   This chapter has introduced you to several methods of putting ideas and facts down on paper in order to begin the writing process. Of equal importance is *applying* the results of such techniques and processes as brainstorming, freewriting, and asking journalists' questions. The effective communicator not only *presents* information, but also *produces* information.

Progress Check

1. Distinguish between primary and secondary research sources. Give an example of each.
2. Describe the prewriting strategies of brainstorming, mindmapping, and freewriting, and explain why they are important in the planning process.
3. What are the six journalists' questions that can assist writers in gathering and organizing ideas?

What's Ahead

Effective planning provides the foundation for the writing process. This process—which includes organizing, composing, and designing business documents—is examined in Chapter 5. Chapter 6 explores the elements of word selection and style.

STUDENT RESOURCE CENTRE

Summary of Chapter Objectives

1. ***Identify the stages in the writing process.***

   The writing process is made up of the following distinct stages: planning, research, organization, composition and design, and revision. Planning involves setting document objectives, assessing audience needs and probable responses, and developing a course of action to accomplish objectives. Research, a planning tool, involves fact finding through the use of primary and secondary sources. Organization focuses on the way in which ideas are presented. Composition and design involve writing a rough draft in a manner that is accessible to readers. Revision focuses on proper word choice, clarity, conciseness, and the elimination of punctuation, grammatical, and spelling errors.

2. ***Describe why the Internet is considered the greatest research tool of contemporary times.***

   There has been an explosion in the number of search systems designed to help Internet users find information about a particular topic, person, or organization. Without having to visit the local library and wade through paper indexes, books, journals, and files, an immense amount of information can be had right at your fingertips. The internet is fast, easy, convenient, and very effective.

3. ***Explain the objectives of a document in terms of its general purpose, specific purpose, and core idea.***

   Document objectives provide a sense of direction as information is gathered and the audience is analyzed. Objectives are defined in terms of the document's general purpose—the overriding reason for which the document is written. The objective may be to inform, to persuade, or to initiate action. The specific purpose briefly summarizes the reason for writing, while the core idea is a one-sentence statement of the document's thesis.

4. ***Define and identify primary and secondary audiences for business documents.***

   Many audiences may read a written document. The primary audience consists of readers for whom the communication is intended and who will use that information in their own work. The secondary audience includes people who may be asked to comment on ideas in the document or those who read it to stay informed but aren't directly affected by the message.

5. ***Identify and briefly explain alternative audience-analysis techniques.***

   Effective audience analysis involves analyzing readers' motivations, and considering the attitudes, knowledge, position, interests, and needs of the audience. It also includes rephrasing the specific purpose in the form of questions and avoiding incorrect assumptions about the audience.

6. ***Describe the role of research in document planning.***

   Research, the first step in implementing a plan, tests the validity of the core idea and directs revision to reflect new information. Research sources can be either primary or secondary.

7. ***Explain the prewriting techniques of brainstorming, mindmapping, freewriting, and asking journalists' questions.***

   Prewriting strategies are techniques for gathering and organizing ideas before actually writing a document. Brainstorming refers to the process of listing ideas as they come to mind and then organizing them into patterns. Mindmapping is a visual technique for grouping information into categories. Freewriting involves a process of uncensored writing. Finally, by asking the six journalists' questions—Who? What? When? Where? Why? and How?—you can present and produce information from different perspectives.

Review and Discussion Questions

1. Name the stages of the writing process. *(Ch. Obj. 1)*
2. Explain the value of spending time on planning before you write. *(Ch. Obj. 1)*
3. List three reasons why the Internet is such an effective research tool *(Ch. Obj. 2)*
4. Distinguish among a document's general purpose,

specific purpose, and core idea. *(Ch. Obj. 3)*

5. Give examples of primary and secondary audiences for a business document. *(Ch. Obj. 4)*

6. Think of an audience that you know—for example, members of an organization to which you belong. Give examples of several questions that you could ask yourself to help you better focus a document addressed to the audience. What about questions you could ask yourself regarding an audience that you don't know? *(Ch. Obj. 4, 5)*

7. Summarize alternative audience-analysis techniques that can help you to focus a document more effectively on a projected audience. *(Ch. Obj. 5)*

8. Explain why research is important in writing effective business documents. *(Ch. Obj. 6)*

9. Describe four prewriting strategies that can help you gather and organize ideas. *(Ch. Obj. 7)*

Application Exercises

1. Refer to the chapter's discussion of informative writing. Then write an informative memo or letter (one to two paragraphs) that relates to a work project or situation in which you have been involved—perhaps on your present job or on a job that you've held in the past. The letter might be addressed to your boss, to a co-worker, or to a customer. *(Ch. Obj. 3)*

2. Write a letter, a memo, or a report (one to two paragraphs) that is an example of writing to persuade. The subject of the document should be a past or present work situation. *(Ch. Obj. 3)*

3. Write an action-oriented letter (one to two paragraphs) that asks your reader either to respond in a certain way or to take certain action. This letter may be a follow-up to your persuasive letter in Exercise 2. *(Ch. Obj. 3)*

4. As the director of the advertising department of a large company, you always try to give your staff enough time to plan documents before they write them. The firm's CEO, however, isn't so well informed, and one day she suggests that your staff speed up production by eliminating the planning phase of your communications. You decide to write a memo that will persuade her of the importance of planning. Write this memo, keeping your audience in mind. *(Ch. Obj. 1, 4)*

5. Apply brainstorming and mindmapping to one of your own writing assignments. The assignment could be a document that you have to write for this class, for another class, for your job, or for a social organization. Try brainstorming, then mindmapping, to help you get started and to organize your thoughts. Do you find these prewriting techniques helpful? Explain your answer. *(Ch. Obj. 7)*

6. Now use the other prewriting techniques discussed in the chapter—freewriting and journalists' questions—to help you get started on another writing assignment. Which of the four prewriting techniques seems most helpful? *(Ch. Obj. 7)*

7. Suppose that your boss has asked you to research and write a report giving your recommendations on whether the company should allow employees to dress casually. Your report should include a recommendation of the days that casual dress be permitted and to what extent. Because this is a controversial topic, you know that your report will require careful research and planning.

    First, the research. Working outside of class, find three articles from different sources that deal with the issue of casual dress in the workplace. After reading the articles, write a brief evaluation of the sources, following the evaluation guidelines given in the chapter. *(Ch. Obj. 2, 3, 6)*

8. Having done your research, you now have a particular recommendation to make. Define your memo's objectives in terms of its general purpose, specific purpose, and core idea. *(Ch. Obj. 3)*

9. Next, analyze your audience (your boss) in order to plan your communication. You know, for example, that your boss has mentioned to colleagues that he would prefer to dress casually himself when he doesn't have meetings. Using the eight suggestions for audience analysis in this chapter, analyze this audience. *(Ch. Obj. 4, 5)*

10. Choose one of the prewriting techniques discussed in the chapter and use it to plan the report. Do this on paper rather than in your head. *(Ch. Obj. 7)*

11. Following the chapter suggestions on writing persuasive memos, write your report on whether casual dress should be permitted in your workplace. *(Ch. Obj. 3, 4)*

12. Your boss liked your report so much that he's asked you to write a memo on casual dress guidelines to co-workers. Write this memo, keeping your audience in mind. *(Ch. Obj. 4, 5)*

ACT: Applied Communication Techniques

Begin by referring to the sections up to and including Adjectives in Appendix II, then correct the grammar, spelling, and usage errors in the following sentences. Check your answers in Appendix V.

1. To be effective, the writer should focus on the specific message and the better way to communicate that message to the audience.
2. Honda's decision to construct an automobile assembly plant in Ontario was so they could become most competitive in the north american market.
3. Think of the specific purpose of a document as a briefest summary of your reason for writing the message.
4. Attached are the regional criminal reports for the six larger budget motels.
5. Readers of corporate anual reports include the general public and interesting employees.
6. His message was more softer than the speaker who lectured in the morning.
7. Primary sources of information contain more new information than do secondary sources.
8. Brainstorming is a planning techneque where you list both the good and poorer ideas.
9. When preparing the final report, take extra percautions with your gramar and proofreed careful.
10. Think quick if you must analyze your audience during a speach.

Building Your Research Skills

Your instructor will assign a topic. Working outside of class, each student should find and read three articles that relate to the topic assigned. Keep notes on what you read. Bring your notes to class and be prepared to summarize the major points of each article from your notes.

Building Your Teamwork Skills

As a class, brainstorm ideas for writing a report on the topic that you researched for the assignment in Building Your Research Skills. Have a volunteer record ideas on the board as they are suggested. Be sure that everyone gets a chance to contribute.

When you have a lot of ideas written down, go on to the next step of organizing this list into patterns.

Again, as a class brainstorm the best way(s) to organize your idea. Select a new volunteer to record your suggestions on the board.

Do you feel that having more people involved in brainstorming generates more ideas than if you had brainstormed all by yourself? Explain.

Building Your Technology Skills

You want to convince your skeptical business partner that you could serve your customers better by using the Internet. You decide to write your partner an informative memo on how other businesses use electronic business forms for communication. An electronic business form may range from a standardized order form to a standardized information request form. You decide to visit the following sites, analyze some electronic forms, and determine how they compare to paper forms.

Shopping Mall Business Sites

Apollo Advertising in England:	http://apollo.co.uk
Branch Information Services:	http://branch.com:1080
Canada Malls International:	http://canadamalls.com
Interactive Super Mall:	http://supermall.com

Financial Services Business Sites

Fidelity Investment:	http://www.fid-inv.com
Mass Mutual:	http://www.massmutual.com
Midland Walwyn Financial Services:	http://www.midwal.ca
Wall Street Direct:	http://www.cts.com/wallst

Now use the prewriting techniques discussed in this chapter to plan your memo.

Weblinks Internet Resources for this Chapter

Using Outlines
http://www.indiana.edu/~wts/wts/outlines.html

Organizing Your Ideas
**http://www.cs.unc.edu/~jbs/sm/
Part1_organizetd.html**

Know Your Audience
**http://www.cs.unc.edu/~jbs/sm/
Part1_analyzeread.html**

How to Get People to Read What You Write
http://www.sideroad.com/writing/column6.html

Getting Ideas
http://www.cs.unc.edu/~jbs/sm/Part1_explore.html

CASE STUDIES

DIVERSITY CASE:

Yen Wong and her *Fortune Generation*

Yen Wong is a Business Administration graduate from your college. She believes there is a need, and therefore a market, for a new type of consumer publication. Her target audience will be 18–40-year-old second-generation Asian Canadians. The name of the magazine will be *Fortune Generation*. The success of her publication will depend on the target readers who no longer see themselves first and foremost as Vietnamese, Korean, Chinese, or Japanese, but rather as having a unique Asian-Canadian identity.

Yen believes that while the first generation is fragmented by culture and language, second-generation Asian Canadians are a much more cohesive group. They have been educated in Canada, have a perspective that is shaped by mass media, and yet have a sensibility that is uniquely Asian Canadian.

Rather than discounting the distinctive Asian languages and cultures that thread Canadian society, Yen chooses to address all Asians—suggesting that a combined Asian culture is the most effective way for this community to gain influence in Canada. Thus, her magazine is written in English, and contains articles, advertisements, fashion, etc. that target all Asian communities within Canada.

Yen is probably unique in her marketing strategy, since many marketing agents target the Korean, Japanese, Chinese,

and Vietnamese as separate communities. Other publications have, for the most part, been printed in these distinct languages.

Whether or not Wong's focus on second-generation Asian Canadians succeeds depends largely on how well she knows her audience and how well she can deliver the magazine they want to read. As a second-generation Chinese Canadian, Wong's audience research comes largely from her personal experience.[12]

Questions and Applications

1. Suppose you were putting together a business plan to raise more capital for *Fortune Generation*. How would you define the magazine's distinctive objectives?

2. Define the unique characteristics of *Fortune Generation*'s target market. In your answer, align yourself with one or two approaches to the target audience described in this case.

3. Plan and draft a cover letter for the business plan that would describe *Fortune Generation*'s unique approach to Asian-Canadian readers. Your goal is to convince people to invest in the magazine.

CORPORATE CASE:

Planning a Firm's Mission Statement

About half of all companies have mission statements that try to capture the company's essence and corporate values. Although some of these statements work, many do not, especially those perceived as misleading or as empty rhetoric. For example:

"We impose on ourselves an obligation to reach beyond the minimal."

This statement neither communicates corporate values nor serves as the organization's guiding light. To be successful, a mission statement must connect words and deeds in ways that mean something to employees and to those doing business with the company. To write a meaningful mission statement requires careful planning.

Many effective mission statements start by encouraging all employees to generate ideas about the company's mission. Gary Edwards, executive vice president of Conoco, explains: "The process needs to cascade down to the individual departments, to the employees themselves. The managing directors identified the values we felt were important. We brainstormed for half a day. Then I asked groups further down to do the same thing. We found threads of consistency. On the core values we got quick agreement."

Planning the right words is often the key to widespread acceptance of the mission statement. Skip LeFauve, the CEO of Saturn, explains why Saturn's number one value is not "commitment to *customer satisfaction*" but a "commitment to *customer enthusiasm*." "We decided 'satisfaction' was just business as usual; 'enthusiasm' raised the bar."

Any well-planned statement must be researched and tested to make sure that its words reflect company policy.

Statements that are out of sync with actions create a skeptical workforce. Thus, Saturn's mission statement includes the promise that employees will not be punished if they alert the company to a defect that prompts a recall, no matter how costly the recall. This linking of words with deeds is the cement of ethical communication.

Planning an effective mission statement requires care so that the statement honestly reflects the company's day-to-day mission.[13]

Questions and Applications

1. How can an effective mission statement serve as a model for ethical communication?

2. Why is it so important to choose exactly the right words to communicate the message?

3. If you were considering a job offer from a company, what standards can you use to evaluate the corporate mission statement and statement of values in order to help you decide whether the company is right for you?

Building Business Documents

Reading maketh a full man; conference a ready man; and writing an exact man.

Francis Bacon
English philosopher and Lord Chancellor

Organize to Communicate

To appreciate the connection between effective organization and effective communication, read the first letter carefully. The recipient of this letter is likely to be confused about just what the writer is trying to accomplish. Is the main purpose a request for travel brochures or a request for a refund? Although, clearly, the latter is the purpose, this request is buried in the body of the letter. In addition, many of the details in the first two paragraphs are irrelevant. To respond to Mr. Lolly's request, Ms. Ericken does not really need to know the Smithingtons' travel history in the letter's opening paragraph. As a result, this letter is more difficult to read than it has to be, especially since it buries its primary purpose. Because of such difficulties, a busy recipient may simply put aside a letter like this one.

ANCHOR *Travel Agency*
1010 Rivercrest Road
Saskatoon, SK S7H 5P7
(306) 555-3333 (phone)
(306) 555-4444 (fax)
wblolly@anchor.com (e-mail)

July 18, 2000

Ms. Diane Ericken
Customer Services Manager
Precision Airlines
2222 Princess Street
Moose Jaw, SK S6H 5P7

Dear Ms. Ericken:

Alice and Andy Smithington have been excellent customers of the Anchor Travel Agency for many years. In fact, they have booked four vacations through our agency in the past two years, including, most recently, a Precision Airlines tour of England and France. When she was in my office yesterday, Mrs. Smithington raved about the tour and asked to see your brochures for African adventures. Can you send these brochures to me?

Although a British Midland flight between London and Paris was part of their European tour package, Mr. and Mrs. Smithington decided not to take the flight because they heard a lot about the Eurostar Chunnel between London and Paris and wanted to try it.

Alice Smithington informed James Rea, one of your customer service representatives, about this change on June 23, the day she confirmed her Chunnel reservations. Mr. Rea told her that a refund would be issued through her travel agent upon completion of the tour. Since the British Midland flight was paid for in advance as part of Precision Airlines' European tour package, please refund the cost of these tickets in the amount of $250.

Thank you for taking care of this matter. By the way, the Smithington's British Midland's flight number was 402, and they were booked to fly coach class.

Sincerely,

William B. Lolly

William B. Lolly
Travel Agent

Now compare this letter with the revised version. This version gets to the point quickly and eliminates irrelevant details. It states clearly and precisely the action that the writer wants Precision Airlines to take. In this revision of his original draft, Mr. Lolly decides not to ask for travel brochures because it would divert attention from his main request. He does not want to give the impression that a request for brochures and a request for a refund are comparable. ▼

ANCHOR *Travel Agency*
1010 Rivercrest Road
Saskatoon, SK S7H 5P7
(306) 555-3333 (phone)
(306) 555-4444 (fax)
wblolly@anchor.com (e-mail)

July 18, 2000

Ms. Diane Ericken
Customer Services Manager
Precision Airlines
2222 Princess Street
Moose Jaw, SK S6H 5P7

Dear Ms. Ericken:

On July 8, Alice and Andy Smithington, customers of the Anchor Travel Agency, did not take the British Midland flight on which they were booked between London and Paris. Two tickets for flight number 402, coach class, were paid for in advance as part of Precision Airlines' European tour package. Please refund the cost of these $250 tickets.

Alice Smithington informed James Rea, one of your customer service representatives, about this change on June 23, immediately after she confirmed her reservations for the Eurostar Chunnel between London and Paris. Mr. Rea told her that a refund would be issued through her travel agent upon completion of the tour.

Thank you for processing this refund. Mr. and Mrs. Smithington have been excellent customers of the Anchor Travel Agency for many years. They raved about your European tour and have already asked to see your brochures for African Adventures.

Sincerely,

William B. Lolly

William B. Lolly
Travel Agent

Chapter Overview _____

In crafting an effective business document, it is important to pay close attention to document organization as it relates to the placement of information. Documents written without organization in mind often fail as communication tools. This chapter will help you develop organizational writing skills as you learn the methods for turning an idea into a first draft. We will begin by stressing the importance of organizing a document and using an outline to achieve the best results. We will also examine the composition process, including guidelines for opening and closing a document, and strategies for choosing an organizational pattern and "building" the middle of a document through evidence. Finally, we will examine design—a critical factor that can mean the difference between a document that is read and one that is put aside.

Organizing a Document _____

In their classic handbook, *The Elements of Style*, William Strunk, Jr., and E. B. White explain why effective organization should be the underpinning of all written messages, including business documents:

> Writing, to be effective, must follow closely the thoughts of the writer, but not necessarily in the order in which those thoughts occur. This calls for a scheme. . . . The first principle of composition, therefore, is to foresee or determine the shape of what is to come and pursue that shape.[1]

In document writing, **organization** refers to the process of arranging information and connecting different ideas to produce a unified, coherent message. In this section we will focus on the crucial link between organization and effective communication.

WHY IS ORGANIZATION SO IMPORTANT?

Business documents require clear organization because a business audience must be able to see at a glance both *what* you are trying to accomplish and *how* it can be done. These goals can be met most efficiently by working according to an organizational plan. A clearly organized document accomplishes the following objectives:

- ▼ It makes its purpose clear and helps the reader respond appropriately.
- ▼ It provides all needed information but no more.
- ▼ It introduces, discusses, and closes the topic.
- ▼ It guides the reader through the arrangement of ideas and logical connections to a precise conclusion.
- ▼ It can help to eliminate any misunderstanding that may result from its message.
- ▼ It reduces the risk that it will not be read. When reading requires too much work, people are likely to put a document aside.

Good organization, therefore, helps the writer as much as the reader. For one thing, having a clear picture—before you begin to write—of what you need to say and how to say it helps to eliminate the fear of facing a blank page. Like a carpenter, a writer builds a structure whose plans are already set. As a writer, your task is to find the right words and tone, not to formulate basic ideas or logical connections. Those tasks should have been accomplished in the planning and organization stages.

WHY SHOULD I DEVELOP AN OUTLINE?

Recall from Chapter 4 our discussion of brainstorming, mindmapping, freewriting, and other prewriting exercises. The purpose of such exercises is threefold: (1) to stimulate the free flow of ideas, (2) to group ideas into preliminary categories, and (3) to form the basis for a cohesive outline—the key to successful organization.

An outline acts as a "road map," guiding the writer from the introduction of a document through to its conclusion. This road map helps produce a logical pattern of connections among ideas *before* the document is written. Also, because whole sections of an outline can be easily shifted, ideas can be rearranged to determine the most effective presentation. Finally, the outline reduces even the most complex material into manageable bits. Deciding whether to use a formal or informal outline depends on the needs and preferences of the writer and the document's requirements.

→ *Cross Reference*
We discussed prewriting techniques in Chapter 4.

FORMAL OUTLINES A **formal outline** follows prescribed rules concerning content and format in order to show the precise relationship among ideas. The form shown in Figure 5.1 is normally used in formal outlines. Notice that the core idea is placed at the top of the outline to guide the document's organization. Although this example illustrates the outline structure for a single main idea, more complex documents are likely to involve two or more main ideas. In that case, the structure shown in Figure 5.1 would be repeated for each main idea to be developed in the document.

Words fly, writings remain.
Latin proverb

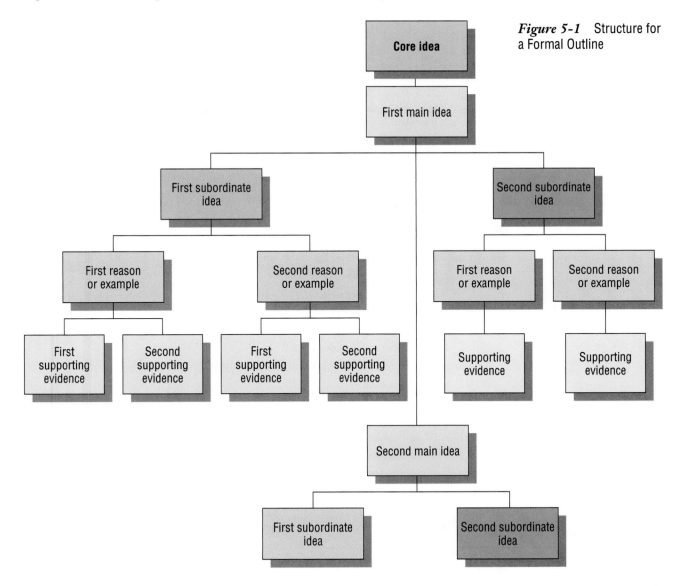

Figure 5-1 Structure for a Formal Outline

Once the outline is completed, the writer can easily revise it by shifting the order of main or subordinate ideas.

INFORMAL OUTLINES   An **informal outline** is a more loosely connected organizational device that need not follow the strict structural rules of a formal outline. Still, it lists main and subordinate ideas as well as supporting evidence. An example of an informal outline is shown in Table 5.1.

Despite their value, most businesspeople resist using informal and formal outlines. Recognizing this resistance, communication consultant Sana Reynolds avoids the term *outline* in her workshops and encourages a more informal style of organizing. Instead of labouring with Roman numerals and indentations, she suggests inserting a word or phrase in the margin and then assigning a number to each notation. This system both connects ideas and identifies them by priority. This informal plan is an effective way to organize short documents, including memos and letters.[2]

For longer documents, formal and informal outlines can be equally effective. Use your outline as a *guideline* but plan to adjust it as your work proceeds. Remember that revision is inevitable during the drafting process.

Progress Check

1. List six reasons why a clearly organized document is important in business writing.
2. How can an outline help you organize a document?
3. List the major differences between a formal and an informal outline.

Table 5-1   Informal Outline for New Business Proposal

I. Core idea

Our inspection of the plants, trees, and grass surrounding your office complex shows growth that needs treatment.

II. Results of our April 4 inspection

    A. Pervasive quack grass

    B. Maple trees with leaf spot and powdery mildew diseases

III. Recommendations

    A. Application of insecticide to destroy insect eggs

        1. Environmental safety of insecticide

            a. Insecticide applications

                i. Type of insecticide

                ii. Amount of insecticide

            b. Department of Health approval

    B. Application of fertilizer to encourage root and foliage growth

        1. Spring application

        2. Fall application

    C. Cost

        1. $250 per treatment

        2. 10% discount available if annual service is paid in advance

Composing a Document

Like a newspaper article or an essay, a business document contains a beginning, a middle, and an end. Depending on the length and purpose of the document, these sections may be as short as a single sentence or as long as several pages. The process of composing a document consists of three distinct stages:

1. creating the opening, middle, and conclusion of the document;
2. deciding on a logical pattern in which to present the information; and
3. integrating evidence to support the core idea of the document.

If you don't get the reader's attention in the first paragraph, the rest of your message is lost.

Public relations maxim

HOW SHOULD I BEGIN?

Because letters, memos, and reports must capture and hold readers' attention from the first word, the opening is as important as the message itself. Indeed, most people read business correspondence in much the same way as they read a newspaper. They glance at the first paragraph and skim the rest. If the document doesn't grab their attention, they go on to something else. The document writer's task, therefore, is much like that of the creator of a television commercial who realizes that the ad must attract the viewer's attention within the first five seconds. After five seconds, the number of viewers always declines; it never goes up.

Except when you must convey bad news, the first paragraph of your document should state the main point in a clear, succinct way. Readers want to know at the start what a document is about and why they should continue reading. If they fail to find that information in the opening paragraph, they may jump to the end or disregard the document entirely. As one communication specialist points out, "We simply don't put up with writing that asks us to slog through fact, fact, fact, logic, logic, logic, to reach that 'perfect' bottom line. If the writer doesn't start with the bottom line, we—as readers—do. We make the bottom line the top line by skipping ahead. We take charge of the organization because the writer didn't."[3]

In both short and long documents many writers tend to bury the main point, forcing the reader to work in order to locate it. Other writers use too many words to make their point. Compare the following opening paragraphs for effectiveness:

Version 1

Our company is extending its sales force by 15 people. We are moving into Moncton, Vernon, and Prince Albert. We are especially excited about this move because our products have never been in these territories before. Because we want to make a good impression on our customers, we decided to go first class, hiring the best people and giving them the best transportation. With this in mind, we think the most prestigious cars are Lincoln Town Cars. That is why I am contacting you. We are interested in leasing 15 luxury automobiles in open-end, 24-month leases.

People don't read today; they flip.

John Lyons
Advertising writer

Version 2

Our company is considering leasing 15 Lincoln Town Cars for use in Moncton, Vernon, and Prince Albert. We would like to discuss the terms for 15 open-end, 24-month leases.

Version 2 is more effective than Version 1 because it states its purpose immediately and omits irrelevant information. It also avoids long, complex sentences.

THE MIDDLE OF THE DOCUMENT

The middle of a business document contains its major points and supporting evidence. As we will see later in the chapter, *evidence* may consist of facts, statistics, examples, or expert opinion. Supporting evidence, however, must also be organized into carefully designed *patterns* that support specific premises. One of the first steps in organizing the middle of your document is to select the most appropriate method for developing your material.

Depending on both the nature of your material and the needs of your audience, you can choose from several organizational patterns. Bear in mind, however,

A QUESTION OF ETHICS

Persuasive Evidence Equals Ethical Evidence

One of the best ways to persuade readers to support a position is to convince them that your evidence meets accepted ethical standards. Apply the following standards to decide if your evidence is effective:

1. *Evidence should be sufficient and representative.* Your goal is to persuade readers that your point of view applies to many actual situations, not to an isolated case.

2. *Evidence should be relevant to the core idea of your document.* It should be used to support or illustrate points made in the document and should be directly related to your subject matter.

3. *Evidence should be accurate.* Not only should your sources be reliable, but you must correctly interpret the evidence that you draw from those sources. Misrepresentations and distortions will produce a document that is inherently flawed.

As you gather evidence, apply these standards as a kind of ethical test. Although the effort will require diligence and disci-

pline, it is likely to yield results in the form of a more effective presentation.

Questions for Critical Thinking

1. Why is ethical evidence likely to be more persuasive than evidence that fails to meet ethical standards?

2. Research the subject of business ethics to find an example of an ethics problem that involves unethical communication. Explain how the ethical standards described in this feature were violated.

3. As a business writer, you will be asked to advocate various positions for your company. What specific measures can you take to ensure that your position has an ethical base?

Source: Lynn Quitman Troyka, *Simon & Schuster Handbook for Writers,* 2d ed. (Englewood Cliffs, N.J.: Prentice Hall, 1990), 141–142.

that your core idea will usually dictate your organizational pattern. For example, if your purpose is to explain a series of events or a step-by-step process, a *chronological pattern* of development might be required. If your purpose is to examine certain events, their causes, and their outcomes, you will probably choose a *cause-and-effect pattern* of development.[4]

We will begin by describing two pairs of organizational categories: deductive and inductive patterns and direct and indirect patterns. We will then analyze the four most common patterns of document development: problem/solution, cause-and-effect, climactic-order, and chronological.

DEDUCTIVE VERSUS INDUCTIVE PATTERNS   Most effective business documents move from a *general* idea to a series of *specific* ideas, thereby providing the most important information first and then supporting it with details. This is the **deductive organizational pattern**—the most common approach used in contemporary business writing. The deductive approach requires that information be presented in the following manner:

- ▼ answers before explanations
- ▼ requests before reasons
- ▼ summaries before details
- ▼ conclusions before discussions
- ▼ general statements before specifics[5]

Using the deductive approach, for example, you might propose that a new women's specialty clothing store would be a financial success in one of the world's

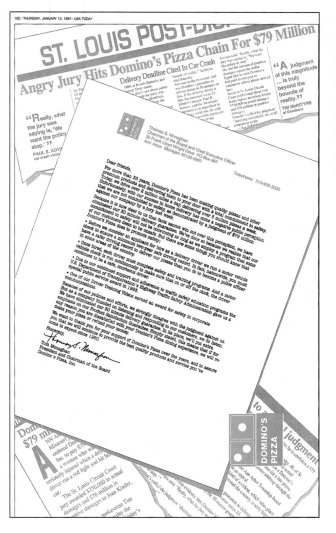

Domino's Pizza CEO Thomas Monoghan used a dramatic introduction to communicate his firm's decision to end its 30-minute delivery guarantee. The newspaper headline announced the $79 million judgment as a result of an accident involving a Domino's driver. It gains immediate attention and draws the reader to the explanatory letter.

largest retail malls—West Edmonton Mall in Edmonton, Alberta. You would then list the reasons supporting your argument. These are likely to include the tens of thousands of shoppers attracted to the mall on a daily basis, the mall's festive atmosphere, World Waterpark, Pebble Beach miniature golf, Galaxyland entertainment centre, and the number of stores that attract your target customers—those shoppers who prefer small specialty stores with quality merchandise.

By contrast, when a discussion begins with a specific idea and moves step by step to a general topic, it follows an **inductive organizational pattern.** This approach assumes that a general or broadly meaningful pattern can be described on the basis of specific facts or observations. For example, you might argue against the idea of opening the proposed outlet in West Edmonton Mall by pointing out specific observations, such as the potential competition posed by five other recently opened stores and the relatively high cost of rent. Using an inductive pattern, you could thus argue that these facts suggest a general pattern that success for a new store in this location is unlikely.

Remember, however, that an inductive pattern is based on a sampling of facts rather than on every possible detail. If you do not consider a sufficient number of facts, your conclusion may be flawed. Perhaps the five recently opened stores offer clothing that is priced too high for your likely customer base. Inductive conclusions must be analyzed carefully in relation to both the quantity and quality of supporting evidence.

DIRECT VERSUS INDIRECT PATTERNS   Selecting an organizational pattern also depends on whether a direct or indirect approach is more appropriate for your message. Like the deductive pattern, the **direct organizational pattern** organizes material so that the main point is presented at the beginning of the message. Documents using direct patterns make the message as clear and straightforward as possible. A direct pattern is effective in direct requests, informative messages, positive correspondence, and persuasive messages.

An **indirect organizational pattern**, much like the inductive organizational pattern, states the main point later in the message. The writer's purpose may be to prepare the reader to accept information favourably or to use supporting information as the best means of persuading the reader. The indirect pattern is often used to convey bad news or when persuasion is an important goal of the message.

PROBLEM/SOLUTION PATTERN   In the **problem/solution pattern** of development, the discussion opens with a particular problem or problems and works toward a solution. The opening statement identifies the problem. The following statements introduce the main idea of the solution by limiting or clarifying the opening statement. This approach is most useful, of course, when you want to persuade someone that you can remedy a difficult situation. You can use a series of steps to illustrate the specific details of your solution. Consider the presentation of problem and solution in the memo in Figure 5.2.

Define the problem before you pursue a solution.

John Williams
CEO, Spence Corporation

CAUSE-AND-EFFECT PATTERN   Some issues lend themselves naturally to an organizaton that focuses on events or consequences and the reasons for them. The **cause-and-effect pattern** is typically used, for instance, to explain a problem and how it affects an organization. It can also be used to identify events and activities that result in opportunities or advantages. For example, if the purpose of a message is to inform a customer that an important delivery deadline will not be met, the message might read: "A wildcat strike at our Chicago plant resulted in a two-week shutdown of the entire plant. As a result, we cannot meet our promised shipment date."

Cause-and-effect analysis must show clear relationships (typically a chronological order of events) and repetitious patterns (every time A occurred, B also occurred). In addition, if you select the cause-and-effect development pattern for your document, you must take definite steps to avoid oversimplification. If the reader can detect that several factors not mentioned in your document could have caused or contributed to the problem or event, you will lose credibility. Let's say that the wildcat strike lasted only two hours and the shipment was delayed two weeks. Most readers will assume you did not disclose all the causes of the delay—and will not believe your explanation.

CLIMACTIC-ORDER PATTERN   As a rule, when dealing with controversial issues, you should order the material in a **climactic-order pattern**—a pattern that presents material that the reader is most likely to agree with first. A climactic-order pattern helps enlist the reader's support for the rest of the document even if what you say next is more controversial. "If the reader agrees with the first argument," say communication consultants Marya W. Holcombe and Judith K. Stein, "you will have established credibility, increasing the likelihood that the rest of your assertions will be viewed positively."[6]

MEMORANDUM

TO: Jonah Billings
          Marketing Director

FROM: Barbara Brofee
          Vice President
          Telecommunications Services

DATE: October 5, 2000

SUBJECT: Upgrading Telecommunications to Meet Increased Call Volume

With next year's summer travel season only nine months away,
we must be prepared for our call volume to increase by 300
percent during the summer months. As you recall from the
numerous system breakdowns that occurred last summer, our
current telephone system and personnel cannot handle this
increased volume. I recommend taking the following measures
to correct this problem:

- Upgrade to an SX27 enhanced telephone system. This
  system is used by three of our major competitors and has
  a proven track record.

- Increase the number of customer service representatives
  handling incoming calls from 50 to 90 between May 1 and
  September 30.

- Upgrade Amalgamated's computer network so that customer
  service representatives have current information on
  rental availabilities as they take orders.

These changes should eliminate the major difficulties we
experienced last summer. Please let me know by next week if
you have additional suggestions.

ltc

Figure 5-2 Problem/
Solution Memo

CHRONOLOGICAL PATTERN   Sometimes it is important to describe a series of events chronologically, either in the order in which they occurred or in reverse sequence. **Chronological patterns** are especially useful in setting out the sequence for a project or process or setting the agenda for a conference or meeting. For example, a letter to a new customer might indicate the steps involved in handling a credit dispute:

Thank you for informing us about your credit problem. The following steps must be taken to settle this dispute:

▼ Within 60 days, we must receive from you a written statement of the problem.

▼ Immediately after we receive your letter, we will issue temporary credit for the disputed amount and initiate a full investigation.

▼ Within 30 days after the start of our investigation, we will issue a letter outlining our findings. If the amount is in error, it will be removed from your account.

George Samoil, Chief Information Officer of the Government of Alberta

There is no greater need for responsible communication than that which flows from public office. Accuracy, discretion, and clarity of design are crucial elements of effective government communication.

As a former cabinet policy coordinator and executive assistant to the premier, George Samoil, Alberta's first Chief Information Officer (CIO), is sensitive to the scrutiny of his readership. His office is responsible for developing high-level policies and strategies that enable all government administrators to fit their information resource plans into the government's broader framework.*

With a passion for clear and concise communication, Samoil has managed to transcend traditional boundaries and develop a government-wide collaborative approach to technology and public access to information. "I probably developed a skill for delivering concise messages when I was growing up," he muses. "As one of seven siblings, with both parents working, the opportunity to engage in individual discussion with our parents was limited. I quickly learned the benefits of delivering concise and meaningful messages!"

Question: What approach do you take to organizing a formal document?

Answer: Whether it's a letter, memo, briefing note, or business proposal, documents that originate in this office have a strong focus on the key issues. However, we also believe that written communication should not only present issues but also suggest solutions. The key, though, is in the diligence and research undertaken before writing—in knowing where you want to go with the document—what you wish to achieve.

Question: How do you hold the attention of the readers of your business documents?

Answer: To hold the attention of the reader, you first have to capture it! Documents should be written like a newspaper story: the first sentence should be clear and concise in identifying what's to follow. Your introduction should, at the very least, help to set the direction and outcome of the document. If you are able to set the direction, you are 75 percent of the way to achieving the desired results.

Question: Given that you have a personal preference in writing style, does your style remain consistent

HOW SHOULD A DOCUMENT CONCLUDE?

The conclusion of a business document serves three important functions. First, it provides a summary of the critical points made in the document. Second, it communicates closure by placing the discussion in a broader context. Finally, it clarifies action to be taken.

SUMMARIZING CRITICAL POINTS Summaries are usually necessary in documents longer than two pages. The main points of shorter documents are usually easy to find, especially if they are visually highlighted with headings and bullets. However, in long letters, memos, reports, and proposals, a summary is an important way of reinforcing your core idea. Remember: the summary is your last opportunity to communicate your message. Here, for example, is a summary of a report on starting a company-wide safety program:

throughout different types of documents intended for different readers?

Answer: Yes, I believe that my style remains consistent. It's concise, clear, and provides solutions along with the issues. I avoid the use of acronyms, since it's a mistake to assume that the reader will know what they stand for. I also use well-marked and referenced attachments, which provide a more detailed review of the material.

Question: How important is the format and design of documents?

Answer: The design is important; it must be easy to read and understand. Keep it simple—less is better in formal texts.

Question: How important is the design of the message when it's in the form of an e-mail?

Answer: In this case the design may not be as much an issue as the content and the source of the message. For example, I get a lot of junk mail from a certain company. I don't even open it any more!

Question: In your role as CIO, how important are statistics in the preparation of business documents?

Answer: I limit the use of statistics in the main body, and include them instead in supporting attachments. I always ensure that they're properly sourced, since my credibility often depends upon such detail.

Question: What are the most common errors in the organization and design of documents that you receive?

Answer: We receive a lot of documents in this office, and you'd be surprised at the problems we have trying to make sense of some of them. The most common errors are those that render the document difficult to read; for example, pages not numbered, key points hidden, or too much extraneous material that should be in the attachment. Problematic documents of this kind tend to distract readers or make them lose interest in the document entirely.

Question: When dealing with the media, are special precautions taken in the organization of your documents?

Answer: No special precautions are taken when dealing with the media, although I often have to provide précis versions of documents. And, as always, I take every precaution to ensure that our communiqué is clear, concise, and delivered with confidence. I am always aware that every letter or briefing I write may be made available to the public, as a result of the Freedom of Information and Privacy Protection (FOIPP) legislation.

* *Information Resource Management in Government.* Office of the CIO, October 1997.

Source: Interview with George Samoil.

As you have seen, a company-wide safety program is necessary for four important reasons: it helps reduce the number of on-the-job accidents, it reduces injury-related employee absences, it reduces workers' compensation claims, and it helps improve employee morale.

COMMUNICATING CLOSURE   When the body of your document focuses on a particular problem, you can add emphasis by placing the problem in a larger context. For example, while Version 1 of the following memo lacks finality, Version 2 places the evidence in a larger context:

Version 1

I believe that instituting a company-wide safety program will help reduce the number of on-the-job accidents.

Version 2

Company-wide safety programs are used by many large corporations to reduce the incidence of on-the-job accidents. Based on the evidence from these companies, we should seriously consider doing the same.

Progress Check

1. Why is the opening of a document so important to the success of the entire document?
2. Distinguish between inductive and deductive reasoning.
3. Describe the three primary functions of the conclusion of a business document.

STATING THE PLAN OF ACTION Many reports, memos, and letters ask the reader to take action. "Action" may mean adopting a recommendation, pursuing the next step in a project, or making a decision, such as hiring an employee. Your conclusion allows you to emphasize once again that a reply is required or that action should be taken. For example:

> The key to reducing the incidence of on-the-job accidents is a company-wide safety program. Adopting the specific program recommendations in this report will help us reach the goal of achieving an accident-free environment.

Integrating Evidence

Documents must offer **evidence**—details that communicate information and support the core idea of the document. In written communication, evidence generally takes one or more of four forms: facts, statistics, examples, and expert opinion.

FACTS ARE IMPORTANT

In the context of business communication, facts clarify why a situation exists in its present form, specify what is being done to change or remedy a situation, and explain why a decision has been made. To be effective, facts must accomplish the following goals:

1. They must clarify the main point.
2. They must define all new terms and concepts.
3. They must present evidence supporting the main point.

Facts can also focus on how something is done. Instructions fall into this category. For example, when a letter is sent to a customer outlining steps for repairing defective merchandise, it contains a factual explanation.

In the early 1990s top management at AT&T decided that something had to be done about the growing number of complaints received from credit card applicants. These prospective long-distance telephone customers of the communications giant reported increasing irritation at the number of errors contained in their credit reports. Internal AT&T memos urging the decision to take action undoubtedly included such *factual* evidence as the number of complaints received, the extent to which such complaints had changed over time, and the nature of these complaints, with particular emphasis on reports of errors in credit reporting. Armed with these facts, AT&T's top management formally requested that the nation's major credit-reporting agencies simplify their procedures when soliciting AT&T credit card applicants, and decided to establish toll-free telephone numbers for applicants to use in resolving problems. The facts assembled in response to the original memos were convincing, and both of AT&T's requests were quickly implemented.[7]

As usual, the best explanations are brief and geared to the needs of the audience. They should supply just the amount of detail needed by readers, and no more. For example, in the AT&T memos referred to earlier, there was little need to explain in detail how AT&T would operate the 800 numbers, the number of employees who

When you have mastered the numbers, you will in fact no longer be reading numbers, any more than you read words when reading books. You will be reading meanings.

Harold Geneen
Former Chairman of the Board,
ITT Corporation

PRACTICAL TIPS

Composing Prototypes

Prototypes are model documents that can be reused. They are commonly created for activity reports, sales reports, and credit-information requests. They can also be used for parts of documents. For example, if your company typically includes background information on company products, services, and key personnel in its documents, sections can be written in advance and filed for future use. Although prototypes save an enormous amount of time and money, they must be used carefully. Here are tips on using prototypes:

▼ *When to use prototypes.* Communication consultant Sana Reynolds encourages people to ask themselves, "Will I ever have to write this again?" If they answer yes, she suggests that they design a prototype and file it. For example, if you have to write an activity report every three months, create a basic prototype to use repeatedly.

▼ *How prototypes save time and energy.* A prototype eliminates the need to rewrite identical or similar documents. Sana Reynolds explains that you won't have to

struggle with how you are going to begin, what to say, and how to motivate the reader. By restricting your phrasing options, you minimize writing difficulty.

▼ *Personalize prototypes.* Although a prototype can store the nuts and bolts of a document, it is not personalized for your reader. Additions and changes are often needed to meet audience and situational needs.

▼ *Review prototypes.* It is important to review prototypes on a regular basis to make sure they still meet audience needs, incorporate updated information, and convey appropriate messages for their intended audiences and uses. It is important to read through each paragraph every time the prototype is used, selecting only those paragraphs that apply to the situation at hand. Fortunately, computer technology makes customizing prototypes as simple as a few keystrokes.

Sources: Telephone interview with Sana Reynolds, September 1, 1995; Jeffrey L. Seglin, *The AMA Handbook of Business Letters* (New York: AMACOM, 1989), 43–44.

would be assigned to answer the calls, and the projected complaint-response times. However, these issues were appropriately included in correspondence between AT&T and major credit-reporting agencies.

Factual explanations are strengthened by specific, concrete language. Instead of responding to a customer complaint with a form letter, for instance, it is much more effective to use a direct, factual explanation of the steps being taken to solve the problem. If possible, it is also helpful to indicate when the problem will be resolved.

WHAT IS STATISTICAL EVIDENCE?

Numerical evidence is presented as statistics—mathematical expressions that describe findings in an objective, uniform way and provide standards for determining whether those findings are valid measurements or chance occurrences. Among the statistical concepts commonly referred to in business writing are measures of central tendency, correlation, and sampling. We will discuss these concepts in detail in Chapter 11, when we discuss planning and researching business reports.

Because the focus of business communication is the clear presentation of information, we will emphasize a few practical guidelines for using statistics as evidence in persuasive messages.

PROVIDE A CONTEXT FOR NUMBERS Numbers often mean very little when presented out of context. Instead of simply pointing to a 17-percent company-wide gain in sales, for instance, place that figure in context—say, of industry-wide sales. What would it mean if industry-wide sales had increased only 12 percent? Comparisons paint pictures for your reader, and your message will persuade when you emphasize the difference in these two numbers.

To convince potential customers of the value of its Scald Guard faucet, Peerless Faucet contacted the U.S. Forest Service and the Shriner's Burn Institute. After learning that people are over 2,000 times more likely to be burned by water than by fire, the firm's marketers developed this chart to communicate the magnitude of the problem and a relatively inexpensive solution. Writers also use statistical evidence in business documents.

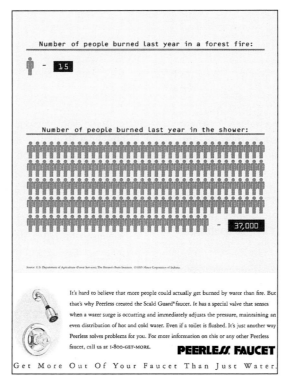

ROUND OFF NUMBERS   Numbers have more impact when they are placed in formats that people can remember. For example, a marketing report issued by a company thinking of expanding operations into Vancouver might cite population figures as "approximately 1.7 million" rather than the exact number (1 746 370). Similarly, fractions such as 41.867 are better remembered as "almost 42 percent" or "about two out of five."

INCLUDE SOURCES   Statistics are credible when attributed to specific sources. Attribution gives your readers confidence in the accuracy of your numbers. However, because statistical studies are constantly revised to provide up-to-date information, it is important to remember that the most current sources lend the most credibility to your document. Finally, by listing sources, you assist interested readers who are seeking more information on a given topic.

LIMIT THE USE OF STATISTICS   Readers have a tendency to skip words—and even entire sections of a document—when too many numbers are presented at once. Numbers, therefore, make their greatest impact when used selectively; that is, when used to focus on a specific point. Because visual aids present statistical information effectively, one way to exercise selectivity is to emphasize statistics through the use of charts. Chapter 12 discusses the use of visual aids in greater detail.

WILL EXAMPLES HELP?

Examples—descriptive stories and specific cases—make information both real and memorable. Even when you are writing to someone with a keen interest in your subject, examples can bring your point home more effectively than a well-reasoned argument. Using an example, of course, is an inductive strategy. One story is by definition a small sample, and your story will be meaningful only if supported by the general reliability of other evidence.

People, including managers, do not live by pie charts alone—or by bar graphs or three-inch statistical appendices to 300-page reports. People live, reason, and are moved by symbols and stories.

Tom Peters
Business writer

Examples may be as short as a phrase or as long as several paragraphs. The following guidelines can help you improve your effectiveness when using examples:

1. Examples should reinforce your point, not come before it. Examples play *supporting* roles. Even if your story is extremely interesting, busy executives want to know the point of your message first.

2. Examples should include only the details necessary to state your case. The amount of detail used should be determined by audience needs.

3. Choose examples that accurately reflect the broader situation. The purpose of an example is to illustrate a point *further*. It should, therefore, be consistent with your point.

As the manager at a nationwide travel agency, the president of the company asks your opinion about reducing the number of on-staff travel agents by 20 percent. You decide to use the following example in your memo:

> A 20-percent staff reduction would cripple our ability to operate, just as it did at Carlson Travel after the company reduced its staff by 17 percent. In one case, an inexperienced and overburdened travel agent booked an important client's trip from Toronto to Hiroshima to Taiwan. After completing his business in Hiroshima, the executive was scheduled to catch a flight to Taiwan for meetings with new clients. Instead, he was forced to take an 18-hour flight back to Toronto because the agent failed to inform him that he needed a visa to enter Taiwan. Errors like this are likely to happen in our organization if we implement the suggested staff cutback.

WHAT IS EXPERT OPINION?

The opinion of a recognized authority or an expert often provides effective support for an argument. Who can be considered an expert? In general, an expert is someone who is more familiar with primary sources than you are. Expert testimony can be gathered from both primary sources—experts themselves—and secondary sources—the media that report on expert opinion. For example, conducting interviews takes you directly to expert opinion through primary sources; quoting from business journals and books, newspapers, magazines, and government reports gives you access to expert opinion through secondary sources. Both avenues can be helpful in supporting your points.

The following guidelines should help you in selecting expert opinions:

1. Be certain that the person you are quoting is a recognized expert. For example, does the name of your primary source appear in other secondary sources?

2. Be certain that your experts are reliable. Are they really familiar with primary source material? Are they being objective? Do they base their opinions on up-to-date information?

3. Avoid distorting testimony. Make every effort to quote sources accurately and in the proper context.

Progress Check

1. Why are examples considered inductive evidence?
2. List the advantages and disadvantages of using statistics in a business document.
3. What guidelines are helpful in evaluating the opinions of experts?

Designing a Document

Because design often determines whether a document will actually be read, it is crucial to the document's success. In this chapter **design** refers to techniques for making business documents inviting and easy to read. We will first survey the goals of document-design techniques and then discuss some of the most important elements of document design.

To emphasize the illuminating capabilities of its new Indiglo watch, Timex managers chose this letter from a product purchaser who supplied expert testimony. The humorous letter, combined with the eerie underwater photo of the alligators, results in a memorable communication.

THE DOCUMENT'S DESIGN WILL AFFECT ITS SUCCESS

Most of us have received one of those sweepstakes letters that announce at least 500 ways to win millions of dollars. Perhaps you noticed that the letter used single-spacing for some paragraphs, double-spacing for others, and boldface or italics for important words. Handwritten notes may appear in the margins, sometimes in colour. Although business documents are typically devoted to different kinds of information, they use many of the same design elements to achieve their objectives.

USING DESIGN ELEMENTS EFFECTIVELY Design decisions are particularly important when a document has more than one audience. A well-organized, effectively designed document makes information readily accessible to everyone who receives it.

As we describe various design elements, keep in mind the following objectives of effective document design:

▼ clarify organization through the use of visual cues
▼ help the writer compose a document in an organized manner
▼ encourage people to read a document instead of setting it aside
▼ make specific blocks of information accessible and easy to find
▼ focus attention on certain parts of a document
▼ give the reader an overview of document content
▼ arrange every element so that the eye moves progressively from one section to the next
▼ make information useful to both primary and secondary readers[8]

Figure 5.3 illustrates how a document can be revised and redesigned to increase its effectiveness. Document 1 [Figure 5.3(a)] is the original letter, and Document 2 [Figure 5.3(b)] is a corrected, revised version of the same letter. We refer to these two documents in the following discussion.

Document 1 is confusing; Document 2 is well organized. While Document 1 discourages reading, Document 2 encourages it through the use of headings, bullets, and short paragraphs that make it easy for the reader to focus attention on distinct units of information. The improved organization is a direct result of the design itself and the decision to exclude unnecessary information, which makes Document 2 significantly shorter than Document 1.

This report, by its very length, defends itself against the risk of being read.

Winston Churchill
British prime minister and author

DESIGN ELEMENTS

Four design elements are examined in this section: short paragraphs, headings, enhanced text, and bulleted lists. Each element has specific functions, and all of these elements can contribute to effective written communication.[9]

SHORT PARAGRAPHS   In today's sophisticated visual environment, it is a mistake to crowd a document with too many words. The layout of a document with wall-to-wall words shouts, "DON'T READ ME!" Notice that Document 1 in Figure 5.3(a) contains too many long paragraphs. To redesign it effectively, the writer should reduce paragraph length.

Try to begin your document with a short paragraph that expresses your core idea or main purpose. Your message will be communicated immediately and the reader will have less trouble understanding your objectives. Note that in Document 2, the writer begins by setting an organizational framework, which tells the reader what the letter will accomplish.

Figure 5-3 Revising Documents for Effective Design
(a) Original Document
(b) Corrected Document

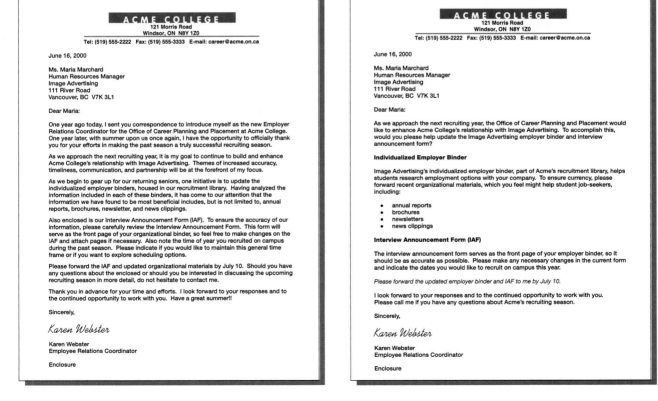

BUSINESS WRITING IN ACTION

Organizing, Composing, and Designing a Business Memo for Cadillac Marketing Employees

THE ASSIGNMENT

This assignment continues where the Business Writing in Action feature in Chapter 4 left off. You are now ready to organize, compose, and design the first draft of an informative memo to employees of Cadillac's marketing department about the steps Cadillac is taking to attract younger buyers.

THE METHOD

Complete the Following Two Steps

Step 1: Organize the Memo Using an Informal Outline

The following informal outline is a mixture of sentences and phrases. References to quotations remind the writer about proper placement of quoted material without requiring the full quotation.

Core Idea: Since the average age of Cadillac buyers is 63, the Cadillac division is taking steps to attract younger consumers and more women to buy its first new model in a decade.

I. The situation Cadillac is facing
  A. Cadillac sales are in a slump
    1. Approximately 350 000 cars sold in 1978. Twenty years later, sales have decreased by approximately 100 000 cars
    2. In 1994 sales still outpaced Lexus, Mercedes, and BMW, but trend is downward
  B. Young consumers are not buying Cadillacs
    1. Average age of consumers buying their first luxury car is 46; average age of Cadillac buyers is 63
    2. Younger consumers don't want to be seen in Cadillacs; too big, bulky, and old-fashioned
    3. Irony is that Cadillacs have never been better; improved quality and power
  C. Women are not buying Cadillacs either
    1. Women account for only three out of ten sales; goal is 37 percent of sales

II. Proposed solutions
  A. Cadillac now understands that new buyers want value more than glamour
    1. Use Chris MacConnell quote
  B. Attempts to attract female buyers are already underway
    1. Meetings with female journalists
    2. Ads are being developed to attract female customers
    3. Female executives now have a greater voice in car development; e.g., Liz Wetzel, interior designer, who insisted designers attach paper clips to their fingertips to see what it feels like to operate buttons with long nails
    4. Cadillac dealers are undergoing diversity training to make them more sensitive to doing business with women
  C. Introduction of the first new model in 10 years
    1. Known as the Catera, the model competes against entry-level luxury cars from Lexus, Mercedes, and BMW
    2. The Catera does not look like older Cadillacs. It is a smaller car, has less chrome, more curves, rounded taillights
    3. Cadillac name appears in small letters on the rear tail lamp, but goal is to separate Catera from rest of product line

Step 2: Compose and Design a First Draft Guided by Your Outline

The Cadillac divisions of General Motors and General Motors Canada are facing a new challenge. If the divisions are to survive, they must attract younger buyers and women as customers.

The Scope of the Problem   Cadillac sales are in a slump, and the trend is in the wrong direction. While the division sold

---

HEADINGS   Visual markers that indicate the organization of your document are called **headings.** Headings make documents easy to use by drawing the reader's eye to distinct sections. Even short letters and memos benefit from the use of headings.

Headings both describe information and break it down into manageable units. The headings in Document 2 focus on three items that require the attention of Image Advertising's Human Resources Manager.

approximately 350 000 cars in 1978, 20 years later sales have decreased by approximately 100 000 cars. While our sales were still outpacing Lexus, Mercedes, and BMW in 1994 the trend is downward, and the demographics of our car buyers is disturbing. While the average age of consumers buying their first luxury car is 46, the average age of Cadillac buyers is 63.

Why Is This Happening? Cadillac is perceived by younger consumers as too big, bulky, and old-fashioned. This prejudice is so strong that young buyers disregard Cadillac's improved quality and power. Our problem is especially serious among women, who account for only 30 percent of sales instead of the 37 percent that we should realistically expect.

Proposed Solutions Cadillac is taking a three-pronged approach to solving this problem. The approach includes:

▼ understanding today's luxury-car buyer

▼ working to attract more female buyers

▼ introducing a new model

An Understanding of Today's Luxury-Car Buyer Marketing surveys have shown us that luxury-car buyers want value more than glamour. Dealers like Chris MacConnell hear this first-hand from customers: "A luxury car used to be whatever was the biggest thing anybody could build," explains Mac-Connell. "It had all the gadgets on it. And everybody would look at it when it went down the street. Now, people in the market for a luxury car aren't comfortable with a purchase unless they know it represents some kind of value to them. They're asking themselves, 'Why should I pay this much for a car?' Our job is to justify the expense."

Attracting Female Buyers For too long, Cadillac engineers, designers, and dealers have ignored women or treated them poorly. We are remedying this situation from the ground up by giving female executives like Liz Wetzel, an interior designer, a greater voice in car development and design. As an in-house advocate for women buyers, Wetzel insists that male designers attach paper clips to their fingertips to see what it feels like to operate buttons and levers with long nails. The result: not a single knob in the new models requires women to bend their fingernails in order to operate it.

Redesign is just the beginning. We must also convince women to enter Cadillac dealerships. We are doing that through new ads and through meetings with female journalists. We also realize that dealers have a lot to learn when dealing with female customers. Many dealers are now taking diversity training workshops to make them more sensitive to doing business with women.

Introduction of the First New Model in Ten Years Because many of Cadillac's older models are not attracting younger consumers, we are introducing a new model, known as the Catera. The Catera competes against entry-level luxury cars from Lexus, Mercedes, and BMW. The Catera does not look like the Cadillacs of old. It is a smaller car with less chrome, more curves, and a rounded European look.

We have made the decision to distance the Catera from other cars in the Cadillac line. If you look hard for the Cadillac name, you will find that it appears only in small letters on the rear tail lamp.[10]

This document is now a first draft that, by definition, is subject to change. We will complete this exercise in Chapter 6, where we will see how attention to audience, language, tone, and intent can change this draft in some dramatic ways. We will also consider whether the draft achieves its intended purpose or whether reorganization and substantial rewriting are necessary.

The types of headings show the reader the relative priority of each section. **Primary headings** indicate titles for major organizational sections. They may be centred or placed flush against the left margin. To further emphasize their importance, business writers often print these headings in boldface or capital letters. **Secondary headings** signal titles for each subsection within a major section. Typically, secondary headings are placed flush against the left margin and underlined, with the

In developing a Web site for the Saturn automobile line, dealerships, and the magazine, the company's advertising agency identified a number of objectives. Both headings and bulleted lists are used in specifying these objectives for the Saturn Web site.

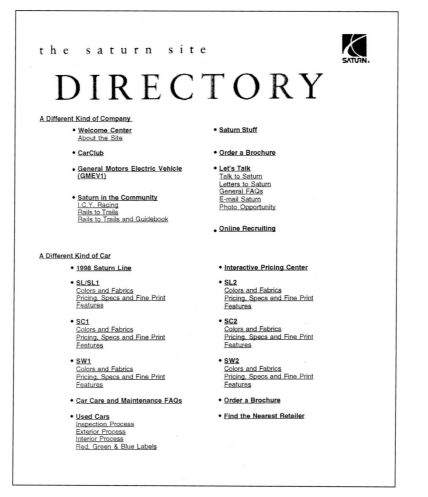

first letter of major words capitalized. Long reports often use third- and fourth-level headings to subdivide sections further.

Headings should enhance the visual impact of a document, so writers should use a consistent style for heading placement and design. Because conflicting styles create confusion, simplicity is the best policy. Remember that the risk of confusion increases as the number of type sizes and fonts increases.

Descriptive headings create expectations. Instead of using headings like "Problem" and "Solution," *name* the problem or solution. By giving the topic a name, headings like "Design Flaws in Model FXW" and "Model FXW Recall and Redesign" can explain the problem more specifically, indicate a solution, or both.

ENHANCED TEXT   Information can also be emphasized through the selective use of enhanced text. These design elements direct the reader's attention to items that the writer chooses to emphasize. In Document 2, for example, the sentence "Please forward the updated employer binder and IAF to me by July 10" is printed in italics for emphasis. Enhancements like italic print, an enlarged or a different font, changed font style, colour, underlining, and capitalization, however, should be used sparingly. Because these enhancements suggest that particular information merits close attention, use these special effects only in headings or critical phrases and sentences.

BULLETED LISTS   **Bullets** are visual cues that indicate critical information by high-lighting items contained in lists. Because business writing often contains lists, bullets can be effective design elements. Document 1 contains no bullets, but Document 2 uses a bulleted list to tell the reader the kind of materials needed for Image Advertising's employer binder.

Bullets transform imposing blocks of text into more inviting units of information. By highlighting information, bullets make it easier for readers to find specific details within the text of a document.

When using bullets to introduce a list of sentences, use a standard sentence format. Start with a capital letter and close with a period. When the bullet introduces words or phrases, use lower-case letters with no closing punctuation. For example:

▼   inspection phase
▼   revision phase
▼   completion phase

Consistency is essential, so avoid mixing sentences and phrases in the same bulleted list, and avoid beginning some bullets with nouns and others with verbs.

Progress Check

1.   Why is document design more important today than ever before?
2.   What two guidelines can enhance the visual impact of headings?
3.   Why is a consistent document design important?

What's Ahead

Having organized, composed, and designed your document, you now have in your hands a completed first draft. By its very nature, however, a first draft is subject to rethinking, refinement, and revision. Chapter 6 will explore the revision process as it examines word selection, style, and tone of voice. It will also examine how to offer and respond to constructive criticism.

STUDENT RESOURCE CENTRE

Summary of Chapter Objectives

1.   *Describe the different outline forms used in organizing business documents.*

An outline guides document writing from the introduction through to the conclusion. It enables the writer to make logical connections among ideas before actually composing, and to rearrange ideas when necessary. It also provides a way of coping with a large amount of information by dividing it into small sections. A formal outline follows prescribed rules concerning content and format in or-der to show the precise relationship among ideas. An informal outline is a more loosely connected organizational device that need not follow the strict structural rules of a formal outline.

2.   *Identify the three parts of a business document and describe their functions in communication.*

The opening of a business document must capture and hold the reader's attention and communicate the purpose of the document in a clear, succinct way. The middle contains the document's main points and supporting evidence. The conclusion summarizes the document's message, communicates closure, and clarifies action to be taken.

3. ***List the alternative patterns for organizing material in the middle of a document.***

The organization patterns that shape a document determine how directly its message will be presented as well as the way in which its ideas are linked together. Business documents can be organized in terms of two general categories that can be described as either deductive versus inductive or direct versus indirect. Within this framework, documents can follow a number of different organizational patterns, including problem/solution, cause-and-effect, chronological, and climactic-order. The core idea of a message generally determines the choice of an organizational pattern.

4. ***Describe the four forms of evidence used in business documents.***

The four forms of evidence are facts, statistics, examples, and expert opinion. Facts are statements that clarify a situation by adding informative details. They clarify your main point, define all new terms and concepts, and demonstrate that you can support your point of view. Statistics, a form of numerical evidence, are mathematical expressions that describe findings in an objective, uniform way and provide a standard to determine the validity of the results. Examples are descriptive stories and specific cases that make abstract information real and memorable. Expert opinion—the testimony of a recognized authority—adds weight to your position.

5. ***Explain the elements of document design and their functions in a document.***

Important document design elements include short paragraphs, headings, enhanced text, and bulleted lists. These elements clarify organization, aid in the composition process, encourage reading, make information accessible, focus attention on certain information, give the reader an overview of the content, and make information usable by primary and secondary readers.

Review and Discussion Questions

1. Why is it important for business documents to be well organized? *(Ch. Obj. 1)*

2. Why is it useful to organize a document in outline form before writing? *(Ch. Obj. 1)*

3. What are the differences between formal and informal outlines? *(Ch. Obj. 1)*

4. Identify the three major sections of a business document. *(Ch. Obj. 2)*

5. What primary functions are served by each of the sections referred to in Question 4? *(Ch. Obj. 2)*

6. Identify the patterns that can be used to organize information in the middle of a document. *(Ch. Obj. 3)*

7. What are the four forms of evidence used in business documents? *(Ch. Obj. 5)*

8. What guidelines should be followed in choosing expert opinions to use as evidence? *(Ch. Obj. 4)*

9. Identify and briefly explain each of the major elements of document design. *(Ch. Obj. 5)*

10. What are the objectives of effective document design? *(Ch. Obj. 5)*

Application Exercises

1. Choose a topic that interests you and that you would like to discuss in a letter to a friend or family member. The topic could relate to a hobby, a class in which you are currently enrolled, or a recent incident. Organize your ideas for this letter by writing a one-page formal outline. Include supporting evidence and/or examples with your outline. *(Ch. Obj. 1, 3)*

2. Write a one-page letter, report, or memo based on the formal outline assigned in Exercise 1. Did you find it helpful to organize your ideas in an outline first? *(Ch. Obj. 1, 3)*

3. Choose another topic that would also be a good subject for a letter. Organize your thoughts for this letter by writing an informal outline. Include supporting evidence and/or examples with your outline. *(Ch. Obj. 1, 3)*

4. Now write another letter, report, or memo following the informal outline that you created for Exercise 3. Which did you find more helpful, the formal outline in Exercise 1 or the informal outline in Exercise 3? Explain your answer. *(Ch. Obj. 1, 3)*

5. Write a letter to a friend describing either a recent or past experience. Organize your letter chrono-

logically. *(Ch. Obj. 3)*

6. Your boss has asked you to write a concise, one-page memo on the importance of good design in business documents. Write this memo and include an opening, middle, and conclusion. Design it to convey maximum visual impact. What organizational pattern would you recommend for this document? *(Ch. Obj. 2, 3, 5)*

7. Write a report describing the layout of your school's campus or major buildings. Use a geographical organization pattern, and design your document to be as clear as possible. *(Ch. Obj. 3, 5)*

8. Write a memo discussing some type of problem at your school or workplace and describing its effects (that is, why it is a problem). Organize your document in a cause-and-effect pattern. Use the design elements described in the chapter to make it more effective. *(Ch. Obj. 3, 5)*

9. Write a memo summarizing the problem that you discussed in Exercise 8 and then present a solution. Organize your memo in a problem/solution pattern and design it to be as readable as possible. *(Ch. Obj. 3, 5)*

10. Suppose the following memo, written by Jack Bunch of Quick Calculators, were to appear on your desk:

> As you know, we've expanded our overseas shipments to England and Germany lately. This requires additional shipments of 5000 units to each country. Demand seems to be rising there. We could start shipping to China as well. Demand is rising for our calculators here in Canada, too. In fact, sales are up 5000 units over last year. Right now, we're selling about 20 000 units a year in Canada alone. Our current supplier, Englewood Electronics, doesn't seem able to meet this increased demand. This past year, Englewood has been late five times in its shipments to us. This in turn makes us late in getting our calculators to customers. I understand that changes in management at Englewood have made it harder for the company to meet its schedules, and things will probably get worse before they get better. I'd recommend that we think about locating another supplier. I'm sending this memo to all employees just to keep everyone informed, but would the employees who are in the shipping department please get back to me as soon as possible with your suggestions for another supplier? Thanks.

(a) Is this an effective memo? Explain your answer.

(b) If your answer is no, outline a new memo that you believe will be more effective using the problem/solution pattern. *(Ch. Obj. 1, 3, 5)*

11. Compose the memo that you designed for Exercise 10. Organize it in the problem/solution pattern, and use design elements to clarify your message. *(Ch. Obj. 3, 5)*

12. Suppose that all the employees in Quick Calculators' shipping department are good friends with the staff of Englewood Electronics. After all, they have been doing business together for years and they enjoy socializing together. Although Jack Bunch still feels strongly that Quick Calculators needs to find another supplier, he knows that he must be very tactful in presenting his case. Rewrite the memo that you composed for Exercise 11, organizing it in the climactic-order pattern. *(Ch. Obj. 3, 4, 5)*

ACT: Applied Communication Techniques

Begin by referring to the sections up to and including Prepositions and Conjunctions in Appendix II. Underline all prepositions once and all conjunctions twice, then correct the grammar, spelling, and usage errors in the following sentences. Check your answers in Appendix V.

1. In crafting a effective business document, its important to pay close attention to document organization as it relate to the placement of information.

2. Because reports must capture and hold attention from the fist word, the opening is a inportant part.

3. Some issues lend themselves naturaly to an organisation that focus on events or consequences and the reasons for them.

4. Useing the deductive approach, your might propose that an new clothing shop would be an financial sucess in west edmonton mall.

5. Many reports asks the reader to take action by either adopting a recomendation or following a work plan.

6. Numbers often meen very little when presented out fo context but are critical to the accuracy of the information.

7. Because design often determine whether a document will actualy be read, its crucial to the documents success.

8. Bullets are visual cues that indicate critical imformation by highlightening items contained in lists.

9. The organization patterns that shape a document determine how direct it's message will be presented as well as the way in which it's ideas are linked together.

10. Importent document design element include short paragraphs, heading, enhance text, and bulleted lists.

Building Your Business Notebook

Carefully read the documents that appears on the following page and assess their communication effectiveness. Next, rewrite the letters, applying what you've learned in this chapter.

Building Your Research Skills

Pair off with a classmate. As a two-person team, choose a business topic that you both would like to research. Then, working independently outside class, read three articles that deal with the topic that you have chosen. Analyze each article to determine whether it follows the guidelines in this chapter for clear, effective writing.

Does each article seem well organized? Do its ideas flow logically? What type of organizational pattern does each article use? What type(s) of evidence does each use to support its points? Are the designs easy to read and follow?

Take notes on your analyses and make a presentation to your partner prior to class. Your partner should then present his or her findings to you. Then select the article that best follows the chapter guidelines for effective writing. Each of you should be prepared to explain whether each article is effective.

Building Your Teamwork Skills

Meet with your partner from the previous exercise. Go over your respective articles and analyses. Determine whether you can explain clearly to your partner why you think each article is effective or ineffective. Does your partner agree with your conclusions? Do you agree with his or hers? Explain your answer. Next, select one article and informally outline a document that summarizes your joint findings.

Building Your Technology Skills

Review your research on business forms for the Building Your Technology Skills exercise in Chapter 4, and select one sample electronic business form, such as a form for obtaining company information. Now analyze the sample form and briefly describe in writing how you would improve its organization and design. Consider whether the form's information is too detailed, missing, or not detailed enough; and whether its organization and design are effective.

Weblinks Internet Resources for this Chapter

Developing an Outline
http://www.researchpaper.com/writing_center/63.html

Writing It All Down
http://www.cs.unc.edu/~jbs/sm/Part1_write.html

Using Statistics
http://owl.english.purdue.edu/Files/87.html

Finalizing Your Document
http://www.cs.unc.edu/~jbs/sm/Part1_verifyrev.html

Design and Style
http://www.cs.unc.edu/~jbs/sm/Part2_format.html

I just read an article in *Business Week* magazine about a
person who was denied credit because of an incorrect credit
rating. When the person checked his credit rating, he found
that the report was for a person whose middle initial was L.
His middle initial was R. The middle initial was incorrect, so
the credit rating was for a different person.

I want to suggest that you should check your credit rating. I
feel that it is important for you to verify that the
information is correct and that you do so before you
experience problems that are not your fault. When you get your
credit report, you should check all the information. Any error
found in the report should be reported on the dispute form
received with the report. Return the dispute form with a copy
of your credit report to the credit-reporting agency that
processed your report. It is a good idea to send supporting
information with the credit report. The three major credit
reporting agencies are listed in the telephone book.

Document 1

```
TO:        Jonna Jonas, HR Director
FROM:      Lee Rocca
DATE:      February 19, 2000
SUBJECT:   Progress
```

You asked me to schedule some training sessions for the
employees. You also indicated that the best days of the week
to schedule these sessions are Wednesday or Friday, so that is
what I have done. You also said Conference Rooms A and B are
the best for holding training sessions, so I have already
scheduled those rooms and have limited the enrollment to 25
for each session.

We already have four sessions that are set up. With three more
I am having some problems getting firm dates with the
speakers. Actually, in one case the speaker isn't certain she
will be able to do it at all, but I think I have a back-up
presenter if the first one won't or can't do it. I'll let you
know later what happens. I don't know for certain how much
information you want, but I'll give you everything I have at
this time. Ms. Ruby Janvier will be speaking on Time
Management on May 14 for three hours in the afternoon in Room
A; Alex Gordon, Sexual Harassment, August 3 for three hours in
the morning; Dr. Rebecca Goldstein, Negotiations, October 23,
three hours in the morning, Room B; and Ron Bert, December 1
for four hours in the afternoon in Room A on Conflict
Resolution.

The sessions for which I'm not certain of all the particulars
will be on Communications, Personal Protection, and
Supervisory Skills. The tentative dates are June 6, September
18, and November 9. In addition to finding out for certain
about these, I am also preparing memos to the supervisors
about the programs and what the employees should do if they
want to attend.

I am also preparing evaluation forms, a suggestion form, and
am ordering refreshments for the session breaks. I will also
contact the speakers closer to the session to see what
equipment they will need. I think I am taking care of
everything—at least I can't think of anything else that needs
to be done right now. I hope this is the information you
wanted. If anything is unclear, let me know and I may be able
to explain it better.

Document 2

CASE STUDIES

DIVERSITY CASE:

Sexual Harassment Charges Are Common in Canada

Sexual harassment is common in Canadian business, industry, education, military—just about any facet of our society. In one documented case, two women in Niagara Falls, Ontario, charged the owner of a steak house with harassment.

According to the Ontario Human Rights Code, an employee is considered to be discriminated against when an employer requests sexual compliance in exchange for maintenance or improvement of workplace benefits.

In the case of the steak house in Niagara Falls, Cherie Bell, a waitress, alleged that the restaurant owner propositioned her when she came to pick up her pay cheque and when she came to the bar to pick up drinks for her customers. According to Bell, the owner fired her when she did not comply with the harassment. Anna Korczak, a second complainant, alleged that the same restaurant owner asked her personal questions, "slapped her 'rear end' on more than one occasion, and invited her to have sex with him."[11]

The Board of Inquiry dismissed both of these complaints, finding Bell's testimony to be inconsistent and Korczak's evidence failing to discharge the burden of proof. When other women came forward to report alleged sexual harass-

ment by the same restaurant owner, the Board of Inquiry did not find their evidence consistent enough with the Bell or Korczak cases to form a pattern.

Questions and Applications

1. Prepare a letter to the Canadian Restaurant Association requesting a copy of their ethics policy and asking how they respond to sexual harassment charges brought against restaurants that belong to their association.

2. Now prepare a letter to the Canadian Human Rights Commission asking for further information about human rights in sexual harassment cases.

3. Compare the organizational pattern of your two letters. What differences, if any, did you make in the opening of the letters? What differences, if any, have you made in the closing of the letters?

Source: Bell v. Ladas (1980), 1 C.H.R.R.D/155 (Ont. Bd. Inq.), Canadian Human Rights Reporter
http://web20.mindlink.net/chrr/sexhar.htm

CORPORATE CASE:

Are Northern Alberta and British Columbia Becoming Chopsticks?

Mitsubishi is one of the two multinational corporations from Japan that are harvesting the boreal temperate rainforest in Northern Alberta and British Columbia. According to environmental advocates, its clearcutting operation is responsible for increasing erosion, polluting natural streams and fisheries, and destroying travel corridors for the animals inhabiting the region. A considerable amount of land being harvested was once inhabited by the indigenous populations (Cree, Algonquin, and Lubicon) for their subsistence by hunting and fishing. The harvesting of this forest has slowly begun to destroy the traditional means of survival in this region. Greenpeace argues that operations like that of Mitsubishi destroy the environment and that the government must "ban the use of chlorine in the pulp and paper industry."[12]

However, reports from Alberta Pacific (ALPAC), the mill owned by Mitsubishi, indicate that their operation is one of the cleanest pulp mills in the world. To support their claim, they pumped their waste byproduct, treated effluent, into a 135-gallon aquarium filled with several species of fish native to the Athabasca River. These fish remained healthy. As well, ALPAC claims to be replacing the forest at a greater rate than they are harvesting it. Further, these Japanese companies have paid the provinces over a billion dollars in forest management agreements in order to gain the right to harvest this land. The land

size covered by these agreements is approximately "10 percent of Alberta's total land mass,"[13] or a land area the size of Prince Edward Island, Nova Scotia, and New Brunswick combined.

But why is this forest so important to Mitsubishi? The Japanese value the aspen tree for paper products, building materials, and disposable chopsticks. These disposable chopsticks from Canadian aspen trees are known as *waribashi* in Japan; over 8 million of them are produced there every day. These *waribashi* are necessary for the "Japanese sushi bars, noodle shops, and fast food restaurants that have become quite common in Japan...."[14] Of course, the production and sale of these chopsticks in Japan is reported to provide Mitsubishi with a huge profit.

Questions and Applications

1. Assume that you are not in favour of Mitsubishi's operation in Alberta and British Columbia. Prepare an outline for a letter you wish to write to your Member of Parliament stating your position.

2. Follow suggestions in this chapter for transforming your outline into a series of headings, with each heading followed by a main point and supporting evidence.

3. Finally, write the letter. Design it to be clearly readable and effective.

Revising and Editing Business Documents

Chapter Objectives

After studying this chapter, you should be able to:

1. Explain the importance of revising business documents.
2. Describe the characteristics of clear, conversational language and identify the qualities of concise, concrete, and correct language.
3. Explain the importance of persuasive and constructive language in business documents.
4. Outline strategies for constructing effective sentences and paragraphs.
5. Explain the relationship between style and writing strategy.
6. Discuss the characteristics of nondiscriminatory writing.
7. Identify ways to evaluate a final draft.

"To improve is to change; to be perfect is to change often."

Winston Churchill
British statesman

The All Too Many Faces of Bad Business Writing

Here are two examples of ineffective business writing—one a compilation of excerpts from actual rejection letters mailed to job applicants and the other an employment inquiry letter. What do these examples have in common? Unfortunately, the answer is poor writing.

The typical rejection letter will include a tactful expression of appreciation to the job applicant for contacting the company, and will attempt to maintain a positive image of the firm even though the job-seeker's application is being rejected. But many rejection letters fail miserably in this area. Imagine how you would feel if you received a letter in response to your application that contained some of the following excerpts from actual rejection letters:

▼ "After most careful consideration of your qualifications and background, we are unable to identify anything you can do for us."

▼ "Unfortunately, we have to be selective."

▼ "We're certain you could be more useful someplace else."

▼ "I'm sorry, but because of the nature of our work, we have to be more careful than others in our hiring."

Our second example, the employment inquiry letter, was received by Maria De Los Olivos, an assistant human resource manager at DDB Needham Worldwide. As you can see, the letter is filled with grammatical and formatting errors as well as errors in logic and common sense. The writer even mangles Maria's last name. If you received a letter like this, how would you respond?

The manner in which many rejection letters and employment inquiries are written is a symptom of a larger problem common to many business documents—the problem of treating a first draft as a final document instead of revising it to present information in a clear, effective way. When documents confuse rather than clarify, when they are filled with errors in language and logic, they are doomed to failure despite the underlying value of the message itself. ▼

Job application rejection examples cited in Malcolm S. Forbes, "How Not to Turn Down Job Applicants," *Forbes* (June 15, 1977): 22; employment letter courtesy of DDB Needham Worldwide, January 5, 1996.

(see example on following page)

Chapter Overview --

This chapter examines revision as a crucial part of the writing process. We will suggest criteria for judging the quality of a draft, choosing appropriate language, and constructing effective sentences and paragraphs. We will discuss the concept of writing style and make use of numerous examples to show how the best writers adapt their style to the needs of their documents. We will also provide practical tools for evaluating your final drafts.

March 20, 2000

Dear Ms. De Sloso Livos:

Misspelled name

I can be an asset to your company. I can envision how to place your client in the media. With research and determination I mastered this feat. While being employed at such noted companies who's President was cited as "Canada's Number Coorporate Sales Trainer", and the agency which was cited in "Who's Who in PR," I conquered the media within its realms by compiling lists and corresponding with the media. I was able to maintain awareness of various media placements.

Ugh!

Spelling and punctuation errors and missing word

What does this mean?

No man can live without bread alone, nor can any company live without the media. Everbody needs to get noticed. There must be some insight established about the client, product or item. I can administer the basics to get started.

Trite, sexist language

Along with my knowledge, I have mastered the feat of reporting, research and profreading. I have the administrative capabilities which helps companies run efficiently.

Grammatical and spelling errors!

In addition, I hold a bachelor of arts degree in English.

Poorly organized

I am eager to meet with you and discuss how I can be an asset to your company. Please call at your earliest convenience to arrange an interview. Thank you for your consideration. I look forward to hearing from you soon.

Sincerely,

Victor Messina

Victor Messina

Revising a Business Document ----------------------------

Although some people use the terms *revising* and *editing* interchangeably, they are distinct processes. **Revising** refers to the process of adding, deleting, replacing, and reorganizing words, sentences, and paragraphs to produce an unedited final draft. **Editing** involves correcting mistakes in grammar, spelling, and punctuation, and producing a document that reflects a consistent style for elements such as numbers, abbreviations, and capitalization.[1]

So whereas editing focuses on technical correctness, revising is a process of evaluating and assessing your meaning and your effectiveness in communicating it.

It is a bad plan that admits of no modification.

Publilius Syrus
Writer of mimes

The processes of editing and revising are illustrated in Figure 6-1, the first manuscript page of Charles Dickens's 1843 classic *A Christmas Carol.* This English masterpiece, written almost 150 years before the use of word processors, offers examples of both tiny and significant modifications that ultimately led to the final, familiar product.

This chapter focuses on the art of revising on every level, from communicating your core idea to choosing your words. (Appendix II offers a detailed guide to help you edit your draft.)

Is revision necessary to produce an acceptable final draft? Absolutely, says William Zinsser, author of *Writing with a Word Processor*. Writing, he emphasizes:

> . . . is not some sort of divine act that can only be performed by people of artistic bent, though obviously a gift for words is helpful. Writing is the logical arrangement of thought.
>
> To clarify what we write, it is important to constantly ask, "Have I said what I wanted to say?" Usually, we haven't. Even for a professional writer very few sentences come out right the first time, or even the second or third time.[2]

How well we communicate is determined not by how well we say things but by how well we are understood.

Andrew S. Grove
CEO, Intel Corporation

Certainly, the importance of lively, concise, and direct writing cannot be overemphasized. Perhaps even more important, however, is knowing how to word the simplest of statements so that the reader is drawn to your perspective and responds to your message. For example, a memo to employees regarding cost control could simply state that the company is taking certain measures to improve profitability and competitiveness. Although there would be no confusion as to what the company is doing, the same memo would probably be more effective if it were written with the reader's perspective in mind: Of what benefit is this to the reader? As

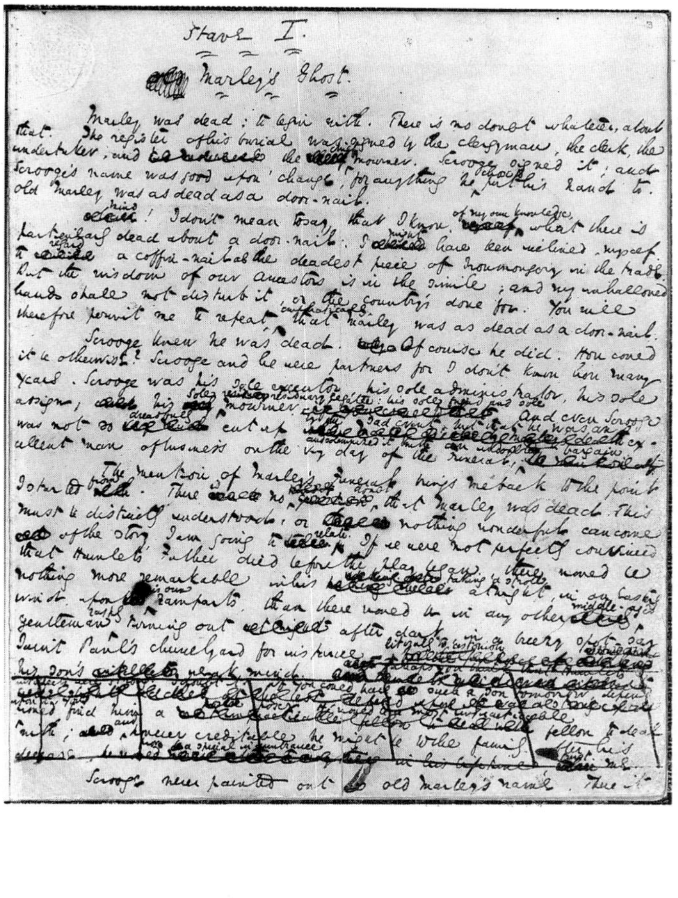
Stave I.

Marley's Ghost.

Figure 6-1 Converting a Draft into a Final Document
Source: The Pierpont Morgan Library/Art Resource, NY

we will see in this chapter, the "you" attitude often plays a significant part in the writing of memos, letters, reports, and other documents.

THE ART OF REVISION

The literal meaning of the word *revision* is "to see again." Even the most accomplished writers spend much of their time rewriting their first draft. Many revised documents, then, differ markedly from their first drafts. Here are some initial suggestions for turning first drafts into final documents that satisfy the needs of the readers, the topic, and the situation.[3]

▼ Effective revision requires a critical read-through to determine whether the document accomplishes its intended purpose and meets readers' needs. It often helps to put the document aside for a period of time so that you can look at it again with fresh eyes. Of course, waiting a few hours or even a few days is ideal, but deadlines and work pressures usually make this impossible.

▼ Reading a draft aloud can ensure that the sound and tone of your language are appropriate. Ernest Hemingway, for example, read his novel *The Old Man and the Sea* aloud several hundred times to be sure that his prose reflected the all-important sounds of speech that he was trying to capture.[4]

▼ You can also use checklists and style sheets as writing guides. While a checklist can remind you to include such key elements as tables and charts, a style sheet can help you focus on a consistent use of language and format.

THE QUALITY OF A DRAFT

Naturally, your revisions will be based on the quality of your first draft. To judge the effectiveness of your document, ask yourself whether it is written in clear, conversational language. Has your core idea been expressed in a concise and concrete way? Is your wording convincing and constructive? Answering these questions will help you evaluate your use of words, sentences, and paragraphs.

Progress Check

1. What is the difference between revising and editing?
2. Why is it especially important to revise and edit business documents?
3. Why should business writers read their drafts aloud?

Choosing Effective Language

Words are the building blocks of communication. They convey information through both literal meaning and tone. Meaning and tone affect the way a message is received and interpreted.

Unfortunately, words are often used ineffectively. Instead of clarifying, they confuse; instead of motivating, they dull the senses. Consider the frustration of Thomas Sobol, commissioner of the New York State Education Department. The Education Department sends over 10 000 letters with his signature each year. The commissioner also receives thousands of interoffice letters, memos, and reports—all requiring responses. Sobol found himself overwhelmed by messages such as these:

▼ "Careful implementation of this policy is needed in order to avoid the pitfall of goal displacement."

▼ "Existing variance procedures should be examined with regard to their potential for extension to circumstances not currently within their scope."

Sobol's solution: He ordered 250 of his highest-ranking department officials—many of whom held doctorates in education—to attend writing classes.[5]

In the following sections, we will examine some basic considerations in choosing effective language. To be effective in business communication, language should be familiar, concise, specific and concrete, correct, persuasive, and constructive.

FAMILIAR LANGUAGE

Consider the following memo excerpt and pity the manager who must read material like this dozens of times each day:

> Our research and storage workload consists primarily of those records which have expired their "In Office" retention periods, therefore, our temporary disruption of service would not have the same direct impact to the customer as would a department that is dealing with customers on a daily one-to-one basis.

A first rule of thumb is that words should be clear and simple enough for readers to understand your message. Simple words echo the language of everyday speech—they are familiar rather than obscure. They are conversational instead of stilted. A document avoids complicated phrases and technical words or terms that are not used by the average person in daily conversation. Even the memo above can be restored to familiar language when simplified as a short sentence:

> Both the research and storage workloads are in-house, so they don't affect customer sales.

Table 6-1 lists several phrases that appear frequently in business writing and compares them with conversational equivalents that are more clear and succinct.

PITFALLS OF OBSCURE LANGUAGE   Obscure, unfamiliar language often confuses rather than clarifies communication. Readers usually skip unfamiliar terms, read on without full comprehension, or get frustrated because the writer has slowed them down. Too often writers use obscure language instead of simple words. Instead of *transpire*, use *happen*; replace *the undersigned* with *I*, *me*, or *you*; substitute *must* in place of *incumbent upon*. The paragraphs in Figure 6-2(a) and (b) illustrate how replacing the italicized obscure words with simple words makes each statement easier to read and understand.

BUSINESS JARGON   Consider the use of language in each of the following business contexts:

▼ A credit company refers your overdue car payment to the "fulfillment office" instead of the collection or billing department.

▼ A bank says "nonperforming assets" when it means "bad debts."

Table 6-1   Conversational Phrases in Business Writing

Instead of . . .	Say . . .
I wish to acknowledge the receipt of your payment.	Thank you for your recent payment.
As per our recent conversation,	As we agreed when we spoke,
Contents duly noted,	I read your comments,
We are mailing the specifications under separate cover.	We are sending the specifications by overnight mail.
We regret to inform you that we are in error.	We apologize for our mistake.

We have *utilized* obscure words so that you can *behold* how they make reading difficult. We *postulate* that you will *concur* and *deem* revision *imperative* to *facilitate* understanding.

(a) *Ineffective Paragraph Using Obscure Language*

We have *used* simple words so that you can *see* how they make reading easy. We *believe* that you will *agree* and *consider* revision *necessary* to *aid* understanding

(b) *Effective Paragraph Using Simple Words*

Figure 6-2 From Obscure Language to Simple Wording

- Instead of referring to company-wide "layoffs," an employer announces "workforce adjustments," "downsizing," and "negative employee retention."[6]

In each case, word choice is characterized by **jargon**—vocabulary peculiar to a specific group, trade, or profession and used to describe its activities. A sort of private language, jargon also consists of unexplained abbreviations and acronyms that leave outsiders puzzled. Does *AMA*, for example, refer to the American *Management* Association, the American *Marketing* Association, or the American *Medical* Association? Is *PC* a *personal computer*, a *professional corporation*, or a reference to being *politically correct?*

Jargon can be useful when the writer is certain that readers understand it. However, a writer should always use plain English when corresponding with people who may not understand the jargon. For example, a recruiter for a large corporation might tell job applicants that the company is not hiring, rather than explain that it is downsizing to increase a return on equity that is below the industry average.

Jargon can be a serious barrier to communication when referring to computer technology. Although terms like *World Wide Web*, *browser*, *Gopher*, and *FTP* are all part of the vocabulary of the Internet, it is a mistake to assume that everyone knows what they mean. If you have any doubts, define the terms or avoid using them.

The following suggestions will help eliminate overly formal language and jargon from first drafts and produce reader-friendly documents:

- Try to imagine an actual conversation with your readers.
- Read your document out loud. Jargon and overly formal language should become obvious. Replace poor word choices with familiar language.
- Substitute personal pronouns, such as *I*, *we*, and *you*, for obscure phrases such as "the undersigned."
- Wherever possible, simplify, clarify, and shorten your message.

CONCISE LANGUAGE

In 1656 French scientist Blaise Pascal added the following postscript to a 20-page letter: "I hope you will pardon me for writing such a long letter, but I did not have time to write you a shorter one." An apparent contradiction, perhaps, but this statement actually explains why so many writers are wordy: a short, uncluttered document

The objective of this message is to increase the number of donations at the St. Francis Church food drive. Instead of a litany of facts about the importance of donations, the message relies on familiar, simple, direct language to make its point. Its visual link to the well-known Campbell soup label reminds people not to forget to donate food.

takes more time and thought than one littered with repetition and unnecessary verbiage. Still, many business writers tend to equate quantity with quality. Perhaps they believe that a document that is four pages instead of four paragraphs will indicate they are more knowledgeable or more productive. However, short, clearly worded messages result in clear, effective communication. Tightening prose is one of the main tasks of revision.

WORDINESS   Given the time constraints most businesspeople face, it is critical to choose vocabulary and sentence structure that make your point directly. Wordy expressions hide your points because they often combine two or more words that mean the same thing, or use passive language that requires three or four words instead of one or two. When unnecessary words are removed and passive constructions revised, statements become more concise and easier to read. The difference between *wordy* and *concise* is clear in the following pair of sentences:

Wordy: A substantial majority of workers are in disagreement over the company's overtime policy, and the workers hope that the problem can be resolved through the process of labour-management negotiation.

Concise: Most workers disagree with the company's overtime policy and hope that negotiations can resolve the problem.

Table 6-2 lists several commonly used wordy and redundant expressions that can be revised to make your writing more concise.

REVISING FOR CONCISENESS   It is important to communicate your message in as few words as possible. First drafts are often wordy, so it is important to revise a document with conciseness as one of your main goals.

Be especially careful about empty words and phrases that pad sentences without adding meaning. Evaluate each word and expression by asking yourself if it's

Table 6-2 Revising for Conciseness

Wordy Expression	Revised Version
at this point in time	today
at a later date	later
the question as to whether	whether
the reason why is that	because
call your attention to the fact that	remind you
during the course of our meeting	in our meeting

Redundant Expression	Revised Version
enter into	enter
new beginner	beginner
past experience	experience
4:30 P.M. in the afternoon	4:30 P.M.
assemble together	assemble
endorse on the back	endorse

necessary. Can your thought be expressed more concisely without changing its meaning? Consider the following sentence, which uses two of the worst offenders among empty phrases:

> *As a matter of fact*, statistics show that *in the case of* the baby-boom generation, Canadians and Americans know more about world events than their parents did.

Revising for conciseness strengthens the following message:

> Statistics show that Canadian and American baby boomers know more about world events than their parents did.

Care should be taken, not that the reader may understand, but that he must understand.

Quintilian
Roman rhetoric teacher

SPECIFIC, CONCRETE LANGUAGE

Imagine words and phrases placed along a continuum running from the most general to the most specific. At the general end, you might find words like *love* and *justice*. These terms represent abstract, intangible ideas. Close to the specific end, words like *hug* and *lawsuit* appear. Specific, concrete terms refer to tangible, real-world items, actions, or people. In business writing, concrete words and phrases are usually more effective because they provide vivid details, are easier to remember, and minimize misunderstandings and mistakes.

Some examples of general words and their specific counterparts are:

General	Specific
change in temperature	the temperature rose five degrees
vehicle	four-door sedan
reading material	*Profit—The Magazine for Canadian Entrepreneurs*
weather disturbance	arctic front

Note that specific words constitute precise information and quantify ideas.

In this ad, United Technologies Corporation promotes simple, concise business writing. The ad reminds us that much of the language that we share most comfortably has been pared down to the essentials.

Keep It Simple

Strike three.
Get your hand off my knee.
You're overdrawn.
Your horse won.
Yes.
No.
You have the account.
Walk.
Don't walk.
Mother's dead.
Basic events
require simple language.
Idiosyncratically euphuistic
eccentricities are the
promulgators of
triturable obfuscation.
What did you do last night?
Enter into a meaningful
romantic involvement
or
fall in love?
What did you have for
breakfast this morning?
The upper part of a hog's
hind leg with two oval
bodies encased in a shell
laid by a female bird
or
ham and eggs?
David Belasco, the great
American theatrical producer,
once said, "If you can't
write your idea on the
back of my calling
card,
you don't have a clear idea."

© United Technologies Corporation 1979

A message as published in the *Wall Street Journal*
by United Technologies Corporation, Hartford, Connecticut 06101

Occasionally, general words may be more appropriate because they downplay negative messages. For instance, in a letter outlining reasons why an employee should be fired, it is probably better to say in closing, "If I can be of any assistance in this matter, please let me know" instead of "If you'd like me to terminate this employee, please let me know."

CORRECT LANGUAGE

Correct language communicates exactly what you want to say in exactly the way you want to say it. Correct language is precise in three senses: it is accurate; it avoids exaggeration; and it avoids miscommunication by following rules of grammar, spelling, and punctuation.

ACCURACY   Inaccurate, imprecise language can cause not only misinterpretation but costly errors as well. For example, writing in a memo that you "suggest" a change is far different than writing that you "recommend" a change. If your purpose is to *recommend*, say so through precisely chosen words.

Accuracy, of course, requires correct word usage. If you write, for instance, that you are a "disinterested observer," do you mean that you "lack interest" or that you are "unbiased"? If you want to say that you lack interest, the correct term is *uninterested*; *disinterested* means *impartial*.

A QUESTION OF ETHICS

Grading the Language of Annual Reports

Nowhere is the precision and honesty of language more important than in the "Letter to Shareholders" that appears in corporate annual reports. Investors make financial decisions based on what they read in these letters, and the company's image and relationship with customers, suppliers, and government officials are affected as well. Recently, business writer Patrice Duggan Samuels analyzed the Letters to Shareholders from eight companies that experienced difficulty in 1994. Hoping to find honest, direct, plain language in all cases, she found a range of candour and clarity. Here is how Samuels analyzed the language contained in five of those letters:

INTEL

1994 was a difficult year for Intel because of problems with flawed Pentium computer chips and angry consumers who wanted an across-the-board product recall. The Letter to Shareholders, written by the company's top three officials, took a candid approach to these problems: "What a year . . . 1994 was the best of times—and the worst of times. We received a crash course in consumer relations when we chose to replace the chip for some consumers but not for others."

NIKE

Philip Knight, chief executive of Nike, was also candid about his company's problems, but Samuels detected a calculated whine that seemed to disguise a hidden agenda. "So, it wasn't such a great year," wrote Knight, referring to Nike's 18-percent decline in net income. "We all know the negatives," and they "get plenty of ink because they make the most entertaining story."

"When Knight sounds like a cranky teenager with a bad report card," observed Samuels, "he conveys to readers exactly what the maker of athletic footwear and apparel wants to convey to its customers, primarily teenagers: it's a company with an attitude."

SCHLUMBERGER

Samuels gives this oil company an excellent grade for tossing out euphemisms and evasiveness and explaining directly why earnings per share dropped by 8 percent. "1994 was a disappointing year," the chairman wrote. "Our improvement in North America . . . was more than offset by problems elsewhere."

PROCTER & GAMBLE

Samuels did not award Procter & Gamble, the personal-care products giant, a good grade for honest, open communication. Their annual report offers little explanation as to why the company lost $102 million in speculative derivatives trading during 1994. The only direct reference to the loss appears in a footnote to the report's financial data. Instead, the Letter to Stockholders refers to the financial fiasco in an oblique way when it states that P&G "has taken steps to substantially increase the oversight of the company's financial activities." P&G's limited explanation failed to impress Samuels. "If shareholders have not followed the saga of the company's loss in the newspapers," she writes, "they won't learn much about it here."

CAREMARK

This health-care company found itself under federal investigation relating to accusations of illegal payments to doctors. Instead of openly dealing with this bad news, Caremark's chairman is evasive. "1994 held significant regulatory and legal challenges for us," he wrote, without offering any specific details.

The general trend is for more openness and honesty in corporate annual reports, but as you have just seen, you cannot assume that you will find it.

Questions for Critical Thinking

1. Why is the choice of language in corporate annual reports often an ethical issue?
2. Why are shareholders and others scrutinizing the language of corporate annual reports more carefully today than ever before?
3. Annual reports are a great research tool for job seekers. Explain how you would evaluate the five companies analyzed here as prospective employers. How does the clarity or evasiveness of each company affect your job-search decision?

Source: Patrice Duggan Samuels, "Annual Reports: Upfront and Unstarched," *New York Times,* 9 April 1995, F5.

MODERATION   Obviously, strengthening the accuracy of your word choice will depend in large part on exercising your vocabulary. Practising moderation in your judgment also helps. Overgeneralization, for example, not only leads to careless word choice but also suggests careless thinking. For instance, you might conclude a report by recommending that your department buy Lotus 1-2-3 because it is "the best value in business spreadsheet programs." Your conclusion may be true—but only with qualification. If you surveyed only three software programs, then Lotus may be the "best value" among the programs in the class that you examined. Moreover, because best value in a product can refer to lowest price, greatest flexibility, or other criteria, that term also requires qualification.

"Absolute certainty, even when justified, can damage credibility,"[7] warns writing consultant John Tarrant. Qualifiers make statements more believable. According to communication authority Roy W. Poe, "Even when you can justify the use of such terms as *most, greatest, largest percentage, overwhelming majority,* and *fewest,* it is usually better to give specific data when you can."[8]

Specificity reduces exaggeration. Refer to actual numbers, examples, and cases, and draw reasonable conclusions. The following statement, for instance, suffers from unnecessary exaggeration: "The vast increase in minorities and immigrants will make them the most important market segment in the next century." If you revised this statement to reflect a more moderate judgment, you could say: "Because 40 percent of the under-30 population consists of minorities, they will become a core market by 2000." Again, note that because it is balanced with specific language, such potential jargon as "the under-30 population" and "core market" contribute to a more precise statement.

GRAMMAR, SPELLING, AND PUNCTUATION   You can spend hours drafting and revising a document, choosing the best words to suit the exact meaning that you want to convey. But if you neglect to correct any errors in spelling and grammar the effectiveness of your document will be undermined. Business writing that contains errors in grammar, spelling, or punctuation is deficient. Indeed, in a recent poll conducted by the executive search firm Robert Half International, 98 percent of executives from 200 large firms reported that grammar and spelling are important factors when interviewing job applicants.[9] Appendix II reviews grammar basics.

Grammatical and spelling errors can also be embarrassing. A business language group called Grammar for Smart People has received about 15 000 written inquiries about hundreds of matters since it began operation. Of these, 15 percent misspelled the word *grammar.* The word was also misspelled by the group's accountant on its federal tax return.[10]

PERSUASIVE LANGUAGE

Words can either enliven writing or reduce its credibility. When language is being used in an effort to persuade, the writer's success or failure may depend upon whether the language used conveys power or weakness. When words are too weak to carry the burden of persuasion, writing consultant Patricia H. Westheimer calls them "hidden dissuaders."[11] We will consider persuasive language from two perspectives: strong verb choice and assertive phrasing.

STRONG VERBS   In each of the following pairs of sentences, a weak first sentence has been improved by revising it with a stronger verb. Main verbs and verb phrases are italicized.

Weak: I *want to give you the authorization* to hire temporary help.
Strong: I *authorize* you to hire temporary help.
Weak: This rule *will have an adverse effect* on new employees.
Strong: This rule will *adversely affect* new employees.
Weak: The plant's hiring policy *is in violation of* federal laws.
Strong: The plant's hiring policy *violates* federal laws.

In each case, the revised sentence features a main verb that is stronger because it expresses *action* on the part of the subject. The most effective verbs move readers along in an action-oriented way. Verbs that communicate action also strengthen a message because they are simpler and more direct (and have the added advantage of reducing sentence length). By contrast, "state-of-being," or "to be," verbs are more static and passive. A sentence is also less effective when it depends on "helping" verbs. The noun form of a verb (frequently ending in *-tion*) also weakens a sentence. For instance, "The manager documented every complaint" is better than "The manager is putting together a documentation of every complaint."

ASSERTIVE PHRASING   What would you say about an individual whose letters and memos consistently relied on such phrases as "If you could possibly," "If I could trouble you," "Perhaps, if it wouldn't be a problem," and "I know how busy you must be"? Some words and phrases lack persuasiveness because they seem too deferential—that is, they suggest that the writer prefers to yield rather than assert opinion or judgment. By implication, then, these words and phrases may tell readers that the writer is in a relatively weak position of power. By eliminating telltale weak phrases, you can communicate greater self-assurance and reflect more accurately the power relationship between you and your readers. As you recall from Chapter 3, using assertive phrasing is often more difficult for women than for men.

CONSTRUCTIVE LANGUAGE

Because it encourages readers to take action that you support, a positive attitude can be one of your most important communication tools. You can communicate a positive attitude by avoiding certain words and phrasing and by focusing your message on constructive action—on what to *do* rather than on what *not* to do.

AVOIDING NEGATIVISM   The first step in communicating a positive approach is to avoid words that encourage negative responses. Some words, such as *blame, wrong, poor, insist, failure,* and *unreasonable,* can cause readers to get angry or defensive—especially when preceded by the pronouns *you* and *your.*

Words like these not only communicate a variety of negative emotions but also suggest unequal positions of power. At their worst, they can embarrass recipients and will almost certainly discourage cooperation. Your goal should be to communicate diplomatically and to establish a partnership between writer and reader based on the mutual need to act toward some goal.

Encouraging your readers to take mutually beneficial action also involves a positive approach that focuses on what you can rather than cannot do. There are times, of course, when every businessperson must communicate negative or unpleasant information. By taking a positive approach, however, you can present this information in ways that will encourage readers to respond in a productive manner. For example, "As soon as we receive the marketing report, we will move to the next project stage," is more positive than, "We cannot move ahead on the project until we receive the marketing report."

Table 6-3 summarizes six criteria for choosing the most effective language for business and most other forms of writing.

> → *Cross Reference*
> We discussed gender and language on pages 86–91.

Progress Check

1. Why is jargon such a detriment to clear communication?
2. Why is it important to be concise and clear in business writing?
3. Cover the right-hand column of Table 6-3. Based on what you have just read, try to describe each category of effective language.

Constructing Effective Sentences _____

Like effective language, effective sentences reflect familiar patterns of speech. Appendix II provides in-depth coverage of sentence construction. In this section we

Table 6-3   Criteria for Choosing Effective Language

Choose Language That Is . . .	How To Do It
Familiar	Use simple, direct, familiar language; avoid business jargon and other language that obscures meaning.
Concise	Use as few words as possible to make a point; replace wordy phrases and passive constructions with language that makes points directly; use qualifiers with care.
Specific and concrete	Use words that provide specific details, balance general phrasing with language that offers precise information.
Correct	Use precise language to be accurate and avoid miscommunication; be moderate in your judgments, avoiding overgeneralization and exaggeration; use correct grammar, spelling, and punctuation.
Persuasive	Choose words that convey enough confidence to persuade readers; rely on strong verbs and assertive phrasing.
Constructive	Avoid words that are likely to encourage negative responses and misrepresent positions of power; communicate a positive approach to working relationships.

will highlight three of the most important strategies for constructing effective sentences in a variety of business documents: use of the active voice, brevity and variety, and concreteness.

ACTIVE VOICE

In the **active voice,** the subject of the sentence performs the action. When you read a sentence in the active voice, you know who is responsible for the action:

> The *manager scheduled* a meeting.

In the **passive voice,** the subject of the sentence is acted upon. In many cases you can identify the person or thing doing the acting because it is the object of the preposition *by:*

> A meeting *was scheduled by the manager.*

In other cases, it is not clear who is taking the action because the subject is not identified:

> A meeting *was scheduled.*

The passive voice focuses on events and situations rather than on people taking action. It lacks the vitality of the active voice and typically has a bureaucratic tone. It also uses more words and can be quite vague (sometimes intentionally so). Here are two examples:

▼ The product *was determined* to be inadequate.
  (Determined by whom? Perhaps the writer does not want to say.)

▼ A commitment *has been made* to finish the project by the end of the month.
  (Who will finish the project? The sentence does not say, even though the issue is critical.)

Note, however, the use of the passive voice in the following sentence:

> A new voice-mail system *will be installed* by next week.

Here, the passive voice is appropriate because the installer is less important than what is being installed.

There are a few other instances in which the passive voice is acceptable—and some in which it can be more effective than the active. For example, while the active voice is a voice of direct action, the passive voice may be appropriate for diplomacy. You may want to use it, for instance, when making direct requests to superiors or to someone outside your company. Similarly, the passive voice may be appropriate when you are delivering a message on someone else's authority. For instance, you can use the passive voice to forward a request or an order without implying that you are exercising responsibility that is not yours. We will discuss the applications of active and passive voice as stylistic strategies in a later section of this chapter.

BREVITY AND VARIETY

Short sentences of between 16 and 20 words command attention because they are easy to read and understand. However, many business writers compose lengthy sentences in an effort to unify related thoughts in sentence units. Although the theory is sound, practice usually demands shorter sentences for greater readability. For example:

> The meeting will be held at 2:00 P.M. on Thursday so that we can discuss the problems on the Albertson account, which, according to Peters, have become more serious in the past few days.

With some slight rewording, this 34-word sentence can be broken down into three parts:

> The meeting will be held at 2:00 P.M. on Thursday. The main topic on the agenda is the Albertson account. According to Peters, the problems on this account have become more serious in the past few days.

As you will see later in the chapter, transitional words such as *however*, *therefore*, *in addition*, and *for example* help connect ideas and reduce sentence length.

While it is generally advisable to limit sentence length, too many short sentences can be choppy and difficult to read because they disconnect related ideas. Sentence variety infuses a conversational tone into written messages and reduces choppiness. Variety adds colour to writing as it mimics the rhythm of speech. For this reason, Version 1 is less acceptable than Version 2:

> **Version 1**
>
> *Canadian Living* is a magazine aimed at women. It includes articles for career women. It includes articles for homemakers. It is an ideal place to advertise products for women in the 20–55 age group.

> **Version 2**
>
> *Canadian Living* is a magazine for women. With articles for career women and homemakers, it is an ideal place to advertise products for women in the 20–55 age group.

CONCRETENESS

Like words, sentences can be either general or concrete. Generalities are usually appropriate when the audience does not require further explanation. However, if you think your readers may not completely understand the abstract version, give specific details.

Brief stories are also effective in describing or illustrating your point. For example, if you are writing to advise a department head on recently approved

1. Describe a situation where sentences in a business document would require use of the active instead of the passive voice. Then describe a situation where the passive voice would be required.
2. What is the advantage of using a variety of sentence structures in business writing?
3. Why is concrete writing particularly important at the close of a document?

sexual-harassment guidelines, you may choose to include the story of a recent incident. When a story is used, however, it should be short and clearly connected to the purpose of the memo. Never tell a story—even a good one—just for its own sake.

Concrete writing is also effective in the close of a document. Even though this approach usually adds several words to the document, it is a good strategy for reinforcing your message at a critical point. It is an especially effective way to close persuasive messages. For example, "I appreciate your help in finalizing the budget" may be better than the more general closing, "I appreciate your help."

Constructing Effective Paragraphs

Think of the paragraph as the basic unit of composition—the unit in which ideas are grouped to communicate your message. In business writing, the most effective paragraphs follow several important guidelines:

- ▼ They are short.
- ▼ They include topic sentences.
- ▼ They use transitional expressions to connect ideas.

The letter shown in Figure 6-3 successfully applies these guidelines.

SHORT PARAGRAPHS

Few businesspeople have the time or patience to wade through "fat" paragraphs, so the shorter the better. Because the eye is drawn naturally to short paragraphs, they are more likely to be read, understood, and remembered.

To keep paragraphs as short as possible, limit each paragraph to a single idea. The best points for paragraph breaks can be identified by determining where one thought ends and another begins. For example, consider the one-paragraph, page-long memorandum in Figure 6-4. Revising a single-paragraph memo into sections helps readers focus on the issues.

TOPIC SENTENCE

A **topic sentence** states the purpose of a paragraph. It is usually the first sentence in a paragraph, and it is crucial in business writing because it "announces" what the paragraph will say. Consider how the topic sentence in the following paragraph sets the stage for what comes next:

> *Your account shows a balance of $4000.* Although we received payments from you in January and February, you also made additional purchases during this period. With these purchases and interest charges, you are approaching your account credit limit of $4200.

The topic sentence also gives readers the option of reading a paragraph in detail or simply scanning it for relevant information. Rather than read every word of every paragraph, people tend to select those paragraphs that satisfy immediate needs. In setting the stage for what follows, the topic sentence "previews" the paragraph for its usefulness to readers.

BMX *Auto World*

1111 Reece Avenue
Chilliwack, BC V2P 5W9
(604) 555-1111 — phone
(604) 555-2222 — fax
ga@bmx.com — e-mail

June 4, 2000

Mr. Jim Matherson, Fleet Manager
Strong Muscle Moving Company
109 Pell Drive
Chilliwack, BC V2P 7M8

Dear Mr. Matherson:

Short paragraphs make it easy to remember information

Thank you for your request for credit with BMX Auto World. We look forward to servicing your fleet of trucks and meeting all your automotive needs.

In order to complete the credit evaluation, we need two business references, preferably companies with whom you have worked for at least two years. We will begin processing your application as soon as we receive this information. You can then expect to hear from us in about a week.

Topic sentences limit paragraph length

While you wait, please review our latest credit policy statement, which explains a mechanism for saving every time you pay your bill within ten business days. For an account as large as yours, these savings can add up to hundreds—and even thousands—of dollars by the end of the year.

I look forward to receiving your references and to servicing your account.

Sincerely,

Greg Avion

Greg Avion
Credit Manager

Figure 6-3 Sample Letter: Effective Paragraphing

TRANSITIONS

In much the same way that a bridge connects two sides of a river, **transitions** are words and phrases that connect ideas to produce coherent paragraphs. Transitional expressions build bridges, both from one sentence to another and from one paragraph to another. Readers need this help as they make their way through the unfamiliar territory of a document. The following excerpt illustrates how transitions help readers follow the writer's sequence of ideas:

> I received the merchandise you returned and your request for credit. *As you know*, our policy is to grant credit for merchandise returned within 30 days. *However*, we do require that the items be in their original cartons and that they have not been used. Two of the three items returned to us do not meet these requirements. *The*

Progress Check

1. List three guidelines for writing effective paragraphs. Why is each important?
2. Explain why the use of short paragraphs can be considered both a design and content feature.
3. Are transitions a tool of persuasion? Explain your answer.

Yesterday's *Globe and Mail* article about Larson's raised several issues about our service and the quality of our merchandise. We should look at these issues now before they become larger problems. The issue of customer service has always been difficult for us. If we want to maintain our low-price policy, we have to provide bare-bones service. But we have to ask ourselves whether a system that requires customers to spend two hours waiting in four lines is reasonable and whether these customers will ever return. The quality issue seems to focus on our housewares. If what the *Globe* points out is correct—if spatulas melt after one use and glasses do not survive a dishwashing—we have to do more than offer customers a liberal return policy. We have to improve the quality of our merchandise. I would like to meet with you, Bill Pierce, Anita Duncan, and Ellen Wolf tomorrow at 2:00 p.m. to talk more about these issues.

Long Paragraph

Yesterday's *Globe and Mail* article about Larson's raised several issues about our service and the quality of our merchandise. We should look at these issues now before they become larger problems.

The issue of customer service has always been difficult for us. If we want to maintain our low-price policy, we have to provide bare-bones service. But we have to ask ourselves whether a system that requires customers to spend two hours waiting in four lines is reasonable and whether these customers will ever return.

The quality issue seems to focus on our housewares. If what the *Globe* points out is correct—if spatulas melt after one use and glasses do not survive a dishwashing—we have to do more than offer customers a liberal return policy. We have to improve the quality of our merchandise.

I would like to meet with you, Bill Pierce, Anita Duncan, and Ellen Wolf tomorrow at 2:00 p.m. to talk more about these issues.

Short Paragraphs

Figure 6-4
Paragraphing for Visual Appeal

first item—a portable telephone—was not returned in its original carton. *The second item*—a clock radio—is scratched and shows other signs of wear.

Table 6-4 identifies many of the most common transitional expressions. At the left is the relationship that each expression signals to readers; at the right are the words and phrases that communicate that relationship.

Choosing an Appropriate Style for a Document

In conversation, it is fairly easy to gauge someone's communication tone or style. Tone of voice, eye contact, and body language send signals that are often as important as the message itself. However, because these cues are absent from written documents, we must look elsewhere for indications of style. In its most basic sense, the **style** of a written document refers to the *way* something is said rather than *what*

Table 6-4   Transitional Expressions

Relationship	Words That Signal the Relationship
Addition	further, furthermore, besides, too, moreover, and, also, in addition, next, then, equally important, finally
Example	for instance, thus, specifically, namely, as an illustration, for example
Contrast	but, yet, however, nevertheless, conversely, on the other hand, on the contrary, still, at the same time, nonetheless
Comparison	similarly, likewise, in the same way, in comparison, in like manner
Concession	of course, to be sure, certainly, naturally, granted
Result	therefore, thus, consequently, so, accordingly, due to this
Summary	as a result, hence, in short, in brief, in summary, in conclusion, finally, on the whole, therefore
Time sequence	first, next, then, finally, afterward, before, soon, later, during, meanwhile, subsequently, immediately, eventually, in the future, currently
Place	in the front, foremost, in the background, at the side, adjacent, nearby, in the distance, here, there

Source: Lynn Quitman Troyka, *Simon & Schuster Handbook for Writers,* 2d ed. (Englewood Cliffs, N.J.: Prentice Hall, 1990), 96.

is said. Put another way, form follows function. It is a reflection of the writer's attitude—the decision to be formal or informal, apologetic or forceful, personal or impersonal, controversial or conservative.

According to management communication professor John S. Fielden, every written document must meet the unique needs of your situation, your audience, and your purpose. The correct writing style, according to Fielden, helps produce the desired reaction and result.[12]

In this section we will survey several stylistic techniques that reflect the writer's sensitivity to situation, audience, and purpose of the message. We will also discuss the importance of the "you" approach as a key to effective reader-centred writing. Finally, we will observe some important principles in nondiscriminatory writing.

Communicate unto the other guy that which you would want him to communicate unto you if your positions were reversed.

Motto of Aaron Goldman
CEO, The Macke Company

STYLE TECHNIQUES

Because writing situations, audiences, and objectives differ, you should develop many writing styles instead of one.[13] The most common business writing situations include: conveying routine information and making direct requests, communicating good news and conveying goodwill, communicating bad news, and attempting to persuade.

Writing style choices also depend on your audience. In business writing, you must consider whether the message is intended for a manager, a co-worker, or a supervisee. "This is where the politics of writing comes in," says writing consultant Sherry Sweetnam. "With a superior, you will probably be diplomatic and tactful. With subordinates, you will probably be more direct and forceful."[14]

In general, the person with the greatest power is the one who will determine your style. If your manager is formal, then you, too, should be formal, even if you normally write in a friendly, open way. The same advice applies to communication with customers and other outsiders with clout: let them determine the style of your correspondence.

The purpose of your message will also affect your style. For instance, if you are trying to convey bad news, you should usually avoid a forceful, confrontational style. In this section we will examine five types of styles: being forceful, passive, personal, impersonal, and persuasive.[15]

BEING FORCEFUL   A forceful writing style is typically used to add emphasis. For example, a memo to company employees regarding safety rules and regulations may warn of life-threatening situations if the rules are not followed. In this situation it is essential to write forcefully.

Forceful writing is defined by several characteristics. It is usually direct in its approach and positive in its tone; there is no need to back into statements. Thus, "I am disappointed by your recommendations" is more forceful than "Your recommendations are not what I had hoped for." Because the active voice enhances directness, it is typically used when writing forcefully. Instead of "This problem should be resolved by Thursday," write "I expect you to resolve this problem by Thursday."

Forceful writing also relies on powerful words and phrases. Seldom are weak words like *perhaps, possible,* and *might* used to express a point. Forceful writing also avoids dependent and subordinate clauses that lengthen messages and weaken emphasis. Thus,

> The accounting system is not meeting the company's current needs.

is better than

> After reviewing our accounting system and comparing it to the systems used by comparable companies, I have concluded that the accounting system is not meeting our current needs.

BEING PASSIVE   When you are writing to individuals in higher positions or communicating negative information, a passive writing style may be the best choice. Passive writing, however, is not a strategy for saying less than you would like. It is a strategy for communicating information that may require some diplomacy on the writer's part. Careful choice of passive language also allows the writer to avoid giving a direct order when such a stance is not appropriate. Here are several examples of an effective passive writing strategy:

Purpose	Example
To communicate negative information without pointing fingers.	Sales quotas are not being met.
Shift responsibility for negative information to persons unnamed.	Your request for an extended line of credit has been refused.
Avoid giving a direct order.	Having the project report by Wednesday will help me prepare for my Thursday meeting.

BEING PERSONAL   A personal writing style is typically used to convey good news or to persuade readers to take some action. A personal writing style tends to be conversational in tone, and short sentences are more conversational than longer ones. Generally, this style includes the use of contractions, personal pronouns, first names, and personal references that make readers feel that the document has been specially written for them.

Personal writing also relies on the active voice, whether to place the writer at the centre of the action or to motivate readers to act. The personal style may include direct questions asking readers about the subject of the document. Here are several examples of effective and ineffective personal writing:

Effective Personal Writing Style	Ineffective Personal Writing Style
Dorothy Solarz suggested that I write to you.	My contact at Canada Safeway suggested that I write to you.
I am pleased to recommend your firm to evaluate our computer system.	Your firm is being recommended to evaluate our computer system.
How would you respond to a new phone system that guarantees better service for less than what you are currently paying?	The phone system I propose promises to be less costly and more effective than the service you currently use.

A good example of a personal writing style is shown in Figure 6-5, an announcement of a personnel shift at DDB Needham.

BEING IMPERSONAL   An impersonal style is almost always used to convey bad news. (Writing bad-news and negative messages is the subject of Chapter 9.) This style removes the writer from the centre of action by using such techniques as the passive voice. Because the writer wants to maintain distance and a level of formality, personal pronouns and first names are generally avoided in impersonal letters. Compare the following examples of effective and ineffective impersonal writing:

The most important words in the English language:

5 most important words: I am proud of you!

4 most important words: What is your opinion?

3 most important words: If you please.

2 most important words: Thank you.

1 most important word: You.

Anonymous

Effective Impersonal Writing	Ineffective Impersonal Writing
A decision has been made to limit your credit line to its current level.	I regret to inform you that I cannot approve additional credit.
Corporate policy restricts us from increasing salaries now.	I cannot provide you with a raise.
Our director of marketing has informed me that he is cutting the advertising budget by half.	James Davies has informed me that he is cutting the advertising budget by half.

BEING PERSUASIVE   The goal of many documents—for example, sales letters—is persuasion. The persuasive approach is characterized by descriptive adjectives and adverbs and creates interest through lively and vigorous writing. Persuasive writing is examined in detail in Chapter 10.

"YOU" ATTITUDE

The best business writing incorporates the **"you" attitude**—a writing style that focuses on readers rather than the writer. A writer can convey the "you" attitude by using the pronoun *you* in place of *I*, and gearing the message to meet audience needs. With the exception of bad-news letters, practise reader-centred writing in almost all your letter writing. Figure 6-6 illustrates how an "I" letter can be revised to create a "you" letter.

The "you" attitude is a natural result of the audience-analysis process that we examined in Chapter 4. To develop a reader-centred style, you must ask yourself questions like the following:

Cross Reference
We discussed audience analysis on pages 111–114.

▼   What do readers need from me?

Figure 6-5 Effective Use of Personal Style in a Letter

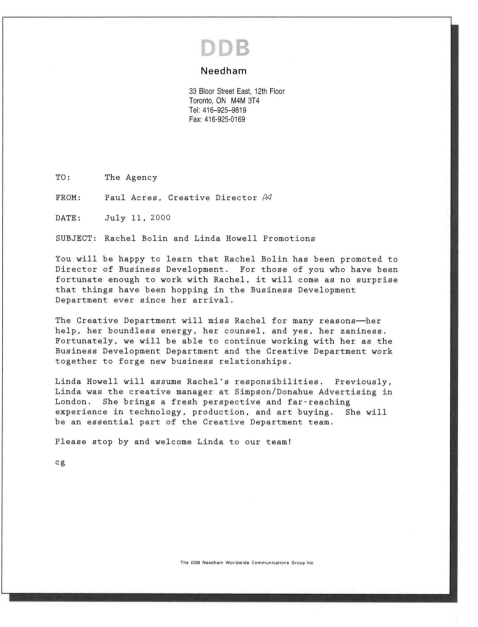

DDB

Needham

33 Bloor Street East, 12th Floor
Toronto, ON M4M 3T4
Tel: 416–925–9819
Fax: 416-925-0169

```
TO:       The Agency

FROM:     Paul Acres, Creative Director PA

DATE:     July 11, 2000

SUBJECT:  Rachel Bolin and Linda Howell Promotions

You will be happy to learn that Rachel Bolin has been promoted to
Director of Business Development.  For those of you who have been
fortunate enough to work with Rachel, it will come as no surprise
that things have been hopping in the Business Development
Department ever since her arrival.

The Creative Department will miss Rachel for many reasons—her
help, her boundless energy, her counsel, and yes, her zaniness.
Fortunately, we will be able to continue working with her as the
Business Development Department and the Creative Department work
together to forge new business relationships.

Linda Howell will assume Rachel's responsibilities.  Previously,
Linda was the creative manager at Simpson/Donahue Advertising in
London.  She brings a fresh perspective and far-reaching
experience in technology, production, and art buying.  She will
be an essential part of the Creative Department team.

Please stop by and welcome Linda to our team!

cg
```

The DDB Needham Worldwide Communications Group Inc

▼ What can I say to motivate readers to respond favourably?
▼ What issues interest readers?
▼ What are the readers' perspectives or positions?

As communication consultant Jeffrey L. Seglin points out, your reader "must be convinced that what you are trying to get him or her to do or react to is of some personal value."[16]

The failure to focus on readers, however, is common. For example, sales communications consultant David Topus believes that overusing the word *I* and failing to explain how a good or service will help the *customer* causes many sales letters to fail. According to Topus, if you simply write that your company has six distribution centres throughout the country, the client may ask, "So what?" But if you add, "so that we can get our product to you faster," clients will better understand how your distribution system can help *them*.[17]

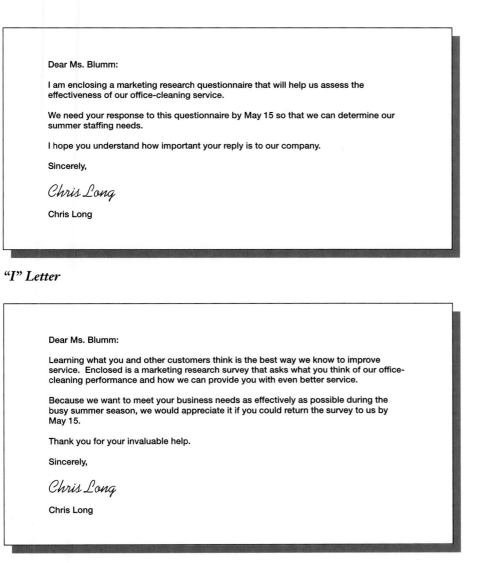

Dear Ms. Blumm:

I am enclosing a marketing research questionnaire that will help us assess the effectiveness of our office-cleaning service.

We need your response to this questionnaire by May 15 so that we can determine our summer staffing needs.

I hope you understand how important your reply is to our company.

Sincerely,

Chris Long

Chris Long

"I" Letter

Dear Ms. Blumm:

Learning what you and other customers think is the best way we know to improve service. Enclosed is a marketing research survey that asks what you think of our office-cleaning performance and how we can provide you with even better service.

Because we want to meet your business needs as effectively as possible during the busy summer season, we would appreciate it if you could return the survey to us by May 15.

Thank you for your invaluable help.

Sincerely,

Chris Long

Chris Long

"You" Letter

Figure 6-6 Converting an "I" Letter to a "You" Letter

The "you" attitude also creates goodwill—an intangible but priceless quality at the heart of every successful business relationship. In effect, this approach reminds readers that you care enough about their concerns to focus your communication on them.

NONDISCRIMINATORY WRITING

A reader-centred writing style is sensitive to the **connotations,** or implied meanings, of words. Because certain language contributes to stereotyping, this sensitivity can be especially acute when you are communicating with women and minorities. It is important, then, to develop a writing style that is nondiscriminatory in its consideration of others' sensitivity to language.

The norm in nondiscriminatory business writing is to let the preferences of others guide your language choices. For example, it is typical to address women as *Ms.* rather than *Mrs.* or *Miss* unless they specifically request that you do so. If you do not know the gender of your correspondent, it is quite acceptable to use "Dear

Progress Check

1. How does the purpose of your writing affect your writing style? List the primary features of a forceful, passive, personal, impersonal, and persuasive writing style.
2. Why do documents that incorporate the "you" attitude tend to be so effective?
3. Does nondiscriminatory writing refer only to the elimination of specific words and phrases, or does it also refer to changes in attitudes?

INTERVIEW   Edmonton TV Host Delivers a Succinct Message

Balan Mathews, Television Anchor for The Risktakers

Few business endeavours demand greater attention to revision and editing than public broadcasting where a precise message must be delivered within a finite period to an expectant audience. For Balan Mathews that challenge is nothing less than stimulating.

Mathews is the anchor of and consultant to an exclusively Canadian entrepreneurial television show that focuses on business activities of small- and medium-sized enterprises. His show, *The Risktakers*, focuses on entrepreneurs who have taken an idea, developed it, and got it working to some measurable degree of success. To maintain the integrity of these success stories, Mathews and his team condense hours of footage into a concise presentable form. "To capture the audience," he says, "your story must be succinct and vital."

Born in Singapore and educated in England and Canada, Mathews has a passion for quality and perfection. He attributes much of his special skill to a strong family work ethic, and to a former television producer Dan Kauffman, who taught him that "brevity is the sole of wit."

Question: How would you characterize your communication style, and why is it successful?

Answer: Getting your message across is a challenging thing. I strive to be very "up close and personal." When someone talks to me I know they are making a real effort to describe the essence of their thoughts. The choice of words and phrases I use in responding to them must reflect the fact that I am listening, and that I care and really understand their point. I often paraphrase what they say, so that the kind of response that is being sought becomes clearer. I also use analogies a lot. It's what I call the parable approach; taking a situation that might have occurred somewhere else and relating it to the situation at hand. This approach works well for me.

Question: Can you describe the parallels between good writing form that focuses on the reader and visual broadcasting that focuses on the viewer?

Answer: Good writing must communicate an idea in a very succinct and vital manner. It's story-telling and it's hard work. It must state your case passionately. Good writing means paying careful attention to the choice of words and to the tone. The reader forms an impression about the author's character and personality, either empathizing and bonding with it quickly, or rejecting it outright. If the impression is

Sir/Madam" or to address the individual by position title—"Dear Director" or "Dear Customer Service Representative." Many companies commonly address form letters to individuals according to good or service. Two examples are "Dear Wireless Phone User" and "Dear GE Appliance Owner." To avoid discriminatory salutations altogether, you may use a simplified letter format that does not include a salutation (see Appendix I).

It is difficult to overemphasize the need to avoid terms that perpetuate stereotypes or that devalue others. It is more appropriate, for example, to say *administrative assistant* than *secretary*, and *physically challenged* is a better choice than *crippled* or *disabled*. Similarly, nondiscriminatory writing avoids terms that imply that only men perform certain jobs. No longer does Canada Post refer to employees as *mailmen*, but rather calls them *mail carriers*. *Chairman* has been broadened to *chairperson* (or

favourable you've succeeded. You've promoted the idea and gained a fan. In the medium of television the presenter must be a conduit, communicating information to an audience with clarity and interest. By presenting information in a warm, passionate, story-telling manner, exuding enthusiasm, confidence, and humour, you will retain your audience.

Question: Why is it important to revise scripts and business documents for a final production or draft?

Answer: My first draft of a script or document contains my initial thoughts on a subject. The mission is to use the facts to tell the story effectively. When I revise the draft, I look at its style and grammar. I read it aloud to make sure that it sounds exactly the way I want it to sound. Although it may make perfect sense to me, will the reader understand what I'm trying to say?

Question: When revising and editing scripts and business documents for your show, what is the relationship between your personal style and the writing strategy?

Answer: *The Risktakers* is about the lives of entrepreneurs, ordinary Canadians who have become extraordinary businesspeople. Our reporters focus on various aspects of their enterprises, reporting on the challenges they've faced and the results they've managed to achieve. We piece together a series of interviews shot at different times in different situations so that it fits within a five- or six-minute time frame. The reporter's goal is to have a finished product in which entrepreneurs tell their own story. Their strategy is to write short pieces that link various parts of the interview, provide background, and set the stage and the direction. My role as anchor is to keep viewers focused on what the program is about, to write leads that will pique their interest, and to provide details that will enhance the reporter's work.

Coming across with a sense of humour, and being enthusiastic, energetic, and interested in each segment are very important parts of the process. Much of that is achieved in the editing, where I take the copy and make it conversational. I shape the facts and tell the story so that the viewer will want to watch—and that's where my personal style plays a large part in editing scripts.

Question: If you were to give students of communication a single piece of advice on editing and revising, what would that be?

Answer: Make sure that the story remains in focus and in concert with your objective. Cut out any deviations from the original goal by asking yourself if each element moves the story along, and if it relates to your purpose. Good editing will ensure that every word, phrase, or picture being used is going to achieve the desired result.

Source: Interview with Balan Mathews.

simply *chair*), and *manhours* are now referred to as *employee hours* or *work hours*.

The general use of masculine and feminine pronouns such as *his* and *her* is also quite limited in today's business world. They are used only when they refer to a specific male or female or when *both* are used, as in "*his or her* work." The *his/her* combination is annoying to many readers, however. In most cases, the writer can eliminate this awkward phrasing by converting the sentence from singular to plural and replacing the *his or her* pronoun with *their*.

Nondiscriminatory writing also avoids allusions that conjure up stereotypes. Ask yourself, for example, whether a man or a woman is being referred to in the following examples:

After accepting the award, the honoree *fainted*.
After accepting the award, the honoree *passed out*.

Some people may conclude that a woman is the subject of the first sentence and a man the subject of the second. The fact that women *faint* and men *pass out* is more than a difference in word choice. Fainting connotes frailty while passing out connotes being overcome despite personal strength. While a tough businessman may be considered *aggressive*, a tough businesswoman may be considered *nasty*. Since aggression is acceptable in business, but nastiness is not, these language choices too often place women at a disadvantage.

Evaluating a Final Draft

With editing completed and revisions in place, you can now evaluate your final draft. As we observed earlier, this process involves evaluating your document against a checklist that reviews the elements of effective style. It also involves carefully proofreading your document.

EVALUATING STYLE

The checklist shown in the Collaborative Communication feature is designed to help you critique the effectiveness of your document by using the revision suggestions covered in this chapter. This checklist can be used independently and with team members who are evaluating each other's work.

PROOFREADING THE DOCUMENT

The last opportunity to evaluate your document is the proofreading stage. **Proofreading** involves checking for obvious errors or inconsistencies in content, grammar, spelling, and punctuation. Although proofreading is a necessary task, it is often overlooked. Communication consultant Sana Reynolds urges writers to view proofreading as time well spent. "I have seen documents," she reports, "that are incomprehensible. They have spelling and typographical errors and include sentence fragments. They make absolutely no sense. When I mention this as gently as I can, I hear: 'I meant to go back and play with it some more, but I never got the time.' I am convinced that making the time is the real issue."[19]

You can take several steps to ensure that spelling and punctuation are correct. Popular word processing software packages include spell checkers that can be used as a preliminary step, but you should not get into the habit of relying on these too heavily. The computer cannot tell whether you wanted to say "manger" or "manager," "sue" or "use." Only a person can decide if word choices and sentences are logical and sensible. To ensure that you are correct, logical, and sensible, you should print out your document and read it carefully.

Depending on the length of your document, the proofreading process may require several readings. For example, the first reading might focus on spelling; a second on facts, figures, and numbers; and a third entirely on content. After you make a change, it is a good idea to proofread the entire sentence or paragraph. Finally, proofread the envelope or mailing label to ensure that it too is correct.

Progress Check

1. How can proofreading help you evaluate your final draft?
2. What steps can you take to make sure that your final draft is technically correct?

What's Ahead

This chapter completes Part II, Writing Basics. So far we have focused on communication fundamentals, the challenges that you face as you write and speak, and the basic skills that you need in order to write effectively. Our next step is to apply this wealth of information to specific written documents.

COLLABORATIVE COMMUNICATION

A Writing Checklist for Team Members

When businesspeople work together in teams, they need a mechanism for evaluating the various documents produced by other team members. The following checklist can be used for that purpose. It is also helpful in uncovering flaws in your own writing. The checklist enables you to judge writing that works and writing that requires revision. It also encourages a positive response to feedback.

When you base criticism on a checklist such as this, you are telling team members that their work meets—or fails to meet—group standards. This depersonalizes the revision process and helps keep the focus on the document rather than on reactions to criticism.

	Yes	No	Suggested Changes
Has unnecessary business jargon been eliminated?	❑	❑	
Is the document written in clear, easy-to-read language?	❑	❑	
Is the language conversational?	❑	❑	
Is the wording specific and concrete?	❑	❑	
Do the words communicate the precise meaning intended?	❑	❑	
Have blanket statements and exaggerated claims been eliminated?	❑	❑	
Is the document grammatically correct?	❑	❑	
Are strong verbs used to communicate the message?	❑	❑	
Is the approach positive and constructive?	❑	❑	
Are sentences short and varied?	❑	❑	
Do the sentences communicate specific information?	❑	❑	
Are the paragraphs short?	❑	❑	
Does each paragraph include a topic sentence?	❑	❑	
Are transitions used to connect ideas?	❑	❑	
Is the style likely to satisfy the needs of readers and the situation?	❑	❑	
Is the "you" attitude employed in the writing style?	❑	❑	
Is the document sensitive to diversity issues?	❑	❑	
Are all sexist references eliminated?	❑	❑	

Questions for Critical Thinking

1. How can a checklist help team members evaluate each other's writing?
2. Why would a checklist make it less likely for team members to perceive feedback as personal criticism?
3. Imagine that you have written a business proposal as part of a team. How would this checklist help you evaluate your own writing?

Part III begins this process by examining the letters, memos, and other short documents that you will encounter when you join a business organization. Each chapter in this part explains how specific documents are written and, more importantly, how to focus on the needs of your situation and audience to produce documents that meet your specific goals.

BUSINESS WRITING IN ACTION

Revising a Draft to Produce a Final Copy

THE ASSIGNMENT

You are now ready to complete the assignment begun in Chapter 4 and continued in Chapter 5. As you recall, you have been assigned to write an informative memo to the marketing department of the Cadillac division of General Motors about the changes that are occurring in the division.[18]

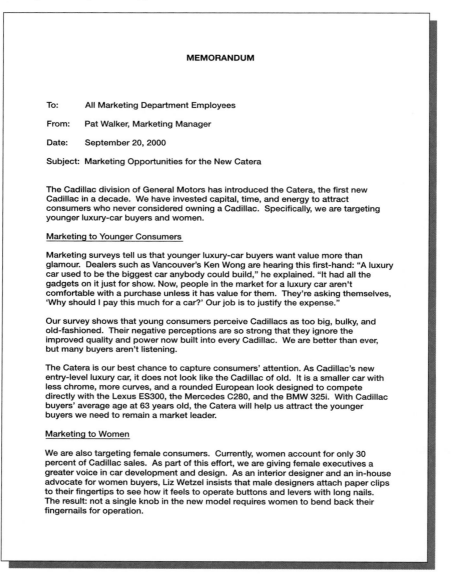

MEMORANDUM

To: All Marketing Department Employees

From: Pat Walker, Marketing Manager

Date: September 20, 2000

Subject: Marketing Opportunities for the New Catera

The Cadillac division of General Motors has introduced the Catera, the first new Cadillac in a decade. We have invested capital, time, and energy to attract consumers who never considered owning a Cadillac. Specifically, we are targeting younger luxury-car buyers and women.

Marketing to Younger Consumers

Marketing surveys tell us that younger luxury-car buyers want value more than glamour. Dealers such as Vancouver's Ken Wong are hearing this first-hand: "A luxury car used to be the biggest car anybody could build," he explained. "It had all the gadgets on it just for show. Now, people in the market for a luxury car aren't comfortable with a purchase unless it has value for them. They're asking themselves, 'Why should I pay this much for a car?' Our job is to justify the expense."

Our survey shows that young consumers perceive Cadillacs as too big, bulky, and old-fashioned. Their negative perceptions are so strong that they ignore the improved quality and power now built into every Cadillac. We are better than ever, but many buyers aren't listening.

The Catera is our best chance to capture consumers' attention. As Cadillac's new entry-level luxury car, it does not look like the Cadillac of old. It is a smaller car with less chrome, more curves, and a rounded European look designed to compete directly with the Lexus ES300, the Mercedes C280, and the BMW 325i. With Cadillac buyers' average age at 63 years old, the Catera will help us attract the younger buyers we need to remain a market leader.

Marketing to Women

We are also targeting female consumers. Currently, women account for only 30 percent of Cadillac sales. As part of this effort, we are giving female executives a greater voice in car development and design. As an interior designer and an in-house advocate for women buyers, Liz Wetzel insists that male designers attach paper clips to their fingertips to see how it feels to operate buttons and levers with long nails. The result: not a single knob in the new model requires women to bend back their fingernails for operation.

THE METHOD

Analyze the first draft that you wrote in Chapter 5, paying attention to all the writing basics you have learned up to this point. Ask yourself whether your draft uses effective words, sentences, and paragraphs; whether it is organized and designed effectively; and whether your writing style is appropriate. Using this first-draft analysis as the basis of your revision, you produce the following final draft.

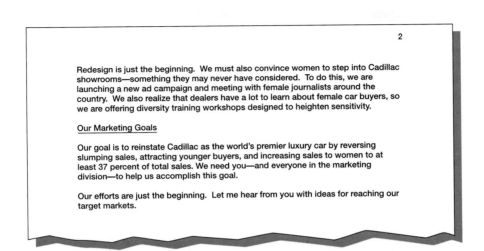

2

Redesign is just the beginning. We must also convince women to step into Cadillac showrooms—something they may never have considered. To do this, we are launching a new ad campaign and meeting with female journalists around the country. We also realize that dealers have a lot to learn about female car buyers, so we are offering diversity training workshops designed to heighten sensitivity.

Our Marketing Goals

Our goal is to reinstate Cadillac as the world's premier luxury car by reversing slumping sales, attracting younger buyers, and increasing sales to women to at least 37 percent of total sales. We need you—and everyone in the marketing division—to help us accomplish this goal.

Our efforts are just the beginning. Let me hear from you with ideas for reaching our target markets.

COMPARING THE TWO VERSIONS

The major difference between the first draft and the final draft is a total reorganization of material. In the process, the memo has been transformed from a negative document to one that communicates a positive message. While the first draft focused on the tremendous problems the Cadillac division has faced, the final draft is more forward-looking as it attempts to excite readers about future changes and opportunities.

The final draft is a more personal document than the first draft. With its pervasive use of personal pronouns, it attempts to make connections between the reader and the writer that will inspire interest and involvement. This connection leads naturally to the closing request for action as the writer asks every department member to become part of a team effort that will ensure the success of the new marketing effort. This appeal was absent from the first draft.

STUDENT RESOURCE CENTRE

Summary of Chapter Objectives

1. **Explain the importance of revising business documents.**

   Revision—the process of adding, deleting, replacing, and reorganizing words, sentences, and paragraphs—moves your document from first to final draft. Revisions are necessary because it is rare that you will produce an acceptable document the first time around. The revision process requires that you keep an open mind, be critical, and take a disciplined approach.

2. **Describe the characteristics of clear, conversational language and identify the qualities of concise, concrete, and correct language.**

   Clear, conversational language uses simple English to communicate in the most direct way. Business jargon—the technical terminology used by members of a group—is acceptable only when the writer is sure the reader will understand it.

Concise writing eliminates extra words and phrases. It makes each point as economically as possible. Concrete language includes words and phrases that provide specific details. It quantifies ideas and minimizes misunderstandings and mistakes. Correct words communicate ideas in a precise way. They are accurate, avoid overgeneralizations and exaggerations, and follow the accepted rules of grammar, spelling, and punctuation.

3. *Explain the importance of persuasive and constructive language in business documents.*

Persuasive language enlivens writing by communicating self-confidence and power. It relies on strong verbs and eliminates weak phrasing. Constructive language takes a positive approach. It avoids words that are likely to create negative responses and emphasizes what to do rather than what not to do.

4. *Outline strategies for constructing effective sentences and paragraphs.*

Effective sentences use the active voice unless there is a strategic reason not to. The passive voice is appropriate when you need to be diplomatic. In addition, effective sentences are short—generally consisting of between 16 and 20 words—and focus on single rather than multiple ideas. Finally, effective sentences are concrete when they provide the specific details that the reader needs in order to understand a message.

The most effective paragraphs have three characteristics. They are short (because short paragraphs are more likely to be read, you should limit each paragraph to a single idea). They have a topic sentence that states the purpose of the paragraph. Finally, effective paragraphs use transitions to connect ideas.

5. *Explain the relationship between style and writing strategy.*

The best business writers learn to vary writing style according to different situations. Style is influenced by your situation, your audience, and your purpose. In general, the most effective business writing reflects a "you" attitude—one that focuses on readers rather than the writer. The "you" attitude reflects a reader-centred approach.

6. *Discuss the characteristics of nondiscriminatory writing.*

Nondiscriminatory writing takes into account the language preferences of readers. In addition, it avoids terms that perpetuate stereotypes at the expense of another individual or group.

7. *Identify ways to evaluate a final draft.*

A checklist will help you evaluate written documents by focusing on words, sentences, paragraphs, and issues of style. Proofreading is also part of the evaluation process. Check for obvious errors or inconsistencies in content, grammar, spelling, and punctuation.

Review and Discussion Questions

1. Why is it important to allow sufficient time to revise your writing? *(Ch. Obj. 1)*

2. How can you judge the effectiveness of a document? *(Ch. Obj. 2, 3)*

3. Explain why it is risky to use obscure language in important business documents. *(Ch. Obj. 2, 3)*

4. Summarize several tips that can help you make your writing more informal. *(Ch. Obj. 2, 3, 4)*

5. Cover the revised version (right-hand column) in Table 6-2. Challenge yourself to come up with your own revised versions of each expression listed in the left-hand column. Can you think of other common but wordy expressions that can be similarly revised? *(Ch. Obj. 2, 3, 4)*

6. Distinguish between the passive and active voice. Give an example of each. *(Ch. Obj. 2, 4)*

7. Define style as it applies to writing. What makes an effective writing style? *(Ch. Obj. 5)*

8. What is the "you" attitude and why is it important? *(Ch. Obj. 4, 5)*

9. What do we mean by "nondiscriminatory" business writing? *(Ch. Obj. 6)*

10. Why is proofreading important? *(Ch. Obj. 7)*

Application Exercises

1. Find an old document you have written—perhaps a class assignment or a work memo. Reread your document and analyze it according to what you learned in this chapter. Can you think of ways to improve it—to make it more concise, readable, and direct? Revise it, using the guidelines in this chapter and the checklist in the Collaborative Communication feature on page 181. What changes do you find yourself making, if any? *(Ch. Obj. 1, 2, 4)*

2. Are there ever times when it might actually be best to write in vague, impersonal terms? What business situations can you think of that might require such a tone? *(Ch. Obj. 5)*

3. Write a description of your job (or a job you have held in the past) for someone who may be replacing you while you are on vacation. Write two versions of this description—one for an employee who already works for the same company, and another for an employee from an outside agency. How do the two descriptions differ? To what extent can you use jargon and other insider language in each? Based on your descriptions, would each person know what to do? *(Ch. Obj. 2, 3, 4)*

4. Could you improve the following sentences? If so, revise each one. *(Ch. Obj. 2, 3, 4, 7)*

   (a) It is to be hoped that we can be of service to you in the future.

   (b) This test is to be administered to all new employees, regardless of the new positions.

   (c) If we follow these new procedures, it would avoid duplication of effort and also facilitate communication among employees.

   (d) We hope the information in this chapter will aid you in monitoring the length of your sentences and, if necessary, making the length shorter.

   (e) As a first step, the number of your potential customers versus non-customers should be identified.

5. Revise each of the following two-sentence statements in order to make them more effective. *(Ch. Obj. 4, 6)*

   (a) We do not know the best way to proceed on this matter. We will ask employees for their opinions.

   (b) Bureaucracy, Inc. has many subsidiaries that operate independently. Maverick, Inc. is a subsidiary with its own chief executive officer.

   (c) Timmy got mad and threw his milk around the room. His father had to clean it up.

   (d) I've been exercising regularly. I feel stronger.

   (e) You are taking Business Communications. You are writing the answers to these questions.

6. Rewrite each of the following sentences in the active voice. *(Ch. Obj. 2, 4)*

   (a) It is greatly feared by employees that many of them will lose their jobs after the merger.

   (b) The new board of directors was approved by the stockholders of the corporation on January 15.

   (c) All of the relevant information should be examined before making a decision.

   (d) It was felt by the committee that the best choice for chairperson would be Margarita.

   (e) Your expense report should be submitted to the accounting office by Friday.

   (f) When he walked onto the stage, the speaker was greeted with a loud burst of applause.

7. Revise the following paragraph, following the chapter's guidelines for transitions, active voice, and nondiscriminatory writing. Does the paragraph have a topic sentence and, if so, is it in the right place? *(Ch. Obj. 4, 6, 7)*

   > Any secretary can lubricate an office chair if she tries. All office furniture is designed by us to be easily lubricated when necessary. Most adjustable chairs have nylon hub tubes that hold spindle rods. Lubricate these spindle rods occasionally. Loosen the set screw in the adjustable bell. Lift the chair from the base so the entire spindle rod is accessible. Apply the lubricant to the spindle rod and the nylon washer. Use the lubricant sparingly to avoid dripping. Replace the chair and tighten the set screw. The secretary can fix her chair and still have plenty of time to see what her boss wants when he calls.

ACT: Applied Communication Techniques

Begin by referring to the sections up to and including Simple Sentences, Compound Sentences, and Complex Sentences in Appendix II. Label simple sentences with SS, compound sentences with CPS, and complex sentences with CPX. Then correct the grammar, spelling, and usage errors in the following sentences. Check your answers in Appendix V.

1. The writer liked his report, but he doubted that the committee would accept his ideas.

2. Appearing at the end, the conclusion summarizes the report.

3. Imprecise language can cause misinterpretation which may lead to cause costly errors.

4. Reports give writers an opportunity to display their work.

5. In order to communicate a positive approach, avoid words that encourage negative responses.

6. Effective writing reflects familiar patterns of speech so try to vary the length of your sentences.

7. By taking a positive approach, you can present information in a way that will encourage readers to respond.

8. Too many short sentences can sound choppy.

9. Sentences can be either general or concrete.

10. There are some instances where the passive voice is acceptable but generally we prefer to use the active voice.

Building Your Business Notebook

Carefully read the following letters and assess their communication effectiveness. Next, rewrite the letters, applying what you've learned in this chapter.

During the last several months, our travel agency had new technology installed at our office. We will have industry representatives from several airlines and some of the technology on display at our office, and we would like for you to come by.

We want you to attend an open house and see the new technology. The open house will be next Wednesday from 5:30 in the afternoon to 8:30.

Some of the technology we will display will be the Apollo Reservation System which is a reservation system for air, car, and hotel bookings. We will show the Cornerstone Information System expert workstation which provides economical and error-free travel. The voice mail installed for all departments will be demonstrated.
  If you have any questions, call us.

Document 1

```
Last week I attended a conference in Montreal. I had received
a travel allowance to attend this conference. The conference
lasted three days, and it was a worthwhile conference. Several
interesting speakers were on the program. I am hopeful that I
will be able to attend more conferences in the future.

You had asked me to give a report when I returned, so I am
reporting. I learned about the importance of security for
electronic mail, the etiquette for using electronic mail, and
some of the newest technological advances for offices. All of
the speakers were experts in their fields and seemed very
knowledgeable about what they were saying. I really enjoyed
getting to meet people from other companies and from listening
to the presentations. My trip was very pleasant.

I also picked up some literature that you may want to see
sometime. Thanks again for approving my travel request to the
conference. I learned much.
```

Document 2

Building Your Research Skills

Choose a topic that interests you—perhaps a hobby, a subject you deal with at work, or a topic you study in school. Go to the library and find two articles that deal with some aspect of this topic. Write a one-page report (keyed and double-spaced) based on these sources, and bring it with you to class.

Building Your Teamwork Skills

Your instructor will divide the class into small groups to read and evaluate each other's reports from the Building Your Research Skills exercise. Each group should work on one report at a time, first reading it and then working as a team to suggest ways for revising it. Follow the guidelines in this chapter in order to analyze the wording of each report, clarifying it, and making it more concise if necessary. Be very careful to be tactful and constructive in your comments—remember, your turn is coming! All team members should feel free to speak up if they feel someone is being too hard on a writer.

Building Your Technology Skills

1. For Building Your Technology Skills in Chapter 5, you critiqued an electronic business form. Customers will need to know how to use the improved form. Create a document that explains how to use your new electronic form, being careful to avoid jargon and highly technical, sexist, or impersonal language. How did your first draft differ from the final draft?

2. Now visit Internet business sites to analyze and evaluate the information presented there. Select one electronic document that you feel needs revision before it's converted to paper form. In revising the document, consider how the use of multimedia (images, video, and sound) contributes to the clarity of electronic information.

Internet Business Links

Yahoo—Business and Economy:	http://www.yahoo.com/Business_and_Economy
EINet Galaxy Business and Commerce:	http://www.einet.net/galaxy/Business-and-Commerce.html
Global Network Navigator—Business Links:	http://gnn.com/wic/wics/bus.new.html
Interesting Business Sites:	http://www.owi.com/netvalue
World Wide Web Business Yellow Pages:	http://www.cba.uh.edu/ylowpges/ycategor.html

Weblinks Internet Resources for this Chapter

Plain English Campaign
http://www.plainenglish.co.uk/

Improving Sentence Clarity
http://owl.english.purdue.edu/Files/116.htm

Reducing Wordiness
http://leo.stcloud.msus.edu/style/wordiness.html

Paragraphs and Topic Sentences
http://www.indiana.edu/~wts/wts/paragraphs.html

CASE STUDIES

DIVERSITY CASE:

Borrowing Circles for Women Only

Would you lend money to Dorothy Wallace? Separated from her husband, Dorothy must support herself and her two teenagers on welfare. She hasn't held a steady job since 1984. She admits that her credit rating has been "ruined by accounts I messed up."

But thanks to the Women's Self-Employment Project (WSEP), Dorothy has turned into a good credit risk. The Women's Self-Employment Project was founded in 1986 to help low-income women who were interested in self-employment as a way out of poverty. Its funds come mainly from contributions and loans by foundations and corporations. Dorothy Wallace borrowed $800 from the Project to set up her own business selling perfumes door-to-door in downtown Chicago offices. Dorothy owes the Project $33.22 every two weeks, but pays $40 to reduce her interest charges. Lately she has started to talk about opening her own office and working her way off welfare.

Over the past three years, WSEP has lent about $60 000 to 60 women, all of whom would be considered a bad risk by any bank. Moreover, although WSEP didn't even check credit histories, the group hasn't suffered a single default on any loan.

What's WSEP's secret? Peer pressure. Borrowers like Dorothy Wallace must participate in "borrowing circles" of five women who meet twice a month. The five members choose the first two of the circle to get loans. These first two borrowers must then stay current on their repayments, and all of the circle members must attend meetings regularly, before the third loan can be made. "Peer support and peer pressure,"

says Connie Evans, WSEP director, "really serve as a good way to lower your risk."

The other members of Dorothy Wallace's borrowing group also hope to start their own businesses. One borrowed $600 for materials to make jewellery that she sells. A retired bank clerk borrowed $700 to buy a sewing machine; she sells hand-sewn lingerie and linens. Another circle member, who borrowed $500, peddles fruit and customer gift baskets in local parks. A woman with four children of her own and four foster children plans to learn to read and to obtain a day-care licence.

Naturally, all of these women appreciate the financial support. The emotional support of the group, however, is often far more important. Indeed, the women in Dorothy's borrowing circle have nicknamed their group, "Too Blessed." As Dorothy says, "They gave me a chance to start all over again."[20]

Questions and Applications

1. Describe the Women's Self-Employment Project and its loan programs.

2. Why has WSEP had such good results getting its loans repaid?

3. Suppose that you're a fund-raiser for WSEP. Write a letter to the board of directors of a large corporation in which you persuade them to provide financial support to the WSEP loan program.

CORPORATE CASE:

Roberto Goizueta: The Coca-Cola Company's Chairman and CEO Is Also a Writing Critic

Roberto Goizueta, chairman and chief executive officer of Coca-Cola, was described in a recent issue of *Fortune* as "formal, ever polite, and always measured—a gentleman CEO who likes a nice predictable schedule and a certain sense of decorum." He may be all this, but he is also known for the caustic letters he writes to industry analysts—letters that make some analysts run for cover when they see Goizueta's return address on the envelope.

According to a recent *Wall Street Journal* story about Goizueta's letter-writing habits, the Coca-Cola CEO "pores over every word analysts write about the company" then writes back. Although many of his letters are filled with praise, some can be best described as negative blasts. For example, Goizueta recently complained to Allan Kaplan, a beverage industry analyst for Merrill Lynch, that the way Kaplan figured Coke's margins was wrong: "How many times have you heard that in a business like ours . . . the gross margin is measured per gallon of syrup sold, not per dollar of revenue?" Goizueta wrote.

Goizueta writes to some analysts as much as ten times a year with the goal of improving the accuracy of their writing. His responses reflect attention to minute detail, including the steps in analysts' calculations. They also reflect scrupulous recordkeeping, which sometimes places analysts in the position of having to eat their own words. For example, Goizueta sent Andrew Conway, formerly an analyst with Salomon Brothers, a year-old newspaper article that contained Conway's prediction that Coke's stock would reach 62 by the end of 1995. After the stock closed around 75, Goizueta wrote "Dear Andrew . . . So much for predictions!"

Why does Goizueta take time out of his hectic schedule to write these letters? In part, because he is dedicated to creating wealth for what he calls the "shareowners" of Coca-Cola. In fact, in one of his top desk drawers, Goizueta keeps the financial characteristics of the businesses Coke owns right next to the company's mission statement. He is dedicated to growing these businesses and increasing shareowner value. He also has an unflinching focus on getting things right and making sure that others get them right as well.[21]

Questions and Applications

1. Suppose you are a beverage-industry analyst. Realizing that if you made any serious errors you might receive a critical letter from Roberto Goizueta, how would you approach the revision process before you issued a report on Coca-Cola?

2. Goizueta's focus seems to be on getting the facts right. Describe the relationship between the presentation of accurate facts and analysis and the way in which a report is written. Is a well-organized and well-written report likely to evoke a different response from Goizueta than a poorly written document? Why?

3. Research the current financial condition of the Coca-Cola Company. Write a report on what you learn, knowing that if you were an industry analyst, Roberto Goizueta might read it.

Chapter

7

Writing Direct Requests

The difficulty is not to write, but to write what you mean, not to affect your reader, but to affect him precisely as you wish.

Robert Louis Stevenson
Author

Chapter Objectives

After studying this chapter, you should be able to:

1. Explain the functions of the opening, middle, and close of a direct request.
2. Explain how to write requests for information.
3. List the characteristics of letters that place orders.
4. Identify the elements of an effective claim letter.
5. Describe two types of request letters associated with personal references.
6. List the essential details included in an invitation.

So Much to Do, So Little Time

Imagine that you are the meeting coordinator for your company's annual sales meeting, which will be held in Toronto this year. The meeting is less than a month away, and you lie awake at night wondering how you will ever get everything done. Here are just a few of the unfinished tasks you face:

▼ Finalize arrangements with the conference centre for more than 300 attendees.
▼ Prepare 25 speakers who will deliver individual and group presentations.
▼ Arrange for the delivery of 20 pieces of audiovisual equipment.
▼ Confirm arrangements for meeting rooms and hotel rooms for every attendee.
▼ Talk to the caterers about the banquet menus as well as the menus for breakfasts and lunches.
▼ Arrange for transportation to and from the hotel.

In the midst of all these demands, you are receiving dozens of letters, memos, and e-mail messages a day from attendees, speakers, suppliers, and, of course, from members of the sales department who want every detail to be perfect. You haven't the time—or the patience—to wade through documents that bury the main point—even if they are requests for important information.

With all this going on, how would you respond to Version 1 of a direct request for information? Do you think you would respond differently to Version 2?

Version 1
I am very excited by the opportunity to speak at your annual sales meeting. Addressing your company's salesforce has been a goal of mine for many years, and the opportunity is finally here.

Thank you for arranging for me to stay at the Palmer House. I hear that it is a classic hotel with all the latest facilities and wonderful restaurants. I especially look forward to spending some time before and after the meeting walking around Toronto's harbourfront area.

I will be flying to Toronto from Victoria on May 3rd. That gives me enough time to get comfortable before the meeting begins on May 5th. Past experience has taught me that it is wise to arrive well in advance of an important presentation.

My plans are set, except for a few details. Will I meet you before my presentation? May I see the meeting room in advance?

May I check the audiovisual equipment I ordered to make sure it is in good working order? Please get back to me as soon as possible about these arrangements.

Version 2
Thank you for the opportunity to speak at your annual sales meeting on May 5th. Although my arrangements are in order, I have several meeting-related questions:

▼ Will I meet you before my presentation?
▼ May I see the meeting room in advance?
▼ May I check the audiovisual equipment I ordered to make sure it is in good working condition?

Please get back to me by April 8th with these details.

I look forward to addressing your corporate salesforce and to my visit to Toronto. ▼

Chapter Overview _____

In fewer than half the words, Version 2 communicates the direct request for information more effectively than Version 1. It does this by taking a "bottom-line" approach. That is, the document purpose is stated immediately, and all unnecessary detail is eliminated. In addition, whereas Version 2 mentions a specific date for action, Version 1 leaves the date open-ended, and therefore the response less certain. Finally, Version 2 uses a bulleted list to help the reader focus on specific requests. In Version 1, these requests are buried in a paragraph. Although Version 1 is more chatty and personal, a busy meeting coordinator would probably view its length and casual organization as an annoyance.

This chapter explains how to craft an effective direct request by beginning with a statement of purpose, adding necessary details, and ending with a courteous close that communicates goodwill. Like Version 2, the most effective direct requests introduce key points early.

We will examine different kinds of direct requests, such as requests for information, orders, credit-information requests, claims, requests for personal references, and invitations. We will also discuss requests made in memo form. As you read, keep in mind that direct requests are written to people both outside and inside the organization, including customers, suppliers and other businesses, government agencies, and employees (both current and potential). These audience groups are the same for all the different types of business correspondence examined in this text.

Although this chapter illustrates direct requests as hard copy letters and memoranda, correspondence is increasingly sent via e-mail. While electronic media may change the format of the correspondence, the content and writing style of a direct request should remain the same.

Cross Reference
We examined types of business audiences in Chapter 4, pages 111–113.

Writing Direct Requests _____

Direct requests are made in both letters and memos and are used to obtain information, order merchandise, gain credit information, file claims, obtain personal references, and extend invitations. A **direct request** is a straightforward written message that asks another individual for information, merchandise, or assistance. The most effective direct requests start with the purpose, add specific details, and end with a courteous close that leaves the reader with positive feelings.

OPENING A DIRECT REQUEST

A direct request is most effective when it gives readers crucial information in the opening paragraph. Business-writing authorities John S. Fielden and Ronald E. Dulek characterize the best approach as "bottom-line" writing. Within the first few sentences, readers should be informed of the reason that you are writing to them as opposed to someone else, the purpose of your request, and the action that you want them to take.[1] This approach is designed to save readers time. Instead of forcing people to read an entire document, you can state your purpose in your opening paragraph—as does the writer of Version 2 in the opening vignette.

The finest eloquence is that which gets things done.

David Lloyd George
British prime minister

MIDDLE OF A DIRECT REQUEST

The middle of the request provides the additional details that readers need in order to take action. When a request is simple, it can be stated in full in the opening paragraph. Nothing more need be said, and the writer can move directly from the opening to the close.

However, when additional information is necessary, the readers' needs should determine what to include and the order in which to provide the information. In the letter in Version 2, for example, the bulleted list specifies the exact information required.

Gear the middle of your letter or memo to the knowledge and sophistication of your audience. Use language that readers will understand, and avoid business jargon that clouds your request. Also use an appropriate tone. A forceful tone might be appropriate if you are requesting action or information from a supervisee, but when writing to a favourite customer a personal tone might be better. To make sure that your document supplies all the needed details, put yourself in the reader's position and then ask yourself whether the letter is complete and understandable.

CLOSING A DIRECT REQUEST

Close your document by focusing once more on the action that you want readers to take. Be as specific as possible. For example, instead of saying "Please send me the information in the near future," write "Please send me the confirmation for my December 12th hotel reservation no later than November 12th."

The close of many business letters is also designed to communicate goodwill. It tells readers that you value their goods, services, or contributions. The close in Version 2, comprising the letter's final two paragraphs, accomplishes both goals—it focuses on the required action and communicates goodwill.

Positive language also helps motivate readers to comply with your request. If you know the person to whom you are writing, a personal comment is appropriate. For example:

> Please send me the information on the model 4567 fax machine. By the time we see each other at the convention in two weeks, I should be ready to place an order.

Memos, on the other hand, typically do not use the same type of close and often come to an abrupt end after the details of the request have been given.

WRITING EFFECTIVE REQUESTS

The following suggestions are designed to help you write effective direct requests. These suggestions also apply to other documents discussed in this chapter that take a direct approach.[2]

- ▼ *State your purpose in full.* When you have more than one purpose in writing a document, make all of your goals clear in your opening paragraph. It is a mistake to begin by stating one purpose and then "hiding" the others somewhere in the middle of your document. Your reader may assume either that you are asking for only one thing or that you attach more importance to your first request.

- ▼ *Provide information in the proper place.* Even when you are convinced that readers need background information, state your direct request at the beginning of the document and then provide details as you proceed. The following example from Fielden and Dulek demonstrates what can happen when you ignore this approach:

> Suppose your company plans to raise prices on October 1st. You want to urge your most important customers to place their orders before that date. But you do not know for certain whether they want to buy or not. You are afraid to bottom-line your purpose and begin your letter with, "Please get your order in before September 30th." You are afraid of appearing too pushy. . . .

In situations like this, most writers start rehearsing the history of price changes in the recent past, leading up to the fact that there is going to be a price change on October 1st. Only then do they feel safe enough to tell the readers that they had better get their orders in before September 30th.[3]

Fielden and Dulek disagree with this strategy. The result, they contend, is likely to frustrate readers who do not understand why you are bombarding them with information and who, as a result, may pay little attention. They recommend that instead of beating around the bush, you state your purpose in the opening paragraph and explain later.

▼ *Seek the action-oriented response.* Focus on the actions that you want readers to take in response to your request. This approach, of course, may be easier in some cases than in others. For instance, you may have no problem making a direct request to a supervisee, but it may be more difficult to be as direct with a manager. Even when dealing with managers, however, the direct approach is often the most effective.

▼ *Seek the useful response.* Try to maximize your odds of getting a useful response by anticipating the details that your reader will need. Here, for example, is a simple but vague request that might be made to a business writing consultant:

> Please send me information about your business writing services so that I can determine whether they fit our business needs.

You are much more likely to get the information you actually need by being more specific:

> The consumer-products division of our company is interested in hiring a business writing consultant to work with a group of 20 customer service representatives, and we would like to learn more about your services. The consultant we hire will provide two one-hour workshops that focus on handling difficult complaint situations.

While the first version provides very little practical information, the second helps readers by informing them of your needs.

▼ *Strike the proper tone.* Remember that being direct is not necessarily the same thing as being overbearing: a nonintimidating request can still get your message across. For example, instead of saying "Call me immediately after you have reviewed this proposal," it may be better to say "I am eager to hear what you think about this proposal." Gear your tone to your purpose and to your analysis of how the reader will respond.

▼ *Reflect your authority to make your request.* Requests are part of everyday business life, and your documents should reflect your position of power in relation to your recipient. Don't apologize for your request even if it involves a great deal of work; unnecessary apologies lessen your perceived power.

▼ *Edit to delete minor points.* Focus on your specific purpose by weeding out unimportant or extraneous points from the middle of your letter. Comments about unrelated events occurring in the company should not be included.

▼ *Design your request for clarity.* Use an effective layout to focus your readers' attention on your request. Use bulleted lists and surround specifics with white space. Italicize key points to add emphasis.

We will turn next to the types of direct requests that are typically required in business today: requests for information, orders,

Progress Check

1. List the functions of the opening, middle, and closing of a direct request.
2. What is "bottom-line" writing?
3. List four suggestions for improving the effectiveness of a direct request.

COLLABORATIVE COMMUNICATION

Delivering Constructive Feedback

As a member of a team, you will be asked to provide feedback on the work of other team members, including their writing. Your feedback may be either positive or negative—you may love what you read or feel that the document has totally missed its mark. How you communicate your thoughts can mean the difference between a successful interaction and one that is perceived as overly critical. Remember that the purpose of feedback is to improve the quality of a document, not to tear it apart or tear down the writer.

The following guidelines will help you provide constructive feedback:

▼ *Use both positive and negative feedback.* Don't focus exclusively on the document's problems while ignoring its strengths. We all respond better to criticism when we feel that what we have done right is also recognized.

▼ *Avoid using negative labels or being judgmental.* Labelling material as "irresponsible," "illogical," "inadequate," or "stupid" is likely to make the writer feel defensive and angry. Instead, try to describe the document's problems in objective, specific terms: "The introduction needs more background information about the company and its key players" is better than "The introduction is all wrong." Similarly, try to avoid words that convey judgment, including "bad," "worst," and "terrible."

▼ *Direct the feedback at the document, not the writer.* No one wants to be subjected to a personal attack. For instance, imagine that a co-worker has written "Our history with Ajax Plumbing Supplies has always been difficult." A suggestion to "rephrase the sentence to convey a more positive tone" is better than "If you knew anything about this customer, you wouldn't have written this."

▼ *Put at least some of your feedback in writing.* When constructive feedback is in writing, the writer can look back at it as he or she revises the document.

▼ *Revise part of the document yourself. Showing* is often more effective than *telling.* When you revise a small section of the document, you provide a tangible model of the effect you want to achieve.

▼ *Encourage the writer to consider feedback as part of the revision process.* The key word here is *process.* First drafts are rarely perfect, and they often improve as a result of group feedback.

Although you cannot control how others respond to feedback, you can control the type of feedback you provide and how you provide it. The best feedback never focuses on the writer. Instead, it focuses on improving the document.

Questions for Critical Thinking

1. You are the co-owner of a small business and your partner just completed a credit application letter. You read the first draft and realize that it is filled with errors and does not convey clearly what your company wants. Describe the steps you would take to improve the letter, including the tone and nature of your feedback.

2. Why does feedback have the potential to strike a raw nerve that makes people respond defensively?

3. How do you think feedback differs when it is directed at written documents versus verbal responses—for example, in a meeting?

credit-information requests, claims, requests for personal references, and invitations. We will focus first on letters to company outsiders and then on internal company memos.

Requesting General Information

Letters requesting information are a common feature of commerce. Providing such information as how to install a computer program or set up a new stereo is an important part of customer service for many businesses. As a result, businesses must make their information readily available. Conversely, many organizations not only supply information but gather and collect information from individuals, businesses, and other organizations.

In this section we will focus on how organizations request general information from business audiences—customers, suppliers and other businesses, and government agencies. Such information is often sent free of charge in brochures, booklets, e-mail, and computer disks, and is often not part of a formal order.

REQUESTS TO CUSTOMERS

There are many reasons to request information from customers. For example, you may need information about an account or a customer's current needs. Or your information request could be part of a company-wide customer survey. In each case customer requests have the same twofold goal: to gather information while maintaining goodwill.

Suppose, for instance, that your information request does not offer the customer an immediate benefit. It will be your job to forge the link between the request and improved customer service and long-term benefits. The letter in Figure 7-1 is a good example of how this sometimes delicate task can be performed.

REQUESTS TO SUPPLIERS AND OTHER BUSINESSES

Information requests to suppliers and other businesses are usually short and to the point. Although goodwill is critical, you don't need to spend much time motivating the recipient to comply with your request. You can assume that the recipient will answer as a matter of good business practice, especially if there is a possibility of

Making a direct request for information may appear to be a simple writing task. However, the managers of Lincoln Life understand that the success of any request—and indeed the success of all business documents—depends on clear, focused writing.

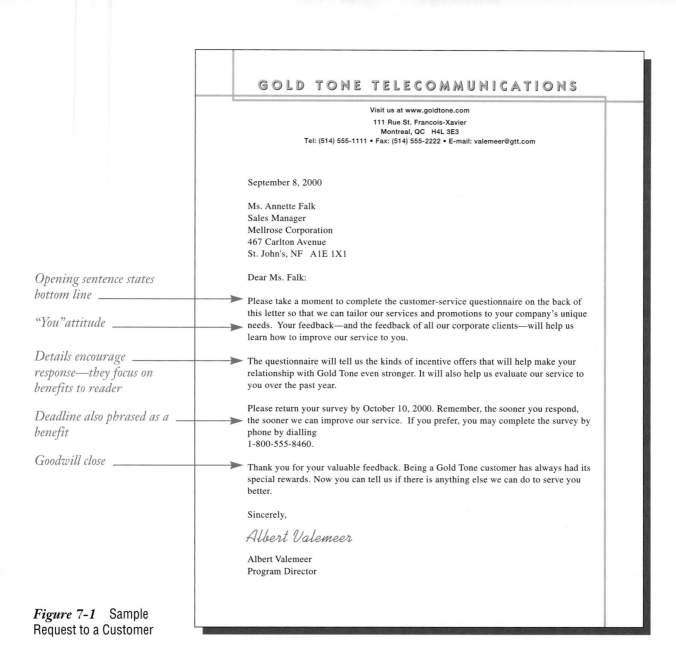

GOLD TONE TELECOMMUNICATIONS

Visit us at www.goldtone.com
111 Rue St. Francois-Xavier
Montreal, QC   H4L 3E3
Tel: (514) 555-1111 • Fax: (514) 555-2222 • E-mail: valemeer@gtt.com

September 8, 2000

Ms. Annette Falk
Sales Manager
Mellrose Corporation
467 Carlton Avenue
St. John's, NF   A1E 1X1

Dear Ms. Falk:

Opening sentence states bottom line →
Please take a moment to complete the customer-service questionnaire on the back of this letter so that we can tailor our services and promotions to your company's unique

"You" attitude →
needs. Your feedback—and the feedback of all our corporate clients—will help us learn how to improve our service to you.

Details encourage response—they focus on benefits to reader →
The questionnaire will tell us the kinds of incentive offers that will help make your relationship with Gold Tone even stronger. It will also help us evaluate our service to you over the past year.

Deadline also phrased as a benefit →
Please return your survey by October 10, 2000. Remember, the sooner you respond, the sooner we can improve our service. If you prefer, you may complete the survey by phone by dialling
1-800-555-8460.

Goodwill close →
Thank you for your valuable feedback. Being a Gold Tone customer has always had its special rewards. Now you can tell us if there is anything else we can do to serve you better.

Sincerely,

Albert Valemeer

Albert Valemeer
Program Director

Figure 7-1 Sample Request to a Customer

new business. Here, for example, is the opening paragraph from a letter written by the recruiting manager of an accounting firm to an employment agency.

> Our firm is looking for a reliable employment agency. Over the next two months, we intend to hire three people for our Fredericton office. Will you please answer my questions about the Bates and Parks Agency and have one of your account executives contact me next week?

REQUESTS TO GOVERNMENT AGENCIES

For the most part, businesses communicate with government bodies through a bewildering array of forms. In fact, agencies like Revenue Canada generate thousands of forms to be completed by large and small firms. Figure 7-2 is a sample of a short information request sent from a small business owner to Revenue Canada.

INTERVIEW   Hostility Only Aggravates a Situation

Mary A. De Vries, Publishing Consultant and Expert on Word Usage

Although direct requests are among the most commonly written documents in business organizations, they are often poorly written. We asked editorial and publishing consultant Mary A. De Vries for her advice on improving the effectiveness of these documents. De Vries has authored more than 30 books as well as professional articles on word usage and written and spoken communication.

Question: Even though direct requests are relatively simple and straightforward, is it important to plan in advance what you want to accomplish?

Answer: Always. Plan what you want to say, how you want the reader to respond, and how you can help the reader provide what you want. For example, would it help to enclose a questionnaire? An outline of your project? A checklist for giving quick answers?

Question: When writing a direct request, how important is it to try to maintain the reader's goodwill?

Answer: It's very important. If you were the reader, would you want to expend extra effort on someone who sounded unfriendly and unappreciative? Remember the old cliché about catching more flies with honey than with vinegar.

Question: What are some of the most serious mistakes writers make when they compose direct requests?

Answer: Most writers are too vague and don't provide specific examples of what they want. They don't focus on the specific request until the second or third paragraph. They don't plan their remarks, so they often aren't stated in a logical order. They are either too abrupt and demanding or too timid and apologetic about bothering the reader. They fail to give a date by which they need the response. They neglect to enclose a stamped, self-addressed envelope. They don't explain how they are going to use the information they need. They sound cold, unfriendly, and unappreciative.

Question: Because claim letters are written when something goes wrong, there is often a tendency to write these letters in anger. Do you recommend a cooling-off period before these letters are written?

Answer: Definitely. Hostility only aggravates a situation. If something needs rectifying, you must sound reasonable and fair if you want to motivate the reader to be willing to correct the problem.

Placing Orders

Because they generate income and profits, orders—written directions to purchase goods or services—are the lifeblood of a business. When a company receives an order, it begins what is often a multipart process. For example, the process could include a credit check, crediting the appropriate sales representative's commission account, entering the sale in the company's accounting ledgers, and shipping goods for delivery.

To avoid confusion or error, use order forms if available. When ordering by letter, include the following details:

▼ name of the item being ordered (use the manufacturer's terminology, not your own)

▼ all relevant numbers pertaining to the item, including catalogue number, style number, model number, and so on

▼ a description of the item, including (if applicable) size, weight, colour, material, finish, and any additional features

Question: Are people less willing to give job references today than years ago because of the possibility of being sued? Are requests for references often ignored?

Answer: Companies have different policies regarding job references, and some won't provide them for legal or other reasons or will provide only basic information such as the length of time employed and job title. But requests for references aren't simply filed in the wastebasket, and you shouldn't hesitate to ask for one unless the company has a stated policy of not providing them.

Question: When writing a direct request in the form of a memo, how important is it to adjust the language and style of the request to your internal audience? That is, should the language and style differ depending upon whether the letter is being written to a subordinate, a co-worker, or a manager? What kinds of changes do you recommend?

Answer: It's very important to tailor a message to the audience. It doesn't matter if it's a memo or a letter or whether the message is going inside or outside the company. For example, address superiors with a title, and don't call them by their first names unless asked to do so. Use courteous, straightforward language with superiors and avoid the casual remarks or personal comments that you might use with a peer. Although you might instruct a subordinate to do something, you would ask a superior.

Question: If you were to give business communication students one piece of advice about writing effective direct requests, what would that advice be?

Answer: Be specific. Don't say, "Please send me any information you have on widgets." Think what that covers—How to build them? Where they're sold? Sales volume per region and country? What type of consumer buys them? Which companies offer competitive products? It could take reams of paper and months or years of work collecting all of the information available on widgets. The reader either has to give a very general response or write back and ask you to be more specific.

Source: Interview with Mary A. De Vries.

- ▼ the number of items in the order (when large quantities are ordered, you may have to specify dozens, cases, or other bulk-quantity measurements)
- ▼ unit price
- ▼ any discounts that apply to the purchase
- ▼ applicable GST and provincial sales tax
- ▼ total price
- ▼ method of order (among the options are cheque, C.O.D., and charge account; if you use a charge, be sure to include your account number)
- ▼ preferred date for merchandise delivery
- ▼ preferred method of shipment (options include shipment via parcel post or overnight delivery)
- ▼ name of the individual to whom the item is being delivered (this may be someone other than the person placing the order)
- ▼ delivery address (which may differ from the billing address)
- ▼ authorized signature

Nails by Beverly

489 Victory Boulevard, Dartmouth, Nova Scotia B2X 4B4
902-555-2266 (phone) 902-555-2267 (fax)   perez@nails.org (e-mail)

April 1, 2000

Revenue Canada
1111 Fundy Street
Dartmouth, NS B3A 1P1

Impersonal greeting is appropriate → Dear Revenue Canada Representative:

Opens with a direct, specific request → Please send me information in the government tax requirements I must comply with to operate a nail salon. I intend to open my salon in Dartmouth on May 15, 2000 and I need information on all tax regulations that will affect my business.

Lots of white space! → Specifically, I would like information on the following:

Bulleted list details specifics →
• Income tax payments, including the schedule of payment for myself and my employees
• GST registration procedures

Appreciative close → Since owning a business is a new venture for me, your guidance is very important. Thank you for your assistance.

Sincerely,

Beverly Perez

Beverly Perez
Owner

***Figure* 7-2** Sample Request to a Government Agency

Although business-to-business goodwill is important, you need not explain what you plan to do with your purchase. There is no need to say, for example, "I am purchasing a new Compaq Pentium computer because I am expanding my accounting business from part- to full-time and need a computer that can handle the increased workload." "Orders," observes business communication authority Andrea B. Geffner, "are routine and handled in quantity. As long as you are a paying customer, your impetus for buying does not interest the seller."[4]

Explanations can be helpful, however, if you lack a catalogue or model number or are trying to describe the purpose to which the item will be put. For example, if you are ordering a staple gun from an office-supply company and you don't have their catalogue, the following statement of purpose will help the company identify the model you need:

The staple gun will be used to bind booklets containing at least 60 pages. Please supply a stapler that will do the job.

Filing Claim Letters

Like all other human endeavours, business transactions are plagued by Murphy's Law—"Whatever can go wrong, will go wrong." As a result, claims and adjustments are a necessary part of business life. A **claim** is a notice from a customer that there is something wrong with a good or service. The most effective claim is a notice sent to the company in letter form. An **adjustment**—the company's response to the claim—is also made in writing. Because claims are letters of request, they will be examined in this chapter. We will look at adjustment letters in Chapters 8 and 9.

Customers write claim letters for many reasons, such as billing errors, damaged or defective merchandise, deliveries containing unordered or incorrect merchandise, and missed delivery dates. Because claim letters are often written when the business has made a mistake, customers tend to write them in the heat of anger. Writers who succumb to anger, however, forget that their purpose is to get results, not to rant and rave. Even if right is entirely on your side, an abusive letter will rarely achieve positive results and can even delay a solution to your problem.

Like all direct requests, claim letters should start by telling the reader what you want and why you are writing. You should then explain the problem and describe all the details that the reader will need to assess the situation. Among the details that you may have to provide are order or invoice numbers; delivery dates (or dates promised); methods of shipment or locations where services were rendered; and descriptions of the items in question (model and style numbers, and so on). It is also a good idea to attach copies of sales slips or invoices.

Finally, your letter should suggest a solution. For example, tell the company that you want a replacement or an adjustment to your bill. At the same time, make every attempt to end your letter on a positive, forward-looking note, expressing confidence that the company will settle your problem fairly. In the sample claim letter in Figure 7-3, note the writer's focus on a clear presentation of both the problem and a possible solution.

When services rather than goods are involved, claims may be more difficult to handle. For example, if you are unhappy with an office-cleaning service, you have nothing tangible to return, nor can you point to a missed delivery. In these cases make your claim in a logical, reasonable way, explaining in detail the nature of the problem and how you would like it resolved.

Progress Check

1. List the information that should be included in a letter that places an order.
2. What is the purpose of a claim letter and what information should it convey?

Personal References

As a job seeker, you must ask someone who knows you for a personal reference—a recommendation stating that you are qualified to perform the duties of the job for which you are applying, attesting to your character, or both. Conversely, as a manager considering a job candidate's application, you may request information from the individuals or organizations identified as references by the candidate.

REQUESTING A PERSONAL REFERENCE

Effective personal references can mean the difference between getting a job and remaining unemployed. With so much at stake, job candidates should make special efforts to line up positive, effective references—a process that often starts with a let-

October 1, 2000

Mr. Enrico Rosario
Better Jeans, Inc.
206 East 32nd Street
Moose Jaw, SK   S6H 3X8

Dear Mr. Rosario:

Opening paragraph states the problem

As the attached invoice shows, the September 30 shipment of women's jeans was to include only 4 pairs of size 2 instead of the 32 pairs of size 2 jeans we received.

This paragraph states how to resolve the claim

I am returning 28 pairs of the size 2 jeans to be replaced with the following items that were ordered but not received in the original order:

8	pairs size	8
10	pairs size	10
5	pairs size	12
5	pairs size	14

White space makes this information easy to read

A mistake was made, but the letter is not angry

If any of these items are not in stock, please credit my account for the amount. Please do not ship any merchandise except the specific items I have indicated. I request that you send the replacements by overnight mail with any additional shipping costs handled by you.

Close tries to re-establish positive feelings

An urgent call to action

As you know, we are in the height of the fall selling season, and your merchandise is an important part of my business. Many of my customers come to my store because they know they always will find a ready supply of jeans. Therefore, I am certain you understand the importance of my receiving the replacements within 24 hours.

Sincerely,

Virginia Harding

Virginia Harding
Buyer, Women's Sportswear

Attachment

Figure 7-3 Sample Claim Letter

ter. The letter has two primary purposes: (1) to ask an individual whether he or she is willing to give you a letter of recommendation, to be contacted by prospective employers at a later date, or both; and (2) to describe the position that you are seeking and explain how this person's knowledge of your background might help get you the job. Consider the sample request letter in Figure 7-4, in which the writer asks a former co-worker if she can use her as a reference on a job application. As you can see, the request takes a direct approach.

Although many requests for personal references are made in person or by phone, many are also written. Written requests are common when people haven't seen each other in several years, or when the prior work relationship was formal, as in the case of a former supervisee asking a manager for a reference. Many written requests are followed up by phone conversations.

In the letter in Figure 7-4, the writer has asked for the recipient's cooperation

O'Hare Consulting

11 Highland Road, Halifax, NS B3M 1X1
Visit us at www.ohare.com
(Phone) 902-555-5555
(Fax) 902-555-4444
(E-mail) kath@ohare.ns.ca

February 12, 2000

Ms. Yvonne Spencer
Technical Writer
Baddington Pierce Computer Software
22 Water Street
Charlottetown, PE C1A 9E1

Dear Yvonne:

Clear, specific request —→ May I give potential employers your name as someone who knows the quality of my work and my work ethic? I recently left my position with Biotech Computers and am looking for a new position as a technical writer specializing in computer software.

Tells Yvonne what job she wants —→
Nice touch to review joint success —→ The position I am seeking involves writing manuals for new software products. As you know, I did just that when we worked together at Baddington Pierce, so I feel comfortable turning to you for a recommendation. I'm sure you remember when we produced a software manual in less than a month, even though everyone said it was impossible.

Stresses value of Yvonne's reference —→ Considering all this, your recommendation would mean a great deal to any software manager. It is my hope that you will hear from managers after my initial job interviews at various companies.

Strong close—restates request as a call to action —→ Please let me know if I may use your name as a reference.

Sincerely,

Kathleen O'Hare

Kathleen O'Hare

Figure 7-4   Sample Request for a Personal Reference

in the event that she should be contacted by a prospective employer. Alternatively, the writer could request a letter of recommendation that can be given directly to a prospective employer, perhaps during an interview. You should be specific about what to include in the reference letter. You know your own background better than anyone else, so offer examples of abilities and job successes to which your reference can attest. We will analyze effective recommendation letters in more detail in Chapter 8.

Among the people typically enlisted as references are former employers and managers, college instructors, clients, and other professional colleagues, including both peers and subordinates. In any case, says outplacement specialist Peter J. Leets, the people you choose as references should be able to sell your skills to others: "Make sure those you select can vouch for you as someone who will contribute added value. They should have the desire . . . to sell your skills, personal qualities and professional attributes."[5]

REQUESTING INFORMATION ABOUT JOB CANDIDATES

Progress Check

1. What are the two primary purposes of a letter requesting a personal reference?
2. How do letters requesting a personal reference differ from letters requesting information about job candidates?
3. What are the three goals of a business invitation?

On the other side of the employment fence is the potential employer who wants to learn as much about a job candidate as possible before making a job offer. The search for information typically begins when the candidate gives the employer a list of references. The list contains the names, titles, organizations, addresses, fax numbers, e-mail addresses, and phone numbers of people who have agreed to discuss the candidate's background.

Most businesspeople telephone or e-mail instead of writing letters to references. Whether verbal or written, however, these are direct requests for information. Written requests should be short, explaining the position the applicant is interviewing for and requesting verification of employment and performance information.

A QUESTION OF ETHICS

Job References, Ethics, and the Law

Asking for a job reference is no longer a simple matter. Ethical and legal considerations have complicated what was once a straightforward, information-gathering process for both companies and individuals.

In fact, during the past decade many companies stopped giving meaningful job references. Afraid of slander and libel suits, companies often supplied references that included only two pieces of information—the former employee's job title and dates of employment. Job performance was never mentioned, and even praise was discouraged for fear that if it were tempered by a slightly negative comment, the company could wind up in court. As a result, honest written references became nearly impossible to find. People tended to tell the truth, whether in person or over the phone, only when they knew their words could not be traced.

This tendency—to tell the truth without committing it to writing—is also motivated by the risk of involvement in *negligent-hiring* lawsuits. These lawsuits, which usually pit one company against another, follow patterns like the following:

▼ Company A is charged with wrongfully hiring someone who has harmed another in the company's employ.

▼ Company A then sues Company B—the worker's former employer—for withholding critical information that may have helped Company A to avoid the incident.

▼ Company A contends that, had it known about the employee's history of drug abuse, sexual harassment, or other problems, it would not have hired the employee in the first place.

Despite these problems, many businesspeople are now determined to tell the truth about employment references. For example, when Peter Scott, an office manager for a telecommunications company in Edmonton, was stung by a dishonest reference that withheld a candidate's criminal record, he vowed never to withhold important reference information from anyone who asked for it.

In addition, businesspeople now realize that withholding information allows dishonest job seekers to say nearly anything on their résumés without fear of being discovered. As a result, many con artists have gone on to bigger and better jobs while honest job seekers have suffered.

Questions for Critical Thinking

1. What are the ethical implications of giving a truthful verbal reference but a meaningless written reference?

2. Why do honest job seekers suffer when meaningful job references are withheld?

3. Knowing about the ethical and legal environment that surrounds job references, how would you respond to a request for a reference from a former employee with a substandard work record?

Source: Adapted from Claudia H. Deutsch, "Psst! References Are Sneaking Back, for Real," *New York Times,* 2 December 1990, F25.

Extending Invitations ————————————————————————

As a businessperson, you may be asked to attend various functions. **Invitations** are requests to attend business or social events, such as receptions and open houses. Although invitations are designed to communicate specific information, they are also intended to communicate goodwill through sincerity and openness.

Every invitation should accomplish three things: (1) request the recipient's attendance at a specific event; (2) explain why the gathering is being held; and (3) provide all the details that the recipient needs in order to attend, including date, time, and location. Many invitations also ask for a response, often by a specific date. Figure 7-5 shows how these elements work in a letter.

Some events require formal invitations, which are written in the third person and are often engraved or printed. Invitations for other social events like parties are more personal and individualized.

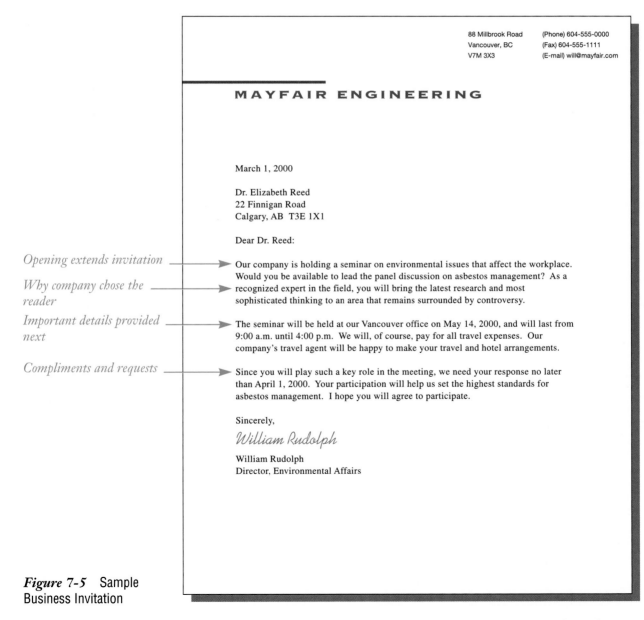

88 Millbrook Road   (Phone) 604-555-0000
Vancouver, BC   (Fax) 604-555-1111
V7M 3X3   (E-mail) will@mayfair.com

MAYFAIR ENGINEERING

March 1, 2000

Dr. Elizabeth Reed
22 Finnigan Road
Calgary, AB T3E 1X1

Dear Dr. Reed:

Opening extends invitation →
Our company is holding a seminar on environmental issues that affect the workplace. Would you be available to lead the panel discussion on asbestos management? As a

Why company chose the reader →
recognized expert in the field, you will bring the latest research and most sophisticated thinking to an area that remains surrounded by controversy.

Important details provided next →
The seminar will be held at our Vancouver office on May 14, 2000, and will last from 9:00 a.m. until 4:00 p.m. We will, of course, pay for all travel expenses. Our company's travel agent will be happy to make your travel and hotel arrangements.

Compliments and requests →
Since you will play such a key role in the meeting, we need your response no later than April 1, 2000. Your participation will help us set the highest standards for asbestos management. I hope you will agree to participate.

Sincerely,

William Rudolph

William Rudolph
Director, Environmental Affairs

***Figure* 7-5** Sample Business Invitation

PRACTICAL TIPS

Why Are Letters and Memoranda Different?

Some of the most important differences between letters and memoranda, usually called memos, can be explained by examining who reads each type of document. Letters are usually sent to people outside the organization—a customer, a supplier, a government official. Memos are generally distributed to people within a company. In fact, the purpose of memos is to maintain a flow of information among people at various organizational levels.

Just as every letter has the potential to create goodwill for a company and its products, every memo has the potential to improve an individual's status within the company. For example, businesspeople who use memos to communicate effectively on critical issues make positive contact with individuals who can contribute to their success within the organization. These and other factors affect the style, language, and level of detail incorporated into each document type.

FORMAT

Memos are formatted more simply than letters. Unlike letters, memos do not include return or inside addresses, salutations, or closings. Rather, most memos start with the four following fill-in-the-blank lines:

To: ________________
From: ________________
Date: ________________
Subject: ________________

On the "TO" line, memo writers put the name of the recipient(s). The "FROM" line should list the sender's name. The "DATE" line contains the date. The "SUBJECT" line should summarize the purpose of the memo.

The subject line needs to be a specific description that informs readers of the subject matter, but not so specific that readers lose interest before they read the memo's content. For instance, "Business Meeting" is too generic. "Agenda for December 15 Meeting in Conference Room B at 9:00 A.M. on Financial, Staff, and Management Performance for Every Department" is too long, too detailed, and too wordy for a subject line. However, "Agenda for December 15 Meeting on Yearly Performance" is descriptive yet brief.

For detailed instructions on formatting business memos, see Appendix I.

LANGUAGE

Whether addressed to co-workers, supervisees, or managers, memos often use less formal language than business letters. After all, people who work for the same company, often in the same building or even the same department, tend to be less concerned about formality with one another than with outsiders. However, this is not always the case, especially when an employee is writing to someone at a higher organizational level. In general, let your relationship with the reader guide your decision regarding formality.

In addition, because most people in a company speak the same business language, memos are often filled with jargon. Used in letters to customers, however, jargon risks alienating readers and causing misunderstandings.

LEVEL OF DETAIL

People in your own company are more likely to be familiar with the subject of your communication than outsiders. As a result, less detail may be needed in a memo than in a letter. When writing memos, you should analyze your audience to find out how much your reader understands. If background is needed, provide it, and use language appropriate to the knowledge and sophistication of the reader.

Sources: See Robert L. Shurter and Donald J. Leonard, *Effective Letters in Business,* 3rd ed. (New York: McGraw-Hill, 1984), 216–220; Andrea B. Geffner, *How to Write Better Business Letters* (New York: Barron's Educational Series, 1982), 103; William C. Paxson, *The Business Writing Handbook* (New York: Bantam Books, 1981), 40.

What's Ahead

As we have seen, the most effective direct requests use the bottom-line approach, delivering the message in the first paragraph. The same approach is used to write good-news, goodwill, and informative messages, which are the subjects of Chapter 8.

STUDENT RESOURCE CENTRE

Summary of Chapter Objectives

1. ***Explain the functions of the opening, middle, and close of a direct request.***

   The opening of a direct request should tell your readers why you are writing to them as opposed to others; it should also explain both the purpose of your request and the action that you want the readers to take. The middle of the request provides any additional details that the reader will need in order to fulfill your request. The close focuses again on the needed action. In letters and many memos, the close also communicates goodwill.

2. ***Explain how to write requests for information.***

   Direct requests for information follow the standard direct approach, with the request stated in the opening paragraph. Informational requests to customers should be "you"-centred and should always focus on maintaining goodwill. Requests to suppliers and other businesses should spend little time motivating recipients. Rather, they should be short and to the point. Requests to government officials should be as specific as possible.

3. ***List the characteristics of letters that place orders.***

   Letters placing orders should include the details found on standard order forms. The letter should be designed to make your order easy to read. Focus on the information needed to place the order rather than on explaining why you are placing it.

4. ***Identify the elements of an effective claim letter.***

   Claim letters are notifications that something is wrong with a good or service. Effective claim letters focus on requesting an adjustment and describing the details that the reader needs in order to assess the situation. The letter should also suggest a solution, such as replacing a defective item or adjusting an erroneous bill.

5. ***Describe two types of request letters associated with personal references.***

   Personal references are recommendations stating that a job applicant is qualified to perform the duties of a job, attesting to the applicant's character, or both. Job applicants often request reference letters from former business associates and instructors. The request letter asks references whether they will write a letter of recommendation or be willing to be contacted by prospective employers. The request letter also describes the type of position being sought and explains how the recipient's knowledge of your background can help. On the other side of the employment fence, reference requests are made by potential employers who want to learn about a candidate's background before making a hiring decision.

6. ***List the essential details included in an invitation.***

   Every invitation should request the reader's attendance at a specific event, explain why the gathering is being held, and provide all the necessary details, including the date, time, and location.

Review and Discussion Questions

1. What are the features of a direct request? *(Ch. Obj. 1)*
2. What are the functions of the opening, middle, and close of a direct request? *(Ch. Obj. 1)*
3. Summarize the chapter's suggestions for writing effective direct requests for information. *(Ch. Obj. 2)*
4. What features contribute to an effective letter placing an order? *(Ch. Obj. 3)*
5. Describe an effective claim letter. *(Ch. Obj. 4)*
6. How would you go about writing an effective letter requesting a personal reference? *(Ch. Obj. 5)*
7. Describe the elements of an effective letter requesting information about a job candidate. *(Ch. Obj. 5)*
8. What information should be included in an invitation? *(Ch. Obj. 6)*

Application Exercises

1. Prepare direct requests covering each of the following situations: *(Ch. Obj. 1)*

   (a) A shipping manager politely asks a new customer to supply further information.

   (b) A shipping manager sends a message to all other managers at a company to tell them about a new computer system.

   (c) A shipping manager sends a message to all of the firm's customers to give instructions and provide details about how to use the new computer system.

   (d) The president of a university sends a message to all of the school's professors, administrators, and students, asking them to stop trampling the grass in the school's quadrangle.

2. Martha Brown, manager of DePaul Memorial Hospital, is writing a letter to General Television, Inc., on April 22nd. Place each the following facts in the appropriate part of her letter—opening, middle, or close. *(Ch. Obj. 1)*

   ▼ DePaul has received seven tuners, all labelled TR-555-2, for the model TV-23 colour receiver.

   ▼ DePaul has been billed three times for tuners that it did not receive.

   ▼ Ms. Brown ordered nine TV tuners (part number TR-222-5) from General Television.

   ▼ When the wrong tuners arrived, she returned them immediately to General Television.

   ▼ She would like General Television to send the correct tuners as soon as possible.

   ▼ She tried twice to call General Television's manager; both times she was put on hold and then the connection was cut off.

   ▼ If General Television cannot fill her order, she would like to cancel it.

   ▼ The original order was scheduled to arrive March 9th.

   ▼ The nine TV tuners that Ms. Brown ordered are for the model TV-20 colour receiver.

   ▼ She hopes that the customer relations manager for General Television will address this problem promptly.

3. Use the information in Exercise 2 to write a claim letter to General Television. *(Ch. Obj. 4)*

4. Find a catalogue that sells products with which you are familiar, such as computer supplies, stereo components, jewellery, or clothing. Using the information that you find in the catalogue, write a letter placing an order from the catalogue. *(Ch. Obj. 3)*

5. Assume that you receive the product from the catalogue company and there's something wrong with it—maybe it's the wrong size or colour or perhaps it's been damaged in some way. Write a claim letter in which you explain the problem and request a replacement. *(Ch. Obj. 4)*

6. Write a letter in which you ask the catalogue company in Exercises 4 and 5 for some type of information—perhaps you'd like to know more about a product in the catalogue or you'd like to ask if the firm carries other brands or sizes. *(Ch. Obj. 2)*

7. Write a letter to a friend or former co-worker whom you haven't seen in a while. Ask this person to write a personal reference recommending you for a job that you would like to have. *(Ch. Obj. 5)*

8. Now suppose that the employer for the job in Exercise 7 writes to your friend to request further information about you. Taking the role of your prospective employer, write this letter. *(Ch. Obj. 5)*

9. As a member of the marketing division at Canuk-Sport, a maker of athletic clothing, you feel it's important to begin a new marketing campaign in South America. You decide to schedule an important meeting to brainstorm ideas and discuss ways to expand CanukSport's markets there. The meeting is set for Thursday, October 22, at 8 A.M. in the Walnut Boardroom. You will invite three co-workers: Craig Culden (from the advertising department); Cindy Sanders (accounting); and Barbara Wadsworth (sales). Craig has good ideas for creating promotional campaigns, Cindy knows the budget that's available, and Barbara knows how to motivate the firm's sales representatives. You know all of these co-workers quite well and frequently get together for lunch. Write a memo inviting Barbara to this meeting. *(Ch. Obj. 6)*

10. In addition to Barbara, Cindy, and Craig, you would like to have your boss, Ramon Esteverria, attend the meeting. Esteverria comes from Peru. Before joining CanukSport, he was director of international marketing for a competing firm, where he headed a successful marketing campaign in Argentina. You feel that his experience and cultural insights would be valuable. You're not sure he can make the meeting because he travels a great deal, but you want to

write a persuasive memo that both invites him to the meeting and expresses how helpful his presence would be. Write this memo. *(Ch. Obj. 6)*

11. You would also like Marianna Bozeman, a market researcher who reports to you, to come to the meeting. Before the meeting, you want her to run the latest computer printouts showing sales data from CanukSport's outlets in South America and then write a brief report summarizing these statistics. Write a memo to Marianna. *(Ch. Obj. 6)*

ACT: Applied Communication Techniques

Begin by referring to the sections up to and including Sentence Fragments, Comma Splices, and Fused Sentences in Appendix II. In addition to correcting the grammar, spelling, and usage errors in the following sentences, in sentences one to five combine the sentence fragments with an independent clause to form a complex sentence. For sentences six to ten correct the comma splices and fused sentences with a semicolon. Check your answers in Appendix V.

1. Like all other human endeavours. Business transactions are plagued by Murphy's Law.

2. Once a company receives a credit request. It tries to determine whether the applicant is creditworthy.

3. Invitations are designed to communicate specific information. Also intended to communicate goodwill.

4. When you need to ask a manager for information. Choose a tone that acknowledges the power differences between you.

5. The complaint focused on wages and hours. Because these issues had the greatest impact on the factory employees.

6. The writer should avoid being too direct, directness is the fastest way to lose customers.

7. Some events require formal invitations these invitations are written in the third person.

8. You may write a direct request to do this only when you are in a more powerful position than the recipient of your memo.

9. The writer from Victoria compiled the research the first part of the project was complete.

10. The writer reviewed all the research, she focused on the qualitative answers.

Building Your Business Notebook

Carefully read the following letters and assess their communication effectiveness. Next, revise and improve the letters by applying what you've learned in this chapter.

```
We are sending you this letter and a questionnaire for you to complete
because your views are important to us. We would like for you to
complete the questionnaire and return it to us as soon as possible.

Once we receive the completed questionnaires, we will evaluate our
banking services to see if they are fulfilling our customers' needs.
We may add additional services if our customers tell us that is what
they want.

Thank you for completing the questionnaire.
```

Document 1

```
I read the article in today's newspaper about your company opening its
own health-care clinic. We are interested in information concerning
this procedure. We are investigating opening our own clinic, and
learning about your experiences could be helpful.

We would like to have any information about your health-care clinic
you think would be helpful. Also, we would like your input on several
issues such as using part- or full-time doctors, general practitioners
or specialists, registered nurses or technicians, services provided,
and so on.

We are eager to learn from your suggestions.
```

Document 2

Building Your Research Skills

Choose a company or product about which you would like to gather more information. Go to the library or seach on the Internet and look up whatever you would need in order to write a letter to that company: name and job title of the right person to receive your letter, address, a description of what you're looking for, and so on. Write a letter requesting information from that person and company. Key the letter and bring it with you to class.

Building Your Teamwork Skills

Your instructor will divide the class into small groups. As a group, take turns reading the letters that each member wrote for the previous Building Your Research Skills exercise. Critique the letters, using the guidelines you studied in this chapter. Working as a team, revise each letter to make it as effective as possible. Be sure to be tactful and to give positive as well as negative feedback!

Building Your Technology Skills

Work in small groups. Individually, each group member should visit several Internet business sites and e-mail a request for information to two or three companies. (You may want to use the Web sites listed in the Building Your Technology Skills exercise for Chapter 6, page 187.) Then send a written request for information by surface mail to the same companies to which you sent e-mail.

When you have received information from the companies, meet in your group and discuss the following:

▼ What are the advantages and disadvantages of using the Internet for customer requests for information?
▼ Is the nature and format of the information returned different from what you might expect by Canada Post Lettermail?
▼ How did your request differ when sent by e-mail compared to Canada Post Lettermail?

Writing Business Correspondence
http://www.algonquinc.on.ca/pilot/twii/apbizw.html

10 Easy Ways To Write More Effective Business Letters
http://www.smartbiz.com/sbs/arts/dir5.htm

10 Tips For Better Letters
http://www.smartbiz.com/sbs/arts/exe195.htm

Writing memos
http://www.csun.edu/~vcecn006/memo.htm

Business Correspondence—Inquiry Letters
http://www.io.com/~hcexres/tcm1603/acchtml/inquire.html

CASE STUDIES

DIVERSITY CASE:

ZhiMeiNai Seeks to Expand

Wang Jia Ying loves fashion—so much so that she left her waitressing job and started her own business in a small town near Shanghai, China. At first, her only employees were herself, her husband, and two retired tailors. Today, her company, ZhiMeiNai, employs 50 people to produce Western-style wedding gowns and formal wear for Chinese movie studios.

ZhiMeiNai pays its employees the equivalent of $1600 to $2200 Canadian in U.S. dollars—triple the national average salary in China. "We are completely self-made people," says Wang. "We had nothing at first and knew nothing about business except what we had read. All I knew was that designing clothes is fun."

Wang Jia Ying wants to buy a heavy-duty sewing machine that will allow her to expand her business by using a wider variety of fabrics. The machine that she would like to buy is made by a U.S. company, and she wants to write to the company to ask for $10 000 in credit.[6]

Questions and Applications

1. Wang knows that she isn't completely fluent in English, and so she asks you to write a letter that she can sign. Write the letter.

2. Explain why you handled the opening, middle, and close of the letter as you did.

CORPORATE CASE:

Lending on Character at South Shore Bank

South Shore Bank specializes in making loans that few other banks would want to touch. Many of these loans help minority business owners in inner-city neighbourhoods. One such business owner is Vivian Wilson, who, ironically, had to get a loan due to too much success. At first, Wilson was ecstatic when her firm, the Star Security & Detective Agency, won a $1-million bid to provide security guards for a large city. Her mood changed as soon as she realized how long it took the city to pay its bills. She had to dip into her own savings to pay her staff, and the bank where she'd had an account for decades refused to lend her any money. By the time she came to South Shore, she was within two weeks of running out of cash.

In situations like this, most banks would demand significant collateral, a detailed credit history, and audited cash-flow statements. David Shryock, South Shore's vice president for commercial lending, relied on character. Shryock knew that Wilson's father had started the Star Agency in 1923 and passed it on to his daughter; Vivian's own daughter, a police officer, helped run the company. "We had confidence she could make the city payment system work," explains Shryock. Within two weeks, he had arranged a $250 000 line of credit for Wilson, and the Star Agency was prospering again.

South Shore continues to work closely with Vivian Wilson, keeping the Star Agency's accounts and receiving copies of all its bills. The bank's relationship with the Star Agency is typical of its personalized lending style: it chooses good risks and follows their progress closely. Unlike many banks, says one South Shore official, "We spend . . . a lot more time . . . working with the borrower one-on-one."[7]

Questions and Applications

1. Compare South Shore Bank's approach to granting credit to that of most banks.

2. Imagine that you are Vivian Wilson. Write a letter to David Shryock requesting a $250 000 line of credit for the Star Agency. Explain why you need credit and mention any facts that you feel will increase your chances of getting the loan.

3. Assume that you are David Shryock and you have just received Vivian Wilson's letter. You're curious to learn more about Wilson, her daughter, and their business. Write a letter to the commissioner of your local police department in which you inquire about the creditworthiness and general history of the Wilson family. (Assume that Wilson's daughter reports to the commissioner.)

Writing Good-News, Goodwill, and Informative Messages

8

Chapter Objectives

After studying this chapter, you should be able to:

1. Describe the use of the direct approach in good-news letters.
2. Explain the importance of expressing goodwill in responses to inquires.
3. Identify three specific types of good-news letters.
4. List the characteristics of an effective goodwill message.
5. Apply the direct approach to writing informative letters.
6. Explain the requirements for writing effective good-news and informative memos.

What is a Customer?
A Customer is the most important person ever in this office . . . in person or by mail.
A Customer is not dependent on us . . . we are dependent on him.
A Customer is not an interruption of our work . . . he is the purpose of it. We are not doing a favor by serving him . . . he is doing us a favor by giving us the opportunity to do so.
A Customer is not someone to argue or match wits with. Nobody ever won an argument with a customer.
A Customer is a person who brings us his wants.
It is our job to handle them profitably to him and ourselves.

Sign posted at the headquarters of L.L. Bean

Intel's Good-News Adjustment Letter

Intel Corp. has a powerful position in the world of computers. Its microprocessor chips power 90 percent of the world's 150 million personal computers, including machines manufactured by IBM, Dell, Hewlett-Packard, Compaq Computer, and Gateway 2000. The trademark "Intel Inside" is a symbol of assurance to computer purchasers worldwide: Intel has a lot riding on the way it responds to business and consumer complaints. Perhaps that is why the computer world responded with shock when Intel mishandled complaints about its prized Pentium chip. As you will see next, the company's actions are a study in poor public relations—especially as the problem could have been avoided with a well-timed, well-written adjustment letter that offered a replacement chip and acknowledged customers' concerns.

The problem began in October 1994 when a flaw was found in the Pentium chip that Intel introduced in the previous year. Intel tried to downplay the glitch, claiming that it affected only users of highly complex mathematical calculations and that these users would encounter the problem only once in 27 000 years of normal use. Customers, including some of Intel's industrial clients, disagreed. IBM pointed to evidence that the flaw could pop up as often as once every 24 days.

When word of the problem became public, thousands of complaints a day poured into Intel's customer service lines. With the Pentium chip powering more than 3 million personal computers, banks and companies requiring precise calculations were particularly alarmed. "We can't afford to be down at all," said one executive of a multimedia training company, who returned two Pentium computers to the manufacturers after a miscalculation was found in a graphics program.

As the brouhaha grew, Andrew Grove, Intel's CEO, took to cyberspace to apologize, but users considered his apology too little, too late. Grove stated that customers who wanted replacement chips would have to convince Intel that the calculations they performed were sophisticated enough to be affected by the flaw in the old chip. Grove was telling them, in other words, that if they wanted a remedy, they would have to prove that they needed it.

The response from computer manufacturers—Intel's direct customers—was swift. IBM suspended sales of all of its personal computers that contained the Pentium chip. "I am not pleased," said a senior executive of another large computer manufacturer. "Intel," he said, "should have acknowledged the problem right off the bat."

What Intel finally did do on December 21, 1994, was publish the following letter in newspapers nationwide. At its heart, the letter is an adjustment letter in which the company tries to establish a fair solution and reestablish goodwill. ▼

Sources: Laurie Flynn, "A New York Banker Sees Pentium Problems," *New York Times*, 19 December 1994, D1–D2; Peter H. Lewis, "IBM Halts Sales of Its Computers with Flawed Chip," *New York Times*, 13 December 1994, A1; Michael Meyer, "A 'Lesson' for Intel," *Newsweek* (December 12, 1994): 58.

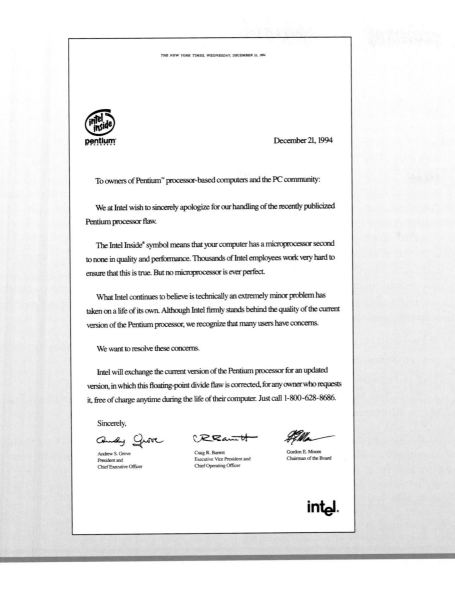

December 21, 1994

To owners of Pentium™ processor-based computers and the PC community:

We at Intel wish to sincerely apologize for our handling of the recently publicized Pentium processor flaw.

The Intel Inside® symbol means that your computer has a microprocessor second to none in quality and performance. Thousands of Intel employees work very hard to ensure that this is true. But no microprocessor is ever perfect.

What Intel continues to believe is technically an extremely minor problem has taken on a life of its own. Although Intel firmly stands behind the quality of the current version of the Pentium processor, we recognize that many users have concerns.

We want to resolve these concerns.

Intel will exchange the current version of the Pentium processor for an updated version, in which this floating-point divide flaw is corrected, for any owner who requests it, free of charge anytime during the life of their computer. Just call 1-800-628-8686.

Sincerely,

Andrew S. Grove
President and
Chief Executive Officer

Craig R. Barrett
Executive Vice President and
Chief Operating Officer

Gordon E. Moore
Chairman of the Board

intel.

Chapter Overview _____

Intel's adjustment letter is not the standard letter you will learn about in this chapter. The problem's solution appears at the end, not the beginning, of the letter. Perhaps Intel believed that a sincere apology was its top priority.

As you will see in this chapter, most adjustment letters take a direct approach to communication, as do other good-news and goodwill correspondence. A good-news message conveys positive information. A goodwill message is designed to forge a bond between the writer and reader. In this chapter we will discuss three types of good-news correspondence: letters of credit, adjustment letters, and positive personnel letters. Then we will examine goodwill messages, including thank-you messages, invitation responses, congratulatory letters, condolence letters, greetings, and informative letters. Finally, we will learn how to communicate good news and information in memo form.

Although this chapter illustrates these messages as hard copy letters and memoranda, correspondence is increasingly sent via e-mail. While electronic media may change the format of the correspondence, the content and writing style of good-news, goodwill, and informative messages should remain the same.

We begin this chapter with the organization plan for good-news correspondence. Similar to direct requests, the key information should be placed first.

Take a Direct Approach to Good News

Most of us want to hear good news right away, so presenting good news first has advantages. For instance, when you know that a message is positive, you are more likely to read the letter and, more importantly, to pay close attention to the details. The direct approach—placing the main point first and the details later—makes the purpose of the letter unmistakable and puts busy readers on your side. Unconsciously, readers may actually thank you for not wasting their time.

The direct approach is usually effective for the following types of correspondence: order acknowledgments; positive credit references and letters granting credit; adjustment letters; personnel-related letters, such as letters of recommendation and employment-related letters; and social correspondence that communicates goodwill.

The following rules of thumb will help you organize information according to the direct approach:

▼ Give your good news and, when appropriate, state what specific steps are being taken.

▼ Explain the details of the news. Refer specifically to any enclosures.

▼ Close with an expression of goodwill that may also summarize and prompt the reader to take action.

As you will see later in this chapter, communicating goodwill is a crucial part of any good-news message and is often part of the close. You may also use your closing to tell your reader what will happen next, to ask your reader for input, or to point to future action, either by asking questions or making suggestions. Table 8-1 summarizes these possible functions and gives an example for each.

Table 8-1   Functions of the Letter Closing

Function	Example
Tell the reader what will happen next.	Now that we have improved our internal mail delivery system, the computer network will deliver internal mail immediately after you send it.
Ask the reader for input.	As you mentioned, we can settle your claim in either of two ways. Please let me know which option you prefer.
Point to future action by asking a question.	Now that your credit line with us has been increased to $100 000, may we talk about how we can better serve your company's needs?
Point to future action through a suggestion.	Thank you for agreeing to meet me next week to discuss your new book. Would you please consider submitting your manuscript on computer disks to save time and avoid errors that may occur if the material is retyped by our production staff? I will be glad to discuss this with you when we meet.

Express Goodwill in Response to Inquiries

Many good-news and informative letters are responses to inquiries. Both businesses and individual customers send letters ordering merchandise, requesting credit, asking for information, making claims, issuing invitations, and so on. Instead of viewing them as demands on your time, consider them opportunities to cement relationships and generate sales.

Goodwill can be communicated in many ways—the tone and language of a letter, the speed with which a company responds to an inquiry, and even the appearance of the reply. Although paying attention to such seemingly small details makes good business sense, many writers fail to do so. As an experiment, business writer Paul Vincent wrote to 50 companies whose ads invited inquiries. Within ten days, he had received only eight responses; nine responses took between 21 and 30 days; 29 responses took more than a month. Four letters were never answered. Not only did most of the responses arrive late, but Vincent's name was also misspelled a dozen times on the return envelopes; six envelopes arrived with postage due; the contents of four envelopes were in bad condition; and two envelopes were empty.[1]

Many companies do recognize that inquiry responses are important. One such company instructed its customer service staff as follows:

1. Answer all inquiries the same day they are received. Strike while the iron is hot! Give inquiries the right of way over all other correspondence.

2. Size up the needs of the prospect and answer his or her inquiry in terms of the advantage of our product to him or her.

3. Don't make the reader wait for information while you refer him or her to "local representatives" or "branch offices." Answer the reader's questions first—and let your local agents follow it up.

4. Allow a reasonable amount of time for an order or a reply to come in, and then follow it up with another letter. Keep on writing at regular intervals as long as the percentage of returns from similar follow-ups makes it profitable.[2]

As you can see, time is regarded as a critical factor in handling customer inquiries. The best advice is to answer every inquiry as soon as possible. In the event of a delay, send a short note acknowledging the inquiry and explaining when you will answer. When an inquiry is better answered by someone in a different department or someone with special expertise, forward it as soon as possible. If you are asked to handle this type of inquiry, it may be necessary to explain the situation to the reader. In your opening paragraph, for example, explain why you are writing rather than the person to whom the inquiry was originally addressed.

In the following sections, we will examine four specific types of good-news and goodwill correspondence: letters of credit, adjustment letters, positive personnel letters, and social correspondence. All are inquiry responses.

> ### Progress Check
>
> 1. Describe what the direct organizational approach to good news means.
> 2. What are the advantages to writers and readers in presenting good news first?
> 3. How do good-news letters give writers the opportunity to express goodwill?

Letters of Credit

Two types of credit letters communicate good news: letters that provide positive credit references and letters granting credit. Such communication is important to businesses and customers alike, since granting credit to responsible applicants is the backbone of Canadian business.

POSITIVE CREDIT REFERENCES

A **credit reference** is a letter that assesses a firm's financial well-being. The business that wants the credit, however, does not give the reference—a third party does. If you are asked to supply such a reference, remember that the recipient may be

PRACTICAL TIPS

The "You" Attitude

The "you" attitude is relatively simple to master: it means shifting your point of view from "I" the writer to "you" the reader. Each of the five sentences below is written from the "I" perspective and could be revised to focus on the reader:

1. We are pleased to announce . . .
2. We are glad you have chosen our firm.
3. We cannot reinstate your service until your bill has been paid.
4. We expect all employees to request their vacation schedule by March 1.
5. We are happy to approve your credit application.

Revised in the interest of reader-friendliness, these sentences now communicate a significantly different attitude:

1. You will be glad to learn that . . .
2. Thank you for giving us the opportunity to serve you.
3. Your service will be reinstated within one day after you pay your bill.
4. Your deadline for scheduling vacation time is March 1.
5. Congratulations on qualifying for our "preferred customer" line of credit.

Is there any time when the "you" attitude is not effective? Perhaps when you must inform a reader that he or she has made a mistake. In these cases, rely on the passive voice. For example, instead of writing, "You failed to send us a cheque this month," write, "No payment was received."

Source: Barbara Lau, "Adding Instant Readership Appeal to Your Business Correspondence," *NRECA Management Quarterly* (Summer 1989): 13–15.

Credit is a system whereby a person who can't pay gets another person who can't pay to guarantee that he can pay.

Charles Dickens
Novelist

looking for reasons to deny credit. As a result, positive credit references must be carefully worded to avoid any suggestion of financial trouble. They should also stick to the facts—speculation can place writers in the middle of a lawsuit.

Because credit references are stamps of approval attesting to the financial health of other individuals or firms, do not give them lightly. State your reference in terms of facts and place it only in the context of specific dealings with an organization or individual. Avoid general impressions or broad statements of confidence in the company's financial health.

Many credit inquiries request that information be supplied either on the inquiry letter itself or on a separate form. However, letters are often necessary. Figure 8-1 is an example of a credit-reference letter. Note the writer's handling of factual details throughout the middle of the letter.

LETTERS GRANTING CREDIT

When a company decides to issue credit, it usually sends a letter to inform the customer of its decision. This letter has four equally important functions:

1. to state that credit has been approved;
2. to summarize the specific terms of the credit agreement;
3. to establish goodwill by welcoming the customer as a new business client; and
4. to encourage future sales.

Tone is critical. Letters granting credit should communicate the company's excitement about the new business relationship and its ability to serve the customer's needs.

Letters granting credit, therefore, should be as positive as possible. For example, try to eliminate negative statements that might suggest the failure of the credit relationship. What strategies does the letter in Figure 8-2 use to strike its positive tone?

July 23, 2000

Mr. Malcolm Washington
Credit Manager
Auto Parts Distributors International
1111 William Street
Winnipeg, MB R2G 1Z1

Dear Mr. Washington:

A direct opener that states the good news first

Here is the credit information you requested on Joanna Baron, owner of Alexandria Auto Supply in Winnipeg. Although this company began only six months ago, it has met all its financial obligations with Manitoba Credit & Savings. In addition, Ms. Baron has an excellent personal credit history with our bank.

Business finances are addressed

Currently, Ms. Baron has a $20 000 business loan on which she has made regular monthly payments. Alexandria Auto Supply has no other outstanding business debt with our bank.

The letter moves next to the subject's personal finances. The focus is on facts rather than opinion

Ms. Baron also has maintained a personal chequing and money market account with us for the past five years. She has always maintained adequate balances to meet her chequing needs and has never overdrawn her account.

The recommendation avoids overgeneralizing

Based on our experience, Alexandria Auto Supply and Joanna Baron have demonstrated a history of creditworthiness. It has been a pleasure working with this company.

Goodwill close stresses confidentiality

I hope this information is helpful, and I am certain it will remain confidential.

Sincerely,

Philip Adams

Philip Adams
Branch Manager

Figure 8-1 Sample Credit Reference

Good-News Adjustment Letters

Written in response to a claim letter, an **adjustment letter** informs the customer how you intend to handle a specific problem. More than anything else, adjustment letters are opportunities to build goodwill by repairing past damage and restoring confidence in a future business relationship.

In writing an adjustment letter, you are often dealing with someone who is annoyed or angry. Even if you concede an error, therefore, the tone of your letter must be conciliatory and your words precise. Handle this situation by responding throughout in a positive manner that shows that you respect the customer's position. Instead of rehashing the details of the problem, focus instead on how your company will correct it in order to satisfy the customer.

Auto Parts Distributors International

1111 William Street   www.apdi.com
Winnipeg, MB R2G 1Z1
(phone) 204-555-1111 (fax) 204-555-2222
(e-mail) mwash@apdi.com

August 3, 2000

Ms. Joanna Baron
Alexandria Auto Supply Centre
100 Main Street
Winnipeg, MB R3B 2X2

Dear Ms. Baron:

Starting today your company has a $5000 line of credit with Auto Parts Distributors International. I am delighted to welcome you as a new credit customer.

Your first order for tires, tail lights, and hubcaps, issued on purchase order 268, totaling $2130.43, will be shipped on August 5.

Your monthly statements are mailed on the 15th of each month and include a 10-day grace period. All outstanding balances are subject to an interest charge of 1 percent per month.

Please keep us in mind for all of your auto supply needs. We carry a complete line of automotive products for both foreign and domestic cars, and when you need a part for an emergency repair, we can have it to you the next day.

Sales Representative Vincent Gower will be handling your account. He will call you on Friday to arrange a meeting to tell you more about the goods and services available to you. Enclosed is our latest catalogue, which shows our complete merchandise line.

We look forward to serving your company for many years and to watching it grow and prosper.

Sincerely,

Malcolm Washington

Malcolm Washington
Credit Manager

Enclosure

Figure 8-2 Sample Letter Granting Credit

If your company is at fault, admit the error. Avoid alibis or excuses when you know you are wrong. At the same time, however, do not make your company look foolish or incompetent in the process. Saying something like "This mistake has plagued our production process for the past two years" will cause the buyer to lose complete confidence in your firm. Although it is acceptable to apologize for the mistake once, offering more than one apology indicates unnecessary weakness.

Try to focus on the way your language will affect the reader. If the customer feels that an adjustment is being made condescendingly or that you are agreeing to terms only grudgingly, you may create further resentment. In addition, remember that business customers making claims do not consider themselves complainers. They regard themselves as people seeking fair treatment. Instead of referring to the problem as a *complaint*, then, call it an error or use the more neutral term *misunderstanding*. Similarly, avoid language that implies you are questioning the customer's truthfulness. Writing "I received your letter *claiming* that four dishes arrived damaged" signals disbelief. Say instead, "I appreciate learning about the problem in the shipment of dishes."

Say nothing to minimize the importance of a customer's claim. If it is important to the customer, it should be important to you. Customers also appreciate genuine expressions of sympathy—for example, "I'm sure this error caused inconvenience and delay. We're working to get the problem solved as soon as possible." Sympathy helps customers feel that you are on their side in your desire to resolve the problem.

Finally, the wording of an adjustment letter should take into account both company policy and legal issues. Do not make promises that your company cannot or will not keep, and avoid language that can be used against your company in court. Admitting, for example, that a product is "defective" is tantamount to admitting liability.[3]

There are two types of positive adjustment letters: letters that grant the requested adjustment and letters that offer a compromise solution. We will examine each type of letter in detail, but we point out first that both types use the following pattern to communicate good-news messages:

▼ Communicate the good news at the start of the letter. Explain that you are granting the adjustment. If necessary, apologize for the problem.

▼ While communicating goodwill and a commitment to customer service, explain the nature of the problem and how you intend to solve it.

▼ Conclude by promoting company goods or services as you continue to rebuild goodwill. Express appreciation for the customer's continued business.

LETTERS GRANTING ADJUSTMENT

Depending on the responsibility for correcting a problem, letters granting an adjustment fall into two categories: letters written when the company is at fault and letters written when the customer is at fault. Naturally, some adjustment letters are offers of compromise. Although each of these uses a good-news approach, the intent of each letter is somewhat different.

WHEN THE COMPANY IS AT FAULT   Every company, of course, enjoys receiving letters of praise from satisfied customers. As a rule, however, companies are subject to human and other forms of error and therefore make mistakes. They deliver wrong or damaged merchandise, miss crucial delivery dates, or provide unsatisfactory service. When customers submit claims, they deserve immediate attention and a fair solution. When the company is at fault, the most important challenge is to reestablish goodwill: you want the customer to return. In the sample adjustment letter in Figure 8-3, the writer attempts to reestablish goodwill through a combination of conciliatory tone and specific details for addressing the problem.

WHEN THE CUSTOMER IS AT FAULT   Customer loyalty is essential to business success. As a result, most companies give the customer the benefit of the doubt in the event of a problem. If you work for a firm that embraces this attitude, you may find yourself in the position of agreeing to customer requests even when you are sure that a customer is at fault. In these cases you may choose—after saying yes—to explain to those customers what they did to cause the problem. Tone is crucial in these instances, since sounding self-righteous or condescending will turn customers away just as quickly as refusing a request.

WHEN COMPROMISE IS NECESSARY   When neither the customer nor the company is entirely at fault, compromise may be the best solution. This is especially true when

July 15, 2000

Mrs. Doris Bower, President
Brookline Senior Citizens United
99-12 Brookline Avenue
Victoria, BC V9E 1Z0

Dear Mrs. Bower:

Opens with good-news adjustment

Enclosed are 20 tickets from the Seasoned Traveller for escorted bus tours to the mansions of Victoria. In addition, we are offering a complimentary lunch as part of the tour. The tickets and lunch are our way of making amends to every member of your group who waited patiently on July 12 for a bus

Reasons for service failure

that never came. With the simultaneous illness of three drivers and the breakdown of two buses, ill fortune seemed to strike us that day, and your group was its unfortunate victim.

Gives overview of tour— brochure gives details

As you can see from the enclosed brochure, the tour we now offer is slightly different from the one you were scheduled to take. While your original tour promised to visit six mansions, we now include guided tours of five mansions. Based on our market research, this is a more manageable number for a day trip.

Request for action tied to specific date

Please let me know by July 22 if the new mansion tour is satisfactory and the exact date you want to book. The tour

A refund offer

must be completed by October 1. If you prefer, a full refund will be mailed to you instead.

Commitment to customer service

We at The Seasoned Traveller pride ourselves on delivering quality tours and exceptional service. When acts of God—and bus breakdowns—stand in our way of delivering this promise, we are committed to finding ways to satisfy our customers.

Sincerely,

Brian Arringten

Brian Arringten
President

Enclosure

Figure 8-3 Sample Goodwill Adjustment Letter

you expect that the customer will not be satisfied with—or your business cannot provide—a replacement. Still, a compromise adjustment letter should offer a good-news solution that fairly compensates the customer. Business communication authority L. E. Frailey uses the following example to make the point. "A restaurant wanted 75 pounds of chicken parts. A meat supply house had 30 whole chickens ready for immediate delivery. The compromise was actually in the customer's favour, and comments about extra meat, bones for stock, etc., further warmed the customer's feelings toward the company."[4] Of course, in the end customers must feel they've been treated equitably. In some cases you may decide to offer the customer choices, such as alternative merchandise, or a full refund.

Progress Check

1. What is the difference between a positive credit reference and a letter granting credit? How do the different audiences for each affect document tone?

2. Explain how letters granting adjustments differ depending upon whether the company is at fault, the customer is at fault, or a compromise is needed.

QUESTION OF ETHICS

The Ethical and Legal Use of Copyrighted Material

When researching and gathering evidence for business documents, you will encounter copyrighted materials, including books, periodicals, tapes, unpublished manuscripts, illustrations, photographs, computer programs, and other original materials. Copyrighted materials are considered the property of the individuals who authored them or the persons or firms who legally hold the copyrights to them. Improper use of these materials may represent a copyright infringement as well as a violation of business ethics.

In Canada, all original creative works are protected by copyright through both federal law and international treaty. CanCopy, a non-profit organization, acts on behalf of publishers, writers, and artists. It does this by collecting a licensing fee or royalty from organizations wishing to copy original work. CanCopy ensures the writers, publishers, and artists their legitimate income by turning the money back to them. With the exception of Quebec, CanCopy has licences with all universities and most community colleges. Quebec has its own organization, Union des écrivaines et écrivains Québécois, that performs a similar function. Among the provisions of CanCopy are:

▼ Electronic materials found on the Web are not copyright-free. These materials must be treated in the same manner as hard-copy documents.

▼ The person who owns the copyright has the right to decide when and how the work may be copied.

▼ CanCopy covers only published work. Therefore, if you wish to cite or copy unpublished materials, you must get the direct approval of the author.

Although copyright law gives authors substantial rights to protect their works and receive compensation for their efforts, these rights are not absolute. They are limited by the doctrine of *fair use,* which gives other writers a limited right to use brief sections of copyrighted material without asking for permission. For example, although quoting a single sentence from a journal article is considered fair use, quoting an entire page is not.

To determine what is fair use and what is not, the law examines various factors. Among these are whether the quoted material will be used for commercial or educational purposes. The intent of the law is to ensure that copyright owners are not deprived of income when others benefit from the use of their material.

Fair use, however, does not eliminate the need to cite sources. Always use footnotes when quoting directly from another work or paraphrasing a work's unique conclusions or research. If you don't use footnotes, especially when quoting directly, you are plagiarizing.

When citing substantial amounts of copyrighted material, you must obtain permission from the copyright owner. Some copyright owners permit the use of their material only for a fee. Failure to obtain permission or pay the fee is considered copyright infringement and is subject to legal action.

Questions for Critical Thinking

1. Is it fair to treat electronic materials located on the Internet in the same way as materials published in hard copy? Why or why not?

2. Why is it an ethical violation to incorporate a substantial amount of copyrighted material without seeking permission for use?

Sources: Copyright protection is discussed in Henry R. Cheeseman, *Business Law: The Legal, Ethical, and International Environment,* 2d ed. (Englewood Cliffs, N.J.: Prentice Hall, 1995), 104–108; William C. Paxson, *The Business Writing Handbook* (New York: Bantam Books, 1981), 247–251; www.athabascau.ca/html/depts/edtech/copyrite; and www.cancopy.com.

Positive Personnel Letters

As a businessperson you may be involved in personnel-related correspondence, including letters of recommendation and other positive employment-related letters. Personnel letters play a crucial role in picking the best people and in starting the employment relationship in a positive manner.

LETTERS OF RECOMMENDATION

Among a job candidate's most valuable assets are well-written letters of recommendation. When candidates can present positive recommendation letters, they help employers do what they will try to do anyway—check each candidate's background. **Letters of recommendation** are reference letters that speak positively about a candidate's background and performance, and may tie the candidate's knowledge, skills, and abilities to a specific job objective (see Chapter 17). If you can attest to a job candidate's background and accomplishments, you may be approached for a written recommendation. Former employers, co-workers, and even subordinates are in positions to write effective recommendation letters.

Every letter should start with an introductory paragraph that names the job candidate and recommends that person for employment. In so doing, the paragraph should state the candidate's full name, the position or field for which he or she is applying, and the relationship between the candidate and the writer.

The letter should continue with one or more *value paragraphs*, which describe the candidate's background and outstanding characteristics and explain why he or she is qualified for the job. Short examples can be an effective way to communicate this information. Finally, a complimentary close repeats the recommendation and may open the door for future contact.

Be truthful as you describe the candidate's background. Not only are embellishments unfair to prospective employers, but they also call into question a writer's integrity. Stick to the facts as you discuss the candidate's knowledge, skills, and personal characteristics, and place the discussion in the context of his or her job history and job objective. If you cannot write a positive recommendation, avoid writing one at all—the letter may create legal problems for you and your company.

Letters of recommendation may either state the candidate's background in a general way or target the candidate's background for a specific job. When a candidate requests a letter that can be submitted to various employers, the letter will be more general than one written at the request of a specific employer. Consider the sample letter in Figure 8-4, where the writer focuses on aspects of the candidate's background that would influence the decision to hire her for a career in advertising.

→ *Cross Reference*
We discussed written requests for recommendation letters in Chapter 7, pages 201–204.

EMPLOYMENT-RELATED LETTERS

Hiring employees involves writing positive employment-related letters. **Employment-related letters** present job offers, acknowledge candidates' applications, invite applicants for interviews, and discuss additional details after an offer has been accepted.

Because employment-related letters often have potential legal ramifications, learn company policy before putting anything in writing. This is especially important in job-offer letters. In many companies, these letters come only from the human resources department, which is charged with having a knowledge of the law. Remember that statements made in job offers can generally be considered legally binding promises. Therefore, include only those facts necessary to communicate your offer. State the offer, the title of the position, starting salary, and the date to report to work. Moreover, in a business environment where change is constant, avoid statements that are in fact speculation—for example, "Within three years, you can expect to be promoted to a manager" or "Although you are starting at a salary of $30 000, within two years you can expect to earn $45 000." Finally, if the ultimate hiring decision depends upon such factors as a background check, medical examination, or drug testing, be cautious about stating categorically that the candidate has been awarded the job.

Progress Check

1. Describe the characteristics of positive letters of recommendation.
2. Why is it important for writers to understand the legal ramifications of employment-related letters? Explain why these ramifications sometimes affect who writes these letters.

APPLEBY & FRANK, Inc.
www.applyby&frank.com
100 Canada Street
Fredericton, New Brunswick E3A 2W2
Telephone: 506-555-1111   Fax: 506-555-2222
E-mail: lceparno@applebyfrank.com

August 13, 2000

Ms. Nicole Bordeaux
Human Resources Department
Image Advertising Inc.
5 Smythe Street
Fredericton, NB E3B 6C6

Dear Ms. Bordeaux:

Strong recommendation → In January 2000, Marissa Samuels began working for Appleby & Frank as an intern. Her performance since that time has been excellent. I highly recommend Marissa to anyone considering her for employment in advertising.

Value paragraphs explain candidate's background and positive qualities → Working within our Account Services Department, Marissa has assisted with market research, compiled reports, and conducted interviews. She brings a positive approach—and a strong desire to learn—to each task, working well in groups or independently.

Informative details support recommendation → Marissa has demonstrated considerable initiative, taking on challenges within our Creative, Media, and Human Resources Departments in order to gain full knowledge of agency operations. Overall, I believe her motivation, talents, and personal qualities make her well-suited for the business of advertising.

Repeats recommendation → These qualities led us to offer Marissa an assistant's position at Appleby & Frank. And that is the most sincere recommendation I can make—that we would hire her ourselves if we had the opportunity.

Powerful final sentence stands alone → She will be a fine employee.

Sincerely,

Laura Ceparno

Laura Ceparno
Chief Executive Officer

Figure 8-4 Sample
Letter of Recommendation

Goodwill Messages

How would you feel if you received a letter from a supplier congratulating you on a promotion? Similarly, imagine how a customer would feel if you sent a birthday greeting or a letter of thanks. In a strict business sense, these messages are not expected or necessary, but they usually leave a residue of good feelings toward you and your company.

Goodwill messages are written to create or maintain bonds of friendship or understanding—personal, professional, or both—between writer and recipient. Goodwill messages are usually written from one individual to another rather than from one company representative to another. But although the exchange of personal messages generally relegates business to a secondary role in the relationship, goodwill messages maintain links, both direct and indirect, with future business activities. According to writing consultant L. E. Frailey, the difference between regularly issued letters and goodwill messages

> . . . is not so much in spirit as in purpose. The regular letters accomplish a double job—they sell, they collect, they adjust, *and* they win goodwill. But the winning of goodwill is the *only* job performed by [goodwill letters]. They can be ignored, and the routines of the business will continue. For some they may be "unnecessary," but you can be sure it is a mistake not to use them.[5]

Goodwill messages fall into five categories: thank-you messages, responses to invitations, letters of congratulations, letters of condolence and sympathy, and greetings. To be effective, these messages must be personal and sincere and should never be form letters. They are generally brief and use a direct organizational approach.

THANK-YOU MESSAGES

The most precious thing a man can have is the goodwill of others. It is something as fragile as an orchid and as beautiful; as precious as a gold nugget—and as hard to find; as powerful as a great turbine—and as hard to build; as wonderful as youth—and as hard to keep.

Anonymous

Many situations in business that have nothing directly to do with business transactions create opportunities to express appreciation. For example, it is appropriate to thank someone for a recommendation, for agreeing to an interview, for spending an hour on the phone explaining information, for making a presentation at a meeting, for providing emergency service above and beyond the call of duty, or for cutting through government red tape. The sample thank-you letter in Figure 8–5 is typical of one that expresses gratitude for extraordinary service.

Say thank you to the individual who helped you and, when appropriate, consider sending a copy to the person's supervisor. Thank-you letters often become part of a worker's permanent personnel file and may affect future raises and promotions.

RESPONSES TO INVITATIONS

Businesspeople are often invited to different functions, such as conferences and meetings. Whether an invitation is made in writing, in person, or over the phone, a written response may be appropriate. Responses to invitations are considered letters of appreciation because they thank someone for a specific offer. In accepting an invitation, express goodwill by making your response forward-looking and positive.

LETTERS OF CONGRATULATIONS

There are many reasons to offer congratulations in business—a promotion, an award for professional excellence or community involvement, a degree awarded after years of night school, a store opening, a new hard-won account. Every letter of congratulation should begin with good wishes and end with a further expression of goodwill. Specific details contribute a sincere, personal tone. Letters of congratulation can be as short as a paragraph or as long as a page.

Word your congratulations according to your relationship with the recipient. For example, when the relationship is not personal or the recipient is in a higher position than you, choose a formal, reserved style. However, when the reader is a professional colleague, it is acceptable to be warm and companionable. Similarly, when you know the recipient well or have a higher professional status, feel free to engage in a light and friendly tone.[6]

LETTERS OF CONDOLENCE AND SYMPATHY

A **letter of condolence** is sent when a business associate or an associate's family member dies. Because letters of condolence arrive during periods of great loss, they should express sorrow and respect in a simple, direct way.

BELLROSE WINDOW TREATMENTS

100 Main Street
Whitehorse, Yukon Y1A 2X2
Phone - 867-555-4444
Fax - 867-555-5555
E-mail - av@bwt.com

October 24, 2000

Mr. Peter Morley, Pesident
Northern Lights Motors
190 2nd Avenue
Whitehorse, Yukon Y1A 2C3

Dear Peter:

Direct approach expresses thanks

Thank you for your organization's extraordinary service during my recent purchase of two Chevrolet Blazers. I have purchased cars and trucks for many years—both as an individual and a businessperson. However, never before have I experienced the attention to courtesy and detail that I enjoyed while doing business with Northern Lights Motors.

Details support the message

Your organization's desire to please started with my first meeting with a sales representative and extended to the help I received when I picked up my new vehicles. I never had an owner take the time to explain his commitment to the customer in the way you did. I felt as if everyone in your organization was there to make me happy.

The highest compliment —telling friends

I have already recommended Northern Lights Motors to my friends and business associates.

Sincerely,

Allen Vallone

Allen Vallone
Owner

Figure 8-5 Sample
Thank-You Letter

Many people have trouble finding the right words to express their feelings. Others fear that contact at such a time may be an intrusion. As a result, many messages of condolence are never sent; many others are sent in the form of commercial cards. To express feelings that give comfort to the bereaved, ask yourself what words you would appreciate if you were in that person's position. Then ask yourself what you would say if you were offering condolences face-to-face. While you should avoid discussing the details of a person's death or alluding to your own religious beliefs, it is appropriate to offer tangible help if you are actually willing to give it.

Use the direct approach in a letter of condolence. Start with an expression of sympathy, and then, if possible, add a personal touch by recalling an incident about the character of the deceased. Close the letter with an expression of goodwill.

Letters of sympathy convey personal concern on such occasions as illness, accident, or other misfortune. They may be written, for example, when someone is in the hospital or has undergone some traumatic experience, such as the loss of home

John Reber, Manager of Public Relations, Air Canada

John Reber develops communications strategies for conveying the wide variety of messages that are sent out from Canada's largest airline. Together with his colleagues in media relations, he supports a diversity of activities, ranging from executive speaking engagements to financial results and product launches. Whatever the news, planned or unplanned, a message must be crafted and conveyed effectively to target audiences. His challenge is to create awareness and enthusiasm for Air Canada in Canada and around the world.

"Defining your objectives is key to effective communications," says Reber. "And you need to know your public. This is fundamental to developing corporate messages and public relations programs. The launch of Star Alliance with our partners Lufthansa, SAS, THAI, United, and VARIG is a case in point. We had a great story to tell—how we created the airline industry's first truly global alliance. We also had a great customer story— how an alliance benefits global travellers. The customer story is the one we chose to focus on. Why? Because our first objective was to create customer loyalty. Crafting the messages and choosing the medium followed naturally from there."

Question: What is the most important skill a writer can bring to crafting an effective good-news communication?

Answer: Being able to synthesize thoughts and write concisely is essential to developing good-news

---

Progress Check

1. What is the primary purpose of a goodwill message?
2. What business situations might call for a thank-you letter?

or business to a fire. Letters of sympathy use the same organization as condolence letters, except that the conclusion offers a note of hope for the future. A sample conclusion might be, "Although the fire destroyed your Mississauga plant, I am certain that you and your staff will be able to rebuild and overcome the loss. The fire destroyed a building; it did not consume your spirit or ability to make things happen."

GREETINGS

Although businesspeople commonly exchange greetings at Christmas, greetings may be extended on other occasions as well. As a supplier of menus and other materials, for example, the owner of a small printing company may send greetings to a local restaurateur on the yearly anniversary of his or her business.

communication. Continually questioning your communication and never allowing yourself to be complacent are also important skills. Otherwise, chances are that not many people will be interested in listening to what you have to say or reading what you have written.

Question: Is a direct approach to good news usually the best choice?

Answer: Yes, a direct approach is best since it conveys credibility to the receiver of the message.

Question: What is your most common method of communicating with the public?

Answer: Press releases are the most common method, and press events and executive speaking engagements are also frequently used.

Question: Is there a right way or wrong way to create goodwill with the public?

Answer: There is both a right way and a wrong way. The right way is to be honest, accurate, and transparent. The wrong way is to be self-serving, in other words, not considering the public by communicating only what is beneficial to your company. Stepping back and analyzing your message from the audience's point of view is always a challenge for communicators.

Question: Does your communication style differ when you communicate good news as opposed to bad news?

Answer: The objective of communicating good news is to create enthusiasm; therefore, you may need to provide more details and a vivid description.

Question: What is the most important factor in writing informative messages?

Answer: Credibility is the most important factor. To achieve this you need a clear, transparent style that avoids conveying misleading information, either through the information itself or the tone in which it is delivered.

Question: Comment on the statement "If you don't give people information, they'll make up something to fill the void."

Answer: This is more often the case for bad news, where it's crucial to set the facts straight. A void in the case of good news usually translates into a missed opportunity.

Source: Interview with John Reber.

Greetings, then, are messages that can commemorate either holidays or special events. They are sometimes sentimental and may thank individuals for their business during the year. Many businesspeople choose commercial cards to extend wishes on holidays and special events, but the best greetings are personal letters and notes.

Informative Letters

Letters that inform use a direct organizational approach, where the main idea is presented first. However, informative messages are neutral, not pleasing like good-news messages, so you may have to work hard to grab and hold readers' attention. This is especially true in a business world of information overload. Organize informative letters in the following way:

- ▼ Open your document with a statement of purpose. Show readers why your information is important by listing how it benefits them.
- ▼ Incorporate details in the middle of your document by relating them to your readers' needs.
- ▼ Close by emphasizing how your information is designed to help readers. Focus as well on communicating goodwill and on laying the foundations for future action. In long documents, a summary may also be necessary.

Informative writing, no matter what information is discussed, must be clear and audience-centred. Be certain that you provide readers with enough detail and context. Use precise, jargon-free language and present points in logical order. The following additional tips will help you write effective informative letters:

- ▼ Let *your readers' needs* determine the priority of information—not your needs.
- ▼ Let your readers' need to know determine whether you include or exclude details. You may present price ranges when you write to a business owner, but provide specific prices when you write to that company's purchasing agent.
- ▼ Even if you are sure that your readers will need background information to understand your purpose, hold clarifying details for the middle of your letter.
- ▼ Be concise by relegating less important information to attachments.
- ▼ Help your readers follow a lengthy or complex presentation by including helpful written signposts—for example, *first, . . . second, . . . third, . . . as a result.*
- ▼ When introducing particularly complex material, consider inserting a short "preview" paragraph that tells your readers how you plan to handle the material. In other words, tell readers what you will do before you do it.
- ▼ Design your document so that your most important points stand out. Use lists surrounded by plenty of white space.

Informative letters are sent for many reasons; for instance, as a reply to an information request, an explanation of an event, an outline or explanation of company policy, a follow-up to a conversation or meeting, or an acknowledgment of documents or information that has been received.

RESPONSES TO REQUESTS

Start your reply with a thank-you for the reader's interest in your company. Then state the type of information you plan to present. The middle of your letter should be devoted to the specific facts that answer the inquiry. Close your letter by telling the reader that you will be glad to answer any further questions. (Do this, of course, only if you are committed to future help.)

As you answer the request, try to place yourself in the reader's position. For example, if an airline is interested in purchasing your company's carry-on luggage for its 5000 flight attendants, would it help to include more information than was specifically requested? Instead of just sending a price list, consider explaining the quality and durability difference between your luggage and competitors' products. This approach can be a valuable business-promotion tool.

ANNOUNCEMENTS OF COMPANY ACTIVITY

There are as many reasons to write letters about events, personnel, and company policies as there are companies—for example, merger announcements, letters announcing an address change, or letters informing customers of their new sales rep-

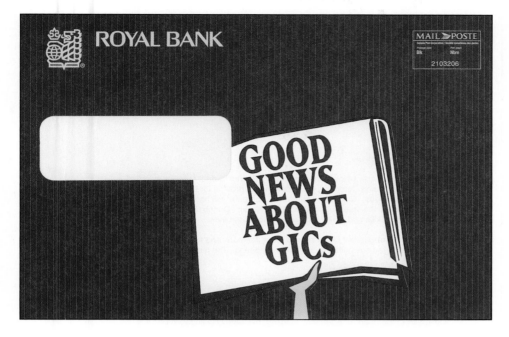

Most of us want to hear good news and advertisers want to provide it to us.

Source: *Courtesy of the Royal Bank of Canada.*

resentative. Remember that announcement letters may also provide the opportunity to promote goodwill.

Consider the letter in Figure 8-6, written by the district manager of a bus company that successfully contracted to provide a school system's transportation service. The letter, written to drivers who worked for the company that used to provide the service, announces the change and offers drivers the opportunity to keep their jobs. Note how the opening attempts to build goodwill.

FOLLOW-UP LETTERS

Many informative letters confirm previous telephone or face-to-face conversations. **Follow-up letters** restate key points of the conversation. Over time, the memory of a conversation decays. A follow-up letter serves as a written record of the conversation for future reference. Follow-up letters also make sure that everyone's version of the information is the same. Some follow-up letters simply state basic facts—for example, confirming the time, place, and purpose of a meeting. Others are more complex—say, written statements to clarify verbal agreements or to set terms for a working relationship.

Bear in mind that follow-up letters pass on information as you remember it— which may or may not be the same way others remember it. The writer of the follow-up letter in Figure 8-7, therefore, is careful to leave the door open to further discussion and clarification.

TRANSMITTAL LETTERS

Transmittal letters, also known as **cover letters,** accompany materials sent from one person to another. They are important because they provide written records that the materials have indeed been sent.

Transmittal letters accompany shipments of materials ranging from literary manuscripts and blank cheques to in-store promotional displays and auto parts. Although most transmittal letters accompany materials sent by mail, they can also accompany materials that are transmitted personally from one individual to another.

GLOBAL TRANSPORTATION COMPANY, INC.
www.globaltransportation.com

2900 Elbow Drive SW, Calgary, AB T3A 4ZA
Tel: (403) 555-1111 Fax: (403) 555-2222
E-mail: rmor@gtc.com

May 20, 2000

Dear Bryant Bus Driver:

Crucial announcements open the letter →

As you probably know by now, the Bow Valley School District recently awarded Global Transportation Company, Inc. a contract to provide for its school transportation needs. Global Transportation Company will hire any Bryant bus driver who meets the safety standards of the district. During this crucial time of transition, your skills and ability are needed more than ever.

To give you the opportunity to learn about our company and to ask any questions you may have, you are invited to a breakfast meeting. The meeting will be held on:

Details set off for easy reading →

Date: June 16, 2000
Time: 9:15 a.m.
Location: Bow Valley Junior High School Cafeteria

Reader-centred goodwill message →

Parents in this community have put their faith in you for seven years. From what I witnessed at the Board of Education meeting, this faith is well deserved. It is obvious that you care deeply for the students you transport. It is our hope that all of you will continue to drive in Bow Valley this coming year.

If you are unable to attend this meeting and are interested in speaking with us, please call my office at 555-6509, extension 16.

Positive look to the future →

I look forward to meeting all of you.

Sincerely,

Richard Morrow

Richard Morrow
District Manager

Figure 8-6 Sample Company Announcement

Transmittal letters that are part of formal business reports will be examined in detail in Chapter 13.

Transmittal letters come in two forms. The brief version identifies and/or describes the item being sent and states the reason for its delivery. The longer version adds explanatory details and may raise questions. Both versions close with expressions of goodwill.

ACKNOWLEDGMENTS

Acknowledgments inform readers that information or materials have been received. Although an acknowledgment is often primarily a matter of courtesy, it can also point toward a future business relationship.

Spencer & Kaplan

Executive Search Professionals
www.spencer&kaplan.com

555 Bloor Street East, Toronto, ON M4W 2Z2
Tel: (416) 555-4444   Fax: (416) 555-3333
E-mail: joan@spencer&kaplan.com

September 5, 2000

Ms. Gail Osborne, CEO
Osborne Publications
51 Metcalfe Street
Ottawa, ON K1P 6N4

Dear Ms. Osborne:

Direct approach summarizes main point

Thank you for speaking with me yesterday about your requirements for a new publisher and your interest in having Spencer & Kaplan conduct this extremely important executive search.

Phrase invites correction of details, if needed

As I recall from our conversation, your ideal candidate should have at least 15 years of experience in trade magazine publishing. Most importantly, you are looking for someone with the vision to reshape your ten trade magazines into more competitive products.

Focus is on what will happen next

By the end of the week, you will receive a draft of the formal search plan, which will reflect the job requirements, compensation, and benefits package Osborne is offering. Once you approve the plan, we will begin the formal executive search.

Request placed in larger context
Promise pledges rapid, responsive service

From what I learned during our talk, your company is in the midst of a major reorganization. The search for a new publisher is an important part of your restructuring efforts. Spencer & Kaplan will do everything it can to conclude this search quickly and present you with several qualified candidates.

Goodwill close

I look forward to working with you during this exciting search process.

Sincerely,

Joan Marks

Joan Marks
Senior Partner

Figure 8-7 Sample Follow-Up Letter

Good-News and Informative Memos

Good-news and informative memos should follow a direct organizational plan. Present your purpose first, follow with essential details, and, if necessary, close with a summary statement or a request for action.

WHAT'S THE PURPOSE?

Among the most common good-news memos are messages of congratulations and hiring and promotion announcements. Figure 8-8 is an example of an announcement memo from Keith Reinhard, CEO of DDB Needham WorldWide. The memo is part of Reinhard's *Any Wednesday* series of weekly good-news memos to all agency

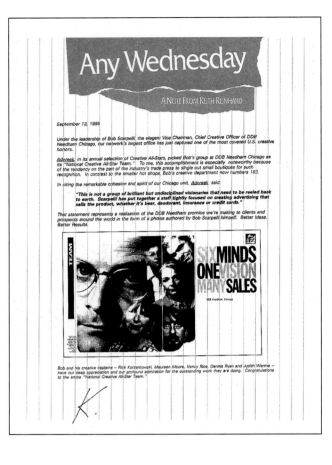

employees. With its creative use of a photo and text design, this memo is more inno-vative than most, but still relies on a direct approach.

Informative memos fall into a number of different categories, including *trans-mittal memos*, which introduce enclosed materials or longer documents; *delegating memos*, which provide the details of assignments; *instructions*, which explain how something works or describe the steps in a process; and *policy announcements*.

STYLE AND LENGTH

Critical to the success of good-news and informative memos is a sensitivity to the issues of style and length.

STYLE As we have seen, in writing direct requests and negative and persuasive mes-sages, it is wise to adopt a style that is appropriate to the position of your reader. Most memos are addressed to co-workers, so they are often filled with jargon and abbreviations. If your memo is going to be sent to people outside the business, be sure to eliminate language that may not be understood.

On the whole, style is less crucial in positive correspondence. Because col-leagues at all levels—managers, co-workers, and supervisees—welcome positive messages for the same reasons, there is little need to distinguish among readers in the style of good-news and informative memos. Style, then, is less important than the message itself. According to one team of communication consultants, "If some-one is told, 'Yes, you got the raise,' the recipient of the message doesn't really pay much attention to the style in which the good news is conveyed."[7]

Similarly, tone is also fairly consistent in informative memos. No matter who you are writing to in the organization, be straightforward and forceful in communicating the details of your message.

LENGTH   The need to focus on the most important information and eliminate unneeded details is crucial in informative memos. A good way to gauge the right level of detail is to analyze how your reader is going to use your information. For example, if you are writing a memo to your manager describing how you plan to delegate responsibility on a project, find out whether he or she wants a detailed account or simply a short overview of your plan. Think about the amount of time and effort that will be required of both you and your reader. While the first memo may take ten pages or more, the latter may require only several paragraphs.

Progress Check

1. Describe the three-part organizational plan for informative letters.
2. Summarize the chapter's guidelines for writing clear, logical, informative letters.
3. How do style and length affect the success of a good-news informative memo?

What's Ahead

Although direct requests and good-news, goodwill, and informative messages all rely on some form of direct organizational approach, this approach is generally ineffective for communicating bad news or critical messages. Chapter 9 will examine the best way to present unpleasant or difficult messages. As you will see, communication in these circumstances is usually more effective when the writer adopts an indirect organizational plan.

STUDENT RESOURCE CENTRE

Summary of Chapter Objectives

1. **Describe the use of the direct approach in good-news letters.**

    Good-news letters should start by telling the reader the purpose of the document, including the good news. The middle of the letter should explain essential details, and the close should express goodwill. The close may also suggest future action, ask the reader for comments, raise questions, or offer suggestions.

2. **Explain the importance of expressing goodwill in inquiry responses.**

    Expressions of goodwill give writers the opportunity to build personal business relationships with their readers—relationships that may ultimately result in increased sales. Language and tone communicate goodwill, as does the speed with which an inquiry receives a response.

3. **Identify three specific types of good-news letters.**

    Good-news correspondence falls into three categories. Credit-related letters include positive credit references and letters granting credit. In good-news adjustment letters, the writer may either grant adjustment of a customer's claim or suggest a compromise solution. Finally, good-news personnel letters include letters of recommendation and such employment-related letters as job offers. Common forms of social correspondence include such goodwill messages as thank-you letters, responses to invitations, and letters of congratulation.

4. *List the characteristics of an effective goodwill message.*

A goodwill message attempts to establish or maintain a personal relationship between writer and recipient. No attempt is made at business promotion. Among the most common goodwill messages are thank-you messages, responses to invitations, letters of congratulation, condolence and sympathy letters, and greetings.

5. *Apply the direct approach to writing informative letters.*

Like good news, information is best communicated through a direct approach. Start with a statement of purpose and include reasons why the information is important to the reader. In the middle of the document, flesh out the information as you continue relating it to the reader's needs. Depending upon the document, the closing may include a statement of goodwill, a summary, or steps for future action.

6. *Explain the requirements for writing effective good-news and informative memos.*

Good-news and informative memos also follow a direct organizational plan. Because everyone welcomes positive messages, there is no need to change the style of the message according to the audience. Memo length should be geared to the reader's needs.

Review and Discussion Questions

1. Summarize the general pattern for organizing an effective good-news letter. *(Ch. Obj. 1)*
2. Why is it important to express goodwill when responding to inquiries? *(Ch. Obj. 2)*
3. Name the types of good-news correspondence. *(Ch. Obj. 3)*
4. Identify the function of the letter closing. *(Ch. Obj. 1)*
5. Compare and contrast credit references and letters granting credit. *(Ch. Obj. 3)*
6. What is an adjustment letter? How should such letters be written? *(Ch. Obj. 3)*
7. Discuss letters of recommendation. What considerations are involved in writing such letters? *(Ch. Obj. 3)*
8. What characteristics make for an effective goodwill message? *(Ch. Obj. 4)*
9. Describe a three-point plan for writing an effective informative letter. *(Ch. Obj. 5)*
10. What characteristics make for effective good-news and informative memos? *(Ch. Obj. 6)*

Application Exercises

1. Cover the right-hand column in Table 8-1. Now write your own example for each of the functions listed. Be sure to make your examples different from the ones in the table. *(Ch. Obj. 1, 5)*
2. La Tanya Johnson buys a pair of jeans from The Clothes Closet, a small boutique in Grande Prairie, Alberta. After taking the jeans home, she decides that she wants to exchange them for another pair of a different colour. The next day, however, she's called out of town on an emergency business trip. When La Tanya returns, she takes the jeans back to The Clothes Closet and asks the salesclerk if she can exchange them. The clerk explains that the boutique has a two-week deadline for exchanges. Thanks to her trip, La Tanya is three days past the limit. La Tanya points out that she's been a faithful customer at the shop, but to no avail. Finally, she storms out of The Clothes Closet, goes home, and writes an angry letter. As the boutique manager, you're the one who receives the letter. Write an adjustment letter in which you try to resolve the problem and keep La Tanya as a customer. *(Ch. Obj. 3)*
3. After the incident with La Tanya Johnson, you decide, as manager of The Clothes Closet, that it would be a good idea for the store to change its policy on returns and exchanges. However, the store's owner, Liz Smith, is worried that a more liberal policy could cost the store too much money. Write an informative memo telling Liz about your experience with La Tanya (who, thanks to your excellent letter, has remained a loyal customer). Relate your memo to Liz's concerns. *(Ch. Obj. 6)*
4. Liz is so impressed by your memo that she agrees to your new policy suggestion. You decide to write a letter to regular customers of The Clothes Closet to tell them about the new policy and its advantages for them. (You also figure that this would be a prime opportunity for a goodwill message and

an announcement of an upcoming sale.) Write the letter. *(Ch. Obj. 5)*

5. Six months later, La Tanya Johnson discovers that a blouse that she bought at The Clothes Closet has shrunk two sizes. She phones you to request a new one. While talking on the phone, you discover that she washed the blouse in hot water even though the label in the garment clearly states, "Hand wash in cold water." What do you do? *(Ch. Obj. 2, 3)*

6. CanukSport, a small firm in Vernon, British Columbia that makes athletic clothing, often gets letters inquiring about its products—sizes and styles available, where customers can buy them, prices, and so on. As a longtime CanukSport staff member, you realize that the company has no standardized policy for responding to such inquiries. You decide that it would be a good idea to write a brief "how-to" manual that explains the importance of handling customer inquiries and describes how to write good responses. Write this manual as an informative memo to CanukSport's staff. *(Ch. Obj. 2, 6)*

7. Suppose that one day the memo below lands on your desk.

    The rest of Ms. Malapro's six-page memo discusses the dangers of wordy, unclear corporate memos. She concludes by referring staff members

MEMORANDUM

```
      TO:  All Staff Members of Worde, Incorporated
    FROM:  Denise Malapro
           Vice President for Internal Communications
    DATE:  August 29, 2000
 SUBJECT:  Long Memos

           The ability to develop effective internal communications is
           a crucial skill that we all should practise consistently.
           Concise, effective memos have always been a priority here at
           Worde.  Indeed, I can safely say that our corporation has
           always been known for the quality of its sentence
           construction, since, as you would no doubt agree, overly
           long and complex sentences can confuse people and disguise
           meanings, leading to misunderstanding on the part of the
           reader and, certainly, frustration on the part of the
           writer, since his or her meaning has been misconstrued,
           whether partially or totally, to the point of almost
           complete obfuscation.

           In a recent conversation with my staff, I learned that over
           50 percent of our internal memos are more than five pages in
           length.  Furthermore many of us use words that the average
           person just wouldn't use in normal conversation.  This is
           simply heinous!  This is why I am announcing a new
           company-wide policy.  From now on, we will write only short,
           effective memos that get to the point quickly.  It is time
           to be more aggressive about length control.
```

to a 160-page style manual entitled "Keep It Brief."

(a)   Does Ms. Malapro's memo follow the chapter's guidelines for writing effective informative memos?

(b)   If not, rewrite the memo to make it more effective. *(Ch. Obj. 6)*

To complete Exercises 8 and 9, pair off with a classmate.

8.   Each of you should think of a job that interests you. Now write a letter of reference for each other, addressed to individuals who might be able to hire you for those positions. Critique each other's letters and tactfully suggest any improvements that can be made. *(Ch. Obj. 1, 3)*

9.   Congratulations! You both got your jobs. Each of you can now write a letter to your partner from the person who hired him or her to inform the candidate of the company's decision. The letter offers the position and mentions the new title, salary, and the date on which work begins. *(Ch. Obj. 1, 3)*

10.   Now that you have your dream job, it's time to extend your credit.

(a)   Write a positive credit reference for yourself, addressing the letter to a company other than your employer.

(b)   Write yourself a letter from this company, informing you of its decision to issue you credit. Follow the chapter guidelines for writing credit-related letters. *(Ch. Obj. 1, 3)*

11.   Things are going so well that you are promoted from the position you obtained in Exercise 9. Write the good-news memo that announces your promotion and your new title and summarizes your new responsibilities. (You can also brag a bit about your past performance, if you wish!) *(Ch. Obj. 4, 6)*

12.   Refer to the chapter's discussion of the five categories of goodwill messages. Now think about real-life situations for which you could write goodwill messages. These situations might arise from a current or former job, a social group to which you belong, or a class. For instance, did a co-worker recently have a baby? Did someone you know win an award, get married, or invite you to a social event? Write five goodwill messages—one for each category—that address these real-life situations. *(Ch. Obj. 3, 4)*

ACT: Applied Communication Techniques

Begin by referring to the sections up to and including up to and including Dangling Modifiers in Appendix II, then correct the grammar, spelling, and usage errors in the following sentences. Check your answers in Appendix V.

1.   In painting four of her pictures, her boyfriend was used as her model.

2.   To find the needed research, the entire library was searched.

3.   Having been delayed by a car accident, the leading role was played by a local actor.

4.   Having moved from Ottawa at twelve, his hometown no longer seemed familiar.

5.   Tossing around in the heavy seas, I felt like our sailboat would sink.

6.   To avoid recognition, sunglasses and a wide hat covered her face.

7.   Wagging his tail, the man fed the dog.

8.   Hearing the horn, the car pulled into the garage.

9.   Plunging from the sky, the Toronto Air Show audience screamed with fear.

10.   Shocked by the high prices, the store offered its customers a discount.

Building Your Business Notebook

Carefully read the documents on the following pages and assess their communication effectiveness. Then, rewrite the documents, applying what you've learned in the chapter.

MEMORANDUM

TO: All Employees

FROM: Jeff Miner, Supervisor

DATE: January 10, 2000

SUBJECT: Attendance

Some of you have been complaining that management never does
enough to reward employees or to build morale. But some people
complain no matter what is done. Those complaining attitudes
seem to be contagious and make it hard for management to want
to do anything.

But management has decided to try to offer something that
should make most employees happy—realizing that there will
still be those not satisfied. Employees will now be eligible
to win awards two ways. The names of those employees who have
perfect attendance for six months will be put in a drawing to
win dinner-for-two certificates and two movie passes. One name
will be drawn every month for this prize. The other way
management has decided to try to reward employees is to award
$100 each month to the employee who submits the best money-
saving idea to management. This award may not be awarded every
month; that depends on the ideas that are submitted and how
workable they are. If they save the company a substantial
amount of money, then the prize will be awarded. But it won't
be awarded if the ideas aren't good ones.

We hope that employees will consider this as management's
attempt to cut down the moaning and groaning about never doing
anything nice for the employees. These benefits will begin the
middle of next month.

Document 1

I have received your letter asking for information about
prices of our fine line of supplies. In reply, I would like
to state that we are glad you are interested in our products
and hope that our answers will answer your questions. I am
writing to give you the information you requested.

Due to the fact that our printing costs have gone up 25
percent during the last six months, the costs for the supplies
you inquired about have also increased. Instead of being
$15.00 per package, they are now $18.00 per package.

Enclosed please find a price chart which also shows billing
options and shipping options. At this point in time, we are
about three weeks behind in our production schedule.
Regardless of this fact, we will soon have all our orders
filled; and you could receive your order in the near future.

Each and every order is handled with the utmost care, concern,
and interest. Kindly advise me if you are interested in
placing an order. Permit me to say that we welcome all
comments from our customers about our products. Per your
request, we will place your name on our mailing list and keep
you advised about new products and sales. Past history shows
that our products are constantly changing to meet customer
demands and needs. If you have any questions, please don't
hesitate to let us know.

Document 2

Building Your Research Skills

Do most letter and memo writers in real-life organizations follow the guidelines given in this chapter? Let's find out.

Collect three examples of good-news, goodwill, and informative messages from actual businesses, your school, or business publications. Analyze each message to see how effective it is. Does it follow the guidelines for communicating its message effectively? If it does a good job, explain why. If it doesn't, how could it be improved? Take notes and be prepared to explain why you think each example is good or bad.

Building Your Teamwork Skills

Your instructor will divide the class into small teams of two to four people. Each group will meet to discuss the examples that students found for the previous Building Your Research Skills exercise. As a group, discuss each example of writing and decide whether or not it is effective. If it is effective, explain why; if it's not, show how it can be improved. Choose "best" and "worst" examples and have one member take notes on the group's suggestions for improving the ineffective message.

Appoint a spokesperson for your team. Your spokesperson will present to the class the group's best and worst messages, along with suggestions for improving the ineffective message. See if the class can come up with additional ideas for improving it.

Building Your Technology Skills

Visit several Internet business sites (see Chapter 6, page 187 for addresses) to see how businesses are using the Internet to communicate goodwill and information. Then form small groups of six to eight people. First, discuss whether e-mail is appropriate for each of the following good-news and goodwill information messages: letters of credit, adjustment letters, positive personal letters, thank-you messages, congratulatory letters, condolence letters, greetings, and informative letters. What are the advantages/disadvantages of using electronic media for good-news and goodwill messages? Do you think goodwill is communicated by the speed in which a company responds to an inquiry request?

Next, divide your group in half. Select one type of good-news or goodwill information message. Group 1 should write the message to be delivered by e-mail; Group 2 should write the message to be delivered by surface mail. Compare and contrast the differences in both types of messages.

Weblinks Internet Resources for this Chapter

Business Letters: Subordinating Negatives in Good News and Neutral Messages
http://owl.english.purdue.edu/Files/92.html

Writing Focused and Organized Memos
http://www.wuacc.edu/services/zzcwwctr/ wrtmemos.txt

Writing & Public Relations Tips: Exciting Newsletters by Paula Wrenn
http://www.thewriteangle.com/tips.htm#news

CASE STUDIES

CORPORATE CASE:

Eaton Corporation Builds a Better Business Through Teamwork

At Eaton Corporation, the morning quiz is underway.

Ten employees sit around a boardroom table. A supervisor asks, "What were our sales yesterday?"

A worker scans a computer printout and replies, "$625 275."

"And in the month?" asks the manager.

"$6 172 666," says another worker.

The quiz continues: What was the cost of materials and supplies used the day before? What was the cost of labour, shipping, and utilities?

Meanwhile, out on the shop floor another employee demonstrates to the plant manager a new technique for making welding electrodes that could save the plant $5126 annually. This marks the 193rd time this year that employees have come up with ideas for improving the plant's operations. Clearly, workers at Eaton aren't just taking tests; they're also doing their homework.

Eaton's business—making gears, engine valves, truck axles, and circuit breakers—may not be glamorous, but its progress is breathtaking. Last year, Eaton lost $12 million. In its first quarter this year, it netted $33 million. The company's productivity (output per hour worked) has risen 3 percent every year during the past decade—compared to 1.9 percent for all U.S. manufacturers. Employees' suggestions have helped the firm save $1.4 million—and earned workers $44 000 in credits toward purchases at the factory store.

How does Eaton do it? Managers attribute much of the company's success to its improved communication with workers. Show employees how the firm's success benefits them, say supervisors, and they'll find creative ways to help. Hence, the daily morning quizzes in which managers and workers assess the plant's progress on a continuing basis. In the company cafeteria, a TV monitor compares the daily performance of each shift and department to its cost and performance goals. Attention to the common cause, says metal fabricator Ricky Rigg, "gives you a sense of direction, and makes you appreciate what you do more." Adds machinist Rodney Romine, "If the company can't make money, you can't expect to have a job very long."

Eaton has also found that communication improves when employees work in teams. Boasting such names as "The Hoods" and "The Worms," worker-led groups constantly look for production bottlenecks and areas where costs can be cut. Sometimes the search pays off in ways that nobody ex-

pected. For example, "Scrap Attack," a team of eight forge-press operators, had long been trying to reduce the plant's scrap-metal waste by 50 percent. Along the way, team members noticed that the dies used to forge gears on one press consistently lasted 25 percent longer than any of the other dies employed to perform the same task. Why? "Nobody knew," recalls team leader Anthony Ourada, "but we got to thinking about it." Eventually, the group discovered that one press operator preheated the dies before using them—a practice that extended their life. Now—at a cost savings of $50 000 a year—every press operator in the plant preheats dies.

Another team responsible for maintaining plant machinery decided that the machines broke down too much. The workers approached their boss with an offer: "You're buying all this on the outside. We can do it for you better." In one instance the team built a new machine for $80 000 to replace a machine for which outside vendors had charged Eaton $350 000. The team's new machines have taken over the most boring tasks in the department and freed workers to handle more challenging jobs. Moreover, the department's output doubled in one year, and the team plans to double it again in another year. "It's nice to start out with a concept and see it through," says Romine, "especially when it gets rid of monotonous work. We're more or less our own bosses."

Office clerk Luci Donaldson sums up the Eaton attitude: "Our opinions matter here. What we say counts—and it's not just to appease us."[8]

Questions and Applications

1. Imagine that you are the CEO of Eaton. Write a letter of congratulations to the "Scrap Attack" team who saved the company $50 000 by preheating dies.

2. Your boss at Eaton asks you to prepare an informative letter to describe for the company's board of directors the plant's new system and its benefits. Write this letter, keeping the needs and concerns of your audience in mind.

3. Eaton's approach requires workers who are comfortable working in teams and who enjoy looking for ways to improve their work. As the plant's head of human resources, you're in charge of hiring new employees. You decide to create an informative memo, addressed to job applicants, that describes the plant's method of operation, how it affects workers' jobs, and the benefits that employees gain from such a system. Write this memo with the needs and concerns of your audience in mind.

CORPORATE CASE:

Why Gannett Considers Newspapers Its Meat-and-Potatoes Business

Anyone who knows anything about the newspaper business will not be surprised to learn that the Gannett Company just won its 40th Pulitzer Prize. The recipient this year is the tiny *Virgin Islands Daily News*, a Gannett paper that was recognized for its public-service journalism.

Fittingly, this award comes to a company that bucked the conventional wisdom that pointed to high-ceiling electronic media as the future of the news business. Instead CEO John Curley decided to keep the bulk of Gannett's money in the newspaper business, which he believes will remain a viable, competitive source of daily information for millions of readers. With 93 daily papers making up an estimated 71 percent of Gannett's profits and 74 percent of its revenues, Curley has wagered that the future lies in newsprint consumers can hold in their hands.

He has also wagered that television will continue to be another important revenue source. To increase Gannett's holdings in both the print and television media, Curley purchased Multimedia Inc. in 1996. This acquisition gives Gannett a total of 15 television stations, cable television franchises serving more than 450 000 subscribers, an around-the-clock cable television news service, and rights to first-run syndicated television programming, including the *Sally Jessy Raphael Show*.

This is not to say that Gannett has completely ignored electronic excursions. On the contrary, Gannett spends about $25 million a year on a few select high-technology projects.

"We may have been criticized for not moving . . . quickly into information vehicles, but we wanted to find the best ones that made the best sense," said Curley. His go-slow attitude won Curley praise after several of Gannett's rivals were forced to pull out of unsuccessful multimedia and electronic ventures they entered too quickly.

Just as Gannett's focus on the old-fashioned media should surprise no one, it should also be no surprise that Curley still uses an old-fashioned IBM Selectric typewriter to communicate to his staff. In fact, he uses it daily to type internal memos to division heads.[9]

Questions and Applications

1. Place yourself in John Curley's position. Under your leadership, Gannett just completed the multimedia purchase. You sit down at your Selectric typewriter to inform your staff of the acquisition. Describe the approach you would take to communicating this good-news message.

2. Now write the memo based on the information you have in this case. Where in the letter would you deal with Gannett's continuing focus on its core newspaper and television businesses? Where would you focus on its online ventures?

Delivering Bad News

Chapter Objectives

After studying this chapter, you should be able to:

1. Explain how to organize bad-news messages.
2. Distinguish between credit refusals to businesses and to individual consumers.
3. Identify the most effective way to refuse a claim.
4. Explain why tact is necessary when declining requests and invitations.
5. Describe circumstances under which bad-news messages are sent to job applicants and why an indirect approach is appropriate.
6. Identify the reasons for conveying unfavourable policies and crisis information.
7. List the special requirements for sending bad-news memos to supervisees, supervisors, and co-workers.

Whenever one has anything unpleasant to say, one should always be quite candid.

Oscar Wilde
Poet, wit, and dramatist

At the Point of No Return

Manufacturers of consumer electronic equipment are mad—and are trying to figure out what to do about it. They are angry with consumers and retailers who return merchandise for no good reason. Here are two examples of what they are dealing with:

▼ A consumer purchases a large-screen television a few days before a Grey Cup party. On the following Monday, he returns the television to the store. With the box in shambles, the retailer then ships it back to the manufacturer as defective merchandise.

▼ After trying for three hours to figure out the instruction book for a new camcorder, a customer throws up her hands in disgust and returns it to the store. Lacking the experience and know-how to help the customer, the salesclerk returns the customer's money and ships the merchandise back to the manufacturer marked defective.

Unjustified returns like these are costing manufacturers millions of dollars a year and are affecting industry profits and viability. At the root of the problem is the money-back guarantee offered by retailers such as Wal-Mart Canada and Kmart Canada Ltd. This policy allows consumers to return merchandise with the *claim* that it is defective and receive a full refund. Retailers then return the merchandise to the manufacturer.

Retailers frequently have to accept the return of goods from their customers. Often these goods bear the CSA (Canadian Standards Association) stamp of approval. Because the Canadian Standards Association is responsible for conducting performance and safety tests on products for sale in Canada, accepting a return on a CSA-approved product can be especially frustrating. However, whether the product is CSA-approved or not, retailers are plagued with questionable returns. For example, why should a customer return a two-year-old cordless phone that clearly has been chewed up by a dog and yet expect a full refund? Or why should a customer return a parka, guaranteed to retain its warmth in arctic temperatures, because the customer determines that, after wearing the parka for a complete winter, the jacket is not warm enough? Why should the retailer accept these goods, and why should the manufacturer have to accept them back? This is why effective retail managers provide their sales representatives with guidelines for handling unhappy customers and for accepting the return of faulty goods their company has sold. ▼

Source: Adapted from Timothy L. O'Brien, "Unjustified Returns Plague Electronics Makers," *Wall Street Journal*, 26 September 1994, B1, B2.

Chapter Overview

It is never easy to tell people something they do not want to hear. In business as well as personal affairs, communicating bad news can create as much discomfort for the writer as for the recipient. Moreover, the stakes are often quite high in business. When business writers bungle bad-news messages, they risk losing the goodwill of valued customers, suppliers, and other business colleagues. Consumer electronics manufacturers understand this as they struggle with ways to stem the tide of unwarranted claims. Although they want to protect their business interests, they also want to ensure that retailers will continue to stock and customers will continue to buy their merchandise.

This chapter will help you communicate bad news effectively by analyzing specific types of bad-news messages: messages involving credit, claims, requests, invitations, and personnel issues. It will also examine methods for communicating negative information, such as price increases, and sending bad news and other negative information in memo form. We begin by focusing on the key to successful communication—the use of a carefully considered organizational plan. We will look at the organization of bad-news messages according to indirect and direct plans, and we will evaluate the importance of tone in maintaining or salvaging goodwill.

Although this chapter illustrates bad-news and negative messages as hard copy letters and memoranda, these and other messages are increasingly sent via e-mail. While electronic media may change the format of the correspondence, the content and writing style of a bad-news or negative message should remain the same. When delivering bad news in person, emotional control may be more difficult to achieve; however, the same rules for effective content in bad-news messages still apply.

Organizing Bad-News Messages _____

In general, a bad-news or negative message can be organized according to either an indirect or a direct organizational plan. The message, the situation, and the relationship between the sender and the receiver determine which organizational plan to use.

USING AN INDIRECT PLAN

Saying no is difficult for many reasons. No one likes to disappoint or anger an associate, for instance, especially when a continuing business relationship is involved. In such a situation, you are faced with a dilemma. On the one hand, you have a good reason for saying no, while on the other, you want to do everything you can to soften the blow.

This dilemma can often be resolved by constructing your message according to an **indirect organizational plan**—a method of organizing documents by delaying bad news rather than announcing it immediately. This plan calls for both an opening paragraph that serves as a buffer and a preliminary explanation before the bad news is announced. It also calls for a closing that tries to maintain or repair goodwill. As you will also see, appropriate language and tone are critical to the success of any bad-news message.

BUFFERS   Imagine having to tell your employees that they will not get a raise this year. Or having to tell customers that their merchandise damage claims are unfounded. Are you likely to blurt out the news immediately on meeting the person? Or will you try to ease the blow with some neutral opening remarks? If you are sensitive to the individual's feelings—and if you recognize the link between personal sensitivity and the success of future business relations—you will begin with a buffer. It makes sense to follow the same approach in written correspondence.

A **buffer** is a protective barrier that helps cushion the shock of bad news. In business correspondence, a buffer generally appears in the first paragraph of a letter or memo. The buffer eases the reader into the bad news, thereby making it less likely that the message will generate a defensive—or possibly angry—reaction. (A

A diplomat is a person who can tell you to go to hell in such a way that you actually look forward to the trip.

Caskie Stinnett
Humorist

word of warning: Although buffers attempt to establish common ground, they should not mislead the reader into thinking that a positive response will follow.)

Among the most frequently used buffers are expressions of appreciation, agreement, and general principle. A chronology of past communications and compliments can also help. Although the temptation to add a sales message may be strong, a buffer is the wrong place to give in to that temptation. Table 9-1 explains the function of each type of buffer and includes examples.

Buffers are often necessary when dealing with customers and job applicants or when writing to someone at a higher organizational level. In such cases, they help to distance the writer from information that cannot always be positive. They are always necessary when politics demands sensitivity to people and situations. For example, if a friend of a senior vice president writes to you for a job, it would be a mistake to turn him down without attempting to soften the blow. Finally, in addition to a conciliatory tone, buffers are especially important when the person to whom you are writing is already angry with you or your company.

DIPLOMACY   When you use a buffer to introduce a bad-news message, you acknowledge the importance of diplomacy in handling difficult situations. **Diplomacy**—the art of handling affairs in a tactful way to avoid arousing hostility—is important in business just as it is in relations among nations. The key to diplomacy is the understanding that people often need help in adjusting to bad or unpleasant information and that being direct in conveying such information may be the worst possible approach.

Words that carry strong negative connotations contradict the purpose of a buffer. You can help your reader adjust to bad news by avoiding unduly negative terms in your opening paragraph. The language in the first few sentences sets the tone for your entire document. Table 9-2 contains examples of negative words,

Table 9-1   Types of Bad-News Buffers

Buffer	Function	Example
Appreciation	Thanks readers for their contributions, thoughts, claims, credit applications, job applications, or inquiries.	Thank you for contacting Maytag about a marketing position. I always appreciate hearing from qualified college graduates who are eager to join our company.
Agreement	Refers to an area of common ground shared by readers and the writer.	Having worked together in the marketing department for five years, we clearly agree on the importance of point-of-purchase advertising.
General principle	Starts with a statement that defines company business practices.	Because you are a regular customer at Barney's, we track your purchases on computer and send notes to inform you of sales items in which you may be interested.
Chronology of past communications	Retraces what has happened to reach this point.	When we spoke on January 2, I agreed to review your credit application in light of the two errors in your credit file.
Compliment	Praises the readers' actions or contributions.	No matter the objective, your efforts have always focused on our goals, and now is no exception. You have given me a thorough, timely proposal.

Table 9-2 Negative Words to Avoid in a Buffer

loss	cannot	nonnegotiable
difficult	never	impossible
forced	unable	unacceptable
emergency	unreasonable	impractical
no	unimportant	unwise
not	unfortunately	unwilling

including words that begin with negative prefixes like "un-," "non-," and "im-." According to business communication authorities Ray E. Barfield and Sylvia S. Titus, these words are "early warning signals [that are] counterproductive to your aim of having the reader take in your whole explanation, not just the opening lines."[1]

THE EXPLANATION   After the buffer, cite your reasons for saying no so that your reader understands your decision. When you begin by presenting these reasons, you set the stage for the announcement of your bad news. You may, for example, explain how time limits, inventory, employment opportunities, or other resources justify what you can or cannot do.

To be effective, use clear language and avoid technical jargon. Choose positive language to describe the reasons for your decision. Avoid sarcasm even if the reader has been an unending source of trouble. Finally, remember that it is petty and short-sighted to try to score points at the expense of your reader. For example, you may be convinced that the reader is completely wrong in making his or her claim, but you should avoid detailing your opinions and stick to the facts.

Direct accusations of any kind are counterproductive. Eliminate expressions like *you claim, your error,* and *you mistakenly did*—that is, phrasing that casts doubt on the reader's actions or motives. In addition, consider using the passive voice or other means of softening the harshness that seems to accompany "personal" criticism. For example, instead of saying:

> Our analysis shows that you chipped your diamond ring, perhaps while gardening or washing pots and pans . . . ,

rephrase your explanation by using the passive voice and nonaccusatory language that removes blame. For example:

> Your diamond has been scratched, perhaps as the result of some accident.

You might further depersonalize your explanation by eliminating the pronouns *you* and *your*:

> Although diamonds are extremely hard stones, they can be scratched, even during everyday wear.

Sometimes one explanation may be all you need to clarify or justify your decision. However, if your explanation has several parts, present each item in the order that you believe is most important to your reader. As a general rule, tell people only what they need to know. For example, it may be sufficient to tell a customer that a part is out of stock but unnecessary to add details about a warehousing problem. In some cases, confidentiality will limit what you say and how you say it. Telling a job applicant why someone was previously fired from the position may breach employer/employee confidentiality, and can create potential legal problems.

Although it is often wise to limit your explanation, it is also a mistake to base

➤ *Cross Reference*
For more on the passive voice, see Chapter 6, pages 168–169.

your explanation on "company policy." As a rule, your reader has a right to know the *particular* reason for your decision, and citing company policy is just not enough.

THE BAD NEWS Communicate the bad news next. Remember that stating bad news is not the same thing as being negative. You are simply telling the reader, for example, about a partial delivery, a credit refusal, or a claim or request that cannot be satisfied. In order to minimize—and possibly eliminate—misunderstandings, it is important to state this news clearly and unequivocally. Depending on the situation, however, the best approach may be to subordinate your bad news to some positive information, perhaps using the passive voice. Although an apology generally weakens a writer's position, it may be necessary to apologize if your company is in the wrong or has made a serious mistake.

More than any other section in your document, your bad-news announcement should avoid negative language and tone, both of which jeopardize goodwill. Readers may perceive words and phrases like *wrong, reject, unqualified, poor credit risk, carelessness*, and *failure to read instructions* as overly harsh. Instead, try such strategies as complex sentences that help to soften the news. For instance:

> Although a hiring freeze is in place for the next six months, I have every hope that after that time we will be able to hire someone with your talents.

Another technique is rephrasing the bad news so that it has a positive dimension. For example, instead of writing:

> Because you clearly damaged the fountain pen, we can only give you a $50 credit toward the purchase of a new pen . . . ,

rephrase the sentence in the following way:

> Because the pen no longer works, we are pleased to give you a $50 credit toward the purchase of a new pen.

In addition, do not make your reader guess what you are saying by burying your bad news in an unlikely place. Even though it is difficult to tell people what they do not want to hear, do not hide your point among generalizations or side issues.

Finally, if possible, try not to end your bad news with a refusal. If there are any alternatives, suggest them here. For example, although it might not be possible to refund someone's money, you may be able to offer a discount or a special service such as free delivery or gift wrapping on a future purchase. "Your reasonable counteroffer," explain Barfield and Titus, "will show . . . that you understand [your reader's] needs and will work within your capacity to meet them."[2] In other words, despite having a legitimate reason for conveying bad news, you are also sending the clear message that you want to help.

THE CLOSING PARAGRAPH   The purpose of the closing paragraph is to refocus on a continuing, positive business relationship. Although it is a mistake to conclude a bad-news message with a sales pitch, you may take the opportunity for promoting goodwill in the business relationship.

First, try to maintain goodwill by not repeating the bad news or referring to it more than once in any way. Avoid words and phrases like *mistake, problem,* or *unfortunate situation,* and do not apologize for having to say no.

In addition, make sure that your close is consistent with the content of your document. For example, it would be a mistake to refuse a request and then close by saying, "Please call me if I can help you in the future." Suggest future contacts only if you are certain you want them. For instance, encouraging job applicants to contact you again may create conditions for further disappointment. Instead, simply reassure applicants that you will keep them in mind if openings arise. Similarly, do not invite readers to tell you what they think of your response. If you close by saying, "Please let me know what you think of this solution," you may be inviting an unpleasant reply.

You may also find it helpful to acknowledge the impact of your bad news by being sympathetic to the reader's situation. You can say, for example, "While you may have hoped for a different decision, I am sure you will do everything you can to continue building the reputation of your department." This approach often requires that you help the reader put bad news in perspective. For example, reminding a client that this is the first delivery problem in a five-year business relationship will help underscore the reliability of your service.

Because an indirect message takes the time to explain bad news in a diplomatic way, it is usually longer than a direct message. Indeed, the more important the message, the longer it may be. For example, if one of your best customers complains about defective merchandise, you may decide that you need a three-page explanation. Although you may not be able to grant a requested adjustment, your explanation can clarify the reasons for your decision. Figure 9-1 presents a sample indirect bad-news letter and identifies each of its major components. In particular, note the comparative amount of space devoted to each section of the letter.

USING A DIRECT PLAN

Bad-news memos can also use a direct organizational plan by starting with a statement of the news. This plan is most often used to communicate bad news to supervisees. Policy memos announcing bad news also use a direct approach. For example, if management is announcing a reduction of vacation time from five to four weeks, the opening paragraph of the memo might state: "Starting May 1, annual vacation time will be reduced from five to four weeks."

Note how the writer avoided naming the manager who decided on the cutback by using the passive voice. Writers can also use the passive voice to soften bad news. For instance, instead of telling a supervisee, "You made a mistake in your budget projections," a manager may indicate the broader implications of the criticism by writing, "A mistake has been made in your budget projections."

BLUE SKY ELECTRONICS, INC.

www.bluesky.com

11 CANADA AVENUE, ST. JOHN'S, NEWFOUNDLAND A1E 1X1

709-555-3333 TEL   709-555-4444 FAX   Kohara@bse.com E-MAIL

October 11, 2000

Ms. Michelle Kwan
99 Cove Road
Fredericton, NB E3B 1X1

Dear Ms. Kwan:

Buffer → Thank you for your request to interview our chief executive officer, Robert Morgan, for your forthcoming book on the country's 50 most successful chief executive officers. We are flattered that you consider Mr. Morgan part of this elite group.

Explanation → In reviewing your interview objectives, I noticed that some of your questions focus on how internal company policy will change due to our just-announced merger with Mitchell Electronics. As I am sure you understand, since the *Bad news* → merger will not be complete for many months, Mr. Morgan's comments would be premature.

Continuation of bad news with suggested alternative → However, Mr. Morgan will be happy to consider your request after the merger is complete. Please write again in six months if you are still interested in the interview.

Goodwill close → Based on your list of other CEOs who have agreed to be interviewed, your book promises to be a great success. I look forward to reading it when it is published.

Sincerely,

Kevin O'Hara

Kevin O'Hara
Corporate Director of Public Affairs

Figure 9-1 Components of an Indirect Bad-News Letter

As we saw in Chapter 6, the passive voice avoids using the personal pronoun *you*. For example, if a manager writes:

> Your plan shows that you have not thought out the consequences of eliminating all regional sales managers . . . ,

she may suggest that the problem exists on some "personal" level between writer and reader. The problem can be more accurately characterized as an organizational issue if the memo reads instead:

> Eliminating all regional sales managers may not prove feasible.

Under certain circumstances, it is also appropriate to use a direct approach with outsiders. For example, if you have a close relationship with a client, you can state directly that a needed part is out of stock. The reader's temperament may also influence your decision. When people want the bottom line in the first sentence, give it to them regardless of whether the news is good or bad. Then there may be times when you want to deliver the bad news in a way that encourages the end of a business relationship. For example, customers who have been an unending source of trouble may no longer be worth keeping. A direct bad-news statement may encourage them to do business elsewhere.

Table 9-3 summarizes the functions and specific uses of the indirect and direct plans for delivering bad-news messages.

Whether you use an indirect or direct organizational plan, read over your completed message several times for content and tone. Make sure that it is both appropriate to the content and sensitive to your reader's feelings. Some bad-news messages—for example, recall form letters—can be composed according to a formula. Because most bad-news messages are written without benefit of a formula, however, writers must decide what to say and how to say it. Naturally, most decisions begin with understanding the type of message to be sent.

Progress Check

1. Describe the parts of an indirect organizational plan.
2. When would you choose to use a direct approach to bad news?
3. Explain why diplomacy is important in bad-news messages and how it influences word choice.

Table 9-3   Using Indirect and Direct Organizational Plans in Bad-News Messages

Type	Function	When Used
Indirect	Communicate bad news to customers, vendors, job applicants, and co-workers by easing the reader into the news with a buffer and an explanation.	Deliver bad-news messages about orders, credit, claims, requests, invitations, and personnel issues.
Direct	Communicate bad news to co-workers and clients when a bottom-line approach is best.	**Internal Uses** ▼ Deliver bad-news policy statements and messages to subordinates. **External Uses** ▼ Deliver bad news to someone the writer knows well. ▼ Deliver bad news to clients and vendors who want every message to start with the bottom line. ▼ Deliver bad news to customers you do not want to keep.

Types of Bad-News Messages

Bad-news business messages fall into five categories. Defined by the subjects that they address, they include messages about credit, claims, requests, invitations, and job applications. All of these messages involve *external communication*—they are messages sent to people outside the organization, such as customers or job applicants. Later we will examine how to communicate bad news within an organization.

WRITING BAD NEWS ABOUT CREDIT

Many business writers believe that letters refusing credit are the most difficult of all bad-news letters to write. In addition to saying no, such letters must also try to encourage the applicant to continue doing business on a cash basis. Methods for accomplishing this twofold task depend both on the applicant's status as a business or individual consumer and on the specific reasons for the refusal.[3]

REFUSING CREDIT TO BUSINESSES When a supplier refuses to extend credit to a business client, the refusal usually results from financial information the client provided to the supplier, rather than what third parties have told the supplier. This distinction is important. Whereas the first situation involves such objective factors as low cash reserves or heavy debt, the second situation often involves a poor track record in paying bills. In addition, a refusal based on the applicant's own information does not question the applicant's character or business skills in the same way as a refusal based on creditors' information.

Most credit refusals to businesses stem from the applicant's own information. With this kind of refusal you can state your case in a straightforward way while still trying to convince the reader to do business on a cash basis. You can offer various incentives, including discounts for cash, the elimination of credit-related interest charges, and making repeated, small cash purchases (which gives the customer access to the most up-to-date merchandise while building a reputation of on-time payment), which may permit you to grant future credit. The applicant, of course, may already be aware of these advantages, but mentioning them in your letter allows you to frame a positive, hopeful response. The letter in Figure 9-2 puts this approach into action by turning a difficult refusal into a business opportunity. Note, too, the tone of the letter—the positive phrasing and the adoption of the "you" attitude.

REFUSING CREDIT TO CONSUMERS Consumer credit is a multibillion-dollar industry in North America. In addition to accepting international charge cards such as Visa, MasterCard, and American Express, retailers may offer customers store credit card accounts. When Eaton's, Sears, or other retailers refuse to issue a credit card, they base their decisions on information from both the applicant and third parties. Credit-refusal letters vary according to the source of negative information.

Refusals Based on Information from Applicants When individuals apply for credit in retail stores, they complete credit applications requesting such information as current income and monthly payments. Just as businesses may deny credit to companies that are overextended, retailers will likely deny credit to individual applicants with shaky financial records. Therefore, when you respond to a consumer who fails to meet minimum credit standards, you can also hold out the hope that the individual's financial situation may change.

In general, follow the pattern that we laid out for the refusal of business credit. Although cash discounts seldom apply to individuals, you can offer other incentives—for example, a layaway plan. While no one enjoys being turned down, your goal is to increase the likelihood that the applicant will become a cash customer.

Refusals Based on Information from Third Parties When a credit bureau or a credit reference provides negative information about an applicant, it means that the applicant has not met certain financial obligations due to late payments or default. In these cases a refusal letter must take a more cautious approach. For instance, if an applicant has a record of numerous unpaid bills, listing those bills will only make the applicant angry and will not benefit your company. Instead, your letter should deal in generalities rather than specifics.

During periods of economic recession or personal financial upheaval caused by unemployment, illness, or divorce, many individuals encounter credit problems.

Yellowknife Medical Laboratory

100 48th Street
Yellowknife, NT X1A 2Z2
www.yellowmedlab.com
(Phone) 867-555-1313
(Fax) 867-555-3131
(E-mail) abbott@yellowmedlab.com

July 14, 2000

Mr. Richard Kryzanowski
Yukon Surgical Supplies, Inc.
200 Range Road
Whitehorse, YT Y1A 3Z3

Dear Mr. Kryzanowski:

Buffer stresses positive credit references → Thank you for your request for credit from Yellowknife Medical Laboratory. According to the three references listed on your credit application, your company has an excellent credit history.

Reason for refusal is explained → Our experience has shown that next to credit references, the most important indicator of creditworthiness is cash on hand. Specifically, it is our experience that a new business like yours needs a six-month cash cushion to cover salary and expenses.

The bad news
Verbs "feel" and "believe" show evaluation is an opinion → Based on your credit application information, we feel that your cash balance is still too low to justify taking the additional monthly payments that are part of an ongoing credit relationship. Although your average cash balance will undoubtedly increase over the next year, we believe it is important to see that cushion in place before we extend credit.

An option with benefits
"You" attitude is strong → With these financial considerations in mind, it makes good business sense to begin our relationship on a cash basis and reevaluate in six months. In the meantime, you will benefit from a 5 percent discount on all your cash purchases. The order form in the enclosed brochure will speed your first purchase. Just fill it out and enclose a cheque. Your order will be on its way.

Optimistic close → In six months, we will reevaluate your application. At that time, I look forward to being able to inform you that your credit has been approved.

Sincerely,

June Abbott

June Abbott
Credit Manager

Enclosure

Figure 9-2 Credit-Refusal Letter to a Business Customer

However, because individual situations often improve, someone who fails to qualify for credit today may be a valued customer tomorrow. Even when denying credit, therefore, treat these potential customers politely and in a businesslike manner. Although you can offer very little in the way of a tangible business relationship, your attitude may sow the seeds for a future business relationship.

REFUSING A CLAIM

Claim refusals often place business writers in the midst of emotionally charged situations. Customers who may have been angry when they first made their claims now learn that they will not get the adjustments they sought. Your biggest challenge is to soften the blow and salvage goodwill.

Self-control is crucial even if you have just received a scathing, accusatory letter; it becomes even harder when the customer is at fault. Correcting the customer

PRACTICAL TIPS

Dousing the Flames

Bad-news and negative messages about company goods and services are sometimes met with angry responses from affected customers. A vocal minority of these customers are expressing their anger online via the Internet, and their voices are affecting how companies are handling bad-news situations. For example, the Intel Corporation fell victim to consumers' electronic fury after it refused to recall its flawed Pentium chip (see Chapter 8). Companies fearing widespread, online critiques are taking steps to douse the criticism, known as *flaming*. If you find yourself on the receiving end of these comments, here are steps you can take to extinguish the flames:

▽ Take immediate action to avoid an escalating online response.

▽ Make sure that everyone at your company is handling the situation in the same way. A one-voice strategy is essential.

▽ Avoid expressing anger online even if you are provoked.

▽ Be reasonable in your response. Assume responsibility for errors your company has made, and do everything you can to correct them quickly.

▽ If your company did nothing wrong and misinformation is the problem, keep repeating the truth in as many places as possible until customers realize that their perception is faulty.

Sources: Helen Roper, "Letters from Cyberhell," *Inc. Technology,* no. 3 (1995): 70; Bart Ziegler and Jared Sandberg, "Online Snits Formenting Public Storms," *Wall Street Journal,* 23 December 1994, B1.

---

may make you feel better for the moment, but you will regret it later. Harsh words guarantee only that your customer is lost forever.

Although there are people who try to cheat businesses with false claims, it is a mistake to approach every claim with the attitude that you are dealing with a cheater. Instead, start with the assumption that the claim resulted either from something that the customer did not understand or from an honest mistake.

Try to communicate sympathy with the customer's request and a desire to be fair. Even when you are forced to say no, customers should believe that they have been treated fairly. And remember that nothing upsets customers more than to be told that a refusal is based on "company policy." Every claimant has a right to know the specific reason for a refusal. These principles are applied in the claim refusal in Figure 9-3, which skillfully subordinates the writer's bad news to her detailed explanation of her company's decision.

REFUSING A REQUEST

Businesspeople often receive letters asking for information they cannot share, favours they cannot grant, or materials they cannot send. These letters require tactful refusals. Your goal is to maintain goodwill while you say no. Refusing the request of an important customer or a business associate with whom you have a close relationship is especially difficult. In any of these cases, it is important to develop a strategy that will accomplish your goal without offending the individual who has made the request.

Be as positive as possible. For example, if two separate items are requested and you can supply only one, say so in your opening paragraph. If you can offer an alternative, suggest it first. Instead of saying, "We cannot send you a tape of the May 6 interview" say, "Although tapes of the May 6 interview are not available, transcripts can be purchased for $6."

Empathy is also critical, especially when the request is important to the reader. As always, expressing genuine sympathy and concern will help maintain goodwill. If

November 1, 2000

Mr. Elliot Scott
11 Ontario Avenue
Sault Ste. Marie, ON P6B 1W1

Dear Mr. Scott:

Buffer refers to earlier letter → Thank you for your October 22 letter. It raised a key issue that deserves a careful and thorough response. Because you describe yourself as committed to purchasing cars built in Canada, I want to do everything I can to keep your commitment strong.

Detailed explanation is objective and well-supported → Your letter noted that the high-gloss finish on your new car has blotches that cannot be washed away. Bart Covington, the service manager at your local dealer, confirmed this. Our researchers tell us that this marring is the result of acid rain. Acid rain is created when factories and power plants spew sulfur dioxide and nitrogen dioxide into the air. When these compounds are in the atmosphere, they turn into sulfuric acid and nitric acid, which fall to the earth as rain or snow. When acid rain hits your car's surface, the sun evaporates the moisture, leaving the acid to mar the finish. The effect is particularly noticeable on cars with dark metallic finishes.

Bad news is coupled with good advice → Although repairing your car is not covered under the warranty, the auto industry offers this advice: wash your car after every rain and keep it garaged, especially during the first six months when the paint is still hardening.

Nice to add this detail → Rest assured that we are doing everything we can to develop tougher clear-coat finishes that are more resistant to the effects of acid rain.

Show commitment to quality → I am glad that your car has met all your other expectations for safety, performance, and comfort. As a company, we are committed to manufacturing the finest automobiles on the road.

Sincerely,

Julia Hagerty

Julia Hagerty
Customer Service Manager

Canadian Automobile, Inc. www.canauto.com
33 Great Lakes Avenue, Windsor, ON N9E 1Z1 Tel - 519-555-1111 Fax - 519-555-2222 E-mail - hagerty@cai.com

Figure 9-3 Sample Claim-Refusal Letter

you need to apologize, do it once and move on. Keep in mind, however, that a reasonable explanation is the most effective apology.

REFUSING AN INVITATION

Invitations are often a formal part of business life. An invitation to speak at a meeting, attend a fund-raising dinner, or write an article for a business publication should be handled like any other important business request. When you must refuse the invitation, employ a tactful strategy. Tact is especially important when the person extending the invitation has a higher position—an important client, for example—or when the invitation puts you in a difficult position. In these situations, an impersonal approach that uses the passive voice to avoid a direct refusal may be the best choice.

Jack Linklater, Warden, Edmonton Institution

Jack Linklater communicates with one of the most problematic sectors of our society. To address this challenge, the team of prison managers at this maximum security penitentiary have built the words "respect, accountability, and cooperation" into the prison's logo. Jack Linklater affirms that team-building and genuine caring for the people in a prison community mitigate the risk of violence.

Although he started out as a registered nurse in Winnipeg, Jack's commitment to human dignity led him down a different path. With both a bachelor's degree and master's degree in social work, he has progressed from parole officer to assistant warden, deputy warden, and finally to the senior position of warden.

Linklater believes that effective communication must be honest and clear, and must include active listening skills. He wants his staff and the inmates to know that he is paying attention to what they have to say. Linklater is often faced with the daunting responsibility of communicating bad-news messages to inmates and their families. "Bad news," he advises, "is best delivered by attempting to focus on the facts of the situation, while keeping your own emotions under control."

Question: What is the most effective method of communication between the warden and the inmates?

Answer: The best way to communicate with an inmate is face-to-face in an environment where both the inmate and the warden are comfortable. Since many incarcerated people are sensitive about communication that takes place between "The

Man" and other inmates, the warden, whenever possible, meets with inmates in the open as a sign that there is nothing to hide.

As a part of successful prison management, I meet regularly with the Inmate Committee, a group of representatives from the inmate population. As well, I communicate individually with many inmates through cell visitations at least once a week. During face-to-face communication, inmates address me in a way that is comfortable for them yet still respectful; "War-

WRITING BAD NEWS TO JOB APPLICANTS

Even experienced businesspeople often have trouble rejecting job applicants. Realizing how difficult it is to find a job and how rejections affect a person's self-confidence, they hesitate to write letters telling applicants that their companies can offer no immediate opportunities. When they finally do write, they often make the mistake of breaking the bad news too quickly, failing to encourage the applicant or soften the rejection.

These letters fail to communicate goodwill—an essential ingredient of most bad-news messages addressed to job applicants. Goodwill is important because the company's ability to attract a continuing supply of qualified job seekers is at stake. If a company gets a reputation as uncaring or overly harsh, the quantity and quality of its applicant pool may be seriously reduced.

den," "Mr. Linklater," or even "Jack" are acceptable.

Question: Does your communication style differ when you communicate with inmates as opposed to the public or federal government representatives?

Answer: No, my communication style doesn't differ. In fact, it's essential that I maintain a consistent style in order to earn people's trust, and to be open and accountable to all. There's no advantage to communicating differently. I don't have a lot of secrets and I'm totally committed to integrity.

Question: As a warden, what circumstances do you encounter that would require you to deliver bad news to your staff, inmates, or their families?

Answer: Life in a maximum security penitentiary is coloured by violence, so sharing bad news is a routine part of my responsibilities. The news may be of a murder, suicide, hostage-taking, assault, or the removal of a prisoner to disassociation. When there's a death or extreme violence, it's not uncommon for prisons to become very quiet, with inmates and staff keeping to themselves.

Question: What role does diplomacy play in communicating bad-news messages?

Answer: Diplomacy is important—but perhaps more important is clarity, so that the receiver understands the facts being communicated.

Question: Are careful language choices critical in bad-news messages? For example, can negative or harsh words have a more potent effect when the message is bad?

Answer: I believe that as a society we do an inadequate job of teaching our children to use language to express themselves. As a result many adults resort to expletives to express their feelings. In the Edmonton Institution bad language is strongly discouraged. I insist that both staff and inmates speak to each other with respect so that our workplace doesn't become mean and unhappy. For example, if this level of respectful language can't be maintained at a meeting, then the meeting is over.

Question: Do you agree with Oscar Wilde that "whenever one has any thing unpleasant to say, one should always be quite candid"?

Answer: Yes, I agree that being candid is the best way to deliver bad news, but you must choose your words carefully, be considerate, and above all, be honest.

Source: Interview with Jack Linklater and Chuck Andrews.

Saying no to job applicants may be necessary when you receive unsolicited résumés, when you decide not to interview an applicant whose résumé you sought, when you must follow up after a disappointing job interview, and when the job has been filled. Figure 9-4 shows how a bad-news letter to a job applicant can still encourage the applicant by pointing to future employment possibilities.

Even when you have either no interest in hiring an applicant or no future employment opportunities to suggest, you can still subordinate your bad news to a positive message of good luck. You can conclude, for example, by saying, "Although the position for which you are applying has been filled, I wish you the best of luck in building a career."

Two additional types of employment-related bad-news messages need a word of warning—letters of reference and termination letters. In short, don't write them if you are at all concerned about legal ramifications. If you cannot write a positive

JUNIORS EVERYWEAR
Youth Sportswear
www.juneverywear.com
100 - 9th Avenue S.E., Calgary, AB T2P 1Z1
TEL (403) 555-0000   FAX (403) 555-1111
E-MAIL mariano@juneverywear.com

March 16, 2000

Mr. Cliff Pendleton
55 Foothills Drive
Calgary, AB T2J 1W1

Dear Mr. Pendleton:

Opening shows goodwill

It was a pleasure talking with you about your background in merchandising. You have impressive experience that is sure to grow in the years ahead.

Explanation first, then the bad news

Pointing to future opportunities softens bad news

The position for which you interviewed was just filled by a member of our own staff. While I am unable to offer you this job, a similar opportunity may be available in the coming months. I hope you will stay in touch so that we can discuss this opening if it arises.

Encouragement and goodwill

As a company, Juniors Everywear prides itself on the talent and motivation of all its employees. We welcome your interest in a career in retailing.

Sincerely,

Betty Mariano

Betty Mariano
Merchandising Manager

Figure 9-4 Sample Bad-News Letter to Job Applicant

letter of reference, exercise one of two options: either provide minimal information in the form of the individual's job title and dates of employment, or don't write anything. Quite simply, the legal environment surrounding reference letters is too delicate for employers and managers to criticize former employees in writing. One executive we know routinely tears up reference requests if he cannot answer positively. If you are called upon to write a letter of termination, follow the guidelines set forth by your company's human-resources or legal departments. Promises in such letters—for example, about the continuation of benefits—may be considered legally binding.

COMMUNICATING UNFAVOURABLE POLICIES AND CRISIS INFORMATION

Negative information consists, in part, of policy and product decisions that specific audiences perceive as unfavourable. Letters are usually sent to inform the specific audience of the decisions. To maintain goodwill, these letters must not only explain changes but also stress the positive things that the company is doing. An example of a negative information letter is shown in Figure 9-5. Although the letter uses a direct approach, it also emphasizes product value and continuing goodwill.

Negative information should face a crisis head-on. Sometimes this means an apology. For example, Steve Case, president of America Online, once offered an online apology to AOL's 600 000 subscribers for serious service delays that had occurred.[4]

A company's effectiveness in responding to a crisis is often measured by the way it communicates negative information. Johnson & Johnson, for instance, received high marks in its handling of the 1983 Tylenol poisoning incident. Intel, on the other hand, suffered a public-relations nightmare after trying to minimize the impact of its flawed Pentium chip.

Progress Check

1. Many business writers feel that messages refusing credit are among the most difficult to write. Why?
2. What can you do to maintain goodwill in various types of bad-news messages?

Group salutation to specific audience

Uses direct approach— bad news and explanation in first sentence

New rates are easy to read

Balances bad news against value of newspaper

Close promotes goodwill, future business

The Kelowna Star

Visit Our Home Page at www.kelstar.com
500 Richter Street, Kelowna, BC V1Y 2Z2
Tel 250-555-5555   **Fax** 250-555-1111   **E-mail** mp@kelstar.com

March 5, 2000

Dear Home Delivery Customer:

Unprecedented price increases in newsprint have shaken the newspaper industry and forced the *Kelowna Star* to raise the price of all home delivery subscriptions, starting August 1. The new weekly rates will be:

7-day delivery	$6.50
Monday–Saturday	$4.50
Monday–Friday	$3.50
Saturday and Sunday	$3.20

Despite this increase, we hope you will agree that the *Star* continues to deliver exceptional value. With our expanded metropolitan section and redesigned business report, we offer complete, accessible new coverage and award-winning regional reporting.

Now more than ever, we value your readership and look forward to bringing you the *Star's* special brand of news coverage.

Sincerely,

Martha Phelps

Martha Phelps
Publisher

Figure 9-5 Sample Negative Information Letter

Writing Bad-News and Negative Memos _____

The organization of bad-news memos, which are used in *internal communication*, depends upon whether the message is being written to supervisees, higher-level management, or co-workers—that is, on whether your communication is downward, upward, or horizontal. Your organizational plan will change according to your need to be sensitive to differences in power and office politics.[5]

SENDING NEGATIVE MESSAGES TO SUPERVISEES

Bad-news memos to supervisees usually communicate the news in a direct way. For example, when John Reed of Citicorp had the unpleasant task of informing 38 000 employees and retirees that the bank had miscalculated the money they had in a Savings Incentive Plan fund, he used a direct approach. "An error was made in the method for computing [Fund H's] unit values," wrote Reed, and this error is "inexcusable."[6]

Although many organizations want their communications to be direct whenever possible, being direct is not the same as being unkind. As in all bad-news messages, criticism should be directed at an act or a product, not a person. Where appropriate, leave the door open for change.

SENDING NEGATIVE MESSAGES TO MANAGERS

By contrast, negative messages intended for readers in positions of greater organizational power usually benefit from an indirect plan. Use a buffer to soften the news and a passive, impersonal, colourless style. If you are asked, for example, to critique a proposal that your manager is about to deliver to an important client, it would be a mistake to make the following statement:

> Your opening is weak. Unless you get the client involved in the first paragraph, you might as well throw the rest of the proposal away.

You should probably phrase your comments like this:

> Although the details in the middle of the document are convincing, a less quantitative approach could be considered in the first paragraph.

Here, the passive voice allows the writer to avoid a direct, negative statement. Similarly, the impersonal style avoids an inappropriate level of familiarity. The opinion is offered without drawing attention to the person offering it.

SENDING NEGATIVE MESSAGES TO CO-WORKERS

When working in teams, co-workers may ask each other for constructive criticism on their work. When you receive a request like this, you take on the role of a superior—at least temporarily. The operative word is *temporarily*. After you give your opinion, you and your co-worker will be equals once more. As a result, even though you may be writing from a superior position, it may be a mistake to be too direct or forceful. It is often wiser to be indirect and diplomatic when conveying negative messages to co-workers. Base your organizational and stylistic decisions on both the situation and the personality of your colleague.

Table 9-4 summarizes the various organizational plans for writing office memos to different audiences. It also gives examples of the circumstances under which each memo might be written.

Progress Check

1. How should a company communicate negative information during a crisis?
2. Discuss how communicating bad news in memo form often differs depending upon whether you are writing to a manager, co-worker, or supervisee.

Table 9-4 Organizing Bad-News Memos

Audience	Organizational Plan	This Message Could Be Sent When . . .
Superiors	Indirect	You cannot meet a deadline.
Supervisees	Direct	You are disappointed with an employee's work.
Co-workers	Sometimes direct, sometimes indirect	A co-worker asks you to critique his or her contribution to a joint project.

COLLABORATIVE COMMUNICATION

A Collaborative Stab at Writing an Artful Bad-News Memo

Many businesspeople believe that a bad-news memo requires a sensitivity to corporate politics, language, and sentence construction. Realizing that memos may succeed only if they take into account the politics of the business, engaging in collaborative role-playing can highlight how difficult it is to write an effective bad-news memo.

H. William Rice at Shorter College divides his classes into three role-playing groups—one group acting as the company president; the second, the administrative vice president; and the third, the manager of day-to-day operations. He gives them the following scenario and lets the groups collaborate on memos and responses.

In an imaginary company, lower-level staff members are commonly asked to work 15–20 minutes late to finish assignments. Although workers comply with the request, they often return late from lunch. The president has to correct this tardiness because of the impending visit of the CEO, who is a stickler for punctuality.

One presidential group in Rice's class devised a memo that focused on the insurance problems created by hourly employees who did not work by the clock. However, with the CEO's visit less than a week away, no one in the vice-presidential group accepted this argument. Furthermore, the vice presidents objected to the memo's insincere language and self-interested tone. Here is a sample:

While many of the workers often work 30 to 40 minutes late at the end of the day without extra pay and without complaining, we as management are placed in a vulnerable position.

This sentence, said the vice presidents, is self-protective as it fails to show real concern for employees. Moreover, the main clause focuses on the vulnerability of company management, with mention of the after-hours work relegated to the sentence's dependent clause. The issue of control is raised in the memo's last paragraph:

Your ideas, your know-how, and your creativity will make the new system a success. You are in control.

This created even stronger objections from the vice presi-

dents, who could hardly ignore the irony. On the one hand, they were being asked to put into effect a policy they did not necessarily support; on the other hand, they were told that they are in control. "Clearly," said Rice, "the presidential group's attempt at creating a 'you attitude' had failed." The vice presidents had such a strong negative reaction to the president's message that they concealed its contents from the day-to-day managers. Instead, they crafted their own memo, suggesting a sign-in, sign-out policy. The memo began with the following buffer.

Are you willing to make a major contribution to keeping Acme Company number one and remaining the leader in the computer industry?

Punctuality, said the vice presidents, is important to company service, and customer service is linked to corporate success. However, they failed to convince the day-to-day managers that their message was correct. The managers argued that because few staff members had direct customer contact, punctuality had little to do with profitability as long as employees worked a full day.

What this exercise accomplishes, says Rice, is a heightened sensitivity to the impact of words—not just their literal meanings—and the effects of sentence structure on communicating bad news. Words used in memos are no longer seen in a vacuum, but in the context of dealing with people in real situations.

Questions for Critical Thinking

1. Why do you think memos are considered politically sensitive documents?

2. In what ways do sentence structure and word choice communicate a political subtext?

3. Given the scenario presented here, write a memo to lower-level staff members that deals with the overtime and tardiness issues in a politically sensitive way and that convinces workers to change their behaviour. Consider other strategies than those presented here.

Source: H. William Rice, "Teaching the Art of the Memo: Politics and Precision," *Business Communication Quarterly* 58:1 (March 1995): 31–34.

What's Ahead

While this chapter focused on writing effective bad-news messages, Chapter 10 will examine the art of writing persuasive messages. Specifically, we will look at the nature of persuasion and how it is used in sales letters. We will also examine the role of persuasion in collecting past-due bills.

STUDENT RESOURCE CENTRE

Summary of Chapter Objectives

1. ***Explain how to organize bad-news messages.***

   Bad-news messages may be organized according to the indirect or direct plan. An indirect organization allows the writer to delay the bad news rather than communicate it immediately. The opening paragraph of the message acts as a buffer that eases the reader into the news. Explanations follow to tell the reader why you must say no. The bad news is communicated next, followed by a closing paragraph that promotes goodwill. The direct plan opens with the bad news and does not attempt to soften it in any way.

2. ***Distinguish between credit refusals to businesses and to individual consumers.***

   Sometimes businesses must refuse to extend credit to other businesses or to individual customers. When a business is involved, the refusal is usually the result of what the applicant has told the creditor about its finances. By contrast, refusals to individual customers often reflect negative information supplied by third parties, such as credit bureaus.

3. ***Identify the most effective way to refuse a claim.***

   The most effective claim refusals avoid emotions while communicating specific reasons for refusing a requested adjustment. The writer's goal is to make customers feel that they have been treated fairly. Citing company policy will probably upset the reader. Every claimant has a right to know the specific reason for a refusal.

4. ***Explain why tact is necessary when declining requests and invitations.***

   Tact is especially necessary when an important customer or business associate is involved. Tact is based on carefully considered strategy. Be positive and, when possible, suggest alternatives. When dealing with someone in a higher position, consider using the passive voice.

5. ***Describe circumstances under which bad-news messages are sent to job applicants and why an indirect approach is appropriate.***

   Businesspeople may have to say no to job applicants when they receive unsolicited résumés, when they decide not to interview an applicant whose résumé they did seek, and when they must follow up after a job interview has failed to produce satisfactory results. Rejection letters should communicate goodwill by using various techniques to ease the blow.

6. ***Identify the reasons for conveying unfavourable policies and crisis information.***

   Companies communicate negative information when they announce "unfavourable" policy changes (such as price increases) to a specific audience. Negative information may also be conveyed during a crisis and may include an apology for mistakes or errors in judgment.

7. ***List the special requirements for sending bad-news memos to supervisees, supervisors, and co-workers.***

   Bad-news memos sent to supervisees usually take a direct, bottom-line approach. By contrast, negative messages intended for readers in positions of greater organizational power generally benefit from an indirect approach. Although you are usually in a superior role when you send messages to co-workers, this role is temporary. Therefore, it is often wise to be indirect and diplomatic rather than direct and forceful.

Review and Discussion Questions

1. Distinguish between the indirect and direct plans for organizing bad-news messages. *(Ch. Obj. 1)*

2. When would you use an indirect approach to present bad news? When would you use a direct approach? *(Ch. Obj. 1)*

3. Distinguish between credit refusals to companies and to individual consumers. Which are easier to write? Why? *(Ch. Obj. 2)*

4. Summarize key guidelines for refusing a customer's claim. *(Ch. Obj. 3)*

5. Why is it so important to be tactful when refusing requests? *(Ch. Obj. 4)*

6. When might you write bad-news messages to job applicants? *(Ch. Obj. 5)*

7. What are the legal issues involved in writing negative reference letters and termination letters? *(Ch. Obj. 5)*

8 When might you write a bad-news message that describes a crisis or an unfavourable policy? *(Ch. Obj. 6)*

9. Summarize the guidelines for conveying bad news to supervisees, supervisors, and co-workers. *(Ch. Obj. 7)*

Application Exercises

1. Cover the right-hand column in Table 9-1. Create your own example for each type of buffer listed. *(Ch. Obj. 1)*

2. The chapter notes that diplomacy is just as important in business as it is in international politics. Do you agree or disagree? Why? Present your point of view in a brief essay and explain why you feel the way you do. *(Ch. Obj. 1, 4, 6)*

3. Which approach would you use—direct or indirect—to convey bad news in each of the following situations? *(Ch. Obj. 1, 2, 5, 7)*

   (a) A supplier with whom you've been working for five years delivers the wrong part.

   (b) You're forced to tell a qualified job applicant that you can't offer him a position due to a hiring freeze.

   (c) As CEO, you decide to send a memo to all employees in which you stress the importance of turning off all copy machines and personal computers before individuals leave each evening.

   (d) You have to turn down a new customer's request for credit because she's been in business for only five months.

4. In an earlier chapter we recommended using the passive voice only sparingly. In this chapter, why do we suggest that it can be both appropriate and effective? *(Ch. Obj. 1)*

5. Ralph Martin orders a Snug-n-Elegant stove, model 2511-S from your company, Tickemeyer Stove Inc. The price is $1500. He asks if he can open a charge account with your company and pay for the stove on credit. Tickemeyer does offer credit to qualified customers, but when Martin's credit application is processed, you learn from the Equifax Credit Bureau that he has a poor credit rating. Apparently he has several outstanding student loans that he hasn't repaid. Now you face the task of refusing credit to Martin while persuading him to go ahead and buy the stove. Tickemeyer has a layaway plan that would allow Martin to make monthly payments toward any purchase. Write this letter to Martin. *(Ch. Obj. 2)*

6. Martin settles for the layaway plan and finally takes delivery of his new stove after six months. However, three months after it's installed, he calls you, angrily claiming that his stove "isn't working right." It seems that waxy deposits are building up on the inside of the stove and coating the inside of the glass door. Martin also claims that the stove isn't putting out as much heat as it did when it was new. In talking with him, you discover that he routinely starts fires in the stove by using a fire-starter log made of pressed-wood by-products and other flammable substances. You recognize the problem. Because they contain waxes and resins that coat interior walls and clog heating vents, fire-starter logs should not be burned in your stoves. When the stove was delivered, Martin also received a brochure that contained instructions and warned users that fire-starter logs would damage their stoves. Martin claims, nonetheless, that the company owes him a new stove. Write him a letter in which you explain the situation and refuse this request. *(Ch. Obj. 3)*

7. Pretty Penny Corporation offers a budget plan to its cellular phone customers. They pay 10 cents

per minute for phone use during peak hours and 1 cent per minute during off-peak hours. Peak hours begin at 7 A.M. and end at 8 P.M., Monday through Friday. Pretty Penny has signed up numerous customers under this plan. After six months, management has reviewed the bills and made a discovery. Many customers are using their phones between 8 P.M. and 9 P.M., when it's not too late to call people but late enough to avoid peak-hour rates. CEO Joe Penny decides to institute a new policy. From now on, off-peak time will begin at 9 P.M. rather than 8 P.M. Because he doesn't like to write bad-news letters, Penny delegates the task to his customer service manager. Write this letter to Penny's customers informing them of the company's new policy. *(Ch. Obj. 1, 6)*

8. The *Globe and Mail* has asked you to write an article on business communications for an upcoming issue. You would love to, of course, but unfortunately you're extremely busy preparing for an international conference in Geneva. Even more important, you have to study for a test that's coming up in your business communications class. Write a letter in which you refuse the *Globe*'s request while explaining that you remain quite interested in writing this piece or another one at some later date. *(Ch. Obj. 4)*

9. As the human resources manager of your company, you've interviewed two applicants for the same position. It's a difficult decision because you were impressed by both candidates. You decide to offer the job to Alicia because her work experience more clearly matches the requirements of the job. However, you want to send a tactful letter to the other applicant, Mohamed. While Mohamed didn't have quite the right experience for this job, you were impressed with his energy and motivation. There are no other openings at the company right now, but you may want to hire him for another position in the future. Write a letter explaining to Mohamed that he didn't get the job. *(Ch. Obj. 5)*

10. The Pacific Research Company has been located in Vancouver since the firm was founded 25 years ago. Most of its employees are Vancouver natives with relatives living nearby. Thus, the company's CEO knew that it would be a big change for employees when he decided to relocate Pacific Research to Saskatoon. Business costs are lower in Saskatoon, as is the cost of living. The CEO suspects that employees will be pleasantly surprised at housing prices in Saskatoon after living in Vancouver. These are selling points that may help reassure employees about moving. Even though Pacific is relocating, it is not planning to lay off anybody—everyone who wants to move will have a job. The CEO asks you to write a memo to all employees that announces the relocation in as positive a manner as possible. *(Ch. Obj. 6, 7)*

ACT: Applied Communication Techniques

Begin by referring to the sections up to and including Punctuation, Period, Question Mark, and Exclamation Mark in Appendix II, then correct the grammar, spelling, and usage errors in the following sentences. Check your answers in Appendix V.

1. The manager asked why the bad news had to be shared with the employees

2. Will the bad news message destroy our employee moral

3. The mayor of Kelowna found it helpful to acknowlege the impact of his bad news message by being sympathetic

4. Stop wasting time now

5. Naturally, most decisions begin with understanding the type of mesage to be sent

6. A small company in Yellowknife could not fill the order immediately

7. Be careful of the falling ice

8. A scarborough supplier refused to extend credit to a business client

9. Why did the fredericton consummer apply for credit in the retale store

10. Would you please draft the bad new memo before noon today

Building Your Business Notebook

Carefully read the following letters and assess their communication effectiveness. Next, revise and improve the letters by applying what you've learned in this chapter.

```
I don't know why so many people think you're a reputable tour
company.  I am appalled at the horrible conditions you expect
your customers to endure.  Not only did I have a terrible
experience on your tour but your customer service
representative refused to refund my money.

I had to wait in hot, humid weather 15 minutes to even get on
the bus, and once I was on it, I wished I had never agreed to
go on the tour.  The seats were too hard and too small.  At
times the bus was hot and then it was cold.  The floors were
dirty and the seats were ripped.

Not only was the bus in terrible condition but when I tried to
express my opinion to the bus driver, he told me that if I
didn't like it, I could get off the bus right there.

You can be certain I will never sign up for another tour from
your company, and I'll make certain none of my friends or co-
workers do either.  I expect a full refund by the end of the
month.
```

Document 1

```
We are sorry to inform you that you will not be able to
receive a replacement for the blouse that shrank when you
washed it.  The instructions clearly state that the garment is
not to be washed.

Our advertisements indicated that the blouse had to be dry-
cleaned, the tag attached to it said the same thing, and the
label also gave the cleaning instructions.  You will agree, I
am certain, that we have done our part in trying to keep you
from ruining the garment by washing it.  If you order anything
else from our company, please be certain to read the
directions carefully so that you won't do it wrong again.

Again, we are sorry that we cannot grant you a replacement.
```

Document 2

Building Your Research Skills

Go to a library and find an article describing a situation in which a business had to give bad news to somebody. This situation could cover a wide range of activities—laying off employees, relocating corporate headquarters, explaining a bad year to the board of directors, dealing with an environmental disaster, and so on. Bring the article (or a photocopy) to class. Be prepared to discuss it.

Building Your Teamwork Skills

Your instructor will divide the class into small groups. Each member of the group should get a chance to present his or her article from the previous Building Your Research Skills exercise and to answer questions about it. Working as a group, create a memo that effectively presents the bad news each company had to convey. Which situations call for a direct approach? Which call for an indirect approach? Can you think of something positive to say in each memo to help buffer the news? Have a volunteer in each group write down each memo as you compose it.

Your instructor may wish to have you read your memos to the class and explain the situations involved.

Building Your Technology Skills

Work in small groups. As most companies are now connected to the Internet, e-mail is rapidly becoming the preferred way to communicate. Begin by discussing the ramifications of using e-mail versus surface mail for bad-news and negative messages. Will messages be perceived differently if sent by e-mail compared to surface mail? When would e-mail be appropriate? Inappropriate? Would your choice for the use of e-mail to communicate bad news be different when writing to a manager, co-worker, or supervisee?

Next, each group member—acting as a business manager—should select one topic from the following list and write a bad-news e-mail message to employees:

▼ the company no longer can provide financial support for a holiday party

▼ an employee's vacation request is denied

▼ a warranty replacement part for a computer is back-ordered for one month

▼ an employee's e-mail message to his work team was inappropriate

Have the group respond to each message, focusing on the organizational plan, tone, language, and sentence structure. How would each message change if it were converted to a business letter?

Weblinks Internet Resources for this Chapter

Designing Bad News Letters
**http://www.wuacc.edu/services/zzcwwctr/
badnews_menu.html**

Writing Claim/Complaint Letters
**http://www.wuacc.edu/services/zzcwwctr/
complaint-intro.txt**

Disappointing-News Letters and Memos
http://www.bus.okstate.edu/quible/jberry.htm

Improving Your Interpersonal Skills: How To Handle Difficult People
http://www.smartbiz.com/sbs/arts/bly59.htm

Business Correspondence—Complaint and Adjustment Letters
**http://www.io.com/~hcexres/tcm1603/acchtml/
complnt.html**

CASE STUDIES

CORPORATE CASE:
Crisis Management at BFGoodrich

Companies in the midst of a public-relations crisis communicate in a variety of ways. Some cover up the facts. Others stall in the hope that the problem will disappear. Still others hide behind their lawyers, claiming that anything they say might lead to litigation. A select few volunteer to tell the truth.

John D. Ong faced these alternatives when he was CEO of BFGoodrich, a specialty chemical and aerospace equipment manufacturer. The crisis involved a health risk from polyvinyl chloride and came to the company's attention after several workers developed a rare form of liver cancer in 1974. At that time, no one knew the connection between exposure to this chemical and human cancer, so the course of action was far from clear. Nineteen years later, Ong explains what happened in 1974, why BFGoodrich decided to tell the truth, and the implications of the decision:

> We told the world—and we did it quickly, without hesitation. We immediately released all available information to the appropriate federal and state health agencies. We told our employees. We contacted local and national news media—and our customers and competitors. . . .
>
> Over the next several years, we continued to communicate regularly on this subject with employees, people in our plant communities, government officials, and customers. . . . In December 1975 we held a major news conference. . . . We unveiled the new technology that we had developed to reduce residual vinyl chloride in our vinyl products and reduce signif-

icantly worker exposure to vinyl chloride. . . .

> We took a great deal of criticism at the time—not for *how* we were communicating the bad news, but for the news itself. However, I could not begin to describe just how negative the reaction would have been if we had not been proactive in our communication of this issue. In fact, I'm convinced that the vinyl industry would not exist today in this country if we had tried to keep this quiet. Or, if we did survive, our credibility would be so low that simply doing business would be almost impossible.

Although ethical communication rarely has such dramatic consequences, the behaviour of BFGoodrich applies to all companies trying to chart a course in the middle of a crisis. In the end, being truthful, open, and accessible are the best and only choices.[7]

Questions and Applications

1. If bad news inevitably generates criticism, why is it important to face the criticism right away? What would the reasons be, if any, for keeping the information quiet? Are they ethical?
2. Assume it is 1974. Write a brief memo to BFGoodrich employees about the health-risk findings.
3. Now write a report to the government health-care agencies stating your findings. How does your memo to employees differ from the report to the health agencies?

CORPORATE CASE:
Morgan Stanley—Deciding When to Invest in Bad News

In this chapter we've talked about the problems that both individuals and companies face in communicating bad news. Investment bank Morgan Stanley seems to have a different problem: it didn't communicate bad news often enough.

Like all investment firms, Morgan has two branches, each with its own goal. One branch competes with other banks to sell stocks for corporate clients; a highly competitive field in which firms do their best to encourage demand for those stocks among investors. The other branch provides research and advises investors on which stocks to buy and sell.

Lately, some Morgan employees claim that these two lines of business have come to constitute a conflict of interest. After all, how can you sell stocks if your own analysts are ad-

vising investors not to buy? "We sit on opposite sides of the table, like a law firm representing both sides of a divorce," admits a former Morgan chemical-industry analyst. "When corporate finance and research clash, it's a real problem."

Several Morgan analysts claim that Morgan bankers have pressured them to change negative research reports on the stocks of Morgan clients. To encourage its analysts to cooperate with its bankers, Morgan management recommended that a bigger part of analysts' pay be tied to how much they contributed to investment-banking transactions. Morgan analysts did not appreciate the pressure. "We were held accountable to corporate finance—playing the game the way corporate finance dictated," complains a former food-retailing analyst. "We shouldn't have been put through the wringer to do our job professionally."

Consider the internal war fought by Morgan over Safeway. When the supermarket chain went public, Morgan won the chance to sell some of its stock. Its corporate-finance group, headed by Robert Matschullat, recommended that Safeway price its stock between $19 and $22 a share. But Morgan analyst Stacy Dutton felt the stock was actually worth only $10 to $13 a share—almost 50 percent less. Thus, while one branch at Morgan was trying to sell Safeway stock at $19 to $22, one of the firm's analysts was advising clients that it was overpriced.

Dutton arranged a meeting with Matschullat to discuss the disagreement. When she began, says Dutton, Matschullat reminded her that her pay would be tied to her help with investment-banking deals. Dutton says she was stunned: "I was coming to him with a strictly objective quantifiable issue, and he wasn't interested at all in the substance of my work. He wasn't interested in debating the merits of one valuation versus another. He was strictly interested if I was going to help him get the deal done."

Other analysts agree with Dutton's story. A few years ago, Morgan Stanley was trying to win part of Occidental Petroleum's stock-underwriting business. When one Morgan analyst concluded that Occidental's stock was overpriced, angry Occidental execs complained to Morgan. The bank quickly removed the offending analyst from the account. When another analyst wasn't sufficiently optimistic about a client's prospects, Morgan shifted him to another division.

Morgan Chairman Richard Fisher feels that his firm knows how to handle a common industry-wide problem: "I guarantee you the tension between investment bankers and research exists at every firm," he argues, "but Morgan Stanley deals with it as well as anyone."[8]

Questions and Applications

1. What situation produces the "tension" between investment bankers and research analysts at Morgan Stanley?

2. Summarize the ethical dilemma faced by Morgan Stanley and its staff.

3. Chairman Richard Fisher asks you to draft a memo to Morgan's staff in which you present the bad news that there are conflicts between the company's two branches. Your main point, he stipulates, should state that the firm's research has not been compromised and that these conflicts have been isolated incidents and are not company-wide. Write this memo.

10

Writing Persuasive Messages

After studying this chapter, you should be able to:

1. Explain the concept of persuasion and the four persuasive goals.
2. Identify and contrast the three major persuasive appeals.
3. Identify and describe the three types of sales letters.
4. Apply the AIDA concept to the organization of a sales letter.
5. List the four types of collection letters and explain the purpose of each.
6. Explain when to use a direct approach in persuasive memos and when to be indirect.

A good business letter can sell your product, get you off the hook, or get you money.

Malcolm Forbes
Publisher

The Success of a Homegrown Letter

For charitable organizations, raising money is big business that often depends on the success or failure of a direct-mail persuasive appeal. However, crafting a successful appeal letter is not easy—and making it work in the marketplace is even harder—due to staggering competition. Nearly 12 billion pieces of third-class not-for-profit bulk mail are delivered each year, and many contain appeals for money.

Share Our Strength (SOS), an anti-hunger organization, understood the difficulty in crafting an effective fund-raising letter when it decided to begin raising money via direct mail. Although about 80 percent of SOS's support comes from corporate sponsorships, the restaurant industry, and special events, the organization wanted to diversify its funding base by attracting more individual donors.

To maximize its chance of success, SOS asked a direct-mail advertising agency to write two different letters, scheduled for delivery prior to Christmas 1994, to learn which was more effective. If either letter drew a 1-percent response rate and an average gift of $25, SOS would use it as the basis of an ongoing fund-raising campaign.

The first letter featured the photo of a smiling child, Anita. Anita's "beautiful smile represents a major breakthrough in the fight to end hunger in America," said the letter. The attention grabber on the envelope was "Photo Enclosed—Do Not Bend." The second letter focused on children in need of a good breakfast. The linchpin for the appeal was the story of Danny, a 12-year-old suicide victim, whose final note explained that his family would now have "one less mouth to feed."

Share Our Strength mailed 75 000 copies of each test letter, for a total development, production, and mailing cost of $50 000. Although the organization's goal was to produce a membership roster of 300 000 names and annual direct-mail income of about $3 million, the results were disappointing. Neither letter achieved the minimum 1-percent response rate SOS had hoped for.

SOS then returned to a fund-raising method that had proven successful in the past. This effort involved tapping SOS's existing donor base. During the 1995 Christmas season, William H. Shore, SOS's executive director, sent a letter to 870 past donors who were personally and professionally involved with the organization. The body of this letter is excerpted on the following pages. Through this letter SOS received 51 contributions (a nearly 6-percent response rate) totalling $28 755. With an average gift of $564, Shore's appeal was a tremendous fund-raising success.

Why did Shore's fund-raising letter succeed and the others fail? Jennifer LaConti White, SOS's corporate sponsorship director, attributes the difference, in part, to the genuineness of Shore's letter and to the fact that it was written by a person who lived and breathed the organization and who was able to communicate his commitment to others. She also attributes it to the quality of Shore's writing, which touches the heart and makes people want to take action. ▼

Sources: Pamela Sebastian, "Charity Tries Two Letters to Melt Cold Hearts," *Wall Street Journal*, 22 November 1994, B1, B4; Interview with Jennifer LaConti White, Share Our Strength, February 14, 1996; Excerpts of William Shore's letter used with permission of Share Our Strength.

Dear Friend:

The best way to thank you for being such a great friend of Share Our Strength is to take you along with me when I see or learn something I know you'd want me to share.

So consider this your trip to The Door, a community center in Baltimore. The after-school classroom for first, second, and third graders is scattered with books, learning tools, and inspirational statements posted on the walls, like "I can be whatever I dream I can be." It looks like my children's suburban classrooms in every way but one. A notice at the entrance to the room is quite different from anything my own Zach and Mollie know. It says: **"If I see a gun or anything that looks like a gun I will not touch it. I will go and get an adult. Because guns can hurt me. And I want to be safe."**

I try to imagine what it feels like to a parent to drop off a child at a place where such a sign is necessary. I ask The Door's president, Joe Ehrman, a former all-star linebacker for the Baltimore Colts who turned to the ministry after his football career, what the neighborhood is like. . . . Joe and I talk about how at this age these kids we're watching at play are nothing but sweet, yet ten years from now, some of the same kids will be bitter, violent, in trouble with drugs, gangs, teen pregnancy. Some are going to slip between the cracks and out of reach.

It seems impossible, looking at their five-year old smiles and innocence, to believe this will happen right before our eyes. Or that we will let it happen. But statistics, experience, and inadequate resources assure us it will. That's the part that always gets me, that really makes me stop and think, whenever I'm with a group of children too young to be anything but happy, unsuspecting of the overwhelming odds they face in single-parent families, below the poverty line, with drugs and guns just steps away on the other side of their playground. What will we allow to happen to them between the ages of five and fifteen? Botanists watch plants grow using time-lapse photography. They can see when and how a plant bends toward the light. They can isolate the moment. But when is the moment a growing child bends toward darkness? And why must we wait to watch it on the 11:00 news?

. . . . What most kids need in their lives, especially kids who are poor and hungry, at-risk or in trouble, what they need more than anything else, more than money, even more than food, is someone to put arms around them, hold on, and not let go. The neighborhood anti-hunger and anti-poverty organizations we're supporting in your own backyard have their arms around kids who are poor, hungry, and at risk. Our commitment to them, and to you, is that we won't let go. Not now. Not a year from now. Not one moment before they are safe, and in a position to support and protect themselves. . . .

Obviously we've got a long road ahead. Stick with us. Come with me. Use your year-end contribution to Share Our Strength to help get our arms around the kids that need us. Don't let go.

Thanks.

Sincerely,

Bill Shore

Bill Shore

Chapter Overview

As the centre of Share Our Strength's appeal for charitable contributions, William H. Shore's letter is a model of effective persuasion. It uses elements common to many persuasive messages: emotional appeals that focus on what the reader can do, a story that motivates the reader, positive rather than negative language, and a call to action.

SOS's letters set the stage for the topic of this chapter—writing persuasive business messages. Many persuasive business messages, including sales letters and collection letters, are aimed at customers and other "public" recipients; others try to convince colleagues to take action. We begin by defining persuasion in terms of specific goals and purposes. We then examine the nature of persuasive appeals in more detail before applying some key principles to sales letters, collection letters, and persuasive memos.

Writers use many formats for persuasive messages. The head of a construction firm may write a letter to a potential client who plans to build a neighbourhood shopping centre in a local suburb. This letter would be a piece of one-to-one correspondence. In other cases the persuasive message may be communicated in a mass mailing. With each of its letters addressed to "Dear Friend," Share Our Strength's direct-mail project is an example of this approach. Finally, persuasive messages may involve mass mailings in which each letter is personalized by using a word processing program to insert recipients' names and individualize messages.

Although this chapter illustrates persuasive messages as hard copy letters and memoranda, an increasing amount of correspondence is sent as e-mail. While electronic media may change the format of the correspondence, the content and writing style of persuasive messages should remain the same.

What Is Persuasion?

Each month our mailboxes seem to contain a growing number of persuasive messages. A political candidate wanting our vote, a not-for-profit organization requesting donations, a business firm trying to market its goods or services, a co-worker who wants a proposal approved—all these are examples of the many types of persuasive messages. **Persuasion** is the process of influencing or changing attitudes, beliefs, values, or behaviours. It is, for instance, a key element in sales contacts that try to convince prospects to purchase company products. Persuasion is also crucial in collecting past-due accounts from customers who have failed to pay outstanding debts. Finally, as businesspeople make recommendations and requests that either support, modify, or reject current activities, their use of persuasion motivates people to change.

We start by describing the broad goals of persuasive messages, and then discuss more specific purposes of such messages.

PERSUASIVE GOALS

Every persuasive message has one of four broad goals: adoption, continuance, discontinuance, and deterrence. The first step in composing a persuasive message is to define what you want your reader to do in terms of one of these four basic goals. You are then in a better position to clarify the specific purpose of your document.

ADOPTION **Messages of adoption** try to persuade readers to start doing something. Adoption is the essence of most sales letters. For example, American Express sends letters to prospective cardholders urging them to apply for various cards. The Hudson's Bay Company sends storewide sales invitations to customers on its mailing lists.

CONTINUANCE **Messages of continuance** urge the continuation of a behaviour. Continuance is the basis for selling any ongoing service. For instance, *Canadian Business* magazine sends letters to current subscribers trying to convince them to renew subscriptions. Near the end of service periods, professionals ranging from consultants to exterminators send letters encouraging customers to renew contracts.

Because both businesses and not-for-profit organizations know the importance of loyal subscribers, customers, and donors, they work doubly hard to retain them.

Messages of continuance are thus sent frequently and in large numbers. Senders face the challenge of making sure their messages break through the "noise" levels created by competing messages of continuance.

DISCONTINUANCE   Collection letters frequently use persuasive messages to encourage credit customers to make payment on delinquent accounts. In effect, they are asking customers to stop avoiding payment. Messages that ask for such behaviour changes are referred to as **messages of discontinuance.** Discontinuance is a common theme in office memos that try to persuade colleagues to cease a given activity—say, to stop using e-mail for personal reasons.

Messages of discontinuance are also used in persuasive letters—for instance, when a competitor successfully attracts another firm's customers, the firm may try to win them back. For example, in the midst of the long-distance telephone wars involving AT&T Canada LDS, Sprint Canada, and Stentor, former customers were offered a special bonus if they returned to their original long-distance provider.

DETERRENCE   **Messages of deterrence** try to prevent an action from taking place. They might be used, for example, when important clients consider moving their accounts to a different company. A deterrence letter might be written to convince the clients that the move is a mistake.

SPECIFIC PURPOSE

Once you have determined the broad goal of your message, you can then define the specific purposes that will accomplish your overall objective. As you recall from Chapter 4, a statement of specific purpose is most effective when it specifies a goal in a way that appeals to a clearly defined audience. In other words, you are more likely to accomplish your goal if you know your audience and can visualize it before you begin writing. Direct-mail marketer Daniel S. Kennedy uses his own writing experience to explain why it is important to address the priorities of the reader rather than those of the writer:

→ *Cross Reference*
We discussed specific purpose in Chapter 4, pages 108–110.

> I was asked to write a corporate fund-raising letter for [an] Arthritis Foundation's annual telethon [. . .] In examining samples of letters other not-for-profit organizations sent to corporate donors, I noticed that they all had this failing in common: they talked at great length about their own priorities—what they needed the money for, how it would be used, how funds were low, etc.—but they hardly addressed the donor's priorities at all. So I visualized myself as the business owner or executive being banged at by all these worthy charities' pleas and asked myself, "If I were to give, what would be important to me?" I came up with this list:
>
>   1.   What benefit to me or my company justifies the cost?
>
>   2.   Who else had picked this drive to contribute to? How can I validate my judgment?
>
>   3.   How would I get the money to give? What budget would it come out of? What other expense would have to be reduced to afford this new one?
>
> With this in mind, I wrote the letter.[1]

Knowing your reader, then, is the key to focusing a broad persuasive goal on a specific persuasive purpose. Although your persuasive purpose must be kept in mind (say, marketing a product or collecting a debt), your document will be effective if you frame the purpose from the perspective of the reader and in terms that the reader will appreciate.

Your purpose in writing a sales letter, for example, is not to tell readers about a wonderful product, but rather to persuade them that the product will help them in specific ways. The purpose of a collection letter is not to express anger at the customer's nonpayment, but rather to persuade the credit purchaser to send money. The purpose of a memo urging the adoption of a proposal is to show how your recommendations will benefit the other people in the company who will be responding to the proposal—how they will improve the efficiency of a department, simplify a task, increase sales, or reduce costs. In each case you should be answering the question that is uppermost in the reader's mind: "How will this help me?"

As we suggested in Chapter 6, the most powerful persuasive word in the English language is *you*. This word underscores the benefits of a message to the individual recipient in the most direct, personal way, as illustrated by Figure 10-1.

➡ **Cross Reference**
We discussed the "you" attitude in Chapter 6, pages 175–177.

Persuasive Appeals

Effectively used, persuasive techniques work on three levels at once. Persuasive messages appeal to the reader's sense of reasoning, establish the credibility of the document, and evoke an emotional response from the reader.

PERSUADING WITH REASONING

Persuasive documents try to convince readers to accept a particular point of view through the logical presentation of evidence. They thus involve the act of **reasoning**—using available evidence to reach a conclusion.

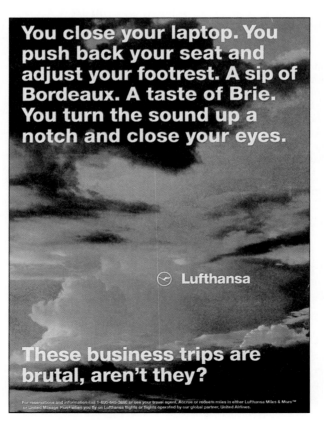

Figure 10-1 A Persuasive Ad That Uses the "You" Attitude

Reasoning involves presenting different forms of "evidence"—nonnumerical facts, statistics, examples and anecdotes, expert opinion, and analogies—that have a direct bearing on the document's specific persuasive purpose. As we saw in Chapter 5, for instance, the use of logical organizational patterns, such as chronological, cause-and-effect, or problem-solution, improves the chances that the reader will accept a document's point of view. Organizational patterns are persuasive, in other words, because they show how a point of view lends itself to logical development.

→ **Cross Reference**
We discussed organizational patterns in Chapter 5, pages 130–140.

To decide which logical pattern will be most effective for a given document, identify and then try to answer questions that the reader is likely to raise. For example, someone who is reading a sales letter for a European tour will probably want to know exactly where the tour will go and when. If you were a travel agent composing such a sales letter, you might use a chronological approach to describe the trip's itinerary.

PERSUADING WITH CREDIBILITY

The ability to persuade is directly affected by the credibility of the document. As we saw in Chapter 1, **credibility** is the degree to which a statement, a person, or a company is perceived to be ethical, believable, trustworthy, competent, responsible, and sincere. Three types of credibility influence whether messages succeed or fail: (1) *initial credibility*—what the reader already knows—is particularly important in sales letters; (2) *derived credibility*—credibility created during the message—is influenced by the logic of the presentation, the strength of the evidence, the emotional appeal, and even the way the information is arranged on the page; and (3) *terminal credibility*—credibility created when readers evaluate the writer, company, and product after reading the message—is the sum total of all previous reactions.

ENHANCING CREDIBILITY WITHIN A DOCUMENT   Although you cannot control exactly how others perceive a message, you can use various techniques to influence how people perceive the document that you write. For example, the language that you choose for the headline and body of your message can be a powerful persuasive tool.

Don't forget that [your good or service] is not differentiated until the customer understands the difference.

Tom Peters
Business writer

You enhance credibility when your document focuses on benefits to the reader instead of dwelling on features of the product, proposal, or idea. For instance, if you are trying to convince your manager to support your recommendations to restructure the department's computerized data system, you are more likely to gain that support by focusing on how the system benefits your manager, not how it will benefit you. A key point in your document might be, "With this change, the department will be able to retrieve information at twice the speed and half the cost."

Although the same document may include brief descriptions of the new system's features, your emphasis should be on the way these features will help the reader solve a problem. Table 10–1 distinguishes the features themselves from their benefits to the reader.

Table 10-1   How Features Differ from Benefits

System Features	Benefits to the Reader
Memory: 64 megabyte RAM	Large memory allows you to run the latest, most sophisticated software.
Internal fax modem	There is no need to buy a separate fax machine, because one is already part of your computer. The high-speed modem also provides online access.
CD-ROM	A library of information and entertainment is now at your fingertips via high-technology laser disks.

Finally, you can increase your credibility through **testimonials**—words of praise for a firm, its products, or its ideas from someone whose name or reputation the reader respects. Many sales letters begin with testimonials intended to establish immediate credibility. An example of a testimonial lead-in paragraph follows:

> Peggy Carpenter, human resources manager at MMM International, is a satisfied customer of BusinessTemps and endorses our service. In her words, "Thanks to the services of BusinessTemps employment agency, we were able to replace absent secretaries on a moment's notice with qualified temporary help."

PERSUADING WITH EMOTION

In many situations emotions are the most powerful persuasive factor. Where logical arguments sometimes fail, emotions often have the power to motivate people to respond and act. Understanding which emotions to tap and which to avoid is one of the most important tasks of a persuasive writer.

→ *Cross Reference*
We discussed motivational analysis in Chapter 4, pages 107–110.

One way to determine the most effective emotional appeal is to analyze readers according to their motivational needs. For example, if *security needs* are most important to your reader, your message should be phrased quite differently than if a person's *social needs*, such as the need to belong, are a top priority. Michael Renz, a Mercedes-Benz salesman in Stuttgart, Germany, questions customers about the features they want in a car and focuses on their underlying needs. When a customer talks about image, Renz focuses on the Mercedes's alloy wheels and state-of-the art metallic paint, both of which enhance esteem needs. When a customer talks about safety, he highlights the car's safety features and the wisdom of choosing a light colour and links both to security needs.[2]

Reader analysis also involves using language that is likely to evoke the responses you seek. Because words like *free*, *new*, *announcing*, and *special* tend to be power words, they are frequently used to enhance persuasiveness. Concrete examples also add emotional power to a message.

Progress Check

1. Define the persuasive goals of adoption, continuance, discontinuance, and deterrence, and provide examples of each.
2. What is the relationship between persuasive reasoning and derived credibility?
3. Why are emotional appeals considered the most powerful of all persuasive appeals?

Emotional appeals can focus on multiple emotions—hope, pleasure, pride, honour, courage, respect, and responsibility—at the same time. For example, in a memo that suggests merging two departments and eliminating 15 jobs, a writer may focus on both the courage that it takes to make such a difficult decision and the responsibility to act in the company's best interests.

In some cases emotional appeals try to arouse negative feelings, like fear or anxiety. An exterminating service, for instance, may highlight how damaging carpenter ants can be to a house and recommend that homeowners invest in prevention rather than repairs. Many last-resort collection letters try to heighten the debtor's fears of legal action.

The following section shows how persuasion can be used to create more effective sales letters. Basically, every persuasive message is a sales presentation—an attempt to sell an idea, a good, or a service to individuals who may not recognize its value.

Sales Letters

The current cost of an average face-to-face industrial sales call is $224; the average consumer-goods sales call now costs $196, the average service-industry sales call $165. Not surprisingly, therefore, an increasing number of businesses are turning to **sales letters** as a relatively inexpensive alternative for both locating prospective accounts and increasing sales to current customers.[3]

A QUESTION OF ETHICS

Logical Fallacies: Illegitimate Persuasion

You can try too hard to be persuasive. The desire to make a sale, collect a bad debt, or convince a manager to take action has led more than one writer down the path of the *logical fallacy*—a flaw in reasoning that can have the effect of manipulating the reader's response. Logical fallacies include *post hoc, ergo propter hoc; red herrings; bandwagoning; card stacking;* and *citing false or irrelevant authorities.*

The Latin phrase *post hoc, ergo propter hoc* means "after this, therefore on account of this." This reasoning technique links a cause to an effect when one may not exist. Suppose, for instance, that a sales letter states: "After the installation of a new inventory system, our sales doubled." In fact, the new inventory system may or may not have been a factor in doubling sales. Other factors (an improving economy, new product introductions, price changes) might have contributed to the sales increase.

A *red herring* diverts attention from an important issue by introducing largely (and even totally) unrelated points. The red herring distracts the reader, usually from an issue or problem. For example, Kellogg promotes its cornflakes with the one-liner "Taste them again for the first time." Although this approach is not necessarily dishonest, it doesn't address the issue of cost or nutritional benefits, which are often the most important concerns of adult consumers.

Writers who use *bandwagoning* urge readers to agree with their position because everyone else does. The implication is that the approval of others, rather than the merits of the argument, should be enough to earn the reader's agreement.

In *card stacking* writers fail to deal with conflicting facts that may contradict their position. For example, if a production as-

sistant is trying to persuade a manager to choose a new supplier on the basis of its excellent service, failing to mention the supplier's high prices would be considered card stacking.

When you cite the opinions of people who have no expertise in a field, you are *citing false or irrelevant authorities.* While it is legitimate for basketball superstar Michael Jordan to be cited as an authority on athletic shoes, his opinion is less credible in the field of computers.

Fallacies that create doubts can cause readers to question the integrity of an entire presentation, and can weaken an argument that might have won the day on its own merits.

Questions for Critical Thinking

1. Why are logical fallacies such an important ethical issue in persuasive documents?
2. Are logical fallacies acceptable if the reader is not aware they are being used?
3. Create specific examples of how each of these fallacies could be used in sales and collection letters.
4. How would you respond if you received a persuasive memo that employed logical fallacies?

Sources: Logical fallacies are discussed in Lynn Quitman Troyka, *Simon & Schuster Handbook for Writers,* 2d ed. (Englewood Cliffs, N.J.: Prentice Hall, 1990), 153–156; Jo Sprague and Douglas Stuart, *The Speaker's Handbook,* 2d ed. (San Diego: Harcourt Brace Jovanovich, 1988), 325; Roy W. Poe, *The McGraw-Hill Guide to Effective Business Reports* (New York: McGraw-Hill, 1982), 49–50.

TYPES OF SALES LETTERS

Sales letters are directed at both individuals and business accounts, including manufacturers, retailers, and wholesalers, as well as government agencies and other not-for-profit organizations. Today, sales letters are increasing in popularity as businesspeople apply them in three distinct ways: as direct-mail messages, as retail-sales announcements, and as inquiry solicitations. We will describe each of these functions and then examine more closely some general strategies for creating these types of letters.

DIRECT-MAIL MESSAGES   On any given day, both businesspeople and consumers receive mail promoting goods, services, and causes ranging from office computer systems to appeals to help save the rain forest. Mail-order retailers now produce 14 billion pieces of mail a year.

Direct-mail sales letters allow businesses to send personalized letters to groups specially selected from mailing lists of target-market customers. Mailings may vary in format and level of detail. Direct mail also offers the advantages of selectivity and speed. For example, direct mailers can select recipients by several methods, including segmentation by postal code, occupation, or past purchases.

The direct-mail letter tries to complete a sale without benefit of either a follow-up sales presentation or a viewing of the product. The customer is urged to make a purchase based only on the sales letter and the product's credibility.

RETAIL-SALES ANNOUNCEMENTS Retailers commonly use sales letters to announce such events as specialized sales. A department store, for instance, may use a sales letter to alert customers to price reductions on mattresses. Retail-sales letters are designed to answer the key questions that customers will have about an event in advance. They may explain when and why a sale is being held, what items are on sale, and prices.

INQUIRY SOLICITATIONS Almost everyone has seen a letter or postcard announcing that "You are a winner"—a common *attention* grabber. To claim prizes, however, readers must fill out and return prepaid responses or call telephone numbers to set up appointments for sales presentations about joining organizations or purchasing products. By opening with the offer of a prize, the writer ensures the reader's *interest*. The reader is then contacted again by phone, in person, or by additional letters in an effort to turn interest into *desire* by pointing out special features or benefits. Then, to increase the possibility of customer *action*, the salesperson may offer a coupon or discount certificate.

When we turn to the discussion of organizing sales letters, we will examine in greater detail the fundamental goal of the typical sales letter: namely, to move the reader through the four steps of *a*ttention, *i*nterest, *d*esire, and *a*ction—the **AIDA concept**—and then to close the sale. Here, however, remember that such goals are unrealistic when selling highly complex products—for example, new communications equipment—whose purchases are frequently made after months of careful evaluation. In such cases writers try to narrow their objectives by attempting to generate inquiries from their readers. Representatives of the sender will then follow up by phone, in face-to-face meetings, or through additional letters.

The nature of the follow-up—whether a personal sales call or allowing the letter to stand on its own—is often determined by the amount of detail in the original sales letter. Because a large percentage of direct mail is allowed to stand on its own, much of it requires a great deal of detail. By contrast, a letter soliciting inquiries to set the stage for a face-to-face sales call will be much less detailed.

DEVELOPING A SALES LETTER STRATEGY

Although sales letters are used often, their success remains mixed because so many people consider them "junk mail." In fact, a 1-percent response rate is often considered a success. To increase the chances of making a sale, then, it is critical to capture and hold your reader's attention. Begin by defining your purpose. Careful planning is the basis of a successful sales strategy. Before writing the first draft of a sales letter, clearly specify what you seek to accomplish in terms of your sales goals, your audience, and your product.

SALES GOALS The first step in preparing a sales letter is to define its purpose. Are you trying to make a sale, encourage an inquiry, prompt a store visit, or promote goodwill? Once you clarify your purpose, you might record it as a purpose statement. For example, the purpose of a sales letter from Merrill Lynch announcing a new municipal-bond offering might be to produce customer inquiries. In their follow-up to an inquiry, account executives can supply detailed information, including a printed prospectus. Before organizing a sales letter, however, you must focus on both your audience and your product.

AUDIENCE Sales letters are mailed to individuals and organizations with shared characteristics. When the people to whom you are writing share common traits, you can personalize your message and increase the likelihood that they will respond. In most instances the first people who receive sales letters are the firm's regular customers, who continue to represent good sales prospects.

PRODUCT All successful sales strategies depend on a thorough knowledge of the product and, more importantly, on understanding why people are likely to buy it. Because benefits create a product-customer connection, it is critical to stress benefits over features.

Organizing a Sales Letter

For most consumers, purchasing a good or service is a process of problem solving. First, the customer focuses attention on a product because of its ability to solve a problem. The customer then becomes interested in the proposed solution and then desires to apply the solution. Finally, the consumer takes action by purchasing the product or subscribing to the service. The four steps that an individual takes before making a purchase decision were referred to earlier as the AIDA concept.

A successful sales letter must take a prospective customer through each of these four steps. First it must gain the *attention* of the reader, and then it must arouse *interest*. Next, the letter should try to stimulate *desire* by convincing the reader to accept an idea or to purchase a good or service. Finally, it should convince the reader to take *action*, usually in the form of a purchase. An indirect approach to these objectives is typically the most effective.

GAINING ATTENTION

Many persuasive documents are unsolicited. They have never been requested and may even be considered nuisances by those who receive them. Knowing that a potential customer is not eager to receive your message means that the opening of your message is crucial. You must find a way to capture and hold **attention** so that your recipient will continue to read your letter.

There are a number of ways to gain readers' attention. You can use startling headlines, ask questions, provide testimonials from credible sources, relate striking incidents or statistics, make readers feel unique or special, and identify needs. In each case your goal is the same—to gain and hold interest in your message so that readers want to learn more. Table 10-2 gives examples of each of these techniques.

Because headlines are such an important part of the typical sales letter, we begin by examining their different uses. We also look at the important connection between headlines and opening paragraphs.

CREATING EFFECTIVE HEADLINES Many successful sales letters use eye-catching headlines that elicit immediate responses. Direct-marketing expert Daniel S. Kennedy explains why:

> What your headline says and how it says it are absolutely critical. You might compare it to a door-to-door salesperson wedging a foot in the door, buying just enough time to deliver one or two sentences that will melt resistance, create interest, and elevate his status from annoying pest to welcome guest. You've got just about the same length of time, the same opportunity.[4]

Table 10-2   Techniques for Gaining Attention in Sales Letters

Technique	Example
Using provocative headlines	You will never miss an important call again!
Asking questions	When is the last time someone offered you a deal you couldn't refuse?
Providing testimonials from credible sources	"Matthew would not have been conceived without the laser surgery I received at Foothills Hospital in Calgary," said May Fenton as she cradled her six-month-old son in her arms. Nearly two years ago, Mrs. Fenton was treated at Foothills Hospital for endometriosis—a condition that prevents thousands of women from having children.
Beginning the letter with a startling incident or statistic	We are defoliating our planet Earth. Each year another 1000 plants become extinct.
Making the reader feel unique or special	Managing your personal finances wisely has its own rewards. You've been pre-approved for a Gold Card.
Identifying a need	With the ebbs and flows of business, you need a weekly publication that will help you navigate the choppy seas.

Headlines may be placed either above the salutation or between the salutation and the middle of the letter. They are often set apart visually by italic or boldface type or by a larger type size. It may also be helpful to categorize headlines according to how they attempt to gain the reader's attention. Four such categories, plus an example of each, are listed in Table 10-3.

CREATING AN OPENING PARAGRAPH   Naturally, an effective headline should encourage the reader to examine the letter's opening paragraph. The best opening paragraphs focus on both the sales purpose and the reader's interests. For example:

The time to stop burglars from robbing you blind is before they get into your home.

Or:

Being a salesperson means you're rarely at your desk to answer important phone calls. The best solution—a full-time administrative assistant—is too costly. Other solutions, like answering machines and voice mail, turn many calls into hang-ups.

THERE IS AN ALTERNATIVE.

Table 10-3   Strategies for Effective Headlines

Headline	Example	Why Is It Effective?
"How to . . ."	How to Live Like a King without Going into Debt	Uses two powerful words in a headline.
"Are you . . ."	Are You Caught in a Dead-End Job?	The question challenges the reader and provokes interest.
"If you are . . . you can . . ."	If You Are 50 or Over, You Can Join CARP	The statement targets a specific reader.
"Warning!"	Warning! Without Estate Planning, Dying Can Be Hazardous to Your Wealth	The announcement focuses on a problem and its solution.

Source: Adapted from Daniel S. Kennedy, *The Ultimate Sales Letter* (Holbrook, Mass.: Bob Adams, Inc., 1990), 57–62.

CREATING INTEREST

Capturing attention is not necessarily the same thing as creating interest. **Interest** implies that the message has tapped a need in the reader—for example, a need to solve a problem or satisfy a desire. Interest is created in two basic ways: by presenting claims that emphasize benefits over features and by making emotional as well as logical appeals. Figure 10-2 shows an example of an appeal to emotion and logic.

Because people tend to scan information in letters and advertisements, maintaining interest is more difficult than attracting attention. Presenting all the benefits of your idea, good, or service increases the likelihood of appealing to a larger audience. For instance, some people like to eat health foods for taste, while others eat such foods because they help minimize health risks. To interest the largest audience possible, it is important to provide both pleasurable and logical reasons for purchasing a good or service.

TRANSLATING INTEREST INTO DESIRE

While interest is largely an intellectual response, **desire** is basically an emotional reaction that propels people to action. Desire and motivation are closely connected. For example, once we make the decision that we want a new drill press to improve factory efficiency (the desire stage), we are often motivated to make the purchase (the action stage).

Although motivation varies from person to person, the satisfaction of basic human needs can trigger responses. For example, sales letters are likely to use one or more of the 25 reasons for spending money listed in Table 10-4 to encourage readers to make purchases. Note how many of these reasons correspond to motivational needs, such as curiosity and safety. Similarly, collection letters focus on delinquent creditors' desire to protect their reputation, avoid trouble, act responsibly, and avoid legal expenses. Persuasive memos may tap into both personal and professional desires—for example, desire for business success, cost reduction, or the ability to simplify a task.

Figure 10-2 An Appeal to Emotion and Logic
This ad appeals to the reader's logic by stressing high worker productivity and low construction costs. It also makes an emotional appeal to those who want access to many golf courses in beautiful settings.

Table 10-4   Why People Spend Money

To make money	To gratify curiosity
To save money	To protect family
To save time	To be in style
To avoid effort	For beautiful possessions
For comfort	To satisfy appetite
For cleanliness	To emulate others
For health	For safety in buying
To escape physical pain	To avoid criticism
For praise	To be individual
To be popular	To protect reputation
To attract the opposite sex	To take advantage of opportunities
To conserve possessions	To avoid trouble
For enjoyment	

Source: Direct Mail Advertising Association.

Last year our customers bought over one million quarter-inch drill bits and none of them wanted to buy the product. They all wanted quarter-inch holes.

Anonymous

To move readers from the interest to the desire stage, the persuasive letter writer must present specific facts. During the attention and interest stages, claims are generally sufficient to capture your readers' attention. To reach the desire stage, however, claims must be supported with facts and statistics organized in a logical, easy-to-understand presentation.

The strategy for many successful sales letters is based on *market research*—a specialized field that attempts to predict purchase behaviour. If your product is an office-cleaning service, market research may tell you that focusing on the need for the service may be the wrong approach—most businesspeople already agree that a clean office is important. You may also learn that a more effective approach is to stress reliability, price, and job responsibility. Offering subscribers a money-back guarantee, then, may produce better results. If market research is unavailable, you can create a "test" by mailing several versions of a letter to identify the version that generates the best response. As you recall from our opening vignette, that is exactly what Share Our Strength did when it tested two direct-mail fund-raising letters.

ENCOURAGING THE READER TO TAKE ACTION

The **action** stage is the most critical step in all sales letters. Readers must be convinced not only to take specific steps to purchase the product but to act quickly. Experienced sales professionals realize that unless most readers respond immediately, they are unlikely to respond at all. Among the many techniques for producing action, we will focus on three of the most common and effective: identifying the specific action you want the reader to take; offering special terms and inducements; and making it easy to respond.

IDENTIFYING SPECIFIC ACTION   It is important to give readers clear purchase instructions. Often the instructions are commands or action statements. To illustrate, a typical sales letter might tell the reader: "To take advantage of this special offer, call NOW!"

What to Say When Your Competitors Have Better Prices

When your company offers a better price than its competitors, you'll probably want to herald the price in a headline and emphasize it in your sales letter. But what do you do when other companies offer the same price or, worse yet, a better deal? The following tips can help you emphasize competitive advantages other than price:

▼ *Focus on the value of the product.* Let's say that your product is reproduction antique furniture that sells at about the same price as that of several competitors. Featuring the price in sales letters offers little advantage. The customer is more likely to respond if you point out that your $150 chair, unlike your competitors, is virtually indistinguishable from an actual antique chair costing $1500.

▼ *Sell bulk.* You can make items seem more substantial by describing them in terms of their component parts. This technique encourages people to focus on product features and benefits that they

might otherwise overlook. For example, if you are selling a reference book, list the number of topics covered, the number of illustrations, and even the number of words.

▼ *Focus on the development costs.* If appropriate, talk about how much time and money your company spent perfecting your product before bringing it to market. Such information makes the selling price understandable and helps people appreciate the item's real value.

When people believe that they are receiving fair value, they are more likely to respond positively to your sales letter. Language can remind people of value—and even create it—through the use of phrases like *special offer, unique opportunity, sensational savings,* and *a small investment for a lifetime of security.*

Source: Techniques suggested by Daniel S. Kennedy, *The Ultimate Sales Letter* (Holbrook, Mass.: Adams Media Corporation, 1990), 66–80.

USING INDUCEMENTS **Inducements** are gifts or other considerations that encourage readers to take immediate action. Inducements are considered positive when they give readers something they want; negative when readers must take action to avoid unpleasant consequences. For example, while premiums, sweepstakes, contests, and discounts are all positive inducements, deadlines and the threat of limited availability ("This offer ends Saturday, and will not be repeated") represent negative inducements. Depending upon your design and strategy, you can announce inducements at the end of your letter or organize the entire letter around inducements as your major theme.

> *The real issue is value, not price.*
>
> Robert T. Lindgren
> Cross & Trecker Corporation

Positive Inducements   One common form of positive inducement is the offer of *discounts* to readers who take immediate action. Besides offering a better price value, discounts encourage readers to respond quickly. Subscriptions and new products are often promoted this way.

Items given free or at reduced cost with the purchase of another product are known as *premiums*. They typically have some relationship with the purchased item. For example, cosmetic companies frequently offer other items from their own product lines as premiums for "any $25 purchase." A car wash might offer an air freshener with a full-service wash, and many magazine and journal subscriptions offer books as premiums for subscribing. To attract customers and introduce new goods and services, many organizations sponsor *sweepstakes* and *contests*. These inducements entice people to respond immediately by offering a chance to win something of value.

Progress Check

1. Why is the AIDA organizational model necessary in a sales letter but not in other types of business letters?
2. What is the role of headlines and opening paragraphs in gaining the reader's attention?
3. Describe the interrelationship among the interest, desire, and action stages of a sales letter.

Negative Inducements   Two common negative inducements are deadlines and limited availability. The use of deadlines is effective in reminding readers that they have "a limited time only" to act. Deadlines are particularly effective when combined with other strategies such as premiums. Some products—say, rare Roman coins or time-share condominiums—lend themselves to limited-availability offers. The reminder that a product is available only in limited numbers also serves as a powerful inducement for prompt action.

AIDING READER RESPONSE   The typical sales letter is just one part of the persuasive message. Most sales letters include pre-addressed postage-paid response cards, order forms, and envelopes requiring readers to take one or more of the following actions: mail cheques; list credit card names, numbers, and expiration dates; or simply check appropriate response boxes, sign, and return. Many sales letters also rely on toll-free telephone numbers that readers can call at any time for immediate service. Obviously, these enclosures and instructions are designed to make it as easy as possible for customers to respond. The letter in Figure 10-3 applies the AIDA concept to a sample sales letter. Notice how all the elements—attention, interest, desire, and action—are designed to encourage a prompt and positive response.

Sales letters, of course, are not the only type of persuasive letter used in business communication. For example, when payment from a credit purchaser has not been received on time, the creditor will make persuasive requests for payment in the form of collection letters. Claims and requests for adjustments to an account are also persuasive letters written by the customer rather than the company.

Collection Letters

Because a sale is not complete unless money has been collected, many companies create their own debt-collection programs to ensure that they will be repaid in full for all credit sales. In general, companies refer past-due accounts to commercial collection agencies only as a last resort. They adhere to this policy for two reasons. They wish to maintain goodwill, and they receive only a fraction of any funds recovered by collection agencies. In fact, after uncollected debts and agency fees are deducted, a company can expect to receive only 12 cents of every dollar owed.[5]

Nevertheless, many companies are heavily involved in credit sales, and many have learned to handle the collection process. Success stories abound. For example, Albany Ladder, a $23-million construction equipment and supply firm, issues credit to home-improvement contractors and tradespeople with no proven credit history, yet is forced to write off an amazingly small 1 percent of sales as bad debts.[6]

Basically, **collection letters** have a dual purpose. They try to persuade debtors to pay the money they owe and encourage continued business. The firm granting credit tries to persuade debtors that if they pay, the firm will work with them. The typical writer of collection letters starts with the assumption that most credit purchasers want to repay their debts and that, with a little time, the firm will be able to collect all or most of what it is owed.

We begin by examining the important question of tone in collection letters and then describe the letters in the collection series.

IMPORTANCE OF TONE
The successful writer of collection letters focuses on three adjectives. Letters should be *persuasive* rather than threatening, *constructive* rather than accusatory, *empathetic* rather than cold. Jim Ullery, customer financial services manager at Albany Ladder,

August 18, 2000

Mr. Robert Deal
Director of Purchasing
Southern Saskatchewan Meat Market
P.O. Box 5000
Regina, SK S4X 1X1

TRY TO RIP APART THE ENCLOSED PLASTIC BAG AND THINK ABOUT YOUR
PACKAGING PROBLEMS.

Dear Mr. Deal:

Go ahead! Try to rip it apart. Give it a good tug and notice
how it's made for rough-and-tumble treatment. The people at
Country Folks Meat are so enthusiastic about our packaging
that they just tripled their monthly order.

WE CAN CREATE A PACKAGE FOR YOU THAT MEETS YOUR NEEDS
PRECISELY.

No matter what products you package, if they are not packaged
properly, you're not going to get the steady increase in sales
you want. Not only must packaging be sturdy, it must attract
the customer's eye, too. The enclosed sample does both.

Take a look at your current packaging. Isn't it time to
explore ways to increase your share of the market through
better packaging? A unique, custom-made package could be the
answer to production and sales problems. Find out how by
asking for our new booklet, "Today's Packaging Solutions."
It's FREE. Simply phone 1-800-123-4567.

Sincerely,

Alice Zeller

Alice Zeller
President

Enclosure

Headline captures attention by posing a personal challenge and relating it to business needs

The first sentence continues to grab the reader's attention. Testimonial enhances product credibility

Promises to satisfy the reader's packaging needs

Interest is turned into desire with focus on increased customer appeal and sturdiness

Closing moves from desire to action by offering free material and a toll-free number

Figure 10–3 Sample Sales Letter Applying the AIDA Concept

Source: *Luther A. Brock*, Sales Lead-Getting Model Letter Book *(Englewood Cliffs, N.J.: Prentice Hall)*, 39.

is convinced that empathy is critical. "Collectors fail to remember that when we make the decision to give customers money, we're buying into it. We really become a co-signer. So now my role in collection is to help."[7] In part, this helping attitude is based on the assumption that many delinquent bill payers are good customers with temporary financial trouble.[8]

A helping attitude, then, is in the creditor's best interest. If you are able to maintain the customer's goodwill during the collection process, you increase the likelihood that you will collect an outstanding debt. This is especially true because debtors tend to pay creditors they like the most. Moreover, you will be working to satisfy your secondary goal—to encourage future business—should the customer's financial situation improve.

You convey a helping attitude through a positive, respectful tone that avoids anger, bullying, sarcasm, or threats. Word choice is critical. Negative words and phrases send a message that the problem cannot be resolved. Words like *irresponsible,*

Guylaine Demers, Consultant and Trainer

With over 17 years of experience in business and training, Guylaine Demers brings a wealth of knowledge to East Coast industry. As a bilingual honours graduate in English and Education, Demers' experience as an instructor at the New Brunswick Community College and as a call-centre consultant positions her well in the telemarketing phenomenon that is sweeping Canada.

From Demers' perspective, persuasion is the process of changing someone's opinion of a product or service. Whether the product is as intangible as a concept or as tangible as an automobile, the fundamentals of persuasion remain the same. "At times, persuasion may be seen as manipulative—but when practised with honesty and integrity, both the sender and receiver of the persuasive message can benefit."

She believes that results can easily be achieved through persuasion, but in order to be successful you must provide a product to suit the consumer's most valued needs.

Question: Given that every persuasive message has one of four broad goals: to adopt an activity, to continue an activity, to discontinue an activity, or to deter an activity, which of these do you employ in your business and how?

Answer: In our business, which is predominantly the sale of new products and services, our primary task is to persuade the potential customer to adopt these. In some cases this involves persuading the customer to continue or discontinue a current activity. So it can be a mix.

Question: How important is it to know the characteristics of the customer when applying persuasion?

Answer: In order to obtain a commitment through persuasion you need to determine the correct approach to use. Ideally, this is achieved by understanding the characteristics of your potential customer. These characteristics include such things as values, needs, and constraints. Not until you understand the customer in this way do you have a real opportunity to obtain commitment.

Question: How do you ensure that honesty and integrity remain an implicit part of your persuasion?

---

embarrassment, and *dishonourable* have a place only in so-called last-resort collection letters.

When the collection appeal is linked to the possibility of future purchases by the delinquent credit customer, the need for a positive, helpful tone becomes especially clear. Consider the following example:

Dear Mr. Dean:

With an unpaid balance of $1879.33, you may be reluctant to order additional merchandise from us even though your business depends on it. This situation harms both of us; we cannot sell to you and you cannot sell to others.

It is in both our interests to resolve this situation. Please mail your cheque in the enclosed postage-paid envelope by June 5 so that you can begin ordering again. We will expedite your first order so that you receive it within days.

The tone you adopt in a collection letter depends on many factors, including the length of time the account has been delinquent; the number of letters that have

Answer: We ensure honesty and integrity among our employees through training and identifying with company values. There is a common understanding that if we respect our customers and provide them with a beneficial product, the customer will trust us with this, and with future business.

Question: Knowing that many of your potential customers are not eager to receive your persuasive message, how do you capture and hold their attention?

Answer: We practise empathy at every opportunity. We put ourselves in the customer's place. We understand they are busy, so we acknowledge the situation; we set a time frame—and respect it. If our persuasion skills are good, even a few minutes can capture their attention and may make a significant difference to them. But those first few minutes of the discussion are critical; they will determine a successful outcome or a loss. As well, we come prepared by knowing both our product and our market. Our skill at linking product knowledge and product application, combined with empathy, will hold the attention of potential customers.

Question: Once you have captured the attention of the potential customer, how do you encourage him or her to take action?

Answer: Once our product has been associated with the customer's need, we use a more specific statement. We say something like, "It might seem costly at first, but remember that within a year you'll benefit, not only in direct savings but in time saved, which will allow you to concentrate on more urgent matters."

Question: In your professional opinion, what are the most critical errors made by developers of persuasive messages?

Answer: There are two critical errors that plague the persuasive message. First, persuaders tend to use an insistent tone. To insist is a big mistake! Readers of, or listeners to, your message may initially concede to your persuasion in order to avoid your perceived demands, but shortly after agreeing they'll reverse their decision. Agreements made under these circumstances are not the way that organizations like to achieve long-term success; they want customer commitments that will endure. The second critical error is dishonest persuasion. Honesty in product delivery is a positive investment in the results of your efforts. So, by being less insistent and less demanding in our persuasion, we develop an enduring customer base and a healthy organization.

Source: Interview with Guylaine Demers.

already been sent; the perception of the debtor as a good, fair, or poor credit risk; the individual's or company's business dealings; and the general state of the economy. For instance, if a debtor is considered a good credit risk, the collection letter will be less aggressive than if the debtor is perceived as a poor risk.

As we will see in the next section, no one letter applies to all credit-collection situations. On the contrary, firms that rely heavily on credit sales realize that they need a series of letters to handle different delinquency situations.

COLLECTION SERIES LETTERS

The letters in the **collection series** can be categorized according to the four types of persuasive appeals used to collect outstanding debts: reminder letters, inquiry letters, aggressive collection notices, and last-resort letters that threaten legal action. Every letter in the collection series should state three pieces of information: the amount owed, the length of time the bill has been overdue, and the specific action the customer should take to remedy the situation.

REMINDER LETTERS The collection process begins automatically in the case of bank card holders, retail credit card holders, and others who are expected to pay suppliers of goods and services. If no payment is received following an end-of-month billing, the next month's billing typically includes a reminder of the unpaid bill and a late-payment fee. Such late-payment fees have been agreed to in writing by both parties, either at the time of card issuance or at the beginning of the relationship between the client and vendor-supplier.

Other agreements involve ongoing contact between seller and credit purchaser. Many of the agreements assume a continuing business relationship. In such a case, the collection process usually begins on a much more informal note. The initial contact typically begins when a bill is more than a month overdue. After sending out a monthly statement informing the customer of the outstanding debt, most companies wait a few weeks for a reply. If none comes, a second statement is sent, perhaps marked "Past Due," or a short **reminder letter** is included with the statement to inform the customer that payment has not been received. Seldom is there a direct request for money—usually just a reminder that the account is overdue.

Although many companies use form letters for their reminders and other early collection letters, most personalize the letters by including the customer's name and the specific amount owed. Write to the name of the person who appears on the bill. At Albany Ladder, Jim Ullery makes a practice of always writing to the company owner or CEO: "It's his cash, it's his reputation and, more often than not with us, it's his personal guarantee. I want it clear I'm talking to *him*."[9]

INQUIRY LETTERS If the combination of statement and gentle reminder doesn't work, the next step is to determine what is preventing the customer from making the required payment. Your tone in the **inquiry letter** should be friendly and conciliatory as you question the customer about whether he or she has forgotten to pay or whether you can help in any way. For example, you might offer to work out a new payment plan. Above all, communicate the message that you are certain the customer intends to pay and stress future business. A sample collection inquiry letter is shown in Figure 10-4.

AGGRESSIVE COLLECTION NOTICES The next letter in the collection process, the **aggressive collection notice,** is firmer and more insistent than the inquiry letter. Starting with the assumption that your method of persuasion must be stronger than in your previous communications, try the following appeals to find one that works:

▼ *Fairness.* An appeal to fairness emphasizes that the customer is already using your company's goods and services and that it is only fair that you receive payment in return.

▼ *Sympathy.* When you appeal to sympathy, you make the point that payment is crucial to your own operations and that late payments put you, the creditor, in a difficult position. This approach is intended to place the customer in the position of helping the supplier who was willing to extend credit.

▼ *Self-interest.* This appeal emphasizes the consequences of continued nonpayment. Future credit problems are mentioned as the writer threatens to notify the delinquent customer's credit bureau and thus jeopardize other lines of credit.

The letter in Figure 10-5 appeals to both self-interest and sympathy.

LAST-RESORT LETTERS If your aggressive collection notice does not produce a telephone call, letter, or cheque from your delinquent accounts, you must assume

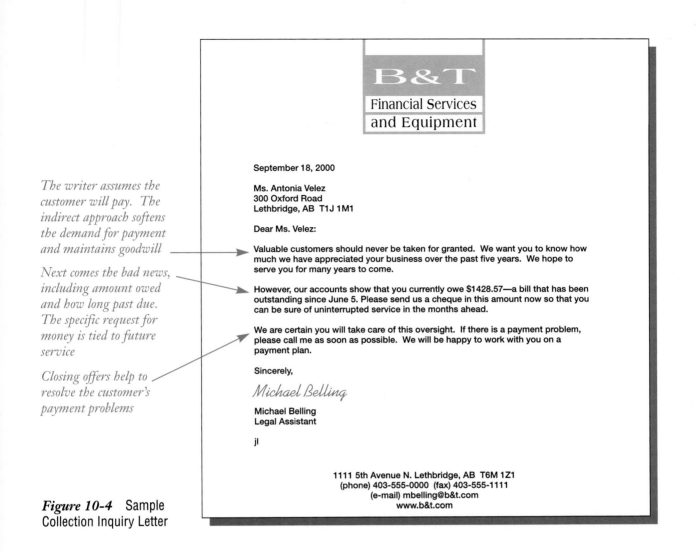

The writer assumes the customer will pay. The indirect approach softens the demand for payment and maintains goodwill

Next comes the bad news, including amount owed and how long past due. The specific request for money is tied to future service

Closing offers help to resolve the customer's payment problems

B&T

Financial Services and Equipment

September 18, 2000

Ms. Antonia Velez
300 Oxford Road
Lethbridge, AB T1J 1M1

Dear Ms. Velez:

Valuable customers should never be taken for granted. We want you to know how much we have appreciated your business over the past five years. We hope to serve you for many years to come.

However, our accounts show that you currently owe $1428.57—a bill that has been outstanding since June 5. Please send us a cheque in this amount now so that you can be sure of uninterrupted service in the months ahead.

We are certain you will take care of this oversight. If there is a payment problem, please call me as soon as possible. We will be happy to work with you on a payment plan.

Sincerely,

Michael Belling

Michael Belling
Legal Assistant

jl

1111 5th Avenue N. Lethbridge, AB T6M 1Z1
(phone) 403-555-0000 (fax) 403-555-1111
(e-mail) mbelling@b&t.com
www.b&t.com

Figure 10-4 Sample Collection Inquiry Letter

that the past-due customer will pay only if threatened with unpleasant actions, such as turning nonpayment information over to a credit bureau, starting legal action, and referring the account to a collection agency. The **last-resort letter** informs the customer that unless the money is received by a specific date, your company will begin taking action.

The tone of the last-resort letter should express a reluctance to take these actions but a determination to do so if the customer does not pay within a stated time limit—usually no more than ten days. To reinforce the seriousness of your message, have a senior executive sign the letter and consider sending it by certified mail, return receipt requested. A sample letter you might send to customers as a last resort is shown in Figure 10–6.

While collection and sales letters are written to customers, persuasive memos are written from one business associate to another. The final section of this chapter examines how this difference—as well as other differences between persuasive letters and memos—changes the way in which the persuasive message is crafted.

Progress Check

1. What are the dual purposes of collection letters, and why is tone important in communicating these purposes?

2. Describe the three persuasive appeals used in collecting outstanding debts. How are they similar and how are they different?

3. List the three pieces of information that every collection letter should include.

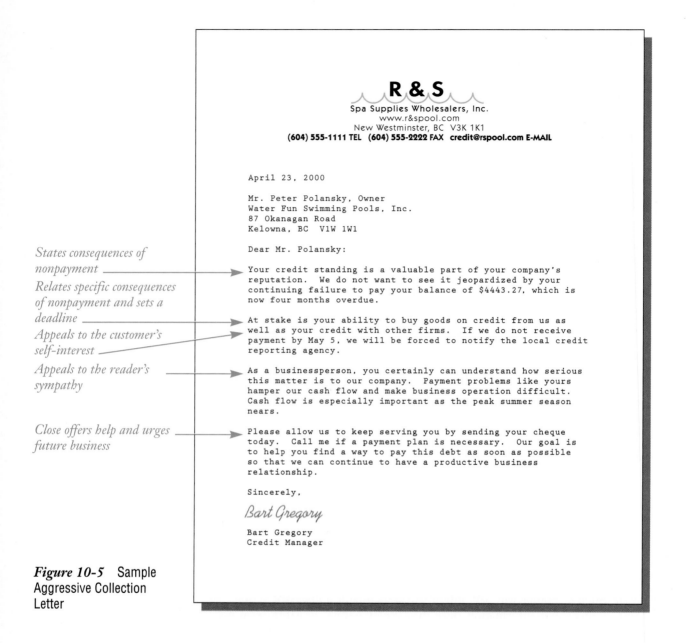

R & S
Spa Supplies Wholesalers, Inc.
www.r&spool.com
New Westminster, BC V3K 1K1
(604) 555-1111 TEL (604) 555-2222 FAX credit@rspool.com E-MAIL

April 23, 2000

Mr. Peter Polansky, Owner
Water Fun Swimming Pools, Inc.
87 Okanagan Road
Kelowna, BC V1W 1W1

Dear Mr. Polansky:

Your credit standing is a valuable part of your company's reputation. We do not want to see it jeopardized by your continuing failure to pay your balance of $4443.27, which is now four months overdue.

At stake is your ability to buy goods on credit from us as well as your credit with other firms. If we do not receive payment by May 5, we will be forced to notify the local credit reporting agency.

As a businessperson, you certainly can understand how serious this matter is to our company. Payment problems like yours hamper our cash flow and make business operation difficult. Cash flow is especially important as the peak summer season nears.

Please allow us to keep serving you by sending your cheque today. Call me if a payment plan is necessary. Our goal is to help you find a way to pay this debt as soon as possible so that we can continue to have a productive business relationship.

Sincerely,

Bart Gregory

Bart Gregory
Credit Manager

Figure 10-5 Sample Aggressive Collection Letter

Writing Persuasive Memos

A **persuasive memo** cannot be written in the same tone or manner as a sales letter. Persuading professional colleagues, whether inside or outside a business organization, rarely involves the typical format of a sales letter. Using the AIDA concept to sell your ideas may be viewed as manipulative and is usually a mistake. Generally, it is best to be direct when writing persuasive memos and letters. Consider the difference between two versions of the same opening paragraphs in a memo. Whereas the first one uses an indirect approach and a tone reminiscent of a sales presentation, the second one is more direct and sober. How do you respond to each?

As in all forms of persuasive communication, it is important to arrange information in a logical, convincing order and to use evidence to support your ideas. Using a direct approach also prompts the reader to take specific action.

ALBANY LADDER

www.albanylad.com
111 Stony Road, Edmonton, AB T5N 1N1
Tel 708-555-0000 • Fax 708-555-1111 • E-mail jull@albanylad.com

August 16, 2000

Mr. Scott C. Debtor
1 Centre Street
Red Deer, AB T8A 1A1

Dear Mr. Debtor:

Headline calls attention to the debt's importance

PAST DUE BALANCE: $4656.32

A direct approach

In a very few days now, our accounts are due for audit, and decisions must be made on those that are seriously past due.

As you might imagine, the choice of whether to place an account with our collection agency is one which we weigh with a good deal of care—especially in your case.

The writer shows respect and empathy for the reader

Your good will, after all, has always been important to us. That is why we are reluctant now to take any action that might jeopardize your credit standing and cause you embarrassment or added expense. Our contract stipulates that you will be responsible for collection and legal fees.

An appeal to the debtor's sense of honour and integrity
The writer adds the possibility of negative action

Yet, I think you will agree that our position is a fair one; we have been happy to extend you credit based on your promise to pay according to our terms. Since then, we have contacted you numerous times without response; and now we must consider the possibility of placing your account with our collection agents or a law firm.

Demand for payment in full

Still, I am hopeful that you will act promptly and forward us your cheque IN FULL IMMEDIATELY. That is why I am going to suspend further action until September 1, 2000.

Starting the ultimatum in the passive voice depersonalizes the bad news

It is important, however, that I hear from you by then. Otherwise, a decision must be made that I am sure neither of us wants.

Sincerely,

Jim Ullery

Jim Ullery
Financial Services Manager

Figure 10-6 Sample Last-Resort Letter
Source: *"The Ideal Collection Letter,"* Inc. Magazine *(February 1991): 59.*

Do you want to increase sales and cut costs? Do you want to motivate the salesforce to push harder to close every deal? Of course you do, and what I am suggesting is the chance of a career—an opportunity to increase sales without increasing operating costs.

The key is a new advanced training program from Murphy & Associates with proven results. Here is how the program works. . . .

Indirect Approach Memo with Sales-Letter Tone

> The increasingly competitive marketing environment requires that sales representatives continue learning about product innovations and new sales techniques. The key to this learning is a program of continuing education. I recommend that we begin using a new sales training program created by Murphy & Associates. This program has a proven track record of success in companies like ours.
>
> The program offers the following benefits. . . .

Direct Approach Memo

Certain circumstances, however, make an indirect approach more effective in persuasive memos. Assume that you are attempting to persuade a reader with whom you do not have a close relationship to take action that is in your mutual best interest. In this instance, an indirect approach may increase the likelihood of success by appearing less pushy.

In addition, an indirect approach is essential when trying to persuade high-ranking managers to do something that they do not want to do. In certain instances this approach may also be necessary to encourage supervisees to take action. "We doubt that [a direct approach] would be effective in a letter where a boss asks you to double your Community Fund pledge," suggest business communication authors John S. Fielden and Ronald E. Dulek.[10]

Progress Check

1. How should the approach to persuasive memos differ from the approach to other persuasive documents?
2. Describe when a direct approach is appropriate in a persuasive memo. When should an indirect approach be used?
3. How does the relationship between reader and writer affect the memo's style?

SELECTING AN APPROPRIATE WRITING STYLE   The most effective persuasive writing style for a memo reflects the relationship between the writer and reader. In general, when writing a negative persuasive message to a supervisee, choose a forceful writing style that uses words like *urge*, *recommend*, and *expect*. Also minimize the use of *I* and *you* to create an impersonal tone. The following versions of the same negative persuasive memo demonstrate how the personal and impersonal approaches differ:

TO: All Sales Representatives

FROM: Al Cuningham, Vice President   *AC*

DATE: September 13, 2000

SUBJECT: Condition of company cars

How would you feel if a client came to your office and found coffee cups and candy bar wrappers scattered on the floor? How do you think your client would feel?

Recently, several clients complained to me that company cars are dirty, both inside and out. To me, this is tantamount to having a dirty office. Both are unacceptable and will no longer be tolerated.

Personal Approach

TO: All Sales Representatives

FROM: Al Cuningham, Vice President *AC*

DATE: September 13, 2000

SUBJECT: Condition of company cars

Company cars are showing excessive signs of wear and tear. Because these cars represent a substantial capital investment, it is important to keep them in good condition. In addition, because they represent the company's image—and the image of every employee—away from the office, I urge you to maintain spotless vehicles both inside and out.

Impersonal Approach

When the situation is reversed and a first-level supervisor is writing to a superior, a passive style is advisable—one that avoids making forceful demands. For example, instead of writing "I want you to do this," it is more effective to say "It would help the department a great deal if this were done." Similarly, an impersonal approach is appropriate for a negative message written to a supervisor.

What's Ahead

This chapter completes Part III, Organizational Letters and Memos. Business communication also includes writing reports and proposals, which is the subject of Part IV. In Chapter 11 we discuss the types and uses of business reports and proposals. We also discuss how to develop and write them, how to create supporting visual aids, and how to prepare the final documents.

STUDENT RESOURCE CENTRE

Summary of Chapter Objectives

1. *Explain the concept of persuasion and the four persuasive goals.*

    Persuasion is the process of influencing or changing attitudes, beliefs, values, or behaviours. It is a key element in sales letters, collection letters, and appeals for action within an organization. Persuasive goals define the nature of the change that the message seeks. Messages of adoption try to persuade readers to initiate action. Messages of continuance urge that a specific behaviour be continued, whereas messages of discontinuance urge that a be-

haviour be stopped. Finally, messages of deterrence attempt to prevent an action from taking place.

2. *Identify and contrast the three major persuasive appeals.*

    The three major persuasive appeals are reasoning, credibility, and emotion. When a business document appeals to reason, it tries to guide the reader to a conclusion by presenting its message in a logical way. The way in which material is organized helps build the writer's case. Persuasive appeals also involve issues of credibility—how readers perceive the writer, company, and message. Document credibility is influenced by language choice, a focus on benefits rather than features, and the use of testimonials praising the company, product, or idea. Often the most powerful persuasive appeal is the appeal to emotion. This appeal can focus on such positive emotions as hope, pleasure, and pride, or on such negative emotions as fear and anxiety.

3. *Identify and describe the three types of sales letters.*
Sales letters represent a relatively inexpensive alternative channel for both locating prospective accounts and increasing sales to current customers. Direct-mail sales letters offer the advantages of personalization, selectivity, intensive coverage, speed, format flexibility, and completeness of information. Retail-sales letters announce such events as special sales and should answer customers' key questions about an event. Letters seeking inquiries are used to generate an inquiry from the person receiving the message. Representatives of the firm sending the inquiry letter will then follow up by phone, in face-to-face meetings, or by additional letters.

4. *Apply the AIDA concept to the organization of a sales letter.*
Most sales letters are organized according to a persuasive plan known by its initials—AIDA, for *attention-interest-desire-action*. The letter opens with an attention grabber that attempts to convince the audience to continue to read. Among the most commonly used attention grabbers are provocative headlines, questions, testimonials, and startling facts and statistics. Attention grabbers continue in the opening paragraph. Sales letters then attempt to create interest by tapping a need in the reader, often through the presentation of specific claims. These claims stress benefits and involve logical and emo-

tional appeals. Writers create desire, the next stage of the sales letter, by presenting evidence about the benefits of a product or service. In turn, evidence motivates action. Finally, every sales letter attempts to convince readers to take specific steps to purchase a product and to do so quickly. Three techniques to produce action are to identify the specific action, use inducements, and make it easy to respond. Inducements to buy include premiums, contests, discounts for immediate action, limited quantities, and deadlines.

5. *List the four types of collection letters and explain the purpose of each.*
Collection letters are persuasive letters that attempt to collect outstanding debts and maintain goodwill. The first letter in the collection series is a reminder. Reminders have a positive tone while gently informing the customer that the debt has not been paid. The next letter in the series, the inquiry, questions whether there is a problem preventing the customer from paying. The tone of this letter is friendly and conciliatory. Aggressive collection notices are sent next. These notices use various appeals to insist that the bill be paid. Finally, last-resort collection letters threaten unpleasant actions if the debt is not paid within a specific time.

6. *Explain when to use a direct approach in persuasive memos and when to be indirect.*
In general, persuasive memos are more direct than sales letters. However, certain circumstances make the indirect approach best. These include trying to persuade a reader with whom you do not have a close relationship to do something in his or her best interest. This approach is also used to persuade people in higher organizational positions to do something that they do not want to do.

Review and Discussion Questions

1. What is persuasion? *(Ch. Obj. 1)*
2. Every persuasive message attempts to achieve one of four major persuasive goals. Describe the differences among these goals. *(Ch. Obj. 1)*
3. Distinguish among the three major persuasive appeals. *(Ch. Obj. 2)*
4. Distinguish among initial, derived, and terminal credibility. *(Ch. Obj. 2)*
5. What are the three major types of sales letters? *(Ch. Obj. 3)*
6. Explain the AIDA concept. Why is it important in organizing a sales letter? *(Ch. Obj. 4)*

7. Name several techniques that can help motivate readers to take immediate action after they have read a persuasive document. *(Ch. Obj. 4)*
8. Name the four different types of collection letters. *(Ch. Obj. 5)*
9. Compare the approaches that a writer might use in each of the four types of collection letters. *(Ch. Obj. 5)*
10. When would you use a direct approach in a persuasive memo to a business colleague? When would you want to be indirect? *(Ch. Obj. 6)*

Application Exercises

1. Write a persuasive letter in which you convince a skeptical friend that it's important to be able to write persuasively in business. *(Ch. Obj. 1)*

2. Suppose that you've decided to write a persuasive memo to your boss, either on your current job or on a job that you've held in the past. You want to persuade him or her that you deserve a promotion. Which of the four persuasive goals are you trying to achieve in this memo? *(Ch. Obj. 1)*

3. Define the specific purposes that will accomplish the goal you identified in your response to Exercise 2. Now write a brief description of your audience, that is, your boss. What are his or her priorities and concerns? How can you persuade your boss that your promotion will also benefit the company? *(Ch. Obj. 1)*

4. Using your notes from Exercise 3, list the statements that you could make in this memo that would help you to establish credibility, appeal to your boss's sense of reasoning, and produce the response you want. *(Ch. Obj. 2)*

5. Finally, using your statements for Exercise 4, write your memo to your boss. Be prepared to explain why you chose an indirect or direct approach. *(Ch. Obj. 1, 2, 6)*

6. Write a memo in which you persuade the president of your school to alter a rule or procedure that you feel needs changing. Be prepared to explain why you chose a direct or indirect approach. *(Ch. Obj. 1, 2, 6)*

7. Think of a fairly expensive good or service that you would like to sell. Now create two lists—one describing the features of this item, the other detailing the benefits that these features provide to customers. *(Ch. Obj. 2, 3)*

8. Apply the AIDA concept to think through the steps that a customer would take before buying the item or service that you described for Exercise 7. What arguments might you use in a sales letter to take the customer through each of these steps? *(Ch. Obj. 3, 4)*

9. Based on your notes for Exercise 8, write a sales letter to potential customers for the item or service that you have selected. *(Ch. Obj. 2-4)*

10. Suppose that Kelly Rowse, a personnel manager at an electronics firm, has bought the good or service that you described in Exercise 9. She bought it on a six-month installment plan that calls for her to make equal payments every month. Kelly made the first two payments on time but has since fallen behind on her payment schedule. Your company has sent her two invoices, and she's now two months late with her third payment. You decide that it's time to write a collection letter. You don't know why Kelly is late on her payments, but you do know that her company is in trouble and has had to lay off 100 employees. Write an effective collection letter to Kelly. *(Ch. Obj. 5)*

11. Larry Laggard has also bought the good or service that you described in Exercise 9. Larry has been late before in paying his bills, and this time is no exception. He is now three months late with his first installment payment on this item, and you have already sent him both a reminder letter and an inquiry letter. Write Larry an aggressive collection notice. How does this letter differ from the one that you wrote to Kelly Rowse in Exercise 10? *(Ch. Obj. 5)*

12. In political advertisements, candidates sometimes resort to making negative allegations and generalizations about their opponents. Why do you think they take this approach? How do such advertisements affect you when you watch them? Explain your answer. *(Ch. Obj. 1, 2)*

Building Your Business Notebook

Carefully read the following documents and assess their communication effectiveness. Next, revise and improve the letters by applying what you've learned in this chapter.

We need your $25 donation to help the community's abused children.

We know how busy you are and how tired you are of irate customers, traffic jams, and late reports. So, we believe that you could use a relaxing evening. We are scheduling five nights under the stars—every third Thursday in May through September.

The Community Action Group has reserved the Community Action Park on those dates so that you and three of your business friends can enjoy the evening socializing in a nonbusiness environment, listening to music, and tasting a variety of refreshments.

We hope you will be interested in watching the sunset and seeing the stars and fireflies flicker in the sky.

So even though you are busy, do consider this opportunity to help children and to enjoy the evening outside—send in the form or call 555-1234 to make your reservation. If you really want to participate in this opportunity, you will probably be able to find the time.

Document 1

TO: M. Lane
FROM: Sara Geralding
DATE: March 18, 2000
SUBJECT: Parking spaces

Why does management get to have special parking places in a half-filled lot when employees can't even find a place to park? We think this is unfair.

Many employees are complaining about the crowded parking lots and how long it takes them to actually find a place to park once they arrive at work in the morning. The number of employees has greatly increased since the employee parking lot and the management parking lot were designed. It seems no one has considered that management-level personnel has declined, while the number of hourly workers has increased. If anyone is interested, several employees have banded together to form LOPS (Lack of Parking Space). If management doesn't do something about this situation, LOPS has suggested that we employees picket to protest our dissatisfaction with the situation. The solution seems so simple—open up the management parking lot to all employees. This would add many more parking spaces. Then have the area on the north side blacktopped and designate it for management's use. That unused area appears large enough to accommodate management.

The LOPS Committee would be glad to meet with management to offer input. We all feel it is about time management does something to solve the horrendous, unfair parking situation.

Document 2

ACT: Applied Communication Techniques

Begin by referring to the sections up to and including Commas in Appendix II, then correct the grammar, spelling, and usage errors in the following sentences. Check your answers in Appendix V.

1. Effectively used persuasive technics work on three levels at once.
2. Reasoning involves presenting facts statistics examples and anecdotes expert opinion and analogies.
3. Wayne Gretsky, a famous canadian hockey stare can send a persuasive message to youth.
4. Although the document may include photographs your text must be writen so that the reader can understand it without the pictures.
5. Sales letters are written by manufacturers retailers and holesalers as well as governmant agencies.
6. Purchasing a product involves a process of prolem solving and often includes the need to be persuade.
7. While interest is largely an intellectual responce desire is basically a emotional reaction.
8. To interest the largest audience possible you must provide both pleasure and logic.
9. "Hear are the pages for the final report" said Amelia as she keyed the last line.
10. We left on our vacation to Halifax Nova Scotia on June 11 1999.

Building Your Reasearch Skills

We all are constantly bombarded by persuasive messages, including advertisements, memos, letters, newspaper and magazine articles, books, even popular songs and movies. Collect four examples of persuasive messages that you have received recently—one for each of the four persuasive goals discussed in the chapter. Analyze each message to determine its effectiveness. If you find it effective, explain why it works. Does it use the AIDA concept? Does it mention benefits as well as features? If the message fails to persuade you, why is it ineffective? Write a brief analysis of each message to present to the class.

Building Your Teamwork Skills

Your instructor will divide the class into small teams. Meet with your team to discuss the four messages that each of you analyzed in the Building Your Research Skills exercise. Do the other members of your team agree with your analysis of each message? Do they have any explanations for effective or ineffective messages that you did not consider? As a group, discuss recommendations for improving the ineffective messages.

Your instructor may wish to have each group present the best and worst persuasive messages to the class.

Building Your Technology Skills

You have been hired to work on the Internet team for a publishing company. Your assignment is to write two persuasive messages to encourage people to visit the company's Web page. The first message will be directed at inexperienced Internet users. It will be distributed in print media, such as a magazine newsletter. The second persuasive message will announce the Web site to current Internet users, such as members of Usenet newsgroups. How will the message change for the different types of audiences?

Weblinks Internet Resources for this Chapter

Persuasive Writing
http://www.mes.umn.edu/~hoefer/web/perwrite.htm

Five Steps to Successful Sales Letters
http://www.so-cal.com/writingbiz/page1.htm

Collection Letters
http://www.commercialcollector.com/ideas.html

Writing Memos
http://www.cs.unc.edu/~jbs/sm/Part3_ltrsmemos.html

CASE STUDIES

CORPORATE CASE:

The Team Approach to Collecting Debts

Many companies are applying the team approach to credit management and finding dramatic improvements in collection rates. The team approach combines credit, sales, and customer service so that all team members have the ability to answer customers' questions, handle sales, and write collection letters.

This approach is used by the Taco Maker restaurant chain, which now has a collection rate of 99.02 percent. It is also used by The Franklin Quest, where the same person takes orders and makes sure they are billed correctly. At Twin Cities Reader, Inc., the person who approves a credit application also collects payment. "The philosophy is, 'If you make the mess, you clean it up,' " says Rich Millerbernd, credit manager. The team approach encourages employees who approve marginal accounts to take a personal interest in collecting outstanding

debts. "If an account does go bad, you're working harder to get that money taken care of," continues to Millerbernd. That includes writing more effective collection letters. As a result of this collaborative approach, bad debt write-offs at Twin Cities Reader have dropped from 4 percent to 1/4 of 1 percent.[11]

Questions and Applications

1. How is collaboration changing the credit and collection process?

2. Why might a team approach improve collection letters? Would it motivate you to write more effective letters?

3. Would you look for a credit management job that also involves sales and customer service? Why or why not?

DIVERSITY CASE:

Women's "Place" in Medicine

Suppose that you are a new member of the medical profession. While you are reading several professional journals, you discover the following facts about the status of female physicians:

▼ Women make up approximately 20 percent of the profession and about 42 percent of medical-school enrollments.

▼ The unadjusted net income of female physicians equals 62 percent of the unadjusted net income of male physicians.

▼ Nearly 75 percent of 2225 female physicians who responded to an informal survey reported that they had been sexually harassed. While most were harassed during medical school or residency, 40 percent were harassed while in practice.

▼ Many female physicians complain that male colleagues exclude them from informal consultations and formal conferences about patients.

An article you read in your medical association journal makes it clear that a variety of factors prevent women from achieving equal status in the medical profession. The "glass

ceiling" affects women's advancement, particularly in academic medicine, as men tend to sponsor and support other men for medical-school posts. However, women's job choices also influence their professional standing. These choices are influenced by the struggle to balance family and career. As a result, female physicians are overrepresented in lower-paid specialties, see fewer patients, and are less likely to be self-employed than men.[12]

Questions and Applications

1. Write a persuasive memo to the president of the Canadian Medical Association. You want to convince the president to start a committee to study these issues further and to appoint you as a committee member.

2. How would you characterize the specific points in your message in terms of the four broad persuasive goals: adoption, continuance, discontinuance, and deterrence?

3. Characterize the persuasive mix in your message. To what extent does your message attempt to persuade through reasoning, credibility, and emotion? Write a short analysis of your findings.

11

Planning and Researching Business Reports and Proposals

Chapter Objectives

After studying this chapter, you should be able to:

1. Identify the characteristics of business reports and proposals.
2. List the steps of the report and proposal writing process.
3. List questions that are used to evaluate primary and secondary research.
4. Identify the major types of secondary business research.
5. Explain how businesspeople use online information to research topics.
6. Compare the two major sources of primary data research.

Writing is an exploration. You start from nothing and learn as you go.

E. L. Doctorow
Novelist

esearching in Cyberspace

Conducting research has become much easier and faster thanks to the World Wide Web. At the Internet Institute in Ottawa, President and founder Gerald Lemay and his staff conduct much of their research on the Web. Lemay reports that the Internet is their primary tool because it is easy to access, fast, and provides the wealth of information necessary to give his company a broad picture of what is going on, not only in their local area, but around the world.

Lemay provides some interesting insight as he shares one example of how he uses the Internet for research:

"A client calls and wants to know more about a new piece of software. To draft our preliminary conclusions we go to the Internet. First, we go to the home page of the manufacturer and read its promotional material. Then we access the "support" area on the site, where the manufacturer posts information about problems that people frequently encounter when using the software. So while the promotional material tells us what the product is supposed to do, the support pages tell us what it doesn't do well—and how responsive the company is to customer complaints.

"Next, we use at least three search engines to access information written by other people about this product. We use more than one search engine because each one possesses different information in its database and allows for different ways of searching for information.

"Typical results from a search include information collected from personal home pages where people report how much they like or hate the product. As well, companies using the product state how they are using it and what success they have had with this product. We also find out what their competitors are saying about the product, and we get reviews from magazines. Now we're getting a better picture!

"Then we go to the archives of newsgroups to find out what users of the product are saying. Newsgroups are the Internet's party line. We listen in to find out how great the product really is, and what its potential problems are. Newsgroups will also tell us about the product's popularity and its applications.

"The wealth of information we're able to compile from these sources enables us to provide the client with a comprehensive report on the product.

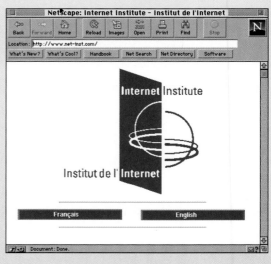

"At the Institute we use the Internet for research every day, every hour. The benefits are many: it's open 24 hours a day and it gives us a perspective from around the world. In today's global marketplace the Internet is a must—and knowing how to use it intelligently is essential for survival."▼

Source: Interview with Gerald Lemay.

Chapter Overview _____

In this chapter we discuss the most effective ways to convert research findings—including those from the Internet—into information for use in business reports and proposals. Reports and proposals play a crucial role in communicating information in profit-seeking businesses, not-for-profit organizations, and government agencies. For example, proposals are used to solicit business from outside the organization, and reports are used to suggest new programs and ideas for internal change. In these ways, reports and proposals are integral to a company's relationships with its business clients, suppliers, government agencies, company employees, and the general public.

This is the first of four chapters on business reports and proposals. Here, we focus on planning and research as two key steps in writing effective documents. This chapter examines information sources and methods of gathering information in the form of primary and secondary research. It also discusses appropriate methods of arranging and interpreting information. Because report writing is often a group effort, the chapter also examines the benefits and potential problems involved in collaborative writing. We begin by examining the nature of reports and the ways in which they are used in business.

What Are Business Reports? _____

Businesspeople often spend hours planning, researching, and writing business reports to their managers, colleagues, or supervisees. A **business report** is a document that organizes information on a specific topic for a specific business purpose. Business reports may be sent to one person or more, inside or outside of the business. Facts—that is, *verifiable data*—are the key to an effective business report. "No matter how far reports go into interpretation and analysis," explains one team of business communication experts, "they begin by presenting and summarizing facts. . . . Reports share the journalist's interest in the fundamentals of who, what, when, where, why, and how."[1]

CHARACTERISTICS OF BUSINESS REPORTS

Although the purpose of all reports and proposals is to inform and/or persuade, we can classify reports broadly as formal or informal. We can also distinguish reports based on six other characteristics: length, distribution, frequency of submission, format, use of visual aids, and method of assignment. Each of these characteristics is briefly described in Table 11-1 and discussed further in this section.

DEGREE OF FORMALITY   Business reports can be formal or informal. **Formal reports** are typically long and highly structured. They include parts such as title pages, tables of contents, and executive summaries. Formal reports usually require extensive research and almost always feature impersonal language. **Informal reports** are typically written in shorter time frames to present findings derived from smaller research bases. They tend to be shorter than formal reports and generally feature a relatively relaxed, personal style.

LENGTH   Short reports are typically one or two pages in length and can be in either letter or memo form. Although they may not fit the common concept of a "report," such memo-type documents can be classified as reports because of their content—they present information to specific individuals for specific purposes. Long reports, meanwhile, may require dozens—and sometimes hundreds—of pages of information in order to analyze complex issues and problems.

Table 11-1   Characteristics of Business Reports

Characteristic	Formal Reports (Impersonal Language; More Highly Structured)	Informal Reports (Personal Writing Style; Less Structured)
Length	Long	Short
Distribution	Circulated outside the organization and/or to superiors, subordinates, and co-workers within the organization	Mostly circulated within the organization
Frequency	Specialized, one-time reports or periodic reports	Specialized, one-time reports or periodic reports
Format	Form reports or narrative reports	Form reports or narrative reports
Visual Aids	Used extensively	Used infrequently
Assignment	Initiated externally, internally, or self-initiated	Initiated externally, internally, or self-initiated

DISTRIBUTION   **Internal reports** can be directed to top managers, to supervisees, or to colleagues. A report sent to senior management, for example, might focus on the results of a meeting with an important client. A manager might send a comparative analysis of productivity among various departments to the supervisees in those departments. A report sent to a colleague might discuss the status of an ongoing project. **External reports** are circulated to interested parties outside the organization, including suppliers, customers, consultants, creditors, and government officials. External reports are more likely to be formal.

FREQUENCY OF SUBMISSION   One-time, or **singular, reports** deal with specific issues and are designed to aid management decisions. For instance, a survey assessing user satisfaction with different long-distance telephone carriers might be the basis for a one-time report to a manager who must decide whether to award the firm's long-distance business to AT&T Canada, Sprint Canada, Stentor, or another telecommunications firm.

Reports submitted at regular intervals are **periodic reports.** Some reports—for example, a comparative analysis of this year's retail sales with last year's—may be issued every day. Other periodic reports are issued weekly, monthly, quarterly, semiannually, or annually. Corporations are required by law to issue both quarterly financial reports and more extensive annual reports detailing financial data and significant business developments. Even market research-based reports may be revised periodically. For example, PepsiCo marketers, fond of competing with rival Coca-Cola by means of consumer taste tests, repeat such tests periodically and release new reports containing the latest findings.

FORMAT   Many reports follow specific formats that can be completed by simply filling in the blanks on standardized forms. Because they focus on specific information, **form reports** discourage narrative. For example, a manufacturer's inventory-control report form might request information on raw materials, work in progress, and finished goods on hand and available for sale. Another section of the form might address particular inventory-related problems that have arisen since the last report.

By contrast, the format of a **narrative report** is largely determined by what the writer decides to say and *how* the writer chooses to say it. In some companies, for instance, the person assigned to write a benefits-analysis report might choose to

Written reports stifle creativity.

Ross Perot
Founder, Electronic Data Systems

use a figure or table to summarize and compare the health-insurance benefits offered by several competing companies. Elsewhere, the person assigned this task may choose to integrate this comparison in the narrative of the report.

USE OF VISUAL AIDS   Longer formal documents—say, reports presenting quantitative findings from company operations or research studies—are likely to make extensive use of visual aids. Short, informal reports may use none. Visual aids (which we will discuss in detail in Chapter 12) range from simple tables, charts, and graphs to more complex computer-generated graphics. They can be extremely effective in long, formal reports to summarize, compare, or emphasize important information.

METHOD OF ASSIGNMENT   Business reports can also be classified according to the way they are assigned. Some reports, for instance, may be assigned to a person because of a one-time customer request. Others may be assigned routinely to a particular individual or department within the company. For example, a firm's sales manager might ask the director of market research to analyze demand for all proposed new products. Still other reports fall within a company's standard operating procedure. Form reports, such as a bank's quarterly loan analysis, fit into this category. Finally, reports may be self-initiated. A compensation manager may discover that one group of workers is underpaid compared to workers holding similar positions in comparable companies. She might decide to analyze the situation in a report to the human resource manager.

TYPES OF BUSINESS REPORTS

When Biomira, an Edmonton-based biotechnology company, interprets information it has collected from studies on cancer patients, it produces an *expert report*. When it decides to suggest a new treatment procedure, it prepares a *recommendation report*. When it reports to its shareholders on its progress in developing a "radioimmunoimaging agent used to detect the spread of cancer,"[2] it gives them a *status report*.

As Table 11-2 shows, reports can be classified according to one or more of five purposes: information, study, expert, status, and recommendation. Although this

Table 11-2   Types of Reports

Type	Purpose	Example
Information	Presents, explains, and interprets historical and new information	New marketing opportunities in Eastern Europe
Study	Focuses on a problem and alternative solutions; includes analyses and recommendations	Analysis of reasons why factory productivity declined during the last twelve months
Expert	Interprets and evaluates information and suggests solutions from an expert's perspective	Analysis of different benefits provided by two companies that have recently merged
Status	Provides updates of a current situation, plan, or project, and recommends solutions to potential problems	Summary of a major product-development project
Recommendation	Suggests a new procedure or policy, changing responsibilities, or different budget allocations to improve productivity or profits	Recommendation that the sales department be reorganized to give greater authority to the nine regional sales managers

Source: Adapted from Michael C. Thomsett, *The Little Black Book of Business Reports* (New York: AMACOM, 1988), 7.

breakdown describes each category separately, remember that many reports include overlapping elements. A status report, for example, may also present new information. Similarly, although recommendations are one type of report, a recommendation section is found in many other kinds (for example, expert and study reports).

What Are Business Proposals?

Almost any business that sells services or goods submits proposals to current or potential customers. Many businesspeople submit proposals to managers or investors who can support their plans with financial aid. **Proposals** are documents that present information about plans to persuade readers to accept and agree to develop those plans. Indeed, the key difference between reports and proposals is that proposals, if accepted, usually require financial investment on the part of their recipients. Like reports, proposals can be either formal or informal, short or long. When compared to the various types of reports, proposals are most similar to recommendation reports.

TYPES OF BUSINESS PROPOSALS

Proposals can be written for both internal and external audiences. Three types exist: internal proposals, sales proposals, and proposals in response to official requests.

INTERNAL PROPOSALS **Internal proposals** are persuasive documents that attempt to convince top management to spend money on specific projects that will change or improve the organization. For example, a proposal written after two companies merge might suggest ways to integrate the two companies' accounting departments.

SALES PROPOSALS **Sales proposals** (also known as **private-industry proposals**) seek to sell a company's goods or services to potential buyers. For example, an outplacement firm may try to sell its services to a corporation's director of human resources. Similarly, the owner of a trucking company may propose a more efficient delivery service to a large retail chain.

RESPONSE PROPOSALS Sales proposals are sometimes submitted to government agencies at the federal, provincial, or municipal level and to corporations in response to **requests for proposals (RFPs)**—detailed, formal documents that request proposals and bids on projects. Government RFPs include projects as diverse as an order for snowmobiles for the Yukon territorial government, an order for highway repairs by a provincial department of transportation, or an order for teaching equipment by a local school board. To ensure equal opportunity in responding, the same RFP is widely distributed throughout an industry.

As we will see next, writing a report or proposal that is useful, well-organized, readable, and persuasive requires careful planning and an understanding of a seven-step writing process.

Steps in the Writing Process

Formal reports and proposals can take months of work hours, involve teams of workers, and often result in documents hundreds of pages long. Undertaking a project of this magnitude without a writing plan often leads to failure. Simplicity and clarity are essential in all reports and proposals, but especially so in lengthy documents. When the federal government of Canada produces its annual Budget Report or its report on bilingualism, these require a team of people because the reports are extensive and need expertise from diverse areas.

Achieving simplicity and clarity involves a step-by-step writing process. As Figure 11-1 shows, this writing process consists of seven distinct steps. These steps move writers from identifying the issue to finalizing and submitting the document: (1) defining the audience and purpose; (2) creating a work plan; (3) collecting and evaluating data; (4) developing the outline; (5) writing the first draft; (6) revising the document; and (7) finalizing and submitting the document. Steps 1, 4, 5, 6, and 7 were examined in detail in Part II, Writing Basics. We will focus now on Steps 2 and 3. First, we examine Step 2, creating a work plan. This step is essential to the success of long reports and proposals.

→ *Cross Reference*
We discussed defining the audience and purpose in Chapter 4, pages 111–114. In Chapter 5 we examined developing an outline and writing a first draft. In Chapter 6 we studied revising and finalizing a document.

Creating a Work Plan _____

After defining their audience and purpose, report and proposal writers often create a work plan. Work plans are especially effective for lengthy or complex reports and proposals. A **work plan** is a document that defines how the work will be done, who will do it, and when each project phase will be completed. Dividing your work into specific tasks linked to deadlines makes the entire project seem less daunting.

To create a work plan, writers must first decide on both the amount and types of research needed to complete the report or proposal. Let's put this in the context of an example. Suppose your manager asks you to prepare a report that evaluates the pros and cons of several sites for a new retail outlet and recommends a specific location. After clarifying your specific purpose and conducting an informal investigation, you create the preliminary outline shown in Figure 11-2. You then decide to obtain data about costs and collect information about the competitive retailing environment by interviewing a variety of people; to review recent census data for population characteristics in each area; and to contact local newspapers and chambers of commerce for statistics on general economic conditions.

CREATING A COLLABORATIVE PLAN

When a report or proposal requires a great deal of research, the work plan must consider various aspects of team communication, as discussed in Chapter 1. During

You can never over-coordinate.

Cle Cox
American Airlines training manager

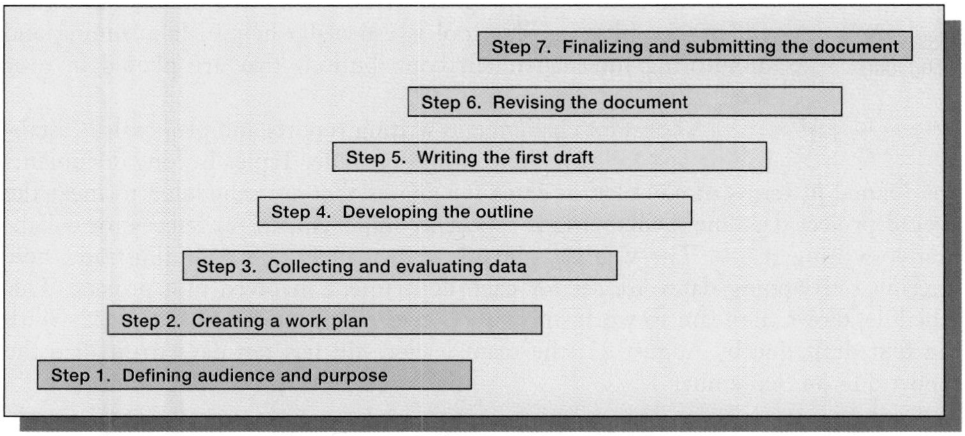

Figure 11-1 Steps in the Writing Process

```
                    Specific Purpose

        To identify for senior management the possible sites for a new
        retail outlet, including the advantages and disadvantages of
        each site, and to recommend a specific site.

                    Working Outline

    I.   Identify at least three possible retail sites, including
         Whitehorse, Montreal, and Charlottetown.

   II.   For each site, discuss:
         A.  Real estate costs for purchasing or leasing the
             property
         B.  Competing stores
         C.  Demographic characteristics of potential customers
         D.  Economic conditions in the community

  III.   Compare the advantages and disadvantages of each
         location

   IV.   Recommend a specific location
```

Figure 11-2 Specific Purpose and Outline

the planning stage, team members develop strategies for conducting research and presenting their findings.

Part of the collaborative plan involves assigning specific areas of responsibility. The team's task is divided into various parts. The team then decides who is likely to be most effective at completing an assignment and divides the work accordingly. In our site-selection illustration, for instance, the work could be divided on the basis of the individual sites. One person would be responsible for evaluating Whitehorse, another Montreal, and a third Charlottetown. Another approach might be to segment the work according to specialty. For example, a marketing analyst might be given the responsibility for analyzing census data, a lawyer might be chosen to examine lease provisions, and a real-estate specialist assigned the task of examining purchasing opportunities.

➡️ *Cross Reference*
See Collaborative Communication in Chapter 1, pages 25–27.

Once team members collect data in their assigned areas, they can begin developing a first draft. Much of this work is accomplished independently. To help keep track of everyone's contributions, however, team leaders typically ask for progress reports at regular intervals. A *status worksheet* like the one in Figure 11-3 can check and record the progress of document submissions at different project phases. This tool is especially helpful in planning and monitoring interdependent contributions that are phased in over time.

A constant challenge in writing reports and proposals is establishing and following a working schedule. Typically, long documents are defined in terms of completion dates for phases that are scheduled to meet the overall project deadline. Scheduling is especially important to the success of collaborative writing teams. The writing schedule shown in Figure 11-4 illustrates how interim, overlapping dates are set for each department involved in a project. This schedule allows the team to work smoothly between August 1 and August 22. With the first draft due by August 22, the team leader still has ten days to finalize the report due on September 1.

Progress Check

1. Explain the seven-step writing process used to develop reports and proposals.

2. In a collaborative project, what specific measures can you take to improve the likelihood of project success?

3. What are the purposes of status worksheets and writing schedules, and why are they important in planning long reports and proposals?

How does a project get to be a year behind schedule?

One day at a time.

Fred Brooks
IBM Corporation systems designer

MANUSCRIPT SUBMISSION SCHEDULE

Chapter	1st Draft Due	2nd Draft Due	Chapter to Production
1	9/1/2000	10/15/2000	10/20/2000
2	9/1/2000	10/15/2000	10/20/2000
3	9/23/2000	10/28/2000	11/3/2000
4	9/30/2000	10/28/2000	11/6/2000
5	10/6/2000	11/11/2000	11/17/2000
6	10/12/2000	11/11/2000	11/20/2000
7	10/16/2000	11/23/2000	11/27/2000
8	10/22/2000	11/23/2000	12/2/2000
9	10/29/2000	12/7/2000	12/11/2000
10	11/4/2000	12/7/2000	12/16/2000
11	11/10/2000	12/21/2000	12/24/2000
12	11/16/2000	12/21/2000	1/4/2001
13	11/20/2000	1/4/2001	1/6/2001
14	11/26/2000	1/4/2001	1/8/2001
15	12/3/2000	1/18/2001	1/20/2001
16	12/9/2000	1/18/2001	1/22/2001
17	12/15/2000	1/18/2001	1/27/2001
18	12/21/2000	1/25/2001	1/29/2001
19	12/29/2000	1/25/2001	2/1/2001
20	1/6/2001	1/25/2001	2/1/2001

Note: Colored areas indicate completed work.

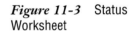

Figure 11-3 Status Worksheet

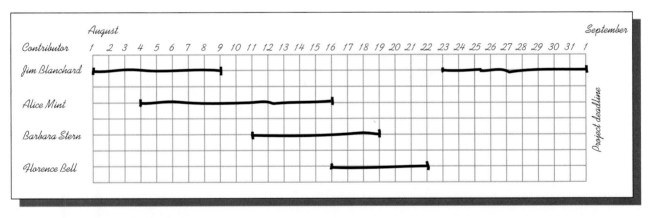

Figure 11-4 Writing Schedule

In the next section, we will examine methods for conducting effective research. Although the specific tools may change with advances in technology and may range from library research to personal interviews, the research strategy remains the same.

Collecting and Evaluating Data

When writing business reports and proposals backed by research, one of the most important factors is knowing where to find data and, once you find it, how to evaluate it. This section examines Step 3 in the writing process—the ways in which primary and secondary research sources are used in collecting data and how to present that data in business writing. We then offer some guidelines for taking effective research notes.

EVALUATING RESEARCH FINDINGS

Not all information is created equally. Although the data collected by your firm or obtained from previously published sources may be perfectly sound, they must also be appropriate for the document you are preparing. To evaluate both primary and secondary research findings, you must ask the following questions:

▼ Is it valid?

▼ Is it reliable?

▼ Is it current?

VALIDITY AND RELIABILITY   One of your first tasks is to evaluate your data in order to find out how useful they will be to you. Research findings typically are evaluated on the bases of validity and reliability. **Validity** is the extent to which a research study accurately measures what it was intended to measure. For example, a study that relies on data from polygraph tests may not be valid because the accuracy of these tests is questionable.

Reliability means that the collected data are consistent, stable, and free from systematic sources of error. Weighing shipments of goods on a bathroom scale, for example, is unreliable if the weights vary according to the positioning of the shipment on the scale.

A continuing concern of writers who rely on published sources of data is that reported findings may no longer be accurate by the time they are gathered for use in a subsequent document. What, for example, could you do with the data derived from a ten-year-old real estate analysis of the city of Vancouver? The upsurge in property values in this city would render the data virtually useless. In short, data sources should be as current as possible. If the data that you need have not been recently collected and published, be prepared to invest the time and money required to collect data that you can use.

EVALUATING DATA

Do not be surprised when your reward for a successful research project turns out to be stacks of undigested data. Turning such data into usable information is one of the most important steps in the writing process—one that requires organization and interpretation.

ORGANIZING DATA   Evaluation depends on organizing data so that relationships, trends, and recurring themes become clear. Organization begins when you group materials according to the topics in your preliminary outline. For example, if you are writing a report analyzing union contracts in the automobile industry, you may decide to group research findings by North American automobile makers (General Motors, Ford, and Chrysler) on the one hand, and imports such as Volvo, Nissan, Saab, and Toyota on the other. Next, you may choose to divide your list of contracts further by specific contract provisions—say, wages, pension funds, health insurance, and other employee benefits. If you use note cards in the research process, separate them according to various subject files. If you use a computer and your document is quite long, create separate computer files to organize data by subjects.

INTERPRETING DATA   Once you begin to interpret your data, your focus moves from organizing to analyzing. Considering your document's specific purpose, you must now evaluate all of your data in terms of your premise. Do your data support your premise? Do they provide strong support or moderate support? Should you modify your premise?

As you analyze your collected data, try to identify logical patterns or draw logical conclusions that will help to structure your report or proposal. Because they will be the basis of your outline, you should consider the strengths and drawbacks of these patterns as you research. Finally, remember that your data will play a critical role in the conclusions and recommendations you will make. Conclusions are the logical results of the evidence presented in your report or proposal. Recommendations are specific actions that you suggest in your report or proposal based on the information and conclusions presented.

DEVELOPING A SEARCH STRATEGY

Knowing how to locate data is as important as knowing what data you need. Success in securing data results from developing a **search strategy**—a systematic method for locating research sources. The most effective search strategies move from general to specific sources in a step-by-step fashion.

As you can see in Figure 11-5, one model of the search strategy starts when you state your specific purpose in the form of a problem; it includes both primary

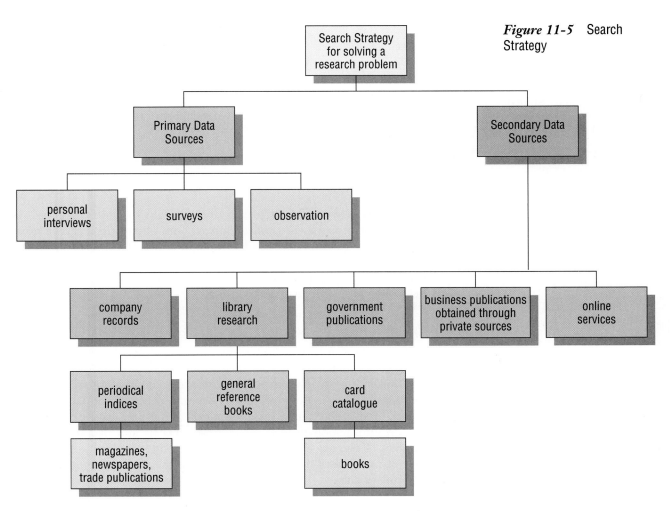

Figure 11-5   Search Strategy

COLLABORATIVE COMMUNICATION

Questions That Help Focus Collaborative Writing

One way to transform individual contributors into team members is to ask a series of questions that help clarify crucial issues regarding content, purpose, audience, organization, development, and design. Ask questions like the following during the planning phase as well as during later stages of document development.

PURPOSE AND AUDIENCE QUESTIONS

1. What do you see as our main point [purpose]?
2. What did you mean by _____? Could you clarify the point about _____?
3. I see a conflict between _____ and _____. How will we deal with it?
4. Who is our intended audience?
5. What does the reader expect to read [learn, do]?
6. How will our reader react to _____?
7. Considering the reader's point of view, what conflicts, inconsistencies, or gaps might be observed?

CONTENT, ORGANIZATION, AND DEVELOPMENT QUESTIONS

1. What more can we say about _____?
2. Have you considered including [excluding] _____?

3. How will we develop and organize this material?
4. What evidence could we use to strengthen our point?
5. Is our emphasis correct?
6. How can we use visual aids to better organize and present the material?

QUESTIONS RELATING TO DESIGN

1. Does the design help readers locate and understand the main points?
2. How can we improve the use of headings, lists, paragraphing, and white space?

Questions for Critical Thinking

1. At which stages during document development should these questions be asked?
2. Why would you ask the same questions at various points in the document development process?
3. Would asking these questions make others perceive you as a team player or as an obstructionist trying to cause problems? Explain your answer.

Source: Checklist based in part on Rebecca E. Burnett, "Benefits of Collaborative Planning in the Business Communication Classroom," *The Bulletin of the Association for Business Communication,* LIII, no. 2, (June 1990): 12.

---

and secondary sources of data. **Primary data** are collected specifically for use in preparing the report or proposal. Interviews, surveys, and observations can be used to obtain primary data. By contrast, **secondary data** have been previously published in company, trade-association, and industry publications; government reports; and books and articles in newspapers, magazines, and journals. Secondary information has already been analyzed, evaluated, and organized.

INTERNAL AND EXTERNAL SOURCES OF INFORMATION

Various company records can be used to generate invaluable data for your report or proposal. **Internal data** may range from sales reports, consultants' evaluations, and wage and salary reviews to analyses of potential markets, information contained in correspondence files, and accounting records. Because much internal data are collected on a regular basis, they can be secured quickly and at low cost.

Much of the information needed for complex reports and proposals comes from external data. **External data** are generated outside the firm. As a rule, researchers seek out secondary data before committing the time and money necessary to collect primary data.

COLLECTING EXTERNAL SECONDARY DATA

Although you can find much secondary data inside your organization, even more are available from external sources. In fact, so much data are available at little or no cost that business writers must be able to locate precisely what they need without being overwhelmed. The four major sources of secondary data are libraries, government publications, private business sources, and online databases.

CONDUCTING LIBRARY RESEARCH   Libraries are used by business writers searching for historical, financial, or other statistical data. Libraries may be public or private and may contain general or specialized information. Increasingly, public library information is available online.

Knowing how to use library resources is vital to the success of any major research project. With the mammoth number of resources available at most libraries, you should conduct your library research systematically, moving from general to more specific sources. To get an overview of your research assignment, it is helpful to consult general reference books like encyclopedias, almanacs, and fact books. An increasing number of these volumes, including the 44-million word *Encyclopedia Britannica*, now appear online or on CD-ROM (compact disc–read only memory) as well as in traditional hard-bound volumes.[3] The researcher should turn next to more specialized reference sources, such as directories of companies in a particular industry or associations and organizations in a specific area. Specialized reference sources are also available in most major fields in bound form, online, and on CD-ROM.

Because business reports must often deal with current information, many researchers turn to *periodical indexes* to find relevant magazine, newspaper, and trade-publication articles. Periodical indexes are found in the form of bound books and, increasingly, in computerized databases. These indexes include the *Reader's Guide to Periodical Literature*, the *Business Periodicals Index*, and the *Canadian Periodical Index*.

Using a Computerized Database   Each item in a computer database includes the article title, authors, journal information (volume, date, and page numbers), key terms and concepts, classification codes (for dividing broad topical areas), and an article abstract. ABI/INFORM, produced by H. W. Wilson Company, contains references to more than 200 000 articles about business and management from nearly 700 journals. Other computerized databases include the Canadian News Index and the Applied Sciences & Technology Index, which contains references to articles in technical journals. Canadian Associations Online is an encyclopedic directory containing detailed information on more than 20 000 organizations. The front-page news in leading Canadian newspapers can be found online at the Infomart Dialog Limited; the site provides extensive Canadian and global information. A great number of databases may be found through Yahoo Canada–Reference; this Internet site will connect you to databases for almanac, dictionary, and encyclopedic information. It also provides databases for maps, phone numbers, quotations, and the Canadian Geographical Name Server.

Computerized databases, containing as many as 250 000 pages of text, are stored on CD-ROMs. These databases allow researchers to quickly and easily read, search, and print information stored on a single disc. Current periodicals are now being translated from books into electronic form. Among CD-ROMs available for business users is *Duns Data*. This CD-ROM contains a database produced by Dun and Bradstreet Canada Ltd. It is a broad listing of Canadian companies, containing about 700 000 company records. These records can be sorted by city, product, range of sales, or range of employees.

Researching via the Internet

Online research tools can help you harness the research power of the Internet. Search engines, discussed in detail in Appendix III, lead to Internet addresses—the strange combinations of letters and sometimes numbers—that, in turn, lead to particular locations on the information superhighway. Here are just a few of the thousands of Internet addresses that may be helpful for business researchers:

▽ Canadian Polar Commission **http://www.polarcom. gc.ca** This site is useful for reading documents relating to cold-climate research and Arctic studies.

▽ Bloc Québécois **http://blocquebecois.org** Through this site you can access literature that the Bloc publishes. This site is available in both English and French.

▽ Government of Canada **http://www.canada.gc.ca** This site contains current listings of every federal government department.

▽ Canadian Resources **http://www.ac.wwu.edu/~canam/ resource.html** This Web site provides connection to many Canadian sites for Canadian cities, history and politics, universities, libraries, current events, government, culture, sports, and provincial information.

Sources: Mary Ann Pike, *Using the Internet,* 2d ed. (Indianapolis, Ind.: Que Corporation, 1995); Harley Hahn, *The Internet Yellow Pages,* 3rd ed. (Berkeley, Calif.: Osborne/McGraw-Hill, 1996); and Jim Carroll and Rick Broadhead, *Canadian Internet New User's Handbook* (Scarborough: Prentice Hall Canada, 1998).

Using a Library Card Catalogue Technology has advanced far beyond the days of actual library card catalogues. Originally, a library's complete inventory was printed on cards filed alphabetically in drawers in large cabinets. Today, most libraries have converted their card catalogues to computerized systems, which save space and provide quick accessibility to information from various locations. Researchers can gain access to computerized public catalogues through online services from work or home, through computer terminals in libraries, or by accessing a library's catalogue via their own portable computers. Despite computerization, however, the organization of the information remains the same. Library card catalogues are generally divided into three categories: authors' names, book titles, and subjects. Entries are listed alphabetically within each category.

So much information is now accessible—and library research is so complex— that many cost-conscious firms are assigning research tasks to not-for-profit libraries that charge on a per-use basis.[4] Other firms are turning to "information brokers," who are adept at navigating electronic databases to find business information. These services save valuable time and money.[5]

CONSULTING GOVERNMENT PUBLICATIONS The federal government is one of the richest sources of business and economic information. Perhaps the most important information source is Census Canada. The Canadian census is conducted once every five years by Statistics Canada. The most current census information is available on the Internet or through hard copy documents published and sold by Statistics Canada. Other information can be accessed through the *Canadian Research Index (CRI). CRI* is an index to publications from all levels of the Canadian government: federal, provincial, and municipal. The database includes approximately 9000 publications in all subject fields.

Each year, Statistics Canada publishes the *Canada Year Book* in both hard copy and on CD-ROM. This book recaps Canadian statistics, and profiles its regions, people, environment, and economy.

The Canadian Almanac and Directory is published annually, and can be used as a desk reference. It lists alphabetically the names and addresses of banks, trust companies, insurance companies, libraries, book publishers, newspapers, associations, law firms, and federal, provincial, and municipal departments.[6]

The Canadian Parliamentary Guide lists the members of the Senate and the House of Commons, of the provincial governments, and of the Supreme Court, as well as other high-ranking public officials. It also contains some biographical material.[7]

OBTAINING INFORMATION FROM PRIVATE SOURCES   Business researchers can also turn to private information sources. For example, one invaluable reference for marketers is *Sales & Marketing Management*'s annual "Survey of Buying Power," which calculates the buying power found in specific cities. This source includes the latest information on population characteristics, household buying income, and retail sales in cities and counties across the country. In addition, trade associations such as the Petroleum Services Association of Canada (PSAC) and the Canadian Chamber of Commerce provide a variety of materials on industry-related topics.

USING ONLINE SERVICES   Online services give researchers access to specialized business topics. For example, a commercial service called Profound gives researchers access to complete marketing research reports, including graphs and charts. Researchers can buy a small section of a report, such as a table, which greatly reduces the purchase price.[8]

A company's Internet site is also an online source of information. A growing number of firms have created *home pages*—specific locations on the Internet where information is available about the company, its products, advertising, recent corporate developments, and other relevant materials. For instance, the Prentice Hall Canada home page shown in Figure 11–6 provides a menu of options that researchers may choose from to find information about the company.

Telecommunications enables companies to move information rather than people.

Erik K. Clemons
Educator

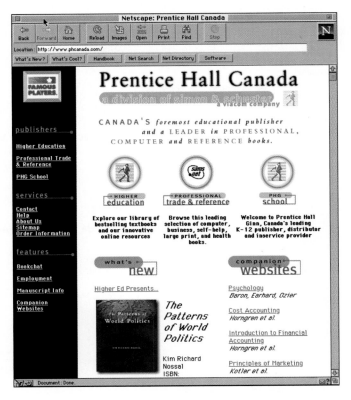

Figure 11-6   The Prentice Hall Canada Home Page
Source: *Courtesy Prentice Hall Canada.*

Other research sources include **online databases**—computerized information-retrieval systems. Electronic databases, including those containing information from Statistics Canada, are available through the Internet (http://www.statcan.ca). Also available on the Internet is the "National Library of Canada's electronic collection, which incorporates formally published Canadian online books and journals. These publications are being acquired, catalogued, and permanently stored at the National Library. Public access is provided through the Internet (www.nlc.ca)".[9] Figure 11–7 shows the National Library of Canada's Web page.

Online databases operated by commercial companies include complete articles and books, not just citations, that are available to users. Among the major business-related online databases are CompuServe, Infomart Dialog Limited, and Yahoo Canada–Reference. Various factors affect the cost of a commercial online search, including length of search, what time the search is conducted, modem speed, and the fee charged by the online service provider. Advances in technology have produced faster modems, decreasing the overall time per search by about 50 percent in the past two decades. However, an explosion in the number and size of databases has kept search costs high.

Progress Check

1. Distinguish between primary and secondary data and name two examples of each.
2. Describe the four major sources of external secondary data.
3. How are online databases changing the nature of business research?

Figure 11-7   Web Site for the National Library of Canada
Source: *Courtesy of National Library of Canada.*

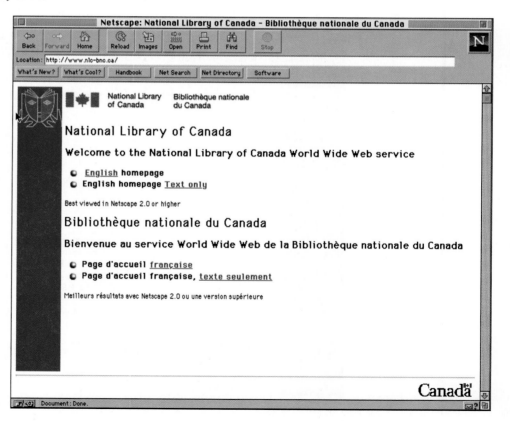

COLLECTING PRIMARY DATA

Usually business writers exhaust all possible sources of secondary data before investing the time and money required to conduct primary research. There will be times, however, when the information you need is not available from secondary sources, is outdated, or comes in a form that is unsuitable for your particular report or proposal. In these cases you may have to collect primary data to secure information. Most primary data is collected by one of two methods: observation or surveys.

OBSERVATION METHOD   **Observational studies** are conducted by actually viewing—either by visual observation or through mechanical devices—the actions of a respondent. For example, a researcher seeking information about the use of the company cafeteria may observe such things as the number of people eating there, the types of meal combinations selected by different groups, and the number of people who take their food back to their offices. Traffic counts may be used to determine the best location for a new fast-food restaurant.

Skillful researchers begin the observation process with a clear idea of what they want to learn. For example, the researcher evaluating the company cafeteria may use a checklist containing the following questions:

▼   What kinds of foods are people eating? Do the choices appear to vary by age, gender, or departments in which the people work?

▼   How much of the cafeteria traffic represents repeat business? Do the frequent users of the cafeteria appear to be similar in age? Are they more likely to be men or women?

▼   Do the same people come back several times a day?

▼   Are people eating in the cafeteria or returning with their food to their offices?

SURVEY METHOD   When primary data cannot be obtained by an observer, either human or mechanical, the researcher must ask questions. For example, when information is needed about *attitudes* or *opinions*, the survey method can be used. **Surveys** are data-collection methods used to gather primary data about the knowledge, attitudes, and opinions of respondents.

As one would expect, problems arise in efforts to interpret the responses to all kinds of surveys conducted in foreign countries. In a recent survey of soft drink sales in Hungary, a large percentage of the respondents reported buying them in drugstores. Susan Hooper, Eastern Europe marketing director for Pepsi Cola International, knew something was wrong. "Drugstores don't exist" in Hungary, explains Hooper. "The information was forced into a structure" developed in the West.[10]

Survey information is rarely gathered from every possible source. Instead, the researcher selects a representative group, called a **sample.** For instance, instead of trying to gauge customer satisfaction by questioning every Volvo owner in Canada, marketers at Volvo may decide to contact a representative sample of 3000 Volvo purchasers.

If the sample is chosen so that every member of the relevant population has an equal chance of being selected, it is called a **random sample** (or **probability sample**). A quality-control check of every fiftieth Volvo of the same make and model produced may provide a representative sample of the overall quality of the production of that car. Similarly, a random selection of student names from the campus directory should provide a probability sample of students at your college. Three types of surveys exist: telephone surveys, mail surveys (which also include e-mail and fax delivery), and surveys obtained through personal interviews.

Telephone Surveys   When researchers want to gather information quickly and inexpensively, they turn to the telephone. In fact, more than half of all primary marketing research is conducted by phone.

Despite the popularity of telephone interviewing, however, it has several important limitations. Subjects contacted by phone are generally reluctant to reveal such personal information as income level and marital status. In addition, because questionnaires must be short and simple, the amount of information from telephone interviews is limited. Because visual contact is impossible, questions that rely on objects, pictures, or product demonstrations cannot be asked. Finally, researchers looking for a representative sample of an entire population may be stymied by the omission of households without phones or with unpublished numbers.

Mail Surveys   Mail surveys are most often used in marketing research but can also be used for other research projects, such as anonymous employee-attitude surveys. Mail surveys allow researchers to conduct national studies at reasonable costs. They also offer several other advantages for the researcher. If the results are anonymous, respondents may be more willing to answer personal and economic questions. However, if the survey is conducted through fax or e-mail, there is less chance of anonymity. Mail surveys also give respondents flexibility to answer questionnaires at convenient times rather than at times chosen by telephone interviewers.

Despite these advantages, mail surveys may be flawed because of differences in the characteristics of those who respond and those who do not. Depending on the respondents' interest in the subject and the skill of the person who prepares the questionnaire and cover letter, response rates for mail surveys are usually between

A QUESTION OF ETHICS

Can Surveys Mislead?

Have you ever completed a survey where you felt forced to respond in ways that weren't completely correct, but were your closest choices? Have you ever completed a ranking question where you were pressured to assign an order of preference to choices you really didn't want to make? Or what about a survey where you desperately needed to explain your answer but the question was dichotomous and left no room for explanation? If so, you'll appreciate that surveys can be misleading.

A business wishing to advertise its product as the number one choice among a certain group—students, women, skiers, etc.—can design its questions or select its population sample such that the desired results are inevitable. Suppose that you wish to market Jamaica as the number one vacation destination for Canadians. You conduct the survey in January and use a small group of people living in Yellowknife as your sample population. You ask the question "What would be your first choice of a vacation destination?" and provide the only possible answers: *Winnipeg, Resolute Bay, Kingston (Jamaica),* or *Edmonton*. No doubt most of your respondents will select Jamaica. All of this is fine, until you advertise that the number one vacation destination choice for 90 percent of Canadians is Jamaica.

Questionnaire design is the source of many survey flaws. Specific questions may have faulty wording or evoke a response that is more human than honest. Moreover, many surveys today are designed to promote a product or service. What was once considered a scholarly research tool has become a vehicle of manipulation.

How do you avoid these pitfalls? Before the study begins, learn the science of questionnaire design and interpretation and understand your own biases. It is also essential to define yourself as a searcher for truth and to be aware that it is difficult to find truth if you or your organization have a vested interest in the survey outcome.

Questions for Critical Thinking

1. Based on what you've learned in the chapter, what other factors can contribute to survey flaws?

2. How can a vested interest in the outcome of a survey compromise your integrity as a researcher?

3. This feature implies that you cannot necessarily take survey findings at face value. If the findings of a specific survey are important to your document, what can you do to confirm their accuracy?

Sources: Adapted from Cynthia Crossen, "Studies Galore Support Products and Positions, but Are They Reliable?" *Wall Street Journal,* 14 November 1991, A1, A9.

10 and 50 percent. For example, people generally respond to mail surveys when they feel strongly about an issue—either positively or negatively. Often, these people do not constitute a representative sample of the entire group. To minimize discrepancies, researchers sometimes mail respondents a second questionnaire to secure additional responses.

Personal Interviewing   The personal interview is the most expensive and most time-consuming survey method. It depends on trained interviewers who must travel to meet with respondents. But it is also a highly effective means of obtaining detailed information. Interviewing encourages the development of a personal relationship between interviewer and respondents and allows the interviewer to explain confusing or difficult questions. The flexibility of this method often more than offsets time and cost limitations.

QUESTIONNAIRE DESIGN   Whether your data are obtained through telephone, mail, or personal-interview surveys, the questionnaire itself will play a major role in the quality and quantity of information that you collect. **Questionnaires** are scientifically designed lists of questions used to gather data.

The following guidelines can help you design a questionnaire. First, every question should be linked to your research objective; questions unrelated to your topic should be eliminated. Second, questions should be designed so that the answers can be tabulated. Although essay questions may provide interesting results, reading and then categorizing 400 essay-type answers is far more difficult than tabulating the results of 400 multiple-choice questions.

Third, to make sure questions will be interpreted correctly, a few potential users should review and edit the questionnaire. When the community relations staff at Ability Inc., an Edmonton-based research company, prepares a survey for its customers, it first pilots the questionnaire with a customer focus group. Using the group's feedback, Ability improves the survey before sending it out into the larger population. Finally, the questionnaire should be user-friendly to both interviewer and respondents. A user-friendly questionnaire begins with a cover letter or brief introduction that explains the purpose of the study and describes the prospective respondents. Your explanation should also include a deadline for returning the questionnaire and express appreciation for the respondent's cooperation.

Survey questions can be categorized as opening or as substantive questions. As you write specific questions, focus on the time it will take to answer the entire questionnaire. The greatest number of survey responses are obtained when respondents can complete the task in no more than five to ten minutes.

Opening Questions   The typical questionnaire begins with questions that are not difficult or overly personal. Such questions are designed to encourage the respondent to continue the interview. For example, demographic questions that focus on such personal factors as marital status and income level are typically asked at the end of the interview. If these questions are asked at the beginning, the respondent may refuse to answer them, and the interview may be terminated. When they are asked at the end, the most important questions have already been answered.

Substantive Questions   Substantive questions can be divided into three basic types: *fixed-alternative*, *scale*, and *open-ended questions*. Fixed-alternative and scale questions are answered with check marks or numbers; open-ended questions allow respondents to say whatever is on their minds.

Fixed-alternative questions limit responses to one or more choices from a list of possible responses. Where the choice is limited to one of two responses (yes/no, male/female, on/off) the question is referred to as a **dichotomous question**. Multiple-choice questions also fall into this category. Questions can also be in list form so that respondents can choose from or rank items according to certain criteria such as preference or use. These questions yield standardized responses and are easy to tabulate. However, they force people to choose among the responses listed and do not indicate the intensity of a response.

Scale questions are a specialized type of fixed-alternative question that structure responses along a continuum. In the Likert Scale, for example, respondents are asked to respond along a continuum like the following:

Strongly Disagree	Disagree	No Opinion	Agree	Strongly Agree
-2	-1	0	+1	+2

Other scales ask respondents to rate answers on a scale of 1 to 5, 1 being the least important and 5 the most important.

Open-ended questions allow respondents to formulate their own answers. Table 11-3 includes examples of the different types of questions used in survey questionnaires.

Table 11-3   Types of Survey Questions

Multiple-Choice Questions

Fixed-alternative questions that allow respondents to choose one or more answers

Example: What health insurance options does your company offer? (Check all that apply.)

❑ dental plan
❑ eye wear vision plan
❑ prescription drug plan
❑ other _____

Dichotomous Questions

Fixed-alternative questions that allow respondents a choice between two answers

Example: Do you use the Internet in your daily work?

❑ yes   ❑ no

List Questions

Fixed-alternative questions that allow respondents to choose among a list of answers

Example: Which of the following have you attended in the last year? (Check all that apply.)

❑ movie
❑ play
❑ concert
❑ ballet
❑ opera
❑ lecture

Ranked-List Questions

Fixed-alternative questions that ask respondents to rank a list of answers

Example: Rank the following items in order of national importance, 1 representing the most important and 5 the least important.

❑ education
❑ foreign affairs
❑ employment
❑ inflation
❑ poverty

Scale Questions

Fixed-alternative questions that allow respondents to rank answers along a continuum

Example: After using Heaven's Air Freshener for a few days, please rank each statement below.

	Agree	No Opinion	Disagree
1. Heaven's Air Freshener eliminates odours.	❑	❑	❑
2. I like not having an air freshener fragrance in the air.	❑	❑	❑
3. I like the hideaway dispenser.	❑	❑	❑
4. The suggested retail price of $3.50 is reasonable.	❑	❑	❑

Open-Ended Questions

Allow respondents to express opinions in their own words

Example: What changes would you like to make in the advertising and promotion of political candidates? Explain your reasons.

Demographic Questions

Focus on factors such as the respondent's age, marital status, occupation, income, or educational background

Example: What is your annual income?

❑ $10 000–$24 999
❑ $25 000–$49 999
❑ $50 000–$74 999
❑ $75 000 and over

CONDUCTING INTERVIEWS   Because of the high cost and the amount of time involved, one of the most important steps in the interviewing process is deciding whom to interview. The answer is usually straightforward: interview the person who is most likely to provide the best information. For example, if you are writing about the need for a more sophisticated office-security system, a likely interview subject is the company's director of security.

Once you have decided whom to interview, you can request an interview by telephone or letter. In your initial contact, explain who you are, the topic of the interview, the projected use to which the information will be put, and the specific type of information you need. After setting a time and place for the interview, prepare a list of questions that you want to ask. However, do not limit yourself to these questions. Depending on the responses, you may want to ask follow-up questions that go into more detail about a topic.

At the start of the interview, repeat what you hope to accomplish and ask a question that focuses on your most important point. Then listen as the subject starts talking. Except for questions, minimize your interruptions. Keep in mind that you are not there to impress anyone with how much you know, but to learn from an expert. As you listen, you will find that certain answers prompt additional questions. Inevitably, however, you will also find that the subject has moved off track. When this happens, ask specific, direct questions that refocus the interview.

In general, make each question short and to the point. If you need help—for example, understanding unfamiliar concepts or properly spelling a name—ask for clarification. At the close of the interview, review your list of questions for any that have not yet been covered. You may also want to ask for leads to other experts in related fields. Finally, ask the interviewee for written materials on the subject that might help you in your work. Because follow-up interviews may be difficult or impossible to arrange, it is important to take accurate and complete notes or use a tape recorder to gather information.

TYPES OF INTERVIEW QUESTIONS   Every interview question should be tied to a specific informational goal and asked in such a way as to yield the most and best results. Questions that are too long or complex are frequently difficult to answer because they usually involve more than one subject, explanation, or point of view. Remember that the wording of a question directly affects the usefulness of the answer and should be an overriding concern when preparing interview questions. Interview questions can be either open-ended or closed-ended.

Closed-ended questions limit responses by encouraging brief, specific answers. They should be used—not overused—to define the details of a story. However, if you are too direct, you may make subjects feel as if they are being interrogated. Closed-ended questions typically ask for specific information, add clarification, probe further into details, or offer a specific set of answers to choose from.

In contrast, *open-ended questions* give the subject flexibility to respond in different ways. For example, "What do you think of the new union contract?" is an open-ended question, while "Do you like, dislike, or have no opinion about the new union contract?" is closed-ended. Open-ended questions that begin with *how* or *why* invite respondents to explain the reasons for their answers. They are intended to produce anecdotes, examples, and in-depth information.

Leading questions are designed to lead the interviewee to a single response. Careful wording is needed to prevent the interview from becoming biased or slanted. Consider the following question: "Were you as excited as everyone else with last month's sales figures and, specifically, with Richard Lau's performance?" The phrase *as excited as everyone else* will probably lead the interviewee to respond with a positive answer.

Matthew Spence, Business Development Manager, Baffin Business Development Centre

Imagine yourself as the manager of the Baffin Business Development Centre (BBDC) in Iqaluit, the capital city of the newly formed Territory of Nunavut. You are responsible for providing advice and support, and administering an investment fund used to help finance small businesses. The BBDC's mandate is to create jobs in an area where unemployment usually runs at between 20 and 30 percent.

Nunavut is an interesting place to work. On any given day you may be required to communicate in English, French, or Inuktitut (the language of the Inuit). Also consider the sophisticated business concepts that your clients may not be familiar with, and the task appears insurmountable.

Such are the challenges facing Matthew Spence, as he deals with the complexities of business reports and proposals in Canada's Far North.

Question: Can you identify the most distinctive characteristics of both the formal and the informal business report?

Answer: Working in an environment where clear communication is hindered by the differences in language and culture, I'm grateful when I receive a written business proposal from a client! A formal business proposal follows the outline of a business plan attached to an application for funding. It contains information under specific headings, such as Background, Proposed Financing, Product or Service Offered, Marketing, and Operations. An informal proposal may not break things down under headings. And rather than answering the standard questions, it's usually a vision of what the business owners are trying to achieve, along with their expectation of the outcome.

Question: Do you have a work-plan format that you employ prior to launching a new project?

Answer: I employ a couple of different work-plan processes depending on whether the project is internal or external (a client's project). Internal projects require an initial assessment, a timeline that outlines the various steps that have to be taken and when, and a budget. An external project work-plan will follow a general business plan format.

Inuksuk is a beacon for Canada's North.

Question: How important is research in a business report?

Answer: Research is very important to most business reports; however, there are difficulties in getting good primary and secondary information about this region.

Question: How do you evaluate this data?

Answer: Most secondary data on this region are provided by government agencies, so while the data may be reliable it's usually dated because the government is slow to compile and assess it. Primary information is generally not very valid because of the small size of the survey group—it's difficult to get 30 respondents, let alone 300. Therefore, I tend to discount the information a survey provides as it may not reflect the views of the majority. There's also a cost involved in compiling primary data, and sometimes it's more cost effective to provide the funding for a business start-up or expansion than to try to get a survey done.

Source: Interview with Matthew Spence.

Multiple-choice questions give the respondent a limited choice of answers. Opinions or explanations are eliminated in this type of questioning. For instance, a human resource manager might be asked a multiple-choice question like "Which of the following do you believe is your company's most pressing employee-relations problem: sexual harassment, limited opportunities for promotions, or low wages as compared with other firms in the industry?"

TAKING EFFECTIVE RESEARCH NOTES

Effective note taking is essential in any research project—especially if you are working with a variety of sources. Taking good notes is important for several reasons. In addition to providing all the publication details necessary for use in the source notes that will appear at the end of your formal report, research notes provide a mechanism for organizing your information. Carefully written source notes also help prevent **plagiarism**—the act of using someone else's words or unique approach without crediting the source.

Writing each note on a separate index card provides flexibility. You can organize the cards in different ways as you build the outline of your report. Therefore, you might collect 20 different index cards from the same book, each card dealing with a different aspect of the topic.

At the top of each card, write all the information that you will need in your footnotes or endnotes (the formatting of source notes is examined in Appendix I). Each card should include the name of the person interviewed and the date of the interview or, in the case of secondary sources, the author's full name, the article title, the publication in which the article appeared, the date of publication, and the page numbers where the information is located. If you are using Internet sources you should begin with the same information that would be provided for a printed source (author, date, title, and publication details) or as much of that information as possible. Then add the Internet address in parentheses. If you are using the same source more than once, only the title and page numbers need be written at the top of subsequent cards. Under this information, paraphrase, summarize, or quote the material taken from the source.

Many researchers write all the information they need on source cards and have little reason to look at the sources themselves as they write. Others use note cards in conjunction with copies of the actual sources. Copies can be either actual books and articles or photocopies of the relevant pages. Using copies, of course, means that you do not need to write as much on each card—the sources themselves will provide all the vital information. If you have a copy of the source, then your source card need only contain minimal information—perhaps a thumbnail reference to a main point in your outline. When you are dealing with photocopies, you will find that underlining critical points and writing marginal notes helps you focus on the important parts without having to reread your entire source.

Progress Check

1. Have you ever been contacted to participate in a telephone or mail survey? If so, were you willing to answer questions? How did you feel about the experience? Compare your reactions with the chapter's discussion of the advantages and disadvantages of these research methods.

2. Describe the differences among fixed-alternative, scale, and open-ended questions. What is the relationship between question design and obtaining meaningful responses?

3. Describe guidelines for taking effective research notes.

What's Ahead

More than any other business documents, reports and proposals rely on visual aids for clear and effective presentation. Chapter 12 examines the effective use of visual aids in business documents, while Chapters 13 and 14 show how these tools are incorporated into short and long reports and proposals.

STUDENT RESOURCE CENTRE

Summary of Chapter Objectives

1. *Identify the characteristics of business reports and proposals.*

   Business reports are documents that provide complete, accurate, and organized information to one or more people inside or outside an organization who will use the information for a specific business purpose. Reports differ in length, formality, circulation, frequency of submission, format, use of visual aids, and method of assignment. Reports, characterized according to what they are trying to accomplish, fall into five major categories: information, study, expert, status, and recommendation.

   Business proposals are documents that set forth ideas and plans for consideration in the hope that readers will accept them and agree to spend money on their development. The three types of proposals are internal, private industry, and proposals to government agencies.

2. *List the steps of the report and proposal writing process.*

   Because report and proposal writing is so complex, it is a multi-stage process. The stages include defining the writing task, creating a working plan, assembling needed resources, evaluating the data, developing a writing outline, writing the first draft, revising the document, getting feedback, and finalizing and submitting the document.

3. *List three questions that are used to evaluate primary and secondary research findings.*

   With so much information available, it is important to evaluate the worth of every research source. The following questions guide this evaluation: Is the research valid? Is it reliable? Is it current?

4. *Identify the four major types of secondary business research.*

   Company records including sales reports, financial statements, and project and status reports can be invaluable research sources. Libraries are used to conduct in-depth research on a variety of subjects. Moving from general to specific sources, researchers consult general library references such as encyclopedias; periodical indexes to find relevant articles in magazines, newspapers, and trade publications; and the library card catalogue for books. Government publications, including those published by Statistics Canada, are also invaluable information sources. Finally, private information sources, including industry trade associations and specific publications, provide helpful data.

5. *Explain how businesspeople use online information to research topics.*

   Online databases, such as Infomart, Dialog Limited, and Yahoo Canada–Reference, are computerized information retrieval systems operated by commercial companies and sold to computer users for a service fee. These systems, which give researchers immediate access to thousands of sources, require the use of a personal computer, a modem, a phone line, and telecommunications software.

6. *Compare the two major sources of primary data research.*

   Interviews allow business writers to gather information from experts. Effective interviews involve understanding the interview stages and knowing how to formulate effective questions, including open-ended and closed-ended questions.

   Another source of primary research is the survey, which involves administering a questionnaire designed to gather specific data. Surveys are conducted over the phone, by mail, and in face-to-face meetings. To be effective, survey questions must be carefully designed to elicit specific information. Among the types of questions asked on a survey are fixed-alternative questions, scale questions, and open-ended questions. Primary research is also gathered through direct observation.

Review and Discussion Questions

1. Describe the important characteristics of business reports and proposals. *(Ch. Obj. 1)*
2. What are the six major categories of business reports? *(Ch. Obj. 1)*
3. Identify the seven steps involved in the report- and proposal-writing process. *(Ch. Obj. 2)*
4. Describe the process of creating a work plan. *(Ch. Obj. 2)*
5. Explain the basic strategy for evaluating primary and secondary research. *(Ch. Obj. 3)*
6. What are the four major sources of secondary business research? *(Ch. Obj. 4)*
7. Explain how an online database can be a valuable research tool. *(Ch. Obj. 5)*
8. Distinguish between the two major methods for collecting primary data. *(Ch. Obj. 6)*

Application Exercises

1. Test yourself on the differences between formal and informal reports. Cover the two right-hand columns in Table 11-1 and supply the information. *(Ch. Obj. 1)*
2. Suppose your boss asks you to write an internal proposal in which your task is to persuade a higher-ranking person in the organization to allot money to a specific project or charity that you feel is important. The proposal could relate to your present job, a job that you have held in the past, or to your activities at school.

   First, research your topic. Use a variety of research sources; collect primary, secondary, internal, and external data. Try to use both the specific sources mentioned in this chapter and other sources as well. Take notes on your research and keep track of the sources that you consult. *(Ch. Obj. 3, 4, 6)*
3. Plan and research a sales proposal in which you try to sell a good or service. Your proposal might relate either to your present or former job or to a product or service that interests you. Use a variety of research sources involving primary, secondary, internal, and external data. Take notes on your research and keep track of the sources that you consult. *(Ch. Obj. 3, 4, 6)*
4. Using an online database, research one of the topics in Exercise 2 or 3. Consult a librarian for information on other databases that are available in your community. Write a brief report in which you compare your online research process with the earlier research. Did you find the online approach more efficient, less efficient, or about the same? What do you like or dislike about the online service? Does it affect your ability to do research and, if so, how? *(Ch. Obj. 5)*
5. Test yourself on the major categories of reports. How many types of reports are there, and what is the purpose of each? Give an example of each type. *(Ch. Obj. 1)*
6. Suppose that your boss asks you to write a brief report summarizing the methods for collecting primary data. Write this report, and include discussions of the advantages and disadvantages of each method. *(Ch. Obj. 3, 6)*
7. Choose a business-related topic about which you would like to learn more. Now choose someone with whom you could conduct a personal interview about that topic. For instance, you might interview a marketing manager about marketing strategies at his or her firm. After scheduling the interview, develop a list of questions that you might ask this individual. Include a good mix of open-ended and closed-ended questions. *(Ch. Obj. 6)*
8. Conduct the interview that you scheduled for Exercise 7. Follow the chapter guidelines for conducting an effective interview. Take careful notes or use a tape recorder. Ask your interviewee to suggest any additional research sources that you might consult for more information. Write a brief report (one page) summarizing the most important information that you gathered from your interview. *(Ch. Obj. 6)*
9. Choose a collaborative writing partner, and select a business-related topic on which you both agree to write a report. Work together to create a brief written work plan that defines your purpose and audience, summarizes your planned procedure for writing your report, and lists the research sources that you plan to use. Do the necessary research; you may wish to divide up the work by having each partner "specialize" in certain sources or topics. Be sure to take notes and to keep track of your sources. *(Ch. Obj. 2, 6)*

10. Working with your partner, evaluate the data that you researched for Exercise 9. Write an outline that organizes the data that you collected into a form that you can use to create a report. *(Ch. Obj. 2, 3)*

11. Working with your partner, write a first draft based on the outline that you created for Exercise 10. Then revise the report to make sure that it is clear and convincing. Include footnotes as needed. *(Ch. Obj. 2)*

ACT: Applied Communication Techniques

Begin by referring to the sections up to and including Semicolons and Colons in Appendix II, then correct the grammar, spelling, and usage errors in the following sentences. Check your answers in Appendix V.

1. A well-written report requires planning it also requires research.

2. When preparing a report you must always take these three actions research, research, and research.

3. The content of your report is very important however format is also important.

4. A chart will add to the appearance of a report nevertheless a chart that contains inacurate information will detract from it.

5. In the annual report the team leader wrote "Our mission is to excede the expectations of our clients."

6. A manager may send a short informal report to her staff she may sent a more formal report to her clients.

7. Table 11 shows a business report that falls into three major catagories information, study, and expert.

8. These three steps move writers from identifying the issue to finalizing the document defining the audience creating a work plan and developing the outline.

9. The colaborative plan forms the basis of writing a extensive report nevertheless independent work is always essential for the completion of the project.

10. Evaluate your research it must be valid, reliable, and current.

Building Your Reasearch Skills

Your instructor will divide the class into small groups. Meet with your team members and choose a business-related topic on which you all agree to write. Compile a list of primary and secondary research sources, and as-sign several sources and aspects of the topic to each team member. Consult your particular sources, taking careful notes and keeping track of any footnotes.

Building Your Teamwork Skills

Bring your notes from the previous Building Your Research Skills exercise to class and meet with your team members to construct a report based on your group's research. The group may wish to develop a brief outline before writing its report. Assign one team member to write the first draft as the group collaborates to develop the report. The group should then work together to revise this first draft into a final version.

Building Your Technology Skills

1. The Internet has stimulated new discussions on copyright. Information is freely available to be downloaded, copied, and reused. Artists, musicians, writers, educators, businesses, and software developers are among the many who express concerns about having their work illegally copied. Some Internet users believe that "If you don't want your product copied, then don't put it on the Internet." Still others hold to "fair-use" standards—if the information used is only two lines from a 400-page book, for instance, this falls into the fair-use category and is acceptable.

Use the research tools (search engines) described in Appendix III and research copyright issues on the Internet. Make a list of the Internet sites you visit that could be research sources for a report on Internet copyright issues, including the Internet address and title of the home page. Begin your research by visiting the copyright Web site (http://www.benedict.com).

2. Visit the following Internet sites where information is made available from a database.

  ▼ National Library of Canada
  http://www.nlc-bnc.ca

  ▼ Statistics Canada
  http://www.statcan.ca

  ▼ PcQuote
  http://www.pcquote.com/aboutus.html

  ▼ Dow Jones News/Retrieval
  http://www.dowjones.com/djnr.html

  ▼ Britannica Online
  http://www.eb.com

After you have visited these sites, write a short report on "Online Information Services." Include information about: (1) the type of information service(s) provided, (2) the types of research services available, (3) the specialized libraries offered, (4) the cost, and (5) the advantages/disadvantages of using each service.

Weblinks Internet Resources for this Chapter

Proposal Development Information
http://www.govsolutions.com/propmnu.html

Business Plan Process
http://www.dtonline.com/writing/
businessplanprocess.htm

Doing Research on the Web
http://www.cohums.ohio-state.edu/english/
People/Locker.1/research.htm

Computer-Mediated Communication
http://www.ascusc.org/jcmc/vol1/issue3/

CASE STUDIES

DIVERSITY CASE:
Reaching Out to Asia

Suppose that while doing some research for your boss, you encounter the following facts:

  ▼ In 1947 almost 75 percent of all first-generation Australians were born in Great Britain or Ireland. By 1989 only 33 percent of all first-generation Australians came from those countries.

  ▼ By the early 1990s, eight of the top ten countries of origin for new immigrants to Australia were in Asia.

  ▼ At present, while only 4 percent of Australian citizens are of Asian origin, the government expects 25 percent of the population to be Asian Australian within 50 years.

  ▼ Trade between Australia and Asia has grown steadily since the 1970s.

  ▼ Australian schools are introducing students to Asian cultures and languages at an earlier age. In the state of Victoria, for example, four of the eight "priority languages" taught in primary schools are Asian (Japanese, Mandarin, Indonesian, and Vietnamese). The Asia Ed-

ucation Foundation has begun a three-year program to introduce Asian themes into Australian curricula. "Two years ago," says Foundation manager Jenny McGregor, "the Australian community did not recognize that Australia was part of Asia, or that it lived anywhere near Asia. Our job is to change that utterly. . . . [The goal is] to make a future generation more prepared for managing the economic ties."

  ▼ Exports to Asia are growing. Telecom, Australia's telephone company, has started a joint venture with the electronics firm AWA to install a new phone system in Vietnam. AWA's exports to Asia are responsible for a quarter of the firm's $172 million in sales revenue. Says AWA manager John Dougall: "Going back five years, we had almost zero exports. . . . We don't think of Australia and Asia anymore. We think of Jakarta just as we think about Perth. . . . We're here in Asia. We're in the same time zone, so if something goes wrong we can pick up the phone and ring them."[11]

Questions and Applications

1. Suppose that you work for an Australian politician who has proposed a plan that would link the 15 separate nations of the Asia Pacific Economic Cooperation group into an integrated economic market. Write a report, using the facts of this case that support the proposal.

2. Now assume that you work for a clothing manufacturer that is considering exporting its products to Japan. You suspect that current research is needed to see whether your business should pursue the Japanese market. Describe how you plan to collect data, and what types of data you plan to use to create a comprehensive recommendation report.

CORPORATE CASE:

How Effective Is Your Questionnaire?

Suppose that you are an employee for Research 2000, a Canadian company specializing in workplace-related research. Besides your research responsibilities, you are expected to analyze questionnaires and make recommendations for their improvement prior to their use.

The following questionnaire has been prepared for the business program at Slave Lake College. The college is wishing to meet the needs of students and industry by offering courses that prepare students for the changing requirements of industry.

Questions and Applications

1. Analyze the effectiveness of this questionnaire. Does it follow the chapter guidelines for effective questionnaire design? Is it user-friendly? Can you find examples of the three basic types of substantive questions (fixed-alternative, scale, and open-ended)?

2. Faxing is an increasingly popular way to send out and return questionnaires. What do you think are the advantages and limitations of this data-collection method for the researchers at Research 2000?

Slave Lake College

What are the Software Needs of our Business Students?

Slave Lake College is dedicated to fulfilling the needs of our community, industry, and students. In order to meet these needs, we rely on expertise from businesses like yours. Your responses to the following questions would be sincerely appreciated. Please answer these questions as accurately as possible and return this questionnaire by fax to us at (403) 555–1111 by May 11.

1. Does your company use a local area network (LAN)?
   ❑ Yes   ❑ No

2. Which of the following responsibilities are your employees required to perform? Please check all that apply.

   ❑ Word Processing   ❑ Spreadsheeting
   ❑ Electronic Records Management   ❑ Desktop Publishing
   ❑ Importing Graphics   ❑ Building Web Pages
   ❑ Electronic Calendaring   ❑ Electronic Project Management
   ❑ Electronic Mailing   ❑ Internet Researching

3. Please explain your method of training employees to use new software that your company may adopt.

   _____

   _____

4. Rate your level of satisfaction with the training method you are employing.
   ❑ Very Satisfied
   ❑ Satisfied
   ❑ Somewhat Satisfied
   ❑ Dissatisfied
   ❑ Very Dissatisfied

Name (Optional) _____ Phone number (optional) _____

Slave Lake College thanks you for your time and assistance in helping us meet our goals.

Visual Aids in Business Reports and Proposals

Chapter Objectives

After studying this chapter, you should be able to:

1. Describe the function of visual aids in reports and proposals.
2. Explain the importance of linking each visual aid to its specific message.
3. List the characteristics of tables.
4. List the kinds of comparisons that charts can illustrate.
5. Contrast pie charts, bar charts, column charts, and line charts, and explain the advantages of each.
6. Explain how business documents use maps, drawings, and photographs.
7. Describe the mechanics of constructing visual aids.

We will draw the curtain and show you the picture.

William Shakespeare

inning the Digital Account

1994 was a terrible year for Digital Equipment Corp. Its losses during the previous five years had grown to $5 billion, including a $131-million loss during the year's first quarter. Conditions were so dire that some stock market analysts predicted Digital's demise. Not surprisingly, customers steered clear of Digital's products; no one wanted to scramble for service from a defunct company.

Despite the bad news, 1994 was also a turnaround year. Corporate executives had no intention of cooperating with doomsayers. Instead, they took the offensive to prove that reports of Digital's impending death were greatly exaggerated. Accomplishing this meant creating a "mission critical," can-do advertising program that would transform the way customers perceived the company.

Among the advertising agencies Digital approached for new-business proposals was DDB Needham Worldwide. Needham was in the running to be one of two agencies that could win the $90-million Digital account. Needham had to convince Digital that it could create a rapid, seamless transition as work flowed from the 42 agencies that had handled Digital's advertising business until then, and that it could communicate an immediate message of corporate health and customer commitment.

The stage for Needham's business proposal was the agency's corporate boardroom. It was there that Needham would show key Digital executives how it intended to handle the Digital account. The presentation took shape in the form of a 40-foot by 3-foot scroll that covered the boardroom table. Accompanying the scroll was an illustrated written proposal that was handed to each client.

Cleve Langton, Needham's Director of Business Development, explains the scroll's purpose. "It showed every step in our 100-day advertising plan. The client could easily see all the integrated steps from day 1 to day 100—what the agency would do, what the client would do, and what suppliers would do. An activity corresponded to each day. For example, day 3 might say, 'Agency contacts clients about research on attitudes.'" Accompanying each description were icons that visually emphasized the message. An ear, for instance, told the client to pay attention.

The scroll, and the written proposal, communicated Needham's master plan by relying heavily on visual aids. It also communicated that Needham was capable of an imaginative, rapid, clear response in a highly competitive environment.

As a result of its work, DDB Needham was one of two agencies to win the Digital Equipment account. Quite fittingly, Needham's first campaign for Digital carried the headline, "Whatever it takes"—a line that conveyed Digital's commitment to making itself indispensable to its customers. ▼

Sources: Information provided by Cleve Langton, Director of Business Development Worldwide, DDB Needham Worldwide, 21 February 1996. Supplementary information from "DDB Teams Up for DEC's $90-Million Biz," *ADWEEK Eastern Edition*, 29 August 1994, 5; David Giantasio and Penny Warnerford, "DDB is on a 'Mission' for DEC," *ADWEEK Eastern Edition*, 24 October 1994, 4.

Chapter Overview

The quality of visual presentations is a function of design and layout—topics that we examined in Chapter 5. That quality also depends on a writer's use of visual aids. This chapter examines how visual aids—in the form of tables, charts, diagrams, drawings, and other illustrations—can help communicate messages, just as they did in Needham's business proposal to Digital Equipment. Specifically, it focuses on the variety of charts that are available in every business writer's arsenal—pie, bar, column, and line charts; as well as tables, maps, and other illustrations. This chapter also presents guidelines for conceiving and creating more effective visuals.

→ *Cross Reference*
We discussed designing a document in Chapter 5, pages 143–149.

How Visual Aids Function in Reports and Proposals

Imagine you are given a class assignment on mother-tongue languages spoken across Canada. While Canadians can speak over 100 of the world's estimated 5000 modern languages, you are asked to present data on the number of Canadians who speak French, English, Ukrainian, Cree, Chinese, and Inuktitut. By referring to the most recent Statistics Canada census data, you are able to locate data revealing that 6 502 865 Canadians speak French; 16 169 875 speak English; 187 010 speak Ukrainian, 73 780 speak Cree; 498 845 speak Chinese; and 24 100 speak Inuktitut.[1]

Although you are satisfied this information is accurate, you want to present it in a more focused fashion than a simple narrative description. You decide to use a pictorial chart as shown in Figure 12-1, which communicates to the reader at a glance the percentages of Canadians who speak the selected mother tongues.

Visual aids—the tables, charts, and illustrations used in reports and proposals—present data in ways that make it both visually appealing and understandable. Visual aids are also frequently used to shorten text. A summary table or chart can present statistics more clearly and concisely than words arranged in paragraph form.

Visual aids relieve the monotony of long narrative passages in a document. They also perform more important tasks, for example, highlighting statistical relationships. A chart can show trends, movements, distributions, and cycles that may not be readily apparent in a completely narrative presentation. In addition, visuals

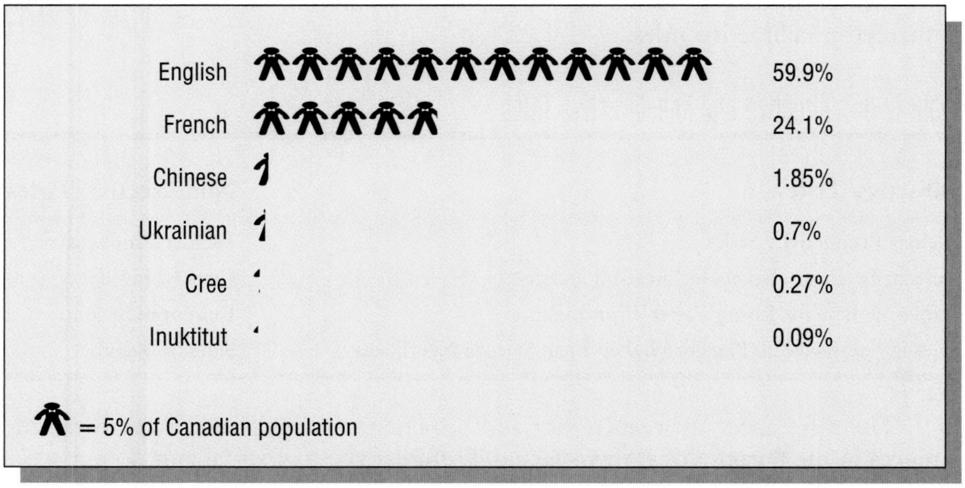

English	🕴🕴🕴🕴🕴🕴🕴🕴🕴🕴🕴🕴	59.9%
French	🕴🕴🕴🕴🕴	24.1%
Chinese	🕴	1.85%
Ukrainian	🕴	0.7%
Cree	🕴	0.27%
Inuktitut	🕴	0.09%

🕴 = 5% of Canadian population

Figure 12-1 Pictorial Chart: Selected Mother-Tongue Languages Spoken in Canada

When you have mastered the
numbers, you will in fact no
longer be reading numbers,
any more than you read
words when reading books.
You will be reading meanings.

Harold Geneen
Chairman, IT&T Corporation

can help readers make sense of difficult concepts. By restating information in different and often lively ways, they encourage meaningful comparisons between pieces of information that may have little appeal to the imagination when presented in dry narrative form.

During the data-gathering process discussed in Chapter 11, it frequently becomes self-evident that a visual aid will enhance reader understanding due to the quantity or complexity of data involved. Although data presented in narrative form may allow for a more detailed discussion, accompanying visual aids foster understanding.

LINKING VISUAL AIDS TO THE MESSAGE

Every visual aid must have a message. Knowing precisely what you want your graphic to communicate enables you to decide on the most appropriate visual aid. "It is not the data—be they dollars, percentages, liters, yen, etc.—that determine the chart," says Gene Zelazny, director of visual communication for McKinsey & Company. "It is not the measure—be it profits, return on investment, compensation, etc.—that determines the chart. Rather it is your message, what you want to show, the specific point you want to make."[2]

Let's say, for example, that as an automobile engineer you are asked to write a report supporting the additional expense of safety features in passenger automobiles. You would almost certainly want to highlight the fact that almost 77 percent of all vehicles registered in Canada are passenger automobiles; thus building a quantifiable case for safety features. You could present your data in a number of ways—in a list embedded in the text of your report, in a formal table set apart from the text with a title and a source note, or in a bar chart. Each alternative is illustrated in Figure 12-2. Although both the in-text listing and the formal table represent the information accurately, the bar chart not only supplies the same specific data but provides a quick visual comparison. As you can also see from Figure 12-2, the bar chart requires less reading to understand the message contained in the data.

DIRECTION IN YOUR TITLE

While **report visuals** let the facts speak for themselves, **presentation visuals** interpret data. When you choose to support your message with a presentation visual, you must tell your reader *why* a table or chart is important. Providing such information is the primary purpose of your title. The best titles, then, are directive titles: simple, clear statements that focus on a relationship between facts that you want to emphasize and about which you have something to say. Directive titles deliver specific, focused messages.[3] Table 12-1 pairs a list of directive headings with a list of unfocused nondirective titles.

Table 12-1 Directive and Non-Directive Titles

Directive Titles	Nondirective Titles
Factory Productivity Soars	Factory Productivity
Current Inventory Level Declines 30 Percent	Current Inventory
Employee Benefits Rising Faster Than Inflation	Employee Benefits
Sales in Southwest 20 Percent Higher Than Sales in Northwest	Sales by Region

The differences between report and presentation visuals reflect the basic differences in the purpose of each visual aid. Different types of visual aids do not serve

Figure 12-2 Alternative
Methods of Presenting Data

In recent years, the overall number of vehicles registered in Canada has increased. From a total of 17 794 773 motor vehicle registrations, 13 639 358 were automobiles; 3 697 792 were trucks and truck tractors; 305 887 were motorcycles; 65 138 were buses; 23 992 were mopeds, and 62 606 were other road motor vehicles.

(b) Formal Table

Types & Numbers of Motor Vehicles Registered in Canada in 1994

Passenger Automobiles	13 639 358
Trucks & Truck Tractors	3 697 792
Motorcycles	305 887
Buses	65 138
Other	62 606
Mopeds	23 992

(c) Bar Chart

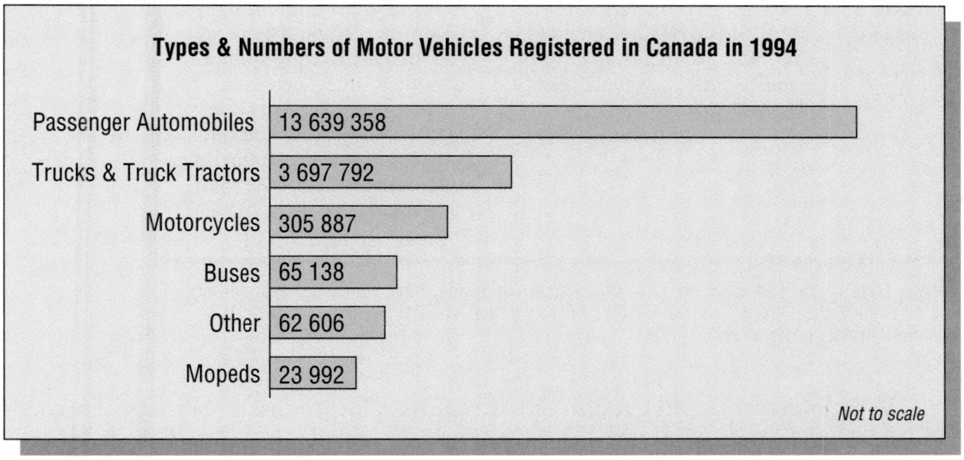

Types & Numbers of Motor Vehicles Registered in Canada in 1994

Passenger Automobiles	13 639 358
Trucks & Truck Tractors	3 697 792
Motorcycles	305 887
Buses	65 138
Other	62 606
Mopeds	23 992

Not to scale

Source: *Statistics Canada, Catalogue no. 53-219.*

the same purposes. Determining which visual aid will best support your message requires an understanding of the specific nature of different types of visuals—in particular, tables and charts. We start by focusing on the function and use of tables in business reports and proposals.

Tables in Reports and Proposals _

Tables are systematic arrangements of data and/or words in rows and columns that provide readers with a fixed reference and a method of comparison. Tables can consolidate large quantities of information in a relatively small space without losing detail. For example, specific (and often complex) numerical information can be conveyed in tables with more exactness than in charts. Two types of tables—data tables and word tables—are illustrated in Table 12-2.

Table 12-2 Comparing Data and Word Tables

(a) Data Table
Comparing Ad Agency Rankings by U.S. Gross Income (in millions)

Agency	1994	1993
Young & Rubicam	$424.0	$406.9
DDB Needham	407.6	378.8
BBDO Worldwide	367.4	346.7
J. Walter Thompson Co.	351.7	331.6
Grey Advertising	332.1	313.6

(b) Word Table
Comparing Fixed and Adjustable Rate Mortgage Agreements

Type	Description	Considerations
Fixed rate	Fixed interest rate; usually long term; equal monthly payments of principal and interest until debt is paid in full.	Offers stability and long-term tax advantages; interest rates may be higher than other types of financing; new fixed rates are rarely assumable.
Adjustable	Interest rate changes over life of the loan; possible changes in monthly payments, loan term, and/or principal; some plans have rate or interest caps.	Starting interest rate is slightly below market, but payments can increase sharply and frequently if index increases; payment caps prevent wide fluctuations in payment but may cause negative amortization; rate caps limit the total amount that the debt can expand.

Sources: Table 12-1a: Data supplied by DDB Needham Worldwide; Table 12-1b: Mortgage descriptions from the Federal Trade Commission, *The Mortgage Money Guide* (Washington, D.C.: U.S. Government Printing Office, n.d.).

Word tables are used extensively in reports and proposals. Writers can consolidate often complex information in one place, making it easier for readers to understand and evaluate material. Instructional materials are frequently listed in word tables. For example, a company safety officer might write a report on workplace safety using a table of various symptoms, remedies, and techniques for administering first aid; a human resources manager might write a report using a table of the various positions in the firm, job descriptions for each position, and salary ranges.

A table can also be classified as either a **spot table,** which runs into the text without title or number, or a **reference table,** which has a title and number but need not appear immediately following the text reference. Spot tables are used for incidental information (such as that in Table 12-1). Reference tables ordinarily contain data that the writer wants highlighted (for example Table 12-2).

Despite their value in consolidating information, however, tables do not always enhance a document. Although they imply relationships—say, growth or decline during a specific period—these relationships are not always clear, and misinterpretations are possible.

Charts in Reports and Proposals _____

When you wish to illustrate your point more dramatically than through in-text description or a table, you can use one of several types of charts. **Charts,** also known as **graphs,** are diagrams that present numerical data in visual form in order to show trends, movements, distributions, and cycles. Because charts are usually less detailed than tables, they are sometimes accompanied by tables that provide exact data. The most common and useful forms of charts are pie, bar, column, line, and flow charts. All charts highlight comparisons, and before we describe different chart forms, it is important to understand the different types of comparisons that they make.

TYPES OF CHART COMPARISONS

Business reports and proposals typically use charts to make four basic types of comparisons: component, item, time-series, and frequency-distribution.[4] The message communicated by a chart is defined by the kind of comparison that it highlights.

COMPONENT COMPARISON   In a **component comparison,** the size of each item in the chart is shown as a percentage of the sum total. For example, each of the following statements indicates a component comparison:

▼ Two sales districts accounted for nearly three-quarters of total corporate sales.

▼ Generic clothing bleaches hold less than 10 percent of market share.

Such topics as market share by company, budget allocations among divisions, and employee population by income also invite component comparisons.

ITEM COMPARISON   An **item comparison** examines relative rankings—individuals, geographic areas, products, production facilities, or a whole host of other variables—in order to determine whether those variables are the same, more than, or less than one another. This comparison analyzes items at a single point in time. For example, the following statements indicate item comparisons:

▼ Employee satisfaction in all four departments is about equal.

▼ Productivity at the Prince Edward Island plant is significantly less than at the virtually identical Quebec plant.

The variables being compared here are different levels of employee satisfaction and productivity, respectively. In general, terms like *equal, larger than, smaller than,* and *less than* indicate that an item comparison is being made.

TIME-SERIES COMPARISON   A **time-series comparison** measures the changes in items over time. This comparison is useful for tracking trends over a specific time period, usually weeks, months, quarters, or years. The following statements indicate a time-series comparison:

▼ Mortgage interest rates have declined over the past four months.

▼ Company exports have risen dramatically since last May, when the dollar started losing value on world markets.

Terms like *increase, decrease, fluctuate, grow, decline, rise,* and *remain constant* indicate the working of a time-series comparison.

FREQUENCY-DISTRIBUTION COMPARISON   A **frequency-distribution comparison** shows how many items fall into a series of defined, progressive numerical ranges. For example, income distributions are often categorized as numerical ranges—less than $20 000; $20 000 to $29 999; $30 000 to $39 999; and so on. A frequency distribution, then, could be used to divide a company's total number of wage earners into progressively higher income brackets. Terms like *range*, *concentration*, *frequency*, and *distribution* characterize frequency-distribution comparisons.

Types of Charts

When constructing visual aids, one of your primary goals is to define and develop a strong relationship between specific comparisons and the type of chart that you intend to use. Four basic types of comparative charts—pie, bar, column, and line charts—are illustrated in Figure 12-3. In some cases one type of chart will be clearly superior to the alternatives. Component comparisons, for example, are best made with pie charts. In other instances, however, you may have several options. For example, in showing age groupings of federal employees (a frequency-distribution comparison), a column chart and a line chart would be equally effective.

In this section we will describe each of the major types of charts by focusing on the kind of relationship that each expresses best.

PIE CHARTS
Among the most common and easy-to-understand visual aids is the **pie chart**—a graph that presents data as wedge-shaped sections of a circle. Pie charts are typically used for component comparisons: The entire circle represents 100 percent of

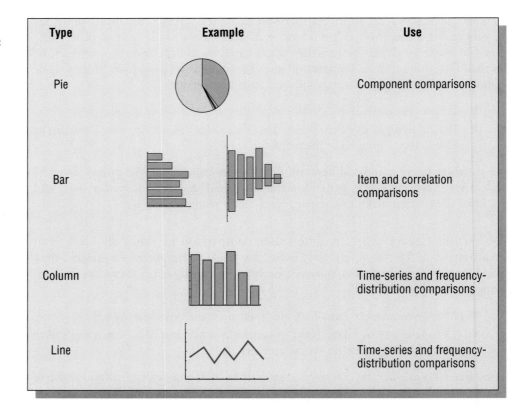

Figure 12-3 Effective Chart Forms and Specific Comparisons

Type	Example	Use
Pie		Component comparisons
Bar		Item and correlation comparisons
Column		Time-series and frequency-distribution comparisons
Line		Time-series and frequency-distribution comparisons

a given whole and each wedge is a portion of the whole. The strength of the pie chart in showing portions of an overall whole is illustrated in Figure 12-4, which shows the distribution of DDB Needham's 187 offices worldwide.

BAR CHARTS

A second type of visual aid frequently found in reports and proposals is the bar chart, or bar graph. **Bar charts** consist of horizontal bars of equal width and varying lengths, each representing a different item for comparison. They are best used for analyzing how items compare with one another rather than as single components of a whole. The bar chart in Figure 12-5 compares the number of multinational clients of six leading advertising agencies.

Depending on their use, bar charts can be subdivided into three categories. A **grouped bar chart** compares various parts of the same item—for example, labour costs with and without employee benefits included. The **subdivided bar chart** divides each bar into components of the same item. For example, a bar chart reporting the number of female employees in your firm might be divided into three sections. The entire length of the bar may represent all female employees; the first subsection may represent full-time employees; the second subsection might represent part-time employees, and the third subsection temporary employees. You could go a step further and emphasize a point by comparing this bar to a similar bar for male employees.

Finally, the **bilateral bar chart** starts from a central point and shows positive and/or negative deviations from that point. It may be used, for example, to highlight a comparison of company territories with net losses and gains in sales. Each of these three types of bar charts is illustrated in Figure 12-6.

PICTORIAL CHARTS   Bar and column charts that use graphic symbols instead of horizontal or vertical bars are known as **pictorial charts.** They are used most often

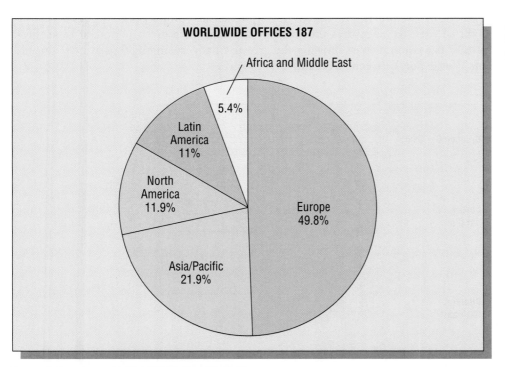

WORLDWIDE OFFICES 187

Figure 12-4   Sample Pie Chart: DDB Needham's Offices Worldwide

Source: *Information provided by DDB Needham Worldwide*

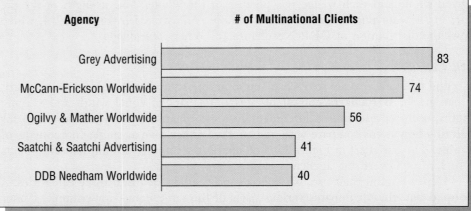

Agency	# of Multinational Clients
Grey Advertising	83
McCann-Erickson Worldwide	74
Ogilvy & Mather Worldwide	56
Saatchi & Saatchi Advertising	41
DDB Needham Worldwide	40

Figure 12-5 Sample Bar Chart: Number of Multinational Clients* of Major Advertising Agencies

*Clients served in three or more countries.

Source: *Information courtesy of DDB Needham Worldwide*

in documents aimed at wide audiences—in reports to company shareholders, for example. The effectiveness of a pictorial chart is directly related to the appropriateness of its symbols. Using pictures of small factories, for instance, is a good way to show the trend in industrial output but a poor way to depict a company's employment trend. The pictorial chart in Figure 12-1 uses symbols to represent the percentage of people in Canada who speak selected mother-tongue languages.

COLUMN CHARTS

Although quite similar to bar charts, **column** (or **vertical-bar**) **charts** are most effective for time-series comparisons that indicate changes taking place over time. They are also useful in frequency-distribution comparisons, in which they highlight a series of items that are part of a progressive numerical distribution.

Column charts consist of vertical bars of different heights, with each height representing a different quantity. In a time-series comparison, for example, the height of each bar measures the value of the data for a given period of time. Figure 12-7 is a column chart showing the growth of advertising billings at DDB Needham Worldwide between 1986 and 1994.

Figure 12-6 Specialized Bar Charts

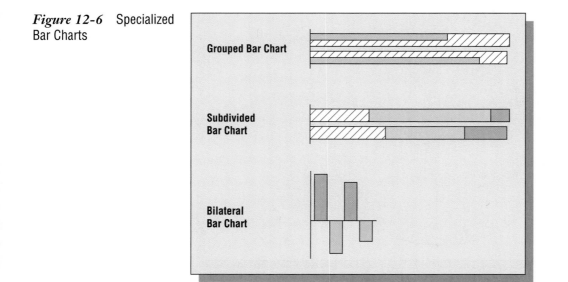

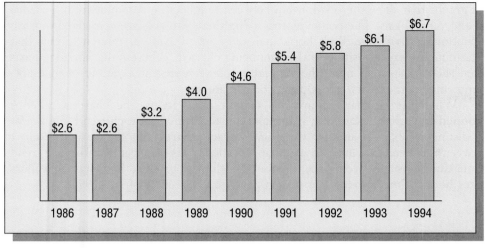

Source: *Information courtesy of DDB Needham Worldwide*

SPECIALIZED COLUMN CHARTS   Two specialized column charts are shown in Figure 12-8. The **grouped column chart** consists of grouped or overlapping columns that can perform two functions at once: they can compare two different items at a given time and demonstrate how the relationship between those items has changed over time. For example, while one bar in a series [say, the purple bars in Figure 12-8(a)] may show advertising expenditures, a second bar (the grey bars) may show company profits. A **subdivided column chart** shows how the individual parts of one whole unit have changed over time. For example, Figure 12-8(b) divides the same data used in Figure 12-7 into international and U.S. advertising billings for DDB Needham Worldwide.

LINE CHARTS

The line chart is the most frequently used visual aid in business reports and proposals. Used to show both frequency distributions and trends over time, **line charts**

Figure 12-8 Specialized Column Charts

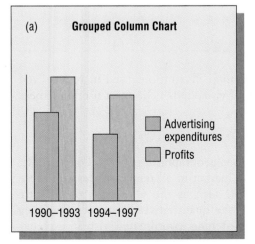

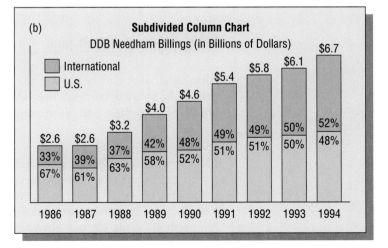

are graphs that show the relationship between numbers on a combination horizontal and vertical axis. The points plotted along these two axes are connected to form a continuous *trend line*. Both horizontal and vertical axes are reference lines that determine the exact position of the data being charted. Whereas the horizontal axis often shows a span of time, the vertical axis may represent a variety of measurements, including dollars, hours, units, or percentages.

When the comparison involves two or more items, the chart is called a **grouped line chart.** Naturally, it is important to ensure that each trend line is easily distinguishable. In another variation, **surface charts,** the surface of the chart between the trend line and the baseline is shaded. This effect emphasizes the trend by making it visually prominent. Figure 12-9 shows a grouped line chart that illustrates hours of media usage per person per year between 1984 and 1997.

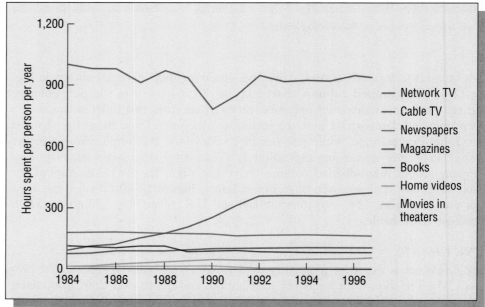

Figure 12-9 Sample Grouped Line Chart: Media Usage, 1984–1997

Source: *U.S. Department of Commerce, Economics and Statistics Administration, Bureau of the Census, Statistical Abstract of the United States, 1994 (Washington, D.C.: U.S. Government Printing Office, 1994),* 564.

Other Types of Visual Aids

Although tables and charts are the most common illustrations used in reports and proposals, many documents use other forms of visual aids. The most useful of these are maps, drawings, and photographs.

MAPS

Maps highlight statistical comparisons of various geographical regions. For example, a map can compare a new product's potential market in all ten provinces and three territories or in a smaller geographic region, such as the Okanagan or Atlantic Canada. Statistical maps are valuable only if the quantitative differences that they represent are clear. Colour, shading, or cross-hatching, coordinated with an explanatory legend, is typically used to differentiate regions on maps.

DRAWINGS AND PHOTOGRAPHS

Custom drawings, often created on a computer, let you focus on exactly what you want the reader to see, omitting all unnecessary information—something that a photograph cannot do. It is important both to tie each drawing to your overall purpose and to keep your reader's needs in mind. For example, in a report describing how to correct a manufacturing problem in an automobile braking system, one or more drawings might be needed to show readers how the system's internal parts interrelate.

Photographs, another popular category of visual aids in reports and proposals, can be the closest thing to reality in presenting facts. Photos are an effective way to bring the reader closer to the idea, person, or product. As an element of design, photographs enhance not only the appearance of a document but also the credibility of the information in a report or proposal. They are also used to increase reader interest and retention. Most corporate annual reports include photos of people, production facilities, and products. Advertising agencies typically use photographs in their proposals.

Designing Effective Visual Aids

To be effective, visual aids must look professional. Above all, your document must be characterized by simplicity, clarity, and consistency of design. Several factors affect these qualities in the design of visual aids: size; titles and numbers; captions, labels, and legends; footnotes; colour, shading, and cross-hatching; borders and rules; grid lines and tick marks; and source acknowledgments. These are the mechanics of design—the factors that determine the final appearance of a visual aid.

SIMPLICITY OF DESIGN AND CONTENT

The best tables and charts have simple, consistent, clear designs that help the reader focus on specifics. Keep in mind that your readers may not have your level of expertise on the subject and may be overwhelmed by visuals that are too complex. Large amounts of data typically result in a crowded, overly complicated visual aid. In such cases you may want to divide your data into two or more visual aids. In general, every visual aid should tell a single story—that is, highlight one important relationship.

A simple design focuses on content over form. When design interferes with the reader's understanding of the relationship being illustrated, it fails as a communication tool. Simple tables and charts contain no unnecessary data. Figures are rounded off, and the level of detail stops when the extra information ceases to be useful. Let's say, for example, that you want to illustrate an employment-growth trend at your company over the past year. Will it be necessary to show the employment of workers in various job categories at the plant? Probably not. This information is irrelevant to your main point that company-wide employment has increased. One way to eliminate excess detail is to select your illustration title first; you can then measure the complexity of your topic against the more modest claims of your title.

CONSISTENCY: SIZE   In general, the size of a figure should be directly related to its importance and complexity. The more important the figure, the larger it should be. Similarly, complex figures require greater space to allow for more detailed explanation. Incidental figures should take only a small portion of a page. Finally, the sizing of visual aids should be internally consistent. Decisions about sizing should be made according to guidelines that take your whole document into account. Two tables of equal importance should be of basically equal size.

Gene Zelazny, Visual Arts Consultant

For the past 30 years, Gene Zelazny, Director of Visual Communications for McKinsey & Company, has helped his colleagues in the firm and members of top management choose and use charts for presentations, reports, and other business documents. In this interview, we asked Zelazny, who is also the author of *Say It With Charts,* to give us his perspective on the art of the chart.

Question: What common elements do the most successful charts share?

Answer: The best charts demonstrate relationships more clearly and more quickly than information in tabular form. They have a message title—a brief sentence that focuses attention on the point you want to emphasize. They are attractive and legible. The fact that charts are decorative or help to break the monotony of a presentation or a page of text is incidental and never justifies using them.

Question: How do you decide when a chart is needed?

Answer: Your message makes the decision for you. If your message is simple—for example, company revenues have doubled—showing a chart with two columns, one twice the height of the other, is not necessary and risks insulting the intelligence of your audience. But if the message is complex—for instance, you need to tell the reader how the mix of market share has changed by quarters for eight companies in the industry over the past five years—then a chart showing the changes will be more effective than words alone.

Question: What are some of the most common chart-making mistakes?

Answer: The most common offence is poor design: the chart is too cluttered or complex to be legible. Aside from this obvious shortcoming, two other mistakes stand out. The first is not choosing the right chart *form* for the point you want to make—say, using pie charts to show changes over time when a line chart would work better. The second is confusing complexity for information. Take a look at the first chart [in the interview]. You see a chart in its early stages of development—many components, data down to two decimal points, footnotes, and so on. The second chart shows what the chart should look like to get its point across clearly and quickly.

Question: Can charts suffer from poor audience analysis?

Answer: I'd turn that question around. After all, it's not the chart that suffers—it doesn't care. It's the audience. The final test of a chart is not what goes into it but what the reader gets out of it. Failure to analyze your audience can result in charts that fail to communicate, no matter how well designed they are. Some people simply do not respond well to charts; either they have difficulty reading graphic representations or they are more comfortable with information in tabular form.

CONSISTENCY: TITLES AND NUMBERS   Consistency is important in the presentation of visual aids, and a key way to ensure consistency is to develop a pattern for titles and numbers. Your pattern will be reflected in your reference system. For example, there are two ways to refer to tables and charts. You can label each item as an "Exhibit" and number them *sequentially* as they appear in the document; or you can separate tables and figures and number *each in order.* In this sense, a **figure**

Question: Should charts be explained in the text?

Answer: Yes. Too often we assume that the chart should speak for itself. Not so. A chart is a visual aid in the sense that it's an aid to the text and not a substitute for words. As such, it's there for the reader to refer to while the text explains how to read it and what point it's demonstrating. The same thing happens in a visual presentation. The chart is on the screen for the audience to look at while the presenter explains it orally.

Question: How has computer technology changed chart making?

Answer: In my career I've seen the rise of visual-aids people, and I'm now witnessing their fall; today they are computer operators who create fin-

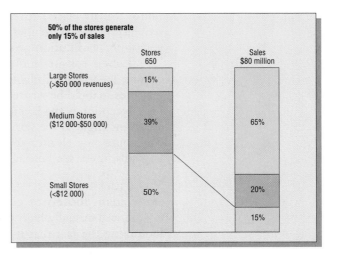

ished charts in the time it takes me to do one rough sketch. Remarkable. I find it fascinating that I can walk into our production department and not find a pencil on anyone's desk. Come to think of it, I can't find a desk; they're now called *workstations.* And it's all for the good. After all, we've drawn enough pie charts to know how thick to make the outline and where to position the chart on the page. Let's face it: today computers are to visual aids what pocket calculators became to multiplication tables.

Question: If you had one piece of advice about chart making, what would it be?

Answer: Remember that *less is more than enough.* Use fewer charts and put less on them. The philosophy that *more is never enough* simply doesn't apply to charts.

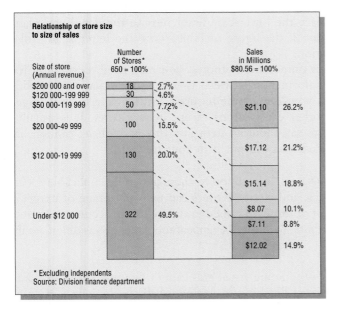

Source: Interview with Gene Zelazny.

is any visual aid other than a table, including charts, maps, drawings, photographs, and other illustrations.

Your narrative should refer to table and chart numbers rather than to the pages or relative positions in which an item appears. For example, the reference "as shown in Table 4" for a numbered visual aid is better than "as shown in the table below." Remember that when your final pages are laid out, each visual aid will be placed as close as possible to the reference in your narrative—that is, as soon as page space permits. The reference to "below," therefore, may be highly variable, ranging from immediately following to the next available space a page and a half later.

CLARITY: CAPTIONS, LABELS, AND LEGENDS In addition to titles, many visual aids require captions. A **caption** is a brief explanatory or descriptive narrative that should support the title as it focuses on the visual's most important point. The caption is usually placed at the bottom of the visual aid and limited to no more than a sentence or two. Often, a phrase is sufficient. If your caption has nothing to add to your title, clarification probably isn't necessary.

Labels consist of all the headings and subheadings that define the parts of the exhibit, including all identifications of the items being compared. For ease of reading, these should be written horizontally, as in the line chart in Figure 12-9. A common exception is the labelling for the vertical axis of a chart, which is often inserted at a right angle to the text. Legends are marginal explanations of chart symbols that contribute to a cleaner appearance than the separate labelling of various elements. Legends, then, are best suited to charts displaying more than one set of data.

SPECIFICITY: FOOTNOTES While captions add information that applies to an entire item, **footnotes** explain specific details. For example, you might want to explain an unusually high pattern in electricity usage during the summer months by footnoting the fact that it was the coolest summer on record.

When a visual aid has only one or two footnotes, asterisks (*) or double asterisks (**) are sufficient to indicate that additional information can be found in the footnote. When footnotes are more numerous, you should use lower-case letters (*a, b, c . . .*) instead of asterisks. Place the lower-case letter next to the detail you plan to expound upon; at the bottom of the figure or table, write the letter again, followed by the footnote explanation.

If your visual aid requires numerous footnotes, you may need to simplify it. Perhaps you could divide the information between two or more visual aids or add a more in-depth explanation in your text. Some business writing experts discourage the inclusion of footnotes or other explanations except in rare cases. It is usually possible to say what you need to say about an item in a title and a brief caption; if further explanation is still needed, you can put it in your text.

PRECISION: OTHER VISUAL TOOLS In addition to these generally applicable tools for design simplicity, consistency, and clarity, writers can take advantage of numerous other design elements. Most of those described in the following section are quite common, and each can contribute to both the appearance and precision of your visual aids.

Colour, Shading, and Cross-Hatching Some visual aids cannot be understood without the use of colour, shading, or cross-hatching to distinguish their elements. Often a necessity rather than a luxury, these techniques highlight and differentiate selected elements by forming visual groupings. Use the colour wheel in Figure 15-8 to choose the most effective colour combinations for your visual aids. Once you have chosen a basic colour scheme—white lettering on a black background, for example—use it consistently throughout your document.

➤ *Cross Reference*
See Figure 15-8, Colour Wheel, on page 436.

If colour is inappropriate or you are unable to reproduce it in your report, distinguish different elements of your visual aid with shading and/or cross-hatching. The specialized bar charts in Figure 12-6, for example, feature shading and cross-hatching. Similarly, for a line chart, differentiate each line by using bold, thin, and interrupted lines.

Borders and Rules   Clarity can also be greatly improved through the consistent use of borders and rules. **Borders** are the lines that frame visual aids and separate them from the surrounding text; **rules** are the internal lines that separate the various elements of an exhibit. For example, horizontal rules are often placed below the title and between the column headings and the body of a table. Similarly, vertical rules are often used to separate columns in a table. In general, writers choose how to use these elements. However, they should be used consistently throughout the document.

Grid Lines and Tick Marks   In some charts a series of solid horizontal and vertical lines, known as **grid lines,** cross one another at 90-degree angles to establish specific values. Other charts mark the same numerical intervals with short broken lines known as *tick marks.* Because it is easy to follow solid lines back to their sources on the horizontal and vertical axes, a chart with grid lines is used to emphasize *exact values.* (The line charts in this chapter's A Question of Ethics use grid lines.) Tick marks, on the other hand, are typically used to show *general trends.* In some charts, such as line charts, too many grid lines make it difficult to distinguish more important trend lines.

Source Acknowledgments   When the material in your exhibit is taken from another document, you must cite that document in a source note at the bottom of your own visual aid. Simply write the word *Source* followed by a colon and then provide the citation. Many of the tables and figures in this text provide examples of the format used in listing source notes.

CONSTRUCTING SPECIFIC TYPES OF VISUAL AIDS

Specific visual aids have special construction guidelines. Just as your choice of a type of visual aid depends primarily on the nature of the information being presented, your design must also be appropriate for the type of visual aid you have chosen. Certain guidelines help you create each of the visual aids that we have discussed so far, including tables; pie, bar, column, and line charts; and drawings.

PRACTICAL TIPS

How to Choose Chart Colours

Choosing the right colours and colour combinations for visual aids is not as simple as choosing what looks best. You should also consider the psychological impact the colour will have on the reader. Research has shown that colours have common associations, including the following:

▽ Blue suggests masculinity and authority (police uniforms are blue). Blue also suggests nature (as in the colour of sky and water) and symbolizes freedom, purity, tranquillity, and clarity.

▽ Red, one of the most powerful colours, suggests excitement, stimulation, and the force of life. It also suggests danger, business loss, malfunction, and prohibition.

▽ Green suggests money, permission (as in a green light), envy, and jealousy.

▽ Yellow, often perceived as a cheerful colour, can also convey caution.

▽ Black is the colour of profit and power in business. It also suggests status and professionalism.

▽ Brown and grey represent conservatism and stability.

Source: "Secrets of Powerful Presentations," *Potentials in Marketing* (March 1992): 27.

TABLES Tables are most effective when they are easiest to read, and they are easiest to read when they follow a consistent format. Figure 12-10 illustrates the parts of a table and their typical arrangement on the page. Below the table title are column titles, which are also known as captions. In some cases tables are divided into several sections that require subcaptions. The captions running along the horizontal rows are known as stubs. Column totals, if any, usually appear immediately following the last horizontal row.

PIE CHARTS As we saw earlier in this chapter, pie charts must be simple and easy to read. For clarity, experts suggest that a pie chart contain no more than six to ten components. Each component's wedge should be accurately represented as a part of the 360-degree circle.

The wedges of a pie chart should start at the top of the figure, with the sections arranged in order according to size or importance. Labels should be written horizontally and, whenever possible, *within* the appropriate section of the pie. If the label will not fit inside the pie section, it can be placed outside the pie with a rule drawn from section to label. This technique is used in the pie chart in Figure 12-4.

BAR AND COLUMN CHARTS The title of each bar in a bar chart should appear either superimposed over the bar or as a stub to the left of the bar (as shown in Figure 12-5). When bar charts or column charts are labelled with individual values (such as 83%, 74%, 56%), no further clarification is necessary. However, when the values of bars or columns must be identified, add a scale on the top, bottom, or at the left side of the chart.

	TABLE NO. **TITLE OF TABLE**			
Stub Head	Caption		Caption	
	Subcaption	Subcaption	Subcaption	Subcaption
Stub	XXXX	XXXX	XXXX	XXXX
Stub	XXXX	XXXX[a]	XXXX	XXXX
Stub	XXXX	XXXX	XXXX	XXXX
Stub	XXXX	XXXX	XXXX	XXXX
Stub	XXXX	XXXX	XXXX	XXXX
Total	XXXX	XXXX	XXXX[b]	XXXX

[a] Footnote
[b] Footnote
Source:

Figure 12-10 The Parts and Arrangement of a Table
Source: *J. Harold Janis and Howard R. Dresner,* Business Writing, *2d ed. (New York: Harper Perrenial, 1991), 272.*

Follow the same basic rules to construct a pictorial chart. Choose a self-explanatory symbol that represents a single unit. Include a legend at the bottom of the chart to explain the value of each unit. For example, each symbol of a worker in an employment-related chart might equal 1000 workers. Rather than increasing the size of each symbol, you indicate increased quantities by adding symbols and portions of symbols to extend each bar or column.

When a chart contains several data sets, it is important to use consistent colours or patterns to connect sets referring to the same category. For example, if a column chart shows a company's profits and losses over a two-year period, all the profit columns should use one colour (black) and all the loss columns should be another single colour (red). The same principle holds for charts that, like the grouped and subdivided bar charts in Figure 12-6, use cross-hatching or shading. It is also important to avoid patterns that clash, especially in simple black-and-white charts; different shades of grey are often more effective.

Colour, shading, and cross-hatching can also be used to distinguish actual data from projected data, different items being compared at a given point, and the components of a subdivided column.

LINE CHARTS   Line charts are relatively easy to prepare. In general, start the vertical axis at zero. If the plotting begins at a high value, you can reduce the height of the axis by inserting a break in the vertical axis. Let's suppose, for example, that a chart should be expressed in increments of 10; the meaningful data, however, begins at 5000 units. To indicate the appropriate increment of 10, start the left axis at 0, then 10, 20, 30. Next, insert a break in the line and continue at 5000, 5010, 5020, and so on.

There is one important exception to starting the vertical axis at zero—charts that include negative values. In this case the vertical axis starts at a negative number and continues into positive numbers to the top of the axis; zero falls somewhere in the middle, with the chart balanced above and below as evenly as the data allow.

Because the purpose of a line chart is to indicate a trend, be sure to emphasize the trend line. In a single-line chart, highlight the trend with a thick line or a bold colour. Try to limit multiple-line charts to no more than three or four lines. Differentiate each line with a different colour or pattern, such as dots versus dashes or bold versus fine lines. Dashed or dotted lines are also frequently used to show projections or estimates.

DRAWINGS AND OTHER ILLUSTRATIONS   With the increasing use of computers in business, more and more drawings, diagrams, and other graphics are computer-generated. Computer-aided design systems for creating such visual aids are especially popular in fields like architecture and engineering. The following guidelines are designed to help you get effective results whether you are drawing an illustration by hand or generating it with a computer.[5]

Any sufficiently advanced technology is indistinguishable from magic.

Arthur C. Clarke
Science fiction writer and scientist

▼ Keep all parts in correct proportion unless you state that a specific part is enlarged.

▼ Show a subsystem in relation to the larger system of which it is a part.

▼ Arrange a sequence of drawings from left to right or top to bottom.

▼ Clearly label all parts. Place the labels on the parts themselves. If the parts are too small, use letter or number symbols with an accompanying key.

Progress Check

1. Describe specific methods for achieving simplicity, clarity, and consistency of visual aid design.

2. List specific guidelines for constructing effective tables and pie, bar, column, and line charts.

Misleading Charts

There are three kinds of lies: lies, damned lies, and statistics.
Benjamin Disraeli
English prime minister and novelist

Although charts depict data in ways that highlight important relationships, charts may also mislead. Whether intentionally or not, writers sometimes distort the relationships shown in various types of charts. As a result, readers often come away with faulty versions of the facts.

Line charts are especially vulnerable to distortion. When improperly drawn, they can exaggerate growth or minimize problems. For example, although the charts in the following illustration are based on the same data, the trend line in the chart on the right suggests a more rapid growth than the one on the left. The distortion occurs because even though time line in both is 1988 to 1996, the horizontal scale on the right is collapsed in comparison to the scale on the left.

Questions for Critical Thinking

1. Why do business writers have an ethical obligation to present accurate charts?
2. We live in an age of visual communication. How does this affect our obligation to present accurate charts?
3. Is it acceptable to use a distorted chart if the surrounding text explains the data accurately?

Sources: Charles T. Brusaw, Gerald J. Alred, and Walter E. Oliu, *Handbook of Technical Writing,* 3rd. ed. (New York: St. Martin's Press, 1987), 277–278; Marya W. Holcombe and Judith K. Stein, *Writing for Decision Makers: Memos and Reports with a Competitive Edge* (Belmont, Calif.: Lifetime Learning Publications, 1981), 137–140; Charts excerpted from Darrell Huff, *How to Lie with Statistics* (New York: W. W. Norton, 1954), 165–166, 278.

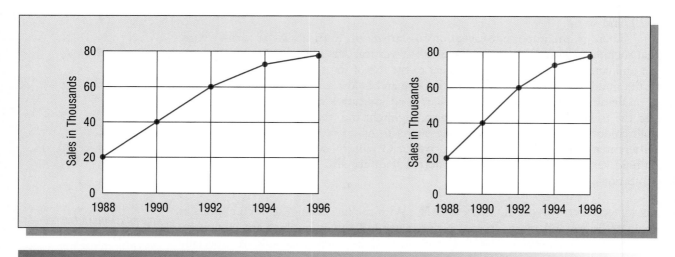

What's Ahead

Chapters 11 and 12 have introduced you to critical functions common to all reports and proposals, including planning, researching, and using visual aids. Chapters 13 and 14 will focus on the specific requirements of short and long documents. We begin in Chapter 13 with guidelines for organizing and writing short and long reports.

S TUDENT RESOURCE CENTRE

Summary of Chapter Objectives

1. *Describe the function of visual aids in reports and proposals.*

   Charts and tables present data in a visual format that breaks the monotony of long narrative documents and helps shorten the text. In addition, visuals help readers make sense of difficult concepts and form meaningful comparisons.

2. *Explain the importance of linking each visual aid to its specific message.*

   To be effective, a visual aid must be linked to a specific purpose and message. This message is often communicated through the chart or table title. The title choice depends on whether the visual aid presents or reports data. While presentation visuals interpret data, report visuals let the facts speak for themselves.

3. *List the characteristics of tables.*

   Tables are systematic arrangements of data in rows and columns that provide readers with both a ready reference and a method of comparison. Composed of numbers, words, or a combination of both, tables can consolidate large quantities of information in a relatively small space without loss of detail.

4. *List the different kinds of comparisons that charts can illustrate.*

   Charts make four basic types of comparisons. In component comparisons, charts show the size of each part as a percentage of the total. In item comparisons, they analyze relative rankings to determine whether variables are the same, more than, or less than one another. In time-series comparisons, charts measure how items change over time. Finally, in frequency-distribution comparisons, they show how many items fall into a series of defined, progressive numerical ranges.

5. *Contrast pie charts, bar charts, column charts, and line charts, and explain the advantages of each.*

   Used for component comparisons, pie charts present data as wedge-shaped sections of a circle that represents 100 percent of a given whole. Bar charts consist of horizontal bars of equal width and varying lengths; each length represents a different quantity. Bar charts are best used for item comparisons. Column charts, which feature vertical rather than horizontal bars, are best used for time-series and frequency-distribution comparisons. Line charts show the relationship of numbers that intersect on horizontal and vertical axes and are used for time-series and frequency-distribution comparisons.

6. *Explain how business documents use maps, drawings, and photographs.*

   Maps show statistical comparisons in terms of geographic regions. Drawings and photographs are illustrations that focus on the structure and function of products and equipment.

7. *Describe the mechanics of constructing visual aids.*

   Effective visual aids have simple, consistent, clear designs that focus on content over form. In general, the size of a figure is directly related to its importance and complexity. Titles and numbers identify each visual; captions, labels, legends, and footnotes clarify information.

   Colour, shading, and cross-hatching distinguish the elements of a chart. These techniques highlight selected elements and form visual groupings. By helping to visually define the parameters of a chart, borders, rules, grid lines, and tick marks make charts easier to read. Finally, source acknowledgments, which are usually placed at the bottom of a chart, tell readers where the data came from.

Review and Discussion Questions

1. Why is it important to give your reports an effective visual presentation? *(Ch. Obj. 1)*

2. What purpose(s) do visual aids serve in business documents? *(Ch. Obj. 1)*

3. Why is it important to link each visual aid to a message? *(Ch. Obj. 2)*

4. What are the characteristics of a good title? *(Ch. Obj. 2)*

5. Describe the benefits of using tables rather than text to present statistical data. *(Ch. Obj. 3)*

6. What are the various types of comparisons that can be made by charts? *(Ch. Obj. 4)*

7. Describe the advantages of each of the following: pie charts, bar charts, column charts, and line charts. *(Ch. Obj. 5)*

8. Summarize the functions of the following visual aids in business documents: charts, drawings, photographs, and maps. *(Ch. Obj. 6)*

9. Describe the mechanics of designing effective visual aids. *(Ch. Obj. 7)*

Application Exercises

1. This chapter notes that every visual aid must have a message. Explain this statement. *(Ch. Obj. 1, 2)*

2. When is it advisable to present information in a table? What are the disadvantages, if any, of using tables? *(Ch. Obj. 3)*

3. Using sources outside class, find four charts used to enhance printed material. Each chart should illustrate one of the four basic types of comparison discussed in the chapter. For each chart, write a brief description of the kinds of data presented. Evaluate the effectiveness of each chart. Does it convey its message well? Why or why not? *(Ch. Obj. 4, 5)*

4. Test yourself on your ability to choose the best type of chart to make comparisons. Cover the centre and right-hand columns of Figure 12-3. Sketch your own example of each type of chart and summarize the comparisons that each type can illustrate effectively. *(Ch. Obj. 4, 5)*

5. Research and design a visual aid that illustrates how your school or employer allocates its advertising budget among various media. Which type of visual aid did you decide to use? Why? *(Ch. Obj. 5, 7)*

6. Research and design a visual aid that compares your school's or employer's current advertising-budget allocation with the budget allocations for each of the last two years. Follow the chapter's guidelines for effective design. Which type of visual aid did you choose to illustrate this information? Why? *(Ch. Obj. 5, 7)*

7. Your school's public relations staff has asked you to compile some brief guidelines for designing effective tables, pie charts, bar and column charts, and line charts. Write these guidelines. *(Ch. Obj. 7)*

8. The public relations staff liked your guidelines for charts, and the director now wants you to write guidelines for designing and using drawings and other illustrations in business documents. Write these guidelines. *(Ch. Obj. 6, 7)*

9. How have various types of bonds performed for investors over the last few years? Using the following data, create a visual aid that compares the yield of these bonds over time. Then write a brief summary of what can be learned by studying this visual aid. *(Ch. Obj. 5, 7)*

Approximate Yields of Short Term Bonds

| 12/31/91 | 7.2% | 12/31/92 | 7.4% | 12/31/93 | 7.8% |
| 12/31/94 | 8.5% | 12/31/95 | 8.1% | 12/31/96 | 7.6% |

Approximate Yields of International Bonds

| 12/31/91 | 8.2% | 12/31/92 | 7.8% | 12/31/93 | 7.2% |
| 12/31/94 | 7.1% | 12/31/95 | 6.8% | 12/31/96 | 6.3% |

Approximate Yields of Money Funds

| 12/31/91 | 6.3% | 12/31/92 | 8.1% | 12/31/93 | 7.9% |
| 12/31/94 | 6.9% | 12/31/95 | 4.8% | 12/31/96 | 3.8% |

10. You have been asked to give a report on the personal-computer software market. You find that there are 95 separate companies with collective shares of 37.1 percent. Here are the market shares of the top five software manufacturers:

Borland, 6.6%   Microsoft, 30%
Lotus, 10.9%   WordPerfect, 7%
Novell, 8.4%

Create a visual aid summarizing this information. Is there a market leader? *(Ch. Obj. 5, 7)*

11. Your school's placement office has asked you to prepare a report entitled "Where the Jobs Will Be." Your research yields the following statistics:

Between now and 2005, the following industries will offer more jobs than they do now. Doctors' offices will add 1 290 000 more jobs by 2005; private hospitals will add 1 058 000 new jobs; and nursing will add 762 000 new jobs. Public schools will add

1 320 000 new jobs; construction will add 923 000 new jobs; computer services will add 710 000 new jobs; restaurants and bars will add 2 147 000 new jobs; retailers will add 2 974 000 new jobs, and wholesalers will add 1 005 000 new jobs.

Prepare a visual aid comparing the number of new jobs to be added in each of these industries between now and 2005. What can you learn from the information presented in this visual aid? (Ch. Obj. 5, 7)

Building Your Business Notebook

Prepare visual aids based on the first-draft text information that follows, applying what you learned in this chapter.

```
Federal spending on the elderly has risen dramatically. This
spending will continue to increase as the aging population
increases. In 1965, 14 percent of the federal budget was spent on
social security and medicare. This amount increased to 34 percent
in 1995. The amount spent on defence decreased from 43 percent to
18 percent. Another major expense, interest, increased from 7 to
15 percent. The category, Other, decreased from 36 to 33 percent.
The budget proportion of these expenses changed dramatically from
1965 to 1995. The source for this information is the
Parliamentary Budget Office.
```

Visual Aid 1

```
Due to improvements in health care and quality of life, the
average life span continues to increase. In the years 1920-22,
life expectancy was 58.8 years at birth if you were a male and
60.6 if you were female. In 1960 these figures had increased by
more than ten years for the male (71.4) and 14 for the female
(74.3). Then the rates continued to increase as follows: 1970,
69.4 for men and 76.5 for women; 1980, 71.9 for men and 79.1 for
women; 1990, 74.6 for men and 81 for women. (Statistics Canada,
Catalogue no. 82-221-XDE)
```

Visual Aid 2

ACT: Applied Communication Techniques

Begin by referring to the sections up to and including Apostrophes and Quotation Marks in Appendix II, then correct the grammar, spelling, and usage errors in the following sentences. Check your answers in Appendix V.

1. The charts vertical bars will be different heights.

2. Youre invited to the boardroom to view our maps and line charts.

3. When the comparison involves two or more items the chart is called a "grouped line chart".

4. Jamess statistical information was included in the pictorial chart.

5. Using a grouped line chart we compared childrens television programs with programs suitable for adults.

6. The team says they arent planning to prepare visual aids for their presentation.

7. Its a surprise that the pictorial chart displays greater poverty in Toronto than in Vancouver.

8. Nova Scotias and New Brunswicks populations were displayed separately on the colourful column chart.

9. Chapter 12 states that manually prepared drawings won't have the same impact as those prepared electronically.

10. During his presentation the prime minister asked Does this graph increase your understanding of the relationship between the budget and the population?

Building Your Research Skills

Using sources outside class, find two articles on topics related to business—one article that you feel is well illustrated and one that you feel is poorly done. Write an analysis of the visual presentation of each article. Explain why you feel the visual aids are better in one article than the other. How could the visual presentation be improved in the poorly illustrated article? Bring your written analysis, plus the two articles, to class.

Building Your Teamwork Skills

Your instructor will divide the class into small groups. Meet with your team to discuss the two articles that you analyzed in the previous exercise. Work together to think of more ways to improve the visual presentation of each team member's articles. Your instructor may want to have a representative from your team present the "best" and "worst" articles from your group to the class.

Building Your Technology Skills

The Internet can be useful for researching visual aids for business reports and presentations. As you visit Web sites, you will find images, charts, and graphs that will enhance your reports and presentations. Select a topic to research for a business report. Use the Internet search engines to research that topic. Find several images you would like to include in your business report during your research. Before you include these images, however, you must examine copyright issues. Expand your research on Internet copyright for information on permission to use the Internet visuals.

The following Web sites may help you start your Internet research:

▼ Canadian Business Media Ltd.
http://strategis.ic.gc.ca/SSG/mi00604e.html

▼ Government Canadian Business Resource Links
http://canada-ny.org/trade/cgbrl.html

▼ Interesting Business Sites
http://www.owi.com/netvalue

▼ Canadian Finance Web Director
http://finance/commerce.ubs.ca/research/canada.html

▼ World Wide Web Business Yellow Pages
http://www.cba.uh.edu/ylowpges/ycategor.html

▼ Canadian Business Links
http://www.spot.ab.ca/~ics/canbiz.html

Weblinks Internet Resources for this Chapter

Business and Workplace Writing—Beyond Words
http://www.rdc.ab.ca/comm250/ld1_7.htm

Using Visual Data in Business Writing
http://raven.cc.ukans.edu/~writestd/bus_visual.html

Visual Data in Business Writing: Organizational Chart
http://raven.cc.ukans.edu/~writestd/bus_orgchart.html

Visual Data in Business Writing: Flow Chart
http://raven.cc.ukans.edu/~writestd/bus_flowchart.html

Graphics and Tables
http://www.io.com/~hcexres/tcm1603/acchtml/graphics.html

CASE STUDIES

DIVERSITY CASE:

Creating a Chart That Shows How Gender Affects Faculty Pay in Canada

You are asked to evaluate an article in the *Canadian Journal of Sociology* that explores the overall gap in pay between Canadian college and university instructors and professors. In the article, "Gender and Faculty Pay in Canada," you find an interesting table showing the salaries of men and women according to their positions. Here is what the table shows:[6]

Questions and Applications

1. Choose the appropriate chart or charts to display these data. Create the chart(s).

2. Write a paragraph explaining why you chose this chart over other chart forms described in the chapter.

3. What does your visual show about the income disparity between male and female faculty members?

Faculty Pay, by Position and Gender

Position Held	Mean Annual Pay			
	Women		Men	
	Number	Mean Pay	Number	Mean Pay
Lecturer	80	$31 000.00	90	$29 900.00
Assistant Professor	308	$35 300.00	683	$36 600.00
Associate Professor	303	$44 700.00	1561	$46 700.00
Full Professor	121	$52 900.00	1573	$59 000.00
Other Ranks	57	$37 000.00	124	$41 300.00

CORPORATE CASE:

Toaster Cuisine

Most of the products in the frozen-breakfast category that are growing and successful right now involve the toaster," says Marc Schwinner, general manager of frozen-breakfast business at Quaker Oats. "In evaluating new products, it is certainly an important factor to take into account." Ellen Perl, head of the breakfast team at rival Pillsbury, agrees: "The toaster is very big right now. We are going to ride it."

The numbers support food-industry executives like Schwinner and Perl. Sales of frozen waffles, for example, grew 15 percent during one year. Sales of frozen bagels, Pop Tarts, and other toaster pastries are also growing. Not surprisingly, sales of toasters are also up by 16 percent.

Currently, the following products are big sellers in the frozen-breakfast market: Eggo frozen waffles (annual sales of $340.2 million, up 18.7 percent from the previous year); Downyflake frozen waffles ($88.8 million, up 31.6 percent over the past year); Lender's frozen bagels ($163.3 million, up 4.6 percent over the previous year); Kellogg's Pop Tarts ($305 million, up 6.4 percent over the previous year); private-label toaster pastries ($45 million, up 41.7 percent over the previous

year); and Pillsbury Toaster Strudel ($50.7 million, up 16.6 percent over the previous year).

Some marketers see this renewed interest in the humble toaster as a reaction against high-tech gadgets. "The toaster," suggests market researcher Ann Clurman, "is an interesting counterpoint to the microwave and all of the technology in the kitchen. It doesn't yell at you. . . . It's like, put up the lace curtains and get out the toaster. It is a wonderfully evocative image."[7]

Questions and Applications

1. As director of new products for your company, you feel that the firm should develop a new line of frozen-breakfast foods that can be cooked in the toaster. Write a report in which you suggest this idea and explain how it could benefit the company.

2. Include at least two visual aids to support the arguments in your report.

13

Organizing and Writing Reports

Report me and my cause aright.

William Shakespeare

Chapter Objectives

After studying this chapter, you should be able to:

1. Identify six differences between short and long reports.

2. List the elements contained in short progress and trip reports.

3. Identify the elements contained in long reports.

4. Explain the functions of executive summaries and introductions in long reports.

5. Describe the types of structural guideposts that can unify the body of long reports.

6. Explain how summaries, conclusions, and recommendations are used in long reports.

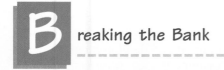

reaking the Bank

Officials at Barings PLC, one of the oldest investment banks in Great Britain, had good reason to hang their heads in shame. Nicholas W. Leeson, a young trader in the bank's Singapore office, broke the bank in 1995 by making an unauthorized $27-billion bet on the direction of the Japanese stock and bond markets. When Leeson lost his bet, Barings lost a staggering $1.32 billion as well as its independence as a 233-year-old financial institution.

To learn how a single, rogue trader could cause the collapse of an institution that counted Queen Elizabeth II among its clients, the Bank of England's Board of Banking Supervision issued a 337-page report on what happened, why it happened, and how to prevent a similar collapse in the future. The report's findings were sobering:

▼ Nicholas W. Leeson was directly responsible for the unauthorized trading that caused the Barings' collapse. However, the report blamed others—including the bank's senior management—for contributing to the failure. Britain's Finance Minister Kenneth Clarke, who presented the report, explained: "It's a picture of the total collapse of management control. It is incredible that such a system of control should exist in a bank like this."

▼ The actions of others outside of Barings also contributed to the collapse. Specifically, the Bank of England—Britain's central bank—made "serious errors of judgment" when it reviewed Barings' practices before the collapse. According to the report, the central bank's "lack of rigour" in overseeing Barings may have set the stage for the problem.

Although the report did not try to spare Barings' management from blame, it took the human factor into account when it concluded: "No regulatory system can provide a 100 percent guarantee against a bank failure, especially when there is a deliberate intention on the part of individual traders to conceal, to deceive, combined with inadequate management controls." With these factors in mind, the report urged procedural improvements, but did not recommend fundamental regulatory change. ▼

Sources: Nicholas Bray and Glenn Whitney, "Barings Collapse Tied to Wide Cast in Special Report," *Wall Street Journal*, 19 July 1995, A5; "Britain Aims Some of the Blame for Barings at Managers," *New York Times*, 19 July 1995, D2.

Chapter Overview

Although relatively few business reports deal with the collapse of one of the oldest financial institutions in Great Britain, they are a critical communications tool for presenting information and recommending action. As we saw in Chapter 11, business reports may be long and formal or short and informal. They may be directed at key decision makers within or outside a company. Finally, a report may be released periodically or issued on a one-time basis.

This is the short and long of it.

William Shakespeare

Reports are as individual as their topics and their writers, but there are certain characteristics that many short reports share. Similarly, most long reports follow specified formats. As we describe the formal report in this chapter, we will examine its specific elements and explain how to format and develop those elements to create coherent documents. Finally, we will examine the use of direct and indirect organizational styles in long reports. We begin with a discussion of how short reports differ from longer ones.

Short Business Reports

The most common type of written report in most businesses is the short report. Short reports may focus on a variety of issues, from employee productivity to project progress. Regardless of their type or length, all business reports share one important characteristic. They take readers on a journey that starts with a statement of purpose and explores findings, conclusions, and recommendations.

Although all reports tell a story, some do it in fewer words than others. Interestingly, the purpose and audience of a report often have a greater influence on its length than its topic. Business communications professors Ray E. Barfield and Sylvia S. Titus use the following example to make this point:

> If an employee has a fender bender in a company truck, a supervisor files a brief accident report, insurance claims are settled, and the matter is soon relegated to the files. On the other hand, a large organization's Director of Transportation, seeing an alarming three-year trend in accident frequency, will ask for a comprehensive report to assess fleet reliability and maintenance needs, employee driver training, and insurance cost containment. The short accident report will pass through only two or three employees' hands, but the lengthy investigative report will be printed (perhaps in dozens of bound copies) and circulated to all interested parties.[1]

In such a case, then, although both reports deal with insurance matters, the long report has not only a broader purpose but also a larger audience.

Short and long reports also differ in a number of other ways. Generally, short reports do not require elaborate front or back matter. They spend little time introducing the topic in the body, and they get to the point immediately; they are usually more personal and require fewer writing devices to aid comprehension.[2] In addition, short reports are often based on prototypes or use printed forms.

FRONT AND BACK MATTER

Most short reports do not include covers, title pages, letters of transmittal, tables of contents, or lists of illustrations. Similarly, appendices, bibliographies, and indexes are rare in short reports. Geared toward simplicity, many short reports are written in letter or memo form.

INTRODUCTORY MATTER

In general, short reports spend little time introducing the topic or providing background information in the body. The writer assumes that everyone reading the document will be familiar with its background. Because most short reports are addressed to relatively few readers, this assumption is usually valid.

Before beginning a short report, then, you should analyze your audience to decide whether introductory materials are necessary. If your topic is discussed often or can be considered common knowledge, a single introductory sentence may be sufficient. Progress and trip reports usually fall into this category. However, if your report will be read by a fairly large number of people (many of whom may be unfamiliar with the topic), or if it is likely to be kept on file for an extended period, a more detailed introduction may be necessary. (Investigative reports usually fall into this category.)

CONCLUSIONS AND RECOMMENDATIONS

The goal of most short reports is to get to the point immediately. Thus, they typically begin with report summaries, which may include general conclusions and recommendations and which may also describe the logical steps that led the writer to make them. The specific details that support the initial summary accompany the conclusions and recommendations made at the end of the report. Material is developed in a logical, analytical way, starting with the introduction, moving to the body of the report, and ending with conclusions and recommendations.

LANGUAGE

Short reports tend to use more personal language than long reports, including such personal pronouns as *I, we,* and *you.* In addition, first names, contractions, and personal references add a familiar tone. This should not be surprising—after all, writers and readers of short reports are likely to know each other and topics are often routine.

Ultimately, the reader's position and preferences will determine whether a personal or impersonal writing style is appropriate in the short report. For example, unless top management sets a more relaxed tone, mid-level managers writing to the CEO or other senior-level executives should use an impersonal style. When the reader is a stranger, the best advice is to err on the side of caution. Use impersonal language until you learn more about the reader's preferences.

WRITING DEVICES THAT AID COMPREHENSION

Because they contain relatively few pages, short reports generally do not require formal writing devices to aid comprehension. These devices, which are common in long reports, include internal summaries and previews placed at key points in the document. We will examine these devices later in the chapter when we describe the long report.

Although short reports must be clearly organized, the connections between sentences and paragraphs can usually be made with simple transitions. Ideas can be sufficiently connected with phrases like *As the previous paragraph demonstrated . . .* or *Based on this information. . . .*

PRESCRIBED PROTOTYPES OR FORMS

As we saw in Chapter 11, many reports, especially short reports such as progress and trip reports, are submitted periodically. To save time, many writers use prototypes such as those we discussed in Chapter 5. These prototypes serve as models for current and future reports written on the same topics.

Cross Reference
We discussed periodic submission of reports in Chapter 11, page 302, and prototypes in Chapter 5, pages 132–137.

The prototype provides a flexible guide for structuring and organizing a report. However, it is important to consider the outline as merely a guide—your situation may very well require adding, deleting, or rearranging information that appeared in previous documents.

Periodic reports may also be written on preprinted forms. Form reports are typically used for routine matters because they save time for the person who must complete them. In general, these reports should be completed in full sentences rather than phrases. In addition, responses should be limited to requested information.

Table 13-1 summarizes the six basic differences between short and long reports.

Table 13-1   Characteristics of Short and Long Reports

Short Reports	Long Reports
no front or back materials	cover, title page, letter or memo of transmittal, table of contents, list of illustrations, and foreword
short introduction	lengthy introduction that describes the report's purpose and scope, organizational plan, and research methods
bottom-line orientation	indirect or direct organizational approach
personal writing style	impersonal writing style
few devices to connect materials	heavy use of internal previews and summaries, transitions, headings, and summary tables and charts to connect report elements
may use a prototype or preprinted form	an original document

Commonly Used Short Reports

→ Cross Reference
For a summary of types of business reports, see Table 11-2 on page 303.

As we saw in Chapter 11, business reports fall into six major categories summarized in Table 11-2: information, survey, study, expert, status, and recommendation. Within these categories we will look more closely at specific types of reports, including progress, trip, investigative, and trouble reports, all of which are frequently written in short form.[3] Progress and trip reports can be considered part of the status or informational report category, whereas investigative and trouble reports are study documents.

PROGRESS REPORTS

No business can afford to leave important project details to chance. Progress reports, then, are among the most common business reports. **Progress reports** provide status information, including updates, on current work.

Progress reports serve many purposes and are written for both internal and external use. For example, in order to summarize what has been done and what remains to be done, an automotive subcontractor developing a new type of seat belt might submit progress reports throughout the life of the project. Because they are timely and current, progress reports help managers allocate equipment and personnel, adjust schedules, revise budgets, and spot potential problems.

ORGANIZING PROGRESS REPORTS   The outline shown in Table 13-2 can be used as a guideline for organizing the information in a progress report to tell the reader what has been done and what remains to be done. A budget analysis may also be included in any of the final four sections. Keep in mind that this and other model outlines presented in this chapter are only guides; your final draft may differ widely in content and form. For example, Figure 13-1 is a sample short progress report in memo form that includes some model outline sections, but not all.

TRIP REPORTS

A second commonly used short report is the trip (or travel) report. Usually written to direct supervisors, **trip reports** summarize the events of a business trip. More

Table 13-2   Model Outline: Progress Report

Section	Description
summary	describes the stage of the project covered in the report, progress that has been made to date, and the future forecast; conclusions and recommendations are also highlighted
work completed	focuses on the items completed since the last report as well as any associated problems and solutions
work in progress	lists work currently being completed; problems are highlighted, as are proposed solutions
work to be completed	focuses on what remains to be done, including any foreseeable problems and proposed solutions
forecast	forecasts progress to be made between this report and the next scheduled report
conclusions and recommendations	focuses on the detail of the conclusions and recommendations; may analyze changes needed to maintain the project's progress, including scheduling, personnel, materials, technology, and funding changes; report concludes with appraisal of the entire project

than listing itineraries and expenses, however, these reports often highlight what the writer accomplished on the trip. Using a direct approach, effective trip reports tell the reader at the start where you went, why you went there, and what you did with your time.

ORGANIZING TRIP REPORTS   Although the temptation is strong to organize trip reports chronologically, most business writers prefer the following model outline. Figure 13-2, a sample trip report based on this model, uses the model as a guide, but does not adhere strictly to it.

▼ *Summary* Include the locations that you visited, the reason for your trip, the dates of your trip, who accompanied you, and a brief evaluation. Your evaluation should mention trip-related conclusions and recommendations.

▼ *Details* Moving from a broad overview to a more specific discussion, review details of your trip. To meet the needs of busy readers, arrange details in order of importance.

▼ *Conclusions and recommendations* Conclusions and recommendations are stated in detail.

▼ *Closing* Close by examining the need for future visits to the same site.

INVESTIGATIVE REPORTS

Let's say that you have been asked to evaluate seven different laser printers to determine which printer will best meet your company's needs. How will you present your findings? This task might require an investigative report.

Investigative reports examine and analyze the details of a particular topic and then present conclusions and recommendations based on that analysis. Depending upon their topic and scope, investigative reports may be short or long. For short documents, you should use a direct approach and organize your material according to the specific needs of your topic.

Progress Check

1. Describe the major differences between short and long reports.
2. What is the purpose of a progress report and how should it be organized?
3. Why do trip reports tend to take a direct organizational approach? Describe an effective way of organizing trip information.

```
                         MEMORANDUM


      TO:      Angela Graves, Director of Human Resources

      FROM:    Mark Megan, Director of Employee Relations MM

      DATE:    November 1, 2000

      SUBJECT: Progress in Drafting New Policy Statement on Sexual
               Harassment

      Billings Technologies is on schedule in revising its company-
      wide policy statement on sexual harassment.

      Work Completed

      The initial phase of this project involved evaluating the
      sexual harassment policy statements of other TSE 300
      companies. Employee-relations specialists analyzed each
      statement in terms of its applicability to the Billings'
      workforce. This evaluation helped us determine what other
      companies are doing so that we can develop an effective
      policy. Based on the information we gathered from this review
      and from other sources, I have completed a policy draft.

      Work in Progress

      We are now evaluating this draft. This process involves:

         • Focus groups (scheduled for November 7)—We want to hear
           how employees at various organizational levels respond to
           the draft.

         • Legal Review (scheduled for November 15)—The revised
           document will be submitted to Joanne Schultz for a review
           of its legal implications.

      Forecast

      The sexual harassment policy statement will be complete by
      December 15, the project deadline. After the policy has been
      approved, Employee Relations will conduct a series of
      communication workshops for managers. These workshops,
      scheduled between January 7 and March 1, will define the
      policy and analyze its workforce implications.
```

Figure 13-1 Sample
Progress Report

TROUBLE REPORTS

When a problem affects a company's day-to-day operations, a trouble report may be written. In addition to determining the cause of problems, **trouble reports** try to present recommendations for preventing and solving the problems. For example, a trouble report may focus on a rash of worker injuries or on the failure of a computer system.

Using the direct approach, trouble reports usually begin with summaries to highlight conclusions and recommendations. Details follow in the next section, where the reader learns what happened, when, where, and how, and who was involved. The report wraps up with details of the conclusions and recommendations.

TO: Jim Powers, Director of Marketing

FROM: Peter Phelps, Manager—Real Estate   *pp*

DATE: September 23, 2000

SUBJECT: Trip to Vancouver to Evaluate Three Proposed Silver's Gym
           Expansion Sites

On September 19 and 20, Jennifer O'Donald and I visited Vancouver to evaluate three real estate sites for a new Silver's Gym (see attached data sheets). Each site offers about 1500 square metres of floor space, which is sufficient for exercise and locker-room facilities and offices.

Conclusions

The presence of Stanley Park, Grouse Mountain, University of British Columbia, Simon Fraser University, Granville Island, Gastown, and the many entertainment facilities continue to draw workers and their families to Vancouver. As a result, downtown Vancouver is filled with young adults who are Silver's target customers.

Sites B and C are not in the downtown area and lack visibility and access to major highways. Thus, these sites do not offer the marketing opportunity of Site A. Site A, at the corner of Elm and Spruce, offers Silver's the greatest marketing opportunity for the following reasons:

- *Visibility and retail environment*—The site is across the street from an established shopping mall that contains three department stores.

- *Access to major routes*—The site is located at the intersection of Pender and Burrard.

- *Neighbourhood*—The site is in a "mixed use" neighbourhood. An office complex, housing 12 midsized corporations, is a block away; and the area is surrounded by a development of luxury townhouses.

- *Lease and renovation costs*—A total of 2200 square metres is available in the building. We could negotiate a lease for the 1500 square metres we need for about $110 000 annually. The building is now under construction, and the owner would build to suit our specific requirements.

- *Availability of parking*—About 200 parking spaces surround the building.

Recommendations

I strongly recommend that Silver's opens a new gym in downtown Vancouver. By choosing Site A, we are placing Silver's at the centre of a growing residential and commercial area that meets our demographic and marketing requirements for short-term and long-term success.

Attachments

Figure 13-2 Sample Trip Report

Long Business Reports

Although short reports are straightforward and relatively simple to write, they are not always appropriate to the needs of the topic, situation, or audience. When a short report will not accomplish your objectives, a longer formal report may be necessary.

Formal reports are usually linked to major projects—the development of new products, a company-wide structural reorganization, a study of competitive products or methods. The decision to write a formal report usually means several things:

▼ The complexity of the subject requires in-depth analysis.

▼ The document requires extensive research that may be time-consuming and costly.

- ▼ The report will be read by various primary and secondary audiences.
- ▼ The document may influence major decisions.
- ▼ The document may become part of an official record that is referred to over time.

Because of the complexity of long report topics and the typical length of the resulting documents, the formal report requires a more prescribed structure than the short report. The basic structure includes front matter, the body of the report, and back matter. The structure also contains internal devices that connect the elements of the report body itself. We will examine each of the elements of the long report in the next section.

Elements of a Model Report

When experienced business readers pick up a formal report, they expect to see certain elements arranged in a specific order. Indeed, many companies and business organizations give employees manuals that detail the "house style" for long reports, including the elements to use and the order in which they should appear. If you receive such a manual, use it as your model. If no manual is provided, use the elements presented here as your composition guide. All the elements that you are likely to find in a formal report are listed in Figure 13-3. While some of these elements are mandatory, such as a table of contents and an executive summary, others are optional and reflect the special needs of your document. For example, a title fly sheet and glossary are not always necessary. Dividing these elements into three main categories—front matter, body, and back matter—we now describe each in detail.

FRONT MATTER

The parts of a formal report that appear before the body are known as the **front matter.** This material describes the document's purpose and gives readers an overview of the information they will find in the body of the report. It also provides a road map for locating specific report sections, figures, and other important information. Because both reports and proposals use many identical front-matter elements, samples of these elements are included both here and in Chapter 14.

It is a foolish thing to make a long prologue and to be short in the story itself.

2 Maccabees 2:32

COVER   To give reports a professional appearance, report covers are often printed on heavy-duty stock paper and may include a company's name and logo. The cover should include the title and subtitle of the report; the writer's name and document submission date are optional.

TITLE FLY AND TITLE PAGE   Some reports open with a page that includes only the report title. This page, which is optional even in the most formal documents, is commonly referred to as the **title fly.** By contrast, the **title page**—which is usually the first page that readers see when they open a report—may include any or all of the following elements:

- ▼ title and subtitle
- ▼ name, title, and address of the person or group for whom the report is intended (precede this information with *Submitted to* or *Prepared for*)
- ▼ author's name, title, company or department, address, phone and fax numbers (preface this information with *Submitted by* or *Prepared by*)
- ▼ date of submission

Figure 13-3 Elements of a Formal Report

The first front-matter page, usually the title page, is considered page i, even though it is unnumbered. Begin numbering the subsequent front matter pages with page ii.

The title, which tells readers what your report is about, is the most important element on both the cover and the title page. Because of its importance, your title should be chosen carefully and should indicate your document's purpose and scope. For example, this title-subtitle combination

Shifting to a Just-in-Time Inventory System at Wayside Industrial Park
Cost-Containment Implications to the Year 2000

is better than the neutral and uninformative

Just-in-Time Inventory System.

Avoid prefacing your title with phrases like *Report on.* Your readers already know that they are about to read a report.

LETTERS AND MEMOS OF TRANSMITTAL The **letter of transmittal** (or **cover letter**) officially conveys the report to the reader. Transmittal memos serve the same purpose in internal reports. Transmittal letters and memos often begin with simple, direct statements. For example:

Here is the report on productivity changes that you requested on December 3.

Note, however, that this statement not only transmits the report but also refers to the authorization under which the document was written. The transmittal document identifies the specific report being sent, the person to whom it is directed, and the reason for sending it. This letter or memo thus provides a permanent document-delivery record for both writer and reader.

The next item in the transmittal document is usually a brief statement of the report's purpose. This statement helps the reader focus on the reason for which the report was written. For example:

> As you recall, you asked me to assess how eliminating administrative support for assistant vice presidents would affect productivity.

Because a formal report will include an executive summary, the transmittal letter or memo need not provide a detailed summary of conclusions and recommendations. Rather, it should orient readers in a general way to the discussion that follows.

The amount of information included in the transmittal letter or memo depends in part on whether the report contains good news or bad news. If it contains good news for the reader, the writer will typically include a short summary of the report's findings and recommendations. Use a direct organizational approach to convey this information: Start with the main idea in the form of a summary statement. If the news is negative, you may choose to provide few details at this early stage.

Transmittal letters and memos are often written in informal, conversational language. They may also use such personal pronouns as *I* and *you* and personal references. These qualities also make transmittal letters the ideal place to acknowledge the work of others who contributed to the report. Finally, transmittal letters and memos generally close with goodwill messages. You can choose, for example, to thank your reader for the opportunity to complete the assignment and express your willingness to conduct follow-up research.

Even though your transmittal document will not be mailed, it should include, where appropriate, the elements of an official letter or memo: inside address, salutation, close, and signature. It is considered page ii of the report, but because it is a letter or memo, the page number is often omitted.

Preface   When a report is written for more than one reader, a preface may be more appropriate than a transmittal letter. Although the preface usually does not include transmittal information ("Enclosed are eight copies of the marketing report"), it does provide a *descriptive narrative* about the document's organization. This narrative may then be followed by a tabulated description in the table of contents. Like the transmittal document, the preface may also focus on the uses to which the report may be put. It is also the point at which the author may thank those who contributed to the document.

TABLE OF CONTENTS   The **table of contents** is a list of the report's primary and secondary headings. Taken from the document outline, these headings provide readers with an overview of the material that follows. The table of contents is like a skeletal system revealing the report's overall structure. It reflects the outline of the report by citing material contained in the body, front-matter material that follows the contents page, and back-matter material, including appendices and other end-of-report sections.

In general, the complexity of your table of contents will be directly related to the length of your report. While the table of contents in shorter documents may cite only primary-level headings, the contents page in longer documents may also include secondary- and third-level headings. Page numbers are usually placed next to each heading, to which they are typically connected by spaced periods known as *leaders*.

LIST OF ILLUSTRATIONS   The list of illustrations—the figures and tables that are included in the document—appears on a separate page immediately following the table of contents or on the contents page itself. As we saw in Chapter 12, figures

Repeating Yourself—On Purpose

Parts of the formal report—including the letter of transmittal, executive summary, and introduction—may convey the same information. These sections prepare the reader for the details of the report as they discuss purpose, scope, background, methods, conclusions, and recommendations.

Because these sections deal with essentially the same material, they often repeat important concepts. Although some repetition is valuable as it reinforces key points, too much can leave a negative, disorganized impression. Here are several suggestions to avoid the appearance of redundancy:

▽ If you are fairly certain that the reader will examine every page of the report, including the front matter, start with the letter of transmittal and present increas-

ingly greater amounts of detail. That is, the letter of transmittal should present the most general discussion, the executive summary should be somewhat more specific, and the introduction the most specific of the three. This method works even if readers skip the front matter and move immediately to the introduction.

▽ If a detailed letter of transmittal is required, use less detail in the sections that follow.

▽ When there is no way to avoid repetition, learn the art of paraphrasing.

Trying to eliminate repetition from business reports is a mistake. Rather, your goal is to make the repetition as palatable—and valuable—as possible.

---

and tables can be grouped together as "Exhibits" or listed separately as "Figures" and "Tables." The first format requires one illustration list, the second two lists. Regardless of the system you use, your list should include the title and page number of every illustration.

➤ Cross Reference
We discussed consistency of titles and numbers in Chapter 12, pages 340–342.

FOREWORD   In some reports, a foreword concludes the front matter. A **foreword** is an introductory statement written by someone who did not author the report. The purpose of the foreword is to provide a context for the report by discussing background information or broad implications.

THE REPORT BODY

The heart of the report is found in the report body. Included in the body are an executive summary, introduction, text discussion, closing sections, and references.

EXECUTIVE SUMMARY   Busy executives are often unwilling to take time to read an entire document without first getting an overview of what it says. This overview is provided in the **executive summary**—a synopsis that condenses the report into relatively few pages. Executive summaries are intended for readers who need digested versions of the information contained in reports. Although most readers will continue reading, some will stop after the executive summary, and the typical reader will refer back to it for key points. Because of its crucial role, the executive summary is one of the most important elements of a formal report.

Executive summaries can be descriptive or informative. **Descriptive summaries** are synopses that act like expanded tables of contents that tell the reader what to expect in the pages that follow. Rather than presenting information, they state what the report is intended to accomplish in terms of its purpose and scope. The **scope** of the report refers to any limitations that define its coverage, including limitations of time and geography. The methodology used to collect data contained in the report may also be mentioned.

An **informative summary** is an abbreviated version of the report that includes conclusions and recommendations as well as descriptions of purpose, scope, and methods. The examples of descriptive and informative summaries in Figure 13-4 will help clarify their differences. Notice that the informative summary shown in Figure 13-4(b) is longer than the descriptive summary in Figure 13-4(a) because the informative summary includes substantive details.

The executive summary presents material in the same order as the report itself. When the report uses a direct approach, the executive summary presents conclusions and recommendations before explanations or methods. When the report is indirect, conclusions and recommendations close the executive summary. Style and tone should also be the same. Your objective here is to prepare readers for what will follow. Because your executive summary is generally read before your text discussion, it is important to avoid unexplained jargon and abbreviations, even if they are defined at a later point. In addition, your summary should not refer to figures and tables that follow later in the document. Finally, although it is considered a part of the report body, the executive summary should not contain exhibits or footnotes.

You should, however, include headings that will help orient the reader to the organization of your material. In addition, use transitional words and phrases such as *therefore* and *in addition* that make smooth, logical connections between ideas. As the first section in the body of the report, the executive summary begins with page number 1.

```
This report contains information on the "sick-building syndrome"—the
indoor air pollution in office buildings with sealed windows that
causes a variety of health complaints.  Included is information on
the causes of the pollution and methods for controlling it.  Special
attention will be paid to the cost and feasibility of installing new
air filtration and circulation systems.
```

(a) Descriptive Summary

```
This report examines the "sick-building syndrome"—the indoor air
pollution in office buildings that causes a variety of health
complaints.  Experts have identified more than 1500 chemicals and
bacteria that contribute to the problem.  Included among these are
the hydrocarbons, ozone, volatile organic compounds, and respirable
suspended particles that are emitted from printers, photocopy
machines, fax machines, and computer terminals.

As many as three out of ten of the nation's 4.5 million office and
public buildings have indoor air pollution problems.  These problems
are often difficult to fix.  One method that proved to be effective
at the headquarters of the Capital City Insurance Company in
Winnipeg, Manitoba, involved installing an air filtration and
circulation system developed by Midland Controls Inc. of Thunder
Bay, Ontario.

Despite the success of systems like this, most building owners are
reluctant to try new air pollution control approaches because of the
cost involved.  According to consultants, fixing a "sick building"
with the best technology can cost as much as $3 per square metre.
```

Figure 13-4 Comparing the Two Major Types of Executive Summaries

(b) Informative Summary

An executive summary can be as long as one-tenth the length of the report body. A 100-page report, therefore, would include an executive summary of about 10 pages. However, some business communicators recommend that it be much shorter, and that it simply list main points and be limited to one page. In order to make the material easy to read, use bulleted and numbered lists.[4]

Finally, although the executive summary is the first element in the report body, it should be written last. Writing a summary requires that you extract the core idea or thesis of your report by reviewing each section. Your next step is to distill this information into a shortened form. Depending on the length of the report, a given section may require no more than a sentence in the executive summary. For other sections, several paragraphs or pages may be needed.

INTRODUCTION   An **introduction** acts as an opening to your entire report, providing your readers with enough information to grasp the significance of the pages that follow. Experienced writers know that effective introductions often begin with attention-getters because the people who read reports must be convinced that the subject holds interest. For example, if you have developed a solution to a chronic problem, that solution should be stated in your opening sentence.

In general, introductions have six basic functions, the first of which is to clarify the subject.[5] Definitions and background information may be necessary to help readers understand the subject. For example, it may be important to explore the historical background of a problem, focusing on how other solutions have failed. Stating the importance of the issue is one way of clarifying the nature of both your subject and your report.

Second, the introduction should state the purpose of your report. Just as the topic sentence tells readers what to expect in the paragraph, the *purpose statement* focuses on the purpose and goals of the report. For example, the introduction may state either that your material provides an overview of existing programs or that it presents a new approach to a problem. Not surprisingly, purpose statements are often problem-centred; that is, they state goals in terms of the need to remedy a problem situation.

Third, the introduction should define the scope of your report. Scope is closely linked to purpose. When you state the scope of the report, you tell readers how broad your coverage will be. For instance, will your proposal for adjusting inventory to seasonal patterns of demand apply to worldwide operations or just to the southwestern region?

Fourth, the introduction should describe your plan for developing your subject. Here the introduction sets the stage for your organizational approach—that is, the *way* your material will be presented and developed in the body of your document. For example, the introduction may tell readers that your report will take a chronological approach or will examine the causes and effects of an issue. Explaining how you will develop your subject at this point also helps readers evaluate how you reached the conclusions and recommendations in your report.

Fifth, the introduction should clarify your research methods. To illustrate, say you conducted a nationwide survey to judge responses to a new product idea. Your introduction, then, should briefly describe the survey as the source of your research data.

Finally, the introduction should set the style of the report. The structure of sentences and paragraphs and the use of personal or impersonal language tells the reader what to expect on the pages that follow.

Perhaps because it serves such an important function, many people consider the introduction the most challenging part of the report to write. Many writers draft the introduction after the rest of the report is complete, but time pressure is usually

A QUESTION OF ETHICS

Plagiarism: The World's Dumbest Crime

Let's not beat around the bush: plagiarism is theft. It is the act of stealing the ideas or words of another writer without crediting the source and, where appropriate, asking for permission. Although it is also against the law, plagiarism remains common wherever words are written, including business settings.

Knowing how to avoid plagiarism is as crucial as knowing the rules of grammar. Here are some guidelines that will help you avoid the problem:

1. Develop the habit of documenting the ideas and words that you obtain from other sources. When citing the exact words of a source, set off the citation in quotation marks and use a footnote for documentation.

2. Develop effective note-taking habits and be very careful in your use of quotation marks. Plagiarism often occurs when, during the research stage, sources are copied verbatim without quotation marks.

3. You are still responsible for documenting your sources even if you rephrase someone else's thoughts in your own words and with your own sentence structure (the essence of paraphrasing and summarizing).

4. Finally, learn when documentation is *not* necessary. First, personal ideas and knowledge require no documentation. Second, "common knowledge"—information known and readily available to most people—is not subject to plagiarism. Thus, when writing a report on a major corporation, there is no need to document the source that gave you the name of the CEO or the location of corporate headquarters.

Plagiarism is a breach of ethics as well as a theft of property. It is also "the world's dumbest crime," said journalist Gregg Easterbrook, who recently discovered that another writer had plagiarized several pages from one of his books. "If you are caught, there is absolutely nothing you can say in your own defence."

Questions for Critical Thinking

1. What is wrong with using the words of another writer without credit or permission?
2. How can understanding some basic concepts of copyright law and fair use help you avoid plagiarism? (See Chapter 8.)
3. What is the relationship between good research habits and the avoidance of plagiarism?

Sources: Trudy Lieberman, "Plagiarize, Plagiarize, Plagiarize . . . Only Be Sure to Always Call It Research," *Columbia Journalism Review* (July–August 1995): 24; James Atlas, "When an Original Idea Sounds Really Familiar," *New York Times*, 28 July 1991, E2; Gregg Easterbrook, "The Sincerest Flattery," *Newsweek*, 29 July 1991, 45–46; Lynn Quitman Troyka, *Simon & Schuster Handbook for Writers*, 2d ed. (Englewood Cliffs, N.J.: Prentice Hall, 1990), 580–583.

---

greatest at this point, so the introduction may not receive enough attention. A more effective approach is to draft an introduction at the start of the report and then continually review and revise it as your report progresses. When the report is complete, your introduction can be refined.

TEXT DISCUSSION All the elements that we have examined so far prepare the reader for the substance of the report contained in the text discussion. This is the discussion in which you record your ideas according to the logical plan developed in your report outline. Recall from Chapter 5 that data may be arranged according to a number of development plans, including deductive, inductive, problem/solution, cause-and-effect, climactic-order, and chronological. Choose the plan that allows you to cover the subject in a logical, ordered sequence that readers will understand.

Although most formal reports close with separate sections devoted to conclusions and recommendations, separate sections of major reports may also include interim conclusions and recommendations tied to the discussions in those sections. The sample report illustrated in Figure 13-5 later in this chapter uses this technique.

Internal Connections: Structural Guideposts   Because your discussion may be dozens—even hundreds—of pages long, readers need help to follow your ideas. Remember that even if your document is logically organized and clearly written, your readers may still be overwhelmed by the sheer volume of information. This problem places a special requirement on report writers. To highlight important connections, writers must provide **structural guideposts** that help readers move smoothly from one part of the discussion to another. These guideposts take different forms, including transitions and headings, which have been discussed in detail in Chapters 5 and 6. They also take the form of internal previews and summaries and summary tables and charts.

➡ *Cross Reference*
We discussed headings in Chapter 5, pages 146–148, and transitions in Chapter 6, pages 171–172.

Internal Previews and Summaries. An internal preview appears at the beginning of a section to preview the material covered in the section. An internal preview may be stated in a simple sentence: "This section will cover points A, B, and C." The section then continues, as promised, with a full discussion of points A, B, and C. At other times, a more extensive preview is necessary. For example:

> Deciding whether to equip all J. B. Hunt trucks with on-board computers depends on a number of factors, each of which will be examined in the next section of this report. The analysis focuses on the relationship between the efficiency gains of the fleet due to on-board computers compared with the cost of those computers.
>
> Efficiency will be examined first. Specifically, the opening section will discuss the application of this technology to long-haul trucking. The second section will examine the cost of IBM on-board computers for the 6000 trucks in the J. B. Hunt fleet.

In both cases the internal preview helps readers to establish key expectations for what they will read in the remainder of the section.

By contrast, the **internal summary** appears at the close of a section, where it reiterates key points and links them both to other report sections and to the report's specific purpose. In effect, internal summaries tell readers what they have just read and clarify the relationships among different pieces of information in the report.

An internal summary usually appears at the end of a lengthy section, often setting the stage for a new direction in the discussion. Indeed, the last sentence in an internal summary may be forward-looking. For example:

> Now that the implications of opening manufacturing facilities in France and Germany have been examined, the next section of the report will focus on the output of Brunswick Corporation's manufacturing facilities in Canada.

In deciding where to place internal previews and summaries, examine your writing outline carefully. Internal summaries should be located at key points in the report, generally where primary-level headings appear. Use them immediately before and after these headings.

Summary Tables and Charts. As summary devices, tables and charts are also important connective tools. They condense various pieces of information from different sections of your report and display them in one location. For example, in a report on the use of wireless phones by sales representatives, the writer may choose to include a summary table that lists the features of various brands. Tables and charts are also useful methods of reinforcing text comparisons.

CLOSING SECTIONS   The close of your report may include a summary and sections offering conclusions and recommendations. Whereas some reports feature all three sections, others may combine these components in a single section. Remember that although your closing sections may offer slightly different perspectives on your findings, they should not introduce new material. On the contrary, every statement made in these sections should be justified by facts already presented.

Summary Informational reports—those that present facts but not interpretations—usually conclude with final summaries. The **summary** condenses the most important information from the report, often recapping the internal summaries from the conclusions of various sections. Summarized information should be presented in the order in which it appears in the report.

Conclusions The logical results of the evidence presented in the report form the report's conclusions. In effect, your conclusions answer the question that is uppermost in your reader's mind: What does all this mean?

In order to be effective, conclusions must be linked to the purpose and methods of your report, as stated in your introduction. For example, if your introduction told the reader that your purpose was to examine the feasibility and cost of installing robots on an assembly line, your conclusion should not focus on the relationship between robots and employee morale. Although this issue may have been mentioned in your report, it is not the problem you promised to explore in your introduction.

Use the following guidelines to write effective conclusions:

▼ Assume that your conclusions will be read independently of the rest of your document. Briefly restate your purpose and methods and avoid unexplained jargon and abbreviations.

▼ Organize your results according to the order in which they are presented in the body of your report. Using this strategy means that you will usually present your most important conclusions first.

▼ Organize your conclusions with the same care that you brought to the body of your report.

Recommendations Following your conclusions, recommendations are the specific actions that you suggest as a result of the information that you have presented. For example, if your report presents options, you should select the one that you think will prove most effective.

Your recommendations, of course, should be financially realistic and appropriate to the problem. Although recommendations are sometimes difficult to make, your reader will expect to find them in your report. If you honestly feel that you cannot recommend any action, say so. Be prepared, however, to explain your position. If the problem requires further study before recommendations can be made, your recommendations should include specific plans for pursuing the problem.

Finally, you should remember two things about the nature of recommendations. First, they must flow logically from the findings of your report. When considering recommendations, many readers will carefully reexamine the specific evidence presented in the report to determine whether it supports your recommended course of action. Second, recommendations are by definition advisory; they suggest courses of action. The final decision to act is made by the person for whom the report is written.

REFERENCES When your report cites material from other sources, these sources are likely to be listed in a **references** section included at the end of the report body. This section, which may be labelled *References*, *Notes*, or *Endnotes*, lists sources according to a consistent documentation style. Various styles are examined in detail in Appendix I. Long reports may include references at the end of each section.

BACK MATTER

Supplemental information is included in the **back matter**—the parts of the report that follow the report body. Depending on the nature and length of your report, your

COLLABORATIVE COMMUNICATION

Report Conferences

Collaboration, or team play, is inevitable in the development of complex business reports. But a group cannot sit around a table and write a document. Rather, the group turns to its individual members to independently draft sections of the report. These assignments and other crucial collaborative activities are determined during report conferences.

Report conferences are meetings of concerned collaborators working on a project. Headed by a knowledgeable leader who is often the senior person in the group or the person who knows most about the project, report conferences have various functions. At a first conference, collaborators discuss the report's purpose, concept, design, and proposed contents. They agree upon a dummy, which defines document design, and accept responsibility for writing sections within constraints of the dummy.

The section that each group member writes should involve his or her area of expertise—say, accounting, finance, or marketing. In general, the best reports are written by people who know their jobs inside-out. These experts may meet at interim conferences to talk over writing strategies and problems. The final report is synthesized at a closing conference when all the copy has been drafted. The group leader, often with the help of an editor, integrates the draft into a single "voice" that expresses a consistent viewpoint and style.

Crucial collaboratives activities are determined through report conferences. They are often lead by a senior person who knows most about the project

Questions for Critical Thinking

1. What are report conferences and for what are they necessary?
2. Why is it necessary to synthesize the work of individual contributors at a closing conference?
3. Why are report conferences likely to produce reports that are usable documents and that give readers the answers they need to complete a job?

---

back matter may include a bibliography, appendices, a glossary, and an index. Each element should start a new page and should be labelled with its appropriate title.

BIBLIOGRAPHY   A **bibliography** is a list of references used in researching the report. While the reference list refers to work actually cited in your text, the bibliography identifies *all* works consulted, regardless of whether you specifically cited them. Naturally, if your reference list contains all the sources that you used, a separate bibliography is unnecessary. The bibliography is usually an alphabetized list.

APPENDICES   An **appendix** supplements material presented in your text. Appendices may be placed in the back matter either because they are tangential to your purpose or because they are too long or detailed to be included in the body. Among the types of material included in appendices are questionnaires, statistical analyses, technical support, and the texts of legal statutes and interviews.

Although you may include as many appendices as you need, each appendix should be limited to one type of supplemental material. When only one appendix is used, simply label it *Appendix*. Label multiple appendices *Appendix A*, *Appendix B*, and so on.

GLOSSARY   When your report includes unfamiliar or technical words or phrases, a glossary may be necessary. A **glossary** is an alphabetized list of words and phrases accompanied by definitions. Remember that glossary definitions are meant to supplement rather than replace definitions that appear when you first introduce terms in your text. Each glossary entry should begin a new line and be followed immediately with a definition written in traditional dictionary style.

INDEX   Finally, a major report may also include an **index**—an alphabetized list of report topics that includes the page on which each topic appears. Many writers find indexes unnecessary when the table of contents also lists topics and pages. However, this alphabetical listing of key words and topics is especially useful in the case of long, complex reports.

Progress Check

1. List the elements that make up the front matter of a report. Are any of these elements optional?
2. What is the difference between a descriptive and an informative executive summary, and which would you be more likely to use in a recommendation report?
3. Describe criteria for judging effective conclusions and recommendations.

A Sample Long Report

Suppose that a school bus accident resulted in the death of an elementary school student. Imgine that residents of a British Columbia town formed a School Bus Safety Advisory Committee charged with recommending ways to improve the school bus transportation system. On that committee were members of the private company that operated and maintained the town's fleet of school buses as well as teachers, parents, police officials, and other town representatives.

After months of work, the committee produced a lengthy report, parts of which are illustrated as Figure 13-5 (adapted from an actual report by the Bus Safety Committee in Westport, Connecticut). Included in the sample are the transmittal memo, executive summary, introduction, and details from the text. The report was submitted by the town's superintendent of schools to the board of education.

Figure 13-5 demonstrates the relationships among diverse groups—businesspeople, government officials, and community members—who got together to work on the solution to a joint problem. Through a collaborative effort, the committee produced a business document that ultimately resulted in the implementation of a paid school bus monitor system. Although businesspeople helped write the report, the document was submitted by a government official (the superintendent of schools) to a government body (the board of education). In the real world, businesspeople play many different roles, including advisers to government officials.[6]

As you read the report, keep in mind that although it follows our model outline in some ways, it deviates in others. Like all effective business documents, it is oriented first toward the needs of the subject and audience and only then toward the requirements of the report form.

More than a year after this report was issued, the town's system of paid bus monitors was working effectively. The School Bus Safety Advisory Committee had accomplished what it set out to do: it made the buses of a British Columbia suburb safer for children.

What's Ahead

As this chapter shows, both long and short reports require careful planning, organization, and writing. As you will see in Chapter 14, the same skills are needed to write effective business proposals.

TRANSMITTAL MEMO

TO:	BOARD OF EDUCATION MEMBERS
FROM:	SUPERINTENDENT OF SCHOOLS
SUBJECT:	REPORT OF THE BUS SAFETY COMMITTEE
DATE:	JUNE 16, 200X

Attached is the report of the School Bus Safety Advisory Committee. The committee was appointed as an advisory group to the superintendent following the tragic death of one of our students in December.

The committee was charged with reviewing all components of the town's school bus safety procedures, bus scheduling and its impact on safety, pupil training, the board of education's transportation policies, and parental responsibility for teaching and reinforcing bus safety. A key charge focused on the merits of a bus monitor program. A voluntary program was put into effect this spring as a result of the committee's preliminary recommendations.

PROCEDURES

The committee report does not constitute a formal recommendation to the Board of Education. Advisory committees such as this make recommendations to the superintendent, and I have been kept informed as the committee's work progressed.

Following tonight's committee presentation, my administrative staff and I will study the recommendations carefully, considering them in the context of feasibility, probable effectiveness, impact on other aspects of the school program, legal implications, and cost. Our review of the report may raise further questions about some of these issues or about the recommendations themselves. Based on this review, I will make preliminary recommendations to the Board of Education regarding implementation of some or all of the committee's recommendations, timing of implementations, and avenues for funding those with cost implications.

The recommendations will then be considered by the Board of Education at a public meeting. Final recommendations for Board action will be developed following this session.

ACKNOWLEDGMENTS

The committee has been working for five months, meeting frequently and doing extensive research. Members have done a real service to the school system, and the administration and Board of Education acknowledge the time and effort that went into producing their thorough report. We thank all the members for their service. There is no doubt that our safety program will improve as the result of the work of this outstanding group.

EXECUTIVE SUMMARY

Getting students to school and home safely and on time is similar to mounting a small-scale military operation on community streets daily. Each day, 32 buses and vans transport an average of 2500 students on 61 arrival routes and 74 dismissal routes. They travel about 2160 kilometres a day, or 393 120 kilometres every school year.

-2-

About 50 employees of the bus company operate and maintain the fleet of 26 Thomas Built diesel-powered buses and seven 16-passenger vans. The locally owned bus company has held the school contract for 22 years. Although operated and maintained by this private company, the vehicles are owned by the town.

Bus safety became an overriding issue for this community after an elementary school child was killed getting off a bus in December 200X. After this incident, the Bus Safety Committee was formed; and this report is the result of the committee's efforts. To improve the safety of the town's school bus transportation system, the committee submits the following recommendations.

Figure 13-5 Selections from a Sample Report

Begin a Full-Scale Paid School Bus Monitor Program at the Elementary School
Committee members agree unanimously that one of the most effective safety improvements that the town could make is a full-scale paid elementary school bus monitor program. The committee recommends that the Superintendent and Board of Education endorse a full-scale paid monitor program and develop a plan and timetable for its implementation.

Hire a Permanent Safety Coordinator to Improve Driver Performance
The position of safety coordinator should be made permanent. This person should monitor, support, and evaluate the job performance of bus drivers and monitors and participate in bus driver and monitor training.

Improve Communication among Drivers, Administrators, and Parents and Standardize School Bus Disciplinary Procedures
All drivers should use the bus conduct report form to report student safety violations. All school administrators should follow the same guidelines for complaints about student behaviour and enforce guidelines uniformly.

Tighten Procedures for Complaints about Drivers
All complaints about drivers should be directed to the Board's transportation coordinator. The coordinator should keep records of complaints and bring them to the attention of the bus company.

Make Elementary Bus Stops Safer and Make All Students Eligible to Ride Buses
All kindergarten through grade six students should be assigned to buses. This assignment of buses will discourage walkers who are at a greater risk than riders of becoming involved in accidents. With fewer walkers, school crossing guards can be eliminated, and crossing-guard funds can be channelled into other bus-safety programs.

Revise Opening and Closing Times
The opening and closing times between middle and elementary levels should be increased by ten minutes to reduce the need for drivers to hurry through their runs.

Make School Loading and Unloading Zones Safer
A professional traffic engineer should be engaged to study the traffic patterns at school grounds and make recommendations for improved safety. Communication with parents regarding parking, waiting, and dropping-off/picking-up procedures should be improved.

Appoint a Permanent School Bus Safety Advisory Committee
A permanent School Bus Safety Advisory Committee should be appointed to review procedures, technologies, and equipment, including seat belts. The committee would make continuing recommendations for improvement.

Improve Student Education Program, Including Standardized Bus Evacuation Drills
Schools should develop and standardize a continuous student-education program about bus safety. Bus and van evacuation drills should be an integral part of the program.

Improve Public Education Regarding Traffic Regulations and School Buses
The schools, in cooperation with the police department, should improve the public's awareness of school bus traffic safety.

Cost to Implement Recommendations
The cost to implement the recommendations proposed by the committee is between $67 000 and $81 000.

INTRODUCTION

The introduction states why the report was written

The superintendent of schools appointed the School Bus Safety Advisory Committee in January 200X following the death of a student in a school bus accident in December 200X.

The charge of this committee was to review school bus safety to ensure that the town and the bus company are operating school buses as safely as possible and to restore the credibility of our transportation program. The superintendent's charge also focused on the specific question of whether the town should begin a school bus monitor program.

Here the document's scope is specified

Bullets highlight this information

Our review was intensive and extensive. It paid particular attention to the following concerns:

- safety of loading zones

- safety of school areas

Figure 13-5 *(continued)*

An explanation of how the committee accomplished its goals provides crucial information: the discussion that follows the introduction is organized according to the findings of each of the three subcommittees

- student education
- driver supervision
- safety of bus equipment
- scheduling of bus runs

In the process of conducting this research, the committee examined findings of national and provincial groups.

To achieve its goals, the committee divided into three subcommittees covering feasibility of monitors, bus equipment and driver training, and student and parent education. As part of its research, the committee held a public hearing and interviewed drivers and parents.

In general, the committee found the town's school bus transportation system to be good. Bus equipment exceeds state and federal requirements. Driver training has been strengthened in recent years, and all drivers have passed new provincial licensing regulations introduced this spring.

General conclusions—both positive and negative—come next

The scope of the report is further defined in the context of report recommendations

However, we found room for improvement. Although a student-education program is in place, it can be standardized further and enhanced. We also concluded that a monitor program would strengthen the safety of elementary school bus riders. In making our recommendations, the committee focused on enhancing the safety of students. The superintendent's charge did, however, include a request to consider the economic impact of a paid monitor program. Thus, the report includes estimated costs.

-4-

An internal preview describes what readers can expect next

The body of the report begins here. All primary-level headings in the report are centred and capitalized. This heading includes a title and subtitle

Research data, including a table, begin the report and establish its credibility. The text explains the table's importance. Notice how closely the table is to the text reference

Figures and tables follow their own numbering systems

The remainder of this report will focus on the specific recommendations made by the three subcommittees to improve the school bus system. The costs associated with the recommendations will then be analyzed and ideas for implementation explored. It is our earnest hope that the Superintendent and the Board of Education endorse our recommendations and implement them without delay.

REPORT OF THE MONITOR SUBCOMMITTEE: BEGIN A FULL-SCALE PAID SCHOOL BUS MONITOR PROGRAM AT THE ELEMENTARY LEVEL

Both provincial and national statistics clearly show that the most dangerous part of a school bus ride occurs when children enter or leave the bus in the area commonly referred to as the loading zone. The Traffic Safety Association of Canada reports that an average of 4 students are killed each year in loading-zone accidents. As Table 1 shows, this number represents more than 65 percent of all fatalities related to school bus accidents.

Children under the age of nine are especially susceptible to loading-zone accidents. As Figure 1 shows, more than half of all fatalities involve children between five and six years of age.

Table 1

Children Killed in School Bus Accidents During Five-Year Period

PASSENGER ON SCHOOL BUSES	AVERAGE DEATHS PER YEAR	PEDESTRIAN AT LOADING ZONES	AVERAGE DEATHS PER YEAR
Passengers on Type 1 School Bus	1	Pedestrians at Loading Zones Struck by Type 1 School Bus	2
Passengers on Other Vehicles Used as School Buses	1	Pedestrian at Loading Zones Struck by Other Vehicle Used as School Buses	2
Total Passenger Deaths	2	Total Pedestrian Deaths	4

Figure 13-5   (continued)

Data follow a geographic organizational pattern. National data are presented first, followed by data for the province

In British Columbia, these figures are even more dramatic. Over the past 20 years, all bus-related fatalities have occurred outside the bus. Since 1972, 20 British Columbia children have died in school bus accidents. One was struck by a motorist passing the bus illegally; 19 were struck by the school bus. Fifteen of the victims (75 percent) were under the age of nine; all of the children were under the age of 13. A report compiled by the British Columbia School Safety Association indicates that 14 of these fatalities, fully 70 percent, might reasonably have been prevented if well-trained safety monitors were riding the buses.

An internal preview

Loading-zone safety can be improved by a staff of paid bus monitors or volunteer monitors. The report will examine the details of these alternatives next.

FIGURE 1

Age Distribution of Children Fatally Injured by School Buses

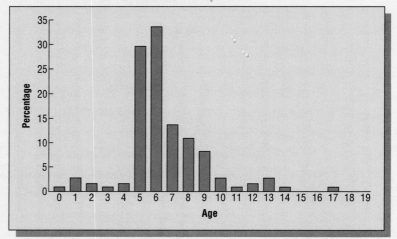

Source: National Highway Traffic Safety Administration

Style of secondary-level heading: flush against the left margin, underlined, upper- and lower-case letters

<u>Programs Involving Paid Monitors</u>
The use of adults as paid school bus monitors is not a new idea. A number of communities, including Peachland, British Columbia; Summerside, Prince Edward Island; and Bedford, Nova Scotia, began using paid monitors in the 1970s. In many instances, the monitors were hired initially to deal with disciplinary problems. Some communities hired them primarily to assist on vehicles carrying special-education students. Still others began their programs as a direct result of a school bus accident. Saskatchewan is the only province to mandate the province-wide use of monitors. It began its program in 1986. In recent months, while a number of communities have scaled back or eliminated monitor programs for fiscal reasons, others have launched studies to start programs. As far as this committee can determine, no school bus loading-zone fatality has occurred in any community with a paid monitor program.

Internal preview is linked to the tertiary-level headings that follow (Vernon's monitor program is omitted here)

In British Columbia, Peachland and Vernon are the only communities with some form of paid monitor program. The report will examine these programs along with the program in Saskatchewan. Each of these programs was initiated as a result of a bus-related fatality.

Headings cite programs in specific localities

<u>Peachland's Monitor Program</u>
In Peachland, monitors trained in procedures to ensure safe boarding and exiting are used on elementary bus trips to and from school. They act as crossing guards when children cross the street and assist the driver in keeping order on the bus. The city and Board of Education continue to support the use of paid monitors after 15 years, believing that it has been responsible for the accident-free record during that time.

Figure 13-5 *(continued)*

The January 200X report of the British Columbia School Safety Association said, "The primary difficulty Peachland has with its program is finding enough monitors."

Saskatchewan's Monitor Program

Saskatchewan began its monitor program after a year in which three children were killed in loading-zone accidents. The Saskatchewan legislature mandated paid monitors on all elementary buses in the province's cities and towns. Some communities also include junior high school.

Monitor training covers procedures in crossing, pupil loading and unloading, behaviour management, and emergencies. The monitor's duties are ensuring that pupils cross the street safely and that the loading zone is clear before the driver pulls away.

After five years, some Saskatchewan school districts continue to have difficulty maintaining a full monitor staff. Few districts have full staffing at all times, and most districts must use variances of emergency procedures allowed under state guidelines. Nevertheless, the latest data indicate that 85 percent of all elementary bus runs were covered by a monitor. See Appendix A for a detailed discussion of the monitor program in Prince Albert, Saskatchewan.

Volunteer Monitors

The committee examined ways to offer the services of monitors without cost. Unfortunately, we did not find any research dealing with specific plans or programs involving volunteer monitors. The committee, therefore, decided to develop, implement, and evaluate its own volunteer monitor plan at the elementary school level.

The plan called for a two-phase approach. In the first phase, volunteer monitors were to ride once each week for six weeks on dismissal runs. One hundred and fifteen volunteers were needed to staff fully all afternoon elementary school bus runs. Parents of the students formed the basis of the volunteer group, and all received training.

The committee evaluated the first phase with a questionnaire and interviews with parents and bus drivers. It concluded that sufficient volunteers could not be obtained for the second phase and cancelled plans to expand the program. The committee also decided to continue with phase one—afternoon dismissal runs—until the end of the school year.

Availability of Volunteers

Seventy parents signed up and served as volunteer monitors during phase one. After signing up, a few dropped out but replacements were found. Approximately 60 percent of the afternoon buses had volunteer monitors ride on them during this phase. During the last week in April, the committee sent a questionnaire to all elementary school parents to determine their interest and availability for phase two. A copy of the questionnaire is included in Appendix B. The survey showed:

- 25 of 70 phase-one volunteer monitors would continue during the second phase

- 31 parents agreed to volunteer during phase two

- 3 community members expressed interest in volunteering; a few senior citizens expressed interest but could not handle the constant up-and-down movement that is required.

The total number of volunteers for phase two (59) was less than the number who participated in the first phase (70).

Conclusions

Before knowing how the initial volunteer monitor program worked, the committee considered how best to staff a volunteer monitor program over a full school year. In what seemed the best way to minimize a volunteer's commitment, the committee assumed that a monitor would ride once a week for nine weeks. This would require 460 volunteers to staff fully an afternoon program (p.m. dismissal) and 920 volunteers to staff fully a total plan (a.m. and p.m. dismissals).

Based on our limited experience, neither goal seemed achievable. The coordination required for a program involving so many volunteers also seemed beyond the community's resources. Therefore, the committee concluded that a safety-monitor program that relies solely on volunteers cannot be successful because of the limited availability of volunteer monitors and the amount of required coordination.

Figure 13-5 (continued)

Recommendations

The committee recommends unanimously that paid safety monitors ride on all elementary school buses.

The committee endorses the findings of the British Columbia School Safety Association that using monitors is the single most effective way to improve school bus safety at the elementary level. The committee struggled with the best way to implement such a program—whether to do it in stages or all at once. A majority recommends every effort be made to begin full implementation by September 200X. Although time is short, other communities have begun their programs in similar time frames. Saskatchewan did it in 35 days, and our town can benefit greatly by that experience.

If it is not possible to have all monitors in place by September, the committee recommends that temporary procedures be developed until positions are filled. These may include use of interim monitors from a list of available substitutes. Such substitutes could be recruited initially from the corps of volunteer monitors used between April and June 200X.

COSTS ASSOCIATED WITH RECOMMENDATIONS

Among the recommendations proposed by the committee, the following have direct cost implications. The figures presented represent costs during the 200X-0X school year.

RECOMMENDATION	COST
Finance the Paid Monitor Program: Elementary Buses	$53 000–$67 000

These costs are based on information obtained from other communities using the monitor system. The lower figure is based on an hourly wage for monitors ($8.50); the higher figure is based on a payment per run ($8.00). This budget allocation would fund 23 monitors for the entire school year.

Hire Safety Coordinator on a Permanent Basis	$7000

The safety coordinator would monitor, support, and evaluate the job performance of bus drivers and paid monitors. The coordinator would report to both the bus company and the school system; and the cost of this position would be shared equally by the two groups. The amount shown represents the school system's portion of the safety coordinator's salary.

-8-

Hire Professional Traffic Engineer	$7000

The committee has significant concerns regarding the congestion and traffic patterns at each elementary and middle school. The committee sees the engineer working with the school administration and the police department in examining and developing the safest traffic configuration at each school. This project will require funding for two years.

Total Cost for All Recommendations	$67 000–$81 000
Average Cost	$74 000

IMPLEMENTING THE RECOMMENDATIONS

The committee has examined how its recommendations might be implemented and presents ideas to consider. Recognizing that the Superintendent of Schools may revise these suggestions, the committee views the following thoughts as a starting point in the implementation process.

The framework for our suggestions is built on the following key ideas:

- The school system and the bus company must work cooperatively in addressing the recommendations. Key personnel within the school system and bus company must be identified and provided with the responsibility to implement specific recommendations.

- Within the school system, the Superintendent of Schools, business manager, assistant superintendent of schools for curriculum, and transportation coordinator must take an active role in implementing specific recommendations.

- Job descriptions and responsibilities for the newly created positions of safety coordinator and bus monitor must be developed carefully.

Figure 13-5   *(continued)*

This short paragraph contains another internal preview

Following are specific details for implementing the committee's recommendations. Included are suggested time frames for each recommendation.

Paid Bus Safety Monitors: Elementary Schools
The committee suggests that the school business manager, working with the bus company, be responsible for implementing this recommendation. The business manager should:

- Write a job description focusing on safe boarding and exiting from the bus, crossing students to the other side of the street, and assisting the driver in keeping order on the bus. This job description, developed by the committee for volunteer monitors, is shown in Appendix C and can be used as a reference.

- Establish payment rates and qualifications for the monitor position, as well as procedures for advertising, hiring, training, and supervising monitors.

- Develop training procedures and schedules for paid safety monitors. The committee sees the training provided in two to three sessions involving classroom and actual time on the school bus. Training can be provided by the bus company.

-9-

TIME FRAME: July–August 200X

Tighten Procedures for Complaints about Drivers
Each school principal should inform parents that all complaints about bus drivers should be reported to the board's transportation coordinator. The transportation coordinator will keep a record of all complaints and bring them to the attention of the bus company. The bus company will investigate all complaints and contact the safety coordinator when appropriate. The bus company will notify the transportation coordinator of the disposition of all complaints, and the transportation coordinator will provide the business manager with a status report on a monthly basis.

TIME FRAME: September 200X–June 200X

Review and Update Driver's Manual
The business manager, working with the bus company and transportation coordinator, will review and update the driver's manual on an annual basis each summer. The bus company will distribute and review the contents with drivers in early September. The business manager will distribute copies of the manual to each principal on an annual basis.

TIME FRAME: July 200X

Prepare an Accident Plan
The business manager, working with the bus company, nursing company, nursing supervisor, and police department, should develop an accident plan to establish procedures that will be used following a school bus accident or other school-related emergency. This plan will then be presented to the Board of Education, bus drivers, school personnel, and parents.

TIME FRAME: September–December 200X

Appoint a Permanent School Bus Safety Advisory Committee
The present committee has spent nearly four months dealing with a very complex topic. We have studied certain issues in great detail. However, other areas need further review and study. Among these are:

- the use of seat belts on school buses;

- the use of coach-type or seatbelt-equipped school buses for student trips on provincial highways;

- new technologies related directly to school bus safety; and

- additional safety measures on school vans.

The committee recognizes that the vans purchased in 200X meet all provincial and federal safety regulations. But because they are frequently used to transport special-education or mobility-impaired students, further study is needed to determine if any other safety measures are required. The British Columbia School Safety Association has made a number of recommendations that merit consideration.

Figure 13-5   (continued)

Corporal Dan MacLean, RCMP Training Academy, Regina, Saskatchewan

The Royal Canadian Mounted Police is a truly national police force, enforcing federal law across the nation and acting as the provincial police force in most provinces.[7] It also acts as the local police force for about 200 municipalities.

The RCMP employs a consistent reporting approach known as the Operational Reporting System, which is designed to provide RCMP members across the nation with clear, concise, factual, and comprehensive information. Overseeing the training and integrity of the ORS is Corporal Dan MacLean, who guides cadets in communication skills from basic grammar to mediation and negotiation. As an officer, teacher, and advocate of lifelong learning, MacLean has become skillful in the ability to articulate his thoughts and ideas both orally and in written report form. His skill is premised in his philosophy "preparation is the key to success."

Question: What type of reports do you train RCMP officers to write?

Answer: As in any service-oriented organization, the RCMP is accountable to its customers. We have to be able to report what we did, why we did it, and what is to be done in the future. Effective reporting ensures that the needs and expectations of the client (public, other police, and partners) have been met.

Cadets learn to complete reports associated with calls for service. These reports can be as simple as the proverbial "cat up the tree" case, or as complex as a serious criminal code investigation. Guided by the standard practices of the ORS cadets learn various forms of internal and external reporting formats. In practice, the intended recipient will determine the format of the report.

Question: Do you prepare investigative reports in which you analize the details of a particular topic?

Answer: There are many types of investigative reports prepared by the RCMP: business plans, quality assurance reports, and human resources reports, to name just a few. They all follow the guidelines and format of consistent with that of the originating department. In preparation for the myriad of reports, cadets are required to prepare a Community Profile. This is the study of a community based on research into its demography and social-economic conditions, for example. When cadets arrive at their detachments they are expected to prepare such a profile of their new community. A research report of this nature will ensure that the delivery of service by the RCMP is consistent with the needs of the community.

Question: Do you use illustrations or graphics in reports?

Answer: Many RCMP reports include illurtrations, graphs,

sketches, scale drawings, and photographs. Their primary function is to give the audience a clearer understanding of the subject matter. The defense or prosecution of many criminal cases use visual aids to give the judge, jury, and others a better understanding of a crime scene or where inverstigators found evidence. One photo can depict what might take hours to explain verbally or in writing.

Question: What are the most common errors an inexperienced report writer might make and how can they be avoided?

Answer: The most common errors I have observed are forgetting who the target readers are, assuming the reader is aware of information not included in the report, leaving the reader with questions due to insufficient detail, and using the wrong report format. These errors can be avoided by identifying the target audience before beginning to write, writing as if you had never discussed the content of the report with anyone, paying constant attention to detail, and following the basic principles of the type of report you are preparing. A final recommendation is to take the time at the beginning of the report to research, analyze, and organize the information that you wish to include. The resulting report will be one you'll be proud to sign as an author.

Source: Interview with Corporal Dan MacLean.

STUDENT RESOURCE CENTRE

Summary of Chapter Objectives

1. Identify six differences between short and long reports.

Short reports typically do not include front or back matter and have short, rather than extended, introductions. Most short reports get immediately to the point and, unlike long reports, are personal and use fewer devices to aid comprehension. Finally, short reports sometimes follow a prescribed outline and may even use printed fill-in-the-blank forms.

2. List the elements contained in short progress and trip reports.

Progress reports—documents that provide status information on current work—often begin with summaries and then focus on work completed, work in progress, and work yet to be done. They may also include work forecasts, conclusions, and recommendations. Trip reports—documents that summarize the events of business trips—often start with summaries highlighting conclusions and recommendations that emerged from the trip. Details follow, then conclusions and recommendations are spelled out. Trip reports often close by examining the need for future visits to the same site.

3. Identify the elements contained in long reports.

A report has three main parts: the front matter, body, and back matter. The front matter of a long report typically includes a cover, a title fly, a title page, a letter or memo of transmittal, a table of contents, a list of illustrations, and a foreword. These elements describe the document's purpose and provide a road map for locating specific report parts.

The body is the heart of the long report. Included in the body are an executive summary, introduction, text discussion, closing sections, and references.

The back matter of a long report may include a bibliography, appendices, a glossary, and an index. This material supplements the information presented in the body of the report.

4. Explain the functions of executive summaries and introductions in long reports.

The first feature usually found in the report body, the executive summary is a digested version of the information contained in the report. It plays a crucial role because many busy executives read only the summary. Executive summaries can be descriptive or informative. Descriptive summaries are report synopses that state what the report is intended to accomplish in terms of its purpose and scope. An informative summary is an abbreviated version of the report that contains substantive details.

The introduction to a long report clarifies the subject and states the report's purpose and scope. In addition, it may describe the plan for developing the subject and clarify research methods. The introduction also sets the style of the report and may begin with an attention-getter.

5. Describe the types of structural guideposts that can unify the body of long reports.

Among the most commonly used guideposts are internal previews, sentences and paragraphs that appear at the beginning of sections and preview the material to come; internal summaries, sentences and paragraphs that appear at the close of sections and reiterate key points; and summary tables and charts, visual aids that are important connective tools.

6. Explain how summaries, conclusions, and recommendations are used in long reports.

The summary highlights the most important information from the report. Conclusions, which embody the logical results of the evidence presented in the report, tell readers what report findings mean. Finally, recommendations are the specific actions that the writer advises as a result of the information presented in his or her report.

Review and Discussion Questions

1. Name six ways in which short and long reports differ. *(Ch. Obj. 1)*
2. Summarize the elements contained in short progress and trip reports. *(Ch. Obj. 2)*
3. This chapter gives several reasons why you might decide to write a long, formal report rather than a short one. What are these reasons? *(Ch. Obj. 1, 2, 3)*
4. What elements are typically found in the front matter of a long report? *(Ch. Obj. 3)*
5. Explain the importance of an executive summary in a long report. *(Ch. Obj. 4)*
6. Summarize the function(s) of an introduction to a long report. *(Ch. Obj. 4)*
7. Describe ways to create internal connections within the body of a long report. *(Ch. Obj. 5)*
8. Distinguish among the functions of summaries, conclusions, and recommendations. *(Ch. Obj. 6)*
9. What components make up the back matter of a long report? *(Ch. Obj. 3)*

Application Exercises

1. For each of the following business situations, would you choose to write a short report or a long one? *(Ch. Obj. 1)*
   (a) A co-worker asks for a quick update on your latest project.
   (b) An important customer—one whom you do not know well—requests more information about a complex group of products.
   (c) You take this important customer to lunch and discuss your report from (b). The customer asks you to write a follow-up explanation of one point in the report that he did not understand.
   (d) Your boss wants a summary of your discussion during the lunch in (c).
2. Using the model outline discussed in this chapter, write a short progress report that summarizes the status of a project in which you are involved. This project could be related to your job, to your classes, or to a social group or hobby. *(Ch. Obj. 2)*
3. Using the model outline presented in this chapter, write a trip report that discusses a trip that you have made. Your subject could be a business trip, a vacation, or a local trip. *(Ch. Obj. 2)*
4. Write a short trouble report that discusses a problem that you have encountered at work or school. This problem might be a faulty piece of equipment, a procedure that doesn't seem to work well, or a negative trend of some type. Use a direct approach and make recommendations on how to resolve the problem. *(Ch. Obj. 1, 2)*
5. Write a short investigative report that summarizes your research and recommendations on a particular topic. Possible topics include buying a new piece of equipment for your job; buying a car, a stereo, a computer, or a bicycle; comparing the merits and drawbacks of several stores; or choosing a dormitory or apartment to live in. *(Ch. Obj. 1, 2)*
6. By surveying several typical business documents, find examples of each of the structural guideposts discussed in this chapter as means of creating internal connections within a document. Your examples can come from the same document or from separate reports. *(Ch. Obj. 5)*

Exercises 7 through 11 deal with writing a long report. If possible, write on a topic related to your present job or to a job you have held in the past. Other possible business-related topics include the role of ethics programs in Canadian companies; the use of diversity training in Canadian firms; the experience of a specific organization in dealing with environmental problems and issues; or important trends in a particular field or job that interests you.

7. Write the text discussion of a long report on the topic of your choice. Your instructor will specify the length. Organize your report in the most effective pattern. Keep track of your references and be sure to use structural guideposts to create internal connections. *(Ch. Obj. 3, 5)*
8. Write the summary, conclusions, and recommendations sections for your report. Set off each section with a separate heading. *(Ch. Obj. 6)*
9. Create a list of references and a bibliography for the report that you have developed in response to Exercise 7. In addition, briefly describe two topics that might be appropriate as appendices to this report. *(Ch. Obj. 3)*

10. Write an introduction and an informative executive summary for the report that you began in Exercise 7. Make the executive summary about one-tenth the length of the report body, including headings. *(Ch. Obj. 4)*

11. Create an appropriate cover, title page, letter of transmittal, table of contents, and a list of possible illustrations for the report begun in Exercise 7. *(Ch. Obj. 3)*

ACT: Applied Communication Techniques

Begin by referring to the sections up to and including Dashes in Appendix II, then correct the grammar, spelling, and usage errors in the following sentences. Check your answers in Appendix V.

1. Student attendance at Aurora College has increased a significant amount about 55 persent since we hired Shawn O'Neil to teach communication courses.

2. It is important to consider the outline as merely a guide your revision may require adding, deleting, or rearranging information.

3. With attendance up, marks are likely to increase, but if you beleive the statistics we may not seen these results until the end of the semester.

4. Formal reports are usually linked to major projects the development of new products, a company-wide structural reorganization, or a study of competitive products.

5. An overview is provided in the executive summary a sinopsis that condences the report into relatively few pages.

6. With company profits rising, our salaries should increase, but if you follow the news from union negotiations we will be lucky to keep the salaries we have.

7. Team-building workshops seminars designed to teach groups to work collaboratively are presented by an number of small organization in St. Catharines.

8. The Canadian Postal Code Directory a book listing all the postal codes in Canada is an essential referance guide for every office.

9. Supplemental imformation is included in the back matter the parts of the report that follow the report body.

10. The document was selected by comunity members civic officials, parents, children, business people who came together to work on the problem.

Building Your Research Skills

Research and write a short report (length to be determined by your instructor) on a business-related topic of your choice. Base your report on sources other than your text and class materials. Include an introduction and conclusion and, if appropriate, your recommendations. Present your completed report to the class.

Building Your Teamwork Skills

Pair off with another student in your class. Read and critique each other's reports from the previous exercise. Pay particular attention to the effectiveness of introductions, conclusions, and recommendations. Are there appropriate transitions and internal connections? Does the report express a clear idea? Try to give each other constructive suggestions for improving your reports.

Building Your Technology Skills

Colleagues in your company are interested in learning more about whether they should establish an Internet presence. You hear the following statements from them:

▼ "Business on the Net is not easy."

▼ "Many dollars are wasted on Internet advertising."

- ▼ "The Internet is a place you can't afford not to be right now. It's not so much that you're going to profit in the near term; rather, you'll lose money in the long term by not being there."
- ▼ "If you're not an active Internet citizen now, you're likely to be out of business by 2000."
- ▼ "A Web site can provide you with a global presence with one click of the mouse."
- ▼ "Putting up a Web site is like setting up shop in the middle of the desert."

Your assignment is to research business practices on the Internet and write a short report for your boss with facts and recommendations regarding your company establishing an Internet presence.

Weblinks Internet Resources for this Chapter

Report-Writing Resources
http://www.lehigh.edu/~incbc/resources/writing/writing.html#mgt311

Technical Reports
http://www.io.com/~hcexres/tcm1603/acchtml/techreps.html

Progress Reports
http://www.io.com/~hcexres/tcm1603/acchtml/progrep.html

Plagiarism and the Art of Skillful Citation
http://condor.bcm.tmc.edu/Micro-Immuno/courses/igr/homeric.html

Strategies for Peer-Reviewing and Team-Writing
http://www.io.com/~hcexres/tcm1603/acchtml/team.html

CASE STUDIES

DIVERSITY CASE:

The European Business Report

Your boss has asked you to create a short report on Europe's most profitable companies. You do some research and find that *Profit* magazine rates the firms in the following table as the "top ten" in terms of their annual increase in market value during one recent year.

Top Ten Firms with Increased Market Value

Company	Country	Market Value (in billions)	Increase in Market Value (in billions)
Glaxo Holdings	Britain	$42.6	$12.6
Wellcome	Britain	15.3	6.9
Guinness Grand	Britain	21.4	6.6
Metropolitan	Britain	19.3	6.2
BTR	Britain	17.2	5.7
Roche Holding	Switzerland	20.8	5.6
Marks & Spencer	Britain	17.0	5.4
J. Sainsbury	Britain	15.2	5.1
Ciba	Switzerland	14.2	4.3
Total Française Petrol	France	9.2	4.3

You also discover these statistics:

▼ In one year, Britain added sixteen firms to *Profit*'s list of the Top Global 1000 companies—more than any other European nation.

▼ During the same year, Britain added $162 billion to its total market capitalization—an increase of 26 percent over the previous year.

▼ The most prosperous British firms tend to be consumer and drug companies that sell to widespread global markets.

▼ Return on equity for investors during the same year averaged 17.7 percent for Britain, 12.8 percent for Germany, 12.9 percent for France, 11.9 percent for Switzerland, and 35 percent for the Netherlands.[8]

Questions and Applications

1. Write a short report in which you summarize the data shown here.

2. Did you include a visual aid in your short report? Explain why or why not.

CORPORATE CASE:

Pride of Ownership

As chairperson of the charitable donations committee at your company, you're looking for a solid, tax-deductible project in which to invest some of the firm's earnings. A co-worker suggests a not-for-profit organization called Workers of Rural Kentucky (WORK). You do some research and collect the following information:

▼ WORK makes loans to low-income residents in rural Kentucky. Many of these loans help residents start their own small businesses.

▼ WORK is one of about 200 programs in 41 states that encourage self-employment as a way to help people living on welfare to become self-sufficient.

▼ A recent study of self-employment concluded that although it is too soon to evaluate the economic impact of such programs, they do improve the self-confidence, self-esteem, and abilities of participants.

▼ The director of WORK is Stella Marshall, who is herself an example of how the program can change lives. Six years ago, Marshall was depressed and suicidal because of poverty and a failing marriage. Says Marshall today: "It was the WORK group that kept me alive and saved my life." Development workers taught her bookkeeping, marketing, and computer skills. Today, she tracks WORK's budget on computer spreadsheets.

▼ One WORK-financed business is the Owsley Cleaning Service, founded by Pam Thornton. Thornton, who was unemployed and almost illiterate, taught herself to strip tile floors and operate a heavy-duty floor buffer. She also learned how to drive a car and began taking classes in reading, writing, and mathematics at a nearby school. Ultimately, she repaid her WORK loan in one year (two years ahead of schedule) and is plan-

ning to open a plant nursery as a second business. Reports Thornton: "If it hadn't been for the WORK group telling me that you can do a lot, I would never have tried anything. I'd still be in a little shack doing nothing."

▼ Another beneficiary is Teresa Bowles. She bought silk-screen equipment, learned how to print letters and pictures on bags, jackets, and shirts, and opened a T-shirt shop. Business is so good that she's struggling to keep up with orders.

▼ Each applicant for a WORK loan must submit a business proposal, including a cash-flow projection and a marketing plan. WORK meets twice a month to monitor the progress of the businesses that it finances. At each meeting, business owners must report their revenues and expenses, as well as any ongoing problems. The support group offers both personal and professional advice.

▼ The WORK group operates on a tight budget and sometimes can't pay all its bills. When that happens, director Stella Marshall doesn't pay herself. "Some nights," she admits, "I can't sleep worrying that all of this is going to fall through the floor."

▼ Teresa Bowles declares that "if this group falls apart tomorrow, what we've all learned here won't be forgotten. It's the greatest thing that's ever happened to all of us."[9]

Questions and Applications

1. Write a report in which you discuss the benefits of your company investing in Workers of Rural Kentucky.

2. Identify what types of evidence you used to support your conclusions.

*O*rganizing and Writing Proposals

Chapter Objectives

After studying this chapter, you should be able to:

1. Explain how logic and reasoning, emotion, and credibility communicate the purpose of proposals.
2. Identify the special characteristics of proposals.
3. Describe the elements of a model proposal.
4. Explain the importance of effective language and style in proposals.
5. Identify the features of successful internal proposals.
6. Identify the features of successful sales proposals.

Changing a Negative Mindset toward Proposal Writing

Patricia Dorazio knew that she had her job cut out for her when the engineers and scientists on her technical proposal-writing team made it clear that they considered writing an annoyance that interrupted their "real" jobs.

Dorazio was hired by a mechanical and electronic systems manufacturer to help a proposal-writing team tackle a request for proposal (RFP). On the team were about ten technical experts, all of whom were highly qualified engineers and scientists. At the kickoff meeting, Dorazio watched the project leader prepare the team. He distributed an outline that listed the topics on which the proposal would be evaluated as well as a schedule that consisted of a single date—the proposal deadline three weeks away. Despite the size of the contract and its importance to the company, there was little attempt to coordinate the team effort and even less emphasis on organizing the writing process.

At the heart of this failure was poor communication and a lack of understanding of the planning activities necessary to make a long proposal a success. These failures are common to many proposal-writing teams and can be remedied during an effective kickoff meeting. After her analysis, Dorazio proposed that another kickoff meeting include the following prewriting activities:

▼ *Information gathering.* Team members meet one another and gain information about the bidding process, the nature of the contract, and the chain of command. A team leader takes charge of the meeting.

▼ *Understanding the RFP.* The team then analyzes the details of the RFP. The goal is for everyone to leave the meeting with the same clear view of what the customer really wants and the points the proposal must make. The kickoff meeting also clarifies how the client's evaluation criteria could be integrated into the presentation.

▼ *Defining the document through an outline and style sheet.* Attention turns to developing an effective outline based on the requirements of the RFP. It is at this point that team members see how the work they will do fits into the framework of the entire document. "A thorough, well-thought-out outline can save everyone a lot of initial chaos and hard work," explains Dorazio. "It's easier (and cheaper) to rearrange and change ideas at this stage than it is during the actual writing and deadline crunch." Style guidelines are also distributed at this time to define page layout and the styling of such elements as section headings, bulleted lists, figures and tables, and captions.

▼ *Defining the schedule.* Working backward from the submission deadline, the project leader presents the group with interim schedules that take into account the time needed for research, writing, review, and revision. Time is built into the schedule for a multiphased editing process. The group is told that the initial edit will focus on technical accuracy, the second edit will deal with issues of style, including clarity and conciseness, and a final edit will analyze such mechanical factors as cross-references and proper figure numbering.

In Dorazio's experience, successful proposals are the result of hard work and a coordinated effort. They occur through solid planning and prewriting activities that focus on meeting the client's requirements. ▼

Source: Patricia Dorazio, "Preparing Technical Proposals: Planning and Prewriting Considerations," *The Bulletin of the Association for Business Communication* (September 1992): 49–52.

Chapter Overview _____

Written proposals are designed to sell ideas—as well as goods and services—to prospective clients. In many cases, of course, verbal communication will set the stage for sales, but deals are sealed by written documents. As we see in this chapter, proposals are used for a wide range of projects, from suggesting internal changes in company operations to making commercial sales pitches. Despite differences in audiences, specific purposes, and final forms, however, all proposals share a common thread: they focus on audience needs to convince readers that the proposal writer can benefit the readers' business.

This chapter will introduce you to the art of writing long and short proposals by focusing on the special characteristics of proposals. We will describe the elements common to many proposals and point to the key roles of language and style. Finally, we will analyze successful sales and internal proposals in both short and long forms. We begin by taking a closer look at the purpose of proposals.

The Purpose of Proposals _____

Problems are only opportunities in work clothes.

Henry J. Kaiser
Industrialist

As we saw in Chapter 11, proposals are sales tools that try to convince readers that you and your organization can solve a particular problem or meet a specific need. Every proposal must communicate the same twofold message: an economically feasible solution to a specific problem and the conviction that the writer is in the best position to implement that solution. A successful proposal is a persuasive document that demonstrates a complete understanding of a problem and solution, audience needs, the market, and the competition.

PERSUASIVE APPEALS

Proposals persuade through appeals to reasoning, emotional needs and self-interest, and credibility. The most effective proposals combine all three appeals.

PERSUADING THROUGH FACT   Every proposal must have a factual base. "Facts," says writing consultant William C. Paxson, "constitute the sales pitch in a winning proposal, not emotional statements or superlative expressions. Proposals succeed on logic, not rhetoric."[1] Successful proposals are both specific and concrete as they try to anticipate the kinds of questions that readers might ask. Proposals should organize facts and figures, including all necessary budget and schedule information, in an understandable and convincing way that supports the writer's conclusions.

The effective proposal, then, requires a well-thought-out organizational plan. Proposals often rely on a problem/solution approach, which defines the nature of the client's problems or needs and suggests mechanisms for improvement. For example, a communications consultant asked to evaluate the writing skills of a company's sales-force may identify a weakness in sales-letter writing (the problem). He may then propose a series of workshops to improve this vital communication skill (the solution).

As you plan your proposal, let the concerns of your prospective client guide your thinking about what to say and how to say it. For example, if your client is particularly concerned about budget requirements, build your proposal around the demonstration that your solution is financially responsible. In fact, proposals written around single themes are among the most convincing—in part because of their simplicity.

APPEALING TO EMOTIONAL NEEDS AND SELF-INTEREST   The goal of a proposal, however, is not merely to present a solution. The successful proposal presents a solution that appeals to the reader's emotional needs and self-interest. After reviewing a proposal, the prospective client should be convinced that its suggestions will result in tangible benefits.

To decide which emotional appeal will work best, recall the needs analysis from Chapter 4 and ask yourself whether you can best meet the reader's needs by targeting physiological, safety and security, social, esteem and status, or self-actualization issues. For instance, an automobile company's proposal concerning the leasing of vehicles could focus on either the status or safety needs of the client. A status appeal might stress that you offer top-of-the-line cars at the same price as the less prestigious models offered by other dealers. If the client is more concerned about safety, you could focus on the vehicle's antilock breaks and airbags and on your company's emergency road service. Both emotional appeals centre on tangible benefits.

SELLING YOUR CREDIBILITY   As you sell your solution, you also sell your personal and business credibility. Indeed, creating a positive organizational image is one of your most important goals when you submit a proposal. Professors John Schell and John Stratton advise proposal writers to "include your firm's successful past record; parade the credentials of key personnel; attach a financial statement that proves your firm's solvency; append managerial documentation that illustrates sound business practices. Do whatever you must to prove your company's strength, resolve, skill, and reliability."[2]

Your credibility is also established by the professionalism with which your proposal is prepared and presented. A well-written document is more likely to be taken seriously than one with organizational, formatting, writing, and other technical problems.

Special Characteristics of Proposals _____

As sales tools, proposals have special characteristics that distinguish them from other documents. Differences in audience define a proposal as internal or external. Differences in the situation that prompts it define a proposal as solicited or unsolicited. Proposals are also distinguished by the manner in which they are evaluated by the reader.

INTERNAL AND EXTERNAL PROPOSALS

The audience for whom a proposal is written determines whether it is an internal or external document. **Internal proposals** are issued to suggest a change within an organization; **external proposals** are issued to prospective clients in business and government. When they deal with relatively minor issues, internal proposals are usually written in memo form. An accountant, for example, may propose ways to elim-

INTERVIEW Clear Thinking in Labrador

Hilda Broomfield Letemplier, President of Pressure Pipe Steel Fabrication Ltd.

Hilda Broomfield Letemplier is an Inuit woman who leads a very productive career in Happy Valley–Goose Bay, Labrador: she is President of Pressure Pipe Steel Fabrication Ltd., Vice President of Finance and Administration for Labrador Industrial Supplies Ltd., and Vice President of Northern Oxygen Ltd. She has been recognized in *Who's Who Among Top Executives*, and was a regional finalist for the *Canadian Woman Entrepreneur of the Year Award*.

Preparing business proposals is one of the many challenges Broomfield Letemplier faces in her professional career. When asked for her general philosophy on the best way to organize and write a proposal, she responded that her success in proposal writing comes from thoroughly thinking through the whole process prior to any formal planning. She believes this *prior* mental planning helps to organize and clarify your thoughts so that an extensive project can become much easier to tackle. "Your thoughts are the framework you need to build on. Once your ideas are organized, you are better able to compile a draft, and finally to apply the finishing touches to the formatting, attachments, and overall presentation." Broomfield Letemplier believes this strategy is the foundation of her many successes.

Question: What do your customers look for when evaluating a proposal you have written?

Answer: Our customers look to see if we have provided precise and satisfactory answers to their requests. If we have additional information that would be beneficial to them we are sure to provide it; this assures them that we know our product and are looking out for their best interests.

Question: What language style do you recommend a proposal writer uses?

Answer: Be very clear in your writing; otherwise your readers will quickly lose interest, put your proposal aside and go to the next one.

Question: Describe the difference between organizing and writing a solicited versus an unsolicited proposal.

Answer: Organizing and writing a solicited proposal can take several weeks of preparation time. Clarity, concision, consistency, and appearance all factor into whether your proposal will be successful. Unsolicited proposals can be less time consuming if you have product brochures, company profiles, and marketing strategies in place. One might send an introductory letter that includes a meeting request with the potential client.

Question: Explain the importance of logic and credibility in proposal writing.

Answer: You have to convince the reader that your ideas are logical. Make sure that you support your statements with facts. If you give the proposal everything you have professionally, your logic and credibility will come through.

Question: What are the most common errors an inexperienced proposal writer is most likely to make?

Answer: Deficiency in research, too lengthy a document, lack of clarity, too general, and not to the point. The writer should be able to feel proud, not only of the contents but also of the overall presentation of the document. Remember, you are representing both you and your company.

Source: Interview with Hilda Broomfield Letemplier.

inate unnecessary steps in a billing procedure. However, internal proposals that suggest major organizational changes as a result of extensive research and work will be lengthy and formal. For instance, the strategic-planning office of a major defence contractor may issue an internal proposal to suggest changes in company operations because of Department of National Defence cutbacks.

Even short external proposals are usually written in letter form. Many small businesses use short proposals to address the problems of prospective clients. A window manufacturer, for example, trying to persuade a homeowner to install insulated storm windows may send a letter to describe the benefits and costs of the work and stress the reputation of the company's product. In such a case, the letter can be considered a proposal.

SOLICITED AND UNSOLICITED PROPOSALS

A **solicited proposal** is a response to a formal or informal request. A prospective client, for instance, might ask an insurance agent to propose a comprehensive disability and health-insurance plan. Formal solicitations are issued by government agencies and large corporations in the form of requests for proposals (RFPs).

→ *Cross Reference*
We discussed RFPs in Chapter 11, page 304.

Solicited proposals put you in the position of satisfying a need identified by the firm to which you are writing. At the same time, they give you the advantage of knowing a great deal about that need before you begin. In addition, they provide some degree of certainty that money is available to pay for the project if your proposal is accepted.

Unsolicited proposals, on the other hand, have not been invited by the potential customer. Indeed, unsolicited proposals may offer something with which customers are unfamiliar, for which they have no need, or for which they cannot pay. Not surprisingly, unsolicited proposals present the greatest persuasive challenge.

EVALUATION

Unlike most other business documents that are considered on an informal basis, proposals are generally evaluated according to predetermined standards. These standards focus on the capacity of your company to solve a client's problem, your financial requirements, and your qualifications to do the job. Your proposal is compared with those submitted by other organizations competing for the same business.

With the special nature of proposals in mind, we will now focus on the features of a model proposal. Later in the chapter, we will apply these features to internal and sales proposals. Many of the same techniques can also be used to answer RFPs.

> ### Progress Check
>
> 1. Explain how proposals persuade through appeals to reasoning, emotional needs and self-interest, and credibility. Why do the best proposals combine all three appeals?
> 2. Why does an unsolicited external proposal present the greatest persuasive challenge?

The Elements of a Model Proposal

Proposals can be as short as a single page or run to hundreds of pages that include front and back matter in addition to the proposal body. In general, the longer the proposal, and the more sections it includes, the more *formal* it is. Like formal reports, formal proposals are often written by collaborative teams that may include members from the various departments who will work on the project if the proposal is accepted.

Although short proposals generally present relatively simple ideas, this is not always the case. Depending on the business being conducted and the relationship between writer and client, multimillion-dollar deals have been proposed on a single page. In most cases, however, the long proposal is the document of choice when a complex deal is presented.

In this section we examine the specific parts of a model proposal as they are identified in Table 14-1. As the table shows, although front matter and appendices are found only in long documents, the elements contained in the proposal body are common to both long and short forms. As you review this model, keep in mind that many proposals do not include all these elements and that even though short proposals do not have appendices, they are often accompanied by related documents.

FRONT MATTER

Certain parts of the proposal precede the body and prepare readers for what follows. Depending on audience expectations and client specifications, a long proposal may include a cover, a title fly and a title page, a letter of transmittal, a table of contents, and a list of illustrations. You may also be asked to include a copy of the RFP.

Cross Reference
We described front-matter elements in Chapter 13, pages 360–363.

When transmittal letters or memos are included with solicited proposals, they are generally short and to the point. The opening paragraph explains that a proposal is being sent and states the reason for its transmission. For example, it might say simply:

> Here is the marketing proposal we spoke about for your company's paint-products division.

The second paragraph might then summarize the nature of the proposal while pointing to sections that will hold special interest for the reader. This paragraph may also explain why the writer or the writer's organization is especially qualified for the work. Finally, many transmittal letters and memos close by expressing the hope that the proposal will meet the reader's needs and extending an offer of additional assistance.

Table 14-1 Elements of Long and Short Proposals

Elements	Long	Short
Front Matter		
cover	✓	
title fly	✓	
title page	✓	
letter or memo of transmittal	✓	
table of contents	✓	
list of illustrations	✓	
copy of RFP	✓	
Proposal Body		
introduction	✓	✓
technical plan	✓	✓
management plan	✓	✓
organizational qualifications	✓	✓
costs	✓	✓
conclusion	✓	✓
appendices	✓	

The document that transmits an unsolicited proposal has a different purpose. Usually it is a letter that tries to persuade the reader to give the proposal his or her attention. The letter summarizes the proposal and the writer's qualifications for handling the prospective client's problem.

In general, the transmittal letter or memo is less formal than the proposal itself. Transmittal documents use conversational English and rely on such personal pronouns as *I*, *we*, and *you* to refer to proposal participants and readers.

THE PROPOSAL BODY

Although all proposals communicate essentially the same type of information, the way that information is conveyed varies considerably, giving writers a certain amount of creative flexibility. As a sign of this flexibility, proposal parts do not feature the relatively standard labels found in most formal reports. For example, whereas reports generally include sections labelled "Executive Summary," "Conclusions," and "Recommendations," proposal terminology varies according to the preferences of the writer. The most common exceptions are proposals that respond to RFPs and those for which the prospective client suggests a specific format.

In general, the best proposals begin by establishing need, provide increasingly greater depth of information, and leave cost until the end. Many proposals thus include the following elements: an introduction; a technical plan or work statement; a management plan; a statement of organizational qualifications; a cost analysis; and conclusions.

INTRODUCTION   The introduction is the first part of your actual proposal that most prospective clients read. It contains your summary of the problem and your proposed solution. Remember that you are trying to "sell" your ideas by creating interest in the detailed solution that will follow, so your introduction must convince prospects that it is worth their time to read the whole document. Many writers use attention-getters that show their solutions are superior to those of competitors. For example, if you propose an innovative solution, part of your introduction should focus on how and why standard techniques (which will probably be proposed by competitors) will fall short. Your introduction should also highlight your company's credentials. Because of its importance, take your time and write the introduction after the rest of your proposal is finished.

As you summarize the content of your proposal, focus on the benefits that clients will enjoy if they agree to do business. Be as specific and as concrete as possible in stressing benefits from increased productivity and profits, decreased absenteeism and injury, and so on. Compare your per-unit costs and success rates with those of your competition—for example:

> While the Acme product costs $1.20 a unit and is 90 percent effective, our comparable product is significantly less expensive at $1.02 a unit and has a 95 percent success rate as proven by extensive factory testing.

Your goal is to show—in no more than a paragraph or two—the efficiency and effectiveness of your solution.

The final section of your introduction defines the proposal's scope and organization by telling readers what to expect in the pages that follow. Avoid reciting the table of contents. Rather, focus the reader's attention on the document's overall organization and key sections.

Finally, the length of your introduction is directly proportional to the length of your proposal. Although a paragraph or two may be all that is needed to summarize a short proposal, five to ten pages may be necessary for a 150-page technical document.

TECHNICAL PLAN   The **technical plan,** or **work statement,** is a detailed description of the work that you will complete if your proposal is accepted. Technical plans are specific and concrete and often include visual aids to illustrate their descriptions of procedures and projected goals. Although the contents of technical plans may vary, they often include the following elements:

▼ *Statement of the problem.* This statement focuses on the purposes of the proposal. It states the prospective client's specific need for your company's offering. In effect, this statement tells your readers that you understand the nature and scope of their problem. At this point, it may also help to define the project in terms of its major and minor tasks.

▼ *Response to an RFP.* If the proposal is in response to an RFP, avoid repeating the language of the RFP. Instead, rephrase and change the language to show that you have thoroughly analyzed the prospective client's needs.

▼ *Technical description.* Here, describe the steps you will take to achieve the proposal's specific objectives. As appropriate, include the following categories of information: the methods, equipment, and materials that you will use to complete the task; specifications for all products produced; the types of data that will be collected; the results that can be expected at each stage of a multistage project; and quality-control techniques. Use subheadings to organize this information.

▼ *Facilities description.* This section describes the facilities and equipment needed to implement your proposal.

▼ *Exceptions.* When you cannot give readers everything they want or expect, it is important to say so in your technical plan. You should always be clear about what the proposal will—and will not—accomplish.

Finally, the technical plan often describes the specific steps in the proposed project according to the order in which they will be taken. It may also describe solutions that have been rejected and the reasons for their rejection, especially if these options are likely to be offered by competitors.

MANAGEMENT PLAN   The **management plan** describes your organization's plans for managing the project once it is awarded. Among the common elements in the management plan are a *functional analysis* (a description of how your company intends to deal with such project functions as subcontracting and accounting), and *flow charts* and *schedules,* which describe the timing and sequence of project phases. Finally, the management plan should present your company's organization chart to indicate the specific people who will participate in the project and the roles they will play.

ORGANIZATIONAL QUALIFICATIONS   This section addresses the capability of your organization and its people to complete the task for which it is bidding. The following elements are often included in this section:

▼ *Company background.* Emphasize the experience that qualifies your company to complete the assignment. The section should list other related contracts as well as the general background and work of your company.

▼ *Personnel qualifications.* Focus on the backgrounds of the individuals who will take part in the project. Whether you devote a short paragraph or an entire résumé to each individual, your descriptions should focus on the match between available skills and project needs.

▼ *Administrative functions.* Cover such necessary details as employee safety and health measures, equal-opportunity and affirmative-action procedures, and security standards. These details are especially crucial when responding to government RFPs. At this point, you may also refer to specific administrative documents. Do not, however, include them in your narrative. When administrative documents are submitted, you can usually place them in appendices.

COST ANALYSIS   Specific project costs, including costs for material, equipment, and labour, are generally listed next. You may want to show how these costs were estimated and the methods that you will use to minimize cost overruns. If the project will continue for several years, consider such factors as the effects of inflation.

CONCLUSIONS   Conclude with a persuasive statement that tries again to convince the reader to accept the proposal terms. Emphasize that your company is better qualified to do the job than its competition and that your proposed solution is the best choice.

APPENDICES

Appendices should contain material that is tangential or too specific to be included in the proposal body. For example, if your client wants to see proof of insurance coverage, include a copy of your company's certificate of worker's compensation insurance. Other supporting materials might include labour-management agreements, your company's affirmative-action plan, additional drawings and illustrations, contracts, résumés, and client lists.

Proposals containing all these elements may still fail because of poor language or tone. In the next section, we examine how language and tone contribute to successful proposals.

> **Progress Check**
>
> 1. What are the front-matter elements of a long proposal?
> 2. Why is an effective introduction important to a proposal?
> 3. What do technical and management plans contribute to a proposal?

The Language and Style of Proposals

Proposal writing is factual writing. Proposals persuade not through the force of overblown language but through the creativity of the solutions and the clarity of the ideas. Language that relies more on adjectives than on hard facts may well persuade readers that you can probably talk about a job better than you can perform it.

Nor will you persuade many readers if you develop the content of your proposal around a series of unsupported generalizations. For example, stating that in the past you have solved a problem similar to the client's could add credibility if you support the claim. Ironically, however, the effect will be the opposite if you fail to provide any details. Instead of bolstering your position, generalizations often cause readers to ask, "Where are the specifics?"

Effective proposals are written in clear, simple, nontechnical language (even when the subject matter is technical) that avoids jargon, defines key terms, and explains abbreviations. Writing above the reader's level of understanding is a sure route to failure, especially when nontechnical readers decide key funding issues. If your material requires the use of technical terminology (as, for example, responses to RFPs often do), you may be required to submit a separate document to describe and explain the technology to a select group of technical readers, such as engineers and scientists. In other cases explain as you proceed.

Because proposals are persuasive documents, it is important to use forceful, direct language that has a positive, forward-looking tone. Avoid qualifying words like *maybe*, *possibly*, and *perhaps*, which minimize the impact of your message. Communicate

Executives who get there and stay suggest solutions when they present the problems.

Malcolm Forbes
Business publisher

selling points with simple sentences that contain few, if any, dependent or subordinate clauses.

In internal proposals directed to superiors, a less forceful, more passive style is often used to avoid the perception of a "hard-sell" approach. This style uses the indirect approach, the appropriate use of the passive voice, and the use of carefully chosen qualifiers.

In general, let your level of formality be determined by your relationship with your reader and the requirements that he or she sets down for the project. Choose an informal style when you know the reader well and when she is comfortable with the choice. Choose a higher level of formality if your reader is someone you have never met.

Long proposals are usually formal. To increase your level of formality, use impersonal language and a third-person narrative. Except in your transmittal letter or memo, avoid first- and second-person references, including *I*, *we*, and *you*. Because brief proposals, in both letter and memo form, are generally less formal, first- and second-person references are generally more acceptable.

We will now examine some specific internal and sales proposals. As you will see, proposals vary in length, organization, and formality. Often they do not include all the model elements categorized in Table 14-1.

WRITING AN INTERNAL PROPOSAL

Internal proposals suggest changes or improvements within an organization. Among other things, such changes might involve new product ideas; proposals for research and development; suggestions for the reorganization of departments; and requests for new machinery and plants. Internal proposals are generally submitted by lower-ranking individuals to managers with the authority to approve their plans. Because every internal proposal asks management to spend money, it must justify the expenditure in terms of the bottom line. Proposals may thus address such questions as:

▼ Will the idea save money? How much and when will the savings occur?

▼ How will this change give us an advantage over the competition?

▼ Will this procedure reduce costs? Increase productivity? Increase sales?

PRACTICAL TIPS

Proposal Power Words

Nowhere are power words more important than in business proposals. As selling tools, proposals must communicate confidence, strength, determination, and clarity. Simple, direct words work best. Here are some examples:

Powerless words can communicate doubt and undermine the reader's perception of your ability to do the job. Once doubts are registered, they are difficult to erase.

achieve	crucial	fast	improved	maximum	productivity	results	trust
advantage	demonstrate	flexible	indispensable	necessary	professional	simple	value
asset	direct	growth	innovative	original	qualified	solution	versatile
benefit	durable	guarantee	knowledgeable	precision	quality	sophisticated	vital
competitive	expert	help	leader	premium	reputation	training	warranty
comprehensive	extensive	important	leadership				

Because the senders and receivers of internal proposals usually know each other, there is no need to mention the qualifications of those involved in the plan, unless the proposal is for something that management might not expect you or your team to possess the capability to do. For instance, if your department deals with planning personnel benefits, suggesting that you also handle employee-relations activities would require that your proposal discuss your ability in this area.

A SHORT INTERNAL PROPOSAL

Short internal proposals are written in memo form. Length is determined by a number of factors, including the subject or the expectations of your audience. Figure 14-1 is a short internal proposal submitted by a sales manager who wants to open a high-end used-car dealership.[3] The proposal contains a short introduction, technical plan, and cost analysis. In-depth financial details are presented in an accompanying document, and details of the management plan are presented separately.

This serves the same function as a transmittal letter, as it takes a direct approach

The introduction starts by focusing on profits, which represent tangible benefits to the reader. To avoid clutter, financial details are presented in an attachment

The marketing environment is examined next

A bulleted list highlights this information

A summary of marketing objectives

The technical plan specifies methods for achieving marketing objectives

---

Automotive Centre of Canada
www.autocentre.com
111 Douglas Avenue, Windsor, ON N8T 1W1
Tel: (519) 555-1111   Fax: (519) 555-2222

TO: Michelle Stoner, President
FROM: Peter Perry, Sales Manager   *PP*
DATE: May 21, 2000
SUBJECT: A business expansion opportunity in the used-car market

As you suggested, I have placed my ideas about expanding our core sales operation into a written proposal.

Introduction

Selling late-model used cars is a profitable business. Statistics from the Candian Automobile Dealers' Association tell the story: While new-car dealers earn less than 1 percent profit on sales, the average net profit of used-car dealers is 2.2 percent of sales. A dealership that offers competitive financing and service can expect net profits to be substantially higher (see the attached financial analysis).

With this profit advantage in mind, we have an opportunity to carve out a niche in the used-car market. The used-car dealership that I propose would market late-model used cars in the same way as other dealers market new cars. The opportunity exists for three reasons:

- Between 1989 and 1995, the average price of North American luxury cars rose nearly $2000 a year, pricing many customers out of the luxury-car market.

- North American and foreign cars are built better today than ever before, which means that they last longer.

- Despite quality improvements, new cars are still depreciating as quickly as ever. The average car loses 28 percent of its value in its first year.

Well-informed consumers understand the financial disadvantages of buying new cars. By giving them top-quality used cars and providing the same—or better—customer service as they now get in new-car dealerships, we can build a financially successful operation.

Goods and Services

To achieve maximum profits, I propose that the used-car operation offer the following goods and services:

- A wide selection of late-model used cars presented in a setting typical of a new-car dealership.

- All cars reconditioned and sold with a 30-day warranty. Consumers must be confident that cars are in top condition.

Figure 14-1 Short Internal Proposal

Peter Perry   May 21, 2000   Page 2

- Full maintenance services delivered in an atmosphere that stresses customer service. I propose that we offer loaner cars, that our facilities be luxurious, and that service managers form personal relationships with customers.

- Attractive financing offered in conjunction with local banks. Our goal is to arrange financing for eight out of ten buyers.

Start-Up Costs

I have calculated the following costs to develop this innovative used-car dealership (additional details are presented in the attached financial analysis):

Property lease	$ 40 000 a year
Property improvements, including an 8-bay service facility	$400 000
Collateral for a $2 million line of credit to purchase an inventory of 150 cars	$300 000

Conclusions

With this substantial capitalization, I project sales of $10 million within four years. This represents an opportunity that cannot be ignored, considering the growing reluctance of middle-class consumers to purchase new luxury cars.

After you review the attached financial analysis, I will be glad to meet to discuss the proposal and to provide additional details.

Attachment

A broad discussion of start-up costs is presented next. Details are provided in an attachment

Underlined and centred headings make information accessible

The proposal concludes with a sales projection and marketing information

Further discussion is welcome

Figure 14-1 *(continued)*

AN EXTENDED INTERNAL PROPOSAL

More complex ideas require extended proposals. An extended proposal is typically submitted along with a transmittal memo that is part of the proposal. The proposal in Figure 14-2 was submitted by the medical director of a major corporation to the head of the company's human resources department.

Writing a Sales Proposal _____

Designed to convince prospective customers that a company has what it takes to complete a project successfully, the best sales proposals focus on solving problems rather than selling goods or services. Developing solutions may require that you investigate your prospective client's needs and identify the client's competition.

For example, when a major soft-drink company asked marketing executive Don Kracke to submit a proposal for handling the licensing of its trademarked name, Kracke's first step was to find out as much as he could about the company and its industry. He read trade newspapers and talked to key parties, including personnel inside the company and current licensees who paid the soda company royalties on the sale of such items as cups, glasses, and T-shirts. As a result of his efforts, Kracke was able to identify a major problem in the company's current licensing arrangement and develop a solution. His research told him that licensees felt that they were receiving very little in return for their royalties, and he was able to convince the manufacturer that this perception had to change if future licensing deals were to succeed.[4]

The length of sales proposals is usually determined by the complexity of the plan and the amount of detail the writer wants to provide. For example, while some

If you think you can, you can. And if you think you can't, you're right.

Mary Kay Ash
Chair, Mary Kay Cosmetics, Incorporated

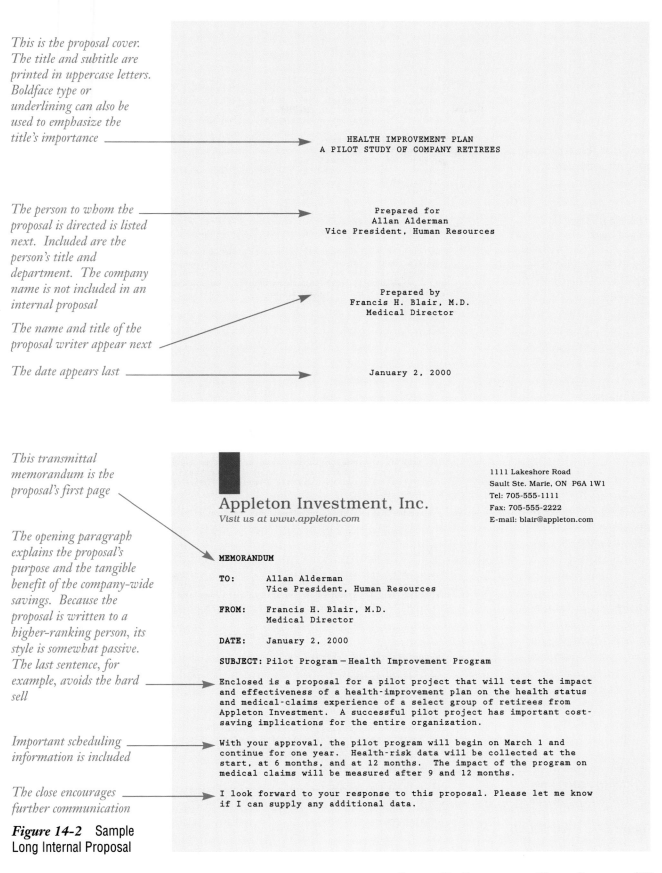

This is the proposal cover. The title and subtitle are printed in uppercase letters. Boldface type or underlining can also be used to emphasize the title's importance

HEALTH IMPROVEMENT PLAN
A PILOT STUDY OF COMPANY RETIREES

The person to whom the proposal is directed is listed next. Included are the person's title and department. The company name is not included in an internal proposal

Prepared for
Allan Alderman
Vice President, Human Resources

The name and title of the proposal writer appear next

Prepared by
Francis H. Blair, M.D.
Medical Director

The date appears last

January 2, 2000

This transmittal memorandum is the proposal's first page

Appleton Investment, Inc.
Visit us at www.appleton.com

1111 Lakeshore Road
Sault Ste. Marie, ON P6A 1W1
Tel: 705-555-1111
Fax: 705-555-2222
E-mail: blair@appleton.com

MEMORANDUM

TO: Allan Alderman
Vice President, Human Resources

FROM: Francis H. Blair, M.D.
Medical Director

DATE: January 2, 2000

SUBJECT: Pilot Program—Health Improvement Program

The opening paragraph explains the proposal's purpose and the tangible benefit of the company-wide savings. Because the proposal is written to a higher-ranking person, its style is somewhat passive. The last sentence, for example, avoids the hard sell

Enclosed is a proposal for a pilot project that will test the impact and effectiveness of a health-improvement plan on the health status and medical-claims experience of a select group of retirees from Appleton Investment. A successful pilot project has important cost-saving implications for the entire organization.

Important scheduling information is included

With your approval, the pilot program will begin on March 1 and continue for one year. Health-risk data will be collected at the start, at 6 months, and at 12 months. The impact of the program on medical claims will be measured after 9 and 12 months.

The close encourages further communication

I look forward to your response to this proposal. Please let me know if I can supply any additional data.

Figure 14-2 Sample Long Internal Proposal

INTRODUCTION

A summary of the proposed program

The plan proposed on the following pages is a personal, confidential health-enhancement program designed to help individuals monitor and change personal health risks and use medical-care services effectively. These factors have a direct impact on the amount of money the corporation spends each year on medical-insurance benefits.

Benefits to the corporation if the proposed plan is adopted

In recent years we have seen company health-care costs skyrocket 300 percent. Although some factors are beyond our control, helping current and former employees control such health risks as high blood pressure, smoking, and high cholesterol and make smart choices when seeking medical advice will reduce substantially medical costs to the company and individual employee.

Additional summary information

The program is administered by mail and consists of sequential health-risk questionnaires, feedback letters, a consumer guide to medical care, and other educational resources.

The summary ends by focusing on the purpose of a pilot study

The pilot project proposed on the following pages is structured to compare participants with a control group of nonparticipants. The population studied in the pilot consists of company retirees. The results we obtain will determine whether to spread the project to the entire population of insured company employees.

GOALS AND OBJECTIVES

The goal of the health-improvement program is to provide motivation and resources for retirees to enhance their health and to use the medical-care system to its best advantage. Specific objectives include:

Part of the technical plan, this section focuses on the proposal's purposes

- reducing unnecessary outpatient visits

- expediting necessary outpatient visits

- motivating and monitoring health-behaviour changes

The goal of the pilot program is to measure the impact and outcomes of the program, test the implementation and administration of the program, and determine how receptive retirees are to providing medical information and modifying behaviours based on the program's suggested advice.

PILOT DESIGN

A more specific technical description begins here as methods for studying the population are examined

Approximately 100 retirees enrolled in Appleton's medical plan during the past two years. These retirees will be randomly placed into three study groups.

Group 1—Full Program

Participants will receive the full health-improvement program intervention consisting of health-risk-assessment questionnaires at six-month intervals; corresponding feedback letters and reports; a medical care consumer's guidebook; and quarterly health newsletter.

Headings and consistent indentation patterns make the material easy to read

Group 2—Questionnaire Only

Participants will receive and complete health-risk-assessment questionnaires at six-month intervals. However, they will not receive feedback or other program materials. This group will provide comparative data on health-risk behaviours.

Figure 14-2 (continued)

```
                                                          Group 3--Claims Only

                                                          Retirees in this group will serve as control subjects for claims
                                                          comparison only.  They will not receive any communications or program
                                                          information.
```

To avoid clutter, the writer
includes tangential letters
in an appendix

```
                                                          Paticipants in Groups 1 and 2 will receive letters from the Vice
                                                          President of Human Resources and the Medical Director explaining the
                                                          project.  These letters are contained in Appendix 1.
```

```
                                                                        PILOT EVALUATION

                                                          The data received on questionnaires from Groups 1 and 2 will be
                                                          compared to the experience of the nonparticipant control group in
                                                          three major areas:

                                                            ● health-risk behaviours

                                                            ● days of hospitalization

                                                            ● outpatient visits

                                                          The medical claims of all three groups will be compared for the year
                                                          preceding the program and the 12 months following program
                                                          intervention.
```

The timeline is part of the
management plan as it
describes the sequence of the
project phases

```
                                                          Timeline for Pilot Program

                                                          March 1        Announcement letter from the Vice President of Human
                                                                         Resources to Groups 1 and 2 retirees

                                                          March 15       Questionnaire package and cover letter from Medical
                                                                         Director to Groups 1 and 2 retirees

                                                          March 15-31    Special phone line available for retiree inquiries

                                                          April          Health-risk-feedback letters to Group 1 respondents

                                                          May            Group health-risk report to company

                                                          September      Second health-risk-questionnaire cycle for Groups 1 and 2

                                                          November       Comparative data analyzed for six-month health-risk
                                                                         changes

                                                          February       Claims data gathered for Groups 1, 2, and 3 for analysis

                                                          March          Third and final health-risk questionnaire.

                                                          May            Final analyses of health-risk and claims data, including
                                                                         changes in the data that resulted from intervention.
```

A discussion of costs breaks
down the total cost into its
component parts

```
                                                          Costs and Potential Savings

                                                          The pilot program proposed here would cost the company approximately
                                                          $160 000 over a 14-month period.  This figure breaks down into the
                                                          following components:

                                                            ● consultants' fees            $100 000

                                                            ● on-staff program specialist  $32 000
```

Figure 14-2   (continued)

- overhead (including office
  space, mailing expenses,
  administrative services) $28 000

The discussion concludes by focusing on how possible benefits far outweigh costs

Based on the experience of our medical-cost containment consultant, potential savings to the company in medical insurance payments could equal more than twice that amount.

CONCLUSION

The conclusion expands the discussion of the pilot to a broader framework as it focuses once more on benefits to the reader

If the pilot proves successful, the company may be in a position to implement it on a broader scale. Involved in this second stage would be active as well as retired employees. A third stage might involve employees' families. As the program expands, so would potential savings to the company in the form of lowered health-care costs.

The last paragraph in the body of the proposal contains a call to action

The first step is approving this pilot project. Once it is approved, I will implement the project according to the timeline just described.

APPENDIX

Appleton Investment, Inc.
Visit us at www.appleton.com

1111 Lakeshore Road
Sault Ste. Marie, ON P6A 1W1
Tel: 705-555-1111
Fax: 705-555-2222
E-mail: alderman@appleton.com

This letter is placed in an appendix. Including it in the body of the proposal would distract the reader from the proposal's purpose

March 1, 2000

Dear Appleton Investment Retiree:

All of us—you and the company—are very concerned about health care. To address this concern at Appleton, we are piloting a program that promotes good health and has the potential to lower health-care costs.

The program is designed to help participants improve their health and become better informed about using medical-care services. It is offered at no cost to you and is not connected in any way with your health insurance coverage or pension.

In approximately two weeks, you will receive a brochure that describes the program and includes a simple, confidential questionnaire. To enroll, complete the questionnaire and return it to us by April 2 using the postage-paid return envelope. Any information you provide is completely confidential. Over the course of the year, you will receive additional material designed to help you maintain your health.

If this trial program proves successful, Appleton Investment may be in a position to implement it on a broader scale. Therefore, this program is not only of personal value to you, but also provides information that can make a difference to all of us. Early next year, we will share the results of our first year with you.

Our hope is that this program can help you lead a healthier, more vital life.

Sincerely,

Allan Alderman

Allan Alderman
Vice President of Human Resources

Figure 14-2   *(continued)*

writers may take a short approach to bidding on an office-equipment service contract, others may map out a detailed strategy for servicing each machine. In general, the more complex the proposed deal, the longer the document.

WRITING A SHORT SALES PROPOSAL

A short sales proposal can accompany a transmittal letter or be written in letter form. If no separate transmittal letter is included, begin your proposal with a statement that clarifies its purpose and scope. Your introduction can then describe why your proposed approach will best meet a particular need or solve a particular problem. It may also introduce your company's credentials.

The body of your proposal letter should provide the details of the technical plan, including a description of the goods and services that you are offering and any procedures that are part of your plan. The body may also refer to certain aspects of your management plan, including time schedules and costs.

The conclusion of your proposal letter may try to reinforce a positive perception of your firm and ideas. You might, for example, list any advantages that your company has over its competition. The proposal can close with a statement that expresses your desire to work closely with the prospective client.

Remember that because there is no set formula for proposal writing, these are only general guidelines. The sample proposal in Figure 14-3 shows how these guidelines take shape in an actual document.

WRITING A LONG SALES PROPOSAL

A long sales proposal may contain all or most of the elements that we discussed earlier in this chapter, including a cover, a title fly and title page, a letter of transmittal, a table of contents, a list of illustrations, an executive summary, a detailed proposal body, and appendices. The sample proposal in Figure 14-4 includes parts of a lengthy proposal from Harris, Rothenberg International (HRI), a consulting firm that provides psychological services to major corporations.

This proposal is for an employee-assistance program (EAP) to help individual employees manage personal problems that can interfere with on-the-job perfor-

Figure 14-3 Sample Short Sales Proposal

DDB

Needham

33 Bloor Street East, 12th Floor
Toronto, ON M4W 3T4
Tel: 416-925-9819
Fax: 416-925-0169

Kevin Conby
Executive Vice President, Client Development

May 4, 2000

Ms. Natalie Rottenberg
Chief Executive Officer
Rottenberg Software Design, Inc.
1111 Great Lakes Street
Mississauga, ON L5J 1X1

Dear Ms. Rottenberg:

At a press conference in Toronto on May 9, 2000, DDB Needham Worldwide will provide details of its new program called:

"Total Creativity. Guaranteed Results."

The introductory paragraph clarifies the proposal's purpose, focusing on client needs

Effective immediately in Canada and the United States, we will **guarantee the results of our creativity** for clients who meet certain minimum conditions. These conditions will vary depending on several factors, including the desired and agreed-upon market results.

A GUARANTEE FOR ADVERTISING RESULTS

Our plan, the first of its type, guarantees that DDB Needham's advertising will be effective in selling your products and services. If our advertising does not produce the agreed-upon results, we will provide you a rebate.

Here the writer focuses on Needham's credibility

After three years' development and application of various techniques to bring precision to advertising goal-setting and preparation, DDB Needham Worldwide will apply the following methods as part of our guarantee plan:

- proprietary methods of strategic planning

- creative approaches to media planning

- cost-effective, reliable market research

- contemporary and innovative ideas to distinguish your products and services

The DOB Needham Worldwide Communications Group Inc.

Kevin Conby   May 4, 2000   Page 2

As you know, marketing factors always remain unpredictable; however, recent experience convinces us that success depends on exploring all communication resources to meet a defined goal. Harnessing all these resources and integrating them to create brand identity in a crowded marketplace is what we mean by "total creativity."

THE GUARANTEE AGREEMENT

The technical plan begins as the letter describes the specific guarantee conditions in a bulleted list

Our guarantee is simple and effective. Because you have individual needs and goals, the details of an agreement will need to be negotiated personally. However, the following provides a broad outline:

- Rottenberg and DDB Needham agree on a precise advertising program result, budget, and schedule.

- Rottenberg agrees to maintain competitive quality and pricing and established levels of support and distribution.

- Rottenberg and DDB Needham agree on compensation for the agency if the agreed-upon results are achieved.

- DDB Needham agrees to rebate a mutually determined amount if the results are not achieved.

YOUR PARTICIPATION

The writer's reassurances that clients have flexibility can be considered part of the technical plan

You may participate in this guarantee program or continue with your current working agreement. You also have the option to choose the guarantee program for part or all of your marketing program. In addition, if you select the guarantee plan and wish to revert to your previous compensation arrangement, you may do so at any time.

The close summarizes the proposal benefits, points to further information, and promises a follow-up

As the enclosed press release and pamphlet show, this new guarantee program addresses your need to receive tangible benefits from advertising, offers more accountability, and links our compensation to performance. Your DDB Needham representative will be in touch with you soon to discuss how this innovative plan will benefit your company. Or, if you prefer, you may contact me directly at 416-925-9819 to discuss details.

Thank you for your thoughtful consideration of this new plan and for your continued confidence in DDB Needham.

Sincerely,

Kevin Conby

Kevin Conby
Executive Vice President

Figure 14-3   (continued)

Enclosure

mance. The proposal is submitted to a hypothetical financial institution. Shown in the excerpts in Figure 14-4 are the table of contents, the introduction, a partial description of the organization's qualifications, a description of the EAP program being offered, and an introduction to the section on program costs.[5]

Compared to the shorter proposal in Figure 14-3, this proposal has a relatively informal tone. Note, however, that it should be considered a formal document because it features such elements as a cover, a table of contents, and various appendices. The tone is set in the opening sentence of Part II, which reminds the reader that "Harris, Rothenberg International is not new on the block." Several paragraphs later, the proposal observes that "HRI has a lot of grey hair." At another point, the proposal asks, "Does HRI understand your business?" and answers its own question: "Absolutely!" This informal tone helps make the proposal reader-friendly. In addition, the proposal itself—especially the introduction—speaks in a highly personal voice.

> ### Progress Check
>
> 1. Why is it risky to rely on unsubstantiated generalizations in a proposal?
> 2. Why is it important for internal proposals to place so much emphasis on justifying the expenditure of money?
> 3. Why do successful sales proposals focus on solutions rather than problems?

This table of contents is organized in the form of a traditional outline with Roman numerals, upper-case letters, and page numbers

Figure 14-4 Sample Long Sales Proposal

Tangential materials are placed in appendices so that the proposal can focus on the selling of services

2

INTRODUCTION

This introduction has several purposes:

- *It makes clear in the first sentence that the document is a sales tool and that HRI is eager to win the business*
- *It summarizes the key advantages of an HRI employee-assistance program*
- *It tells the reader how the proposal that follows is organized. This technique is helpful in long proposals*

Harris, Rothenberg International (HRI) wants very much to be XYZ Bank's provider of choice for its national employee-assistance program (EAP). We believe that our high quality and expertise will be a good match for XYZ's business and culture. One of the goals of this proposal is to explain the experience of HRI professionals, not only in the EAP field, but also in the financial-services business. This varied experience will be discussed in Part II.

Harris, Rothenberg International efficiently and professionally delivers integrated EAP services nationwide. We can do the same for XYZ. The high quality in delivery will be the focus of Part III.

XYZ has moved to its leadership position through sound financial management. HRI will deliver a quality EAP at a modest cost for the service that is sensitive to XYZ's fiscal concerns. Cost will be reviewed in Part IV.

At the conclusion of your reading of HRI's proposal for an employee-assistance program, we hope you will agree that HRI should be your provider choice.

Figure 14-4   *(continued)*

Because qualifications are important in choosing a psychological consulting firm, HRI establishes its credibility to deliver EAP services

6

HARRIS, ROTHENBERG INTERNATIONAL IS A HIGH-QUALITY PROVIDER

In choosing an EAP provider, XYZ is certainly concerned about the quality of the overall organization and the quality of the employees at HRI.

Getting Bigger With Quality

It then establishes expertise in the financial-services and legal industries. Using an appendix avoids clutter

Harris, Rothenberg International is not new on the block. We have been delivering employee-assistance-program services to businesses since 1982. The partners made a decision at the time of HRI's creation to hold its growth to a rate that would ensure HRI's position as a quality provider.

HRI grew by word of mouth. As you can see by our partial client list (Appendix A), businesses talk to each other, especially when they deliver the same services. As a result, HRI has been providing services over the years to many financial-service businesses and law firms. Some turned to us after disappointing experiences with other providers. HRI, in contrast, has never lost a client. . . .

Employing High Quality People

This part of the proposal describes the experience and credentials of HRI staff

HRI has a lot of grey hair. In our business, we believe that a seasoned professional is the most effective professional. Garnering experience, then, has been part of HRI's strategic plan. All our professionals have an in-depth understanding of business and how people's psychologies affect their work behaviour.

This section focuses on staff qualifications and how these qualifications enable HRI to perform effectively

HRI's professional staff of highly skilled senior practitioners has considerable business experience managing employee-assistance programs on site for client companies. In addition, partners and staff of HRI are therapists who are either licensed psychiatrists, psychologists, or certified social workers. Many hold doctoral-level degrees in their fields.

The complexity of workforce diversity makes this statement important

HRI maintains a multicultural workforce with language capability in French.

Because HRI is an international orgnization, the proposal also focuses on the process of selecting affiliate professionals

8

Worldwide Affiliates. The quality of HRI extends to its associates and affiliates worldwide. This quality is important because so many of XYZ's population are distributed among many sites. The selection of our affiliates demonstrates HRI's ongoing attention to quality.

An appendix is used once again to present tangential material

Affiliates are referred to us by experienced professionals in our own network. If he or she has the required educational and professional credentials, an extensive interview is held; the affiliate is assessed, in depth, on clinical expertise; intervention skills; knowledge of EAP work; and knowledge of community resources. A contract is then set up with the affiliate. He or she is paid on a fee-for-service basis (see Appendix C). The fees paid to affiliates are consistent with the high level of expertise that we mandate.

Figure 14-4   (continued)

HARRIS, ROTHENBERG INTERNATIONAL
DELIVERS THE HIGHEST-QUALITY SERVICE

A company's reputation and the credentials of its providers determine the quality of service XYZ can expect to receive.

The technical plan, or work statement, describes the specific services that HRI will complete if the proposal is accepted. The plan moves from overall strategies to services to individual employees

Description of the EAP Program
HRI offers assessment and referral, short-term treatment (when a need is indicated), and follow-up for all EAP clients.

Keeping in mind that HRI services are always specifically tailored to the unique needs of the client, the following describe the overall components and strategies for a full-service EAP.

Full-Service Assessment and Referral Model

- Comprehensive employee-assistance program development to include assistance in drafting policies, procedures, and publicity material.

- Assistance in the development of written information for all employees, including brochures and business cards.

- Orientation meetings with key managers and supervisors.

- Management training for all supervisory personnel with focus, content, and method jointly determined by Harris, Rothenberg International and the client.

- Annual and quarterly statistics and reports on program use and information regarding corporate climate. . . .

Variety of Services Available
Employees/dependents who are referred or who find their own way to the Employee Assistance Program can expect a variety of services. These programs include:

- As many counselling sessions as required to make proper assessment and referral for a variety of personal, family, career, or marital problems.

- Short-term treatment when indicated.

- Referral of those employees who need longer-term professional care to appropriately qualified and competent practitioners.

- Referral of those employees needing in-patient treatment for substance abuse and for psychiatric problems.

- Referral of employees with special needs, such as financial, addiction, or family problems, to appropriate private or public service agencies. . . . Over the years HRI has maintained a high success rate in returning a significant majority of impaired employees to their jobs. . . .

Figure 14-4   (continued)

This section describes the specific steps that will be taken to achieve the proposal's objectives. Details and procedures are introduced here that have not been addressed before

A Walk through the Process
It may be helpful to walk through one possible process. The actual events will be determined jointly by XYZ and HRI. . . .

When an employee contacts the EAP, he or she will speak directly with a professional counsellor. The system operates 24 hours a day, seven days a week. Our phones are initially answered by our receptionists during business hours or by a bonded medical answering service during evenings, weekends, and holidays. Such calls are immediately turned over to a professional counsellor. . . .

A brief discussion of the problem and an orientation to the EAP occurs during the initial phone contact. Employees are offered an appointment with a counsellor within a 24-hour period. Emergencies, of course, receive immediate attention. . . .

After the counsellor completes the assessment process with the employee, he or she carefully considers the nature of the problem, the diagnosis, treatment plan, and the client's insurance coverage. This information determines the best referral source.

When an employee comes to the EAP for the first visit, he or she is given HRI's Statement and Policy of Confidentiality (see Appendix K). . . .

One of the first tasks of the account manager is to familiarize him- or herself with the health-insurance policies and benefits of XYZ Bank. The account manager then sees to it that all associates and affiliates are familiar with the policies. Whenever a referral is made, the counsellor always takes the individual's health-insurance coverage into consideration. We are dedicated to informing the individual of the most cost-effective form of treatment. In this way, we are also able to monitor insurance plans. . . .

We structure our relationships with providers so that there is collaboration in developing treatment plans. We review this treatment plan with the providers periodically to ensure that the treatment is proceeding as originally designed. We strive to ensure that the overall objectives are obtained. . . .

The EAP counsellor maintains ongoing contact with each employee who is referred and the referral source at one-month intervals. The purpose of follow-up is to make sure that the employee has received the required services offered by his or her treatment plan. Follow-ups stop once we are certain that the employee has received the appropriate services and is functioning successfully on the job.

The proposal spends several pages introducing how much the services will cost. The section begins with the key concept that spending money on an EAP actually saves money

HARRIS, ROTHENBERG INTERNATIONAL OFFERS A COST-EFFECTIVE PROGRAM

The cost of any EAP program must be analyzed in terms of the benefits.

Having an EAP Saves Money

Employees bring their problems to work, which affects how they work.

Preventing and Treating Problems that Interfere with Work. An employee in a major company experiences a great deal of stress in today's business climate. Add to that the fact that one in five employees has significant personal problems, and that in half of these situations productivity is negatively affected.

Figure 14-4 (continued)

- Alcoholism and drug abuse exist in the workplace as never before. The Canadian Centre on Substance Abuse estimates that substance abuse costs more than $18.4 billion in Canada in 1992, representing $649 per capita.

- One out of four Canadians suffers from a mental-health problem, such as depression or anxiety. When left unattended, such problems will not only cause employees' productivity to decline progressively, but also will have an expanding negative impact on co-workers and supervisors.

- Nearly half of all couples currently married will at some point undergo marital discord resulting in separation or divorce. Workers affected by this problem will experience difficulties in concentrating, executing routine responsibilities, and maintaining stable business relationships.

- Although alcohol consumption continues to decline, 72.3 percent of Canadians reported drinking in 1994; nearly one in ten Canadians (9.2%) said they have problems with their drinking.

HRI clients have recognized that it makes good business sense to help their employees resolve their personal problems as quickly as possible. They are accomplishing this by sponsoring employee-assistance programs. . . . These companies have clearly seen the cost/benefit advantages of an EAP. They also report that many employees use the EAP when they feel their personal problems will result in deteriorating job performance. As a result, the company and the employees are simultaneously helped.

Figure 14-4   (continued)

What's Ahead

Chapter 14 concludes Part IV, Report and Proposal Writing. Part V moves the discussion from written to oral communication. Specifically, Chapter 15 will focus on Delivering Speeches and Oral Presentations. As we will see, oral communication, like written communication, is more an art than a science.

STUDENT RESOURCE CENTRE

Summary of Chapter Objectives

1. *Explain how logic and reasoning, emotion, and credibility communicate the purpose of proposals.*

   As sales tools, proposals communicate through appeals to reasoning, emotion and self-interest, and credibility. Appeals to reason rely on an organized presentation of facts and figures that make the document specific and concrete. Emotional appeals mould this information so that proposed solutions are perceived as tangible benefits that will help the reader. The appeal to credibility helps to sell you and your company's ability to do the job.

2. *Identify the special characteristics of proposals.*

   In part, proposals are defined by whether they are internal or external, solicited or unsolicited, and by the manner in which they are evaluated. An internal proposal is submitted within an organization to bring about change; external proposals are sent to both private and government clients. Whereas solicited proposals respond to formal or informal requests, unsolicited proposals have not been invited.

3. *Describe the elements of a model proposal.*

The front matter of a model proposal contains a cover, title fly and title page, letter of transmittal, table of contents, list of illustrations, and a copy of an RFP. Many or all of these elements are included in most long proposals. By contrast, short proposals normally do not include these materials.

The introduction should state the problem and the proposed solution. It may also highlight the credentials of the writer's company and define the scope and organization of the proposal that follows. Next, the technical plan often includes a detailed description of the work that the writer's company will complete if the proposal is accepted. The management plan describes how the writer's organization intends to manage the project. Included are a functional analysis, flow charts and schedules, and a description of participants. Organizational qualifications may also be included to describe the qualifications of the company and the individuals who will work on the project if it is awarded. This section is often followed by a description of costs. The body ends with a conclusion, a persuasive statement that attempts to sell the proposal's main ideas.

Appendices help reduce potential clutter in the proposal body. Appendices include materials that are either tangential or too specific to be included in the proposal body.

4. *Explain the importance of effective language and style in proposals.*

The most effective proposals rely on specifics rather than generalizations; they use simple, clear language, a forceful style, and an appropriate level of formality. In general, successful proposal writers gear their language and style to the needs of their readers.

5. *Identify features of successful internal proposals.*

Internal proposals are typically written to higher-ranking individuals in an organization. To be successful, these proposals must emphasize the ways in which suggested changes will improve the bottom line. While short internal proposals are often written in memo form, long proposals may include many or all of the model proposal elements.

6. *Identify the features of successful sales proposals.*

The most effective sales proposals focus on solutions as they demonstrate the writer's grasp of the prospective client's problem and the writer's ability to handle it. Short sales proposals, written in letter form, include an effective introduction, details of the technical and management plans, budgets, and a strong conclusion. Long sales proposals contain all or some of the elements of a model proposal.

Review and Discussion Questions

1. What are proposals? *(Ch. Obj. 1)*
2. How might you make appeals to logic, reasoning, emotion, and credibility in writing an effective proposal? *(Ch. Obj. 1)*
3. Identify the four special characteristics of proposals. *(Ch. Obj. 2)*
4. Which would present a greater challenge—writing a solicited proposal or an unsolicited proposal? Why? *(Ch. Obj. 2)*
5. What elements are inclued in the front matter of a long proposal? *(Ch. Obj. 3)*
6. What are the components of a proposal body? *(Ch. Obj. 3)*
7. When might you include appendices with a proposal? *(Ch. Obj. 3)*
8. Describe some guidelines for the effective use of language and style in proposal writing. *(Ch. Obj. 4)*
9. What characteristics contribute to successful internal proposals? *(Ch. Obj. 5)*
10. What are the characteristics of a good sales proposal? *(Ch. Obj. 6)*

Application Exercises

1. Why is it important to be able to write an effective proposal? *(Ch. Obj. 1, 4)*
2. Suppose that your boss (at your present or former job) has asked you to write an external proposal to sell a skeptical businessperson on a product offered by your company. Describe some specific ways in which you could appeal to logic, emotion, and credibility in order to make your proposal more effective. *(Ch. Obj. 1)*

3. Write the technical plan (work statement) for the proposal that you planned in Exercise 2. What visual aids, if any, might be helpful? *(Ch. Obj. 3, 4, 6)*

4. Write the management plan to accompany the technical plan that you wrote for Exercise 3. *(Ch. Obj. 3, 4, 6)*

5. Write the organizational qualifications section and the costs section to accompany the management plan that you developed for Exercise 4. *(Ch. Obj. 3, 4, 6)*

6. Write a persuasive conclusion to the proposal you created for Exercises 2–5. *(Ch. Obj. 3, 4, 6)*

7. Finally, write an effective introduction for the sales proposal that you prepared for Exercises 2–6. Convince your readers that your solution is the best one for their purposes. *(Ch. Obj. 1, 3, 4, 6)*

8. Write the front matter that might accompany the proposal that you crafted for Exercises 2–7. What front-matter elements would be most appropriate? *(Ch. Obj. 3)*

9. Think of a problem that exists at your present or former workplace. Now prepare to write an internal proposal, addressed to your boss or other appropriate readers, in which you will suggest a solution. How could you appeal to logic, emotion, and credibility to make your proposal more effective? Be specific. *(Ch. Obj. 1, 5)*

10. Write a short internal proposal based on your answer to Exercise 9. Be sure to address your audience's concerns and show how and why your solution would be effective. *(Ch. Obj. 3, 5)*

11. Think of a need for training at your present or former job. For example, perhaps you feel that the staff would benefit from a business communications class. Write a short internal proposal, addressed to your boss, in which you suggest this additional training and convince him or her that it's important. *(Ch. Obj. 4, 5)*

12. The admissions office at your school has asked you to write a sales proposal for prospective students. Write this proposal designed to persuade prospective students to attend your school. *(Ch. Obj. 4, 6)*

ACT: Applied Communication Techniques

Begin by referring to the sections up to and including Parentheses in Appendix II, then place the parentheses in the correct locations and correct the grammar, spelling, and usage errors in the following sentences. Check your answers in Appendix V.

1. Wining the sports championships soccer and volleyball the team's self-esteem bolstered.

2. A sample trip report will contain: 1 summary, 2 details, 3 conclusions and recomendations, and 4 closing.

3. Imformational reports also known as summary reports present facts but not interpratations.

4. The bill listed the cost of preparing the report at three thousand dollars $3,000.

5. She originated from the West Coast Whistler, British Columbia and was proud to promote tourism in the region.

6. Effective proposals are written in clear, simple, nontechnical language even when the subject matter is technical that avoids jargon and explains abreviations.

7. Will this project 1 reduce costs, 2 increase productivity, or 3 increase sales?

8. Many Total Quality Management TQM programs are intended to imporve customer service and thereby improve profits.

9. As illustrated Table III the employees are payed on an hourly wage basis.

10. Canadians are required to speach one of our two official languages English and/or French.

Building Your Research Skills

Interview a businessperson whose job calls for him or her to write proposals frequently. This individual might be someone in sales at a local company or even someone at your school who writes proposals for funding projects. Ask this professional for tips on writing effective proposals. What style guidelines and research sources does this person favour? What usually works and what usually doesn't? Write a report on your interview, summarizing the major points of your conversation.

Building Your Teamwork Skills

Your instructor will divide the class into small groups. Each group will choose an issue at your school that you feel could be solved. Working as a group, write a short proposal, addressed to the school's president, in which you describe your solution and explain why it would im-prove matters. Select one group member to coordinate and write out the group's proposal as you create it.

Your instructor may wish to have your group present its proposal to the class.

Building Your Technology Skills

Recall the short report you wrote for Building Your Technology Skills in Chapter 13 assessing whether your company should establish an Internet presence. After reading your report, management is very interested in setting up a Web site for the company. You have now been asked to write an internal proposal for the establishment and maintenance of a Web site. This proposal will include three new positions: Web programmer, graphic artist, and company content expert. Each of these positions does not need to be full-time. Include in your proposal the following:

- ▼ introduction (be sure to refer to your previous research)
- ▼ technical plan
- ▼ management plan including cost analysis
- ▼ persuasive conclusion

Weblinks Internet Resources for this Chapter

Business Writing: Proposals
http://raven.cc.ukans.edu/~writestd/ bus_pro2.html#proposal

How to Write a Letter of Proposal
http://www.dsu.edu/departments/liberal/english/ techwrit/parkprop.html

Designing Business Proposals
http://www.io.com/~hcexres/tcm1603/acchtml/ props.html

Writing Business Plans
http://www.io.com/~hcexres/tcm1603/acchtml/ busplan.html

CASE STUDIES

DIVERSITY CASE:

Canadian Internet Users and the Music Business

During your reading one day, you encounter the following statistics in the *Toronto Star*:

- ▼ Use of the World Wide Web has increased from 9.7 percent to 19.3 percent of Canadian adults during the past year.
- ▼ While the number of male users increased by 70 per-cent, the number of female users increased by 182 per-cent.
- ▼ Canadian men still outnumber Canadian women on the Net by 2 874 000 to 1 655 000.

- ▼ Usage in the 18- to 34-year-old group doubled; the number of Net users over 45 tripled.

Questions and Applications

1. Imagine you are the vice president of advertising for a company that sells CDs. Your company hasn't used the Internet for advertising its product and you feel that it should take advantage of the Net's explosive growth. Write a short internal proposal addressed to the CEO in which you discuss the importance of making a strategic shift to advertising on the Internet.

2. Now imagine that you are the product and promotions manager for the country music division of the same company, and you have to compete (with other divisions) for advertising space on your Web site. You have to ensure that your division gets the space you believe it deserves, so you create a new marketing idea. Write a short external proposal to Country Video, a small video distributor, proposing a joint venture in which you market a combination CD/video package.

CORPORATE CASE:

McKinsey & Company Preaches the Joy of Going Horizontal

McKinsey & Company, a well-respected business consulting firm, advises its clients on how to organize: try horizontal.

McKinsey principal Douglas Smith notes that vertical (hierarchical) organizations are traditional in corporate America. This vertical organizational structure is also predominant in Canada, where such firms are organized around functional areas such as accounting and human resources.

By contrast, so-called horizontal organizations group workers into self-managed teams with the authority to solve customers' problems as they arise and to change work procedures as needed. "The people who do the work," observes one consultant, "should have in their hands the means to change to suit the customer." Some companies that have switched from hierarchy to self-management have seen double-digit productivity increases.

Ford is one company that has experienced these changes firsthand. After a $2\frac{1}{2}$ year study, the automaker ripped up the organizational chart for its 6200-employee customer service division. In its place, Ford announced an organizational structure that centred on four key customer-satisfaction processes: fixing cars right the first time, on time; supporting dealers and handling customers; engineering cars with ease of service in mind; and developing service solutions more quickly. Functional job categories were retained in critical areas such as employee relations.

McKinsey consultant Frank Ostroff believes that many companies will find it difficult to discard their traditional functional organization in favour of a horizonal structure. He believes that managers contemplating this change should ask themselves, " 'Where do we need functional expertise above all else?' If it's more important than anything, keep strict functions. [They should also ask themselves] 'Where are we better served by working in a real-time parallel way?' That's where you go horizontal." In-between solutions include creating technical pools from which skilled people can be pulled. "The trick," says Ostroff, "is getting the balance right."[6]

Questions and Applications

1. Suppose that you've just joined the staff at McKinsey & Company. Your boss asks you to write a sales proposal geared to prospective corporate clients, in which you persuade them to sign up for McKinsey's latest series of seminars, "The Horizontal Workplace." Describe how your writing task would change if the proposal were solicited or unsolicited.

2. Draft a proposal introduction, keeping in mind that it could be used as a critical marketing tool.

Chapter

Delivering Speeches and Oral Presentations

15

Chapter Objectives

After studying this chapter, you should be able to:

1. Identify the characteristics of a speech and an oral presentation.

2. Explain ways to organize a speech or oral presentation and to conduct effective audience analysis.

3. Describe the purpose and characteristics of an effective introduction, body, and conclusion for a speech or an oral presentation.

4. Describe three special requirements of oral communication.

5. Identify the importance and characteristics of a planning outline and speaking notes.

6. Describe the different types of visual aids used in speeches and oral presentations, and identify elements of effective visual-aid design.

7. Describe methods for avoiding speech tension.

8. Analyze techniques for handling audience questions.

9. Discuss how to cope with presentation hazards.

I've seen a lot of people who are smarter than I am and a lot who know more about cars, and yet I've lost them in the smoke. Why? Because I'm tough? No. You don't succeed for very long by kicking people around. You've got to know how to talk to them, plain and simple.

Lee Iacocca
Auto industry executive

F lood of the Century

They knew it was coming—but the rate at which the Red River flood of 1997 engulfed Manitoba's Red River Valley surprised even the most seasoned flood watchers. The previous year's wet fall, coupled with a record snowfall in the United States, gave rise to the probability that Canada's only major south-to-north flowing river would produce severe flood conditions. When the big blizzard of April hit Manitoba, the regional population prepared themselves for the worst.

Larry Whitney, the manager of Water Planning and Development for Manitoba Natural Resources, not only predicted that peak levels would be higher than officials had expected, but also reported that the water south of the floodway would spread further. Ultimately, the flood waters dampened the very fabric of their community. In an unprecedented move, both the province and the city of Winnipeg declared a state of emergency. Officials mobilized 8500 soldiers, evacuated entire communities, and proceeded to build more than 30 kilometres of new diking in order to contain Mother Nature.

Billed as the flood of the century, water volumes far exceeded the previous emergencies of 1979 and 1996. However, the lessons learned from those experiences better enabled officials to prepare for the big one. Effective management and an open and honest communication policy were the critical elements of control and recovery. The world was watching as moment-by-moment developments were beamed around the globe—and into the homes of those flood victims still fortunate enough to receive a broadcast. "In the flood of '96," Whitney said, "it was tougher to deliver current and consistent information to the community. In those days, I would have to deal with 30 or 40 individual members of the press on a one-on-one basis whenever time permitted. This time," he confessed, "we are better able to provide the important information that people want to hear through scheduled press conferences, media sheets, and public news releases, as well as fewer one-on-one interviews each day."

Whitney, a 30-year veteran of the Water Resources Department, has spent the most recent years of his career focusing on flood outlook, a challenging and critical role in his part of central Canada. Quite apart from his day-to-day responsibilities of dealing with water, natural disasters, regulations, and international and interprovincial water issues, he became the primary provincial media contact for the flood of '97. Armed only with a light theoretical understanding of dealing with the media, his broad experience and integrity won the respect of more than 400 accredited reporters, and the confidence of the community.

For seven weeks, Whitney and his dedicated team met daily with the operations personnel, and with the Premier and Cabinet. They gathered current flood information through a fan-out reporting system that represented their ears and eyes in the community; the resulting daily press release was both accurate and factual. "In my 30 years' experience in this business, I have found that the only approach to reporting these kinds of emergencies is an honest approach. These situations are usually charged with emotion, where victims are anxious, frustrated, angry, and often desperate for support and information. People expect reliable communication to help them through their crisis. That's where accurate and professional news reporting plays an essential part. I attempt to help reporters do their job by furnishing timely and factual information and by interpreting that information for them to explain evolving events and situations."

With an arsenal of maps of the flood area, radar-satellite pictures, and his up-to-the-minute information-gathering system, Whitney presented understandable facts for public consumption in a fashion not unlike that of the Gulf War. He says, "Facts are not only easy for people to understand, but they are also defensible and tend to minimize sensationalism. However, delivered without compassion, empathy, and a meaningful rationale no number of facts can comfort the soul of a flood victim." ▼

Source: Interview with Larry Whitney, Manager of Water Planning and Development, Province of Manitoba.

Chapter Overview

The story of how Larry Whitney handled the press throughout the Red River flood is an excellent example of how important effective oral presentations can be. Whitney's role as primary media contact, required well-planned oral presentations, accurate audience analysis, effective use of visual aids, impromptu speaking, the ability to handle tough questions from his audience, and to be at ease in the spotlight. All these elements will reappear throughout your career as a business speaker. These and other elements are discussed in this chapter as we focus on the increasing importance of public speaking in the business world.

What Is a Speech? What Is an Oral Presentation?

A common tool in business communication, a **speech** is a highly structured form of address in which a speaker addresses an audience gathered to hear a message. Most feedback comes after the speech is over, although nonverbal feedback can occur at any time.

By contrast, **oral presentations** are almost always less structured than speeches, are delivered with the help of visual aids, and are participative. As you will see later in the chapter, *extemporaneous presentations* are delivered using only notes and visual aids to guide the performance. Audiences often participate in oral presentations with comments and questions that may occur at any point. Because such participation shows involvement and interest, it is both expected and welcome.

Oral presentations play important roles in both a company's internal and external communication systems. Internally, for example, they are used to present budget requests and sell programs. A redesigned benefits package, for instance, will probably be presented to top management through an oral presentation. Externally, oral presentations are used to win and keep new clients. When small business owners present a company's credentials as a supplier to a major corporation, they make an oral presentation. Both internal and external oral presentations often combine oral and written material. In many cases companies that are bidding for new contracts must first submit detailed written proposals that must then be summarized in oral presentations.

A talk is a voyage with a purpose, and it must be charted. The man who starts out going nowhere, generally gets there.

Dale Carnegie
Writer and speaker

From General Purpose to Core Idea

In all forms of formal communication, it is essential to focus on your purpose and message. You can accomplish this by identifying your *general purpose*, defining your *specific purpose*, and clarifying your *core idea*. Chapter 4 defines these concepts as they apply to both written and oral communication. In addition to the general purposes of informing and persuading, speeches are also delivered for special occasions.

Special-occasion speeches are those of presentation, acceptance, or commemoration. Businesspeople are often involved in award-ceremony presentations. They may be asked to introduce speakers, present eulogies or toasts, or deliver keynote or commencement addresses. An effective special-occasion speech targets the specific needs of the occasion. As a special-occasion speaker, you speak for yourself and your company. In the truest sense of the word, you are a company spokesperson.

As you move from general purpose to specific purpose to core idea, you develop written statements of the main point you hope to communicate. Your goal at this stage is to plan your oral message, just as you plan the message of written documents.

Who's the Audience?

→ ***Cross Reference***
We discussed audience analysis in Chapter 4, pages 111–114.

To improve communications, work not on the utterer, but the recipient.

Peter F. Drucker
Business philosopher

As you recall from Chapter 4, *audience analysis* is the process in which speakers try to understand who the members of their audiences are and what those members know and feel about them and their topics. Because audience analysis gives speakers tools to link their specific purposes to audience interests and needs, it is at the heart of any successful speech or oral presentation.

Knowing your audience requires that you ask the same audience analysis questions posed in Chapter 4. Your goal is to learn what the audience knows—and feels—about you and your organization and topic. Audience analysis also requires that you define the context for your presentation. When presenting a business proposal, find out who else is competing for the business. When delivering a speech, ask if you are the first speaker or the last, the one right before lunch or the one at the end of a conference. This information will help you predict audience response and adjust your information, delivery, and approach. Finally, find out the power of your listeners to close the deal. If they are not key decision makers, learn what role they may play in influencing the decision-making process.

THE DIVERSE AUDIENCE

Although audience members often have roughly the same level of interest and knowledge in you, your company, and your topic, many audiences are diverse, with wide variations in information, attitudes, and responsibilities. To address such a diverse group, start by believing that the response of each person in the room may be crucial to your objective. Consultant Jim Elms explains:

> Suppose I had an audience of 80 people and am sure that ten [people] in the front row have 99 percent of the power and that the others are there because it's something to do. . . . The guys in the back row may have more to do with it than you think. They can tell [a manager] your proposal is all [wrong] technically and that he shouldn't have anything to do with it. . . . If those guys in the back row . . . say the presentation by XYZ Company (your competitor) was satisfactory, but they haven't the foggiest idea what those guys from ABC Company (you) were talking about, you had an ineffective presentation.[1]

When the needs of audience members differ greatly, divide the audience into smaller subgroups and give separate presentations to each group. For example, one group may deal with technical issues, another with budgetary constraints, a third with production or design issues. When it is not possible to separate the group, keep everyone's interests in mind as you decide what to include and what to omit, focusing always on the best way to communicate your core idea.

However, it's best to be careful when judging the needs of the audience. One of the greatest traps we can fall into is stereotyping our audience by their race, age, gender, or apparent disability. Some of these common stereotypes are listed in Table 15–1. Such generalizations can be grossly inaccurate and may form the foundation of your failure as a group presenter. For example, you might believe that your presentation to seniors should be factual and dry; however, Myrtle Hansen, a Canadian senior shown in Figure 15–1, loves a speaker who is active, full of fun, and humorous.

CROSS-CULTURAL CHALLENGES Most Canadians live and work in a unilingual environment; only 16 percent of Canadians are comfortable in both English and French, our two official languages.[2] Contrast this with a European setting where diversity of languages and cultures is the norm. Diversity of language is only one of many challenges you face when presenting information to a cross-cultural audience. Personal space, achievement, time orientation, and socialization must also be

→ *Cross Reference*
We examine communication challenges in a diverse world in Chapter 3 on pages 69–101.

Table 15-1 Stereotyping Your Audience

Who Do We Stereotype?	How Do We Stereotype?
A. Gender Stereotyping	
Women	Feel they are not listened to
	Are offended by sexist language, sexual innuendo, or harasment
	Receive watered-down feedback
	Feel excluded from male-dominated subgroups
B. Age Stereotyping	
Older People	Dislike being compare with one's mother or father
	Are assumed to be less technologically literate/skilled; out of touch with the "new"
	Are assumed to be less physically fit or less mentally alert
Younger People	Are uncomfortable supervising older workers
	Are assumed to be careless, impatient, with a short attention span
	Are assumed to be immature, inexperienced
C. Alternative Lifestyle Stereotyping	
	Are subject to offensive terminology (e.g. "sexual preference" implies a choice; "sexual orientation" implies an innate condition)
	Are not recognized for their diversity
	Feel judged, disdained by others

Source: Adapted from *Communication Skills for Business and Professionals,* Paul R. Timm and James A. Stead, (Upper Saddle River, Prentice Hall), 1996, p. 170

Figure 15–1 Senior's Speaker Preference Myrtle Hansen, a Canadian senior who was born in 1901, prefers a speaker who has clarity of voice, a dynamic topic of interest, and a great sense of humour.

considered. As a part of your planning for an oral presentation, research the demographics of your audience and then build your delivery around their needs.

TOOLS FOR AUDIENCE ANALYSIS

Among the most common—and most useful—tools for researching an audience are the questionnaire and the interview. Using a well-constructed questionnaire, you can learn how much your audience knows or cares about your topic, the job titles and responsibilities of your listeners, the environment in which your presentation will be delivered, the impressions that people have of you and your company, and the goals that different people hope to achieve as a result of the event.

You can also gather this information through personal interviews. Before a major presentation or speech, for instance, find out what the members of your potential audience need from you. The information that you gather through questionnaires and other research tools should lead to a clear idea of your audience's needs and of the ways in which you can help your listeners. "Every presentation," says Ron Hoff, a leading business speaker in advertising and marketing, "begins in this way." He continues:

The audience *needs* something—usually *help*. . . . By coming to your presentation, by simply showing up, your audience is expressing a need for help, counsel, wisdom, inspiration—maybe even something that can change its life. Not its collective life— its personal, individual lives. If truth be told, the audience arrives on the scene with the ardent hope that the presenter knows something that it does not know.[3]

Progress Check

1. Define the major differences between speeches and oral presentations.
2. Explain why identifying the general purpose, specific purpose, and core idea of a speech or oral presentation is critical to communication success.
3. Why is addressing a diverse audience particularly challenging?

Major Parts of Speeches and Oral Presentations

Like written documents, speeches and oral presentations have beginnings, middles, and ends. In this section we describe some specific techniques for shaping a speech or an oral presentation with an effective introduction, body, and conclusion.

THE INTRODUCTION

In the first sixty to ninety seconds—the time it takes to make a first impression—listeners decide whether a speech or presentation has any value, whether the speaker is credible, and whether they should pay attention. If you make a bad impression during your introduction, you will probably spend the rest of your time trying to regain the good graces of your audience.

Some suggested techniques for introducing your subject effectively follow. Bear in mind that despite its importance, an introduction should take no more than 10 percent of your entire speaking time.

ESTABLISH YOUR CREDIBILITY Through your words and delivery you must convince your audience that you are qualified to speak. Although speakers are typically introduced before they begin, making a low-key statement about your expertise enhances credibility. Here is how T. Boone Pickens, general partner in Mesa Limited Partnership, established his credibility when he spoke before the Japan Society:

> I've been asked to talk about my recent experiences in Japan. . . . As a geologist and an oil and gas producer, I've done business in the United States, Canada, the United Kingdom, Australia, and Africa.
>
> In the past few years, I've given hundreds of speeches where I've talked about the importance of free trade and the critical need for competition in the global economy.[4]

Although most of his audience could identify him, Pickens nevertheless began by establishing his credibility as an expert on free trade and global economics.

CAPTURE ATTENTION The main purpose of your introduction is to capture the attention of your audience and make them want to hear more. Whether you choose humour, a startling statement, an anecdote, rhetorical questions, a quotation, or a demonstration, there must be a clear link between your introduction and the subject of your speech. A joke or a story with little or no connection to your core idea will reduce credibility.

The need to capture the audience's attention is actually a novel idea to many business speakers, especially speakers who deliver routine presentations to the same audience. Instead of opening with an attention-getter, they often proceed as if business as usual means putting people to sleep. Consider the impact of these two opening statements:

Version 1

My subject today is the introduction of Weight Watchers meals to Burger King Restaurants. I would like to talk about test-marketing the idea in one Ontario restaurant.

Version 2

When does offering less mean getting more? Think in terms of calories and you'll have the answer. Offer consumers meals like this with fewer than 300 calories [the presenter holds up a Weight Watchers meal] and count the customers we attract—even those who never ate at Burger King before. I recommend test-marketing the Burger King/Weight Watchers combination in one of our Ontario restaurants.

By asking a question and holding up a prop, the speaker in Version 2 succeeded in capturing audience attention. The speaker in Version 1 promised nothing more than a routine presentation.

HUMOUR Humour is one of the most effective ways to capture audience attention because it establishes an immediate bond between the speaker and the audience. According to Melvin Helitzer, a journalism professor and an expert in humour, "a joke

INTERVIEW   Powerful Communication in the Yukon

Sally Ross, President, Yukon College

Sally Ross heads up one of Canada's exceptional small colleges. As the only post-secondary school in the Yukon, and with one of the highest enrolment rates in North America, Yukon College's importance in the emerging new economy and social structure of Canada's North is enormous. Her job consequently entails extraordinary communication pressures and opportunities.

Ross believes that the symbolic elements of the role of president are of great significance to effective leadership. Symbols are powerful motivators of collective action, inspiring and energizing organizations. They are a vital part of the responsibility of good leaders, who embody the dream of the organization in their demeanour, dress, and spoken and written word. To be conscious of this is to honour a deep human need to respect leadership.

According to Ross, an effective oral presentation seizes the imagination of the listener, provides valued information, and leaves the audience with something memorable to "take away." This requires that the presentation be authentic, creative, cleanly articulated, and powerful. Symbolism, metaphor, and connection with the audience's deeper values are the paths to powerful communication.

Question: How do you define a successful speech or oral presentation?

Answer: Success in this context is the achievement of the desired outcomes. Have you accomplished the goals you set out for yourself? In fact, defining the desired outcomes at the outset can help to bring your presentation into focus.

During presentations, I attend to the signals provided by the audience. Eye contact, listening postures, flashes of recognition and response are all evident in an engaged audience. When a good presentation is over, there are individuals who want to connect in a personal way with comments or questions. When people are touched, they are reluctant to let go of the event. There is a certain sparkle in the air.

Question: Are visual aids always helpful for speakers?

Answer: The decision to use visual aids should be based on your assessment of the subject matter, the audience's need for graphic affirmation of the information, and the appropriateness of the context. Usually, your audience will enjoy the

---

at the start says, 'I'm confident. I've got a smile on my face. I want you all to relax and enjoy yourself as you also learn something from my remarks.' "[5]

THE STARTLING STATEMENT   Say the unexpected: surprising your audience is a good way to capture and hold its attention. For example, Richard D. Parsons, president of Time Warner, opened his remarks to a graduating university class with the following unexpected twist:

> I wish I had all the advice and wisdom you need to succeed in the future. I don't. But I do have some suggestions, which may be of help.
>
> In offering these suggestions, I'm mindful of something a schoolchild wrote as an answer on a history test. He wrote, "Socrates was a Greek. He lived 2000 years ago. He told people what to do. He was poisoned."
>
> So I'm not here to tell you what to do.[6]

Question: What are the most common mistakes made by business speakers?

Answer: Here are some really irritating speaker errors: 1) not matching the voice level to the acoustics in the room and the comfort of the listeners; 2) not using visual aids that can be readily seen by all members of the audience; 3) overusing clichés and/or language relating to a particular profession; 4) speaking for too long; 5) rambling presentations; 6) underestimating or overestimating the sophistication of the audience; making jokes that are not funny, are offensive, or are forced; 7) using a packaged presentation and reading from the projected images; and 8) having a monotonous voice modulation.

Question: How do you prefer to open and close your speeches?

Answer: I like to start out with a "from the heart" kind of statement that introduces my interest in being there, and gives the audience a chance to get to know me. I like to close with the "headline" that I hope they will take away with them.

Question: What circumstances, if any, would make you feel uncomfortable or nervous during your delivery of a speech?

Answer: A feeling of discomfort might occur if I: 1) was not prepared; 2) had to use a poor sound system and/or inadequate technical support for visual materials; and 3) had to compete for attention with other events. Who was it who said "Never perform with kids or dogs!"?

Question: How do you combat your nervousness?

Answer: Nervousness is natural, inevitable, and even desirable at a certain level. If you aren't just a little uncomfortable, you aren't tuned into the situation! To bring my anxiety to a productive level, I remember that any audience is composed of ordinary people, just like me, whose genuine hope is that I do well. To reaffirm this fact, I maintain extensive eye contact. I also wear comfortable clothing.

Question: What advice would you give to students who want to "knock the socks off" their audience during an oral presentation?

Answer: Be genuinely passionate about your subject matter. People recognize truth when they hear it, and can detect a phoney at ten paces. Reach into their hearts with your message. Maintain eye contact and stay focused. Above all, know who the heck they are.

Source: Interview with Sally Ross.

There is a difference between the effective startling statement and the offensive shock tactic. Pounding the lectern for no reason but to gain attention, using profanity, or telling offensive jokes reduces credibility.

ANECDOTES Few of us can resist an **anecdote**—a short, entertaining account of some event—especially if it has personal meaning. Jerry Greenfield, co-founder with Bennett R. Cohen of Ben & Jerry's Ice Cream, started a university commencement address with the following anecdote:

I'm Jerry. Graduation is a time for words of wisdom, thought-provoking words, challenging words, and that is why we have Ben with us today. I will be speaking to you about how we have reached our august positions as true ice cream magnates.

Ben and I are old friends from junior high school. We met at Merrick Avenue Junior High School in seventh grade when we were the two slowest, fattest kids running around the track together. And Coach Phelps was yelling at us, "Gentlemen, you've got to run the mile in under seven minutes. If you don't run the mile in under seven minutes, you're going to have to do it again." And there were Ben and I in this little pack way behind the rest of the pack, and Ben would yell back, "Gee coach, if I don't run it in under seven minutes the first time, I'm certainly not going to run it in under seven minutes the second time."

And that's when I realized that Ben was someone I wanted to get to know.[7]

This story succeeds because it leads naturally to Greenfield's core idea about the relationship between him and Cohen that was at the heart of his remarkable business success.

RHETORICAL QUESTIONS   A rhetorical question excites involvement in a subject without requiring an actual answer. For example, when speakers ask listeners questions like the following during the course of their remarks, they are asking rhetorical questions:

▼   "How can we ignore changing technology?"
▼   "Is it good business to ignore the needs of the inner cities?"
▼   "How can we help our employees communicate more effectively?"

In a sense, then, rhetorical questions create involvement by encouraging listeners to question themselves and thus be better prepared to examine certain answers. Generally, speakers pose rhetorical questions because they intend to propose their own answers to them.

QUOTATIONS   Quoting someone who is well-known or who is an authority on your subject can add credibility to your speech or presentation. Here John Cady, president of the National Food Processors Association, invoked the words of Mark Twain to open a speech on a crisis of public confidence in the food industry. "Mark Twain," Cady began, "had a rule about food. 'Eat what you like,' he said, 'and let the food fight it out inside.'" Cady then moved quickly from the humorous quote to his core idea:

> These days the idea of some seems to be to fight it out with our food and its producers to keep it from ever getting inside....
>
> Let me suggest that the first step to restoring public confidence in our food supply is for us in the industry to recognize that these special interest groups would not be so prominent if the public were not receptive to their message. Dealing with those public attitudes is the challenge for us.[8]

Similarly, a quote from the CEO adds authority to an in-house presentation on sexual harassment and makes it clear that the behaviour will not be tolerated.

DEMONSTRATIONS   Bring in prototypes of new compact-disc packaging. Demonstrate how a defective five-cent part can cause a $100 tool to fail. Demonstrations are attention-grabbers and lead naturally into the body of your speech or presentation.

PREVIEW YOUR MAIN POINTS   Your introduction should also preview things to come. In no more than a sentence or two, your preview can give your audience reasons to keep listening.

Never promise more than you can perform.

Publilius Syrus
Writer

Previews that promise too much may, of course, set up false expectations that ultimately result in lost credibility. Similarly, too much detail in the preview obliges you to spend much of the body of your speech repeating yourself rather than saying something new. Tell your audience what to expect in general, but relevant, terms and then proceed to the body of your message.

THE BODY

The body of a speech or oral presentation uses common organizational patterns to present main points and supporting materials. These patterns—including *problem/solution, cause and effect, climactic order,* and *chronological order*—were examined in Chapter 5. Choose an organizational plan that suits your purpose, the nature of your material, and, most importantly, the needs of your audience. Because listeners have no chance to "rehear" points once they have been made, avoid saying too much; as a rule, limit yourself to between two and five main points.

→ **Cross Reference**
We examined common organizational patterns in Chapter 5 on pages 130–137.

It is within the context of these main points that you present your *evidence*—the material, drawn from firsthand observation, outside sources, or both, that supports your opinion or position. You may support your specific purpose and main points through such evidence as factual information, statistics, brief or extended examples, narratives that involve the audience in a story, testimony and quotations, or analogies. As you move from point to point, your goal is to lead listeners to accept a particular point of view or to understand the information that you are presenting.

Always remember that listeners have a limited ability to absorb spoken information. Don't overload people with too many details—they will forget at least some of them. Choose your supporting materials carefully and develop them so that they are easily and clearly interpreted. Make your points concrete. For example, instead of talking in general about a store-wide shoplifting problem, talk about the theft in one month of 40 pairs of shoes, 10 suits, and 50 sweaters.

Some speakers make the mistake of spending too much time introducing and concluding their presentations and too little time developing their main points. The body is the heart of your speech or presentation and should receive the most speaking time. For example, if you are developing three main points in a speech whose body is fifteen minutes long, you have three options.

1. *Start with your strongest point first.* Allot eight minutes to the first, five minutes to the second, and two minutes to the third.
2. *Use a progressive pattern to build power as you move from point to point.* Allot two minutes to the first, five minutes to the second, and eight minutes to the third.
3. *Treat all points equally.* Allot each five minutes of time.

THE CONCLUSION

The conclusion of a speech or an oral presentation serves four important functions. It summarizes your message, places your message in a broad context, personalizes your message, and calls for specific future action. The same techniques used to introduce a speech or presentation—anecdotes, humour, quotations, rhetorical questions, startling statements, demonstrations—can conclude it as well. Like the introduction, the conclusion should take about 10 percent of your time.

The conclusion contains the final words your listeners will hear—words that should leave a lasting impression. The conclusion also tells listeners that your remarks are completed, so it is not the place to make a new point. All your points should have been introduced and developed earlier. Finally, even if you are disappointed in your performance, don't conclude by apologizing for your failure.

SUMMARIZE YOUR MAIN POINTS   Follow the advice of Winston Churchill, who once said, "If you have an important point to make, don't try to be subtle or clever. Use a pile driver. Hit the point once. Then come back and hit it again. Then hit it a third time—a tremendous whack." Think of your summary as an opportunity to tell people once more what you have already told them.

Restatement—recasting rather than just *repeating* your point—is essential to an effective conclusion. For example, a presentation recommending the initiation of an employee-assistance program to aid troubled workers might conclude like this:

> With stress a fact of life for almost all of us, an employee-assistance program can help us all function better. In summary, it promises to:
>
> ▼ deal with drug and alcohol problems;
> ▼ help employees cope with crises at home like illness and divorce;
> ▼ intercede when workers do not get along; and
> ▼ deal with emotionally disturbed workers.
>
> I recommend that we begin an immediate search for an employee-assistance consulting firm. Our employees deserve it and so do our stockholders.

If you are forced to abbreviate your speech or presentation, your summary may be even more critical. Even when details or visual aids are omitted, your summary can still make your point. The formula becomes in this case "Tell 'em, in brief, what you would have told 'em in full if you hadn't run out of time."[9]

PLACE YOUR MESSAGE IN A BROAD CONTEXT   Use your conclusion to look ahead—to tie your ideas to a broader framework of goals and ideas. In the following excerpt, for instance, Linda Winikow, a vice president of Orange and Rockland Utilities, Inc., uses her conclusion to broaden her thoughts on cultural diversity in the workplace:

> Now, as much as I enjoy singing Orange and Rockland's praise, let me close my talk not with what we're doing, but rather what remains unfinished.
>
> I began my talk by saying that cultural diversity—as complex as it is and as threatening as some find it—is the thing that can make . . . business even greater. Our challenge is to . . . put that great force to work for us.[10]

In an oral presentation, the broader context may include a summary of conclusions or recommendations.

PERSONALIZE YOUR MESSAGE   Your conclusion should also refocus on listeners' needs. Listeners who perceive themselves as the focus of your final remarks are more likely to receive your entire message in personal terms. Notice that in the following commencement address on career success, corporate executive and author Harvey Mackay uses an effective concluding story to personalize his remarks:

> Being rich isn't about money. Being rich is a state of mind. . . . One of the best examples of what I'm talking about comes from an experience I had with my mentor, Curt Carlson [a very wealthy man]. . . . It happened the day . . . [we were] hit with the worst blizzard in 50 years. [The] airport . . . was closed for the first time in years. I had to go to a meeting in New York that day, and Curt had generously offered me a ride in his jet. Our prospects of getting out of town seemed exceedingly slim.
>
> Although the storm continued to pummel us, the airport inexplicably provided a short grace period and opened a runway for small craft only. . . .
>
> As we were taxiing down the runway to take off, Curt turned to me and said gleefully, "Look, Harvey, no tracks in the snow!"
>
> Curt Carlson, 70 years old at the time, rich beyond anyone's wildest dreams, could still sparkle with excitement about being first.
>
> From my standpoint, that is what it's all about. . . .
>
> ▼ never stop learning,
> ▼ believe in yourself, even when no one else does,

Progress Check

1. List ways to capture audience attention during an introduction.
2. Describe three strategies for organizing main points in the body of a speech or oral presentation.
3. Why are summaries so important during speeches and oral presentations?

- ▼ find a way to make a difference, and ...,
- ▼ then go out and make your own tracks in the snow.[11]

MAKE A CALL TO ACTION   Asking your listeners to do something is a task best left to the end of your message. Many persuasive speeches and sales presentations conclude with appeals that urge action, such as George V. Grune's concluding remarks urging support for the Magazine Publishers Association (MPA):

> If you belong to companies or organizations that are not MPA members, I urge you to encourage them to join. We must put aside our partisan interests and work together to support our industry—your industry.
>
> To those of you who are MPA members, I urge you to get actively involved. We need your contributions, your suggestions and your help.
>
> Let's leave here today rededicated to that mission—and above all, believing in the power of magazines.[12]

In concluding an oral presentation, you may also talk about the steps that come next. For example, talk about responsibilities or tasks that must be accomplished and the people responsible for them. Leave your audience with a mission and a sense of energy.

Table 15-2 summarizes the various purposes of the introduction, body, and conclusion in a speech or an oral presentation. It also lists techniques for accomplishing these purposes.

Table 15-2   Purpose and Techniques in the Formal Presentation

Element	Purpose	Techniques
Introduction	establish credibility capture attention	refer to your personal background use humour tell a story ask rhetorical questions use quotations demonstrate
Body	preview main points present main points present supporting material	briefly tell what is to come rely on common organizational patterns use facts, statistics, examples, narratives, testimony, and quotations
Conclusion	summarize main points extend message to broader context personalize message call to action	use repetition form conclusions and recommendations focus on the needs of your audience focus on the future and what must be done

Special Requirements of Oral Communication

In Chapter 6 we analyzed elements of word selection and style for written communication. Although oral communication shares most of these characteristics, differences naturally emerge when words are spoken. Among these differences are the need for repetition, verbal signposts, and word pictures.

REPETITION

Recall Winston Churchill's emphasis on the importance of *repetition*—the reminder that saying something once may not be enough to communicate meaning. Repeating

A QUESTION OF ETHICS

Celebrating a Corporate Blunder

It is human nature—and good business sense—to avoid calling attention to a long-gone corporate blunder, especially if the blunder was termed a "fiasco" by marketing mavens in Canada and the United States. Thus, few people expected Roberto C. Goizueta, chairman and chief executive officer of the Coca-Cola Company, to mark the tenth anniversary of the introduction of New Coke with an hour-long presentation billed a "celebration." Goizueta, who was in charge when New Coke was introduced in 1985, addressed 600 employees in an auditorium in the company's Atlanta headquarters.

He recalled the series of marketing miscalculations in which the Coca-Cola Company replaced its 99-year-old formula with New Coke and then brought back the old Coke (as Classic Coke) 77 days later after consumers rebelled. He focused on what the company learned from the mistake and how far it has come in 10 years. "Today," said the chief executive, "we are in the best shape as a company in many decades, and our stock price and our earnings are at an all-time high."

Goizueta's remarks were also filled with self-deprecating humour as he showed a video segment from *The Simpsons* television program in which a hobo was portrayed as the developer of New Coke; video highlights from news programs that criticized the breakdown of Coke's well-oiled marketing machine; and a narrated list, on slides, of the "Top Ten Favourite Blunders of the Coca-Cola Company," David Letterman-style.

At the end of the presentation, two other company officials joined Goizueta to answer audience questions. In response to one question, Goizueta acknowledged that the Coca-Cola Company was "rocked to the heels" by the error. "Obviously, this was a blunder and a disaster, and it will forever be," he said, despite Coke's financial turnaround. Asked if the entire episode was a brilliant, carefully planned marketing ploy, Goizueta responded with disarming candour that put the episode in perspective: "We are not that smart and we're not that dumb."

Questions for Critical Thinking

1. Was it appropriate for Roberto Goizueta to draw attention to the Coca-Cola Company's blunder its anniversary celebration? Why or why not?
2. Why would Goizueta show that particular video segment from *The Simpsons*?
3. Do you believe that the New Coke episode was a well-planned marketing ploy to increase sales? Why or why not?

Sources: Glenn Collins, "Ten Years Later, Coca-Cola Laughs at 'New Coke,'" *New York Times,* 11 April 1995, D4; Leah Richard, "Remembering New Coke," *Advertising Age* (April 17, 1995): 6; and Jack Honomichl, "Missing Ingredients in 'New' Coke's Research," *Advertising Age* (July 22, 1985).

---

key points not only gives listeners time to understand your message but communicates the value that you place on a thought. The second time around, your message clearly begins with the appeal to "PAY ATTENTION."

Repeating key thoughts at strategic places is not the same thing as being wordy. Tight, concise language is as important in speaking as it is in writing. Examine the two hypothetical presentations made by a sales manager from Ralston Purina to A&P buyers, urging the grocery chain to introduce a new line of natural pet foods:

Version 1

I am here to tell you about our new line of pet foods, which we have named Nature's Course, that every one of your nutritionally oriented customers will want. These pet foods are targeted at people who do everything they can to avoid fat and a wide range of additives and artificial colourings in their own diets. Foods like these, manufactured for years by small companies like Natural Life and Nature's Recipe, lack the marketing strength of the Ralston Purina name. They are sold through veterinarians' offices, health-food stores, and pet-supply boutiques. It is my proposal that natural pet foods should go mainstream and appear on A&P's shelves.

Version 2

People who care about their own nutrition are beginning to care what their pets eat. For years, small companies like Natural Life and Nature's Recipe have marketed low-fat pet foods with few additives and artificial colourings through veterinarians' offices, health-food stores, and pet-supply boutiques. We propose to place Nature's Course, our own line of natural pet foods—with the marketing appeal of the Ralston Purina name—on A&P's shelves.

Version 2 communicates the same message using only 66 percent of the word total required by Version 1.

VERBAL SIGNPOSTS

Brief statements that give listeners "clues" to the organization and structure of a speech are known as **verbal signposts.** They include transitions, internal previews, and internal summaries.

TRANSITIONS   As you recall from Chapter 6, the words, phrases, and sentences that connect ideas are called *transitions*. Verbal transitions fall into four categories. First, they *show the relationship* between a new idea and a previous idea:

> On the other hand, small-appliance sales were strong in the last quarter.

They *enumerate:*

> First, Revenue Canada is telling us that our lunchroom subsidy may be a taxable benefit to employees.

They *repeat*, or *restate*, key words or phrases:

> These opportunities are important enough for us to take action.

Finally, they *communicate emphasis:*

> The opportunity open to us in the over-65 market cannot be overemphasized.

INTERNAL PREVIEWS   Transitions that tell listeners what you intend to say before you say it are called *internal previews*, similar to those used in written reports. These verbal signposts are especially important if the point that you are introducing is long and complex. In helping your audience to anticipate your remarks, internal previews also prepare the listener to follow their development. For example, the following preview prepares listeners for a sequence of major ideas:

Cross Reference
We described internal previews and their use in written reports in Chapter 13 on page 367.

> First, I am going to talk about why our line of natural pet foods is superior to competing brands. Second, I will examine our marketing approach. And finally, I will look at possible distribution problems.

INTERNAL SUMMARIES   Unlike the summary delivered at the end of a speech or presentation, *internal summaries* occur at key points within a message. Their purpose is to restate and emphasize what you have just said and to connect internal elements. They are also used in written documents. For example:

Cross Reference
We discussed internal summaries in written documents in Chapter 13 on page 367.

> In review, action figures are the toys of the season, with sales exceeding expectations. However, as I have shown, sales have been limited by the manufacturers' inability to ship the quantities we need.

Internal previews and internal summaries may also act as transitions to connect the major points within your speech or presentation.

Outline Your Oral Presentation

As you will see later in the chapter, extemporaneous speaking is the most effective delivery form for speeches and the only acceptable form for business presentations.

Two formats used for extemporaneous presentations can also be useful in preparing other forms of presentations: the planning outline and speaking notes.

PLANNING OUTLINE

The **planning outline** is a full-content outline that includes every part of a speech or presentation—the introduction, the body (including main points and supporting materials, internal previews, and summaries), and the conclusion. It also includes statements of your specific purpose and core idea. The traditional outline form that we examined in Chapter 5 enables you to see the connections among ideas as quickly and clearly as possible.

The planning outline also helps you think in terms of language choices. Because it is composed of full sentences rather than words or phrases, it lets you judge how your speech or presentation will sound. The example in Figure 15-2 is a planning outline for a presentation on selecting the right career. Note how the verbal signposts are found throughout the presentation.

SPEAKING NOTES

An abbreviated key-word outline designed to guide a speaker's actual *delivery* is known as **speaking notes.** Unlike the planning outline, speaking notes are short and to the point. Complex sentences have been reduced to key words, phrases, and simple sentences; transitions, internal previews, and summaries appear in an abbreviated form.

The advantage of speaking notes is that although they provide structure, they allow you to deliver your speech or presentation extemporaneously and, in the process, to maintain contact with your audience. Remember that there is an important difference between *extemporaneous speaking* and *impromptu speaking.* Impromptu means without preparation—offhand. *Extemporaneous* means that you prepare the content of your presentation in the form of speaking notes, but do not rely on a complete manuscript or on memorization.

In preparing speaking notes, follow the same form that you used in your planning outline. You want to see at a glance the structure of your speech or presentation. Write legibly and large because you will be glancing at your notes for guidance as you speak.

The planning outline from Figure 15-2 is presented in the form of speaking notes in Figure 15-3. Notice that neither the specific purpose nor the core idea is included because these points are never put directly into words.

In the margin of your speaking notes, you may want to include instructions for improving your delivery. For example, at a key point you might write, "SLOW DOWN" or "LOOK AT AUDIENCE." You can also indicate the exact spot where you want to introduce a visual aid—"SHOW MAP HERE" or "TRANSPARENCY #2 GOES HERE." As we will see in the next section, visual aids can also be used not merely to complement your presentation but also to *organize* it.

Progress Check

1. Describe the three special requirements of oral communication and how they function.
2. Are internal previews and summaries transitional statements? Explain.
3. What are the differences in form and function between a planning outline and speaking notes?

Visual Aids Success

Visual aids may be the only notes you need during a speech or presentation. Business speakers often structure their presentations around a series of slides that provide both visual appeal and content, interest, and clarity. Other business speakers may use many types of visual aids in one speech. For instance, when Keith L. Reinhard, CEO of DDB Needham Worldwide, addressed the GTE Directories Leadership Conference about the changes in the advertising industry, he used 42 slides,

8 video clips, and 1 audio segment in his multimedia presentation.[13] We begin by taking a closer look at the types of visual aids available to speakers and then offer some guidelines for both designing and using them.

TYPES OF VISUAL AIDS

Business speakers have a broader selection of visual aids than those available to writers. Freed from the constraints of paper, speakers can think in terms of such media

---

Planning Outline

Selecting the Right Career for You

I. SPECIFIC PURPOSE
    A. To inform students that there are working requirements for individual careers, and to have them identify their talents, skills, and interests with these particular requirements.

II. CORE IDEA
    A. Work is a necessary fact of life. For most people, some form of career will occupy their lives for approximately 50 years.
    B. Therefore, it is important to have a fulfilling career that will be a rewarding experience.

III. INTRODUCTION
    A. What is a perfect career? What you consider to be the ideal career is probably not the same as that of the person sitting next to you. The ideal career for each of us is the one that allows us to meet our needs and realize our goals.
    B. It is imperative when planning your future to be able to define what is ideal to you, and not to simply follow in the footsteps of someone who has influence, perhaps a family member or friend.
    C. *Internal Preview*
        1. Career planning is closely connected with personal career satisfaction and productive contribution to your community.
        2. Therefore, I will define the four main categories of working requirements that all students should consider.
        3. All students should then be able to measure themselves against the requirements for a particular job to determine if their career is suitable.
    D. *Transition*
        1. "So," you ask, "what are these magical four categories that can make or break my career success? I've already determined what I want.' First, let's examine the four categories and then you can reassess your suitability for your chosen career. You might be surprised by the results.

IV. BODY
    A. *Education and Training*
        1. Every career requires unique training, some being far more intense and lengthy than others. Are you prepared for the four to seven years of university education necessary to become a doctor or lawyer? Or would you prefer a college diploma that would allow you to get a job after only two years of training?
        2. If you believe that engineering is your field of interest, have you studied the course requirements for math and science? If you dislike these subjects you are quite possibly not suited for four years of university in engineering.
    B. *Physical Prerequisites*
        1. Have you ever considered that computer programming, for example, is a career that has physical prerequisites? This particular job can be responsible for neck and eye strain as well as repetitive action conditions such as carpal tunnel syndrome.
        2. Consider if your chosen career will require you to stand on your feet for prolonged periods, to lift heavy objects, or to continually reach and bend into awkward positions.
    C. *Internal Summary*
    Conducting serious research into the eductaion and training requirements of your chosen career is your first step toward career discovery. You may discover ceratin prerequisites that you hadn't previously considered.

Figure 15-2 Sample Planning Outline

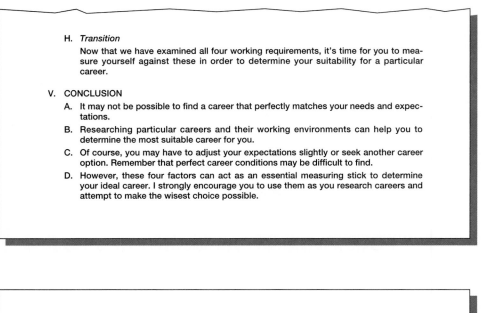

> H. *Transition*
>
> Now that we have examined all four working requirements, it's time for you to measure yourself against these in order to determine your suitability for a particular career.
>
> V. CONCLUSION
>
> A. It may not be possible to find a career that perfectly matches your needs and expectations.
>
> B. Researching particular careers and their working environments can help you to determine the most suitable career for you.
>
> C. Of course, you may have to adjust your expectations slightly or seek another career option. Remember that perfect career conditions may be difficult to find.
>
> D. However, these four factors can act as an essential measuring stick to determine your ideal career. I strongly encourage you to use them as you research careers and attempt to make the wisest choice possible.

Figure 15-2   (continued)

> *Speaking Notes*
> *Selecting the Right Career for You*
>
> I. *Introduction*
>
> The perfect career for you may not be a perfect career for someone else.
>
> A. *Internal Preview*
>
> 1. Career planning—connection with career satisfaction and contribution
> 2. Consider main categories of working requirements
> 3. Measure yourself against these requirements.
>
> B. *Transition*
>
> What are these categories?
>
> II. *Body*
>
> A. *Education and Training*
>
> 1. Each career requires unique training
> 2. Engineering
>
> B. *Physical Prerequisites*
>
> 1. Neck and eye strain
> 2. Repetitive action syndrome
> 3. Standing, lifting, reaching, bending
>
> C. *Internal Summary*
>
> Research— the first step toward career discovery

Figure 15-3   Sample Speaking Notes

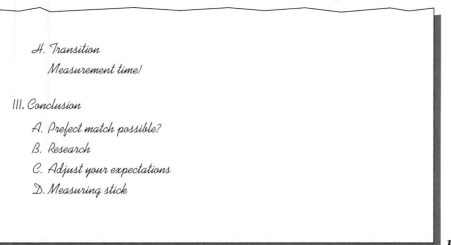

H. Transition
  Measurement time!

III. Conclusion
  A. Prefect match possible?
  B. Research
  C. Adjust your expectations
  D. Measuring stick

Figure 15-3   *(continued)*

as computer presentation software; interactive electronic whiteboards; objects and models; flip charts, chalk- and writing boards, and posters; handouts; overhead transparencies; slides; and videos. As shown in Figure 15-4, according to a recent survey of 69 000 sales managers, speakers prefer to accompany their verbal sales presentations with bound-paper presentations far more than any other medium.

COMPUTER PRESENTATION SOFTWARE   A number of presentation software packages, like Microsoft PowerPoint and Corel Presentations, are available to enhance your oral deliveries. These packages allow you to create and manipulate coloured slides with animated graphics and text, as well as audio. They are compatible with many independent graphic packages, making the availability of suitable graphics very impressive. The use of such presentations can have an awesome effect.

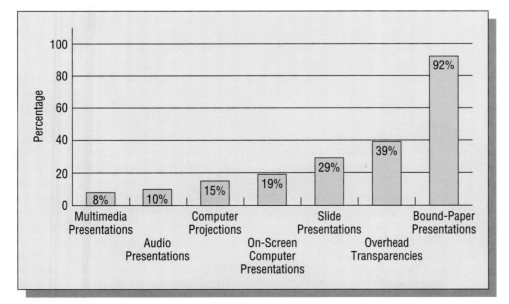

Figure 15-4   Visual Aids Preferred by Sales Managers

Source: *Simmons Research Survey in* Sales & Marketing Management, *(March 1995), 49.*

These software packages are easy to learn. They require a computer and projection system suitable for large audiences. When the computer-enhanced presentation is delivered to a small group, a computer screen may suffice in place of the larger projection system.

INTERACTIVE ELECTRONIC WHITEBOARDS   The **electronic whiteboard** is an extremely effective medium for sharing ideas with a group of people. Although it has the appearance of a simple whiteboard, it combines the power of software, a computer, an electronic pen, and a projection system into a large and intelligent touch screen. As a presenter writes on the screen with a finger or the electronic pen, the information is stored in the computer and may be printed as handouts for the audience. Just as you would normally use a mouse to indicate menu choices on your computer screen, the presenter simply uses a finger to pull down menus and make selections. With the support of such a visual aid, the presenter can enhance audience understanding and support comments with visual demonstrations.

This interactive presentation tool, shown in Figure 15–5, adds a professional and highly sophisticated appearance to an oral presentation.

OBJECTS AND MODELS   If you are presenting the prototype for a new hammer, your best visual aid is the hammer itself. If you are involved in the manufacture of a new airplane, a scaled-down model enables you to demonstrate its characteristics. You may use objects creatively to add interest and clarity to your presentation, as shown in Figure 15-6 where students use Lego blocks during a presentation to emphasize a point. As objects and models are passed around the room, they encourage active, hands-on interaction. However, you may find yourself competing with your own visual aids for audience attention.

FLIP CHARTS, WRITING BOARDS, AND POSTERS   These media are effective in presenting information to small interactive groups. Flip charts are the most common

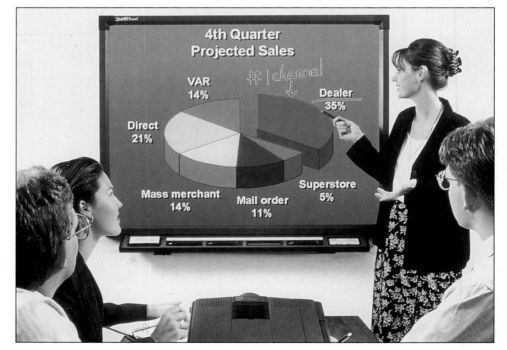

Figure 15–5 An interactive whiteboard acts as an effective presentation tool during a meeting.

Photo courtesy of Smart Technologies, Calgary, Alberta

Figure 15–6 Using Objects in a Speech Presentation
Lego blocks grab attention and aid understanding in this student presentation.

way to display visuals in a business presentation, allowing you to show a sequence of graphic information with the turn of a page. Because flip charts can be prepared in advance, your presentation can be neat and exact. In addition, advance preparation eliminates the need to turn your back as you speak or to pause while you draw or write. If you choose this medium, be sure that an easel is available in the presentation room. In Figure 15–7, a speaker uses a flip chart to present to a small group.

Figure 15–7 Flip charts are an effective tool for presenting information to small groups.
Photo by Rosina Solylo

In certain situations, however, you may actually prefer to write as you speak. When used in this manner, aids like flip charts and writing boards are excellent group-interaction tools. In a problem-solving situation, for instance, you can record key ideas as they are contributed. For an informative presentation, you can list your most important points in the order in which you want to make them.

HANDOUTS Many speakers hand out printed materials such as agendas, reports, and letters and such visual aids as charts and tables so that the audience can refer to them during the presentation. Handouts are especially useful in small working groups because they encourage interaction. However, they can divert the audience's attention. Some speakers prefer to save their handouts until the end of the presentation. Indeed, many speakers consider it essential to leave a copy of the presentation, especially if they discussed complex data that requires more than one quick look.

OVERHEAD TRANSPARENCIES Overhead transparencies, a popular presentation medium, allow an image to be projected without darkening the room and without losing touch with the audience. They are easy to use and flexible, allowing you to add or highlight a concept while it is being shown. High-quality transparencies can be produced in-house on photocopy machines that handle transparent film. To really catch the audience's attention, colour could be used in the transparency. Where the intent is to stimulate the audience, vibrant colours used along with attractive graphics can be quite effective. However, many transparencies call for conservative use of colour, since its overuse can detract from the professionalism of the presentation.

SLIDES Both colour and black-and-white slides can add a professional touch to a presentation. Slides can be used to display any type of two-dimensional visual aid, including photographs, maps, lists, tables, and charts.

Remote-control slide projectors allow you to change slides without stationing yourself next to the machine. You can stand in front of the room where the audience can pay attention to you as you point out important details on the slide. However, slides require a darkened room, thereby decreasing audience interest and eye contact.

VIDEOS Videos are an integral part of many business presentations. Video has the advantage of easy recording and instant playback. If videos are shown on television screens, they are only effective for small audiences. However, large projection screens and equipment expand the range of the audience. Many presenters are now showing video clips with sound via CD-ROM and a computer.

Table 15-3 compares the features of some of the visual aids that we have examined in this section.

DESIGNING VISUAL AIDS

The following are some design guidelines for effective visual presentations. Because visual aids are used to give graphic dimension to presentations, design is critical to their successful use.

SIMPLICITY Visuals that try to communicate too much risk overloading the audience. Communicate your message in a simple, direct way by limiting each visual to a single point. If you want to show a series of related concepts, use a series of visuals. If something must be written out, use bullets and key words, not sentences, and eliminate all unnecessary detail.

→ Cross Reference
We discussed designing visual aids for reports and proposals in Chapter 12, pages 329–336.

Table 15-3 Using Visual Aids in Formal Presentations

Format	Audience	Advantages	Disadvantages
flip charts, chalk- and writing boards	small	helps organize, summarize; high flexibility; informal	low-impact
overhead transparencies	medium/large	portable; no high technology needed; high flexibility	can be distracting; complex charts and graphs are ineffective
slides	medium/large	flexible/modular; minimum equipment needs; type serves as outline	do not show motion; lights must be dimmed
videos and CD-ROMs	small–large	high-impact; instant replay; easy assembly; provides change of pace	requires equipment; availability
computer presentation software	small–large	flexible; high impact; sophisticated appearance; easy to learn	requires specialized hardware and software
interactive electronic whiteboards	small–large	high impact; sophisticated appearance	requires specialized hardware and software

Source: Adapted from material supplied by Burson Marsteller, 230 Park Avenue South, New York, NY 10003.

SIZE   Use print large enough for everyone to read. If necessary, bring your visuals to the presentation room in advance and read them from the back of the room. Also use plenty of white space to reduce clutter.

COLOUR   When used correctly, colour can make visuals more attractive, exciting, and easier to read. By the same token, carelessly chosen colours can make visuals more difficult to read. If you examine the colour wheel in Figure 15-8, for instance, you can see that orange lettering against a red background would be extremely difficult to read because the contrast between the two colours is so low. The pairing of colours that are adjacent to one another on the colour chart, therefore, may produce subtle, harmonious effects but little contrast. Not surprisingly, white images on dark backgrounds provide the greatest contrast, followed by images in yellow, orange, green, red, blue, and violet. Black images show up best on light backgrounds, followed by images in red, orange, green, blue, violet, and yellow.

In addition to using colours for the strongest contrasts, you can select colours for their so-called temperatures. While "warm" colours like red and orange highlight visual presentations because they "advance" toward the audience, "cool" colours like blue and green, which tend to "recede," make excellent backgrounds.

DESIGN FOR CONSISTENCY   Develop a consistent format and style for your visual presentation. For example, avoid mixing colour with black-and-white slides. Use the same style and size of lettering and the same palette of colours on every visual.

GUIDELINES FOR USING VISUAL AIDS
Depending on how they are used, visual aids can enhance or detract from a speech or an oral presentation. The following guidelines will help you select and design effective visual aids.

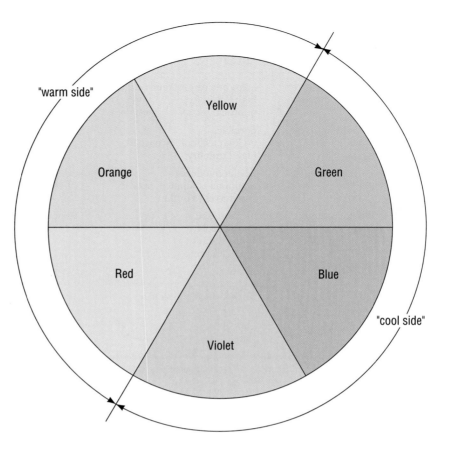

Figure 15-8 Colour Wheel

Opposites give the strongest contrast, whereas adjacent colours blend. The "warm" side advances toward the audience; the "cool" side retreats.

▼ *Choose the right visual aid.* Your choices should be based on the purpose of your speech, the size of your audience, the needs of the occasion, and your skill and experience in using the medium. Ask yourself whether each visual belongs in your presentation or could be eliminated.

▼ *Remember that your audience wants to see you, not your visuals.* Beginning your presentation with slides projected in a darkened room will prevent you from connecting with your audience. Ending with a visual will encourage your audience to remember the visual instead of you.

▼ *Don't repeat the content of the visual when you comment on it.* Resist describing every detail, but explain what is being shown. For example, "This slide shows how workforce reduction has reduced company overhead in the last three years."

▼ *Stop after your main point and allow the audience to scan the information projected on the visual.* If you speak "on top" of a visual, you will force your audience to choose between you and it. Pause for several seconds after displaying a visual aid and then continue.

▼ *Avoid turning your back on your audience.* Maintain eye contact throughout your presentation, even when displaying a visual. Do not talk to your visual; talk to the audience.

▼ *Work on your timing.* Never display a visual before talking about it; remove it when you finish the thought.

▼ *Rehearse.* Integrate your visual and oral presentations before your performance. Rehearsal is especially important if you use more than one medium. Moving from a flip chart to a slide projector to a VCR requires familiarity with the equipment (and a back-up plan if something goes wrong).

Delivery

Delivery refers not only to your method of speaking but to your voice quality and body language. Next, we examine the ways in which voice quality and nonverbal language influence what people hear and how receptive they are to your message.

VOICE QUALITY AND NONVERBAL LANGUAGE

The quality of your voice and the way you move during a speech or presentation are also elements of your delivery. A variety of voice elements, including loudness, pitch, rate, pauses, articulation, and pronunciation are known as **voice quality** (sometimes called *paralanguage*). These elements make important and lasting impressions, as do several other forms of nonverbal language.

LOUDNESS   Your audience must be able to hear you. In order to speak loudly but without shouting, project your voice from the diaphragm—the flat respiratory muscle in your chest wall—not from the throat.

PITCH   Pitch refers to how high or low your voice sounds. Because speaking in a monotone can make listening difficult, try varying the pitch of your voice as you emphasize key words or phrases.

RATE   Varying your rate of speech can make your delivery more interesting. Slow down to emphasize important points; speed up when recounting familiar material.

PAUSES   When used effectively, pauses add emphasis, power, and effective timing. They can influence the impact of a dramatic story, a joke, a series of rhetorical questions, a quotation, even a visual aid. Plan your pauses in advance for maximum impact.

Remember, however, that unplanned vocalized pauses are verbal annoyances. The *umms*, *ers*, *you knows*, *ahs* and the *ehs* of everyday speech can reduce credibility. To perfect your timing and eliminate these pauses, rehearse your presentation with a tape recorder. You might also jot down reminders, such as "DON'T SAY 'YOU KNOW,' " in the margins of your speaking notes.

ARTICULATION AND PRONUNCIATION   The clarity and distinctiveness of vocal sounds is determined by a process known as **articulation; pronunciation** refers to the formation of the proper sounds to create words. Saying *dint* instead of *didn't* is an articulation mistake; saying *hunnert* instead of *hundred* is usually an error in pronunciation. Both types of error can reduce credibility. Many articulation and pronunciation mistakes are childhood habits, and changing them may require considerable practice. A tape recorder can help identify undesirable speech habits.

NONVERBAL LANGUAGE   As we saw in Chapter 1, communication takes place nonverbally as well as verbally. Nonverbal communication is critical in public speaking because it conveys an overall impression of your competence and credibility. You undercut your message through such visual cues as poor posture and darting eyes.

> *I do not object to people looking at their watches when I am speaking. But I strongly object when they start shaking them to make sure they are still going.*
>
> Lord William Norman Birkett
> British lawyer and judge

→ *Cross Reference*
We discussed nonverbal communication in Chapter 1, pages 9–13.

PRACTICAL TIPS

Overcoming Speech Tension

Speech tension (more commonly known as "stage fright") is the body's "fight-or-flight" reaction to the stress of delivering a speech or oral presentation. Sensing "danger," the heart rate zooms, the palms sweat, the mouth becomes dry, hands and knees shake, and breathing becomes laboured. These symptoms cause many people to consider public speaking the "public equivalent of a root canal."[*]

The following advice will help you minimize the tension associated with public speaking:

▼ *Be prepared.* Know your material, your audience, and the reason for your presentation. Organize your thoughts into speaking notes. Memorize your first sentence. Then put it all together in practice.

▼ *Rehearse in front of a mirror.* Use a tape recorder or video camera. Ask a friend to watch a practice session with all your visual aids. If possible, practise in the actual presentation room.

▼ *Visualize your own success as a speaker.* Veteran business speaker Ron Hoff suggests that you rehearse by "letting the words sink into your consciousness. . . . The verbal and the nonverbal begin to blend together, reinforcing each other. . . . You hear what you sound like. You visualize what you look like. And you're familiar with the environment. . . . Relax. Glide."[†]

▼ *Breathe deeply and drink water.* Right before you begin speaking, breathe slowly several times; deep breathing will relax your entire body. Be sure to have a glass of water available during your presentation in case your mouth becomes dry.

▼ *Use gestures and movements as natural outlets for nervous tension.*

▼ *Use visual aids.* When you are actively involved with visual aids, your nervous tension will seem less evident, both to you and to your audience.

▼ *Look at people.* People want to see you succeed, not fail. Look people straight in the eye for enormous positive feedback.

▼ *Don't let a mistake shake your confidence.* Perfection is not possible. If something goes wrong, just keep going. Your audience may not even know what happened.

[*]Deirdre Fanning, "The Public Equivalent of a Root Canal," *New York Times,* 2 December 1990, F25.
[†]Ron Hoff, *I Can See You Naked: A Fearless Guide to Making Great Presentations* (Kansas City, Mo.: Andrews and McMeel, 1988), 216.

EYE CONTACT   As you speak, briefly look at individuals in different parts of the room but avoid darting your eyes back and forth or looking above heads. Choose people who are smiling or who appear receptive. Speakers who make eye contact are perceived as more confident and open to feedback than speakers who look at their notes.

> *All the great speakers were bad speakers at first.*
>
> Ralph Waldo Emerson
> Essayist and poet

GESTURES   Gestures, both voluntary and involuntary, play an important part in every speech and presentation. Displaying a chart and pointing to it, using your fingers to count critical points, and clenching a fist to emphasize a point are all natural outgrowths of your message and communicate involvement and self-confidence. By contrast, gestures that appear forced call attention to themselves by suggesting speaker discomfort.

MOVEMENT   Natural, relaxed movements also communicate self-confidence. Instead of holding on to the lectern for dear life, it is more effective to cross the room and point to visual aids, circulate in the audience, then walk back to the lectern. Movements tell your audience, "I'm involved. You are, too."

A NOTE ABOUT CLOTHING   Finally, remember that before you speak your first word, your clothes communicate whether you are part of the group in the room.

COLLABORATIVE COMMUNICATION

Developing and Delivering Team Presentations

The best team presentations function like well-oiled machines. Each segment supports the presentation's overall purpose and is linked to—but does nor repeat—the functions of other segments. In addition, performances are coordinated as each person acts according to a carefully crafted plan intended to maintain the focus of the final presentation.

The most successful team presentations involve three stages; predesign, design, and delivery. The techniques used in each stage are intended to shape the team into a unified whole.

PREDESIGN

Unless everyone knows in advance exactly what the teams is trying to accomplish and focuses on that purpose, wrong decisions are inevitable from that point on. The predesign stage also involves identifying channels of communication and the person who will lead the team's effort. It is the leader's responsibility to coordinate individual segments and to ensure that everyone knows what everyone else is doing. Among the leader's tasks are dividing the presentation into distinct segments and assigning speakers for each.

DESIGN

During the design stage, general themes are translated into concrete, specific presentation plans. To coordinate the presentations of all groups members, it is often helpful to develop storyboards for each speaker that define what he or she will cover, the visuals that will be used, and the time needed to complete the presentation. Completed storyboards may be prominently displayed—for example, taped to a wall—so that every presenter can see exactly what will be said at each point in the presentation. This information minimizes duplication.

Visuals are created during the design stage. To produce a coordinated effect, they should all have the same type and art style.

DELIVERY

Here are some factors that contribute to a successful delivery:

▼ *Strict adherence to time.* Practise to make sure you can deliver your speech in the allowed time.

▼ *Focus on organizational clarity.* Speakers who use previews, transitions, and summaries help the audience understand how presentations interrelate.

▼ *An effective team leader.* The leader introduces speakers, provides transitions from one speaker to another, and makes sure that the group maintains its focus.

▼ *Mutual team support.* Team support is demonstrated in many ways— for instance, deferring to another team member's expertise and being flexible enough to accommodate another contributor's last-minute changes that affect your presentation.

Although team presentations are undoubtedly more complex than single-person presentations, they can be successful if they are carefully if they are carefully planned and executed.

Questions for Critical Thinking

1. How could a coordinated effort to be arguably more important to the success of an oral team presentation than a written presentation?

2. Can a team presentation be delivered effectively without predesign and design work? Explain your answer.

3. Why is organizational clarity so important to an audience viewing a team presentation?

Sources: "The Art of Business Presentations," *Managing Office Technology* (March 1994): 83; and Thomas Leech, *How to Prepare, Stage, and Deliver Winning Presentations* (New York: AMACOM, 1993).

While artists might wear casual clothes during a presentation to an advertising agency, colleagues should wear a suit for presentations to bankers.

At Ease in the Spotlight

"The bad news is that it is quite likely that your knees will turn to water, your voice will rise to a shrill squeak, and your pores will leak profusely, even at the prospect of climbing to the platform. The good news is that nervousness on the speaking platform is not a rare disease, and there are cures that will work for you too."[14]

The fear of speaking to groups—**laliaphobia**—is often reported as being our number-one phobia. There is no general cure for laliaphobia. A solution for one person may not be useful for another. However, here are some suggestions that many people find helpful.

▼ Standing behind a barrier is an excellent way to separate you from the audience. A podium will hide shaky hands and knees.

▼ The use of presentation aids takes the focus off you. As well, they help the audience to understand your key points.

▼ Being unprepared may cause you to panic. Well before the date of your presentation, ask yourself if you have prepared your outline, your cue cards, and your presentation aids. Ask yourself if you have rehearsed until you feel confident. The greater your sense of security, the more confidence you will have on the stage.

▼ Don't be thrown into doing a major presentation your first time out. Begin with smaller audiences and shorter speeches.

▼ Get your feet wet by public speaking on a panel. It's much less intimidating to be speaking as part of a group.

▼ Attend to all the logistics well ahead of your presentation. Are your handouts assembled? Will the projector be in place? Will there be pens for the flip charts?

▼ Perform relaxation exercises before beginning your presentation, for example, breathing exercises, taking a brisk walk, or allowing your muscles to go limp. You can psyche yourself up by thinking of all the excellent qualities of your speech, such as colourful illustrations, sound data, or a lively conclusion.

▼ Become an evangelist for your subject. If you have a passionate opinion on a topic, your enthusiasm will override your nervousness.

▼ Allow yourself plenty of time to arrive at the venue of your presentation.

▼ Speakers who announce that they are nervous are inviting the audience to look for the signs. This just compounds feelings of anxiety.

As a speaker learns to cope with nervousness, confidence replaces anxiety and eventually the speaker becomes completely in tune with the needs and reactions of the audience.[15]

Handling Audience Questions

Most business presentations include question-and-answer periods. Depending on the type of presentation, questions may arise at any point or only at the end. According to Sarah Weddington, the lawyer who argued the landmark abortion case *Roe* v. *Wade* before the Supreme Court, handling questions can be an art form. "I remember watching President Reagan handle hostile questions during the Iran-Contra scandal," she recalls. "In response to a question about whether he thought Oliver North was still a hero, the President answered that you could not take away from North the medals he had won in Vietnam. He sidestepped the question in an extremely effective way, which is a technique all speakers need to learn."[16]

In a formal speech, questions begin when the speaker asks for them. Be sure to take questions from every part of the room, including the back. When your presentation is in a large room, repeat each question so that everyone can hear (rephrasing also gives you time to think).

Knowing your audience can help you to anticipate questions. According to Ron Hoff, "People ask questions about the issues of greatest concern to them—their positions in the organization, the problems affecting them that day. Sales managers ask about sales promotions. Corporate communications directors ask about images. . . . And everybody asks about costs. If you've done your homework, you'll be able to anticipate at least 70 percent of the questions you actually get."[17] Practice answering anticipated questions with a tape recorder and listen critically to your response.

Although you will be able to anticipate many questions, there will be others that you cannot answer. Say so in a direct way. But also tell the questioner that you will try to find the answer and respond as soon as possible. Of course, there may also be questions that you do not want to answer. Use finesse or redirect the question to a colleague. Sometimes you can maintain your credibility by saying something like, "Public relations is Ann's area, so I'll turn that question over to her."

Try to turn hostile questions to your advantage by remaining calm and recasting questions in a less confrontational style. For example, if someone asks, "How could you have approved that ridiculous policy?" repeat the question in a less inflammatory way: "I've been asked about the policy of dressing casually on Fridays. Our research shows that . . . ."

Finally, always be conscious of the individual who is asking a question. Is it the CEO or a lower-level employee? As you might expect, you may get the toughest questions from top managers who are looking for both broad implications and specific data. To handle such questions, you must be prepared and be able to think on your feet.

Coping with Presentation Hazards

Murphy's Law tells us that "Anything that can go wrong will." Hence, a speaker should never leave anything to chance. When something does fail, keep calm and don't let your audience see your frustration. Here are a few possible scenarios:

▼ Your host gives you a very brief or poor introduction. However you proceed, don't let your audience believe you are bitter. You may wish to re-introduce yourself or make a humorous remark about your host's introduction.

▼ Your flight has been delayed and you will arrive late for your presentation. In order to avoid this sitation, plan to arrive early. Then if your plane is delayed you can take a less direct route but still arrive on time. Or if it's not too far consider driving your car; this may turn out to be more reliable than making connections with airlines.

▼ Technical equipment opens all sorts of opportunities for hazards. Herman Holtz, best-selling author and consultant, suggests keeping the equipment simple and always having a backup plan just in case your primary plan fails.

▼ You don't know your audience. Researching your audience prior to a presentation can avoid unnecessary embarrassment. Before preparing your presentation, find out your audience's needs and interests.

▼ A heckler in the audience is compromising your presentation. If you ignore the first couple of comments from the heckler, he or she may not persist. Dottie Walters, an experienced international speaker suggests a light-hearted semi-putdown, such as 'Excuse me, sir; I work alone,' said with a grin."[18]

▼ The time allotted for your speech is expanded or reduced. Stretching a presentation may be as simple as adding a question-and-answer session at the end. Shortening it may be more difficult. Look for areas where you can shorten topics; Herman Holtz suggests not omitting any topic, especially one your audience is expecting to hear.[19]

What's Ahead

Speeches and oral presentations are characterized according to how formal the speaker-audience interaction is. In Chapter 16 we will examine a number of informal, often daily, interchanges in both group and one-on-one exchanges.

STUDENT RESOURCE CENTRE

Summary of Chapter Objectives

1. **Identify the characteristics of a speech and an oral presentation.**

   Speakers delivering formal public speeches address audiences that give no verbal feedback until after the speech is over. By contrast, oral presentations are characterized by an interchange between speaker and audience that may occur at any point during or after the presentation. Oral presentations also rely heavily on visual aids and are almost always extemporaneous.

2. **Explain ways to organize a speech or oral presentation and to conduct effective audience analysis.**

   Speeches and oral presentations can be organized with statements of general and specific purpose and a core idea. The general purpose may be information, persuasion, and meeting the needs of a special occasion.

   Effective audience analysis requires an understanding of what your audience knows and feels about you and your topic. Questionnaires and interviews are often used to gather this information. The goal of audience analysis is to gather a clear picture of what the audience wants and needs from a speech or presentation.

3. **Describe the purposes and characteristics of an effective introduction, body, and conclusion for a speech or an oral presentation.**

   The introduction establishes the speaker's credibility; captures attention by means of humour, startling statements, anecdotes, rhetorical questions, quotations, and demonstrations; and previews the main points. The body presents the speaker's main points and supporting material. The conclusion summarizes the speaker's message, places the message in a broad context, personalizes the message, and, when appropriate, calls for future action.

4. **Describe the special requirements of oral communication.**

   Oral communication requires the repetition of key ideas to aid audience recall. It also requires verbal signposts—in the form of transitions, internal previews, and internal summaries—that signal the organization and structure of a speech or presentation.

5. **Identify the importance and characteristics of a planning outline and speaking notes.**

   The planning outline is used in the preparation of a speech or an oral presentation. It is a full-content outline that includes what you plan to say in the presentation as well as statements of your specific purpose and core ideas. Speaking notes, which are used during the actual delivery, are key-word outlines based on the planning outline.

6. **Describe the different types of visual aids used in speeches and oral presentations, and identify elements of effective visual-aid design.**

   Among the visual aids commonly used in speeches and oral presentations are objects and models; flip charts, writing boards, and posters; handouts; overhead transparencies; slides; computer software presentations; and videos. Visual aids are most effective when they have a simple design, when they are large enough for everyone to read, when they use colour effectively, and when they are consistently designed.

7. **Describe methods for avoiding speech tension.**

   Laliaphobia, the fear of speaking to groups, is common among even the best speakers and performers. Some suggestions to oversome this difficulty might be to use presentation aids, stand behind a barrier, prepare diligently, attend to the logistical details, work on your sense of security, and perform relaxation exercises.

8. **Analyze techniques for handling audience questions.**

   Start by anticipating the questions that might be raised. If you cannot answer a question, say so in a direct way. Learn to finesse questions that you do not want to answer. Rephrase hostile questions so they are less confrontational.

9. **Discuss how to cope with presentation hazards.**

   Doing detailed preparation in advance, allowing yourself plenty of time to travel, keeping the technical equipment to a minimum, as well as remaining calm are some of the critical behaviours for coping with presentation hazards.

Review and Discussion Questions

1. Distinguish between speeches and oral presentations. *(Ch. Obj. 1)*

2. Explain the terms *general purpose*, *specific purpose*, and *core idea* in speeches and oral presentations. *(Ch. Obj. 2)*

3. Explain the importance of audience analysis. *(Ch. Obj. 2)*

4. List several questions that you can ask yourself to help in analyzing an audience. *(Ch. Obj. 2)*

5. Name the three basic components of an oral presentation. What are the functions of each? *(Ch. Obj. 3)*

6. What are the three special requirements of oral communication? *(Ch. Obj. 4)*

7. Distinguish between a planning outline and speaking notes. *(Ch. Obj. 5)*

8. As a business speaker, what types of visual aids are available to you? *(Ch. Obj. 6)*

9. Suggest five activities to avoid speech tension. *(Ch. Obj. 7)*

10. Summarize some basic techniques for handling audience questions. *(Ch. Obj. 8)*

11. Suggest five ways to cope with hazards that may occur during a presentation. *(Ch. Obj. 9)*

Application Exercises

1. Write a script for an oral presentation in which you discuss the importance of good communication skills, both oral and written, in business. You might include examples of businesspeople whose good communication skills you have seen in action. *(Ch. Obj. 1)*

2. Imagine that someone whom you admire has been invited to receive an award from your school. You've been asked to give a speech in which you introduce this person, describe why the award is being presented, and explain why you admire the recipient. Write down the general purpose, the specific purpose, and the core idea of your presentation. *(Ch. Obj. 2)*

3. Prepare a short (three to five minutes) special-occasion speech based on your preparation for Exercise 2. Your instructor may ask you to deliver this speech to the class. *(Ch. Obj. 1, 5)*

4. Choose a product you enjoy. Plan a five-minute oral presentation in which you persuade your audience (the class) to buy that product. For example, you could sell your favourite performer's latest CD, a stereo system, software, or backpacking gear.

   Write an outline that lists the three major sections (introduction, body, and conclusion) of your talk. Under each heading, briefly describe how you might accomplish the functions of that section. For instance, how might you establish your credibility and capture your audience's attention during your introduction? *(Ch. Obj. 3, 5)*

5. Prepare and give the presentation that you planned in Exercise 4. Use visual aids; you might even want to bring in an example of the product to demonstrate. Give your audience time to ask questions at the end. *(Ch. Obj. 1, 6, 8)*

6. You have been asked to give a presentation to all 32 employees of a small company. Included in the audience will be the firm's president, the human resources staff, the accounting staff, clerical workers, salespeople, advertising copywriters—the entire spectrum of organization members. Describe the challenges involved in giving such a presentation. Write a plan for analyzing your audience and defining its needs. *(Ch. Obj. 2)*

7. Prepare and give an informative presentation to the class on your job or a favourite hobby. If you wish, you may use visual aids. Make the presentation interactive by allowing the audience to ask questions throughout your talk rather than just at the end. *(Ch. Obj. 4)*

8. Attend a speech or an oral presentation. Write an evaluation (approximately two pages) of the speaker's performance. Did the speaker follow the guidelines suggested in this chapter? Did the speech contain an effective introduction, body, and conclusion? Did the speaker use visual aids and handle audience questions effectively? If you feel the speaker could have done a better job, state why you feel that way and suggest specific improvements. *(Ch. Obj. 1, 3, 6, 7, 8, 9)*

9. Research two major business publications for information and forecasts about the Canadian economy for the upcoming year. (Possible sources include *Canadian Business, Profit—The Magazine for Canadian Entrepreneurs, The Financial Post Magazine*, or the Canadian edition of *Time*. A reference librarian can suggest others.)

   Prepare a script for a summary oral report. Your audience is the CEO of the company at which you're presently working or one for which you have worked in the past. What types of visual aids would make this presentation more effective? *(Ch. Obj. 3, 5, 6, 8)*

10. Research and prepare an oral report that discusses the job outlook for students graduating from college and university this year. What are the "hot" jobs? What are the growing areas of the economy? What qualifications do employers look for? Discuss and compare the outlook for at least three different majors. What types of visual aids would make your presentation more interesting? Work on avoiding speech tension and presentation hazards. *(Ch. Obj. 3, 6, 7, 9)*

11. Research and prepare an oral report that advises your classmates on how to conduct an effective job search. Include such topics as researching employers, conducting informational interviews, designing good résumés, performing well in job interviews, and following up after job interviews. What types of visual aids would be good for this presentation? Work on avoiding speech tension and presentation hazards. *(Ch. Obj. 3, 6, 7, 9)*

12. Choose a piece of legislation that has a big impact on business (possibilities: human rights; tax laws; environmental regulations). Write the script for an oral presentation that discusses the provisions of this law and the ways it affects business. Be sure to present all sides of the issue along with the appropriate evidence. Include effective visual aids. Your instructor will determine the length of your presentation and may ask you to present to the class. *(Ch. Obj. 2, 5, 6)*

ACT: Applied Communication Techniques

Begin by referring to the sections up to and including Capital Letters, Italics, and Underlining in Appendix II, then correct the grammar, spelling, and usage errors in the following sentences. Check your answers in Appendix V.

1. Living near weyburn, saskatchewan the children learned all about farming.

2. As a geologist, I've worked in the northwest territories as well as labrador and southern ontario.

3. My subject today is the introduction of weight watchers meals to burger king restaurants.

4. We met at lorne akins junior high school in st. albert, alberta.

5. The book was titled you've got what it takes.

6. His consistently high marks qualified him to recieve summa cum laude on his degree.

7. Premier Smith gentley put his arm around me and said, "don't let him upset you."

8. mark twain said "eat what you like and let the food fight it out inside."

9. The poor presentation was due to two reasons: (1) she lacked knowledge on the topic. (2) the technology was not operating properly.

10. All canadians who earned gold medals at the olympics were guests at the canada day parade.

Building Your Research Skills

Research a business-related topic that interests you. Your research should include reading at least three different articles or chapters from books, not including this textbook. Prepare a short (three to five minutes) oral presentation summarizing your research. Be sure to include an introduction, a body, and a conclusion.

Building Your Teamwork Skills

Your instructor will divide the class into pairs or small groups. Each member of the group should take turns presenting the topic prepared in Building Your Research Skills. After each presentation, the group should critique the presentation and make constructive suggestions for improvement. For instance, was the introduction effective? If not, how could it be improved? Remember to state your criticism tactfully; after all, your turn is coming up.

Building Your Technology Skills

You have been asked to prepare and deliver a presentation to the CEO, vice president, managers, and sales staff of your company on your research findings and proposal for the company to establish a Web site. Prepare a five-minute oral presentation. Include the visuals, including handouts, that you will be using to speak about the importance of establishing a Web presence and your proposal for doing so. Be prepared to give the presentation to the class.

Weblinks Internet Resources for this Chapter

Business Presenters' Home Page
http://www.busicom.com/

The Ten Commandments of Client Presentations
http://www1.tagonline.com/~strategy/ tencommpres.html

The Key Steps to an Effective Presentation
http://www.access.digex.net/~huance/ keystep1.html

Good Presentations: Hints and Tips
http://www.csun.edu/~vcecn006/hintspre.htm

CASE STUDIES

DIVERSITY CASE:

Struggling with the Federal Employment Equity Act

The Federal Employment Equity Act requires businesses to demonstrate fair employment practice to women, Aboriginal people, members of visible minorities, and persons with disabilities. It also prohibits discrimination against these groups. Despite the Act, many businesses are still struggling with creating fair employment practices and accessible work environments for employees with disabilities.

Questions and Applications

1. Research and prepare a script for a three- to five-minute talk that discusses the steps that companies must take to meet the needs of persons with disabilities in order to comply with the federal Employment Equity Act. Focus on recruitment, hiring, and training issues. You could also discuss changes in physical facilities (parking lots, building layouts) that would be required by this Act.

2. What visual aids, if any, would be useful in your speech? Explain.

CORPORATE CASE:

When in Rome

In ancient times, the Romans stole wonderful ideas from the Greeks. For years, corporate North America has acted like the Romans, but it calls the practice of using others' ideas "benchmarking." According to a *Fortune* magazine article, benchmarking is the "art of finding out, in a perfectly legal and aboveboard way, how others do something better than you do so you can imitate—and perhaps improve upon—their techniques." Firms like Toyota, AT&T, IBM, and Xerox use it as a standard tool for improving productivity and quality.

As an example, suppose a Canadian bank targets its procedures for handling credit card billing disputes as an area in need of benchmarking. The bank appoints a team of eight employees from different departments, including four who ordinarily handle such disputes, and gives them the authority to change the process. Meeting once a week, the team benchmarks seven other companies, including several credit card firms, an airline, and a competing bank. By visiting three of its benchmark companies and talking to representatives from the others on the phone, the team picks up several ideas about improving the bank's credit card service.

One ongoing service problem is locating documents when customers register complaints. Because clerks have had to search numerous possible sites, this step alone often takes three to four days. At other banks, better software enables clerks to view all relevant documents at once on a computer terminal. Benchmark companies also maintain "help desks"

staffed by experienced employees who tell customers the exact status of their complaints.

The Canadian bank adopts these improvements and several others. The result is a drastic fall in complaints outstanding from 5000 in December to 2000 in June in one fiscal year. Borrowed procedures also reduce the amount of time necessary to resolve complaints from an average of 45 to 25 days.[20]

Questions and Applications

1. Plan and research an oral presentation on benchmarking; your audience will be the CEO of the company for which you work (or one for which you have worked in the past). Research the benchmarking procedures of various firms, learning what they've gained from the strategy and what they've determined to be the best ways to use it. (Be sure to consult other sources in addition to this textbook.) Develop specific suggestions on how your employer could apply benchmarking. What procedures or problems would you target first? Draft a general purpose, a specific purpose, and a core idea for this presentation.

2. Write a script for your presentation. Be sure to tell your audience what benchmarking is and how it can benefit a company. What visual aids would be effective for this talk?

*O*ral Communication in Groups

The ability to deal with people is as purchasable a commodity as sugar and coffee. And I pay more for that ability than for any other under the sun.

John D. Rockefeller
Oil magnate and philanthropist

Rider pride runs deeper than fans' memories of the last successful game or the energy of a fund-raiser between seasons: it's more a way of life. For Saskatchewan's most prominent professional sports franchise, pride in their football team is an imperative. It's both a mission and a vision; a metaphor and a reality.

It all started back in September of 1910, when a displaced rowing club donned old gold and purple jerseys and promptly lost its first football game 7-6 to Moose Jaw. There is something about those prairie players that keeps them hanging in because today, in green and white and with a centennial anniversary rapidly approaching, the Saskatchewan Roughriders are still very much in the game.

At the helm of this progressive organization is Alan Ford, the club's twelfth modern-era General Manager and Chief Operating Officer. Ford's tenure with the club spans more than three decades. It links the legendary management of Eagle Keys and the Roughriders' first sweet Grey Cup victory of 1966 to today's big-budget football club, where strong leadership, fiscal responsibility, and effective communication are as much part of the club's success as the game itself.

Recent evidence of effective communication in action came when the Roughriders entered the 1997 play-off season with a less than stellar point average and a devastating home loss to Winnipeg. Undoubtedly, club revenue, fan support, and team morale were in jeopardy. The club's partnership-management philosophy empowered the coaching team and players to identify the root cause of their malady and to develop a more synergistic team through selective player trades. The rejuvenated Roughriders went on to defeat the Calgary Stampeders and Edmonton Eskimos in exciting play-off action. They also won the Western Conference Championship and a berth at the Grey Cup.

The Roughriders mostly communicate orally; after all, six months of close proximity, the privacy of locker-room planning, and game-play calling rely on the most fundamental of human communication skills. However, "There is always room for improvement," says Ford. "The more prepared we are to learn of the other person's position, the more valuable will be the exchange."

"The key to successful team building is honest and consistent communication," reflects Ford. "When done well, it can make or break confidences; it can provide encouragement and motivation; and it certainly helps shape a winning team."

Clearly, synergy and effective communication paid off. Their memorable Grey Cup challenge took the host town of Edmonton by storm, with more than 40 000 visiting Rider fans demonstrating unconditional support of their team. That was the day Rider pride gave way to Prairie pride. ▼

Source: Interview with Alan Ford.

Chapter Overview _____

Alan Ford is a communication enabler. As a modern-era General Manager, his management style has incorporated principle-based leadership, empowerment, and consensus. As a club leader, he has inspired those around him to achieve success. He's achieved this through determination, the ability to focus on a goal no matter what was happening outside of his club, an understanding of the business, and a willingness to listen.

As you will see in this chapter, business communicators can learn a great deal from Ford as they engage in meetings, negotiations, and other forms of formal and informal oral communication in groups. Indeed, there are parallels between Ford's leadership style and the style of any other business leader. In business, as in football, a quarterback has to take emotion out of the huddle. Although the definition of a "business touchdown" will vary from situation to situation, team success is always linked to successful communication.

The ability to work and communicate with groups sounds so simple. Yet, working and communicating as a team is a serious challenge to many people—and one of the skills most in demand.

According to Nuala Beck, Canadian economist and best-selling author, it's difficult for a lot of employees to consider themselves as problem-solvers. This is because managers have traditionally made all the decisions while employees simply waited for their directives. "But all of a sudden, there's no more 'they'; there's just 'us.' We are now responsible for executing plans—and, in most cases, for thinking up plans in the first place."[1]

Formal Business Meetings _____

Depending upon your company and position, you may spend between 25 and 40 percent—or more—of your time in formal meetings. It is not surprising, then, that a recent survey of 2000 business leaders found that considerably more time is now spent in meetings than it was five years ago.[2] **Formal meetings** involve a leader and participants, are prearranged, and have specific stated goals. Formal meetings may be internal or external. While **internal meetings** involve only company personnel, **external meetings** also include outsiders.

All meetings, of course, take time to prepare, to meet, to pursue agreed-upon tasks. According to George David Kieffer, an authority on business meetings, "When someone in your office asks if you're available for a half-hour meeting this afternoon, don't be fooled. In all likelihood you will be allocating at least two hours of your time and forgoing far more than one-half hour doing something else. Every meeting leverages your time, so you must make sure you leverage it wisely."[3]

As a result, meetings are focusing increasingly on bottom-line business. Companies like Microsoft "don't ask their salespeople after a conference if they liked the main speaker," explains Hugh K. Lee, president of the Center for Organization Development. "They ask how the salespeople will use the information they got to improve their work."[4]

One way to ensure that meeting time is well spent is to decide whether a meeting is really necessary. Before scheduling a meeting, ask yourself whether the work can be accomplished without it, whether an informational memo will suffice, or whether the same result can be achieved by calling two or three people on the phone. Bennett Cerf, co-founder of Random House, was famous for leaving the room every time a meeting was called—he believed that working alone was the only way to get things done in a creative field like publishing.[5] Although there are good reasons to call meetings—even in publishing—Cerf's point is well-taken: if you can accomplish something on your own, don't call a meeting.

When you do call or attend a meeting, remember that the way you communicate in group sessions tells others how competent you are. During every meeting you attend, whether as a leader or a participant, others judge your communication and people skills. They also judge your knowledge and ability to solve problems while working as part of a team. Most importantly, they judge your ability to get the job done—to work with people who have diverse opinions but who are trying to reach the same goal.

Meetings are a kind of theatre where managers observe and evaluate the performance and progress of key players. Even in the most ordinary meeting (a weekly staff meeting, for example), what you say and how you say it demonstrates whether you are ready for more responsibility—or less.

The group communication that takes place within meetings can be defined by each individual's role as leader or participant. In this section we will discuss the nature of these roles in some detail. We will also describe the role played by meeting minutes and the nature and function of meeting mechanics.

LEADING A MEETING

Leading a meeting involves the ability and responsibility to communicate in a variety of ways. While many of the following leadership responsibilities apply to all meetings, some apply only in special situations.

DEFINING AND LIMITING TASKS   Much as you define a general purpose for written documents, speeches, and oral presentations, you must define the function of the meetings that you chair. Believing that group activities will somehow find their own focus may well be your first—and biggest—mistake. It is the leader's responsibility to make sure that each participant understands the purpose of a meeting. "I'm stunned," says television producer David Corvo, "by the number of people who don't know what kind of meeting they're in. One of the best examples is when the boss convenes a meeting to convey a decision that has already been reached, and a staff member persists in debating the decision. The time for that is past! You're in the wrong meeting. This meeting is informational and delegatory. By continuing to question the decision, you are only showing your own poor judgment and insensibility to the boss's purpose and needs."[6]

Being an effective meeting leader also means recognizing what the group can and cannot do. For example, entry-level managers do not develop company policy because it is not within their province. Similarly, corporate directors generally do not gather information—this job usually is done at a lower organizational level.

Task definition also requires task limitation. Because trying to do too much almost always ensures failure, it is critical to limit the purpose of a meeting. Each of the following types of meetings has different basic goals. Although two or more of these goals can be combined under certain conditions, it is generally wise to call separate meetings when goals get too broad or prove incompatible.

To Give or Exchange Information   In **informational meetings** information is delivered to participants by means of oral reports. Reports are most effective when they clarify written information that participants have already received rather than present information for the first time.

To Develop New Ideas   In **brainstorming sessions** new ideas are suggested in an open, nonauthoritarian atmosphere. For example, after the merger was announced between Wardair and Pacific Western Airlines, employees performing similar functions for both companies met in brainstorming sessions to determine how the new combined company would operate. These recommendations took into account differences in the way Wardair and Pacific Western did business as well as the needs of the new, larger corporation.

To Make Decisions   Decision-making meetings bring people and companies together to debate issues and make decisions, often by taking votes. Decision-making meetings are usually held to reconcile conflicting views and generally should not be used to gather information. In most cases information should be collected as advance preparation for the decision-making stage.

Cross Reference
We discuss brainstorming further on page 461, and decision making on page 463 of this chapter.

To Delegate Work or Authority   Even when job responsibilities have already been assigned (perhaps over the phone or by memo), a delegating meeting may be necessary to clarify specific details. In **delegating meetings** specific tasks are assigned to individuals or groups who are then responsible for their completion. Meetings to delegate are often followed by informational and decision-making meetings.

To Collaborate   In **collaborative meetings** participants work together to prepare memos, letters, or reports, or to develop projects. Collaborative efforts, however, usually succeed only when participants work together as teams. Efforts may be doomed if group members have trouble completing joint assignments.

Don't let your vision get diluted, but don't be afraid of teamwork.

James B. Patterson
CEO, J. Walter Thompson

To Persuade   **Persuasive meetings** involve oral presentations designed to achieve group consensus or support for a course of action. Purchasers and office managers, for example, may hold persuasive meetings to discuss and debate the merits of several competing office-equipment suppliers.

To Inspire and Build Enthusiasm   **Inspirational meetings** attempt to build enthusiasm for the company and its products, encourage teamwork, or generally improve organizational morale or interaction. Inspiration, argues Mary Kay Ash, founder and chair of Mary Kay Cosmetics, is the heart of her company's many sales meetings:

> The most important weekly events in our organization are the sales directors' unit sales meetings. Monday morning is the best time for these meetings, because it marks a "new beginning. . . ." In addition to being informative, these meetings provide both inspiration and motivation. Even if the last week's sales were poor, here's a new week to start fresh. . . . When a consultant leaves a sales meeting full of enthusiasm, she has an entire week to let that enthusiasm work for her.[7]

CHOOSING PARTICIPANTS   Group communication works best when everyone in attendance has a reason for being there and can contribute to the discussion. For example, when more than one person has the same expertise or point of view, it may be wise to simplify communication by inviting only one. For the best results, limit the group to no more than ten to twelve people. A meeting half that size makes communication even easier.

In highly structured companies, meetings are usually attended by people from the same organizational level. For example, all seven attendees at a planning meeting might be vice presidents. In less structured firms, there is often less emphasis on seniority and position, with participants more likely to span the entire organization.

SETTING MEETING TIMES   Meetings are often defined by how long they take as well as by what they accomplish. Establish as soon as possible times when a meeting will begin and end, and send this information to participants in memo form. This

INTERVIEW High-Flying Communications

Major Darryl Shyiak, Commanding Officer, Snowbirds Team Leader

Major Darryl Shyiak of the Canadain Forces is responsible for leading the 24 personnel and 11 jet aircraft that make up the 431 Air Demonstration Squadron—otherwise known as the Snowbirds. This highly skilled team weaves its way across North America, thrilling crowds at more than 60 air shows each season.

In Shyiak's world of fast jets and dependency on communication, he has developed a profound belief that the collective strength and effectiveness of teams cannot be assessed by looking solely at the talents or shortcomings of individual members. Rather, he suggests, any great team must be evaluated on how well the individuals work together as professionals to achieve team goals, and by how successfully they motivate each other to overcome obstacles encountered as a team.

When Shyiak works with highly skilled teams of professionals, such as those in the Canadian Forces, his first imperative is to listen and understand the information being communicated. In this way, he can ensure the safety and success of his squadron through a clear, concise, and accurate exchange of information.

Question: How important is effective communication when the Snowbirds are in flight?

Answer: With nine jets flying within four feet of one another at speeds of up to 300 nautical miles per hour there is little tolerance for error. A thorough briefing is conducted before each flight; manoeuvres requiring improvement are discussed, and any potential problems are resolved. When in flight, cues for formation changes are transmitted by radio in short-phrase form, for example, *Smoke on now!* Short phrases ensure that all pilots are clearly aware of the next manoeuvre, for in formation flying each manoeuvre has to be executed precisely at the same time for all aircraft. Any breakdown in communication would compromise the flight safety of the team and choreography of the performance.

Question: Can you describe a situation where effective communication makes a critical difference to the Snowbird team?

Answer: During the performance, each pilot uses visual references from one aircraft while cross-checking with another to stay in formation. Since the pilots cannot see all the other eight aircraft, each communicates via radio transmission to advise others in the formation of potential problems. An example may be from the pilot in aircraft number five who transmits *Five Power*. This communication advises me that I must reduce power to provide the second line astern aircraft with enough power to stay

practice encourages punctuality and pressures people to close meetings on time. Placing time limitations on specific agenda items may also better focus the discussion.

Most meetings last too long. The longer the meeting, the greater the likelihood of distractions. When people are called away for phone calls or begin focusing on other things, real communication is over. The best way to shorten a meeting is to remember why the meeting was called in the first place. Stay focused on the agenda, and help others to maintain the same focus.

CREATING AN AGENDA   An **agenda** is a written document that defines the meeting by telling participants why it was called and what it should accomplish. By forcing people both to prepare in advance for a specific type of discussion and to focus on it

Question: How does your communication style motivate people to work as a team?

Answer: Motivation is best achieved by encouraging and respecting each member's opinions. By seeking their input and implementing it whenever possible, members are assured they have a valuable contribution to make to the team.

Question: As a leader, do you need to communicate in a style that will inspire confidence in members of the team?

Answer: These highly skilled team members already have a high degree of confidence in themselves. I don't consciously communicate in a style to inspire confidence, however there are times when inspiration may be required. By reviewing the significant contribution of each member, the team as a whole is re-energized. Sharing disappointment and, through discussion, finding their own solutions, also reinforces the team's confidence.

Question: Is the communication style of the Snowbirds unique?

Answer: I believe the Snowbirds communicate in a similar fashion to many companies employing the teamwork approach. Members are encouraged to support the team in daily operations by providing input from their specific areas of expertise. I have final responsibility in all matters, but use the team's input as the basis for my decisions.

Question: As a leader, do you require good listening skills?

Answer: Leading the Snowbirds in a nine-plane, military-jet aerobatics performance is a multifaceted task requiring the full support of all aircrew and groundcrew. It's essential that I listen and comprehend all issues brought forward by the team before a performance. Inadequate listening skills would most certainly jeopardize safety and compromise the performance.

Question: If you were to give students of communication one piece of advice regarding team communication, what would that advice be?

Answer: Leaders must develop their own style of communication based on the type of group they're working with. For me, the most appropriate communication approach is one of consensus, but this is made possible by working with a highly professional and skilled team such as the Snowbirds. For others, a different approach may be more suitable. However, effective communication in groups is so much a critical factor of success that one must consciously adopt a style that will not compromise the capabilities of the team.

Source: Interview with Major Darryl Shyiak.

---

while the meeting is underway, the agenda exerts a powerful force both before and during the meeting. In a sense the agenda is the leader's promise to the participants that the meeting will deal with specific issues. Regardless of the size or length of a meeting, an agenda is needed. Generally speaking, agendas may be simple or formal.

Simple Agendas   Typically used for short meetings with few participants, **simple agendas** are written documents that outline meeting goals without describing the sequence of meeting events. Say, for example, that you and three other members of your department are assigned the task of investigating the Internet as a marketing tool. As the group leader, you call a short meeting to discuss the idea and to set idea development and approval schedules. You announce the meeting in a memo, along with the date, time, and place. Although the meeting is short, the project is important, so you also include an agenda like the one in Figure 16-1.

Formal Agendas   When you call a larger meeting, you'll probably need a formal agenda. **Formal agendas** are written documents that schedule the order of business and the approximate time allotted to agenda items. When you distribute a memo to call the meeting, place the formal agenda on a separate sheet and send it to participants several days in advance to give everyone time to prepare. Figure 16-2 is a sample formal agenda for a meeting of the board of directors.

In a meeting that involves various presentations, talk with all presenters in advance to find out how much time they will need. The final agenda should reflect input from everyone participating in the meeting.

CONVENING THE MEETING   You should show direction and purpose when convening a meeting. Open the meeting by restating the specific tasks you hope to accomplish. Although this information is part of your agenda, repetition will focus group attention. Your statement should be positive and forward-looking even if you anticipate problems. Convening the meeting on time shows determination to get the job done.

Let's suppose in the next few sections that you are the leader of a decision-making meeting called to explore the possibility of a reserved-ticket policy for a chain of movie theatres.

FOCUSING THE GROUP'S PROGRESS   Use your agenda to focus the direction of the meeting. Problems arise when participants fail to stay on the topic—when attention drifts to peripheral issues or personal concerns. For example, if one of your participants starts voicing personal concerns or experiences, it may be necessary to say something like, "Nick, I'd really like to hear about that restaurant—after the meeting. Right now, let's talk about. . . ." Be polite and friendly but determined to keep

Figure 16-1   Sample Simple Agenda

Image Worldwide Communication

505 Burnard Street, Vancouver, BC V7X 1R8

Tel: (604) 451-8000 • Fax: (604) 451-8005 • E-mail: imageworld@m-wave.com

Meeting of the Board of Directors

Friday January 21, 2000
12:00 noon - 6:00 p.m.
Board Room 5 on Second Floor

Time	Agenda Item	Presenter
12:00 noon	Lunch	
12:30 p.m.	Previous Minutes	Michelle Carlston
12:35 p.m.	Officer Elections	Michelle Carlston
12:40 p.m.	Overview and Perspective	Michelle Carlston
1:00 p.m.	Report on Finances — Year of 2000	Shigeru Mizuno
1:30 p.m.	Report on Profit Strategy — Year of 2001	Shigeru Mizuno
1:50 p.m.	Impact of Lorenzo Policy	Peter Romanchuk
2:30 p.m.	Health Break	
2:50 p.m.	Solutions in Canada East	Wayne Caroll
3:10 p.m.	Solutions in Greece	Steve Ioannides
3:30 p.m.	Solutions in Australia	Carolyn McLelland
3:50 p.m.	Solutions in Japan	Shigeru Mizuno
4:10 p.m.	Solutions in Italy	Maria Giordano
4:30 p.m.	Cost Benefit of Lorenzo Policy	Peter Romanchuk
4:50 p.m.	Improved South American Marketing	Carlos Viano
5:30 p.m.	Dinner and Guest Speaker	Mario Pucci

Figure 16-2 Sample
Formal Agenda

the group on track. Take the same tack if someone leads the group down an unrelated business path.

Participants who ramble waste precious meeting time. Instead of making statements in concise, focused ways, some people talk around a subject, never quite getting to the point. When you encounter ramblers, summarize what you think they have said and, if necessary, pose a question designed to point them in a specific direction. For instance:

> John, you've been telling us about Odeon Theatre's early experience with advance movie ticketing in Montreal. With only 6 percent of all purchases made in advance, the system seems shaky at best. What does Odeon project for the future?[8]

If the question is focused and direct, the answer should be, too:

> My sources tell me that Odeon is working on the assumption that when word gets

out about the service, one out of four people will reserve their movie tickets in advance.

Summaries can also be used to move the group forward. An effective group leader looks for signs of confusion—puzzled looks, questions asking for clarification, signs of drifting attention. Whenever necessary, the leader can interject a summary, restating what the group has accomplished, what is now being discussed, and where the discussion is heading.

ENCOURAGING ACTIVE PARTICIPATION   In many groups a few people seem to dominate the conversation while others rarely say a word. A group leader typically tries to balance these contributions—to encourage ceaseless talkers to say less and quiet types to say more. Without intervention, the meeting could become a platform for one person's point of view and a true consensus might never be achieved.

Participants who say little can be encouraged to participate by means of specific direct questions. To illustrate:

> Yen, you are our computer expert. Will adding a reserve-seat policy tax our existing computer system? Will we have to upgrade?

Often, when people start talking about an area they know well, they participate more.

Handling an overzealous contributor may be tougher. Start with the direct approach:

> Mohamed, as you can see on the agenda, we have a lot to cover in two hours. I can only give you five more minutes to discuss these survey results.

If this approach fails, redirect the discussion to another person. If necessary, interrupt the person and say something like:

> Your survey demonstrates the need to communicate our policy shift to consumers. Pierre, can you fill us in on the advertising plan?

SETTING THE TONE   As the leader, you set the tone for the meeting through your fairness, work ethic, and control. The following strategies usually contribute to successful meetings.

Recognizing Everyone's Contribution   Not surprisingly, participants who feel that their contributions are valued will contribute more and better work. Even if a proposal is questionable, focus on its positive aspects and lead the group forward. For example, you might say something like:

> Michelle, your idea of using a service like MovieFone, which provides free hardware and software to theatres for advance credit card purchases, is a good one. But I can't get past the $1 fee they charge for every ticket. How much are people willing to pay for a movie? Brian, what does your research tell you about pricing?

Maintaining High Standards   Don't accept slipshod work or opinions that masquerade as facts. You may have to confront people whose statements lack support:

> Brian, what you've just given us is the story of one woman who said she wouldn't pay extra to call ahead and charge her tickets on her MasterCard. What I'm looking for are broader research results. Have you conducted any surveys?

When participants are unprepared with the information that the group needs, you may need to postpone the meeting.

Maintaining Order   Follow your agenda as the discussion moves through the various meeting stages. At the conclusion of each item, summarize points of agreement and disagreement, including any actions that will be taken. These internal summaries improve communication and make it likely that everyone will leave the meeting with the same message.

Maintaining order also involves silencing whisperers. Allow only one person to speak at a time and discourage private conversations.

HANDLING DIFFICULT PEOPLE   Unfortunately, handling difficult people may be the greatest challenge faced by any meeting leader. Because you do not often get to hand-pick participants, sooner or later you will find yourself face-to-face with an **obstructionist**—someone whose personality or hidden agenda threatens group success.

According to various observers of business-meeting behaviour, obstructionists tend to fall into different categories, including blamers, boilers, or know-it-alls. The following suggestions are designed to help you control situations involving these people.

Blamers   Criticizing ideas and even making personal attacks, **blamers** are participants who focus on problems rather than solutions. To counter this aggressive behaviour, try sitting next to a blamer at a meeting and make him or her part of the group's "inner circle." When a blamer makes cutting remarks, resist the temptation to strike back. Wait a few seconds and then try responding in a positive, conciliatory way. If you know that you will be dealing with a blamer at a meeting, plan a strategy for best results.

Boilers   Participants who typically respond with anger when they do not get their way are known as **boilers.** Justified or not, these outbursts can destroy a meeting. Whether the anger is directed at you or someone else, your job as meeting leader is to depersonalize the attack. Business-negotiation experts Juliet Nierenberg and Irene S. Ross believe that self-control is a key element in handling anger:

> You can protect your self-esteem by reminding yourself that the tantrum is a matter of style, and doesn't indicate a particular antagonism toward you. [The person] probably persists because explosions always get results for him, and so he is not likely to change. Your problem is to stand up to him without upping the ante. Adopt good eye contact and a firm stance. Calmly allow him to wind down before you speak, and then deal in unemotional facts on a corrective basis. [Say something like], "What would you like me to do to correct the error?"[9]

Remember that anger can be a method of manipulation—boilers may rant and rave until someone gives in. Resist the temptation, then, to restore peace at a high price. Instead, promise angry participants that you will discuss the problem later when tempers have cooled. When you refuse to make on-the-spot concessions, you rob them of their control and initiative.

Know-It-Alls   Believing they have all the answers before the meeting begins, **know-it-alls** are participants who try to control meetings, often by leading participants in directions that they prefer regardless of group goals. Deal with know-it-alls by establishing in advance equal speaking time for everyone in the room; you can also try to make allies of know-it-alls before the meeting begins.

Dominating or Reluctant Team Members   When one or more members of a team monopolize discussions, or when you have a member who is reluctant to discuss the team's issues for whatever reason, you need to work at balancing the participation. While treating all members with courtesy and respect, you should point out a meeting ground rule that states that communication should be balanced. As well, you

Stand up, speak up, then shut up. The human mind can absorb only what the human seat can endure.

Hugh Shantz
Former Speaker, British Columbia
Legislature

could encourage a balanced discussion by interjecting with comments such as "Carole, thanks for sharing that information. Rima, we haven't heard from you. What are your feelings on the . . . ?"[10]

Lacking Direction   When team members lack direction, the team flounders; members do not know how to get started or what the next step should be. If the team establishes an action plan in the early stages of the process, the members will find it easier to stay on track. As well, a method of project planning such as a Gantt chart or deployment chart will help team members stay focused and ensure that they complete tasks on time.[11]

Digressing   Not staying on topic is a common team problem. When the topic starts to drift, tactfully make the team aware of it, and ask the members to focus on the topic at hand.[12]

Quarrelling   When two or more team members begin to argue, the other team members are left feeling uncomfortable, and frustrated by the team's lack of productivity. If this should occur during your team work, act as the mediator. Mediation may take the form of speaking privately to the members involved; however, if you have already established meeting ground rules, you can reiterate the ground rule discouraging quarrelling and remind them that their actions are unproductive. Remember, however, that the disagreement may be deeper than it seems on the surface. Have these members had difficulty working together before?[13]

Discounting   People sometimes discount the work and opinions of others through their unkind criticism, lack of attention, poor body language, and so on. However, every team member deserves respect and attention. If you sense that some of your team members are being discounted, support them with comments that show consideration and attention. In the hustle and pressure of trying to meet deadlines and quality expectations, it is sometimes easy to slip into this unproductive behaviour yourself, without even realizing you are offending others. Be aware of this possibility and remain diplomatic in all scenarios.[14]

HELPING TO IMPROVE DECISION MAKING   When participants are reluctant to make decisions, the leader must try to move them forward. For example, you might start by asking a probing question:

> Does anyone need more information about how the reserve-seat system works?

Very often, those who persist in making requests for further information—or in otherwise going over ground that you have already covered—are also preventing a decision. When the information is available, the leader can summarize it as succinctly as possible:

> Now that the volume-pricing issue has been clarified, we can make a decision.

When the information is not readily available, you may have to postpone the decision for another meeting. If allowed to go on too long, requests for additional information or debating time can cripple a group. If you sense that this is happening, force a decision.

The opposite problem occurs when the group makes a decision before the leader feels it is ready. In such cases, with perhaps one aggressive faction stampeding the whole group toward a premature vote, you might find facts to be less important than emotions. Some experts recommend delaying tactics to postpone action. For instance:

> I've listened carefully to all the information, but I still have some questions. Bill, tell me again why you think moviegoers are ready for a reserve-seat plan.

You can also tell the group quite bluntly that you think a decision is premature:

> We need more cost information before we can take a vote. I know this is an attractive plan, but we have to justify it to the CEO. Let's get more solid data and meet again next week.

Even if the group does not agree with you, your hesitation will probably delay a decision by generating further discussion.

ENDING THE MEETING At the end of the meeting, summarize what happened and move the group ahead to future action. Your summary should review the discussion so that everyone understands how the group progressed from thought to action. Summarize items needing further consideration, review assignments and deadlines for future work, and set the time and place for the next meeting. Your goal is for every participant to leave the meeting understanding what is expected.

Table 16-1 summarizes the responsibilities of meeting leaders. It also focuses on some of the common failures that result from insufficient leadership control.

Progress Check

1. List seven broad goals for meetings. Is it best to limit a meeting's goals or to try to accomplish as much as possible in as many areas as possible?
2. What is the relationship between distributing an agenda and having a successful meeting?
3. Explain why you agree or disagree with this statement: A meeting leader must have well-developed people skills.

Table 16-1 Responsibilities and Common Failures of Meeting Leaders

Responsibilities	Failures
define the task	trying to accomplish too much
choose participants	including too many people; choosing the wrong people
define the meeting time	allowing meetings to last too long
create an agenda	being poorly focused and producing a disorganized agenda
convene the meeting	starting too late; failing to restate goals
focus the group's progress	permitting the discussion to stray from the topic
encourage active participation	allowing some people to dominate the meeting and others to say nothing
set the meeting's tone	failing to make participants feel valued; allowing slipshod work; permitting disorganization
handle difficult people	losing control
help improve decision making	failing to reach a decision; making a premature decision
end the meeting	permitting participants to leave the meeting room unclear as to what is expected of them and what will happen next

PARTICIPATING IN A MEETING

Let's suppose that the head of your company's human resources department has asked you to participate in a meeting to explore cost-saving options in employee benefits. Although you are not running the meeting, you are a group member because of your expertise on medical insurance and your reputation for active involvement in the human resources activities of the company.

BEING AN ACTIVE PARTICIPANT   Active participation means that each person is a "part owner" of the meeting. The leader's goal is the group's goal—even when there are different points of view. Joining the leader in being responsible for success requires participants to look forward, not backward, and to channel group energy into accomplishing the task.

This type of participation requires *involvement*—a process that begins before you enter the meeting room. For example, when you receive an agenda telling you that new information about your benefits program will be presented, you can make a list of questions that you would like to ask. In this case you might ask the following: Are insurance deductibles increasing? Will premiums rise? How will retired employees be affected by these changes? If you learn that the meeting has been called to make a decision, you should come prepared to support your point of view.

Taking part ownership, therefore, does not mean agreeing with everything that is said by your "partners"—even the managing partners. In fact, with the high cost of pulling people away from their other duties, few managers want to be "yes'd." They feel that if they must bear the expense of a meeting, they should accomplish something that could not be accomplished without the give and take of a meeting.

MAKING AN IMPACT   The following suggestions are designed to improve your value as a group participant. They not only reflect an appreciation of organizational and interpersonal skills but also call upon common sense.

1. *Take a position but be willing to change it.* Groups work best when participants are open to new information and different points of view. If you change your mind, explain why—others who share your view may be convinced if they understand the reasons behind the new position.

2. *Be brief, simple, and organized.* Speak in a direct, clear way so that others will want to listen. Clarity increases when you connect your comments to what has already been said. For example: "I agree with Jim that our health-insurance costs are more than we can afford, but I'm not sure that passing the total increase on to our employees is the right decision."

3. *Engage in discussion, not argument.* While discussion involves an exchange of ideas, argument often results from heated emotional reactions that leave reason behind. Arguments often start when people put their ideas ahead of group objectives and refuse to listen to differing points of view. Worse, they become defensive, suggesting that every expression of disagreement is a personal attack. Even when you believe that the group is making a costly error, remain calm as you state your point of view. The moment you begin shouting is the moment you lose credibility. It is also the moment the group stops functioning.

4. *Avoid personal attacks.* Mutual respect is the key to positive group dynamics. When one person says something like, "Only a fool would make that statement," it becomes impossible for two or more people to work together. When you disagree, criticize the idea, not the person, and try to make your criticism palatable. Being too negative will make it impossible for the group to move forward. Consider the following two statements. Although they both express the same sentiment, the first is inflammatory, the second productive:

> If you had bothered to prepare for this meeting, you would have realized how costly our current medical insurance plan is. It's stupid to suggest continuing with this dinosaur.

Yes, I agree that our medical plan has worked so far. But our costs have skyrocketed and our needs are changing. Our benefits have to change, too.

Resist the temptation to blame others for mistakes or problems. Pointing a finger only gets people angry and obstructs group goals.

5. *Engage in fair play.* Don't dominate the discussion. Give everyone the opportunity to speak. Ironically, participants who try to seize control undermine their own positions when their behaviour is perceived as inconsistent with group goals.

6. *Use nonverbal language to your advantage.* Make eye contact when you begin speaking, speak slowly and calmly even when you are excited, and make sure that your posture communicates authority and confidence. Equally important is paying attention to the nonverbal cues of others—they may tell you what people are really thinking.

Table 16-2 summarizes the responsibilities and failures of meeting participants.

Table 16-2   Responsibilities and Common Failures of Meeting Participants

Responsibilities	Failures
actively participate	failing to regard the goals of the meeting as personal goals
state your position	remaining uninvolved; choosing not to share your views with the group
be organized	rambling from topic to topic; speaking for too long
discuss ideas willingly	arguing with people who disagree
focus on the topic	engaging in personal attacks
engage in fair play	dominating the discussion and otherwise acting unfairly

KEEPING TRACK—MEETING LOGS

The written record of what occurred orally at a meeting is known as meeting minutes or a meeting log. Minutes review group activities (the positions of individual members are recorded), measure productivity (the number of decisions that were made is noted), highlight participation (group members with the greatest influence are cited), and summarize the proceedings (a single, cohesive report adds strength to the group's conclusions).

Minutes are written by the recorder of the group and distributed to participants and others who request them. The most effective minutes are brief but thorough summaries. They begin with the date, time, and place of the meeting.[15]

BRAINSTORMING

When a group of people are expected to solve a problem or simply provide issues for discussion at a meeting, brainstorming is often an effective tool for getting results. Brainstorming, either structured or unstructured, will help a group develop as many ideas in as short a time as possible.

▼ *Structured.* The structured method works well if the point is to avoid having one or two people dominate the meeting. It also works to encourage more introverted members to share their ideas. Every person is given a turn to express opinions, concerns, or ideas. The opportunity to speak rotates so that people wishing to express their ideas must wait their turn.

COLLABORATIVE COMMUNICATION

Collaborating in a Nonterritorial Office

The private office is dead! Although this proclamation may be a bit premature, many companies are rapidly tearing down walls and removing closed doors and other barriers that get in the way of open, collaborative communication.

For example, a package manufacturer invested nearly $1 million to create a "nonterritorial" work environment. At this company, cubicles are the norm as are 250 data ports, located throughout the building, that allow workers to access computer files via portable computers or unassigned computer terminals. When one of the company's account executives learned that a client was dissatisfied with the colour quality of a package proof, he called a spur-of-the-moment meeting in the film production department with the production planner, print supervisor, and a finishing supervisor. Then, using his portable computer, he accessed the client's file to compare the client's request with final in-house specifications. The team quickly solved the problem and called the client for approval.

In contrast to the conventional network of hallways and closed offices, open environments enable workers to see one another on a regular basis and respond together to problems without regard to rank or title. To foster collaborative communication in an open environment, rely on the following communication guidelines:

▼ *Think of open work spaces as environments that encourage communication rather than as intrusions on your personal space.*

▼ *Be focused and disciplined.* Casual conversation can disrupt those around you and it may get in the way of collaboration.

▼ *Take advantage of technology, such as laptop computers and cellular phones, to create communication links.*

▼ *Move away from the group to your small private area only when you must*—for example, when you need a quiet environment for writing. Use special private phone rooms to make or take confidential phone calls.

Nonterritorial work spaces are intended to encourage communication and collaboration.

▼ *Respect the privacy of your co-workers who signal that they want to work alone.* And demand the same respect from others.

Experts believe that technology-equipped open spaces may be here to stay because of their link to teamwork and office productivity.

Questions for Critical Thinking

1. What do you think are the pluses and minuses of an open work environment?
2. Why is the latest communication technology necessary for the success of a nonterritorial work environment?
3. As a new employee, would you prefer a conventional office or an open work space? Why?

Sources: Joshua Macht, "When the Walls Come Tumbling Down," *Inc. Technology* no. 2 (1995): 70–72; Raju Narisetti, "Executive Suites' Walls Come Tumbling Down," *Wall Street Journal,* 29 June 1994, B1, B12; and Kirk Johnson, "In New Jersey, IBM Cuts Space, Frills and Private Desks," *New York Times,* 14 March 1994, B1, B2.

During the rotation, any member may forfeit the opportunity to express an idea. Each of these ideas must be recorded by the facilitator (or the facilitator's assistant) and by the person responsible for preparing the meeting log.[16]

▼ *Unstructured.* This method engenders a freer atmosphere; participants are allowed to express their ideas as they think of them. No ration or waiting for turns is involved. While this creates a very relaxed atmosphere, the problem of domination by one or two members may arise.[17] Peter Scholtes, author of *The Team Handbook*, refers to unstructured brainstorming as the "popcorn" method.

DECISION-MAKING TOOLS

Although there are many tools that can be used to help a group reach a decision, the following three work well with oral communication.

▼ *Multivote.* Once all the issues or suggestions, generated through brainstorming, have been placed in full view of the group, group members often request some clarification or even full discussion of some items. Once the discussion has been satisfied, each member is then given a number of votes that equal one-third the total number of items. All members silently complete their voting by placing a mark next to their top preference; a show of hands may be used as each item is read out by a team member. The votes are then tallied. To reduce the list, those items with the fewest votes are eliminated. The process of voting is repeated as often as necessary until the list is reduced to a manageable size.[18]

▼ *Nominal Group Technique.* NGT is a fairly well-structured method of generating a list of ideas and narrowing it down. Begin the process by brainstorming a list of options; clarification and discussion may take place on any of the issues. The group is then asked to vote on each idea. Voting is based on the following.

3 This issue is of high priority to me.
2 This issue is of medium priority to me.
1 This issue is of low priority to me.
0 This issue is of no priority to me.

Once the votes are tallied, the topics are rearranged according to the numeric priority.[19] Refer to Figure 16-3 for a sample Nominal Group Technique voting sheet.

▼ *Cause-and-Effect Diagrams.* A cause-and-effect diagram is a tool for identifying and organizing the possible causes of a problem in a structured format. It is sometimes called an *Ishikawa diagram* after Kaoru Ishikawa who developed this tool. It is also referred to as a *fishbone diagram* because it looks like the skeleton of a fish, with a head, spine, and bones. Cause-and-effect diagrams help people organize their ideas about the causes of problems.

To prepare a cause-and-effect diagram, begin by drawing the fish (head, spine, and bones) in a location where it can be viewed by the whole group. Write the general problem, inside the head of the fish. At the edge of each large bone, write a category that represents the possible causes for the general problem, for example, *people, procedures, external influences, equipment, materials,* or *policies.* Now the group is ready to brainstorm possible causes that could be contributing to the problem or what we call the effect. These diagrams show only the potential causes.[20] However, they act as an excellent foundation for group discussion and problem solving. Refer to Figure 16-4 for a sample cause-and-effect diagram.

MEETING MECHANICS THAT WORK

When trade talks or treaty negotiations are in the news, someone behind the scenes is planning the mechanics of those meetings. In politics, technical decisions about

ITEM NO.	ISSUES FOR DISCUSSION	TOTAL VOTES				WEIGHTED AVERAGE
		3	2	1	0	
1.	Ticketing of cars parked in the south lot should be reviewed.	7	3	4	1	2.0
2.	New payment schedule for per diem expenses should be reviewed.	12	1	1	1	2.6
3.	Criteria for Employee of the Month award should be reviewed.	10	2	3	0	2.4
4.	Lack of nutritious food in the staff cafeteria should be reviewed.	0	3	9	3	1.0
5.	Purchase of more voice mail boxes should be reviewed.	10	3	2	0	2.5
6.	Upgrading of fax machine should be reviewed.	12	1	1	1	2.6
7.	Purchase of a color photocopier for the Repro. Dept. should be reviewed.	5	8	1	1	2.11
8.	Extension of LAN services for office support staff should be reviewed.	12	2	1	0	2.7
9.	Further TQM training for administrative assistants should be reviewed.	9	3	3	0	2.4
10.	Dissatisfaction of customers due to delayed billing should be reviewed.	14	1	0	0	2.9

REMEMBER:
3 = This problem is of high priority and should be dealt with now.
2 = This problem is of medium priority and should be dealt with as soon as possible.
1 = This problem is of low priority and should be dealt with when possible.
0 = This problem does not affect me or my work.

CALCULATION OF WEIGHTED AVERAGE:
(3 × No. of Votes in Priority 3)
Plus (2 × No. of Votes in Priority 2)
Plus (No. of Votes in Priority 1)
Divide the sum by total number of votes on the problem.

Figure 16-3 Voting Sheet for Nominal Group Technique

scheduling, location, and table and seating arrangements become crucial. Although the mechanics of a business meeting may not have the same urgency as in world politics, they are important because they set the tone for what is to come.

SCHEDULING Although meetings can be scheduled at any time during the day, some times are preferable to others. The first thing in the morning and right after lunch are popular times to schedule meetings. As business becomes more hectic, many more businesspeople now hold working breakfasts, lunches, and dinners. These meetings are often conducted in offices with meals brought in.

Often, meetings are scheduled to accommodate personal working styles. Whereas early risers hold 8:00 A.M. meetings, late workers may hold meetings after hours. When scheduling your meeting, consider also the travel needs of meeting

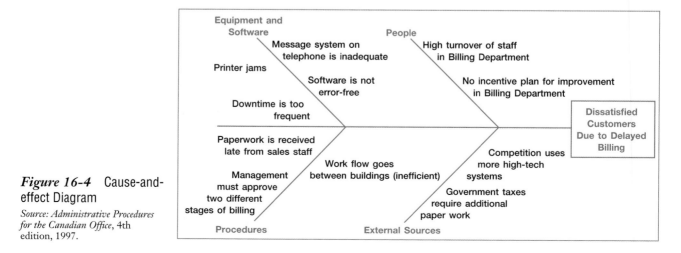

Figure 16-4 Cause-and-effect Diagram

Source: Administrative Procedures for the Canadian Office, 4th edition, 1997.

Conducting Successful Negotiations

We asked Tessa Warschaw, Ph.D., President of the Warschaw Group and best-selling author and corporate consultant, for her views and some practical advice on conducting successful negotiations. An advocate of the win-win negotiating style, Warschaw presents negotiating seminars in Canada, the United States, Asia, and Europe.

▼ Skilled negotiators try to get what they want while helping the other person come away with something, too. Their goal is to win the dollar on the table while leaving the loose change. I learned very early in life that this win-win strategy keeps options open. If you go for the jugular and try to destroy someone, you leave that person little choice but to try to destroy you, too.

▼ Everyone has a different negotiating style, and successful negotiators are always aware of the style of the person with whom they are dealing. They realize that while a passive person is unlikely to attack, a hardball player will go for the game winner. Thus, when negotiating with a hardballer, it is a mistake to mention anything personal because it will be used against you. The key to successful negotiating, especially with a person like this, is being willing to walk away from an idea or even a job.

▼ You can strategize your part of the negotiation, but you can't strategize what the other person will say. That's why it's important to develop contingency plans. If things go in a direction that you don't expect, you can abandon Plan A and go with Plan B or C. Physical preparation is also necessary. Don't eat or drink heavily before a negotiation. It takes energy away at a time when you want to feel lean. And get enough rest. The Japanese realize this. They often fly to North America a week in advance of a meeting. This gives them time to get acclimated, relax, and take care of last-minute details. By contrast, North Americans are on the plane for 20 hours—eating and drinking all the way—get two hours sleep, and walk into the meeting. They think they are ready to negotiate, but they're not.

▼ Recognize that negotiating is really about relationships and about people with different styles trying to make a deal. Start by looking at your own negotiating style. If you are the type who takes care of others at the expense of yourself, you may wind up forgetting your own agenda. You may have to fight against your inclinations in order to be successful. Then analyze your opponents. If they play hardball, be ready for the attack. You can't be shaken or forget your own bottom line.

Source: Interview with Tessa Albert Warschaw.

participants. An 8:00 A.M. meeting that forces people to get up at 5:30 A.M. may be counterproductive. Even if participants do arrive on time, they may be too tired to accomplish much.

If you are having a series of meetings, set the time for the next meeting at the end of the current meeting. Because almost everyone is present, this procedure is the most efficient way to coordinate schedules. To schedule an initial meeting, write a meeting memo instead of using the phone. Trying to work out a schedule by phone can literally take two or three days as you call and recall participants with conflicting schedules.

It is not unusual for employee teams to meet to discuss problems, suggest solutions, and make proposals to management. Nor is it unusual for firms to award prizes for successful teamwork. Motorola, however, has taken the idea of effective teamwork a step further by organizing an international event called the Total Customer Satisfaction Team Competition. Teams are evaluated on the basis of ideas for saving time and money and increasing overall productivity. Interestingly, some team members come from outside customers and suppliers, and all are judged on their ability to share their innovations with other units of the company.

LOCATION   Deciding where to hold a meeting—in your office, in a conference room, in someone else's office, at an outside location—depends on how much space you need and the kind of environment that is best for the group. For example, even if your office is large enough to seat five, you may need a table to spread out papers; perhaps the data projector is available only in the conference room.

Political considerations also affect meetings with clients. Going to a client's office, for example, delivers the implicit message that you are committed to his or her needs.

TABLE AND SEATING ARRANGEMENTS   Table and seating choices can either enhance a meeting or create communication barriers. Here are some considerations:

1. The natural place to sit during a meeting in your office is behind your own desk; your papers are there and so is the phone. However, the desk sends an implicit message that you are in charge. To remove the signal of power, move to a separate space where people can sit across from one another as peers.

2. Position yourself at a conference table so that you can make easy eye contact with influential people—the meeting leader, for example, or a key ally.
   At a rectangular table, sitting across the table rather than side by side makes eye contact possible. At a circular table, all positions are equal. With no "good" seats or "bad" ones, there is no obvious seat of control and the discussion can get intense. At a semicircular table, the leader maintains control by virtue of sitting in the centre.

3. Even when seating is informal, certain people have traditional places at the table. The leader, for example, usually sits at the head of the table while a key ally or the department manager may sit directly across. To avoid mistakes, wait for key players to be seated before choosing your place.

Progress Check

1. Describe the behaviour and attitude of an effective meeting participant.
2. Outline the major discussion categories contained in meeting minutes.
3. What can you learn from the nonverbal cues that surround meetings, including those that involve meeting location, table choice, and seating arrangements?

4. Choose your seat with your own purposes in mind. If you intend to provide input, choose a controlling position (say, toward the head of the table). If you have little to say, choose a spot that will allow you to remain relatively unnoticed.

5. Consider also where "troublemakers" will sit. When you expect dissension, arrange the seating to separate troublemakers from one another. Figure 16-5 shows two alternative seating arrangements.

The Art of Negotiating

Many meetings are held for the specific purpose of making a deal. You negotiate with suppliers for more favourable prices, with prospective clients on contract terms, with your counterparts in other departments to divide the workload on important projects. In every case the goal is mutual benefit. A negotiation is a process of give and take in which both parties try to leave the bargaining table with what they perceive as a "good deal."

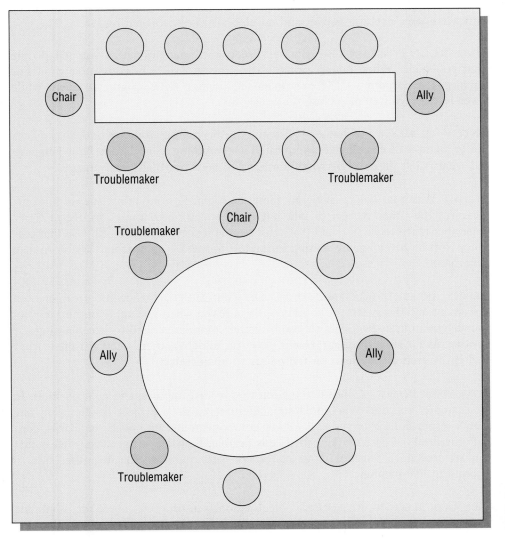

Figure 16-5 Seating Arrangements for Effective Meetings

Admittedly, negotiations often involve people who personally dislike one another and may even take place between bitter adversaries. When the atmosphere is professional, however, opposing positions and negative feelings are beside the point—ultimately, all participants are trying to achieve something that benefits them by finding a common ground that is acceptable to everyone.

Mutual benefit, for example, characterized negotiations between a United Way fund raiser and a group of truckers. At a 6:00 A.M. meeting, the fund raiser handed out pledge cards and pencils to the truckers and asked for contributions. A particularly grumpy driver stood up and told the fund raiser what he could do with the pencil. Keeping his negotiating goal in mind (raising money), the fund raiser calmly replied, "I'll be happy to do whatever you like with that pencil after you sign the pledge card." The comment disarmed the group and convinced everyone—even the disgruntled driver—to make a pledge. In the end, both sides won.[21]

NEGOTIATING STRUCTURE

Although negotiating styles and tactics develop with experience, there is a basic structure to most negotiations. The key elements in the process combine common sense with important communication skills.[22]

KNOW YOUR OBJECTIVES BEFOREHAND   Decide what you want to come away with when your meeting is over and develop a strategy for getting it.

STATE YOUR POSITION   Be concise, direct, and unemotional as you tell people what you want. When it will expedite the process, use team communication. For instance, the corporate CEO may begin negotiating with a potential client while lower-level executives may close the deal.

→ **Cross Reference**
We discussed listening in Chapter 1, pages 14–19.

LISTEN   As we saw in Chapter 1, listening means paying attention both to the facts and to nuances of meaning communicated in everything from tone to body language and what is left unsaid. Use what you learn to your negotiating advantage.

THINK   When no one is saying anything, be silent. For one thing, silence not only pressures the other person to talk but gives you time to think. In negotiations, remember that silence is a void that most people feel compelled to fill. Use that tendency to your advantage by waiting for people to speak—and perhaps say more than they intend.

DEFINE AREAS OF AGREEMENT AND DISAGREEMENT   Define the areas of both agreement and disagreement as you see them. Even when you agree on nothing but your negotiating goals, establish goodwill and common ground by accentuating the positive. As for areas of disagreement, don't try to debate them—just list them. Your goal is to reach a consensus on the points to be negotiated.

CONCEDE A POINT   Concede the point that is least important to your position. If, for example, you and a potential supplier disagree on a project deadline, on one party's responsibility for supplying a key component, and on quality standards, concede the deadline date if your schedule is flexible. Be positive but make it clear that you are making a sacrifice. Your concession sets the stage for the other side to respond in like manner.

Don't negotiate with yourself. Have the patience to wait for the other fellow to make a counteroffer after you've made one.

Richard Smith
Partner, Smith, McWorter & Pachter

SEEK CONCILIATORY RESPONSES   Negotiations can proceed only if the other side is as willing to compromise as you are (or should be). For example, if your opponent

QUESTION OF ETHICS

Unsuccessful Communication at General Electric

Robert Lemire, an engineer for General Electric, was mesmerized by the words of John F. Welch, GE's chairman. Sitting in a darkened auditorium, Lemire was transformed when Welch spoke, on a videotape, of GE as a "boundaryless company," where ideas were more important than bureaucratic red tape. Managers, said Welch, were ready to listen to anyone with a new idea because GE "ignores hierarchy and functional boundaries and cares only about the value of an idea, rather than the title of its source."

Taking the words of this speech to heart, Lemire became a man with a mission—a corporate gadfly committed to doing everything possible to improve General Electric's products and productivity. Committed to new ideas rather than traditional channels of upward communication, Lemire's first suggestion was a Department of Creativity and Innovation, which would report directly to Welch. Under his plan, employees would be given an 800 number and encouraged to call in new ideas. A life-size photo of Welch, along with the slogan "Tell it to Jack," would personalize the program.

Lemire wrote a letter directly to Welch describing his vision. Although Welch rejected the idea, Lemire was undeterred. He decided to take a different approach to convince top management to adopt the plan. This time Lemire worked his way up the chain of command, starting with his boss and his boss's boss. Ultimately, his letter reached Tamir Hamid, general manager of GE's power-plant systems, who called Lemire in for a two-hour meeting. According to Lemire, Hamid's goal was to convince him that he was pursuing a "stupid idea" and that he should drop it. In a subsequent letter to Lemire, Hamid wrote: "During the past months this suggestion has been reviewed by no less than four managers at three different organizational layers, as well as with our patent counsel, and each has come to the same conclusion. . . . It does not warrant further discussion. . . . I

can only recommend that you reexamine your suggestion's merit, and move on to other challenges facing our business."

Although Hamid's response disappointed Lemire, he did not abandon his idea. He made his next big move at General Electric's annual meeting. He flew, at his own expense, to the site of the meeting, where he once again heard Welch talk about General Electric as a company without boundaries. Inspired by the rhetoric, Lemire stood up and nominated himself to GE's board of directors. He told shareholders that although Welch had some brilliant ideas for improving GE, he was like "the naked emperor . . . who needs an honest lieutenant to tell him when he is naked." With no one willing to second his nomination, Lemire left the meeting with yet one more plan.

He sent a 35-question survey on creativity over General Electric's electronic mail system in an attempt to collect hard data on the company's current innovation program. Lemire's e-mail was cut off as soon as his supervisors realized what he was doing. Lemire was fired two weeks later and escorted by security guards out of the General Electric plant. His two-year crusade to establish a Department of Creativity and Innovation had ended in failure.

Questions for Critical Thinking

1. What was wrong with Lemire's communication style? Was he seen as a *part of* the group or *apart from* the group?
2. Was Lemire performing an important service for GE? Was his problem one of style rather than content?
3. Do you think GE gave Lemire's suggestion a fair hearing? What more, if anything, should managers have done to improve communication? Was GE justified in firing Lemire?

Source: William M. Carley, "A Corporate Gadfly Takes Boss Seriously—A Serious Mistake," *Wall Street Journal,* 14 April 1995, A1, A10.

---

counters your concession by saying, "Okay, I can supply the component without additional cost," you have made progress. If no concession is offered, try to learn more about the issues dividing you by asking questions. You may discover, for instance, that your quality expectations are the problem. In your opponent's view, you may be asking for so much that further negotiation is impossible. Ironically, just defining the key stumbling block may put the negotiation back on course—there may now be room for movement on both sides.

When no concessions are made and no explanations given, negotiations have broken down. Resist the temptation to concede too much just to get a deal—in the end you will probably be dissatisfied. Instead, suggest another meeting after both parties have had time to think.

So far, the main theme of this chapter has been the principle that successful group communication during meetings means defining your personal communication style in each role that you play. Remember, however, that you will frequently be limited by corporate cultural expectations. Each firm's unique personality determines which individuals attend meetings and what is expected of them, the setting and frequency for meetings, and even the shape of the table and where people sit. While some companies require daily meetings, others meet once a month; while some companies encourage active involvement, others use meetings as slide theatres where everyone sits back and watches the show.[23] In the next section, we will explore informal business conversations.

Progress Check

1. Describe the overriding goal of negotiation and a model road map for achieving that goal.
2. Explain how silence and compromise are effectively used during negotiations.

Informal Business Conversations

If formal meetings occupy one end of the oral communication spectrum, brief, informal business conversations occupy the other. **Informal business conversations** are unscheduled meetings held on the spur of the moment, with as few as two and as many as four people. Some phone calls are also included in this category. Many observers believe that the real business of a company takes place during these conversations. They point out that when conversation time is limited and agendas narrow, communication must be focused and productive. Indeed, some companies design their buildings with these meetings in mind. Corning Glass, for example, designed an engineering building with escalators rather than elevators to encourage conversation.[24]

Like other forms of business communication, the most productive brief encounters benefit from preparation. In a basic sense, being prepared means having a personal agenda—a mental list of what you want to accomplish. It also means having at your disposal the questions and documents that you will need during conversation. Before you see a colleague in the hall and ask, "Do you have a minute to talk about the production problem?" you should know what you want when the conversation is over.

The success of brief encounters also depends a great deal on your attitude. You must be as committed to getting something done in this setting as you are in a formal meeting. Give the conversation your undivided attention. If you divide your time between it and reading phone messages or giving instructions to an assistant, you are sending a clear message that you do not consider the conversation important.

IMPROVING INFORMAL MEETINGS

Here are some suggestions to maximize the effectiveness of brief, informal conversations. We will then examine some additional requirements for phone communication.

▼ *Keep a limited agenda.* You are squeezing important business into unscheduled time, so don't try to accomplish too much.

▼ *Be sensitive to other people's schedules.* Unless it is urgent, don't interrupt managers when they are facing deadlines. Wait for a more opportune time. And don't be put off if a colleague tells you to come back later. This is not a brush-off, just good business.

▼ *Be sensitive to other people's feelings.* If a co-worker seems angry or upset, postpone your conversation. Your idea won't get a fair hearing.

▼ *Follow basic conversation etiquette.* Don't monopolize the conversation (people will stop listening); don't interrupt (let people finish before you begin speaking); stick to the topic (it's the only way you will get anything done); and keep your emotions in check (make your points through solid argument and support, not anger).

▼ *Be conscious of your colleague's position in the organization.* Think twice before criticizing your supervisor. Even when a supervisor asks for feedback, open criticism may put you in the middle of a minefield with no safe ground in sight.[25]

▼ *Send follow-up memos.* Some conversations require follow-up memos to summarize what was said and what actions will be taken. For example, if during a meeting with a co-worker you agree to conduct a marketing survey but discuss no details, write a memo stating exactly what you will do.

▼ *Learn to deflect conversations.* There will be times when you do not want to divulge information—perhaps a co-worker asks you about a new project before you have presented it to your manager. In these cases, resist the pressure to respond to direct questions. Instead, deflect the question by saying something like, "I'm reporting to Bill about this next Tuesday. I'll be glad to discuss it when I pass that stage." Deflection may be necessary if an issue is politically sensitive or a project is someone else's responsibility.

▼ *Listen for the subtext.* Nonverbal cues can create misunderstandings or communicate such positive attitudes as attentiveness and interest.

COMMUNICATING BY PHONE

Conversations that take place on the phone are crucial to business success. Mary Kay Ash explains how two of her sales managers make the phone an integral part of business communication:

> I know one national sales manager who calls each of his 35 sales representatives at least once a week. Although he no longer personally makes customer calls, constant communication with his salesforce keeps him abreast of what's going on in the field. [Another sales manager] makes it perfectly clear to each [sales representative] that he's never too busy to accept a call. When he's not available, he makes a point of returning every call from his salespeople before he goes to sleep each night.[26]

The following suggestions are designed to help you improve the effectiveness of your telephone communication:

▼ *Identify yourself.* When placing a call to someone who does not know you, clearly identify yourself and the organization you represent. When answering a call, identify yourself with your full name ("Good morning. This is customer service. Amy Quin speaking").

▼ *Leave clear messages.* When you cannot reach someone, leave your name, title, company name, and phone number as well as a specific time to return your call ("Don, you can call me back anytime after 3:00"). With voice mail, you should leave a complete message. Messages improve efficiency because the person you are calling can follow up on the problem before returning your call.

▼ *Realize the subtext.* Each of the following behaviours sends a clear message of control: waiting a week to return a call (or not returning it at all), carrying on a conversation with someone in your office while on a call, or interrupting an important meeting to take calls.

▼ *Prioritize your phone calls.* If you have four phone calls to make in the next fifteen minutes, start with those that you can finish quickly. By getting your short calls out of the way, you will be able to devote full attention to your final—and most important—call.

▼ *Return every phone call or redirect it elsewhere.* When you are away from your desk, forward your calls to your voice mail. Because delays in responses imply that the caller is unimportant, try to return calls promptly even if the message is "Thanks for your call, Matthew. I don't have the information you requested, but as soon as I do, I'll get right back to you."

▼ *Handle interruptions properly.* When you are on one call and another comes in, put the first party on hold—but just long enough to get the name and number of the second caller. It is rude to carry on an extensive conversation with a second caller while the first is put on hold. In general, avoid putting people on hold for long periods. When you have to pause in order to look for information, offer to call the person back.

▼ *Think about the impression you make.* It is easy to make a poor impression on the phone. Some cases in point:

> "I'm sorry. Tracy isn't here. She's in the bathroom."
> "That's not my department. I can't help you."
> "Why are you calling me for this?"

Say instead:

> "Tracy is not at her desk right now. May I take a message?"
> "Although I can't handle that problem, I will transfer you to Chris Anderson, who can."
> "I would like to help you get to the bottom of this, but I'm not sure how."

▼ *Build goodwill with customers.* When a customer calls with a complaint, take down the facts, promise to follow through, and call back. And don't be defensive. Instead of saying, "We've never had a complaint before on that item," tell the customer that you will investigate the problem and get back with an answer.

During peak selling season, more than 400 telephone agents handle as many as 20 000 calls a day to the Neiman Marcus Christmas Book. With this volume of calls, phone agents must have patience, wisdom, impeccable manners, common sense, and a rapid-fire response. The latter quality was particularly important when phone agent Betty Ortega handled a call from a Latin American customer who wanted to buy one of the *actual* fashion models who appeared in the catalogue. "I'm sorry, the models are not for sale," said Ortega. "Could I help you with something else?"[27]

▼ *Make calls when others are likely to receive them.* When you call people on a regular basis, keep track of the most convenient times to reach them. Then call only during those times. For example, the best time to reach many busy executives is before 9:30 in the morning.

▼ *Learn to end a conversation.* Ending a conversation when the other party wants to continue talking can be difficult. "Usually when I'm late for an appointment, it's because I don't know how to cut people off on the telephone," admits Michele Ateyeh, president of jewellery manufacturer Angela Cummings, Inc. "I'm afraid to be rude."[28]

How do you end a phone conversation that has gone on too long? Interrupting, summarizing, and promising to help often works. Say something like, "Let me restate what I think you're saying." Another way to

Employees must be with Heath at least three years before they can answer the phone. The policy ensures that customers are greeted by someone who knows the ropes. It's had a very positive effect.

Janice Heath
President, Heath Electronic
Manufacturing Company

end a conversation is to focus on a solution rather than a problem: "I hear the problem. What do you think we should do to solve it?" This technique is especially helpful when people describe a problem in detail, forgetting that what they really need is a solution. When these techniques fail, be honest: "I'm swamped with work, so I'll have to speak with you next week."

What's Ahead

Knowing how to communicate effectively in both speech and writing will help prepare you to meet the challenge of finding a job. We will turn next to the subject of employment communication, as we explore writing résumés and cover letters in Chapter 17 and employment interviewing in Chapter 18.

STUDENT RESOURCE CENTRE

Summary of Chapter Objectives

1. *List the responsibilities of a meeting leader.*

    Meeting leaders define and limit the task of meetings, choose participants, set meeting times, and create agendas. The leader also convenes the meeting, focuses the group's progress on stated objectives, encourages active participation, sets the tone for the meeting, facilitates decision making, brings the meeting to a close, and manages difficult people.

2. *Classify formal meetings according to seven general purposes.*

    The primary purposes of meetings are (1) to give or exchange information, (2) to develop new ideas, (3) to make decisions, (4) to delegate work or authority, (5) to collaborate, (6) to persuade, and (7) to inspire and build enthusiasm. The leader has the primary responsibility for defining the meeting's purpose.

3. *Describe a simple agenda and a formal agenda.*

    The agenda is a written document that tells participants what a meeting hopes to accomplish. Simple agendas are used for short meetings with relatively few participants. They inform participants about general goals without listing the sequence of events. Formal agendas, which are used in larger, longer meetings, list the order of business and the approximate time allotted to each agenda item.

4. *Identify the responsibilities of meeting participants.*

    Effective participants work with the leader to accomplish the group's goals. The contributions of meeting participants can be improved if they are willing to take and change positions; to present ideas in simple, organized ways; to avoid arguments and personal confrontations; to commit themselves to fair interchanges with other group members; and to understand nonverbal cues.

5. *Explain the purpose and content of meeting minutes/logs.*

    Meeting minutes provide a written record of what occurred at a meeting. Minutes record the positions of individual members on key issues, state the number and nature of decisions that were made, highlight individual participation, and summarize the proceedings and conclusions.

6. *Explain how brainstorming and decision-making tools work for teams.*

    Brainstorming, multivoting, the nominal group technique, and cause-and-effect diagrams are effective methods for communicating orally and sharing concerns, preferences, and solutions. With the assistance of a facilitator, these methods can be very effective.

7. ***Describe the mechanics of a meeting and their influence on a meeting's outcome.***

The mechanics of a meeting involve technical decisions about scheduling, location, the meeting table, and seating arrangements. These decisions set the subtext for the meeting and often establish who is in control. Mechanics provide nonverbal cues that are often invaluable to achieving group and personal objectives.

8. ***Explain the steps in the negotiating process.***

Negotiation is a process that involves give and take between two or more parties at a bargaining table. As a negotiator, you must know what you want to accomplish before you begin. At the start of the session, state your position and then listen to the response. Remaining silent gives you time to think and pressures the other parties to talk. When positions are clear, define agreements and disagree-

ments and be willing to concede a point that is not critical to your position. Look for similar concessions from your negotiating partner and, if you do not find them, try to encourage conciliation.

9. ***List ways to improve informal face-to-face and telephone business conversations.***

To improve the quality of informal business conversations, limit goals, be sensitive to the scheduling problems and feelings of others, learn the art of deflecting conversations, and be alert to nonverbal cues. Conversations that adhere to the rules of etiquette and are followed up with summarizing memos are more likely to succeed.

To improve telephone communication, identify yourself at the start of the conversation, be conscious of the impression that you make, and learn how to end conversations. Poor impressions are made when interruptions are handled badly, when phone calls are not returned, and when messages are unclear. In every phone call, focus on what is said, what is left unsaid, and on the opportunity to establish goodwill.

Review and Discussion Questions

1. Why is it important to communicate effectively at meetings? *(Ch. Obj. 1, 4)*

2. When you lead a meeting, what are your responsibilities? *(Ch. Obj. 1)*

3. What are seven general tasks that meetings can accomplish? *(Ch. Obj. 2)*

4. Distinguish between simple and formal agendas. *(Ch. Obj. 3)*

5. What are the responsibilities of a meeting participant? *(Ch. Obj. 4)*

6. What are meeting minutes, and what function(s) do they serve? *(Ch. Obj. 5)*

7. Summarize the mechanics that can affect the outcome of a meeting. *(Ch. Obj. 7)*

8. Describe the steps involved in effective negotiation. *(Ch. Obj. 8)*

9. How can you improve your communication effectiveness during brief, informal business conversations? *(Ch. Obj. 9)*

10. Summarize tips for improving telephone communication. *(Ch. Obj. 9)*

Application Exercises

1. Think of a meeting in which you participated that didn't seem to accomplish much (perhaps a meeting at your present job, a former job, at school, or at a club). Analyze the failure of the meeting: Why didn't it "work"? What might the leader have done differently to make it more effective? What could you have done? *(Ch. Obj. 1, 4)*

2. Now think of a meeting in which you participated that accomplished a great deal. Analyze the success

of this meeting: Why was it more effective than the one you discussed in Exercise 1? What did the leader do differently, if anything? What did you do differently? What tools were used to reach these decisions? *(Ch. Obj. 1, 4, 6)*

3. Exercises 3–5 deal with an actual meeting in which you are a leader or participant. Classify this meeting according to its general purpose. What do you hope to accomplish? *(Ch. Obj. 2)*

4. Create a formal agenda for this meeting. Be as specific as you can regarding participants and the order of business. If you are a participant rather than the leader, create what you feel is a probable agenda. *(Ch. Obj. 3)*

5. During the meeting or immediately afterward, write out the minutes to record what happened. Make your minutes concise but thorough; if it's applicable, use the outline format discussed in this chapter. Make sure that your recorded minutes fulfill all the functions discussed for meeting minutes or meeting logs in this chapter. *(Ch. Obj. 5)*

6. During meetings, there are nearly always some people who dominate the conversation while others sit there and say very little. As a meeting leader, how can you deal with this situation? *(Ch. Obj. 1)*

7. Think of meetings that you've either attended or led in which there were one or more blamers, boilers, or know-it-alls. Using the suggestions made in the chapter, list some specific statements that you might have made to help deal with these obstructionists. *(Ch. Obj. 1, 4)*

8. According to legend, King Arthur of Britain held regular meetings with his nobles at a circular table—whereby they became known as the "Knights of the Round Table." Why do you think Arthur chose a round table for his meetings? What are the advantages and disadvantages of this arrangement? *(Ch. Obj. 7)*

9. Suppose that you want to ask your boss (current or former) for a raise. You honestly feel that you deserve a raise, but you also realize that because money is tight, getting your raise will require good negotiating skills. Write a detailed description of each stage that you might encounter during this negotiation. What are your boss's objections likely to be? How might you counter those objections? What are

you likely to agree or disagree about during the course of negotiation? *(Ch. Obj. 8)*

10. Your instructor will ask for two volunteers to role-play a negotiation in front of the class. The participants may choose the subject about which they will negotiate; possibilities include a promotion, a new job, or a conflict over a work-related issue. If they wish, they can take a few minutes to prepare by thinking about their respective positions and objectives. Then they will conduct the negotiation while the class listens. (Unless one of the participants actually feels that the other has successfully negotiated a concession, it is not necessary to resolve the issue.)

   After the participants have finished their negotiation (or your instructor has called it a tie), the class should give the two negotiators feedback about their techniques. Did they listen to each other well? Did they do an effective job of listing similarities and differences, conceding points, or seeking responses? What advice would you give to each? *(Ch. Obj. 8)*

11. Why is it important to communicate effectively even if you just happen to encounter a business colleague in a hallway? *(Ch. Obj. 9)*

12. Phil calls Nancy because he wants to update her on a project that he's working on. Nancy's assistant takes a message because Nancy is in a meeting. Phil waits a week, gets no response, and dials Nancy again. This time, she answers the phone herself and seems a bit flustered when Phil identifies himself. "Oh, uh, I'm sorry I didn't call you back earlier," she mumbles. "But I knew we were late sending those reports to you, and I thought you were going to complain about it. I thought I'd let Sam [her boss] call you back instead; I don't get paid to listen to people yell about late orders."

   What is your opinion of Nancy's telephone communication skills? How could she improve them? *(Ch. Obj. 9)*

ACT: Applied Communication Techniques

Begin by referring to the sections up to and including Abbreviations and Numbers in Appendix II. Change all underlined words to abbreviations, and correct any errors in the way the numbers are written. Then correct the grammar, spelling, and usage errors in the following sentences. Check your answers in Appendix V.

1. Eleven employees formed the audience for the manager's twenty-minute presentation.

2. An article about team comunications was sent to us

through the facsimile machine.

3. 75 percent of the audience stood and cheered for an encore.

4. The company printed their profit and loss statements so the executive team could discuss the future direction for the company.

5. 15 participants is to large of a team for productive brainstorming to ocurr.

6. During the oral presentation, the group displayed a graph showing the <u>wholesale</u> operation.

7. The <u>manuscript</u> (<u>copyright</u> 1998) was accepted by the publisher.

8. Can 7 people reach a concensus?

9. Why are there only ten people on this team and twelve people on the opposing team?

10. Glassmith <u>Incorporated</u> is the finest stained-glass shop in Scarborough.

Building Your Research Skills

Set up an interview with a businessperson in your community to discuss the role(s) that meetings play in his or her organization. What types of meetings does this person attend most often (informational, brainstorming, and so forth)? Do the meetings seem constructive? Why or why not? Ask this individual to recall effective meetings and to explain why they seemed more worthwhile than others.

Write a one- to two-page summary of your discussion with this person. What conclusions can you reach regarding the ingredients of an effective meeting? Your instructor may ask you to present your conclusions to the class.

Building Your Teamwork Skills

This chapter discusses the importance of paying attention to the "subtext" of a conversation. Subtext, for example, can include a wide variety of nonverbal cues, such as eye contact, gestures, posture, and tone of voice. This exercise will help you think about the ways in which subtext has influenced conversations that you yourself have had with others.

Your instructor will divide the class into small groups. Each team member should think of conversations in which he or she has participated and in which subtext has played a role, either in making the conversation more or less effective. One member of each team should list everyone's experiences.

Now have someone from each team present the team's list to the class as a whole. Explain the role, whether positive or negative, played in each instance by subtext. What conclusions can the class draw about nonverbal cues that facilitate or block communication?

Weblinks Internet Resources for this Chapter

Three Most Important Secrets of Effective Meetings
http://www.openthis.com/secrets.htm

Better Brainstorming
http://cgi.amcity.com/louisville/stories/032497/smallb3.html

Recording the Minutes of a Formal Meeting
http://www.cowan.edu.au/secretariat/policy/ad/ad009.html

How to Handle Difficult People
http://www.smartbiz.com/sbs/arts/bly59.htm

Negotiating Skills
http://www.humber.ac.uk/su/leader/negotiation.htm

CASE STUDIES

DIVERSITY CASE:

CEO Holds Meetings of a Different Kind

Reuben Mark, chairman of Colgate-Palmolive Company, does something different with his Saturdays: he spends them in a community centre in New York City's tough Lower East Side. There, Mark and his wife, Arlene, tutor, praise, scold, and, in general, mentor a group of teenagers from the ghetto. Their goal: to persuade the teens to stay in school.

Since the late 1980s, the Marks have spent their Saturdays hanging out with a group of kids, all of whom have special educational or emotional needs. Group members do homework, play board games, discuss problems, or just horse around. The Marks circulate among the group, talking to the kids about their progress and their goals. Get-togethers are occasionally followed by trips to neighbourhood restaurants.

Meetings, of course, were not always friendly; in the beginning, fights broke out frequently. Progress began when students realized that the conflicts were self-defeating and ultimately developed their own code of conduct. Among the rules: no weapons, no violence, and no insults (each insult incurs a 25-cent fine).

Says Maritza Pineiro-Hernandez, one member of the group: "At first I didn't think the Marks would make a difference, but they did. I would have quit by the seventh grade." Instead, Maritza plans to enroll at university.[29]

Questions and Applications

1. Do you think the Mark's informal communication approach would change if the group size were 5, 10, 20, or 30? If so, explain how it would change.

2. How would you prepare to become a communication leader for a group of similar kids?

3. Describe how a group similar to this one should decide on and negotiate rules for group meetings.

CORPORATE CASE:

The Gift of Good Communication Pays Off

When Phil Tumminia first called on Henry Rowan, a businessperson who had graduated from M.I.T., Tumminia had no idea that this simple visit would end up breaking records.

Tumminia was the director of the Glassboro State College Development Fund; Rowan was the founder and head of Inductotherm Industries, an industrial furnace maker with $468 million in annual sales. Tumminia's cold call was the beginning of a two-year series of visits and discussions between the two men. The ultimate result was that Glassboro State College received one of the largest donations ever given to a public institution: $100 million. The college changed its name to Rowan College in honour of their prime benefactor.

To say the least, Tumminia's success demonstrates the importance of good communication. In fund-raising, as in many other sales-oriented jobs, success often comes only from a long, patient interchange between fund-raiser and client.

After his first visit, Tumminia stayed in regular contact with Rowan. That meeting led to more than 50 other meetings. Much of their rapport resulted from the fact that Tumminia focused on Rowan's interests and needs. Says Tumminia: "We talked a lot about what we were doing and what [Mr. Rowan's] interests were. I would make very specific suggestions about what we could do to try to address what he wanted."

Their discussions revealed, for example, that Rowan liked the idea of endowing a new engineering school. Although he could have donated money to an existing engineering department, "building one from scratch," says Rowan, was "much more exciting." Clearly, Rowan wanted to make a difference. When Tumminia realized the source and nature of Rowan's enthusiasm, they started planning the creation of a new school at Glassboro. Ultimately, Rowan agreed to provide the $100-million endowment.

Although Henry Rowan's gift makes him a star in fund-raising circles, Phil Tumminia is modest about his own accomplishment: "You can only do what you're capable of doing. In this case, I listened to what he was saying."[30]

Questions and Applications

1. Why do you think Tumminia was successful in obtaining this large donation?

2. What was Tumminia's personal agenda? What was Rowan's?

3. Explain this case in terms of the principles of person-to-person communication discussed in this chapter.

Chapter

17

Targeting Your Career: Résumés and Cover Letters

The best career advice given to the young is, "Find out what you like doing best and get someone to pay you for doing it."

Katherine Whitehorn
Columnist

After studying this chapter, you should be able to:

1. Describe eight distinct stages of the job search.
2. Describe the process of targeting career opportunities that link to your interests, skills, traits, and accomplishments.
3. Describe a résumé layout that is computer-scanner-friendly.
4. List the elements and types of effective résumés.
5. State suggestions for faxing a résumé.
6. List the elements of an effective cover letter.
7. Describe specific networking techniques.
8. List formal sources that can assist you in finding a job.
9. Describe how the Internet can be an effective job search tool.
10. Explain the basic approach to answering help-wanted ads.

"We Want You to Be Our CEO"

No one would ever call Ben & Jerry's Homemade, Inc., ice cream maker of such gourmet flavours as Cherry Garcia, a traditional business. Rather, they're known as those wacky ice cream makers with the '60s philosophy. Founded in 1978 by boyhood friends Ben Cohen and Jerry Greenfield, Ben & Jerry's marched to its own corporate drummer as it grew from a storefront operation to a nationwide business.

Starting out in 1977 as a homemade ice cream parlour in a renovated gas station, they have grown to 132 scoop shops in three countries and three ice cream manufacturing plants. In the company's early years, Greenfield and Cohen did a remarkable job of creating a brand identity and expanding the company. The firm prospered as Ben & Jerry's gourmet flavours took hold of America's imagination—and its sweet tooth. By 1994, however, the pair realized that the company needed an infusion of professional management talent to handle $140 million in annual sales and plans for overseas expansion. Plagued by shrinking sales and increasing competition, a slumping stock price, and the public's growing fear of fat, Ben Cohen made the decision to step aside as CEO—to hand over power to an outsider who could handle a maturing business in the midst of financial crisis.

Not unexpectedly, Greenfield and Cohen undertook a very special kind of job search to find the new CEO. They announced a contest inviting Ben & Jerry's customers to explain, in 100 words or less, "Why I would be a great CEO for Ben & Jerry's." The "Yo! I'm your CEO" contest yielded more than 22 000 applications, including résumés written on the icings of cakes.

As a back-up, Ben & Jerry also retained the services of an executive search firm, which convinced them that they would have to remove the CEO's salary cap in order to attract the kind of manager they needed. (The cap limited the salary of the highest paid executive to seven times that of the company's lowest paid worker.)

However, other things were not open to negotiation: Greenfield and Cohen required that the new CEO be committed to the company's "community focused culture," which championed social causes affecting children and families; have broad managerial experience and "the skills and vision to see around the corners of our future business development;" and a burning desire "to wear jeans to work."

The person who fit the bill was Robert Holland Jr. Discovered by the search firm (he did not enter the contest), Holland got the job because of his "character, experience, and passion for social causes," said Cohen. He also got it because of his vision to turn the company around through the introduction of new products and overseas expansion. ▼

Sources: "No Rocky Road; as Ben & Jerry's New CEO, Robert Holland Will Get His Licks In," *People Weekly* (February 20, 1995): 554; Joanne S. Lublin, "Ben & Jerry's Scoffs at Tradition, Hires Some Suits to Find a CEO," *Wall Street Journal*, 10 August 1994, B1; Nancy Hass, "Squares Need Not Apply," *Newsweek* (June 27, 1994): 44; Barnaby J. Feder, "Ben Leaving as Ben & Jerry's Chief," *New York Times*, 14 June 1994, 44; William M. Bulkeley, "Ben & Jerry's Is Looking for Ben's Successor," *Wall Street Journal*, 14 June 1994, B1; and Claudia Dreiful, "Ben & Jerry: Passing the Scoop," *New York Times Magazine*, 18 December 1994, 38–41; "Ben & Jerry Write Book on Corporate Behaviour," *Edmonton Journal*, 21 June 1997, 10.

Chapter Overview ---

Although you can't expect to apply for too many jobs via a nationwide contest or write your résumé on cake icing, you can expect that every job search will be different and that every company will have a unique personality that you must recognize and learn if your search is to be successful. With uncertainty and change as facts of business life today, flexible, responsive employment communication is critical—as is the ability to tailor your communication to the needs of both specific employers and the general job market.

This chapter explores eight distinct stages of the job-search process, which are summarized in Figure 17-1. This process starts with self-analysis and moves quickly to targeting first a field and then a specific job. It involves creating a hard copy résumé and an electronic résumé—a statement of your career objectives, experience, and education—a cover letter to capture attention and interest, and follow-up correspondence to assist in the successful job search. It requires that you cultivate a network of people who can help you find a job and identify sources of employment counselling and job leads. (Remember that even Ben & Jerry's turned to an executive search firm.) It also teaches you such skills as focusing on newspaper help-wanted ads, communicating via "cold" letters and calls, and searching the Internet for career positions.

The job search may be your first business communication experience. It may also be your hardest. Through letters, résumés, and conversations, you will give prospective employers reason to hire you—or pass you by. Your communication skills may very likely mark you as distinctive or ordinary, as the best candidate for the job or as just another also-ran.

Although we will present the components of the job-search process in sequential stages, it is important to remember that many of these "stages" usually occur simultaneously. Moreover, some that we present as "late" stages in the process may actually occur before those presented as "earlier" stages. For example, networking, which we have detailed at Stage 5, should occur throughout the job search.

Figure 17-1 Stages in the Job Search

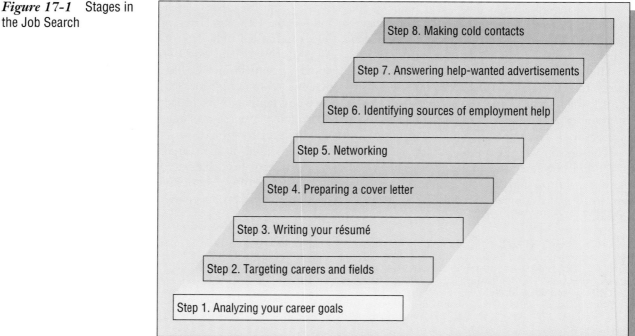

Step 8. Making cold contacts

Step 7. Answering help-wanted advertisements

Step 6. Identifying sources of employment help

Step 5. Networking

Step 4. Preparing a cover letter

Step 3. Writing your résumé

Step 2. Targeting careers and fields

Step 1. Analyzing your career goals

Analyzing Your Career Goals _____

The process of defining your interests, skills, personal qualities, and accomplishments is known as **self-analysis.** This process is the first step in building your résumé—the most important employment communication tool in the job-search process.[1] In order to appreciate the likelihood of career mistakes and the need for early and careful self-analysis, consider the findings of a recent survey: fewer than half the senior executives who were interviewed said that they would pursue the same career if they had a chance to start over.[2]

As a practical matter, however, analyzing your career goals should begin early in your college or university career as you choose a major—the field that you intend to study in depth while you are a student. In many ways deciding on a major is a prelude to deciding on a career and should involve the same process of defining your interests, skills, personal qualities, and accomplishments.

As Canadian author and economist Nuala Beck observes, there is "a world full of golden opportunities awaiting people of ambition, brains, energy and enthusiasm and armed with ... the tools to put them to work."[3]

WHAT INTERESTS ME?

According to Nuala Beck, we are living in a high-knowledge economy where it is more important than ever to get the education and training that will give you a head start. And it doesn't matter what you study, as long as you apply your learning in an industry with a future.[4] Table 17–1 shows the various career possibilities in Canada for seven areas of study.

Table 17-1   Where Are the Jobs?

Topic to Study	Associated Field in Business or Industry
Urban Geography	Waste management industry, environmental consulting
Business Administration	Software industry, waste management, pipeline transportation industry
Marine Biology	Motion pictures & video industry, ecotourism
Health Sciences	Registered nurse practitioners, chiropractors
Computer Studies	Libraries, museums, elementary and secondary schools
Manufacturing Technology	Steel pipe and tube manufacturing, plastics and synthetic resins manufacturing, agricultural chemicals and fertilizers manufacturing
Social Work	Community social services, elder care

Source: Adapted from Nuala Beck, Excelerate, (Toronto, 1995), Harper Collins Publishers Ltd., p 17.

Start by analyzing what you like to do best—so that you can look for a job in a growth industry that will allow you to do it. For example:

- ▼ write for the student newspaper
- ▼ listen to opera music
- ▼ "surf" the Internet
- ▼ exercise an hour a day
- ▼ play the piano

After creating your list, ask yourself one of the classic questions of career fulfillment. What would you do with your life if you were independently wealthy and did not have to work? You might answer, for example, that you would write novels, start your own company, or do fund-raising for the Canadian Cancer Society. You are looking for the same thing in both exercises; namely, the activities that reflect your *values* and that give you the greatest personal satisfaction. Identifying these activities is the first step in finding a way to make them part of your work.

As you list your interests, also make a list of the things that you would rather *not* do. This list might include activities like the following:

▼ working outdoors;
▼ working with your hands;
▼ managing people; or
▼ dealing with budgets.

In finding the right career, understanding what you *don't* like is just as important as understanding what you *do* like.

WHAT AM I GOOD AT?

Your next step is defining your skills—the abilities and talents that can give you an edge in the workplace. Make an inventory of your skills, just as you did your interests. Be as specific as possible, and ask yourself whether you would be willing to use each skill in your work. Here, for example, is one person's list of job-worthy skills:

▼ selling products;
▼ managing a team of workers;
▼ working with customers;
▼ analyzing human resources; and
▼ public speaking.

Another person's list looks very different:

▼ analyzing financial data;
▼ working on a computer;
▼ budgeting and keeping financial records; and
▼ writing financial proposals.

To evaluate your own skills, ask yourself the following questions about each of them:

▼ Do I enjoy performing the skill?
▼ Am I able to perform the skill at a professional level?
▼ Do I have experience performing the skill, either at work or in other activities?
▼ Is this something that I would be willing to do in the future?

WHO AM I?

Next, compile a list of the qualities that define your personal character. As much as your skills and interests, these qualities influence the kind of job you should seek. Many of these traits, including those on the following list, may be obvious during job interviews:

creative	self-starting	detail-oriented
hard-working	determined	intense
sensitive	warm	efficient

COLLABORATIVE COMMUNICATION

Know Yourself—Collaborate with a Canadian Counsellor

Self-evaluation is a personal and often a difficult process to undertake. When done in isolation, we tend to evaluate information we believe others would *need* to know—often at the expense of redeeming characteristics that a potential employer would like to know: your hobby expertise; your latent potential; your artistic talent. A collaborative analysis with a vocational counsellor may help in presenting the best in you.

Beverley McLachlan, the principal of LNI Group Inc., Vancouver, B.C., understands the rigour of self-evaluation. Specializing in helping others to master their careers and relationships, McLachlan collaborates with her clients, offering advice on making balanced decisions.

According to McLachlan, the work of analyzing your career goals includes consideration for additional and less obvious factors. We often choose a career to satisfy someone else, for example our parents or spouse. Unfortunately, when we put ourselves in the position of seeking the approval of others, we always limit personal choices.

Choosing a career solely on the basis of its high financial return is another way to play it safe. However, when you play safe you again limit your choices.

Personality typing is a powerful tool to assist in analyzing yourself and aligning the results with a career choice. *Typing* is based on the theory that different personality types are predisposed to particular careers. Self-evaluation type testing is available, for example, through the Myers-Briggs Type Indicator, and True Colors®. If you are able to identify your personality type *and* a matching career choice, you are on track. Otherwise, consider reassessing your career choice.

Yes, it is possible to find your passion, to avoid the interim steps, and go directly to the career of your choice. It has everything to do with knowing yourself. Consider the job interview. If you are not yourself at the interview, the prospective employer may not get to know the *real* you. And yet that's the purpose of the interview—to let the employer get to know you. Therefore, the best advice is to let the potential employer see you as you really are. When you are being yourself, you are better able to:

▼ understand yourself

▼ express to others who you are

▼ appear sincere, and

▼ be your passionate, creative, powerful, and personal best.

Remember, strive to make your own choice of career—one that will give you the opportunity to become the *real* you.

Questions for Critical Thinking

1. List the potential outcomes of a successful career choice for you. Prioritize these outcomes.
2. Who has influenced your career choice? Allow your intuition to ask for whom is your career choice intended. Is this really what you want to do? Could you be excited about this career over the long term?
3. Will your chosen career allow you to perform in a passionate way and at your personal best? Will it support a balanced lifestyle? If not, what needs to change?

aggressive	friendly	intuitive
analytic	funny	visionary
flexible	responsible	open to risk

Your résumé should also reflect these traits. For example, writing that you created a plan to raise advertising revenues for the campus newspaper shows creativity, analysis, vision, aggressiveness, and determination.

WHAT HAVE I ACCOMPLISHED?

In business, nothing impresses more than results—the tangible products or accomplishments that stem from your efforts. You may have already achieved results in a number of areas—in school, in part- and full-time jobs, in community and leisure activities, in the military, and at home. Results are the building blocks of your résumé. They are also the references that most impress employers during job interviews. For instance, each of the following accomplishments tells an employer that you have achieved results:

- took a public speaking course and delivered five speeches;
- organized the local chapter of Students Against Drunk Driving;
- ran in the Jasper-Banff relay;
- supervised seven mechanics while stationed with the Canadian Armed Forces in Bosnia; and
- conducted a computerized financial analysis of four home mortgages to choose the most favourable option.

Results like these tell employers what you have done in the past and the kind of work that you are capable of doing in the future. Note, too, that results can be obtained in a wide variety of activities.

Because results reveal skills, you also can work backward from your accomplishments to define marketable skills. For example, the accomplishment just described as conducting "a computerized financial analysis of four home mortgages to choose the most favourable option" demonstrates the skills of analysis, computer competence, and problem solving.

Self-analysis is the process used by most vocational counsellors to help people narrow options and choose careers. Counselling also includes job targeting, the next step in your personal job-search plan.

Targeting Careers and Fields

By combining the interests, skills, and personal qualities that you defined in Stage 1 of the job-search process, you can create tangible job possibilities. Targeting careers and fields is Stage 2 of the job-search process. For example, a skill in sales, an interest in computer games, and an orientation to detail may make computer sales an ideal career. Similarly, good communication skills, an interest in people, and a warm, open personality may be the starting points for careers in public relations, employee relations, and convention planning.

To get a better sense of the kind of job possibilities that exist in today's market, there are numerous places to start. For example, you can:

- read the employment and career sections of newspapers;
- check job postings on the Internet;
- speak with your college or university counsellor; and
- read magazines such as *Career Options* published by the Canadian Association of Career Educators and Employers (CACEE)

As you read job descriptions, remember that many careers apply to different industries. Your interests, therefore, can also be a guide to various industries from which to choose. Let's say, for example, that your career choice is compensation and benefits administration. If you are also interested in fashion, you could decide to apply your career choice to the field of retailing and, specifically, to job openings in organizations like Sears Canada Inc. and Wal-Mart Canada. If you are interested in sports, you may decide to apply your career choice as a systems analyst to the business of running a minor league hockey team.

Once you familiarize yourself with the general terrain of employment opportunities, you can begin to target specific types of work. This involves analyzing the work environment and job market.

WHERE DO I WANT TO WORK?

Targeting a career and an industry involves analyzing the **work environment**—the physical, social, cultural, and economic conditions that define the workplace and its surroundings. To get a better idea of how your environment can affect your choice of career and industry, ask yourself questions like the following:

▼ Do I want to work indoors or outdoors?

▼ Do I prefer a small business or a large corporation?

▼ Do I prefer a job with regular hours or one that involves evening and weekend work? (Shift work, for example, is often required in retailing and in the hotel and restaurant industries.)

▼ Do I prefer to work for a manufacturer or a service business (the difference between General Motors and Merrill Lynch)?

▼ Do I want a job with constant deadline pressure (say, a printing plant manager for a newspaper) or pressure that varies by season (a tax accountant)?

▼ Do I want to work for a unionized company like Ford of Canada or a nonunionized company like Nissan Canada?

▼ Am I willing to relocate? (Similarly, do I want to work in a small town like Morinville, Alberta, or Maple Creek, Saskatchewan? Do I want to work in a large city like Vancouver or Toronto? Do I want to work in a northern community like Yellowknife, Northwest Territories? Do I want to work on the East Coast, West Coast, or the Prairies? Would I be willing to work wherever the company sent me, even a foreign country?)

Canadians used to be told to head for the big city if they wanted good jobs. However, the information revolution has made it possible to live and work almost anywhere. In 1995 the Globe and Mail's *Report on Business* magazine conducted a national study to determine where the most educated people in Canada live. Based on postsecondary educational credentials, their research indicated that the five urban centres with a clear edge in brainpower were:

▼ Saskatoon

▼ Halifax

▼ Edmonton

▼ Toronto

▼ Ottawa-Carleton

The runners-up were:

▼ Calgary

▼ Kitchener-Waterloo

▼ Montreal

▼ Victoria

▼ Fredericton[5]

WHAT'S THE CURRENT JOB MARKET?

Targeting a career also requires that you analyze the forces of supply and demand that affect the job marketplace. These forces are both short- and long-term. From a short-term perspective, we have all read headlines about layoffs at such computer giants as IBM. From the long-term perspective, however, these same jobs may show employment growth. In fact, Nuala Beck lists software and computer services as one of the top industries in Canada's new economy.[6]

Some published information may even suggest salaries or the speed at which you are likely to climb a chosen career ladder. Remember, however, that when a popular field becomes saturated with qualified applicants, the salaries may decrease, you will wait longer for promotions, and changing jobs will be harder than it is when opportunities abound.

While looking into the career crystal ball, it is important to recognize that the *exact nature* of anticipated job growth in any particular field is not totally predictable. While, for example, the government predicts that computer programmers will be in demand in 2005, some industry analysts think differently. Paul Saffo, an industry analyst at the Institute for the Future, believes that programming will become automated over the next decade, placing programmers out of work. "The real trick," said Saffo, "is staying skills-relevant. If you bet on artificial intelligence in 1980, which was then a hot field, you either retrained or you're in another industry."[7]

In all of this uncertainty, one thing is known—employers want to hire applicants who can "hit the deck running." Therefore, prepare yourself by getting the most up-to-date education and training possible.

Writing Your Résumé

A résumé is a balance sheet without any liabilities.

Robert Half
Personnel-agency executive

With the information that you have collected in your self-analysis and career targeting, you are ready for Stage 3 of the job-search process: creating your résumé—the written document that will be your primary job-search tool. A **résumé** is a personal marketing tool through which you try to convince employers to grant you an interview. Your résumé performs this task by relating your education, work experience, and personal accomplishments to the needs of prospective employers.

Moreover, your résumé can actually create opportunity in the job market. Many employers will view your résumé both as tangible evidence of your ability to communicate in written form and as a statement of how you see yourself. As your first work project, your résumé will be evaluated on its merit. As a result, it will either increase or decrease your opportunities.

Your résumé will be an integral part of the employment-interviewing process. If you are granted an interview, your résumé will be on the employer's desk during the interview session. Questions about your background that are not answered on your résumé will be addressed directly in the interview. Therefore, although you may decide to omit from your résumé an employment gap that lasted two years, you should be prepared to explain that gap during the interview.

BUILDING A RÉSUMÉ THAT GETS ATTENTION

When employers receive a résumé, they expect to see specific blocks of information, including your name, address, phone number, education, and work experience. Some résumés also mention job objectives, community and professional activities, and employment references. The most effective résumés deliver specific information. Write, for example, that you are interested in a statistical analysis of survey data, not just marketing or market research.[8]

NAME, ADDRESS, PHONE NUMBER, FAX NUMBER, AND E-MAIL ADDRESS Open your résumé with your name, address, phone number, fax number and e-mail

A QUESTION OF ETHICS

A Plague of Lying

Many job seekers lie on their résumés. According to the Executive Search Review, 20 percent of candidates for executive positions "inaccurately state their educational credentials." When another source randomly surveyed 200 résumés, nearly one-third of job seekers misstated dates of employment by three months or more.

People who lie on their résumés justify their actions to themselves, says Michael Josephson, president of the Joseph and Edna Josephson Institute for Ethics. "Typically we hear that an applicant says, 'I can really do the job—I just have to convince them.'" But, Josephson points out, telling lies on your résumé hurts those who tell the truth and lose out on the job. And it robs the employer of the ability to choose the best-qualified applicant based on accurate information.

Lying also sets you up for being discovered. "If you're starting a job on a foundation of dishonesty, you will spend your entire time worrying that the truth is going to come out at some time," says Barbara Ley Toffler, principal of a management consulting firm specializing in ethical management. And when the truth does emerge, through formal and informal background checks, you face the possibility of being fired, no matter how many years have passed since the transgression.

How do you navigate the fine line between stretching the truth to your best advantage and telling a lie? One way is to write selectively, omitting details that may place you in a less than favourable light. For instance, if you never received a col-

lege or university degree, writing "degree program" or indicating your years of attendance states the matter truthfully. However, if you attended for four years but never received a degree, stating outright that you did not complete your degree is the best way to avoid confusion. If the reason will help explain the situation—for example, you took time off after a death in the family—include this information as well.

With employers now sensitized to the plague of résumé lying, you can bet that they are alert for signs of trouble. You can also be sure that if they learn the truth—as they almost surely will—you face the difficult prospect of having to restore credibility as you apply for your next job.

Questions for Critical Thinking

1. What factors do you think contribute to the epidemic of résumé deception?
2. Is it reasonable for an employer to dismiss an employee of one year after learning that he or she lied to get the job? Is it reasonable after five years? After ten? Should there be a statute of limitations on this issue?
3. If you have something in your background that you want to hide, how would you choose to handle it on your résumé?

Sources: Joyce Cohen, "To Tell the Truth . . . ," *Wall Street Journal*, 27 February 1995, R14; Gilbert Fuchsberg, "Managing," *Wall Street Journal*, 4 May 1992, B1; and Joan E. Rigdon, "Deceptive Résumés Can Be Door-Openers but Can Become an Employee's Undoing," *Wall Street Journal*, 17 June 1992, B1.

---

address. This information identifies you and gives employers a way to reach you if they are interested in your qualifications. Because accessibility is critical during a job search, it is a good idea to have an answering machine or voice mail to receive calls when you cannot. If you are currently employed, listing your work number may be risky—a co-worker may pick up the phone. Instead, direct all messages to your home number or address or to another phone number at which messages can be received. For example:

Joanne McTavish
1111 Borden Avenue
Kelowna, BC V1Y 6A5
(250) 555-1111 (tel—home)
(250) 555-2222 (tel—messages)
(250) 555-2121 (fax)
jmctavish@v-wave.com (e-mail)

Place this information at the top of the first page. There is no need to identify your résumé with a label like "Résumé," "Qualifications Brief," "Curriculum Vitae," or "Background Sheet"—it will be clear at a glance what the document is.

JOB OBJECTIVE   The next heading is often "Objective," which reflects the job target you defined in Step 2 of your search. For instance:

▼ Objective—Production editor for print media
▼ Objective—Entry-level compensation and benefits administrator
▼ Objective—Credit manager in a retail firm

This information helps prospective employers pinpoint a slot into which you might fit. However, by including it, you run the risk of restricting how an employer sees you. If a job opening does not precisely match your stated objective, an employer may assume that you would not be interested or that you are not qualified. Nevertheless, a job-objective statement is often valuable and is necessary on a targeted résumé, which will be examined later in the chapter.

EDUCATION   Until now, your greatest accomplishments may have occurred in school. The skills and abilities that you have acquired, major career-related courses and projects, grades and awards, and extracurricular activities all point to your ability to achieve results. Your résumé should tie your accomplishments to your job objective. For example, if your objective is an editorial job in publishing, you can point to the fact that you majored in English, that you had a 75 percent average in your major, that you were the editor of your school's student newspaper, and that you were part of a course-related volunteer program to teach English as a second language to local high school students. Such activities will become less important over the years, but before you have accumulated a body of work experience, they will form the core of your résumé.

Include the names and locations of all the higher-education institutions that you have attended, including technical schools, community colleges, four-year colleges and universities, and graduate schools; the dates you attended; and the degrees you received. Mention awards, special projects, and grades if they are job-related or show distinctive personal qualities.

In recent years more and more firms have been checking educational claims for accuracy. This check may be conducted prior to employment or within the first few months of work. If inaccuracies are found after you start working, you may be subject to dismissal.

WORK EXPERIENCE   Your résumé also lists your previous work experience. At this point, of course, it might be limited, but it will eventually make up most of your résumé. Be sure to include part-time and summer jobs, especially those that are related to the kind of work you want to do. For example, if your job target is to become a management trainee in a nationwide chain of child-care centres, note that you worked for three summers as a teacher's aide in an elementary school.

Whether you use a chronological, functional, or targeted format, your résumé should list the names and locations of organizations, dates of employment (if you are still employed, write "19XX–Present"), and job titles. As we will see, formats for listing and explaining accomplishments vary according to different types of résumés.

COMMUNITY AND PROFESSIONAL ACTIVITIES   You may also decide to mention community and professional activities tied to your job target. For example, if you are applying for a job as a fund raiser, mentioning that you recently raised $5000 for the Canadian Cancer Society is a significant credential. Even activities unrelated to your job target can show such qualifications as initiative, the ability to lead, or aptitude for working as a team member. For instance, Steve Rosenbaum, president of Broadcast News Networks, a company that produces and distributes television programming, once hired an employee based on the fact that he had unicycled across the country and had the guts to include the information on his résumé. "As a CEO of a creative company," said Rosenbaum, "I look for pieces of paper that reflect spirit and energy," and unicycling across the country certainly showed both.[9]

REFERENCES   Your résumé may also include references—a list of people whom an employer may call to learn about your ability, character, and background. References may be previous employers, college professors, community leaders, or even well-known or influential friends. Many résumés include a standard tag line like "References available upon request." Most employers, however, assume that you will provide a reference list when they ask. Be prepared to provide this list with the résumé or during the interview. In a format like that of a résumé, where every word counts, the tag line adds nothing and may detract from more important items like your statement of achievements.

➤ **Cross Reference**
Recall that we discussed writing requests for personal references in Chapter 7, pages 201—203.

When employers request references, give the names, titles, organizations, addresses, and phone numbers of all references. Type the list neatly on a separate sheet of paper. Before including people on your personal-reference list, be sure to tell them about your intention and ask permission. If possible, explain your job objective so that when they are called, they can focus on those aspects of your experience that are tied most closely to your employment objective. For example, if you are applying for a job as a market researcher and use your marketing instructor as a reference, remind her about your class project survey to assess student reaction to tuition increases. Because your goal is to highlight accurate information about your past, such nudges in the right direction are ethical.

Table 17-2 shows the qualities that matter most to employers. Many of these qualities are reflected either directly or indirectly on an applicant's résumé, including communication skills, previous work experience, various recommendations, skills-related credentials, and years of schooling completed.

MASTERING YOUR RÉSUMÉ WRITING STYLE

Résumé writing requires a clipped, action-oriented style that focuses on results. Rather than sentences that elaborate on sometimes unnecessary details, use phrases that start with action verbs. For instance, instead of writing,

> I was chosen by a committee to coordinate the college blood drive that resulted in the donation of 100 pints of blood

write,

> Coordinated college blood drive. Increased donations by 50 percent.

The subject of your résumé is what you have *done*, and such action verbs as *coordinated* and *increased* stress successful activities. Here are some other action verbs that will help you emphasize your activities and accomplishments:

wrote	solved	managed
produced	maintained	translated
prepared	proposed	taught
sold	tested	transferred
founded	enhanced	interviewed
built	expanded	planned
simplified	saved	organized
implemented	collected	improved
decreased	succeeded	structured
strengthened	upgraded	adapted
devised	established	programmed

Table 17-2 Qualities That Employers Consider Most Important

"When you consider hiring a new non-supervisory or production worker, how important are the following in your decision to hire?"

(Ranked on a scale of 1 through 5, with 1 being not important or not considered, and 5 being very important.)

Factor	Rank
attitude	4.6
communication skills	4.2
previous work experience	4.0
recommendations from current employees	3.4
recommendations from previous employer	3.4
industry-based credentials certifying skills	3.2
years of schooling completed	2.9
score on tests administered as part of interview	2.5
academic performance (grades)	2.5
experience or reputation of applicant's school	2.4
teacher recommendations	2.1

Source: Census Bureau survey of 3000 employers nationwide, 1994. From "Qualities That Count with Employers," *New York Times,* 20 February 1995.

Try to limit your résumé to one or two pages by eliminating repetitions and unnecessary personal data. For example, if you performed the same function for three different companies, describe your common responsibilities only once. Don't waste space mentioning your age, height, weight, marital status, number of children, religious affiliation, hobbies, or the names of high school, college, or university fraternities or sororities. Including this information makes you appear unfocused and detracts from your professionalism.

CHOOSING AN EFFECTIVE LAYOUT

Résumés that are too long, contain "fat" paragraphs, or require close reading to find essential information may never be read. The following suggestions will help you design a résumé with visual appeal.

▼ *If possible, limit your résumé to one or two pages.* Break this rule only if it is absolutely necessary. Similarly, limit the amount of space devoted to each item in the résumé. As a rule, no paragraph or section should contain more than ten to twelve lines.

▼ *Expect companies to use computerized key-word searches.* An increasing number of organizations, including Nortel, Bank of Montreal, Canadian Imperial Bank of Commerce, and Canadian Tire are using technology to scan, retrieve, and store résumés in order to lighten the workload of examining and cataloguing high volumes of these applications.

▼ *Use plenty of white space.* To produce a feeling of openness and readability, you should use one-inch margins and also double-space between major sections. Remember that many employers read résumé information in sections, starting first with what interests them. Coupled with headings, white space enables readers to find information quickly. At the same time, single-space within sections.

▼ *Use upper-case letters.* Type headings and important titles in UPPER-CASE letters. Use this and other techniques consistently throughout your résumé.

▼ *Use underlining and bullets effectively.* <u>Underline</u> results or accomplishments that you want to emphasize. Because the reader's eye is normally drawn to underlined sections anyway, remember to use the technique sparingly and with your job target in mind. Punctuate specific accomplishments with bullets that look like ■ or ● .

▼ *Use consistent indenting.* Arrange information in the body of the résumé in visible columns. For example, in a chronological résumé like the one in Figure 17-5, dates appear at the left margin and job descriptions are indented to the right. At the top of page one, of course, your name, address, and phone number should be centred in order to catch the reader's eye.

▼ *Produce a perfect final copy.* Crossing or whiting out mistakes is unacceptable on a résumé. To eliminate spelling, grammar, and punctuation errors, draft your résumé on a word processor and proofread the final copy several times. Make sure that all names and companies are spelled correctly. Take the same care in addressing envelopes.

Despite the wisdom of this advice, employers are reporting that the spelling skills of job applicants are dropping. Take the example of a letter that was supposed to be addressed to the Boeing Aerospace Corporation. Instead, the envelope read Blowing Air & Space Company. Miraculously, the letter reached its destination.[10]

→ **Cross Reference**
The Corporate Case on page 525 of this chapter lists common errors found in résumés.

▼ *Print your résumé on high-quality paper.* Use a laser or ink-jet printer. If you wish to use coloured paper or ink, make your choice conservative. Remember, the message you wish to relay is that you are professional and your interest in the position is a serious one.

▼ *Never fold your résumé.* Instead, treat it like a work of art. Use a full-sized envelope that allows you to lay it flat.

▼ *Clip or staple your cover letter to the résumé.* Remember that the employer may be receiving hundreds of cover letters and résumés; if this is the case, you don't want your pages to become separated in the pile.

FORMATTING A SCANNER-FRIENDLY RÉSUMÉ

"Over 50 Canadian companies, among them high-tech organizations with specialized skill set needs, executive search firms, contract, temporary and permanent employment agencies, have adopted the procedure"[11] of electronically scanning résumés.

This process allows the recruiter to scan hundreds of résumés in only a few minutes. When recruiters wish to retrieve or short-list a group of appropriate candidates, they supply key words that are essential for the right applicant. These key words will identify expertise, experience, and education. For example, they might include such words as *bilingual, entrepreneur, desktop publishing, total quality management, supervisor,* and *teams.*

Electronically scanned résumés save the recruiter an inordinate amount of time. However, an applicant who is unaware that his or her résumé is being electronically scanned may be preparing an ineffective document. Although the applicant may have extensive credentials, those credentials may go unnoticed if the

→ **Cross Reference**
We provide more information on electronically scanned résumés in the Corporate Case on page 68 in Chapter 2.

scanner cannot identify them. Here are some tips for maximizing the computer's ability to read your résumé:

▼ Use a standard typeface. Do not use italics.

▼ Do not bold any of the text.

▼ Do not use the underline feature.

▼ Describe your personal traits in nouns, not verbs.

▼ Use the key words found in the job ad.

▼ Use straightforward words to describe your experience. Embellished terms will not be in the list of skills the recruiter is searching for.

▼ Use multiple pages if necessary. Unlike humans, computers do not tire of reading.

▼ Use common résumé headings such as Objective, Education, Experience, and Interests.

▼ Do not print your résumé on coloured paper.

▼ Increase your lists of key words. Include specific software names such as Corel WordPerfect and Microsoft Word.[12]

▼ Left-justify the entire document.

▼ Use a sans serif font in 10 point size.

▼ Avoid using tabs.

▼ Avoid hard returns.

▼ Avoid script fonts.

▼ Avoid graphics.

▼ Avoid shading.

▼ Avoid horizontal and vertical lines.

▼ Avoid parentheses and brackets.

▼ Avoid compressed printing.

▼ Avoid faxed copies since they may be unclear."[13]

Figure 17-2 demonstrates an example of a résumé formatted for electronic scanning. Figure 17-3 illustrates a résumé and summary displayed side by side on the computer screen using the Resumix System, which gives users the advantage of a complete picture of the candidate on one screen. The applicant's complete file may be scanned and stored electronically; Figure 17-4 shows an application for employment form that has been scanned and displayed on the screen. One advantage of an electronic scanning system is that electronic storage takes so much less space than paper storage. This means that résumés may be kept on file for an extended time.

If applicants are not aware of the electronic scanning process and submit attractive yet traditionally formatted résumés, some of the information may not be identified by the computer. The best approach when you do not know whether electronic or human screening will be used is to submit two résumés. The résumé intended for human scrutiny should be printed on attractive paper, using highlighting features, graphic lines, and so on; the résumé destined for electronic scanning should follow the format described in the bulleted list above. The reason you have included two résumés should be briefly explained in your cover letter, with a comment like "In the event that your company electronically scans résumés, I am also enclosing a résumé designed to be scanner-friendly."[14]

REMINDERS FOR A SCANNER-FRIENDLY
RÉSUMÉ

So that the computer scanning system does not omit any of your valuable informa-

Figure 17-2 Sample Résumé Suitable for Electronic Scanning.

Mark Hoffman
11 Alphonse Crescent
Mississauga, ON L5M 5B6
Tel 905 555-3434
Fax 905 555-9999
E-mail mhoffman@m-wave.com

Objective:

To contribute my marketing skills to a progressive team.

Employment History:

October 97 - present
Marketing Manager at Palmer Ross Advertising
Increased client base by over 90%
Created marketing plan for international team
Managed 40 marketing agents
Earned 120% of quota for last 2 years

August 95 - October 97
Associate Marketing Manager at Kaye Hunter Advertising
Supervised design of all advertising materials
Represented company at international advertising symposium

Education:

B.A., Major in Foreign Studies, Simon Fraser University, Vancouver, 1993
M.B.A., Major in International Marketing, University of British Columbia, Vancouver, 1995

Interests:

Chairperson, Special Olympics, Vancouver, 1995
Team Leader, Fundraising, University of British Columbia, 1994

tion, it's essential to prepare your résumé in a scanner-friendly format. The following list of reminders will assist you in this preparation.

APPEARANCE
❑ You have used a standard san-serif font in a 10-point size, without italics, bolding, or compressed print.
❑ You have used as many pages as necessary to list your skills and experience.
❑ You have avoided coloured paper and coloured inks.
❑ The entire document has been left-justified and tabs have been avoided.
❑ You have avoided graphics, vertical and horizontal lines, and shading.
❑ Parentheses have been avoided.

Figure 17-3 Scanned
Résumé and Summary
Courtesy of Resumix

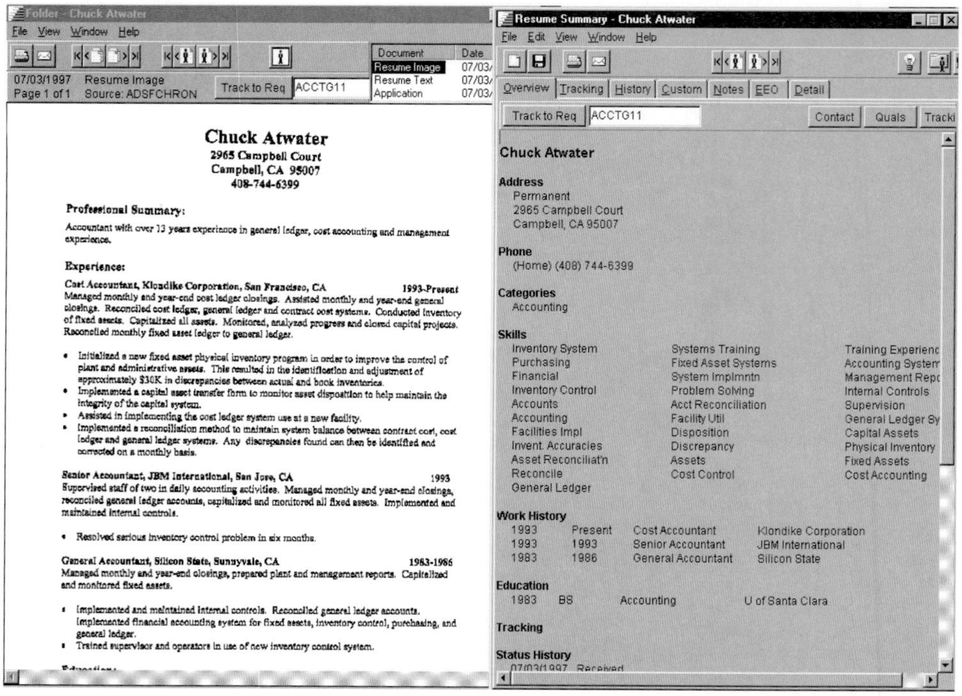

Figure 17-4 Scanned
Application for
Employment
Courtesy of Resumix

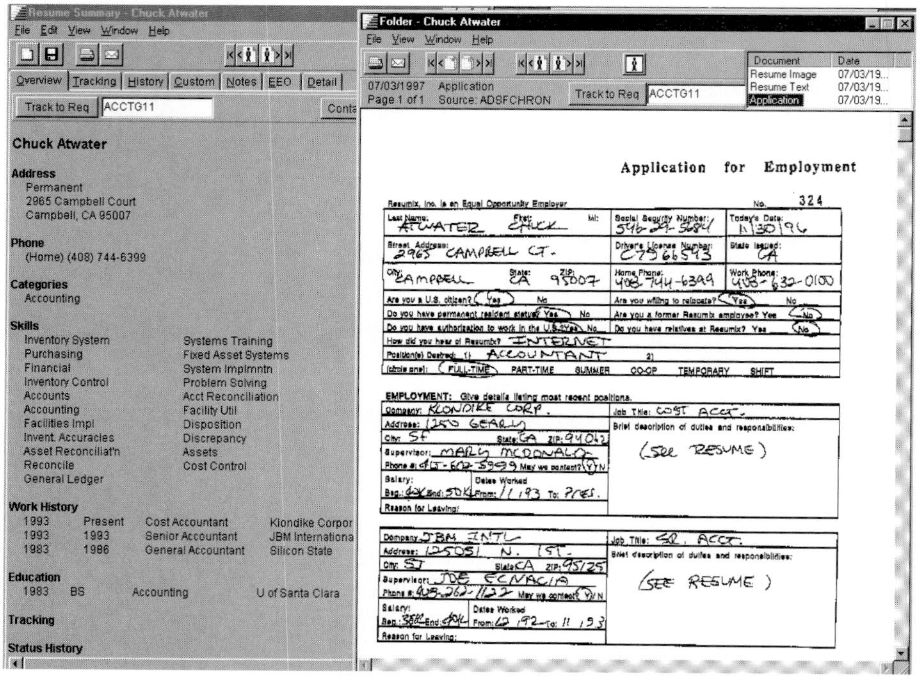

CONTENT

❑ You have described your personal traits in nouns instead of verbs.

❑ You have described yourself using the key words found in the ad.

❑ Complicated words have been avoided and clear words have been used to describe your skills.

- ❏ The suggested headings have been applied.
- ❏ You have included specific software names.

Accuracy
- ❏ You have proofread the document several times for typos, grammar, spelling, punctuation, and content.
- ❏ The spell-check function has been applied to ensure that your résumé is free of spelling errors.
- ❏ You have checked your résumé for spelling errors that the spell-check cannot detect.
- ❏ A reliable person has proofread the document and given you constructive feedback.

Other
- ❏ The document has not been folded.
- ❏ You have avoided faxing the document.
- ❏ You have delivered your résumé in an appropriate way.
- ❏ You have delivered your résumé on time.

ORGANIZING YOUR RÉSUMÉ

Organize your background into one of three résumé formats: chronological, functional, or targeted. Your choice depends on your previous experience and your job target.

Chronological Format   A **chronological résumé** arranges your work experience, education, and personal history in a *reverse* time sequence—that is, with the most recent experience in each category listed first. The chronological résumé has the advantage of highlighting your work experience and career growth as it focuses on names of employers, dates of employment, and specific job titles and responsibilities. Employers report a preference for the chronological résumé since it provides a very clear record of what the applicant has actually done. It is the résumé of choice when you have an impressive job history that shows movement up the career ladder. The chronological résumé may not be the best choice when your history shows major employment gaps, repeated job changes, or little or no career progress. Chronological résumés may be less effective when you are applying for your first job. Follow these guidelines to organize a chronological résumé:

1. Devote the greatest space to your most recent work experience. *Working backward* from that point, detail each of the positions that you have held in the past. Include company names, locations, dates of employment, titles, and responsibilities. Make sure that there are no time gaps—account for all of your time from your first to most recent job.
2. If you are a recent graduate, vary the format by listing your education before your work history.
3. Do not describe your experience in neutral terms. Rather, describe your work history with your job objective in mind. Focus on the accomplishments and responsibilities that will impress prospective employers.
4. Describe only your major achievements and responsibilities. Don't mention the routine parts of your jobs.
5. If you have held the same job for several employers, describe it only as it applies to your most recent position.

Figure 17-5 is a typical example of a brief chronological résumé. Note how the consistent use of white space, capitalization, spacing, and underlining gives this résumé a clean, open appearance. Note that no references appear on this résumé. In this case, the applicant would prepare a list of references on a separate page and submit the references with the résumé or be ready to present them at an interview.

FUNCTIONAL FORMAT   A **functional résumé** highlights your accomplishments and abilities rather than your work history. The flexibility of this format allows you to focus on your strengths in ways that support your job objective. Because you can emphasize functions rather than jobs, this format is excellent for recent college graduates with little or no work experience. Under various functional headings, school and community activities and volunteer and part-time work can all take on added importance.

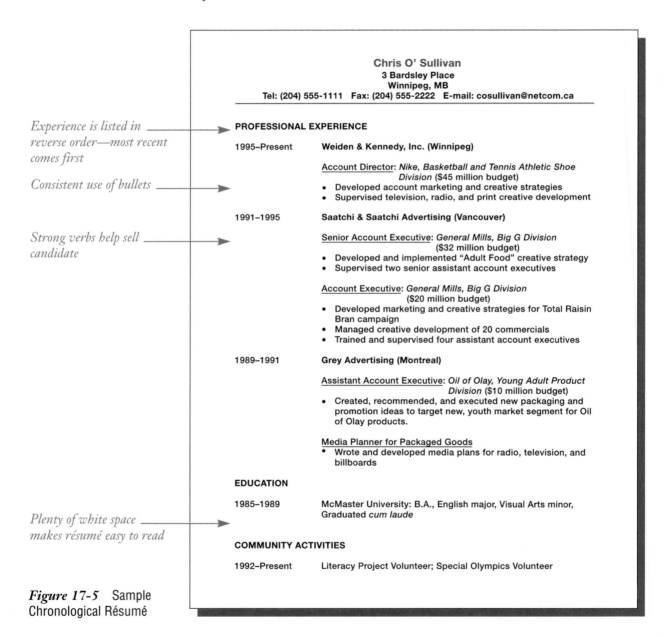

Experience is listed in reverse order—most recent comes first

Consistent use of bullets

Strong verbs help sell candidate

Plenty of white space makes résumé easy to read

Chris O' Sullivan
3 Bardsley Place
Winnipeg, MB
Tel: (204) 555-1111   Fax: (204) 555-2222   E-mail: cosullivan@netcom.ca

PROFESSIONAL EXPERIENCE

1995–Present   **Weiden & Kennedy, Inc. (Winnipeg)**

Account Director: *Nike, Basketball and Tennis Athletic Shoe Division* ($45 million budget)
- Developed account marketing and creative strategies
- Supervised television, radio, and print creative development

1991–1995   **Saatchi & Saatchi Advertising (Vancouver)**

Senior Account Executive: *General Mills, Big G Division* ($32 million budget)
- Developed and implemented "Adult Food" creative strategy
- Supervised two senior assistant account executives

Account Executive: *General Mills, Big G Division* ($20 million budget)
- Developed marketing and creative strategies for Total Raisin Bran campaign
- Managed creative development of 20 commercials
- Trained and supervised four assistant account executives

1989–1991   **Grey Advertising (Montreal)**

Assistant Account Executive: *Oil of Olay, Young Adult Product Division* ($10 million budget)
- Created, recommended, and executed new packaging and promotion ideas to target new, youth market segment for Oil of Olay products.

Media Planner for Packaged Goods
- Wrote and developed media plans for radio, television, and billboards

EDUCATION

1985–1989   McMaster University: B.A., English major, Visual Arts minor, Graduated *cum laude*

COMMUNITY ACTIVITIES

1992–Present   Literacy Project Volunteer; Special Olympics Volunteer

Figure 17-5 Sample Chronological Résumé

Handling Background Problems in Your Cover Letter

Because things left unsaid often raise questions, it is a good idea to address problems in your background in an open, honest way. Any of the following situations may require explanation in a cover letter.

POOR GRADES

Poor grades can harm your chances of getting a job unless you craft explanations recruiters can accept. For instance, telling a recruiter that a class was outside your major will help explain a poor grade. Similarly, explaining that you changed majors after doing poorly for several semesters indicates flexibility and self-awareness. Finally, pointing to a trend of improving grades also helps.

REASON FOR YOUR JOB SEARCH

If you are one of the thousands of people who have lost their jobs after a merger or company downsizing, chances are that your job loss had little to do with your competence. You must nevertheless anticipate the question "Why is this person looking for a job?" You can do so by writing:

> Due to the recent merger between the Royal Bank of Canada and Royal Trust and the staff reductions that resulted from it, I am now looking for a position as a mortgage lender.

There is no stigma attached to this type of layoff, and mentioning such circumstances in your cover letter will also eliminate any suspicion that you were dismissed for cause.

EXPLANATION OF GAPS

If there is any way to explain a gap in employment or education, do it. If you explain nothing, employers may create their own worst-case scenarios ("Who needs people who spend a year after high school searching for themselves and then take six years to finish college?"). Ironically, the right explanation, as in the following excerpt, can make you a more attractive candidate:

> I spent a year between high school and college caring for a sick family member, and these responsibilities delayed my college graduation.

Many employers believe that this kind of dedication is transferable to the workplace.

There are times, of course, when the only explanation for a gap does not reflect well on a candidate's activities or experience. If such is the case, do not mention the explanation. If it is brought up in an interview, tell the truth and hope that your skills, qualifications, and attitude will overcome any negative impact.

FREQUENT JOB CHANGES

Although it is common in many fields to change jobs frequently, it is generally not a good idea to highlight job changes in your cover letter or résumé. Focus on your job skills and past accomplishments and downplay job-hopping by using a functional rather than a chronological résumé format.

Finally, remember that the first thing employers focus on when they receive your cover letter is what is *not* right—the obvious negatives that eliminate you from the running immediately. Only when they find no negatives are they likely to look for positive traits. Your writing challenge, then, is to anticipate negative reactions by taking a positive approach. For example, if you did not work during college because your parents paid your expenses, anticipate a negative reaction to your lack of job experience by indicating in your cover letter that you were able to devote all your time exclusively to your studies.

Sources: Timothy D. Schellhardt and Tony Lee, "Hints for Hunters," *Wall Street Journal*, 27 February 1995, R6; and Richard H. Beatty, *The Perfect Cover Letter* (New York: John Wiley, 1989), 87–97.

A functional résumé is also useful to people who want to change career direction, have employment gaps, have job-hopped, or who have made little career progress. It is not suggested, however, when you want to emphasize steady job growth and promotions, when your work experience involves a limited number of functions, and when you are applying for work in such traditional fields as education and government.

Follow these guidelines for constructing an effective functional résumé:

1. Choose three to five functional headings to highlight not only your accomplishments and responsibilities but also your job goal. Choose descriptive functional headings like these:

Management	Public Relations
Sales	Training
Writing	Fund-Raising
Accounting	Purchasing

2. Prioritize these functions in terms of your job objective. For example, if you are trying to get a job in sales, list this function before all others—even if you have more experience doing other things.

3. Do not link functions to employment by stating where your accomplishments took place. This information will emerge in the job interview.

4. List employment and education at the bottom of the résumé and include relevant names, dates, locations, and titles. If you have little or no prior work experience (many recent graduates fall into this category), eliminate the employment section. The same advice holds for people with major employment gaps.

Progress Check

1. Why is your résumé the most important persuasive document you will ever write?
2. Knowing that the reader is likely to look at your résumé for only a few seconds, how should you write and design it to capture attention?
3. As your career progresses, are you likely to use the same résumé format you used when you were looking for your first job? Why or why not?

Figure 17-6 is a sample functional résumé. Note that the major headings have been created to categorize and highlight the nature of the candidate's accomplishments, and not the employers for whom she achieved results. "Work Experience" is thus reserved for a separate functional heading.

TARGETED FORMAT   If you have a specific job objective, a targeted résumé highlights abilities and achievements that relate to a specific goal. However, because targeted résumés apply only to specific jobs or types of jobs, you will need a different résumé for each target.

Targeted résumés emphasize capabilities over job history and are excellent for people who have accomplished a great deal outside the work setting (for example, unpaid fund raisers). Generally, they are not very valuable when you are trying to start a career.

Follow these guidelines to write an effective targeted résumé:

1. State your specific field and job target at the top of the résumé.

2. Learn as much as you can about your job target and tie your capabilities and accomplishments to that target.

3. Your list of capabilities should emphasize the things that you can do to fulfill the responsibilities of your targeted career. Use the present tense to stress the fact that your capabilities apply to present and future work.

4. Your list of achievements should focus on the specific accomplishments that relate to your job target. Use the past tense to stress the fact that these are things you have in fact done.

5. Include work history and education at the bottom of your résumé. Include appropriate names, dates, titles, locations, and degrees.

Figure 17-7 is a sample targeted résumé. This candidate has worked from the general to the specific, describing her "capabilities" and then itemizing the "achievements" that enabled her to gain them through her work experience.

Table 17-3 compares the advantages and disadvantages of chronological, functional, and targeted résumés. As we have seen, deciding which format to use depends upon your own background, job history, and career goals.

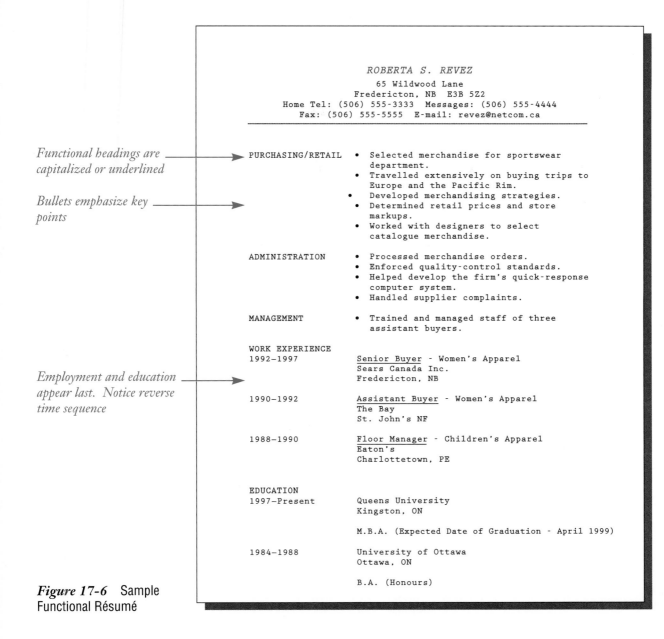

Figure 17-6 text annotations:

Functional headings are capitalized or underlined

Bullets emphasize key points

Employment and education appear last. Notice reverse time sequence

ROBERTA S. REVEZ
65 Wildwood Lane
Fredericton, NB E3B 5Z2
Home Tel: (506) 555-3333 Messages: (506) 555-4444
Fax: (506) 555-5555 E-mail: revez@netcom.ca

PURCHASING/RETAIL
- Selected merchandise for sportswear department.
- Travelled extensively on buying trips to Europe and the Pacific Rim.
- Developed merchandising strategies.
- Determined retail prices and store markups.
- Worked with designers to select catalogue merchandise.

ADMINISTRATION
- Processed merchandise orders.
- Enforced quality-control standards.
- Helped develop the firm's quick-response computer system.
- Handled supplier complaints.

MANAGEMENT
- Trained and managed staff of three assistant buyers.

WORK EXPERIENCE
1992–1997   <u>Senior Buyer</u> - Women's Apparel
            Sears Canada Inc.
            Fredericton, NB

1990–1992   <u>Assistant Buyer</u> - Women's Apparel
            The Bay
            St. John's NF

1988–1990   <u>Floor Manager</u> - Children's Apparel
            Eaton's
            Charlottetown, PE

EDUCATION
1997–Present   Queens University
               Kingston, ON

               M.B.A. (Expected Date of Graduation - April 1999)

1984–1988   University of Ottawa
            Ottawa, ON

            B.A. (Honours)

Figure 17-6 Sample Functional Résumé

Preparing a Reference Sheet

Many applicants place a single line at the bottom of their résumé stating "References available upon request." This allows you to control access to your employment history until you have been interviewed. Although this is a valid point, keep in mind that since employers are busy people, you should make it easy for them to hire you. As well, if an employer chooses to call one of your references before contacting you, his or her referral should serve to help you get an interview. Therefore, you may decide that providing references along with your résumé is the best approach.

When choosing your references, use past or present employers as well as your educators. Never use your relatives! List three or four people who will provide

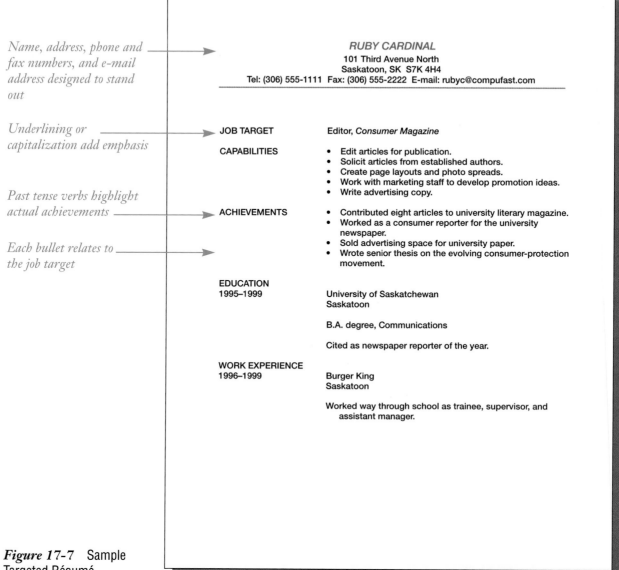

Name, address, phone and fax numbers, and e-mail address designed to stand out

Underlining or capitalization add emphasis

Past tense verbs highlight actual achievements

Each bullet relates to the job target

RUBY CARDINAL
101 Third Avenue North
Saskatoon, SK S7K 4H4
Tel: (306) 555-1111 Fax: (306) 555-2222 E-mail: rubyc@compufast.com

JOB TARGET   Editor, *Consumer Magazine*

CAPABILITIES
- Edit articles for publication.
- Solicit articles from established authors.
- Create page layouts and photo spreads.
- Work with marketing staff to develop promotion ideas.
- Write advertising copy.

ACHIEVEMENTS
- Contributed eight articles to university literary magazine.
- Worked as a consumer reporter for the university newspaper.
- Sold advertising space for university paper.
- Wrote senior thesis on the evolving consumer-protection movement.

EDUCATION
1995–1999

University of Saskatchewan
Saskatoon

B.A. degree, Communications

Cited as newspaper reporter of the year.

WORK EXPERIENCE
1996–1999

Burger King
Saskatoon

Worked way through school as trainee, supervisor, and assistant manager.

Figure 17-7 Sample Targeted Résumé

positive information about your work habits and skills. You will need to know their working titles, full business addresses, telephone and fax numbers, as well as e-mail addresses. Refer to Figure 17–8 for a sample reference sheet.

It's essential that you contact the people you wish to use as a reference. This is best done in person or over the telephone. Be certain that the people you place on your reference sheet are enthusiastic about providing a reference for you. Follow the meeting or telephone call with a letter that confirms their agreement to stand as your reference. If your job search continues over an extended period of time, occasionally check back with your references to make sure that you may continue to use their name. When you do get a job, be certain to let your references know and thank them for their support.

Astute employers will not rely on reference letters; therefore, do not send them along with your résumé. Rather, present them during the interview. However, if you

Table 17-3 Advantages and Disadvantages of Three Résumé Forms

Advantages	Disadvantages
Chronological	
gives clear picture of work background	may be ineffective when applying for first job
is useful for showing an impressive job history	shows employment gaps, job changes, and poor career progress
Functional	
highlights accomplishments and abilities	does not show history of steady job growth and promotions
focuses on strengths	is not useful when experience involves limited number of job functions
excellent for recent graduates, job-hoppers, and career changers	
Targeted	
highlights abilities and achievements that relate to a specific goal	minimizes specific job history
allows job hunter to target specific types of jobs	forces job hunter to write different résumés for different job objectives

Reference Sheet
for
Roberta S. Revez

Dr. Benjamin Ross
Chair, Statistics Department
Queen's University
85 Leeward Avenue
Kingston, ON K7M 2Y1
Tel: (613) 555-7777
Fax: (613) 555-7878
E-mail: bross@netcom.ca

Mr. Edward Kaye
General Manager
The Bay
500 Bonaventure Avenue
St. John's, NF   A1C 4Z4
Tel: (709) 555-1212
Fax: (709) 555-4141
E-mail: kaye@bay.nf.ca

Ms. Amelia Taylor
Marketing Manager
Sears Canada Inc.
800 Bayshore Drive
Fredericton, NB E3B 5M5
Tel: (506) 555-8888
Fax: (506) 555-8989
E-mail: taylor@sears.nb.ca

Mrs. Lilian Mundee
Senior Vice-President
Eaton's
555 North River Road
Charlottetown, PE   C1A 3M2
Tel: (902) 555-9898
Fax: (902) 555-6565
E-mail: lil_mundee@eatons.pe.ca

Figure 17-8 Sample Reference Sheet shows how references should relate to résumé.

have a letter that will help explain a gap in employment or a job termination, you may wish to attach it to your résumé. Above all, apply good judgement.

FAXING YOUR RÉSUMÉ

If you've spent hours printing your résumé on bond paper of perfect quality and colour, and perhaps have even used coloured ink for just the right amount of accent, then faxing your résumé will seem like an anticlimax. However, it does have the advantage of expediency. Employers will often request that résumés be faxed in order to save time. If you are requested to fax your résumé or simply determine yourself that faxing is appropriate, consider the following:

▼ A faxed résumé will probably not be confidential. In fact, it may be seen by several people before being collected by the designated receiver. You may be able to avoid this disclosure by telephoning the recipient just prior to sending the fax and asking him or her to collect the faxed document.

▼ A faxed résumé should always include a cover letter, just like the résumé you mail or hand deliver.

▼ If your résumé is attractive enough to earn you points, mail an original paper copy immediately after you send the faxed copy. In order to avoid any confusion, make reference in your cover letter to the fact that you have sent both a faxed and original copy. If the regular postal system is not rapid enough, use an express delivery or courier.

REMINDERS FOR A HUMAN-FRIENDLY RÉSUMÉ

Before submitting your résumé, use the following checklist to ensure that your document will work for you. Remember that any poor work may cause an employer to send your résumé to File 13!

APPEARANCE

- ❑ The spacing is attractive.
- ❑ You have plenty of white space.
- ❑ You have used quality paper that is white or of a conservative colour.
- ❑ Excessive enhancements have been avoided.
- ❑ A proportional-space font has been used.
- ❑ Your format is consistent throughout.
- ❑ Your headings are emphasized.
- ❑ Your information is in point form and uses bullets.
- ❑ You have followed the format described in this textbook.
- ❑ Your résumé is free of creases or folds.

CONTENT

- ❑ Résumé headings shown in this textbook have been used.
- ❑ Your résumé emphasizes skills and mastery of software.
- ❑ Your résumé shows your most recent education first.
- ❑ Your résumé shows your most recent experience first.
- ❑ You prepared a reference sheet that includes three or four former employers and/or educators.
- ❑ Your references are complete. (courtesy titles, working titles, company names, full addresses, telephone, fax, and e-mail addresses)

ACCURACY

- ❑ There are absolutely no typographical errors in your résumé. It has been proofread repeatedly by you and by someone else who gave you constructive feedback.

- ❏ You have used the spell-check function to ensure your résumé is free of spelling errors.
- ❏ You have checked your résumé for spelling errors that the spell-check function would not detect.
- ❏ Your lists are consistent in wording as well as format.
- ❏ You have clearly stated your expected date of graduation if you have not already graduated.

OTHER
- ❏ Your résumé has been delivered in an appropriate way.
- ❏ Your résumé has been delivered on time.

Preparing Your Cover Letter _____

With each résumé send a **cover letter**—written correspondence to a prospective employer aimed at convincing the employer to grant an interview. Cover letters, in other words, are sales letters intended to sell your value. Writing an effective cover letter is Stage 4 in the job-search process.

The best cover letters are written from the employer's perspective. When they have jobs to fill, employers are looking for people who will help them once they have been hired. You should tailor each letter to the unique requirements of the job, the company, and the industry. Form letters (which are usually easy to spot) get few results.

Gathering the information that you need to write an effective cover letter often requires research into both industry trends and developments within your targeted company, such as personnel changes. We will talk about specific research techniques in Chapter 18. Here, we will focus on the components and format of the cover letter itself. It is important to note at the start that every detail in your cover letter must be accurate or you will be eliminated from consideration. As an example, consider how an editor of a newspaper would feel about receiving a cover letter that read "I would like to be considered for a photography position..." when the newspaper has never used photographs.

As you examine the components of an effective cover letter, adopt an audience-centred approach. Your value to a prospective employer exists only if the employer perceives it as she reads your cover letter and résumé. With this in mind, we suggest a visualization exercise before you begin writing: Picture a busy manager with dozens of résumés on his or her desk; the phone is ringing and piles of other work wait to be done. Now picture this manager as he throws out letters (and accompanying résumés) that ramble on for several pages in search of a point. Finally, picture this manager reading your letter, which is short and focused. The moral: Write every cover letter with the idea that you have only a few seconds of reading time to capture and hold audience attention and no time to make a poor impression.

WHAT MAKES A GREAT COVER LETTER?

Effective cover letters include no more than four or five paragraphs. Each paragraph has a purpose as a selling tool.

INTRODUCTORY PARAGRAPH   Open your letter with an attention-getter—a statement that convinces the employer to read on. Create interest. You might begin by naming a person either within or outside the company whom the employer knows, by citing specific knowledge of the company's business, or by using a compliment.

The last sentence of your introduction should state directly your interest in employment with your reader's company.

USE CONTACTS   The best way to stand out from the crowd is to mention a personal contact—a professional colleague, a friend, or a relative—whose name the reader will immediately recognize. For instance:

> Albert White, an employee in your accounting department, told me about an entry-level opening in accounts payable. I am interested in talking with you about this position.

> Andrea Swain, a close family friend, suggested that I contact you about a position in sales. As a recent business graduate with several years' experience in retail sales, I believe that my background is right for your company.

CITE KNOWLEDGE OF COMPANY BUSINESS   Another effective technique is to demonstrate knowledge of the company and, if possible, tie new business developments to your personal qualifications. Current knowledge comes from research—from reading local papers and national publications like the *Financial Post* and *Maclean's* magazine and from reviewing annual reports and other corporate documents. For example:

> I read in yesterday's paper about the size of DDB Needham's international advertising business. With 52 percent of billings coming from Europe, Asia, and Latin and Central America, your firm has a need for qualified managers who know the advertising business and who have lived and worked abroad. Because I am qualified in both areas, my background should interest you.

COMPLIMENT THE COMPANY   In business as elsewhere, compliments never hurt—especially if they are sincere and reflect your knowledge about a company and its achievements. Use the compliment as a springboard to ask for an interview. To illustrate:

> Ever since I began studying advertising in college, I have been impressed by the work DDB Needham Worldwide has done, especially your campaigns for Volkswagen and McDonald's. As a copywriter, I would like to be part of such a creative, forward-looking organization. I am enclosing my résumé for your consideration.

MIDDLE PARAGRAPH #1: SELL YOUR VALUE   Turn next to answering the question on the mind of every prospective employer: "How will hiring this person help me do my work and improve company profits?" By describing your value, you can give employers an answer to that question—and a reason to invite you for an interview.

Sell your value through results—the achievements in school and the workplace that demonstrate a "track record." Remember, however, that although these results are indeed tangible evidence of your ability to perform, they will create interest only if they tap into company need. For example, telling a bank that just closed its consumer-banking division about your expertise in retail banking is a waste of time. Despite the value of your accomplishment, the need is just not there.

Writing this paragraph requires application of your research to your own background. For example, recall the excerpt of the cover letter to DDB Needham Worldwide that cited knowledge of DDB Needham's international business. The second paragraph of that letter might read as follows:

> For the past five years, I have worked for Young & Rubicam as an account executive in its Paris office. While there, I gained experience dealing with the cultural differences that can foil even the most creative ad campaigns. My fluency in French—as well as in Spanish and Italian—and my ability to handle these cultural differences are readily transferable to your operation.

Here is how another recent college graduate communicated personal value to a prospective employer:

> As you can see from my résumé, I am graduating with a degree in accounting. Because of financial need, I worked my way through school, maintaining a job throughout the school year. Despite this, I graduated with honours and participated in such extracurricular activities as the college band and chorus. I also created an advertising campaign for band concerts that raised attendance by 70 percent. I bring to you an enormous energy for work and an ability to organize my time to get things done.

Even without work experience, this person's competence, work ethic, and dedication would be attractive to most employers.

MIDDLE PARAGRAPH #2: SUMMARIZE YOUR BACKGROUND   Take the opportunity here to summarize additional aspects of your background that will help you get an interview. Focus attention on anything that the employer could find valuable. Remember, however, that because your résumé is attached, it is unnecessary to repeat everything that you have done. In fact, if you feel that the previous paragraph gave a complete picture of your background, you can omit this paragraph completely.

CLOSING PARAGRAPH: A CALL TO ACTION   Like other persuasive letters, a cover letter should close with a call to action. Your call to action can take two forms: it can ask employers to call you to arrange an interview or it can tell employers that you will call them to determine interest and arrange a meeting time. Here is a sample of each closing form:

> I would like the opportunity to explain my background and qualifications to you in a personal interview. I look forward to hearing from you and to arranging a meeting in the near future.

> I will call you during the week of May 21 to learn if my background interests you and to arrange an interview time.

Figure 17-9 is a sample cover letter written by a recent college graduate. As you can see, this writer has emphasized his value and background in a single paragraph, but otherwise adheres closely to the guidelines we have discussed. With the writer's résumé, it is ready to be mailed. Before mailing a cover letter, however, make sure every name is spelled correctly and that job titles are up-to-date (you may have to call the company to gather information). Don't forget to proofread the envelope as well.

TIPS FOR A WINNING COVER LETTER!

If you want your cover letter to attract attention to your suitability for the job, use the following tips as a guide.

▼ Use key words from the job posting.
▼ Keep it short and simple. This is often referred to as the KISS principle.
▼ Always key your cover letter unless specifically asked to handwrite it.
▼ Use high quality bond paper that matches the paper used on your résumé.
▼ Use the same font as that used in your résumé.
▼ Be certain that your letter is *letter perfect*! It must be typographically correct, without grammar, punctuation, or spelling errors.
▼ Be enthusiastic and sincere when constructing your letter.[15]

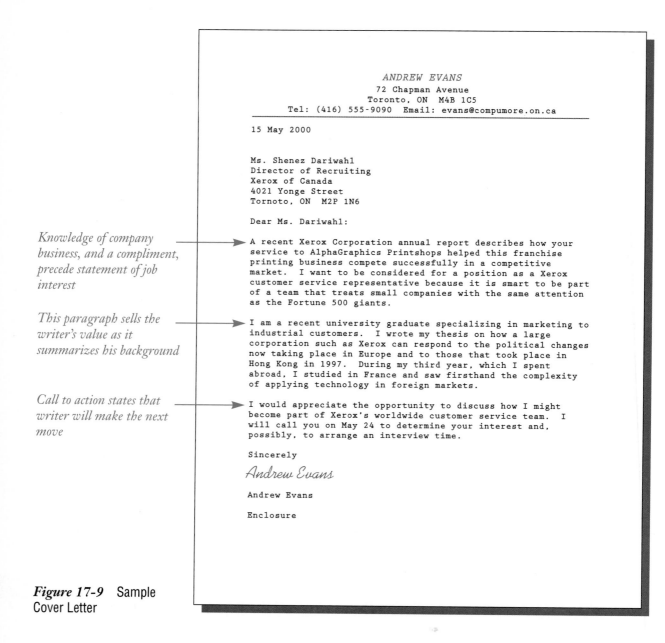

Knowledge of company business, and a compliment, precede statement of job interest

This paragraph sells the writer's value as it summarizes his background

Call to action states that writer will make the next move

ANDREW EVANS
72 Chapman Avenue
Toronto, ON M4B 1C5
Tel: (416) 555-9090 Email: evans@compumore.on.ca

15 May 2000

Ms. Shenez Dariwahl
Director of Recruiting
Xerox of Canada
4021 Yonge Street
Tornoto, ON M2P 1N6

Dear Ms. Dariwahl:

A recent Xerox Corporation annual report describes how your service to AlphaGraphics Printshops helped this franchise printing business compete successfully in a competitive market. I want to be considered for a position as a Xerox customer service representative because it is smart to be part of a team that treats small companies with the same attention as the Fortune 500 giants.

I am a recent university graduate specializing in marketing to industrial customers. I wrote my thesis on how a large corporation such as Xerox can respond to the political changes now taking place in Europe and to those that took place in Hong Kong in 1997. During my third year, which I spent abroad, I studied in France and saw firsthand the complexity of applying technology in foreign markets.

I would appreciate the opportunity to discuss how I might become part of Xerox's worldwide customer service team. I will call you on May 24 to determine your interest and, possibly, to arrange an interview time.

Sincerely

Andrew Evans

Andrew Evans

Enclosure

Figure 17-9 Sample Cover Letter

REMINDERS FOR AN EFFECTIVE COVER LETTER

Your cover letter is your personal introduction. That's why it's critical that the letter markets you in the most effect way possible. Use the following checklist to be certain your cover letter is working for you.

APPEARANCE

❑ The letter is keyed.

❑ You have used high-quality bond paper.

❑ Your paper and font match those on the résumé.

❑ Your cover letter is stapled to the top of your résumé.

❑ The documents have been placed in an envelope large enough that they may lay flat without folding.

CONTENT

❑ You have opened with an attention-getting statement.

❑ You have demonstrated knowledge of the company.

❑ Your letter complimented the company.

❑ Key words have been used that were included in the job posting.

❑ You have described what would make you valuable to the company.

❑ Your background has been summarized.

❑ You closed with a call to action.

❑ The letter has been kept short.

❑ The letter has been kept simple.

❑ The letter sounds sincere.

❑ The letter sounds enthusiastic.

ACCURACY

❑ You have proofread the letter several times for typos, grammar, spelling, punctuation, and content.

❑ Another reliable person has proofread it and given you feedback on it.

❑ The letterhead contains the correct information (full address, telephone and fax numbers, and e-mail address).

HOW SHOULD I FOLLOW UP?

Unfortunately, it is a common practice for employers to complete the hiring process without ever informing the unsuccessful applicants of their status. Applicants often report mailing out 30 to 100 résumés and receiving only a handful of form rejection letters. The rest of their cover letters are not even answered by a form letter. This should be an unacceptable business practice, however, applicants can expect this to occur and should not let it dissuade them in their employment search.

If you have not received a reply after two weeks, consider calling the company. Your purpose is to ask if your letter and résumé have been received, not to restate your job qualifications (pushing may eliminate you from consideration). If your employment application is lost, the employer will probably ask you for another copy.

You can also follow up in writing, asking about the status of your application and communicating any new information that might enhance your chance for an interview. If you just learned, for example, that you will be graduating cum laude, say so in the follow-up letter. Similarly, you would tell an advertising agency if a campaign you developed in your current job just won an award. If you still hear nothing, assume that you are not being considered for the job or that it has been filled and go on to more fruitful possibilities.

While you are preparing your résumé and sharpening your letter-writing skills, you should begin looking for actual job openings. Start by building and refining your employment communication network.

> ### Progress Check
>
> 1. Describe the attributes of both an effective and ineffective cover letter.
> 2. Describe the different techniques you can use to craft an effective introductory paragraph for a cover letter.
> 3. List some guidelines for following up on an employment application.

Networking

In simple terms, networking means exchanging information. Information is the most powerful asset a business professional can have. If you have information and are willing to share it, you will be viewed as a valuable person to have on staff. Remember

INTERVIEW Job Seekers Hit the Net

James C. Gonyea, Founder of the Career Center on America Online

Online technology is changing the way people find jobs and the way companies look for new employees, says James C. Gonyea, founder and director of the country's first electronic career and employment guidance service—the Career Center on America Online. The Career Center gives job seekers the opportunity to connect online with professional career counsellors, to refine and electronically distribute their résumés to employers and employment agencies worldwide, and to search through thousands of electronic help-wanted ads. Similar resources are found on other online services and bulletin boards, and through CD-ROM.

We asked Gonyea to describe the online help available to job seekers and why so many corporate recruiters are electronically plugged in. You can learn more about online career services by contacting Gonyea directly at America Online (address your e-mail message to CareerDoc) or via the Internet at Careerdoc@aol.com.

Question: How do electronic career services differ from traditional career services?

Answer: Both use the same strategies of effective career planning. The difference lies in the way these strategies are delivered. Using traditional methods, career counsellors have face-to-face meetings with clients and talk about career objectives and ways to reach them. Using online

services, these "conversations" take place electronically.

Question: What do employers and job seekers think of online recruiting?

Answer: Posting help-wanted notices electronically gives companies access to instantaneous global communication; companies can let the world know about job opportunities and receive responses as soon as their ads are posted. The same process can take days and

that networking should not be a one-way effort. The more information you give, the more information you are likely to get back.

Studies have shown that networking, Stage 5 in the job-search process, is the most effective way to find work. **Networking** involves talking and writing to people about your job search. When job holders are asked how they found work, approximately half reported that they relied on person-to-person contact. Other sources claim that networking is responsible for about 70 to 80 percent of successful job searches.[16]

MAKING YOUR CONTACTS WORK FOR YOU

Developing a network and using it effectively takes time and practice. It also means understanding that networking is yet another form of business communication. The following general suggestions are designed to help you communicate effectively in a network. We will also offer more specific advice on preparing for and making the actual networking call.

▼ *Ask everyone you know for advice.* Discuss your job search with family, friends, former co-workers, teachers, and community businesspeople. If they can't

even weeks to accomplish using traditional newspaper advertising.

By connecting online, job seekers have access to thousands of employment listings from all over the country. Right now, for example, you can log on to America Online and browse through more than 10 000 help-wanted ads.

Question: Isn't this too much to digest?

Answer: It would be impossible to digest without the ability to narrow a search. Fortunately, our databases are key-word searchable, which means that someone looking for an accounting position in Calgary can type *Accounting Calgary* and the computer will list only those jobs that contain these words.

Question: How do online career services help job seekers prepare and distribute their résumés?

Answer: We help people shape their résumés to fit the electronic medium by inserting the key words employers are looking for. We also provide help getting résumés online and show job seekers how to e-mail their résumés and cover letters to employers within minutes of reading an electronic ad. This gets candidates through the employer's door well ahead of the competition.

Question: Is the number of help-wanted ads growing?

Answer: There is no question in my mind that electronic career services are becoming the mainstream medium for employers, employment recruiters, and job candidates. When we started posting ads about two years ago, we listed only about 1000 ads a week. There's been a tenfold increase since then, and I expect this number to double within six months.

Question: What place should an online job search have in the entire job-search process?

Answer: Job seekers should spend 50 percent of their time on traditional job-search methods such as monitoring classified ads, contacting employers to inquire about employment opportunities, networking, and using placement and employment services. They should spend the other 50 percent online. This requires keeping up with changing technology and being open to new methods.

Source: Interview with James C. Gonyea.

help, ask for the names of other people whom you might contact. In networking the more contacts you have, the more likely it is that you will find a source of help. Keep in mind, however, that your best resources are likely to be people with whom you have an ongoing relationship.[17]

▼ *Be prepared and be specific.* Be ready with a short summary (no longer than two to three minutes) of your background and career objectives. And be specific about the type of help you want.

▼ *Don't ask for a job.* Asking directly for a job is one of the fastest ways to end a conversation—it puts your contact in a difficult position. Instead, ask for job-hunting advice. If a job is available, your contact can make the first move. This approach makes your intentions clear without creating an awkward situation.

▼ *Develop an organized database of your contacts.* Keep a file of meeting dates and conversations. Include the name, title, company, phone number, fax number, and e-mail address of each person you contacted, and the person who introduced you. Also record any personal information that will assist your communication with your contact.

- ▼ *Become involved in activities that will enlarge your network.* Join clubs at school; attend professional conferences; become involved in community activities. Activities like these increase your number of potential contacts.

- ▼ *Send letters of introduction to new contacts.* The purpose of the letter is three-fold:

    1. To establish the source of the reference. For instance:

        > Professor Abigail Andrews, of Memorial University in St. John's, Newfoundland, suggested that I contact you for information about entry-level career opportunities in accounting.

    2. To introduce yourself and your background.
    3. To make a request. For example:

        > I would like the opportunity to meet with you in your office to talk about the accounting field, my background, and career objectives. I will call you next week in the hope of setting up a time we can meet.

- ▼ *Call new contacts.* When you call a new contact, your primary goal is to make a favourable impression so that the contact will remember you when she hears of a job opening. A secondary goal is to come away with other networking contacts.

- ▼ *Make follow-up calls (but don't abuse people's time).* Keep in touch with your networking contacts on a regular basis even after you have found work. An occasional phone call will ensure that your contacts will be there for you if you need them again. The best way to guarantee a continuing relationship is to become part of their professional network. The most successful networker that management consultant Craig E. Schneier knows is a lawyer who "focuses on what someone needs and provides them with tips and leads and ideas. It's the godfather philosophy of networking. When she needs something, she has plenty of chits to call in."[18]

- ▼ *Make yourself visible.* Becoming a leader of a professional organization or volunteering to serve on a committee will open networking doors.

- ▼ *Purchase a telephone message machine.* Missed messages may mean lost contacts.

- ▼ *Increase your reading of business materials.* Remember that information is power and reading will build your information base.

Identifying Formal Sources of Employment

Your job search will bring you in contact with such sources of employment assistance as college or university placement officers, on-campus recruiters, and employment agencies. Another source, online career services, are discussed in detail in the interview with James C. Gonyea, founder and director of the Career Center on America Online. The importance of various job-search methods are shown in Figure 17-10. Learning to communicate with each source and understanding what each can and cannot do will help you to use these resources more efficiently. Acquainting yourself with available employment-assistance resources is Stage 6 of the job-search process.

COLLEGE PLACEMENT ADVISORS

College placement advisors are job-search professionals hired by colleges and uni-

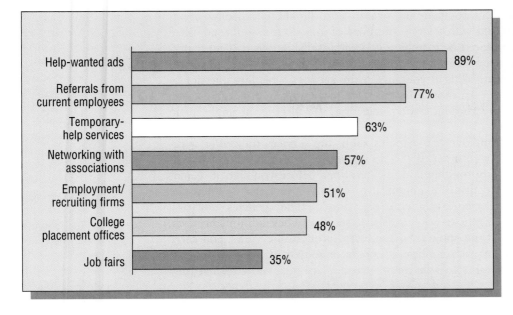

Figure 17-10 The Most Popular Recruitment Tools
Source: *Olsten Corporation. From Robert L. Rose, "A Foot in the Door,"* Wall Street Journal, *27 February 1995, R7.*

Help-wanted ads — 89%
Referrals from current employees — 77%
Temporary-help services — 63%
Networking with associations — 57%
Employment/recruiting firms — 51%
College placement offices — 48%
Job fairs — 35%

versities to help students and alumni find jobs. They offer personal career counselling and testing as they help students analyze their career goals and guide them through the job market maze. College placement advisors usually work closely with on-campus recruiters and so act as college-based employment agents who match students with jobs brought to them by employers. This is often done through *job fairs* in which numerous employers talk to students about available job opportunities.

An increasing number of placement centres are also offering computerized job-matching systems for graduates, which put them in touch with both small and large employers.[19]

ON-CAMPUS RECRUITERS

When companies like Motorola and General Motors have job openings, they often send representatives to college and university campuses. These representatives, known as **on-campus recruiters,** are trained professionals in the company's human resources department who interview students for jobs.

On-campus recruiters also look for candidates interested in summer internships—unpaid or low-paid positions held by students while they are still in school. These positions give students the opportunity to learn about a company and give the company the opportunity to evaluate the student for a job after graduation. Apple Computer, for example, uses student interns in marketing, finance, computer design, and manufacturing. Internships are especially popular in tight job markets.[20]

EMPLOYMENT AGENCIES

There are, of course, employment-help choices outside college and university campuses. Private and federal government employment agencies match job candidates with specific jobs. Employment agencies fall into three categories: private agencies, federal government agencies, and executive search firms. Each is geared to different populations with different employment needs.

PRIVATE EMPLOYMENT AGENCIES   Both temporary and longer term positions are available through private employment agencies. Interviewers at employment agencies sift through the applicant pool—reviewing résumés and references—to present a handful of qualified people for company interviews. With hundreds and often thousands of business contacts and with a large inventory of jobs on file, well-established agencies can shorten your search by matching you with available jobs that meet personal career and financial needs. Working with an employment agency also allows you to fine-tune your interviewing skills as you answer the agency's screening questions.

Employment agencies earn money by charging the company a markup fee to cover the agency's cost for recruiting, testing, selecting, and placing the applicant in the company.

You can ask private employment agencies about the services they offer without being obligated to sign a contract. If you do register with a private employment agency, study the contract thoroughly and ask questions before you sign it. Canadian employment agencies consider it unethical to use a contract that restricts the applicant's right to hold other contracts with other employment agencies.

Private employment agencies give excellent service. They administer tests, scrutinize the appearance of the applicants, conduct thorough interviews, and carry out a complete job hunt for each applicant. Private employment agencies make a sincere effort to refer applicants to jobs for which they are qualified and that they are likely to accept.

Employment agencies sometimes specialize in specific fields—accounting, sales, legal, or engineering, for instance. To find a qualified agency, "determine that the agency belongs to the Employment and Staffing Services Association of Canada (ESSAC). The mission of the ESSAC is to promote the advancement and growth of the employment industry in Canada. This association has adopted rigid standards of ethical practice, which member agencies are required to follow. Membership in the ESSAC ensures that these agencies are reputable."[21] The classified ads in your local newspaper or the Yellow Pages will also point you to agencies that specialize in your field.

When no jobs are immediately available, call the agency once a week, both to get status reports and to express continuing interest. Remember that it is in the agency's best interest to find you a job—that's the only way it earns a fee unless it is one of the few agencies licensed to accept fees from applicants. But also remember that it is to the advantage of the agency to steer you toward as many jobs as possible—some of which will be further removed than others from your ideal employer.

When permanent and long-term positions are not available, or when the applicant prefers a more flexible work schedule, temporary work may be the answer. When you work as a "temp," your employer is the temporary employment agency that provides your services, for a fee, to companies in need of short-term help. Such work may be a profitable stopgap until you find a permanent position. It may also be a stepping stone to a permanent job with the company for which you are working. The business managers see you in action and can judge the quality of your work to determine whether you would fit into the organization. Temporary contract work has become a very popular means of employment for both the employer and the employee.

FEDERAL GOVERNMENT   Canada Employment Centres list openings for all kinds of work—industrial, commercial, technical, and professional. Their services are free to any job seeker and to any employer.

Job information for your region is available from computerized Job Information Centres (JICs). These centres are located in federal government buildings as well as at kiosks in public areas such as some shopping centres. All new job orders are posted at the same time daily. All JICs throughout a city are connected to the same computer terminal; this way, all centres receive the same job information at the same time.

Before qualifying to work in the offices of the Public Service Commission (federal government), the applicant must take a keyboarding test. This test is available in both French and English and may be taken in most Canada Employment Centres. Most positions for employment with the federal government are never posted in the newspapers. Only when the job requires special skills that are difficult to find will the federal government advertise in the newspapers. In all cases, Canadian citizens are given preference when applying for federal government positions in Canada.

The Public Service Commission has a Web site that posts job positions within the federal government. It also publishes a telemessage number in local telephone directories. This message provides a menu of options; among the choices is the current job information selection.

Human Resources Development Canada (HRDC) also has a Web site, which provides information on the labour market and employment insurance. The following e-mail address connects the user to Human Resources Development Canada: http://www.culturenet.ca/hrdc.[22]

EXECUTIVE SEARCH FIRMS Also known as "headhunters," executive search firms are specialized employment agencies that work for companies rather than individual job applicants. Used primarily to place high-level personnel, they often earn a percentage of the first year's salary for each job placement—a fee always paid by the company. Like private employment agencies, search consultants screen candidates with the right qualifications and arrange for the most qualified to interview for the job. They are often given exclusive listings—a certain agency is the only one screening candidates for a particular position. Your chance of success, then, is much greater if you pass the screening stage.

Executive search consultants do not work for recent college and university graduates with limited job experience. As their name implies, they are geared to the executive job market and often contact employed executives with good reputations in the hope of enticing them with more attractive offers. Some of the largest executive search firms in Canada are Western Management Consultants and The Caldwell Partners.

Table 17-4 compares formal sources of employment assistance. Included are the functions, advantages, and disadvantages of each.

Online Career Services

The computer is a valuable job-searching tool. Searching the Internet for job opportunities will not eliminate the need to practise traditional job-hunting techniques, but it will add another dimension to your job search.

Job announcement databases are available for browsing. The National Association of Colleges and Employers (NACE) has a home page called JobWeb, on which job opportunities are published as well as useful career search information. By browsing through Web sites you will reach many online Canadian job-search facilities, such as

▼ CACEE (College and Career Educators and Employers)
▼ Career Bridge
▼ Rostie & Associates Inc.
▼ NetJobs
▼ JobMatch

Table 17-4   Comparing Sources of Employment Assistance

	Functions	Advantages	Disadvantages
College or University Placement Advisor	offer career counselling and testing	provide assistance to students and alumni	have relatively limited number of job listings
	act as employment agents	can shorten the job search by matching students with actual jobs	
On-Campus Recruiters	are company interviewers	have inventories of actual jobs that must be filled	may arrive with few jobs to offer
Private Employment Agencies	match applicants with actual jobs for both temporary and permanent employment	can shorten the job search	applicants may have to pay high fees
		give applicants repeated opportunities to interview	may steer applicants to unsatisfactory jobs just to collect fees
		provide opportunities in tight job market	temporary jobs are often short-lived and do not include benefits
		temporary work may lead to permanent	
Federal Government	offer free placement service	same as for private agencies	deal primarily with jobs at the low end of the pay scale
Executive Search Firms	place executives in relatively high-paying jobs	work for companies and have exclusive listings	do not work with recent college graduates
		fees paid by hiring companies	
Online Career Services	provide electronic access to potential employers	speed job search with electronic searches and résumé transmittal	no face-to-face career counselling
		low cost access to potential employers worldwide	should combine with other job-search methods
			concern for confidentiality

▼ Canadian Job Exchange

▼ David Aplin & Associates

▼ WebJobs Nova Scotia

In the highly competitive search for work, the Internet has become a new job market. It is also useful for sending your résumé to one of the online career services. However, you should ask yourself if you want your personal information to be so publicly available.

Some online career services remove the résumé's heading (your name, address, telephone number, fax number, and e-mail address), so that only the body is left for display. Employers search the online résumé listings using words that represent the key competencies required to perform the job, for example *supervisor, team leader, executive assistant, records management, diploma*, and *degree*. When an employer believes that your credentials match a job opportunity available, the employer will offer to purchase the identifying header. With your permission, the online career service will release the header to the paying customer—the potential employer. This high-tech method allows you to protect your identity.

As a job search tool, the Internet has a strong advantage: it enables you to reach a vast audience in almost no time at all. As the candidate database grows, more and more companies are subscribing to the Internet as a recruiting tool.

Responding to Job Opportunities

Stage 7 of the job-search process involves learning how to answer help-wanted advertisements. The classified-ad sections of such newspapers as the *Vancouver Sun*, *Whitehorse Star*, *Winnipeg Free Press*, *Ottawa Citizen*, and the *Halifax Chronicle Herald*, as well as trade publications, contain help-wanted ads for available jobs.

A company can choose to name itself in an ad or use a postal box number. You can assume that if a name is used, the ad describes a legitimate position. Companies also place ads with box numbers when they want to keep the search private. However, many of these ads do not describe real jobs. Often, they are placed by employment agencies and search firms trying to amass stockpiles of qualified candidates for particular kinds of jobs. Companies may also place ads to test the job market for certain positions. Responses not only tell them how many people would respond if a job were actually available, but also indicate the range of current salary requirements.

In most cases responses to company-placed help-wanted ads are screened by assistants in human resources departments. To make your application stand out, then, you will need a distinctive cover letter and résumé. One way to set yourself apart is to send your résumé via overnight mail or to fax it.

Answering an ad, however, is not the end of your effort. After a week or two, follow up with a phone call to express active interest. You can also send a second letter in response to an ad that does not mention the company's name, asking when you might hear from the company and requesting an interview. Include another copy of your résumé. This type of persistence often creates results.

To use help-wanted ads, you need to learn the shorthand that saves companies advertising dollars (because newspapers charge advertisers by the line, brevity is a virtue). For example, "sal. $25K" means "salary $25 000"; "college grad w/excel . . ." means "college graduate with excellent . . ."; "strong wp, database mgmt & willingness to take on addit responsibility" means "strong word processing, database management and willingness to take on additional responsibility." In most cases help-wanted shorthand is common sense, but sometimes knowledge of the field is needed to figure it out. For example, it would be difficult to translate "WWW" into "World Wide Web" without a knowledge of this communication technology.

Making Cold Contacts

Because most job opportunities are never advertised, you may want to make a series of cold contacts after you exhaust your networking ties. **Cold contacts**, Stage 8 of the job-search process, are unsolicited letters in which you introduce yourself and ask about job openings. Cold contacts are sales efforts in which you attempt to convince a firm that you are a valuable, although unknown, commodity deserving an interview. Figure 17-11 is a sample of a cold-contact letter.

Before writing a cold-contact letter, research the company and, if possible, learn something about recent corporate developments. By reading the business section of a newspaper, you may learn, for example, that Ben & Jerry's Homemade, Inc., is expanding its operation abroad (recall the chapter's opening vignette). With a major in marketing, an interest in international food sales, and fluency in Italian, French, and Spanish, you thus decide to write a letter to the

Progress Check

1. What is networking, and why is it such an important job-search tool?
2. List three formal sources of employment. Describe the career assistance that you can expect from each.
3. Why is a cold-contact letter perhaps the most difficult job-search letter to write?

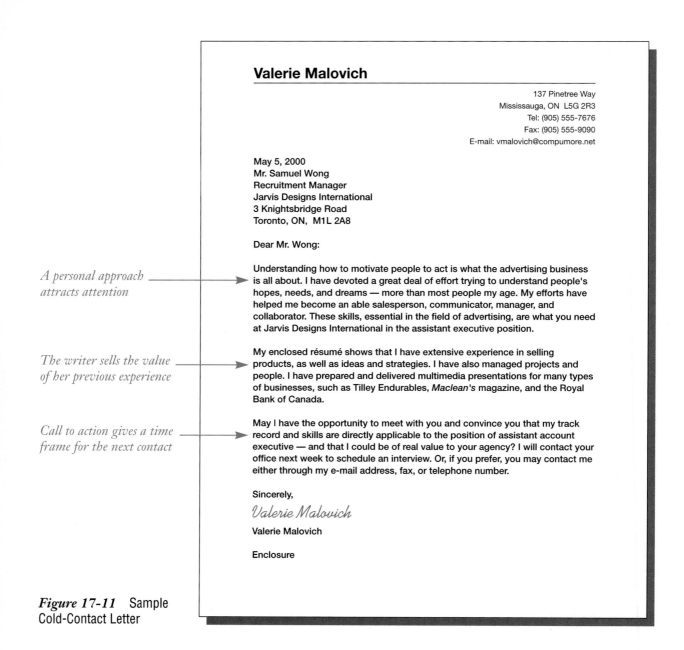

Valerie Malovich

137 Pinetree Way
Mississauga, ON L5G 2R3
Tel: (905) 555-7676
Fax: (905) 555-9090
E-mail: vmalovich@compumore.net

May 5, 2000
Mr. Samuel Wong
Recruitment Manager
Jarvis Designs International
3 Knightsbridge Road
Toronto, ON, M1L 2A8

Dear Mr. Wong:

A personal approach attracts attention

Understanding how to motivate people to act is what the advertising business is all about. I have devoted a great deal of effort trying to understand people's hopes, needs, and dreams — more than most people my age. My efforts have helped me become an able salesperson, communicator, manager, and collaborator. These skills, essential in the field of advertising, are what you need at Jarvis Designs International in the assistant executive position.

The writer sells the value of her previous experience

My enclosed résumé shows that I have extensive experience in selling products, as well as ideas and strategies. I have also managed projects and people. I have prepared and delivered multimedia presentations for many types of businesses, such as Tilley Endurables, *Maclean's* magazine, and the Royal Bank of Canada.

Call to action gives a time frame for the next contact

May I have the opportunity to meet with you and convince you that my track record and skills are directly applicable to the position of assistant account executive — and that I could be of real value to your agency? I will contact your office next week to schedule an interview. Or, if you prefer, you may contact me either through my e-mail address, fax, or telephone number.

Sincerely,

Valerie Malovich

Valerie Malovich

Enclosure

Figure 17-11 Sample Cold-Contact Letter

director of human resources. Even though it is a cold-contact letter, the letter's message may be convincing enough for the recipient to grant the writer an interview.

What's Ahead

From all this effort, one or more interviews will emerge. Chapter 18 will examine how to communicate effectively during an interview so that you will improve your chances of receiving a job offer. We will also examine the various forms of written communication associated with the job-interviewing experience.

STUDENT RESOURCE CENTRE

Summary of Chapter Objectives

1. **Describe eight distinct stages of the job search.**

   Eight stages characterize an effective job search. These include analyzing your career goals, targeting a field and a specific career, writing a résumé, preparing a cover letter, networking, identifying formal sources of employment assistance, answering help-wanted ads, and making cold calls.

2. **Describe the process of targeting career opportunities that link to your interests, skills, traits, and accomplishments.**

   Using the process of self-analysis, you can identify your interests by listing the things that give you personal satisfaction as well as the things that you would rather not do. Next, personal-skills assessment involves listing the abilities and talents that can give you an edge in the workplace. You can then define the personal qualities that influence your own job choice. Finally, list your accomplishments—the concrete results of your experience and activities that will impress prospective employers. The information that you compile in this process will lead you in one or more specific career directions.

3. **Describe a résumé layout that is scanner-friendly.**

   In general, the résumé should be plain, without embellishments. Avoid the use of bolding, tabbing, graphics, lines, script fonts, coloured paper, and coloured inks. Lists should state nouns instead of verbs.

4. **List the elements and types of effective résumés.**

   An effective résumé lists your name, mailing address, telephone number, fax number, and e-mail address; education; employment experience; and community and professional activities. It may also include a job objective and references. Résumé style features abbreviated, action-oriented language and focuses on results. A clean, open layout invites prospective employers to focus on the résumé items to which you want to draw attention.

   There are three types of résumés. A chronological résumé lists work experience, education, and personal history in a reverse time sequence. It focuses on names of employers, dates of employment, and specific job titles and responsibilities. A functional résumé makes your specific work history secondary to your accomplishments and abilities. A targeted résumé ties your abilities and achievements to a clear and specific job objective, which is stated at the top of the résumé.

5. **State suggestions for faxing a résumé.**
   - ▼ Remember that faxing a résumé may mean lack of confidentiality.
   - ▼ Always include a cover letter.
   - ▼ Mail the original copy of your résumé and indicate the duplicate mailing in your cover letter.

6. **List the elements of an effective cover letter.**

   An effective cover letter is made up of no more than four or five paragraphs. The introductory paragraph attempts to capture the reader's attention by mentioning a personal contact, citing knowledge of company business, or complimenting the company. The body of the letter describes your potential value to the business as it summarizes your background. The letter closes with a call to action that attempts to arrange an interview time.

7. **Describe specific networking techniques.**

   Networking involves talking and writing to people about your job search. It means asking everyone you know for advice, being prepared with a short summary of your background and career objectives, becoming involved in activities that will enlarge your network, writing to new contacts, and following up with phone calls and letters on a regular basis.

8. **List formal sources that can assist you in finding a job.**

   Formal sources of employment assistance include college placement advisors, on-campus recruiters, employment agencies, and online services. College and university placement officers are school employees who provide employment assistance for students and alumni. On-campus recruiters are company representatives who travel to campuses to interview students for jobs. Employment agencies link job hunters with jobs, sometimes for a fee.

Employment agencies fall into four categories: private, public, and temporary agencies, and executive search firms. Online services provide low-cost electronic access to career counselling services and employers around the world.

9. ***Describe how the Internet can be an effective job search tool.***

The Internet may be used to search out job opportunities by browsing through Web sites for online job search facilities. The Internet may also be used for sending your résumé to one of the online career services.

10. ***Explain the basic approach to answering help-wanted ads.***

Because help-wanted ads often bring in hundreds of responses, you will need a strong cover letter and résumé to make your application distinctive. To communicate the importance that you place on an opportunity, you may decide to fax your résumé or send it by overnight mail. If you have not heard anything after several weeks, send a second letter expressing active interest. At this point you can also contact the company by phone.

Review and Discussion Questions

1. Name eight stages that make up the job-search process. *(Ch. Obj. 1)*
2. Explain the importance of self-analysis to your career. *(Ch. Obj. 2)*
3. How might you go about analyzing yourself to choose a career? *(Ch. Obj. 2)*
4. Describe how you could target a particular field and specific career. *(Ch. Obj. 2)*
5. State five tips for preparing a résumé to be computer-scanned. *(Ch. Obj. 3)*
6. What elements help to make an effective résumé? *(Ch. Obj. 4)*
7. Distinguish among chronological, functional, and targeted résumés. *(Ch. Obj. 4)*
8. State three tips for faxing a résumé. *(Ch. Obj. 5)*
9. Describe the characteristics of a good cover letter. *(Ch. Obj. 6)*
10. Summarize some important tips that can help you network effectively. *(Ch. Obj. 7)*
11. In addition to networking, what sources are available to help you find a job? *(Ch. Obj. 8)*
12. State two ways the Internet may be used to search for a job. *(Ch. Obj. 9)*
13. Describe the approach that you would take in responding to a help-wanted ad. *(Ch. Obj. 10)*

Application Exercises

1. A major component of self-analysis involves knowing your interests and skills. First, make a written list of your interests, whether job-related or not. Second, develop a list of your skills and abilities. In writing the lists, consider activities in which you're presently active as well as past activities that you enjoyed. *(Ch. Obj. 1, 2)*
2. Analyze your personal qualities. Compile a list of the characteristics and personality traits that make you the person you are. To remind yourself of additional items, you may wish to discuss this list—and the ones that you developed in Exercise 1—with a friend. *(Ch. Obj. 1, 2)*
3. Analyze your accomplishments and experiences. Develop a list that describes your achievements, whether at work, at school, in athletics, in hobbies, or simply as personal goals that you have achieved in some tangible way. Be sure to use phrases and action verbs. *(Ch. Obj. 1, 2)*
4. Choose a field or an occupation that interests you. After consulting some references, describe the ways that supply and demand have affected that career path during the past decade. Is this occupation currently in demand? Why or why not? What is the outlook for jobs in this field for the next five years? Ten years? Write a brief report summarizing your findings. *(Ch. Obj. 2)*
5. Convert your résumé to a format that is compatible for computer scanning. *(Ch. Obj. 3)*
6. The placement office at your school has asked you to write a concise guide for your fellow students on how to write effective résumés. In addition to presenting overall tips for writing a good résumé, your brief manual will explain when one should use chronological, functional, and targeted résumés. Write this guide. *(Ch. Obj. 4)*

7. Working from the lists that you created in Exercises 1–4, write your résumé using a chronological format. Be sure to follow the guidelines described in the chapter for effective format, layout, and writing style. (Ch. Obj. 4)

8. Now, write your résumé using a functional format. Follow the guidelines given in the chapter. Don't just copy what you wrote in your chronological résumé; as you rewrite, evaluate your résumé to find ways of improving style and layout. (Ch. Obj. 4)

9. Write your résumé using a targeted format. Target your résumé either to a job that you hold now or to a job that you would like to have. Which of the three résumé types do you find most appropriate for your needs? Why? (Ch. Obj. 4)

10. From Exercises 7–9, select the résumé that you prefer and write a cover letter to accompany it. Address your letter to someone who is in a position to hire you for the job you targeted in Exercise 9. (Ch. Obj. 6)

11. How good are you at networking? In the next week, develop three new contacts whom you can add to your present network. Introduce yourself in person, call, or write a letter of introduction. Follow the guidelines given in the chapter for communicating with these people. Write a brief description of the means by which you contacted each person, what you talked about, and how the conversation went. Do you feel that you handled each contact well? Can you think of ways to improve your networking skills? (Ch. Obj. 7)

12. Check an online service for job information. Did you find any new sources of employment assistance? Outline what you found out from the service. (Ch. Obj. 8, 9)

13. Are you looking for a job? If so, scan the classified-ad section of your local newspaper or a trade publication in a field that interests you. Find two to three ads that sound interesting; send your résumé and a cover letter to each. The ads do not have to be in the same field. If you're seriously interested in these positions, you may wish to customize your résumé and/or the cover letter to suit each job.

If you don't receive a response within two weeks, follow up with a phone call or another letter and résumé. Take notes on your experience with each ad. What can you learn from each experience? For instance, did you do a better job of customizing your résumé to one ad than another? Did you express yourself better in one follow-up phone call than in another? Use this information to help you in future job searches. (Ch. Obj. 10)

Building Your Notebook

Carefully review the cover letter and résumé that follow. Assess their communication effectiveness. Next, revise and improve the letter and résumé by applying what you've learned in the chapter. Consider, for instance, what type of résumé format would be best-suited for the applicant, given his experience, and add or remove information as needed.

```
I am writing to apply for the accounting position advertised
in yesterday's newspaper. After reading the job requirements,
I feel I am the person for the position.

My résumé is enclosed. I have done well in all my college
classes. I do have an accounting educational background which
would enable me to work well at your company.

I work well with people and am a natural leader. In addition,
I enjoy accounting work and have experience in accounting. I
have held several accounting positions.

I look forward to discussing my qualifications with you.
```

Document 1

```
RICHARD SMOTHERS

911 Borden Avenue
Kelowna, BC  V1Y 6A5
(604) 555-6767


Career Objective

A challenging position in sales.


Education

Okanagan University College, Kelowna, BC, B.B.A., Marketing,
May 1997
GPA 83%


Activities and Honours

Student Ethics Committee: Member
Marketing Club: Presentations Committee
Intermural Sports: Softball, Volleyball
Campus Crusade: Participant


Experience

CCR Supply, Inc., Vernon, BC, Summer, 1997
Responsible for counter sales and developing delivery schedule
for construction supply firm.

Xerox Corporation, Vancouver, BC, 5/98 - 8/98
Aided in trouble-shooting for the introduction of new product
line. Assembled magnetic products for disk drive, and
performed quality control inspections for Xerox copier
components.


References

Mr. John Smalley, President, CCR Supply, Inc., 8436 Taylor
Road, Vernon, BC, V1T 3L9, Fax: (250) 555-3456, E-mail:
smalley@ccr.bc.ca

Amanda Lupert, Assistant Vice President, Xerox Corporation,
Vernon, BC, V7T 1S6, Tel: (604) 555-7890
```

Document 2

ACT: Applied Communication Techniques

Begin by referring to the sections up to and including Abbreviations and Numbers in Appendix II. Change the spelling of any homonyms that have been used incorrectly, then correct the grammar, spelling, and usage errors in the following sentences. Check your answers in Appendix V.

1. I except your offer for employment at the West Edmonton Mall security office.

2. After an employment interview, it's difficult to have patients to wait for the results.

3. Whose been shortlisted for the interview for the Office Manager position?

4. Karen called the company to determine weather or not she was the successful applicant for the job.

5. Our organization was built on the principal of equal opportunity employment.

6. Applicants reported four incidence of unethical questioning.

7. The applicant respectively requested an interview for the marketing position.

8. He printed his letter of application on personal stationary.

9. Don't loose your confidence when an employer asks behavioural questions on an interview.

10. The interviewer wrote comments about the applicant's lack of presents.

Building Your Reseach Skills

Set up an appointment with someone with a great deal of experience in reading résumés from job applicants. This individual might be a human resources professional, a manager who hires staff members for a company, or someone in academia who hires staff or faculty. Interview this person about what he or she looks for in résumés and cover letters. According to this individual, what characteristics make an effective résumé? Does this person prefer chronological, functional, or targeted résumés? What traits doom résumés and cover letters to the wastebasket? What advice does this person have for job applicants?

Building Your Teamwork Skills

Your instructor will divide the class into small groups to work with résumés and cover letters that each member developed for Applications Exercises 7–10. Make enough photocopies of your best résumé and cover letter to distribute to each member of the group. Using the guidelines offered in the chapter, take turns evaluating each other's résumés and cover letters. Assess the format, layout, and writing style of each. What elements are effective? What elements seem less effective? Can the group members suggest changes or improvements?

Building Your Technology Skills

Many employers believe that those candidates who communicate using the most current information technology are superior candidates. Visit these Web sites and review online résumés and job search information. Print examples of five different résumés that you feel best use the electronic medium. Be prepared to discuss online résumés in small groups and to design your own résumé for Internet distribution.

▼ Monster Board
http://www.monster.com/home.html

▼ Yahoo (Career & Employment)
http://www.yahoo.com/Business/Employment

▼ Career Mosaic
http://www.careermosaic.com

▼ Online Career Center
http://www.occ.com/occ

▼ CanWork Net
http://canworknet.ingenia.com/canworknet

▼ Canadian Job Source
http://www.irus.rri.uwo.ca/~jlaw/job_can.html

▼ JobLink Canada
http://peace.netnation.com/joblink/welcome2.html

▼ Canadian Résumé Centre
http://netaccess.on.ca/resume/index1.html

In small groups discuss how the résumés you found on the Internet compare to paper résumés. Focus on design, content, organization, and delivery issues. What advantages and disadvantages are there in using an electronic medium to distribute résumés? After the small group discussion, each group member should design an online résumé for a job that interests him or her and transmit it via the Internet.

Weblinks Internet Resources for this Chapter

Cover Letters
http://www.rpi.edu/dept/llc/writecenter/web/text/coverltr.html

Purdue OWL Resume Workshop
http://owl.english.purdue.edu/Files/resume.html

Writing an Effective Application Letter
http://www.wuacc.edu/services/zzcwwctr/applicationletter.wp51.txt

Career Bridge, Welcome to E-cruiting
http://www.careerbridge.com/

Netjobs Information Services
http://www.netjobs.com/

CASE STUDIES

DIVERSITY CASE:

Proving That You Have *Neyaka*

If you wanted to work for Sony, Japan's large consumer-electronics firm, you'd have to prove that you have *neyaka*.

Neyaka is a Japanese term meaning "optimistic, open-minded, and interested in many subjects." Sony executives believe that it is a vital personality trait in successful engineers and other employees. "There is a spiritual side of the world," says Sony founder and honorary chairman Masaru Ibuka, "that is very unpredictable, vague, and abstract, that is the source of human creativity. Creativity comes from looking for the unexpected and stepping outside your own experience." Senior managing director Minoru Morio agrees: "A good engineer is not necessarily young, but new in terms of his experience. We believe that having continuous success in the same area makes you believe too much in your own power, and harms your creativity."

The emphasis on *neyaka* guides project assignments at Sony. "If you want to lower the cost of an existing product or find a better way to manufacture it," explains one upper-level manager, "you assign it to experienced engineers who like what they are doing. If you are designing something new that is higher-priced, with lots of features, you give it to the rookies."[23]

Questions and Applications

1. Suppose that you are interested in a job with Sony. Prepare a résumé that would appeal to a hiring manager there. Use your own experience or create a fictional résumé based on the experience of people you know.

2. Write a brief memo explaining why you chose to organize the résumé in Question 1 in either the chronological, targeted, or functional format.

3. Now prepare an accompanying cover letter for the résumé you crafted for Question 1.

Source: *Brenton Schlender, "How Sony Keeps the Magic Going,"* Fortune *(February 24, 1992): 76–84. © 1992 Time, Inc. All rights reserved.*

CORPORATE CASE:

From the Wastebasket

Because typographical errors and poor writing style will condemn your résumé to the wastebasket, proofreading it is crucial. The following excerpts are from actual résumés sent to employment agencies. Test your proofreading skills. Can you spot the mistakes? Revise each example so that it's correct (or at least makes sense).

1. Education: Curses in liberal arts, in computer science, in accounting.
2. My résumé shows my critical career developments. I'm also including other important parts of me.
3. Auditing for small manufacturing companies since 1877.
4. An obsession for detail; I like to make sure I cross my I's and dot my t's.
5. Self-Image: An octagon with smooth, radius angles versus a plain square with sharp corners.
6. Referees available on request.[24]
7. I am an excellant speller.
8. The following are my relevant qualities for you to overlook.
9. I was in the Honour Roll at my high school.
10. Yours truely
11. You will find that I am imminently qualified.
12. Extra curriccular activities
13. I was responsable for issueing official reciepts.
14. I play the guitar, violen, and paino.
15. My strength is in schedulling staff.
16. Through my education I have exposed myself to ...[25]

Effective Employment Interviewing

Learning how to look for and secure a job is the most critical life skill we can acquire.

Jennifer Young
University College of the Cariboo

(*Source:* Stephen J. Kaplan, *Don't wait 'til you graduate,* CACEE, Toronto, 1995, 17)

Facing a Gauntlet of Corporate Recruiters

M.B.A. students Ernest Blazzard and Mary Kowenhoven learned both the good news and the bad news at the same time: the good news was that they would have the opportunity to interview with a host of companies that might never travel to their university campuses; the bad news was that they would face these recruiters at a gruelling mass-interviewing forum—some would call it a pressure cooker—sponsored by 15 graduate business schools.

The day-long event was attended by 403 candidates and 62 employers. Candidates had just 30 minutes with each employer—time enough to make a positive impression or a career-damaging blunder.

Both Blazzard and Kowenhoven prepared extensively for their scheduled interviews. Blazzard sought the help of the university career services office to hone his interviewing skills. Working with consultants hired by the office, he took part in mock interviews that would help him obtain a job in corporate finance. Kowenhoven, also interested in a finance position, did extensive research: She studied articles about the seven companies she would interview with as well as corporate annual reports. She also grilled students who had already interviewed with these companies. She was particularly interested in the brainteasers used by interviewers from high technology firms to test candidates' ability to reason under pressure.

Both candidates handled themselves well. Kowenhoven was asked to analyze business cases for interviewers from consulting firms and to predict how changing economic conditions would affect interest rates. Blazzard was asked a number of time-tested interview questions: Tell me about last summer's internship, asked the Lotus interviewer. Where do you see yourself in five years? Why are you interviewing with Lotus? He successfully manoeuvred around subtle questions from a financial company about the ethics of aggressive stock traders.

Inevitably, both performances had flaws. When one interviewer asked Kowenhoven about her weaknesses, she was mortified to hear herself blurt out, "chocolate." As Blazzard linked his past experience with Lotus Notes to the requirements of the position offered by Lotus, he seemed uncomfortable when talking about technical systems. The interviewer picked up on this and quizzed him further, forcing Blazzard to assure him that although his knowledge was thin, he was a quick study. Blazzard also faced an unethical question that had nothing to do with his ability to do the job: As a family man, could he handle Lotus's heavy workload and travel schedule? Without hesitating, he said yes.

When the forum was over, both candidates assessed what they had been through. They hoped for choices and for good matches. Kowenhoven focused on finding people she would be comfortable working with, because she would probably be spending more time with them than with her own family. Blazzard would analyze each offer's compensation package, growth opportunities, potential for on-the-job satisfaction, and time left for family. "I'm looking at what emphasis [companies] place on your time," he explained. "It speaks volumes about how they value their employees." ▼

Source: Hal Lancaster, "Business Students Get 30 Minutes to Launch a Career," *Wall Street Journal,* 5 December 1995, B1.

Chapter Overview

The experiences of Ernest Blazzard and Mary Kowenhoven feature many of the elements that define employment interviewing: preparing for an interview, handling stressful questions, dealing with difficult and sometimes illegal questions, making silly mistakes and less than perfect impressions, and analyzing choices and lifestyles. These and other elements are the focus of this chapter, in which we will describe the employment-recruiting process. The common thread that ties all the elements together is the need for effective communication.

Defining the Job Interview

At the heart of this stage of the job-search process is the job interview. A **job interview** is generally a face-to-face encounter between a recruiter and a candidate in which the recruiter delves into the candidate's background, skills, job objectives, interests, and attitudes; in turn, the candidate asks questions about the position and the recruiting company. Typically, recruiters ask a series of probing questions to learn if the candidate is right for the job. Here are the ten most common qualities for which interviewers are looking when they question job candidates:

1. Intelligence and analytical ability
2. Creativity and flexibility
3. Communication skills
4. Work experience and required technical skills
5. Leadership qualities/team-playing ability
6. Initiative and entrepreneurship
7. Energy and stamina
8. Maturity
9. Interest in the position
10. Personal qualities and personality[1]

While the interviewer is assessing the candidate for these qualities, the candidate is conducting an assessment of his or her own to determine if the job is really desirable. If you think of the interview as a form of courting, you realize that the job choice is as much yours as the company's. It is a process in which job candidates and interviewers judge *each other* to decide whether they want to work *together*.

Those Challenging Behavioural Interviews _____

An applicant can prepare thoroughly for an interview; however, it is impossible to anticipate all possible interview scenarios. Behavioural descriptive interview questions are commonly used by recruiters to sort facts from exaggerations. These interviews use a domino questioning technique, in that each question leads to the next and probes deeper into an experience or scenario described by the applicant. Here is a typical set of behavioural interview questions:

1. Describe a situation where you were a team leader in a professional environment and conflict arose within the team.
2. What did you do to resolve this conflict?
3. What did you learn from this experience?
4. Since the conflict, how have you applied what you learned?
5. Where and when have you applied what you learned?
6. Who has benefited from your ability to resolve conflict?
7. May we call this person and verify your leadership in conflict resolution?

Another example might be:

1. Tell us about a situation when you have had criticism directed toward you.
2. Who criticized you?
3. What was the topic of the criticism?
4. What exactly were you criticized for?
5. How did you respond to the criticism?
6. What actions did you take following the criticism?
7. How would you handle the same criticism if it occurred again?
8. What did you learn from the incident?
9. Where have you applied this learning?

Often the interviewer reviews your résumé and asks questions to see whether you are qualified for the position.

10. Who has witnessed the results of what you learned?

11. May we contact this person to verify your ability to deal with criticism?

Many applicants feel threatened and almost interrogated by the probing nature of these questions. However, these questions, if presented in a diplomatic manner, are highly successful in determining the best candidate. Because many people embellish their résumés and then perform well at exaggerating their talents during the interview, the best candidate is not always selected for the job.

Behavioural descriptive questions are not difficult to answer if the candidate has the experience the recruiter is seeking. If you are asked a behavioural descriptive question and simply don't have the experience necessary to answer the question, be honest. The best policy is to tell the interview that you have no experience in this particular area. If you have related experience, ask the recruiter if you might refer to a similar situation in perhaps a different type of environment.

Relax—It's Only a Telephone Interview

Every employee is expected to practise excellent telephone techniques, which is why telephone contact with a potential employer may be a critical determining factor in the selection process.

In fact, when the potential employer and the applicant are located at long distances from each other, the employer may use only a telephone interview to make the employment selection. Be ready for the telephone interview by preparing a set of organized notes containing your questions and the attributes you wish to emphasize. Of course, it is essential to speak clearly, at a moderate pace and volume, with an enthusiastic tone, and with a great deal of courtesy.

Successful applicants will usually be placed on a probationary or contract status, since not having the opportunity to meet with the applicant has put the employer at a disadvantage when making the selection.

Preparing for an Interview

Nowhere are first impressions more important than in job interviews. Presenting an insecure or uncertain image may eliminate you as a candidate. Surveys tell us that more than six out of ten interviewers decide whether or not to hire a candidate within the first fifteen minutes.[2] It is not surprising, therefore, that interviewing training workshops are now helping job candidates learn how to present themselves effectively to potential employers. These workshops focus on the verbal and nonverbal communication skills needed to make an immediate, positive impression and land a job.[3]

Following some basic rules, however, can help you build a positive impression from the start. These include doing your homework by finding out as much as you can about the company and the position before the interview begins, generating a list of questions, choosing an effective presentation style, being ready to handle difficult interviewers, dressing for business, arriving on time, using effective nonverbal communication, and coming prepared with your résumé and recommendations.

Remember that everything you say and do communicates a powerful subtext that can influence the interviewer's perception more strongly than your skills or education. Keep this subtext in mind as you prepare for the interview.

COLLABORATIVE COMMUNICATION

Oh No! I'm Being Interviewed by the Whole Team.

A growing number of companies are using teams to interview and hire potential employees. It is commonly thought that better hiring decisions are made when more than one person is making the decision. The team should be **cross-functional** so that each person on the team provides a unique expertise and perspective.

As a job candidate you may encounter hiring teams, and after you are hired, you may become part of a team yourself. In either case, it is important to understand what companies value in team members and what makes hiring teams work. Here are some of the most important qualities and skills teams need to successfully evaluate job applicants:

▼ *Teams need people from various organizational levels who will interact with job applicants.* "Involvement in the hiring process gives employees [at all levels] a feeling of buy-in."

▼ *Teams need people with strong interviewing skills.* For hiring teams to function effectively, every team member must be trained in the skills of interviewing candidates. Interviewers must be able to ask behavioural-style questions that probe for in-depth answers in order to expose the candidate's experience and knowledge. Many companies offer interview-training programs to improve the skills of team members and to help members avoid the pitfalls of illegal questions.

▼ *Teams need individuals who have a positive attitude, who can articulate what they see in a candidate and what they need in a position, and who can remain objective.*

The process of making a joint hiring decision brings team members together, as they take ownership of the decision and try to make it work. An unexpected by-product: the team creates a support system for newly hired workers as it helps them adjust to the company, the company culture, and the work.

Questions for Critical Thinking

1. What are the main advantages of hiring teams? What might be the disadvantages?
2. Do you think hiring teams need a team leader to make the final decision? How do you think the leader would handle a situation in which half the team liked the candidate and the other half did not?
3. As a job applicant, would you approach an interview with a hiring team any differently than an interview with a single interviewer? Explain.

Sources: "How to Form Hiring Teams," *Personnel Journal* 3 (August 1994): S14; and "Teaming Up on a Problem," *Sales & Marketing Management* (July 1993): 36+.

RESEARCH, RESEARCH, AND THEN RESEARCH

Researching the company before the interview has several advantages. First, it helps you equalize your relationship with the interviewer, giving you information to ask questions as well as answer them. Second, it allows you to formulate a list of specific questions that will influence your thinking and responses. Third, and most important, it allows you to judge whether or not you want to work for the organization.

Despite the importance of pre-interview research, only about 5 percent of job applicants take the time to learn anything about a company, says Manchester Partners International career consultants.[4] John Sculley, former chairman of Apple Computer, bypassed company research when he took the job as chairman of Spectrum Information Technologies. Sculley quickly learned what he should have known at the start; namely, that the firm was being investigated by the Securities and Exchange Commission for financial and accounting irregularities.[5]

Begin your research well before you schedule any specific job interview. As we saw in Chapter 17, learning as much as you can, both about a specific field and about specific companies, will help you target a career. Among the information you can gather is the following:

No More Library Books—Using the Electronic Career Search

Searching through online databases and CD-ROM products can save you hours when researching industries and careers. Most libraries provide free access to CD-ROMs, but they generally charge online search fees. Here are some valuable electronic career information sources:

▼ *Canadian Business and Current Affairs* (CBCA, CD-ROM). Updated every six months, this CD-ROM provides current information on Canadian businesses and their affairs.

▼ *American Business Disc* (American Business Information, CD-ROM). Includes a database of over 10 million businesses nationwide.

▼ *Canadian News Disc* (CD-ROM). This disc, updated quarterly, provides current Canadian news articles and allows the user to search for information by company name.

▼ *Company ProFile* (Information Access Company, CD-ROM). Offers information on more than 150 000 private and public companies. A valuable feature allows you to use the industry code or geographic area to retrieve the top 100 companies ranked by sales.

▼ *Dun's Electronic Business Directory* (Dun & Bradstreet Information Services, online directory). Updated quar-

terly, this directory contains information on more than 8 million companies divided into 15 business categories. The directory is available through Dialog Information Services.

▼ *Dun's Million Dollar CD-ROM Collection* (Dun & Bradstreet Information Services, CD-ROM). Three separate databases focus on large companies, midlevel companies, and service-industry and public administration companies.

▼ *ABI/Inform Ondisc* (Data Courier Inc., CD-ROM). Updated monthly, this database contains citations and article abstracts from some 800 business publications.

▼ *Business Index—Public Edition* (Information Access Company, CD-ROM). Indexes more than 700 business and trade journals.

▼ *Business Periodicals Index* (H. W. Wilson Company, CD-ROM). This database is known for its thorough indexing of business subjects.

▼ *The Wall Street Journal Index* (Dow Jones and Company, online and CD-ROM). Includes indexes, abstracts, and articles from the *Wall Street Journal.*

Sources: Timothy D. Schellhardt and Tony Lee, "Hints for Hunters," *Wall Street Journal,* 27 February 1995, R6; and Richard Lathrop, *Who's Hiring Who? Find That Job Fast!* (Berkeley, California: Ten Speed Press, 1989), 203–205.

▼ the goods and services that the organization sells

▼ the company's organizational structure, including the functions and locations of subsidiaries and divisions

▼ employment trends (has the company been hiring or cutting staff?)

▼ industry trends (are new products changing the field?)

▼ earnings (in public companies, this number has a strong effect on stock price)

▼ external pressures affecting business operations (which may be exerted by government or by the general economic climate)

Your basic sources of information are:

▼ company Web sites posted on the Internet

▼ the company itself (for example, annual reports, brochures, newsletters, news clippings)

▼ business and industry groups like local chambers of commerce

▼ business publications like the *Financial Post, Maclean's, Profit—The Magazine for Canadian Entrepreneurs, Canadian Business, Time—Canadian Edition*

- ▼ Canadian Key Businesses (Dun & Bradstreet) and V.I.P. Business Contacts (both discuss Canadian businesses, are organized by the name of the company, are updated annually, and are available in the public library)
- ▼ local and financial newspapers

In order to learn all you can about the organization, research:

- ▼ the organization's products and services
- ▼ how profitable the organization is
- ▼ the number of employees the organization has
- ▼ how long the organization has been operating
- ▼ the extent of the company's operations
- ▼ any recent expansion the company may have experienced
- ▼ any mergers or name changes the company has undergone
- ▼ the company's competitive standing in the industry, and
- ▼ the organization's hiring practices.[6]

Personal resources are also valuable. In your network of contacts, for example, you may find people who have worked or currently work for your target organization or who are connected with one of the firm's clients or suppliers. In addition, the placement office at your college or alumni association may help you to locate people with firsthand knowledge about a company. Finally, you can be your own detective. If you wanted to work for Northern Images Greeting Cards, for example, you could interview the managers of stores where the greeting cards are purchased in order to learn what they think about the product.

Most sources of employment research information are available at your library. Using such online services as CompuServe, you can tap into information databases to find business and trade information from hundreds of sources specializing in particular fields (for example, *Advertising Age* and *PC Magazine*); company financial statements, including annual reports, press releases, and the reports of financial analysts; and current-events coverage of the business climate.

Upon request, virtually all companies provide not only annual reports but also sales and marketing brochures, which define company products and their potential in the marketplace. Another valuable source is a company's employee handbook, which explains both employees' obligations to the company and its commitment to them. You can ask to see a copy of the handbook at your interview.

→ *Cross Reference*
We discuss job descriptions later in this chapter on pages 536 and 537.

Keep in mind that although your research will tell you a lot about a company and its industry, it will tell you very little about the specific job for which you are applying. For this reason, you might request a job description (if one is available) from the company. A job description provides much more specific information than just the job advertisement. Information about career opportunities, travel requirements, and relocation possibilities may be requested during an interview. However, information about salaries and benefits should be requested only after the position has been offered to you.

GENERATE INTELLIGENT QUESTIONS

From your research, compile a list of questions that you want the interviewer to answer. Write these questions on a sheet of paper and bring them with you. As you formulate your questions, remember that most interviewers respond favourably when a candidate takes an active part in the interview. Naturally, they consider questions a sign of intelligence, assertiveness, and involvement. Appropriate questioning also demonstrates your ability not only to analyze the company's situation from your own perspective but to use what you have learned to communicate your strengths and qualifications.

Table 18-1 lists a number of questions that, as a job candidate, you might want to ask a prospective employer. As you can see, although some of the questions are straightforward requests for information ("What are the job responsibilities?"), others are attempts to analyze the job opportunity. Do not, however, waste time asking for detailed information that you can find in other sources. Questions like the following are a clear sign that you did not do your homework:

▼ What are your major products?

▼ How many people work for your company?

▼ How long have you been in business?

Table 18-1 Questions That You May Want to Ask an Interviewer

Job-Content Questions

▼ What are the job responsibilities? May I get a copy of the job description?

▼ To whom would I report and how many people would report to me?

▼ What do you consider ideal experience for this job?

▼ What personal qualities improve the likelihood of job success?

▼ What is the most serious problem facing this department?

▼ Are there any unusual job demands that I should know about?

▼ What have been some of the best results produced by people in this job?

▼ What would be my primary job challenge?

▼ Was the person who last held this job promoted? If so, may I speak with him or her about the position? May I speak to any team members?

▼ I noticed in [name any appropriate business publication] that you are expanding your _____ division. How will that affect my job responsibilities?

▼ Can you tell me about your performance review system?

▼ Do you have a training program for this position?

▼ Why do you think this job would be right for me?

Job-Opportunity Questions

▼ What is the typical career path for someone who takes this position?

▼ Do you provide career counselling?

▼ Is opportunity more likely if I am willing to relocate?

▼ I noticed that your international division produces the same products in [name the appropriate parts of the world]. Does my background lend itself to working in those locations?

▼ What is the company's policy regarding in-house transfers?

▼ From which areas do your company's top executives come?

Questions about Unique Company Characteristics

▼ Where is the organization going? What products are being developed to increase market share?

▼ Can you describe the corporate culture?

Sources: Richard Lathrop, *Who's Hiring Who? How to Find That Job Fast!* (Berkeley, Calif.: Ten Speed Press, 1989), 203–205; and Timothy D. Schellhardt and Tony Lee, "Hints for Hunters," *Wall Street Journal,* 27 February 1995, R6.

DEVELOP A KNOCKOUT
PRESENTATION STYLE

The first step in adopting an effective presentation style is to consider the interview as yet another communication interaction involving a sender, a receiver, a message, a channel, a context, and feedback. The following guidelines should help you to implement this strategy.

▼ *Be a careful listener.* Listen carefully to all questions and give concise, direct answers. Occasionally, you may not get the opportunity to give any answers at all. Debbie Ng, a McGill University grad, states, "I had an interview in which the interviewer did all the talking."[7]

▼ *Be organized and goal-directed.* Keep in mind that your purpose is twofold—to be offered the job and to evaluate the opportunity. Don't ramble or provide irrelevant background information. Ask questions that will help you make your decision.

▼ *Provide specific examples.* Concrete examples tell a story better than any generalization. Telling an interviewer that you have the skills to "increase sales" or "reduce production costs" is far less effective than supporting your claims with a descriptive anecdote. Paul Green, a management consultant who developed Hewlett-Packard's interview system, tells the following story: "I was interviewing a plant manager and needed confirmation that the individual had a strong commitment to task completion. The candidate described a time when he had his appendix removed on a Thursday and was back in the office on Monday—to the shock of everyone at the plant. This story provided very strong evidence that he was a driven, hard-working person. He got the job."[8]

▼ *Practise your delivery.* Annoying speech mannerisms—such as repeating *you know, okay, um,* or *eh* throughout your conversation—can compromise the impression that you make.

▼ *Be conscious of your tone as well as your words.* Convey the feeling that you welcome the opportunity to talk about yourself and the position. Be enthusiastic and eager as you describe your background and ways that you can help the company. However, don't make the mistake of telling managers what their companies are doing wrong and then enumerating the changes you would make. Even if you did considerable research, this approach is presumptuous—you don't have inside information. Instead, focus on the employer's concerns and describe how your background qualifies you to deal with them. As Noni Wright, Recruitment and Selection Coordinator at TransAlta Utilities Corporation remarks, "Extremely pushy, persistent students really turn me off."[9]

▼ *Never let your guard down.* Millington F. McCoy, managing director of a New York executive search firm, remembers how one job candidate ruined his chances of being offered the job by making inappropriate remarks *after* the formal interview was over. "We were casually talking and this anger came up," recalls McCoy. Complaining about his former company, the candidate said, " 'Those damn guys never do reports in the format I want.' " McCoy was stunned. "That remark showed his true soul. I hadn't detected his need to control. Boy, that finished the interview."[10]

BE READY TO HANDLE THOSE TOUGH INTERVIEWERS

An interviewer's personal style can interfere with the normal exchange of information. At their worst, personal idiosyncrasies can hinder communication. Interviewers who are extremely formal, disorganized, uninterested, arrogant, or obviously overworked may make your presentation difficult or give you less attention than you deserve. Regardless of the situation, focus on your communication objective. Try to maintain control of the interview, and be conscious of presenting yourself in a positive, forceful way.

DRESS TO MAKE A PROFESSIONAL STATEMENT

Although first impressions rarely win jobs, your appearance—your clothes, hair, shoes, cosmetics, and jewellery—can certainly cost you a job before you ever open your mouth. Your goal is to look the part by adopting the traditional "uniform" of business. Your appearance should make the statement that you are a professional and you want to be taken seriously. This is true even in companies that have a dress-down policy. Kathi Henderson, a recruiter for retailer Eddie Bauer, explains: "Even though we wear shorts and jeans around the office, if a candidate wore that to an interview, I wouldn't like it. I look for a certain professionalism in an interview."[11]

Spend the extra time it takes to look well groomed. Dress conservatively since you want the interviewer to focus on your answers without being distracted by your appearance. By applying the following checklist to your interview preparation, you may be able to convey the proper message.

- ❏ Your hair should be neat, and away from your face.
- ❏ If you wear cosmetics, apply them sparingly.
- ❏ Your nails should be well manicured and clean.
- ❏ Your jewellery should be simple, minimal, and yet complimentary. Since you don't know the nature of the interviewer, it is best to play it safe and wear limited and conservative jewellery.
- ❏ Your professional attire should include a suit jacket.
- ❏ Your clothing should not be revealing; skirts should be of a comfortable length and blouses should never reveal cleavage or camisole.
- ❏ Shoes should be clean, polished, and conventional.
- ❏ White blouses or shirts must be very white. Cuffs or collars that have a grey appearance are a sign that grooming is less than perfect.
- ❏ Ties should complement a suit rather than be flamboyant.
- ❏ Cologne should be avoided. A fragrance that is attractive to you could be offensive to another person.
- ❏ For men, the most appropriate choice of colour is a variation of black, navy, brown, or grey. Acceptable business clothing for women tends to be more colourful than that of their male counterparts, although still conservative.

Whatever you determine will be your style for an interview, consider the strong nonverbal message that your image portrays.

BE PUNCTUAL—BE READY

Make it a point to arrive on time for job interviews. Keeping an interviewer waiting sets a negative tone that will be difficult to overcome. To make sure that you will arrive on time at an unfamiliar location, take a dry run to measure the length of the trip. And always give yourself a cushion—a half-hour or so of extra time that will enable you to get through the worst traffic jams.

Being "punctual," however, does not mean arriving too early. Announce yourself to the receptionist five minutes before the interview—no sooner. In business, where meetings are often held back to back, making a premature entrance may mark you as an amateur. You should arrive ten to fifteen minutes before your scheduled interview. The first five minutes should be spent in the washroom making last minute adjustments to your appearance. Do your best to relax. If the reception area has other applicants waiting for their interviews, try to avoid the area until the last possible moment because the tense atmosphere will only increase your anxiety. "Spend the time thinking about the particular position for which you are being interviewed. Reread those key factors on the job advertisement. Keep thinking about the skills required for the position and how you are going to convince the interviewers you're the best candidate."[12]

PERFORM THE GREAT CANADIAN HANDSHAKE

In a job interview, the handshake initiates the communication that will last throughout the meeting. At the same time, it says something about who you are. As you enter the meeting room, give a clear signal that you are indeed initiating a handshake—extend your hand in the direction of the interviewer. Grasp the interviewer's hand in a relaxed, firm manner and shake hands for no longer than a second or two. Women use handshakes in the same way as men, although some women make the mistake of believing that a strong handshake marks them as too aggressive. On the contrary, a weak handshake marks them as unbusinesslike and ineffectual.

Make eye contact with the interviewer as you are shaking hands. Momentarily holding the interviewer's gaze communicates confidence. *Initiating* eye contact—rather than simply *responding* to it—is the most effective way to begin because it says that you are unafraid to make the first move.

Progress Check

1. If company research is such an important part of interview preparation, why do you think so few people do it?
2. What is the relationship between effective research and effective questioning?
3. List critical aspects of nonverbal communication that can affect how others see you during an interview.

WHAT SHOULD I BRING TO THE INTERVIEW?

You will need only a few important materials for the interview. The following items can be essential or at least useful:

❑ Always bring your best attitude and enthusiasm. The nonverbal communication conveyed by your attitude is transparent and powerful!

❑ A portfolio is a collection of samples of your best (and perfect) work. The work should be organized into sections, such as reports, spreadsheets, tables, and graphics, that you have created by yourself. You might want to include related certificates and diplomas, as well as transcripts if they are impressive. At least one letter of reference is an asset. Your work should be packaged into an attractive case with rings to hold the pages and plastic covers to protect your work samples.

During the interview, find an appropriate opportunity to introduce the portfolio and discuss your work with the interviewer. Remember, the portfolio is not intended to be an information tool; rather, it is a sales tool, and the product is you.

- Be prepared with a pen and paper to write down important facts you learn during the interview. Your pen should be attractive and in a good writing condition.

- To demonstrate your preparedness, bring along extra copies of your résumé and offer one to the interviewer just as the interview is about to begin. You should also have a copy for yourself.

- If references do not appear on your résumé, you should bring a list of three or more references (including their names, titles, company names, company addresses, and company telephone, fax, and e-mail numbers). The list should be attractively keyed on a single sheet. Be prepared to leave this sheet with the interviewer.

- If this interview is a result of your response to a posted job advertisement, bring a copy of the advertisement to the interview. Highlight the key responsibilities listed. Don't be afraid to refer to the advertisement during the interview; this shows that you know exactly what type of job you are applying for and that you have prepared for the interview.

- It is wise to prepare a crib sheet and bring it along to the interview. Your crib sheet can list the key responsibilities for the job and cite specific examples of how you have demonstrated competence. It should also include any questions you anticipate asking. The sheet should be attractively keyed and organized.

- With desktop publishing, you can prepare personal business cards. You can produce your own professional-looking cards by printing them on card stock. Or, for a nominal charge, you can have a professional printer produce a small number of business cards. The applicant who leaves a business card makes a professional statement.

WHAT SHOULD I AVOID BRINGING TO THE INTERVIEW?

Although some items in the following list seem like common sense, employers often report that applicants do bring these items to an interview. Under all circumstances, avoid the following:

- Never bring packages. If you've been shopping immediately prior to the interview, leave your packages in the car or in the store.

- Large and heavy handbags and briefcases detract from a professional appearance. Keep it simple!

- As ridiculous as it may sound, you should never bring another person to the place of the interview. Naturally you wouldn't bring anyone into the interview room, but many applicants do make plans to meet friends or relatives immediately after the interview. The applicant needs to concentrate on the interview, not on other people who may be waiting in the lobby, reception area, or a circling car outside. Demonstrate your independence by arriving alone and leaving alone.

Table 18–2 summarizes the steps in preparing for an interview. It also highlights some of the problems that arise when these steps are mishandled.

WHAT DOES A MODEL INTERVIEW LOOK LIKE?

Most interviews for entry-level positions follow a general pattern that includes six distinct parts: an introduction, questions about work experience, questions about education, a discussion of current activities and interests, an analysis of strengths and

Table 18-2   Summary of the Steps in Interview Preparation

Preparation	Value	Problems When Poorly Handled
Conduct thorough research	provides information to question the interviewer enables applicant to evaluate an organization equalizes relationship with interviewer	candidate may be perceived as uninterested, unmotivated, and unprepared
Prepare questions	demonstrates an active, assertive approach enables candidate to ask questions as well as answer them	inappropriate questions may influence the interviewer's perception of the applicant
Choose an effective presentation style, dress, and body language	can provide a subtext of competence the *way* applicants talk is just as important as *what* they say	negative first impression is difficult to overcome
Handle difficult interviewers	enables applicant to salvage a difficult situation	inability places applicant at the mercy of the interviewer's idiosyncrasies
Prepare to be on time	communicates that applicants are serious about the opportunity and understand the importance of punctuality in business	lateness sets a negative tone that is difficult to overcome
Bring résumé and references	demonstrates forethought and preparation can save the interview when interviewer misplaces critical documents	absence demonstrates lack of preparation and an unprofessional approach to the interview

weaknesses, and closing remarks.[13] As we analyze each part of this pattern, remember that variations in this model are not only possible but likely. For example, an interviewer would probably ask recent graduates about education before work experience. In this section we will describe the basic parts or stages of a "model" process by focusing on the nature and pattern of questions that are typically asked. In the next sections, we will focus more specifically on the content of some of these questions and ways of responding to them; namely, strategies for handling difficult questions (including unethical questions) and negotiating salary and other compensation.

As we mentioned earlier, your goal throughout the interview is to get interviewers to talk about their department, needs, and problems so that you can demonstrate why you are the best candidate. When managers are specific, you too can be specific in describing how something in your background applies to the present situation. If you are reluctant to probe, remember that most people—including businesspeople—love to talk about themselves and their problems. Your questions should begin after the introductory phase of the interview.

THE JOB DESCRIPTION   During the interview, the manager may refer to a **job description** which, like the one in Figure 18-1, outlines the requirements of the job. Included are the job title, general objectives, specific duties, the individual to whom the employee will report, supervisory responsibilities, and required education and skills. Because it describes in detail the job to be done and the qualifications of the ideal candidate, this document is especially important during screening interviews

JOB DESCRIPTION
ENTRY-LEVEL CLAIM REPRESENTATIVE

General statement of duties
Investigate claims, negotiate settlements, and authorize payment to claimants for losses covered under homeowner and automobile policies.

Supervision received
Report to a department manager who is responsible for 10 claim representatives.

Supervisory responsibilities
None.

Typical duties
(List includes most of the duties required by the job.)
- 30% 1. Work with policyholders who file claims for damage or loss covered under their homeowner or automobile policies.
- 25% 2. Contact claimants by letter or telephone to obtain information on repair costs or other records requested by the company.
- 15% 3. Input data into central computer.
- 10% 4. Keep written records of information obtained from claimants in order to process claims.
- 10% 5. Work with supervisors to negotiate a settlement with claimants and close cases.
- 5% 6. Analyze repair bills submitted by claimants according to standards set by company.
- 5% 7. Work with accounting department to request payment cheques.

Minimum qualifications
Education: Basic degree. Courses in insurance, economics, business, or accounting preferred.
Experience: No prior claim representative experience necessary.
Knowledge, skills, and abilities:
1. Communicate effectively with claimants in writing and over the phone.
2. Strong analytic ability.
3. Understand and apply federal and provincial insurance laws and regulations.
4. Use a word processor.

Desirable qualifications
Good memory, observant, detail-oriented; excellent working knowledge of computer applications; knowledge of home and automotive repair terminology helpful.

On-the-job training
Provided by company. Job holder must pass a written examination after completing an approved course in insurance adjusting. Licensing required by the province.

Prepared by:_____
Date:_____

Figure 18-1 Sample Job Description

with company recruiters. It is less important during the in-depth interview, where the interviewing manager knows and can explain the requirements of the job in much better detail.

THE INTRODUCTION   In the first few minutes, a good interviewer has one overriding goal—to establish rapport and relax the candidate. Nonverbal language is important at this stage. A firm handshake, eye contact, and a smile all tell the interviewer that you welcome the opportunity to exchange information and demonstrate your worth.

Many interviewers engage in small talk to reduce tension. They may, for example, ask if you know a common acquaintance at a company listed on your résumé. During this stage, an experienced interviewer lets you do most of the talking, realizing that the act of speaking will make you feel less self-conscious.

General job-related questions follow. The interviewer may ask, "Tell me about yourself," delve into how you learned about the job, or explore your job expectations. The following are a few popular introductory questions:

▼ Why are you interested in this job?
▼ What do you know about this company and this particular job?
▼ What do you see as the purpose of this interview?

These questions are important because they establish whether you and the interviewer share the same assumptions about the interview's purpose and the job.

EMPLOYMENT EXPERIENCE   Next, most interviewers turn to the body of the interview, expecting to learn about you and to answer questions that you may have about the job and the organization. According to Kelly Smith, Regional Manager, London Life Insurance Co., "Come prepared to blow your own horn. Tell employers about past success—it will be your only chance."[14] The first area of interest is usually work experience. The interviewer may begin by saying something like the following:

> Let's talk about your background and experience—both what you've done and what you hope to do. Then we can judge whether opportunities in our organization suit your talents and interests. Perhaps the best place to start is with your work experience.[15]

A series of probing questions usually follows, often focusing on the specifics of one or more of your previous jobs. The primary purpose of these questions is to determine if your experience qualifies you for the present position. However, the questioning is also aimed at judging your adaptability, productivity, motivation, and leadership, and assessing the development of your career over the years. You may be asked common work-related questions like the following:

▼ How does your previous employment experience prepare you for this job?
▼ Describe the most difficult problem you faced in your last job and how you solved it.
▼ What were you best at? Give me specific examples.
▼ What things did you do less well?
▼ Tell me about your on-the-job people skills. Describe a situation in which you handled people effectively. How do you know you were effective?
▼ Were there incidents when your people skills were less effective?
▼ Tell me about your team projects.
▼ When you work on a team would you prefer to be a leader or a team member? Why?
▼ Were deadlines a problem? How did you prioritize your responsibilities when working under pressure?
▼ What is your career goal? How have the jobs you've held in the past helped you pursue that goal?
▼ What work accomplishment are you most proud of?
▼ Why did you leave your last job?
▼ Why do you want this job?
▼ The job advertisement requested someone with several years experience; however, your experience is limited. How would you expect to compensate for this deficiency?

Practise responding to these questions as you prepare for the interview. Later in the chapter, we will examine specific responses to difficult questions.

INTERVIEW Seeking Employment Abroad

G. Frederick Reinhardt III, International Private Banker

As the son of the U.S. ambassador to Vietnam, Egypt, and Italy, G. Frederick Reinhardt III learned European languages and cultures by living and attending schools abroad. Reinhardt's knowledge was put to the test when he interviewed for an executive position with Merrill Lynch International Bank in London. We asked him about the series of interviews that led to a job offer and for advice to others seeking employment abroad.

Question: Why do you think you were offered the job?

Answer: There were three key factors. First, my experience with the international division of Chemical Bank in New York and Italy gave me a solid background in banking. Second, I knew the investment side of finance. And third, I spoke the languages and knew the cultures.

Question: Were you interviewed in languages other than English?

Answer: Although English was used most of the time, my American, German, and English interviewers would occasionally shift to French, Italian, and German. Because business requires a different vocabulary than conversational speech, they wanted to know whether I could use these languages in a business context. At the time, my Italian business vocabulary was the strongest because I had spent a number of years in Italy.

Question: Did the interviewers focus on your knowledge of European cultures?

Answer: They looked at my ability to adapt to the cultures of Italy, Switzerland, and Germany because I would be doing business in those countries. Specifically, they wanted to be sure that I understood the vast differences between the Italian and German cultures, one being Latin-based and the other Germanic. They also focused on my knowledge of each country's business practices.

Question: Your family background gave you the opportunity to live all over the world and to learn different languages and cultures. Because few North Americans have this opportunity, how can they prepare themselves to work abroad?

Answer: They can start sensitizing themselves at an early age to different languages and cultures. They can take part in exchange programs during high school and college. Spending a year in Asia, Europe, or South America is an invaluable

learning experience. For those already in the job market, it's a good idea to spend time travelling abroad and to join an international club run by a foreign chamber of commerce. These clubs, found in large Canadian and U.S. cities, have programs for citizens who want to study foreign cultures. To learn about the global marketplace, they should read publications like the *Economist* and the *International Herald Tribune* and study international business news in the *Wall Street Journal.* They should master geography and international current events. While many Americans can't identify the Prime Minister of England, every English person knows the President of the United States. They should raise their consciousness about international affairs well before the interview begins.

Finally, they should learn as much as they can about the interview process as practised abroad. Many North Americans don't realize that foreign interviewers are not governed by the same employment laws or practices. For example, while interviewers in North America are not allowed to ask about marital status, age, or disability, interviewers in foreign countries can delve into these personal areas. As a result, interviews often centre around your family as well as your ability to do a job.

Source: Interview with G. Frederick Reinhardt III.

EDUCATION   Having explored your work history, interviewers usually turn next to education. Their interest lies not so much in your grades, major, or extracurricular activities as in the way your school accomplishments relate to your ability to do a job. Bear this fact in mind as you analyze the interviewer's questions and focus your answers accordingly. Provide the link between school and work by highlighting the specific knowledge and skills that will help you succeed. Demonstrate motivation by pointing to such items as extracurricular activities and volunteer work. Finally, be sure to describe all connections in a direct way—for example:

> When I was editor of the student newspaper, I handled weekly deadlines as well as 18 credits. The paper won two awards that year, and I maintained a B+ average. This demonstrates my ability to juggle my responsibilities and do them all well, which I think would suit the needs of your fast-paced office.

During this stage of the interview, you may also be asked common education-related questions like the following:

▼ How has your education prepared you for this job?
▼ Why did you choose your major field of study?
▼ What were your most and least favourite subjects?
▼ Did you work while in school? How did you manage your time?
▼ Describe the toughest problem you faced while in school and how you solved it.
▼ Describe your extracurricular activities.
▼ What did you learn in school that will help you succeed on this job?
▼ Do you plan to continue your education? How?

Be prepared to deal with these questions in the same way that you deal with work-related questions. Be detailed in describing your activities and focus your responses—that is, tailor them to highlight the link between your past experience and the current needs of your potential employer.

ACTIVITIES AND INTERESTS   In an attempt to learn what your leisure pursuits reveal about you, many interviewers turn next to your activities and interests. This discussion is often considered optional, especially if there is limited interview time. As you will see, many activities-and-interests questions are designed to explore not only the skills that give you the most satisfaction but, perhaps more importantly, your ability to deal with people, both as a leader and a team member. Follow the strategy of continually trying to tie your answers to the job opportunity and the employer's needs. Here are some typical activities-and-interests questions:

▼ Your résumé indicates that you are involved in various community activities. What do you do in these activities?
▼ Do your activities place you in a leadership role? Describe how you work with other people. What type of leader do others believe you are?
▼ With so many community ties, how would you feel about relocating?
▼ Do any of your community activities involve skills that you could also use on this job?

STRENGTHS AND SHORTCOMINGS   As interviewers explore your strengths and weaknesses, they ask themselves three key questions:

▼ Can this person do the job? (Do you have the right skills, knowledge, talents, and experience to work effectively?)

▼ Will this person do the job? (Will your interests and personal characteristics motivate you to do the work?)

▼ Will this person fit comfortably in the organization? (Are your personality, character, work ethic, and people skills compatible with the corporate culture?)

In order to tie the discussion to your ability to do the job, most interviewers start with your strengths. For example, they may start by turning the interview in the following direction:

> Now let's try to summarize our discussion. As you think about what we've covered, what would you say are some of your chief strengths? What are some of the assets that would make you a good prospect for an employer?[16]

At this point, you may be asked follow-up questions such as:

▼ What do you believe are your special qualifications for this job?

▼ List three of your most outstanding qualities. How would your previous employers respond to this list?

▼ What in your background makes you the ideal candidate for this job?

Moving on to your shortcomings, the interviewer may then lead with comments and questions like these:

> You've shown me some real strengths. Now, what about some of your qualities that aren't so strong? All of us have a few areas we'd like to improve. In the past you may have had constructive criticism from friends, supervisors, or other people who have come to know you well. Thinking of the future, what areas or what personal qualities need improvement for you to be fully effective in your job or career?

CLOSING REMARKS   In closing, the interviewer thanks the candidate for discussing his or her background and job qualifications and asks if there are any unanswered questions about the job or the company. When interviewers are extremely interested in the candidate, they may take this opportunity to try to "sell" the company by describing such inducements as its market strength and employee benefits. Finally, interviewers will usually tell you what will happen next—for instance, "You can expect to hear from me within a week."

A CLOSING DESIGNED TO NAIL THE INTERVIEW

The last few activities of an interview may be the critical ones that determine your success.

Watch for clues that the interview is coming to an end. The interviewer may thank you for coming, suggest that you schedule a time to take employment tests, invite you to arrange for a second interview, tell you that you will hear by a certain date if the organization is interested in your application, or offer you the job.

A good closure to an interview would include one or more of the following:

▼ Firmly shaking hands.

▼ Restating your interest in the position. Example: "I hope you will consider me for the job. I feel confident I would make a positive contribution to your organization."

▼ Checking the follow-up procedure that will be employed by the organization. Example: "When might I expect to hear from you? If I don't hear from you by that date, may I call you?"

Progress Check

1. List some work-related questions you can expect an interviewer to ask.

2. Why is it important to link answers to interview questions to the employer's needs? How does this relate to the concept of audience analysis?

3. Why would an interviewer ask you about your activities and interests?

Table 18-3   A Guide to Screening and Selection in Employment

Subject	Avoid Asking	Preferred	Comment
Name	about name change: whether it was changed by court order, marriage, or other reason maiden name		ask after selection if needed to check on previously held jobs or educational credentials
Address	for addresses outside Canada	ask place and duration of current or recent address	
Age	for birth certificates, baptismal records, or about age in general	ask applicants if they are eligible to work under Canadian laws regarding age restrictions	if precise age required for benefits plans or other legitimate purposes, it can be determined after selection
Gender	males or females to fill in different applications about pregnancy, child bearing plans, or child care arrangements	can ask applicant if the attendance requirements can be met	during the interview or after selection, the applicant, for purposes of courtesy, may be asked which of Mr./Mrs./Miss/Ms. is preferred
Martial status	whether applicant is single, married, divorced, engaged, separated, widowed, or living common-law whether an applicant's spouse is subject to transfer about spouse's employment	if transfer or travel is part of the job, the applicant can be asked if he or she can meet these requirements ask whether there are any circumstances that might prevent completion of a minimum service commitment	information on dependents can be determined after selection if necessary
Family status	number of children or dependents about child care arrangements	if the applicant would be able to work the required hours and, where applicable, overtime	contacts for emergencies and/or details on dependents can be determined after selection
National or ethnic origin	about birth-place, nationality of ancestors, spouse, or other relatives whether born in Canada for proof of citizenship	since those who are entitled to work in Canada must be citizens, permanent residents, or holders of valid work permits, applicants can be asked if they are legally entitled to work in Canada	documentation of eligibility to work (papers, visas, etc.) can be requested after selection
Military service	about military service in other countries	inquiry about Canadian military service where employment preference is given to veterans by law	
Language	mother tongue where language skills obtained	ask if applicant understands, reads, writes, or speaks languages required for the job	testing or scoring applicants for language proficiency is not permitted unless job-related
Race or colour	any inquiry into race or colour, including colour of eyes, skin, or hair		
Photographs	for photo to be attached to applications or sent to interviewer before interview		photos for security passes or company files can be taken after selection
Religion	about religious affiliation, church membership, frequency of church attendance if applicant will work a specific religious holiday for references from clergy or religious leader	explain the required work shift, asking if such a schedule poses problems for the applicant	reasonable accommodation of an employee's religious beliefs is the employer's duty
Height and Weight			no inquiry unless there is evidence they are genuine occupational requirements

Table 18-3 [continued]

Subject	Avoid Asking	Preferred	Comment
Disability	for listing of all disabilities, limitations or health problems	ask if applicant has any condition that could affect ability to do the job	a disability is only relevant to job ability if it:
	whether applicant drinks or uses drugs	ask if the applicant has any condition that should be considered in selection	- threatens the safety or property of others
	whether applicant has ever received psychiatric care or been hospitalized for emotional problems		- prevents the applicant from safe and adequate job performance even when reasonable efforts are made to accommodate the disability
	whether applicant has received worker's compensation		
Medical Information	if currently under physician's care		medical exams should be conducted after selection and only if an employee's condition is related to job duties
	name of family doctor		
	if receiving counselling or therapy		offers of employment can be made conditional on successful completion of a medical
Pardoned Conviction	whether an applicant has ever been convicted	if bonding is a job requirement ask if applicant is eligible	inquiries about criminal record/convictions are discouraged unless related to job duties
	if an applicant has ever been arrested		
	whether an applicant has a criminal record		
Sexual Orientation	any inquiry about the applicant's sexual orientation		contacts for emergencies and/or details about dependents can be determined after selection
References			the same restrictions that apply to questions asked of applicants apply when asking for employment references

Source: *A Guide to Screening and Selection in Employment,* Canadian Human Rights Commission, 1995.

A QUESTION OF ETHICS

Is the Interviewer Discriminating Against You?

The Canadian Human Rights Commission tells employers how to conduct job interviews without violating the law. Their guidelines are listed in Table 18-3.

Questions for Critical Thinking

1. Critics of these guidelines say that they focus too much on semantic differences and that the distinctions between legal and illegal phrasing is slight. Do you agree or disagree? Why?

2. Do these guidelines fully protect persons with disabilities against this type of discrimination? Explain your answer.

3. How much do you think the employer should know about job applicants' religious convictions?

→ **Cross Reference**
We discuss thank you letters in this chapter on page 551.

▼ Leaving a business card.[17]

▼ Delivering a thank-you message to the office within 24 hours. This message may be in the form of a letter, card, or an e-mail note.

How to Handle Difficult Questions

Handle difficult questions by being positive. Positive responses give interviewers little reason to focus on the negative, and, as a result, they are less likely to look for problems. Negativity is often displayed when people say the first thing that comes to their minds. These responses may encourage the interviewer to probe deeper for further signs of negative behavioural patterns. To avoid this tendency, develop a strategy based on the following guidelines:[18]

▼ *Prepare for difficult questions.* Start by expecting that difficult or negative questions will be asked. Prepare for them by confronting them in advance. Make a list of all the questions that you would find difficult to answer. Then prepare the answers by focusing on positive outcomes—what you learned from a situation, how you grew, what you did to solve a problem.

▼ *Learn to identify negative questions.* Often included in these questions are words like *weakness, problem, conflict, difficulty, criticism,* and *least.* Remember, however, that experienced interviewers often couch negative questions in positive terms as they focus on a candidate's deficits—for example:

> If you had the opportunity to start your last job over again, what would you do differently?

or

> If you had the chance to go back to school to improve your job performance, what would you study?

▼ *Turn negative questions into positive responses.* For example, you might describe what you learned from a difficult situation, how you grew professionally, or how you transformed a problem into an opportunity.

> In response to the question, "If you had the opportunity to start your last job over again, what would you do differently?" you might say:

> I would have encouraged my manager to give me feedback about my work as soon as possible after I was hired. Pointing out the pluses and minuses of my work at this early stage would have helped me learn the company's expectations within a shorter period of time.

▼ *Don't blame others for problems or rationalize negative situations.* Like most people, employers respond poorly when candidates minimize serious problems or shift responsibility for problems. For instance, don't blame your previous manager for the department's poor productivity or try to say that the problem was unimportant. Instead, describe problems in specific, concrete terms and offer suggestions for remedying them—for instance:

> Our computer system couldn't handle the volume of work the department produced. As a result, we had weeks of orders backing up. After analyzing the problem, I wrote a report to my manager suggesting an upgraded system—similar to your company's system.

▼ *Don't reveal proprietary information about your previous employer.* Proprietary information is confidential information owned by a company. Revealing it in an interview marks you as untrustworthy and unethical. Rather than winning points for providing secrets, you lose credibility—not surprisingly, interviewers will conclude that you would do the same thing to them.

DIFFICULT QUESTIONS AND EFFECTIVE ANSWERS

Many of the questions posed by employers can leave the applicant surprised and unprepared. According to Jason Toledano, a York University graduate, "The first question I was asked in an interview was if I could play goalie for their hockey team."[19] Remember that interviewers often use many of the same questions to elicit information and put job candidates off balance. Although there are many "right"—or at least standard—answers to the most common difficult questions, it is still valuable to analyze several successful approaches to some of them. Here, for example, is a series of typical difficult questions. Each is paired with a suggested approach for responding.[20]

> *Questions:* What do you like most about your current job? What do you like least?
> *Approach:* Focus on the things that you like rather than those you dislike. If you paint a negative picture, the interviewer may wonder why you are still in the job or whether your negative comments reflect a poor attitude. Avoid talking about personal differences you had with co-workers.

> *Question:* What are your most serious weaknesses?
> *Approach:* Turn weaknesses into positive traits. Try saying, for instance: "I tend to get so wrapped up in what I'm doing that I can't think of anything else till it's done." Or, "I can't stand to see people waste time." Offer one or two weaknesses and then stop. If the interviewer presses for a third weakness, explain that nothing else comes to mind.

While being honest, you should emphasize the steps you are taking to overcome your weaknesses. State, for example, "Sometimes I miss a deadline because I try to turn in quality work. I'm now learning to rely more on team members to get the work done on schedule."

> *Question:* Describe a time you failed.
> *Approach:* Don't tell interviewers that you never failed; they won't believe you. Instead, tell them about a specific business failure, what you learned from your mistakes, and what you are doing differently now.

> *Question:* Does your grade-point average reflect your ability?
> *Approach:* If your grade-point average was mediocre, you can say something like, "I'm a results-oriented person. Schools test how well you show what you know, while work judges you on what you do with what you know. Although my grades were average, I was very successful in the jobs I held in college and I can achieve the same results here." Poor grades can also be explained by personal problems; a poor choice of major in your early college or university years; taking classes outside your major; and a heavy load of extracurricular activities.

> *Question:* How much direct supervision do you need?
> *Approach:* Interviewers look for candidates who are self-starters and who motivate themselves throughout a project. An effective answer gives this impression while showing that you are nevertheless willing to ask for help. To illustrate, you might respond by saying, "In most cases my manager has to tell me something once, then I'm on my own. When a problem arises, I try to be creative and consult with others involved in the project. When I encounter a problem I can't solve, I ask my manager for help. I try to come prepared with suggestions for handling the problem, so that the manager can see my thinking."

Mike Tuff, who was Coordinator of Education and Training for the Toronto-Dominion Bank, advises that when you encounter difficult questions you should "relax—don't be nervous, be prepared to answer questions about why we should hire you. Close the sale—make us love you."[21]

ISN'T THAT ILLEGAL?

There are certain questions that employers cannot ask job applicants without threatening their equal opportunity for employment. Equal opportunity in the workplace is protected by both provincial and federal employment equity laws. According to both the provincial/territorial Individual Rights Protection Acts and the Federal Employment Equity Act, candidates cannot be discriminated against on the basis of age, gender, sexual preference, colour, race, creed, national origin, religious persuasion, marital status, political beliefs, physical well-being, or disabilities. As a result of these laws, any questions relating to these areas and unrelated to work are illegal. Yet *Maclean's* magazine reports that "despite the federal government's employment equity law, most employers have done little to hire more women, aboriginals, members of visible minorities, and people with disabilities."[22]

Canadian federal equity laws protect people employed in nationally operated companies such as Air Canada, while provincial and territorial laws protect employees in all other companies. Table 18–4 illustrates the prohibited grounds of discrimination both federally and provincially/territorially.

In general, questions are considered legal when they relate directly to the applicant's ability to perform job duties. They are illegal when they probe into areas unrelated to job performance. Questions like the following are generally considered illegal or unethical:

- ▼ Are you married or single?
- ▼ Do you plan to become pregnant soon?
- ▼ Are you HIV-positive?
- ▼ How much time do you spend with your family?
- ▼ How much does your spouse earn?
- ▼ You look forty pounds overweight. Do you think you have the stamina to do this work? (This question is illegal if there is no weight requirement for the job.)
- ▼ Has your driver's licence ever been revoked? (This question is valid only if driving is part of your job.)
- ▼ How have you arranged your child care?
- ▼ What political party do you support?
- ▼ How old are you?
- ▼ What church do you belong to?
- ▼ Where does your spouse/father/mother work?
- ▼ What gender is your roommate?

Although all of these questions are or can be regarded as unethical or illegal, job applicants report encountering these questions on a frequent basis. According to Gary Goldstein, president of an executive search firm, although most recruiters are subtle, they still ask illegal questions. "Companies want to know," explains Goldstein, "why a woman isn't married, or if she is, why she'd want to spend so much time travelling."[23]

There are at least two ways to deal with illegal hiring questions. First, refuse to answer. Every applicant has the right to refuse to answer illegal questions. You must understand, of course, that refusal will probably eliminate you as a candidate. Second, you can choose to answer illegal questions that do not compromise your application. For example, if you are not HIV-positive or have no problem with child care, you may wish to answer these questions truthfully even though you know that the interviewer is asking an illegal question.

Table 18-4   Employment: Prohibited Grounds of Discrimination*

Prohibited Grounds	Federal	British Columbia	Alberta	Saskatchewan	Manitoba	Ontario	Quebec	New Brunswick	Prince Edward Island	Nova Scotia	Newfoundland	Northwest Territories	Yukon
Race or colour	•	•	•	•	•	•	•	•	•	•	•	•	•
Religion or creed	•	•	•	•	•	•	•	•	•	•	•	•	•
Age	•	19-65	18+	18-64	•	18-65	•	•	•	•	19-65	•	•
Gender (incl. pregnancy or childbirth)	•	•	•	•	•¹	•²	•	•	•³	•	•³	•	•
Marital status	•	•	•	•	•	•	•⁴	•	•	•	•	•	•
Physical/Mental handicap or disability	•	•	•	•	•	•	•	•	•	•	•	•	•
Sexual orientation	•	•	•†	•	•	•	•	•		•	•³		•
National or ethnic origin (incl. linguistic background)	•		•⁵	•	•	•⁶	•	•	•	•	•	•⁵	•
Family status	•	•	•	•⁷	•	•	•⁴			•			
Dependence on alcohol or drug	•	•³	•³	•³	•³	•³		•³,⁸	•³		•⁸		
Ancestry or place of origin		•	•	•	•	•		•				•	•
Political belief		•		•	•		•		•	•	•		•
Based on association				•	•			•	•	•			•
Pardoned conviction	•					•	•					•	
Record of criminal conviction		•					•						•
Source of income			•	•⁹	•						•		
Assignment, attachment or seizure of pay												•	
Social condition/origin							•					•	
Language				•³			•						

Harassment on any of the prohibited grounds is considered a form of discrimination.

Threatening, intimidating or discriminating against someone who has filed a complaint, or hampering a complaint investigation, is a violation of provincial human rights codes, and at the federal level is a criminal offence.

* Any limitation, exclusion, denial or preference may be permitted if a bona fide occupational requirement can be demonstrated.
† Sexual orientation is now a prohibited ground for discrimination—April 1998.
1) includes gender-determined characteristics
2) Ontario accepts complaints based on a policy related to female genital mutilation in all social areas on the grounds of gender, place of origin and/or handicap
3) complaints accepted based on policy
4) Quebec uses the term "civil status"
5) defined as nationality
6) Ontario's Code includes only "citizenship"
7) defined as being in a parent-child relationship
8) previous dependence only
9) defined as "receipt of public assistance"

Source: Canadian Human Rights Commission, 1996.

SHOW ME THE MONEY!

Naturally, such employment conditions as salary, bonuses, vacation time, medical insurance, pension plans, and company savings plans are on every applicant's mind. However, bringing them up prematurely during an interview will weaken your bargaining position. As a rule, your strategy should be to wait until the company offers you the job before you request this type of information. Asking about money prematurely may also send the message that the job is less important than what you will earn. However, if you know someone who works for the organization, you may be able to learn this information before the interview.

This is not to say that you should go into the interview with no idea of the job's fair-market value. On the contrary, your sources may tell you a great deal. For example, newspaper ads often list salary ranges, and employment agencies have similar information. Members of your business network may also tell you what comparable jobs pay in the industry. *Occupational Profiles*, published by provincial departments of Advanced Education and Career Development, show salary ranges for occupations; the *Career Directory* published by Edcore Publishing of Toronto lists names of Canadian companies and the salaries they pay; and Canadian books such as *Excelerate*, written by Nuala Beck, describe Canadian occupations and their employment requirements.

If an interviewer presses you for a salary figure at the start of the interview, try postponing the answer by saying something like the following:

> I really would prefer to make that determination after I've had a chance to explore the potential of working here and the opportunity for advancement.[24]

Or:

> The starting salary is not my most important consideration. As you know I'm earning $_____ a year now. If you don't mind, let's postpone this discussion until you have a better idea of what I can do for you and I have a chance to know a little more about the job and the company.

When you finally start talking money, remember that you are involved in a high-stakes negotiation. While most of us no doubt feel that we are entitled to every penny we can get, the hiring manager has a responsibility to hire people for the least money possible. As a result, the negotiation may follow a pattern something like this:

> *Interviewer:* What starting salary would you accept?
> *Interviewee:* I was thinking of $_____ (you quote a figure 5 percent higher than you realistically think you can get).
> *Interviewer:* We can't go that high. The position doesn't warrant it.
> *Interviewee:* Then what is your best offer?

At this point, the employer may decide to go higher than originally planned and offer you about what you expected in the first place. If the interviewer doesn't budge—and often he or she cannot because of budget restrictions on starting salaries—explain that although you are reluctant to go that low, you might compromise. You might reply, "Does $_____ sound more realistic?" If the interviewer still refuses to change the original figure, do not feel forced to make a decision on the spot. Instead, say something like, "I would like to think about it overnight. May I call you tomorrow?" Base your decision on opportunity as well as money. If you think there is a future in the company, consider accepting the job. Remember, however, that verbal promises of future compensation may evaporate.

If you think the company *really* wants you, your best bet is to press hard before you start your new job, because that is when the company loves you most. However, pressing *too* hard may be a mistake. Remember that if you are successful in earning the job, you will be expected to live up to the standards you promised the employer during your job campaign.

Pricing yourself requires a healthy dose of reality testing—testing of the economic climate (is Canada in a recession or experiencing an economic boom?), of the specific marketplace for your skills (the industry and company), and of the way in which your past translates into today's dollars. Always remember that your job search takes place in a particular marketplace. If you are fortunate enough

Progress Check

1. List and explain five guidelines for handling difficult interview questions.
2. List some unethical questions that you may encounter during an interview.
3. When is the right time to talk about salary and benefits? When is the wrong time?

to be in a hot industry, such as computer software, you may find soaring salaries and bonuses simply because talent is scarce.[25]

When talking about money, it is critical that you also consider **employee benefits**—the benefits that employers provide to individual employees to cover costs for such services as medical insurance and *perquisites* such as vacations and company savings plans. The importance of benefits cannot be understated. They often amount to as much as 30 percent of the total compensation paid to workers.

Pre-Employment Testing

The decision to hire workers can be costly in terms of employment agency fees, job training, time spent interviewing, and time lost when new employees prove unfit. An increasing number of companies, therefore, use some form of pre-employment testing to screen workers. **Pre-employment testing** is a process of evaluating job candidates through the use of skills tests, physical examinations, and drug tests; reference checks are also considered part of the pre-employment screening process.

SKILLS TESTS

Skills tests measure the aptitudes and abilities of job applicants. For example, you may be asked to prepare a memo on a given topic using Microsoft Word software. Or, if you are applying for a managerial position, you may encounter an "in-basket" type of simulation where you must respond to a variety of memos on such topics as staff complaints, scheduling conflicts, financial advice, and strategic planning.

Because the federal Employment Equity Act prohibits the use of discriminatory hiring tests, the courts have ruled that all pre-employment skills tests must be limited to helping employers predict job success. Tests that are culturally biased or unrelated to job performance are considered discriminatory.

PHYSICAL EXAMINATIONS

A physical examination may be given only to determine whether an applicant can fulfill the duties required by a job. However, it is unlawful to ask applicants if they are disabled, to inquire about the nature or severity of a disability, or to require an applicant to take a physical examination before a job offer is made. However, after you have received an offer, your employer may require a physical examination.

If the examination shows the presence of a disability that would affect your ability to perform the job, the employer can choose not to hire you. For example, a candidate for the position of executive chauffeur could be refused employment if a physical exam revealed that glaucoma limits his or her peripheral vision.[26]

DRUG TESTS

Pre-employment drug testing—screening for illegal substances such as cocaine and marijuana—is legal in Canada. An employer may test applicants for illegal drug use before making a job offer. The Canadian Human Rights Act does not prohibit drug testing, but if an employer uses the results of these tests against the applicant, this action may be considered discriminatory. Further, the employer must establish that drug testing is relevant in determining whether an applicant can perform the job safely, efficiently, and reliably. Of course, this is very difficult for an employer to prove since most drug testing is not reliable enough. It can only indicate that the applicant has been exposed to a particular drug days prior to the test. Therefore, the link between a positive test result and the ability to perform the job safely, efficiently, and reliably is a tenuous one.

The Canadian Human Rights Commission recommends that drug testing be applied only when on-the-job deficiencies are obvious in employees. Even where the employee tests positive, the employer may be required by law to avoid discrimination against him or her. In other words, the employer may have to support an employee assistance program, counselling, and rehabilitation. However, if in the eyes of the Human Rights Commission the employee has not overcome the dependency, the employer may dismiss the employee. The Human Rights Commission is responsible for determining what constitutes reasonable accommodation on the part of the employee.[27]

REFERENCE CHECKS

Finally, the screening process often includes a **reference check**—an effort to verify a candidate's educational claims and work history. Verification techniques range from a careful reading of reference letters that applicants bring with them to calling references to gather or confirm background information.

Employers are adamant about checking references because many candidates misrepresent or lie about their backgrounds, as we saw in the Question of Ethics feature in Chapter 17. Among the information most frequently misrepresented are degrees and grades. You should expect all your references to be checked every time you apply for a job.

Executive recruiter John A. Coleman remembers a candidate for a senior vice presidency who was asked about his accomplishments in high school. He said he won an Olympic gold medal in swimming, but when Coleman checked his references, he discovered that he had never even participated in the Olympics. Worse yet, the reference check showed that he had not gone to college. Although he was one of the top candidates before the reference check, the man was never offered the job.[28]

Table 18-5 summarizes various pre-employment tests. It also highlights some of the problems commonly associated with these tests.

Table 18-5 Pre-Employment Testing: Purposes and Common Problems

Test	Purpose	Common Problems
Skills Test	determines ability to function in a simulated job situation or in other situations requiring actual job skills	test may not reflect actual job situation candidate may respond poorly to pressure
Physical Examination and Drug Test	determines if candidate is physically able to perform a job identifies individuals who have recently taken drugs	exam may be used to discriminate illegally against applicants may be unreliable
Reference Checks	verifies that applicant's claims are correct	references provided by the candidate may be perceived as self-serving

Following Up the Interview

Your job-search task is not complete when the interview is over. To reinforce a positive impression, it is a good idea to follow up with a letter of thanks. Other letters may also be necessary, including inquiries to check on the status of your application, time-extension requests, and resignation letters, if you are leaving one job to take another.

THANK YOU!

Use your thank-you letter to reinforce the employer's impression of both your value and your interest in the position. A thank-you letter may do any or all of the following:

- ▼ thank the employer for the interview
- ▼ state clearly that you want the job
- ▼ restate how you can help the company and why you are qualified
- ▼ clear up any mistaken impressions that you may have made (optional)
- ▼ provide information that you did not have at the time of the interview (optional)
- ▼ request action in the form of a decision

The sample letter in Figure 18-2 is brief and personal. Thank-you messages can also be communicated over voice mail or e-mail. Or the candidate may choose to send a personal message in a greeting card.

WHAT'S HAPPENING?

Many interviewers inform applicants when they will make a hiring decision. For instance, if the interview is held on May 1, you may be promised a decision by May 10. When the promised date has passed—or about two weeks after the interview if no date was mentioned—you may want to write a letter inquiring about the status of your application. If you have received another offer but would prefer the one in question, the letter of inquiry is essential. Your letter should mention the following:

- ▼ the time lapse that created the need to write the letter
- ▼ your continued interest in the position
- ▼ the presence of another job offer (optional)
- ▼ your potential value to the organization
- ▼ the request for a decision by a specific date

Figure 18-3 is an example of an effective letter of inquiry.

LET ME THINK ABOUT THIS!

If you have interviewed with more than one company, the situation may arise in which one company offers you a job before the others. In that case a letter or phone call requesting additional time may be necessary. If you want to consider all your options, you will want to ask the company that has made an offer for more time to decide. Your request should include the following elements:

- ▼ an acknowledgment of the company's job offer and a statement that you are interested in the position
- ▼ a statement that you are interviewing with another company and that you expect an offer within a short time
- ▼ a statement that you would appreciate the opportunity to let the company know by a certain date
- ▼ a restatement of your potential value to the company
- ▼ a request for an answer

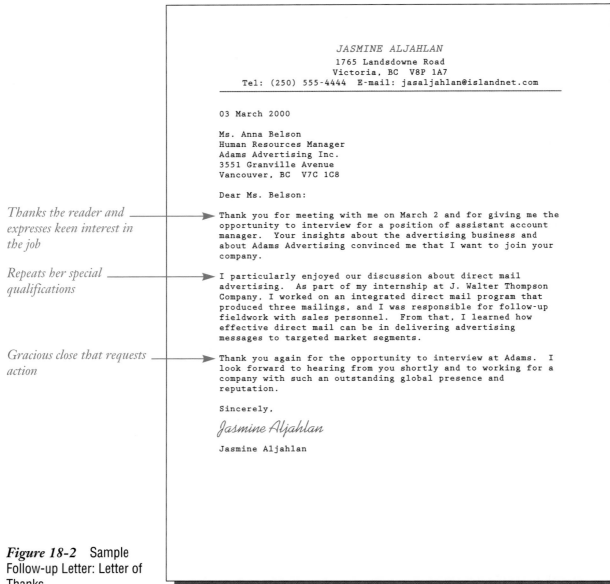

Thanks the reader and expresses keen interest in the job

Repeats her special qualifications

Gracious close that requests action

JASMINE ALJAHLAN
1765 Landsdowne Road
Victoria, BC V8P 1A7
Tel: (250) 555-4444 E-mail: jasaljahlan@islandnet.com

03 March 2000

Ms. Anna Belson
Human Resources Manager
Adams Advertising Inc.
3551 Granville Avenue
Vancouver, BC V7C 1C8

Dear Ms. Belson:

Thank you for meeting with me on March 2 and for giving me the opportunity to interview for a position of assistant account manager. Your insights about the advertising business and about Adams Advertising convinced me that I want to join your company.

I particularly enjoyed our discussion about direct mail advertising. As part of my internship at J. Walter Thompson Company, I worked on an integrated direct mail program that produced three mailings, and I was responsible for follow-up fieldwork with sales personnel. From that, I learned how effective direct mail can be in delivering advertising messages to targeted market segments.

Thank you again for the opportunity to interview at Adams. I look forward to hearing from you shortly and to working for a company with such an outstanding global presence and reputation.

Sincerely,

Jasmine Aljahlan

Jasmine Aljahlan

Figure 18-2 Sample Follow-up Letter: Letter of Thanks

Remember: If the company to which you are writing is your first choice, communicate this fact so that no one mistakes your intent. If you are undecided, you can be more vague but still express genuine interest.

If you are a highly desirable candidate, an effective extension request may spur the company to improve its offer for fear of losing you. When this happens, you are in the enviable position of negotiating with two or more companies for the best offer. However, if the first company replies that it cannot wait while the second company is still deliberating, you will be forced to choose between the offer that you have and the existing offer that you may or may not yet receive.

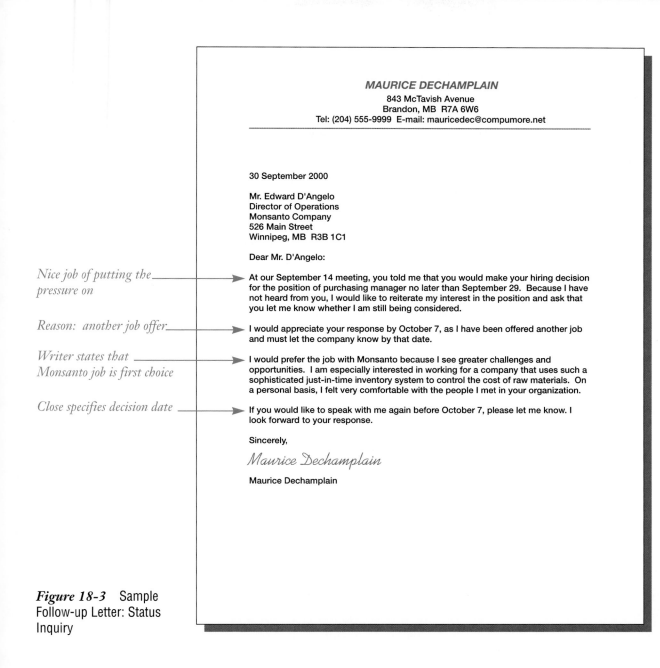

MAURICE DECHAMPLAIN
843 McTavish Avenue
Brandon, MB R7A 6W6
Tel: (204) 555-9999 E-mail: mauricedec@compumore.net

30 September 2000

Mr. Edward D'Angelo
Director of Operations
Monsanto Company
526 Main Street
Winnipeg, MB R3B 1C1

Dear Mr. D'Angelo:

Nice job of putting the pressure on → At our September 14 meeting, you told me that you would make your hiring decision for the position of purchasing manager no later than September 29. Because I have not heard from you, I would like to reiterate my interest in the position and ask that you let me know whether I am still being considered.

Reason: another job offer → I would appreciate your response by October 7, as I have been offered another job and must let the company know by that date.

Writer states that Monsanto job is first choice → I would prefer the job with Monsanto because I see greater challenges and opportunities. I am especially interested in working for a company that uses such a sophisticated just-in-time inventory system to control the cost of raw materials. On a personal basis, I felt very comfortable with the people I met in your organization.

Close specifies decision date → If you would like to speak with me again before October 7, please let me know. I look forward to your response.

Sincerely,

Maurice Dechamplain

Maurice Dechamplain

Figure 18-3 Sample Follow-up Letter: Status Inquiry

Responding to Job Offers _____

In everything you have done up to this point, you have had a single goal—to get a job offer. Once you have received one or more offers, your next communication task is to respond in writing. Naturally, your response depends on whether you accept or reject the job.

YES—I ACCEPT!

You may receive an offer anytime from one day to six weeks after your final interview. Realistically, you can expect to wait about two weeks. Offers often come over the phone, with the manager repeating your salary, bonus potential, benefits, and starting date. When the conversation is over, you should understand fully the terms of the deal that you have made.

Do not feel pressured to respond right away: it is well within your rights to tell an employer that you want to think about the offer for a short time. Simply ask when the company needs a decision. Delaying your response may also give you a psychological advantage—you may well be perceived as an independent person who is not begging for the job. When you finally make your decision, communicate it with enthusiasm—let your employer know that your commitment is 100 percent. You can accept the offer on the phone or by letter. An acceptance letter has several important goals:

- ▼ stating officially that you will take the job
- ▼ repeating your enthusiasm for the offer
- ▼ restating the basics of the offer, including your title, salary, and starting date
- ▼ stating any miscellaneous details
- ▼ looking forward to the future

The letter in Figure 18-4 is an example of an acceptance letter.

NO THANKS!

Every job offer is not an offer you should accept. Indeed, there are any number of realistic reasons to consider refusing an offer:

- ▼ *The job requires skills that would take too long to master.* Some jobs require so much learning that they put a great deal of stress on the skills and experiences you actually possess. If it looks as if it will take more than a year to master a job, consider turning it down.
- ▼ *You have negative feelings about your prospective manager.* If a manager is difficult or has a style that makes you uncomfortable, you may find working conditions similarly intolerable.
- ▼ *The employer is offering a "low-ball" salary.* If you should learn that others with similar experience and background are being paid more for the same job, your resentment may hinder performance. It may be wise to refuse the job before you experience trouble in performing it.
- ▼ *The offer is merely the best in a series of bad offers.* An offer may be the best you've received but still not be what you want. Evaluate every job on its own merits, not by comparing it to other prospective jobs.
- ▼ *You are sick of job hunting and the company is eager to hire you.* Job hunting is often stressful. However, accepting a job that you really don't want because you are tired of the process is often a mistake. Focus on what you want, not on who wants you.[29]

Of course, refusing an offer is inevitable if you receive more than one offer at the same time. To decide between jobs, return to the objectives that you developed at the start of your job search. Before you consider money, benefits, or even job titles, focus on job duties, the people with whom you would work, and location. Ask yourself which job would be more challenging. Are you uncomfortable with any of the responsibilities entailed by a prospective job? When you make a decision, communicate your refusal in writing. Your letter should contain the following elements:

- ▼ your decision not to take the job

```
                    Grete Klippstein
                    101 Greenlees Drive
                   Kingston, ON  K7K 6R2
          Tel: (613) 555-8787 Fax: (613) 555-8888
             E-mail: greteklipp@prime-wave.ca
_____

October 4, 2000


Ms. Rochelle Rasch
Director, Accounts Payable
3M Corporation
121 Laurier Avenue W.
Ottawa, ON  K1P 5J2

Dear Ms. Rasch:

I accept your offer of employment as a supervisor in your
accounts payable department.  I am delighted to be joining 3M
on October 20 and look forward to the challenge and the
opportunity that lie ahead.

As we agreed, my annual starting salary will be $38 000, with
the possibility of a bonus after a year.  I plan to visit your
human resources department on October 15 to complete all the
pre-employment paperwork, including insurance and tax forms,
and to have my picture taken for my photo I.D.

Thank you for this opportunity.  I look forward to being part
of the accounts payable team.

Sincerely,

Grete Klippstein

Grete Klippstein
```

Direct, enthusiastic opening mentions start date

Restates specific offer to avoid any miscommunication

An optimistic look ahead

Figure 18-4 Sample Letter of Acceptance

- ▼ your main reason for refusing the offer
- ▼ a statement that you will be taking another job (optional)
- ▼ a statement of appreciation for the offer and the time and effort made to consider your application
- ▼ a statement of thanks to all the people involved in the interview process
- ▼ a window left open to the future

Address the letter to the person who officially offered you the job. In addition to communicating your refusal, your goal should be to build bridges to the future. Parting with friendly enthusiasm and grace makes it possible for you to contact the firm again in the future. Figure 18-5 is an example of a job-refusal letter.

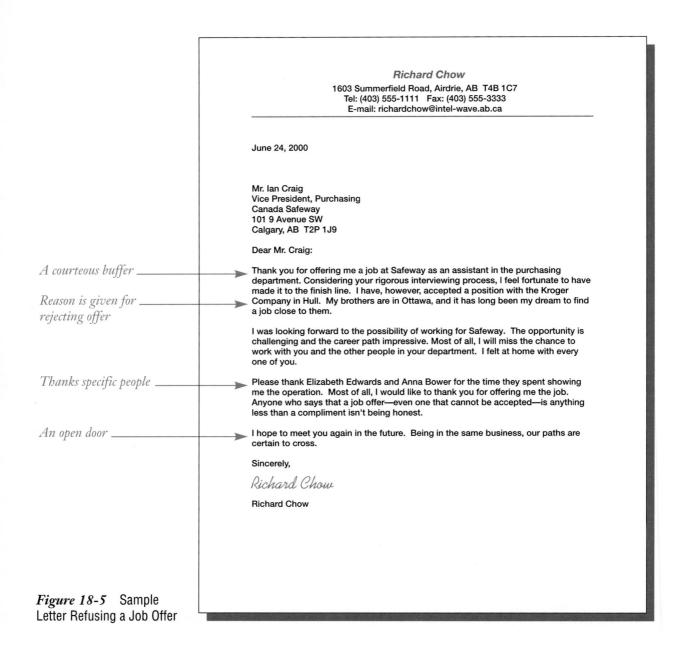

A courteous buffer

Reason is given for rejecting offer

Thanks specific people

An open door

Richard Chow
1603 Summerfield Road, Airdrie, AB T4B 1C7
Tel: (403) 555-1111   Fax: (403) 555-3333
E-mail: richardchow@intel-wave.ab.ca

June 24, 2000

Mr. Ian Craig
Vice President, Purchasing
Canada Safeway
101 9 Avenue SW
Calgary, AB T2P 1J9

Dear Mr. Craig:

Thank you for offering me a job at Safeway as an assistant in the purchasing department. Considering your rigorous interviewing process, I feel fortunate to have made it to the finish line. I have, however, accepted a position with the Kroger Company in Hull. My brothers are in Ottawa, and it has long been my dream to find a job close to them.

I was looking forward to the possibility of working for Safeway. The opportunity is challenging and the career path impressive. Most of all, I will miss the chance to work with you and the other people in your department. I felt at home with every one of you.

Please thank Elizabeth Edwards and Anna Bower for the time they spent showing me the operation. Most of all, I would like to thank you for offering me the job. Anyone who says that a job offer—even one that cannot be accepted—is anything less than a compliment isn't being honest.

I hope to meet you again in the future. Being in the same business, our paths are certain to cross.

Sincerely,

Richard Chow

Richard Chow

Figure 18-5   Sample Letter Refusing a Job Offer

I RESIGN!

If you are already working, accepting a job offer means that you will be leaving the company you now work for. This requires that you write a resignation memo to your current employer. In effect, you are delivering bad news (you are resigning your position), which requires the indirect approach explored in Chapter 9. As you write this memo, keep the following in mind:

▼   Open with a positive, appreciative buffer.

▼   The reasons for your resignation should precede the resignation itself.

▼   State the date you intend to leave.

- ▼ Your tone should be positive, regardless of circumstances; avoid "burning your bridges."
- ▼ Close with further expressions of appreciation.

Figure 18-6 is an example of a resignation memo.

MEMORANDUM

To: Abby Adams, Sales Manager

From: Paula Zender, Sales Representative *PZ*

Date: July 30, 2000

Subject: Resignation

Appreciative comments serve as a buffer →
Since I graduated from college, Salisbury Computer Supplies has been my home away from home. You, Nick, and Taylor taught me everything I know about selling—and more than I would like to admit about working with people.

Reason for resignation precedes bad news →
For the past year, it has been my goal to move into sales management. An opportunity has just been offered to me by Global Electronics, and I will be joining Global on August 15 as an assistant national sales manager. Jobs like this don't come around too often, and I found myself in the position of being unable to refuse.

Close tries to maintain positive relationship →
I appreciate the support and encouragement you gave me over the years; it means more to me than you will ever know. Most of all, I appreciate your belief in me when I was an inexperienced—but eager—college graduate.

Salisbury Computer Supplies, Inc.
www.salsup.com
73 Queen Street, Charlottetown, PE C1A 4A8
(902) 555-0000—phone (902) 555-1333—fax
scs@master-wave.pe.ca—email

Figure 18-6 Sample Resignation Memo

What's Ahead

This chapter marks the end of the text. Following, you will find five appendices on Preparing Business Documents, Basics of Grammar and Usage, Internet Research, Proofreader Marks, and Answer Key for ACT Questions that will serve as valuable resources as you prepare business documents.

STUDENT RESOURCE CENTRE

Summary of Chapter Objectives

1. ***Explain the process involved in behavioural interview questions.***

   These interviews use a domino questioning technique. Each question leads to the next and probes deeper into the experience or scenario described by the applicant. The final question may ask the applicant if information can be verified by calling people the applicant has made reference to. These questions are not difficult to answer if the applicant is honest and has the experience that the employer is seeking.

2. ***Explain how to prepare for a telephone interview.***

   Prior to the telephone interview, prepare a set of organized notes containing your questions and the attributes you wish to emphasize. Practise your best telephone techniques by speaking clearly, courteously, and enthusiastically.

3. ***Describe the most effective ways to prepare for a job interview.***

   Effective preparation begins with research about the company and its industry. Company and general business publications are useful sources. Research leads to a list of questions that a candidate can and should ask an interviewer about a company at different stages of the interview process. Preparation also includes thinking about presentation style, including such forms of nonverbal communication as dress and eye contact. Preparation also means developing techniques for handling difficult interviewers. To be properly prepared, you must also arrive on time and bring your résumé and references.

4. ***Develop effective questions to ask the interviewer.***

   Questions indicate that you have spent the time and effort to analyze the company and that you are taking an active part in the interview. By indicating that you want to know as much about the company as the company wants to know about you, questions also help to place you on an equal footing with the interviewer.

5. ***Outline the six stages of a model interview.***

   During the introduction, the interviewer attempts to establish rapport with the job candidate. Work experience is examined in the second stage, in which the interviewer focuses on the specifics of previous employment. Interviewers generally turn next to education in order to determine whether school experience has provided applicable skills. Activities and interests are then examined to learn what leisure pursuits reveal about the applicant's personality, skills, and interests. Interviewers turn next to candidates' strengths and shortcomings in order to learn whether they can do the job, whether they would like to do it, and whether they would fit comfortably within the organization. Finally, closing remarks establish expectations for what will occur next.

6. ***Describe an effective interview closure.***

   An effective closure includes firmly shaking hands; restating your interest in the position; checking the follow-up procedure; and leaving a business card.

7. ***Identify strategies for handling difficult and illegal questions.***

   Make every attempt to answer negative or difficult questions in positive ways. Prepare for difficult questions by making a list of all the questions that you would rather not be asked; then design answers that focus on positive outcomes. Keep in mind that interviewers often ask difficult questions to put job candidates off balance. Handling illegal questions starts with a knowledge of both how to identify such questions and how the law protects job applicants from discrimination.

8. ***List strategies for negotiating salary and benefits.***

   Always save the discussion of salary and benefits for the end of the interview process. You may be at a negotiating advantage if you wait until the company decides that it wants you. Before you begin talking about money, make every attempt to learn what comparable positions pay. Remember that during the negotiations, it is your goal to get as much money as possible, while it is the employer's goal to hold down salaries. Always consider the value of such employee benefits as health insurance and vacation time.

9. ***Outline different types of pre-employment testing.***
Pre-employment testing may involve skills testing to measure the aptitudes and abilities of job applicants. Physical examinations may be required after a job offer has been made and only if they measure the applicant's ability to perform the job. Pre-employment drug testing or screening for illegal substances is legal in Canada. However, under the Canadian Human Rights Act this action may be considered discriminatory if an employer uses the results of drug tests against the applicant. Finally, reference checks are made to verify that educational claims and work histories are accurate.

10. ***Describe types of interview follow-up documents.***
The purpose of thank-you letters is to thank the interviewer for the opportunity to interview with the company and to state interest in the job. Letters inquiring about the status of an application may be necessary if you have not heard from the company by a promised date (or after about two weeks if no date was mentioned during the interview). Requests for additional time may be needed when one company offers you a job before others with whom you have interviewed. Letters of acceptance inform the company that you will take the job; letters of refusal inform the company of your decision not to take the position. Resignation memos inform your current employer that you will be taking another job.

Review and Discussion Questions

1. State a sample behavioural question and possible follow-up questions. *(Ch. Obj. 1)*
2. What are two items you might prepare prior to a telephone interview? *(Ch. Obj. 2)*
3. Describe the basic steps in preparing for a job interview. *(Ch. Obj. 3)*
4. Name several sources that you can use to research a company before a job interview. *(Ch. Obj. 3)*
5. During an interview, why is it important for you to ask questions of the interviewer? *(Ch. Obj. 4)*
6. What are the six stages of a model job interview? *(Ch. Obj. 5)*
7. State four actions you should take during the closure of an interview. *(Ch. Obj. 6)*
8. During an interview, how might you handle questions that are difficult or illegal? *(Ch. Obj. 7)*
9. Describe effective strategies for discussing salary and benefits. *(Ch. Obj. 8)*
10. What types of pre-employment testing do companies use? *(Ch. Obj. 9)*
11. What possible steps might you take to follow up a job interview? *(Ch. Obj. 10)*

Application Exercises

1. Your school's placement office has asked you to write a brief manual for your fellow students in which you offer guidelines on how to prepare for an interview. Write this manual (one to two pages). *(Ch. Obj. 3, 4)*
2. The school's placement director likes the interview guide that you developed for Exercise 1 so much that she asks you to write a brief guide to negotiating salary and benefits. Write this guide (one to two pages). *(Ch. Obj. 8)*
3. This chapter notes that research is crucial to doing well in job interviews. Explain why. *(Ch. Obj. 3)*
4. Choose a field or an occupation that interests you. Find out as much as you can about this field by doing research outside of class. Answer the following questions about the field you have selected:

▼ What are the leading companies?

▼ Where do they tend to be located?

▼ What background and training are generally required for professionals who enter the field?

▼ What are the salary levels?

▼ What is the outlook for jobs in this field?

Take notes on your research and keep track of which sources you find most useful. *(Ch. Obj. 3)*

5. Choose a company for which you would like to work (perhaps one of the firms that you read about in working on Exercise 4). Find out as much as you can about this firm by doing research outside of class. What types of jobs are available at this company, and what background and training do they require? What is the corporate culture? Is the

company successful, and if so, why? Use sources mentioned in the chapter, and talk to anyone you know who is familiar with the company. You may also wish to check with a librarian to see if other research sources are available. Take notes on what you find out. *(Ch. Obj. 3)*

6. Use the information you gathered from working on Exercises 4 and 5 to write a report on the company you researched. Describe the firm, the role it plays in its industry, and its outlook (short- and long-term). Explain why you feel this company is or is not successful, and summarize the career path of company employees. Your instructor will determine the length of your report and may wish to have you present it to the class. *(Ch. Obj. 3)*

7. Based on your research and report for Exercises 4–6, draw up a list of questions you would like to ask if you were interviewing with that company. *(Ch. Obj. 2, 3, 5)*

8. Refer to the list of questions that interviewers frequently ask about work experience and educational history. Suppose that you're being asked these questions during a job interview. Write an effective answer for each. If you wish, you may relate your answers to the industry and company that you researched for Exercises 4–6. *(Ch. Obj. 5)*

9. Refer to the questions itemized in the Strengths and Shortcomings section of this chapter. Write effective answers for each. If you wish, you may relate your answers to the industry and company that you researched in Exercises 4–6. *(Ch. Obj. 5)*

10. We're all better at some things than at others. An important part of preparing for a job interview is anticipating any reservations that interviewers may have about you based on your résumé or other information. Look at your background from an interviewer's point of view, and think about what questions may come up. (You may also refer to the questions listed in the section "How to Handle Difficult Questions.") Draw up a list of questions or issues related to your own background, and then write effective responses that you could use during an interview in which any of those questions might be asked. *(Ch. Obj. 7)*

11. Suppose that you interview for a position with the company that you researched in Exercise 5. Write a follow-up letter thanking the interviewer and asking about the status of your application. *(Ch. Obj. 10)*

ACT: Applied Communication Techniques

Begin by referring to the sections up to and including Words with Misunderstood Meanings in Appendix II, then correct the grammar, spelling, and usage errors in the following sentences. Check your answers in Appendix V.

1. The decision to advertise the position was made between the three managers.

2. The applicant faced continuous questions interrupted only by his own short answers.

3. Catherine was released from her employment because the manager believed she was disinterested in her work.

4. During his presentation, the manager inferred that ten percent of employees would be laid off.

5. Mitchell's father loaned him an expensive suit for the interview.

6. Prior to an interview, you should do some research for practicable information.

7. Irregardless of the outcome, the interview will give you excellent experience.

8. The names of the job candidates are confidential and should be kept among the two of you.

9. From the lack of enthusiasm on the employer's face, the applicant implied that the position was already filled.

10. Because the company was an equal opportunity employer, the interviewer was uninterested in the gender of the successful applicant.

Building Your Research Skills

Research and locate two articles that discuss some aspect of the job search, the interview process, or both. (Both articles should come from sources outside class.) Did you find the articles useful? Why or why not? Write a brief report that summarizes their major points and suggestions and evaluates their usefulness to most job hunters.

Building Your Teamwork Skills

Your instructor will divide the class into small groups. Meet with your group and take turns role-playing job interviews and salary negotiations. One volunteer should be the interviewer, another the applicant (everyone should role-play the applicant at least once). The other team members should observe each interview and offer feedback to the participants. What did they do well? What might they do to improve? Try to offer constructive feedback regarding classmates' body language, tone of voice, posture, and other factors that can influence interviewers' decisions.

Building Your Technology Skills

You are preparing for an interview with a company. Your preparation includes learning as much information as possible about the company.

Select one company that interests you by researching Internet sites that have business links. Visit the company's home page and write a paper that describes the company and includes important information for your interview.

The following Web sites have links to businesses on the Internet:

▼ Yahoo, Business and Economy
http://www.yahoo.com/Business_and_
Economy

▼ EINet Galaxy Business and Commerce
http://www.einet.net/galaxy/Business-and-
Commerce.html
▼ Global Network Navigator, Business Links
http://gnn.com/wic/wics/bus.new.html
▼ Interesting Business Sites
http://www.owi.com/netvalue
▼ World Wide Web Business Yellow Pages
http://www.cba.uh.edu/ylowpges/
ycategor.html

Weblinks Internet Resources for this Chapter

HotSeat: Can you survive the mock interview and land the job?
**http://www.kaplan.com:8000/miniapps/
hotseat/index.html**

Employment Interviewing
http://www.crc.ufl.edu/Employment.html

Employment Interviewing Tips
http://www.mricincy.com/general.html

CASE STUDIES

CORPORATE CASE:
Why Corporations Test Employees for Drugs

Employers sometimes receive "wake-up calls" about the effects illegal drugs are having on their companies. A case in point: although Daniel Burke, president of Capital Cities/ABC, Inc., could recite chapter and verse about the growing national drug problem, he never considered drugs to be a problem in *his* company. That changed when an ABC employee died of a cocaine overdose in an office stairwell. Similarly, Joy Hawley, co-owner of a boat manufacturing company, never suspected there was a drug problem in her company until an employee described the problem after checking into a substance-abuse program. Hawley then traced a $6000 mistake to one employee's on-the-job drug use.

In tangible terms unchecked drug and alcohol abuse results in increased accidents and absenteeism, high employee turnover, low employee morale, and a corporate culture that discourages the best people from working for the company.

These factors help explain why some companies institute pre-employment drug testing.

Although companies realize that pre-employment drug testing will not solve the problem of on-the-job substance abuse, they also realize that there is tremendous wisdom in weeding drug abusers out of the pool of potential applicants. A drug-free environment attracts the best people, explains Joy Hawley. "Although it may be harder to get employees, the ones that we do get are of a higher quality, with better skills, and more loyalty."[30]

Questions and Applications

1. Would you apply for a job in a company that required a pre-employment drug test? Why?

2. Critics consider drug testing an invasion of applicants' privacy. How do you feel about this criticism in light of the heavy toll on workplace productivity?

3. Suppose you are the head of recruiting in a midsize manufacturing firm. Draft a persuasive memo advocating—or discouraging—a new program of pre-employment drug testing.

CORPORATE CASE:

Wanted at Magna International: Employees Who Never Want to Go Hungry

Once it was just another tiny tool and die manufacturer. Today, however, Magna International is one of the top auto-parts makers. It is Chrysler's biggest components supplier, and Magna workers helped invent the fold-out child-safety seat for Chrysler's profitable minivans.

Magna's fast-charging growth reflects the gung-ho attitude of its founder and majority owner, Frank Stronach, who announces that "I never want to go hungry and I never want to crawl for anybody." Stronach's company is changing. While car makers once wanted their suppliers simply to make and deliver parts like door handles, today they're expected to design and produce entire "door systems," complete with armrests, interior trim, latches, and wiring. Explains Thomas Stallkamp, chief of procurement for Chrysler: "We want component makers to be the experts in technology—to keep us current in trim, motors, and stampings."

To stay competitive, Frank Stronach believes in motivating his employees with incentives. Nearly the entire pay of all Magna managers is tied to the success—or failure—of their factories. Each year, every production worker in those factories shares equally in 10 percent of the pre-tax profits. All Magna factories are kept small and feature the latest in manufacturing technologies.[31]

Questions and Applications

1. Describe Magna's changing role in the automobile industry.

2. Suppose that you're interviewing with Frank Stronach for a managerial position at Magna. What needs and concerns is Stronach likely to have? What qualities will he probably look for in you?

Preparing Business Documents

Preparing business documents requires a knowledge of the *mechanics* of business writing:

▼ using the parts of a letter correctly
▼ addressing business envelopes
▼ preparing memos, reports, and proposals
▼ formatting letters
▼ documenting sources

Mechanics are the "technical" aspects of preparing a document, and are designed to improve communication by setting up clear *standards* for written documents. These standards are used consistently throughout the business community.

Appendix I describes the business writing mechanics that apply to the letters, memos, reports, and proposals examined in this text. We begin by focusing on the importance of document appearance.

The Appearance of Business Documents

Before your reader reads a single word you have written, the appearance of your document has communicated a message. It has told your reader how much care and concern you have put into your document, and it has testified to the professionalism of your approach. First of all, the appearance of business documents is influenced by paper quality and the accuracy of your word processing.

PAPER

Paper quality is usually taken for granted—unless it is substandard. Paper that is transparent, too light, coloured, or oddly sized may not be acceptable for business purposes. Here are the basic standards that all business paper should meet:

▼ *Weight.* Paper is categorized by the weight of four 500-sheet reams of letter-size paper. Most businesses use 20-pound paper for correspondence, reports, and proposals. Stationery used for business letters may be heavier; 24-pound paper is common. Lighter paper, especially if it is transparent (onion skin falls into this category), is not acceptable for business use, although it may be used for file copies or overseas mail.

▼ *Colour.* The standard colour for business paper is white, although off-white stationery in ivory or grey tones is also acceptable. Unless there is a special reason to use them, pastels—including green, blue, yellow, and lavender—are generally not appropriate for business correspondence. Coloured paper is sometimes used in mass mailings as a way of attracting attention.

▼ *Size.* The standard size for North American business stationery and paper is $21\frac{1}{2}$ cm by 28 cm ($8\frac{1}{2} \times 11$ inches). Reports, proposals, and most business letters are written on paper this size. Stationery also comes in two other sizes:

> Baronial (used for notes, memos): 14 cm by $21\frac{1}{2}$ cm ($5\frac{1}{2}$ by $8\frac{1}{2}$ inches)
> Monarch (used by some executives for personal business correspondence): $18\frac{1}{2}$ cm by $26\frac{3}{4}$ cm ($7\frac{1}{4}$ by $10\frac{1}{2}$ inches)

▼ *Cotton Content.* The best stationery has 100-percent cotton content; inexpensive paper bond is used primarily for routine mailings and documents.

MANUSCRIPT QUALITY

Manuscript errors are red flags that identify documents as unprofessional. Guidelines here are in fact quite straightforward: Run every document through your word processor's spell checker. Then, proofread a hard copy of your document as well.

Parts of Business Letters

Business letters may contain as many as 17 individual elements. As you can see in Table I-1, while seven of these elements are included in all business letters, ten others may be considered optional. We have arranged these items in the order in which they appear in business letters.

HEADING

The *heading* of the business letter, which often consists of the *business letterhead*, usually contains the following elements:

Table I-1   Elements of a Business Letter

Standard Elements	Optional Elements
heading	reference line
dateline	personal or confidential notation
inside address	attention line
salutation	subject line
middle	identification line
complimentary close	enclosure notation
signature	mail notation
	copy notation
	postscript
	continuation-page heading

- ▼ the complete legal name of the business
- ▼ full street address and/or post office box number
- ▼ city, province/territory, and postal code
- ▼ telephone number
- ▼ fax number
- ▼ e-mail address
- ▼ Web address (if applicable)

The letterhead may also contain a *business logo* and may specify the department or division to which the letter writer belongs. Letterheads may also be personalized to include the writer's name and title.

DATELINE

The *dateline* should appear two to four lines beneath the letterhead. Leave one line space after the dateline if a *reference line* (see next section) is used. If the next element of the letter is the *inside address*, the dateline should be followed by between two and five line spaces. The varied spacing accommodates letters of different length.

As you will see later in this appendix, the position of the dateline in relation to the left margin depends on the *letter format* you are using. In full-block and simplified formats, the dateline appears flush against the left margin; in the modified-block format, it appears two to three character spaces to the right of the centre of the page and is aligned with the complimentary close. Another option is to place the dateline flush against the right margin.

REFERENCE LINE

Reference lines are designations referring the receiver of a document to a relevant file number or code. If your stationery does not include a printed reference line, place the reference line two lines below the dateline; align it immediately under the first character of the dateline. Again, placement of the reference line depends upon your letter format. Dual reference lines designate the reference codes of both writer and recipient. In this case the sender's reference line should appear before the recipient's reference line. Figure I-1 features dual reference codes.

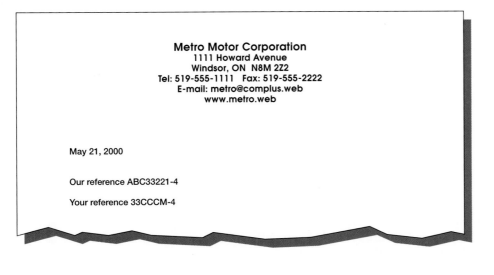

Metro Motor Corporation
1111 Howard Avenue
Windsor, ON N8M 2Z2
Tel: 519-555-1111 Fax: 519-555-2222
E-mail: metro@complus.web
www.metro.web

May 21, 2000

Our reference ABC33221-4

Your reference 33CCCM-4

Figure I-1 Sample Letter: Dual Reference Codes

PERSONAL OR CONFIDENTIAL NOTATION

When a letter contains personal or confidential material intended only for the addressee, the writer usually makes a special notation on the envelope. The writer may make a notation in the letter as well. In letters, the notation *Personal* or *Confidential* appears two lines below the reference line. Following the notation are about four line spaces and then the inside address. Notations always appear flush left and may be capitalized or underlined:

PERSONAL   CONFIDENTIAL
<u>Personal</u>   <u>Confidential</u>

INSIDE ADDRESS

The inside address, which identifies the person and/or company to whom the letter is being sent, is an obligatory part of all business letters. It can be between two and twelve lines after the last element—dateline, reference line, or personal or confidential notation—of the letter. The most common spacing allows four lines before beginning the inside address.

The inside address is always single-spaced and appears in upper- and lower-case letters. It is positioned flush against the left margin. As a rule, the inside address is usually no longer than five lines. Omit the recipient's title if necessary to maintain this length. Here are some additional guidelines for composing the inside address:

▼ No line in the address should cross over the centre point of the page. Lines containing too many characters should be broken in half and continued on the next line after an indent of two spaces.

▼ The inside address should begin with the person's *courtesy title*, followed by his or her full name. If the recipient's *professional title* is short enough, it can be included on the same line as the name. For example:

Ms. Alexandra Bennington, Treasurer

Longer titles should appear on separate lines. For example:

Mr. Arthur Hawley
Vice President and Director of Human Resources

▼ The name of the recipient's company should precede the name of his or her department.

▼ Write the company's name in the same way it appears on its letterhead. For example, if the company abbreviates words like Corporation (Corp.), Incorporated (Inc.), or Limited (Ltd.), you should do the same.

▼ When you are addressing a company rather than an individual, the inside address should include the name of the company, the department to which the letter is being sent, and the company's full address.

▼ When both a post office box and a street address appear on a company's letterhead, letters addressed to that company should use the post office box on both the envelope and inside address.

ATTENTION LINE

The *attention line* is used when a letter is addressed to a company but directed to the attention of a specific individual. Whenever you know the name of the person who should receive the letter, use it. The purpose of the attention line is to prevent delays and ensure immediate attention: if the person named in the line is not available to receive the letter, it will be opened by someone else in the company.

An attention line should always be placed flush left; it may be keyed in all capital letters, or with a combination of capital and lower-case letters. It should be placed either a double line space below the last line of the inside address or within the address, as shown in the two examples that follow.

Atlantic Bell Telephone Company
11 Canada Drive
St. John's, NF A1E 1Z1

ATTENTION: FINANCE MANAGER

or

Atlantic Bell Telephone Company
Attention: Mrs. Rudy Schendel, Finance Manager
11 Canada Drive
St. John's, NF A1E 1Z1

SALUTATION

The official greeting that appears immediately before the body of the letter, the *salutation*, follows either the inside address or the attention line. As you will see later in this appendix, salutations appear in all letters except those using the simplified format.

In most cases writers should double-space (leaving one blank line) before and after the salutation. Salutations usually begin with the word *Dear* followed by the proper form of address for the recipient. The specific salutation that you use will depend on three factors: whether the recipient of the letter is known or unknown to you, whether a title precedes the recipient's name, and whether you are writing to one or more than one person. The salutation in a business letter is always followed by a colon unless the writer is using *open punctuation*. Open punctuation is a punctuation style in which the writer does not use a colon after the salutation or a comma after the complimentary close. Examples of salutations punctuated with colons follow:

Dear Mr. Vanelli:
Dear Dr. Vanelli: (not Dear Dr. Vanelli, M.D.)
Dear Leslie Adams: (gender unknown)
Dear Customer Service Manager: (name unknown)
Dear Sir: (name unknown but gender known; a less preferred option)
Dear Madam: (name unknown but gender known; a less preferred option)
Ladies and Gentlemen: (a salutation to a company; a less preferred option)
Dear Mr. Vanelli and Ms. Bloom:
Dear Mr. Vanelli and Mr. Deaver:
Dear Messrs. Vanelli and Deaver:
Dear Ms. Vanelli and Ms. Deaver:
Dear Mss. Vanelli and Deaver: (both women are Ms.)
Dear Dr. and Mrs. Vanelli: (titled husband)
Dear Dr. Vanelli and Mr. Vanelli: (titled wife)
Dear Drs. Vanelli: (both spouses are titled)
Dear Friends: (group address)
Dear Stockholders: (group address)
Dear Employees: (group address)
Dear Neighbours: (group address)

SUBJECT LINE

The *subject line* summarizes the purpose of the letter. In most formats writers use a double-space before and after the subject line, leaving one blank line after the salutation and one blank line before the body of the letter.

The subject line begins flush against the left margin. It may begin with the word *SUBJECT* followed by a colon, or it may state the subject without introduction. To emphasize its importance, some writers capitalize all or part of the subject line. (In the simplified format, the subject line is usually capitalized.) For example:

Dear Ms. Kohut:

ANNUAL SALES MEETING

Here are preliminary plans for the annual sales meeting scheduled for February 1. Included are . . . .

Or:

Dear Ms. Kohut:

SUBJECT: Annual Sales Meeting

Here are preliminary plans for the annual sales meeting scheduled for February 1. Included are . . . .

BODY

The *body* of the letter contains the letter's message. It follows the salutation or subject line and is separated from the previous element by a single line space. Line spaces also appear between each paragraph and before the complimentary close. Paragraph lines are almost always keyed in single-spaced format.

In the full-block and simplified formats, paragraphs begin flush left. In the modified-block format, writers may choose to begin paragraphs flush left or indent paragraphs. If indented, start paragraphs five to ten character spaces from the left margin.

COMPLIMENTARY CLOSE

The *complimentary close* appears one line space after the body of the letter. It is used in all letter formats except the simplified format. It appears flush left in the full-block style; in the modified-block style, it appears two to three character spaces to the right of the centre of the page. The complimentary close is always aligned directly beneath the date, except when the date is flush with the right margin. In that case align the close directly beneath the inside address.

The first word of the complimentary close is capitalized and the last word of the close is followed by a comma. Note, however, that the comma is omitted when using open punctuation. Depending on your relationship with the reader, the close can be formal or informal. The most commonly used closes in business letters are those in the "Less Formal" category of the following example closes:

Formal	*Less Formal*	*Least Formal*
Very truly yours,	Sincerely,	Best wishes,
Respectfully,	Sincerely yours,	Best regards,
Very sincerely yours,	Cordially,	Regards,
	Cordially yours,	Kindest regards,

SIGNATURE

The letter writer's *signature* appears directly under the complimentary close. The writer's name is then keyed below the signature—usually four line spaces after the complimentary close. When the letterhead does not include the writer's business title, a second line may also be added to include this information. In all letter styles, the keyed name and title are aligned directly below the complimentary close. For example:

Sincerely,

Alice P. Fenton

Alice P. Fenton
Vice President, Recruiting

Most signature blocks do not include courtesy titles such as *Ms.*, *Mrs.*, *Mr.*, and *Miss*. An exception, however, can be made when the title is needed to clarify gender (*Mr. Fran Barron* or *Ms. Billy Diamond*). In business the preferred title for women is *Ms.* That title is assumed unless the signer indicates *Miss* or *Mrs.*

If the writer's letterhead does not identify the name of his or her company, the company name should be keyed in capital letters two lines below the complimentary close. Four lines below this is the keyed signature. For example:

Sincerely,

ELVIRA ELECTRONICS

Jonathan J. O'Brian

Jonathan J. O'Brian
Vice President

If someone signs the letter for the writer—administrative assistants often do this for their employers—that person should sign using his or her own name and write the word "for/" to the left of the writer's name.

IDENTIFICATION LINE

The *identification line* indicates who wrote the letter and who keyed it. This optional element is keyed two lines below the signature block and flush against the left margin. When a personal signature is shown in the signature block, the writer's initials are optional. Indeed, the most common practice today is to omit the writer's initials.

If the writer's and administrative assistant's initials are used, the writer's initials usually appear in capital letters, the assistant's initials in lower-case. The two sets of initials are separated by a colon. If only the assistant's initials are included, they are keyed in lower-case. For example:

DAB:jw

or:

jw

ENCLOSURE OR ATTACHMENT NOTATION

If an enclosure is included with the letter, an enclosure notation should be keyed in immediately after the identification line or the signature line. If an item is stapled or clipped to the letter, an attachment notation is used. It is acceptable to write these notations in any of the following ways:

Attachment
Enclosure
Enc.
Encl.
enc.
encl.

The notation may also tell the reader something about the enclosed or attached item(s). In the following examples the enclosure notation has been used; however, an attachment notation would work in the same way.

Enclosures: two cheques

Or:

Enclosures
1. contract
2. meeting agenda

Alternatively, the notation may simply indicate the number of items enclosed:

3 enclosures

MAIL NOTATION

A *mail notation* may appear after the enclosure notation. This entry indicates that the letter was mailed in a special way or in a way that is of interest to the recipient. For example:

fhb

Enclosures

Certified

Here are some other commonly used mail notations:

By Canada Post
By Federal Express
By United Parcel Service
By fax

Mail notations are frequently left off original copies and added to file copies.

COPY NOTATION

Often, the person to whom a letter is addressed is not the only person receiving a copy of the letter. When copies are sent to individuals other than the addressee, a *copy notation* may be added at the end. This notation appears flush left after the enclosure and mail notations. When several people receive copies, the names are stacked on top of one another. Many writers place check marks after names on a list to indicate which copy goes to which individual. In the past most companies used "cc:", which stand for "carbon copy." Because carbon copies are no longer used, companies have switched to copy notations that accurately reflect today's copying technology.

The copy notation can be made in several ways:

Copy to
Copies to:
copy:
c:
pc: (stands for "photocopy")
ec: (stands for "electronic copy")

The following examples show various combinations of identification lines and enclosure, mail, and copy notations:

br

Enclosures
 1. cheque
 2. contract

By Federal Express

c: John McCoy

btt

ec: Ann Hastings

WAA:ma

Enc.

Copies to: Carolyn Miller
             Ronald Yang

Sometimes copies of a document are distributed to people whose names are not listed on the original document. *Blind copies* are copies sent to individuals without the knowledge of the addressee. The initials *bc* should appear on both the copy of the letter sent to the blind-copy recipient and the file copy. The notation must *not* appear on the copy sent to the addressee.

Regardless of format, all notations, including the enclosure notation, mail notation, and copy notation, appear flush left. Double- or single-spacing may be used between notation items. Double-spacing is generally preferred.

POSTSCRIPT

Some letters end with *postscripts*—afterthoughts about subjects essentially unrelated to the main topic of the letters themselves. Postscripts should not contain comments directly related to the topic of the letter: Relegation of relevant material to a postscript may be perceived as an indication of a poorly organized document.

A single postscript begins with the initials *P.S.* If a second postscript is necessary, use the initials *P.P.S.* All postscripts should end with the typed initials of the writer. For example:

P.S. The budget meeting has been rescheduled to May 1. MRB
P.P.S. Call me next week to talk about the Anderson deal. MRB

CONTINUATION-PAGE HEADING

Long letters require *continuation sheets*—blank, quality stationery used for second and all subsequent pages of the letter. Each continuation page includes a heading with the addressee's name, the date, and page number. This information is usually placed flush against the left margin, with each item starting a new line. The continuation-page heading may also be spread out on a single line. For example:

Edith Sakura
Page 2
April 14, 2000

Or:

Edith Sakura   Page 2   April 14, 2000

     The continuation-page heading should appear two to six lines from the top of the page and at least two line spaces should be allowed before resuming the body of the letter.

Addressing Business Envelopes

     First impressions are formed not when your recipient begins reading your letter, but when he or she receives the envelope containing it. To make the best impression, be sure that your envelope looks professional, with every element correctly formatted in its proper place.

     Canada Post uses computerized systems that can scan a wide range of addressing styles; this includes both handwritten and keyed addresses. To increase the speed and efficiency of mail handling, Canada Post has designed a consistent format for users. Canada Post requests that we use this *optimum* format whenever possible, but recognizes some other formats as acceptable for computerized scanning. This is especially important for mail addressed in some languages other than English. Especially important in Canada is the fact that the *acceptable* formats encompass the accents, upper and lower case characters, full spellings, and punctuation used in the French language. For the sake of brevity, this textbook deals only with the *optimum* format as defined by Canada Post. The optimum format is described below and illustrated in Figure I-2.

▼ The bottom lines of the address are the most critical, since the automated equipment scans from the bottom lines upwards.

▼ Attention or information data must always appear at the top of the address block.

▼ Delivery address information, municipality, province, and postal code must always be the bottom three or four lines of the address block.

Figure I-2 Six Simple Steps for Addressing a Standard Envelope

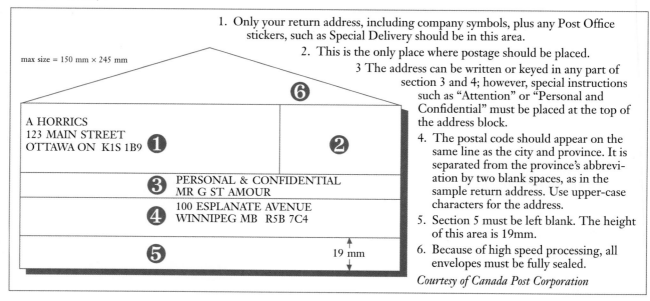

1. Only your return address, including company symbols, plus any Post Office stickers, such as Special Delivery should be in this area.

2. This is the only place where postage should be placed.

3 The address can be written or keyed in any part of section 3 and 4; however, special instructions such as "Attention" or "Personal and Confidential" must be placed at the top of the address block.

4. The postal code should appear on the same line as the city and province. It is separated from the province's abbreviation by two blank spaces, as in the sample return address. Use upper-case characters for the address.

5. Section 5 must be left blank. The height of this area is 19mm.

6. Because of high speed processing, all envelopes must be fully sealed.

Courtesy of Canada Post Corporation

- ▼ Address components and elements on the same line will be separated from each other by one blank space. The postal code, however, must be separated from the province by two blank spaces.

- ▼ Province and state names should always be written in the two-letter abbreviation format.

- ▼ All lines of the address should be formatted with a flush-left margin.

- ▼ Upper-case letters are preferred on all lines of the address block.

- ▼ Punctuation should not be used between address elements (for example, VANCOUVER BC). Use punctuation marks only where they are part of the place name (for example, ST. ALBERT AB).

- ▼ The name of the addressee is the last line scanned; this means that the automated equipment has already determined the destination before it reads the addressee's name. Therefore, punctuation is acceptable on this line. However, for consistency it is best to adhere to the rule of all capital letters, and no punctuation, except where these are part of the name (for example, MR W ROSS).

- ▼ The return address should follow the same format as the main address. Although the return address is of little value in the original scanning for sorting and delivery of the item, if the address cannot be deciphered, the item may need to be returned to the sender.

Preparing Memos

Just as companies print stationery for use in business letters, they print memo forms for internal use. Memos come in various sizes and may even include tear-off forms. In some cases the company's name and address is printed at the top of the memo. Just above or below the address may be the printed title *MEMO* or *MEMORANDUM*.

PARTS OF A MEMO

Memos are simpler than letters and include fewer elements. Unlike a letter, for example, a memo has no inside address, complimentary close, or signature line. In addition, many memos are not signed; instead, writers may simply initial their keyed names after the *From* guide heading, which is described below.

Word processing software packages provide templates where the user simply keys in the variable information. A variety of formats is available, allowing numerous options for the users. These electronic templates represent a saving to the company since no preprinted paper is required. In a business where a software template is not used, the company may provide preprinted memo sheets.

Many memos begin with four fill-in-the-blank lines: *To, From, Date,* and *Subject*. These elements, or *guide headings*, may be arranged on the page in different ways. Two examples are shown in Figure I-3. Although many companies include guide headings on printed memo forms, others expect writers to key in the headings themselves.

Allow two to three line spaces after the last guide heading before beginning the memo body, which consists of single-spaced paragraphs placed flush against the left margin. A line space appears between each paragraph. Some memo forms include the word *MESSAGE* after the printed headings. In this case, begin the body of your memo about two or three lines below that.

To help readers scan documents for vital information, many writers incorporate headings into their memos. Although the style of your headings is largely a matter

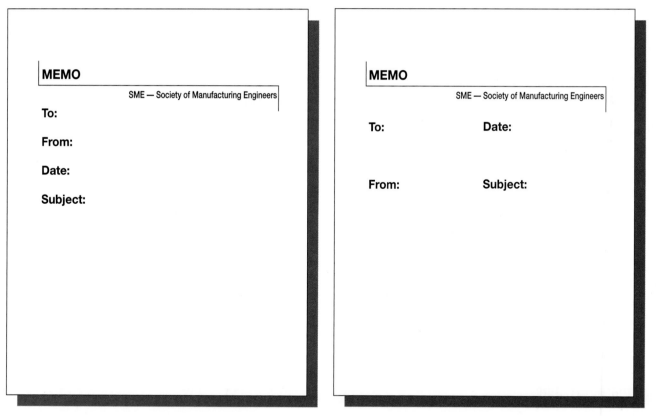

Figure I-3   Memo Guide Headings

of preference, be consistent in creating headings throughout your document. Here, for example, is one way to style memo headings.

▼ *Primary-level headings.* Capitalize and centre; use upper- and lower-case letters.
▼ *Secondary-level headings.* Underline and place flush against the left margin.
▼ *Third-level headings.* Begin headings at the left margin. The heading is followed by a period and two spaces; the opening sentence of the paragraph begins on the same line as the heading. In fact, this paragraph is an example of a third-level heading.

The same heading styles can be used in reports and proposals.

Set off primary- and secondary-level headings from the body of your memo by triple spacing (leaving two blank lines) before the heading and double-spacing (leaving one blank line) after the heading. If the body of your memo is more than a page long, use continuation sheets. *Continuation-page headings* in memos should follow the same style as that suggested for business letters.

Many memos close with notations like those used in standard business letters. Notations should be placed at the end of the memo, flush against the left margin, consistently spaced, with or without line spaces between each item.

Because there is no signature block in a memo, notations begin either two lines after the last line of the memo body or two lines after the sender's handwritten initials. A distribution list may appear at the bottom of the notations, indicating who receives the memo in addition to the people listed at the head of the memo form. For example:

dh

Enclosure

<u>Distribution</u>
  Anna Serrell
  May Albright

Preparing Reports and Proposals ─ ─ ─ ─ ─ ─ ─ ─ ─ ─ ─ ─ ─ ─ ─ ─ ─ ─

A report or proposal that takes weeks or months to research and write can still make a bad impression if the appearance of the document is sloppy or inconsistent. A professional appearance comes from the consistent and correct use of margins, headings, line spacing, and page numbers.

MARGINS

Unless your report is bound, all margins in the body of a report should be $2\frac{1}{2}$ cm (1 inch) wide, except for the first page of a chapter or a section. This page requires a 5 cm to $6\frac{1}{2}$ cm (2- to $2\frac{1}{2}$-inch) top margin.

If binding is used, about $1\frac{1}{4}$ cm ($\frac{1}{2}$ inch) of paper is lost in the binding process. As a result, margins must be adjusted for the loss.

▼ *Top-bound:* In top-bound manuscripts, leave a $3\frac{3}{4}$-cm ($1\frac{1}{2}$-inch) margin at the top of each page *except* the first page of a chapter or section. After binding, the page will show $2\frac{1}{2}$ cm (1 inch) of top margin space. To ensure that a 5-cm or $6\frac{3}{4}$-cm (2- or $2\frac{1}{2}$-inch) margin remains after the binding, allow a $6\frac{1}{4}$- to $7\frac{1}{2}$-cm ($2\frac{1}{2}$- to 3-inch) margin for the first page of a chapter or a section.

▼ *Left-bound:* In left-bound manuscripts, use a $3\frac{3}{4}$-cm ($1\frac{1}{2}$-inch) left margin so that a $2\frac{1}{2}$-cm (1-inch) margin remains after binding.

HEADINGS

Like those in letters and memos, the headings in reports and proposals must be planned in advance and must be implemented consistently. Headings should also use parallel structure. You can use any clear and reasonable heading system, but remember that you have one goal in mind: to make information easy to find.

LINE SPACING

Depending upon either your personal preference or the chosen style of your organization, your report or proposal can be single- or double-spaced. Single-spacing is more common. In double-spaced documents, paragraphs are indented five spaces; in single-spaced documents, paragraphs usually begin flush left and sometimes are indented; however with single spacing the paragraphs are always separated from one another with a double line space.

Proper spacing around primary, secondary, and paragraph headings makes them more noticeable—and more effective. Here are some general guidelines for spacing around headings:

▼ Triple-space before and after primary headings.
▼ Triple-space before secondary headings; double-space after secondary headings.
▼ Do not add any extra line spacing before or after paragraph headings.

Whereas quotations of fewer than four lines are generally incorporated into the text, quotations longer than four lines are typically set apart from the text. They appear below the regular text and are indented five to ten spaces from both the left and right margins. When the text is double-spaced, the excerpt is generally single-spaced. In addition, at least one blank space is added above and one blank space below the excerpt to separate it further from the regular text.

PAGE NUMBERS

Obviously, page numbers are crucial in long reports and proposals. Placement depends on whether your document is left-bound or top-bound.

- ▼ *Left-bound.* Page numbers are usually keyed at the top right of the page, approximately $1\frac{1}{4}$ cm ($\frac{1}{2}$ inch) from the top edge and $2\frac{1}{2}$ cm (1 inch) from the right edge; alternatively, they can be centered $1\frac{1}{4}$ cm ($\frac{1}{2}$ inch) from the top edge of the page. The first page of the report text, however, is unnumbered.
- ▼ *Top-bound.* Because top binding makes numbers at the top right of the page difficult to read, they are usually centred at the bottom of the page, $1\frac{1}{4}$ cm ($\frac{1}{2}$ inch) from the bottom edge.

The front matter of reports and proposals is numbered with lower-case Roman numerals (*ii*, *iii*, *iv*, and so on). Although the title page is technically the first page of the front matter, it remains unnumbered. Similarly, the letter of transmittal is considered *page ii*, but the page number is often missing because it is considered a letter rather than text material. The actual page numbering begins after the table of contents, which is often *page iii* of the front matter. Arabic numbers begin with the first page of report text.

Page numbers should stand alone and should not be set off by dashes, parentheses, or periods.

Formatting Letters _____

The *format* of a letter refers to the way in which the elements of a letter are placed on the page—for example, whether paragraphs are indented and where the dateline, inside address, and salutation are placed. Three different formats are used in business letters: *full block*, *modified block*, and *simplified*. Your choice of format depends on personal preference and on the style adopted by your organization.

FULL BLOCK

Every line in a full-block format—from the dateline to the postscript—begins at the left margin. Paragraphs are single-spaced, and a double space separates one paragraph from another. Figure I-4 depicts a letter in full-block format.

MODIFIED BLOCK

Unlike the full-block style, writers using the modified-block style may or may not choose to indent paragraphs. If paragraphs are indented, writers should indent them five to ten character spaces.

Also in contrast to the full-block style, the position of the dateline, reference line, complimentary close, and signature block are not flush left. Instead, they are usually keyed starting at the centre point of the page. These elements may also be

Billows Real Estate
Commercial Real Estate Department
1111 Sunnyside Road
Abbotsford, BC V2T 2Z2
Tel: 604-555-1111
Fax: 604-555-2222
E-mail: Jeafilippe@billows.web

March 22, 2000

Mr. Samuel Jenkins
Western Trust
1000 Mountain View Street
Abbotsford, BC V2T 1W1

Dear Sam:

Congratulations on your promotion to executive vice president in charge of real estate. I am delighted, but not surprised, by your success. Western Trust had the good sense to choose the most qualified person for the job.

Call me once you get settled. We'll have lunch and discuss several deals that look like opportunities for both our companies.

Cordially,

Jeanette Filippe

Jeanette Filippe
Executive President

mm

All the elements in a full-block format begin flush against the left margin. Allow at least two to four line spaces above and below the date. Exact spacing depends on the length of the letter. The writer limits the inside address to four lines by eliminating a separate line for the addressee's title

Figure I-4 Sample Letter: Full-Block Format

placed flush against the right margin or somewhere between the right margin and the centre of the page. As you can see in Figure I-5, all the other letter elements are placed flush against the left margin, and the paragraphs are not indented. Figure I-6 shows a sample letter in modified-block format with indented paragraphs.

SIMPLIFIED

Letters using a simplified format look somewhat different from letters using the other two formats. There are three main differences:

- the absence of a salutation and complimentary close
- the inclusion of a subject line in every letter; keyed in all capital letters, the subject line appears three lines below the inside address and three lines above the body of the letter

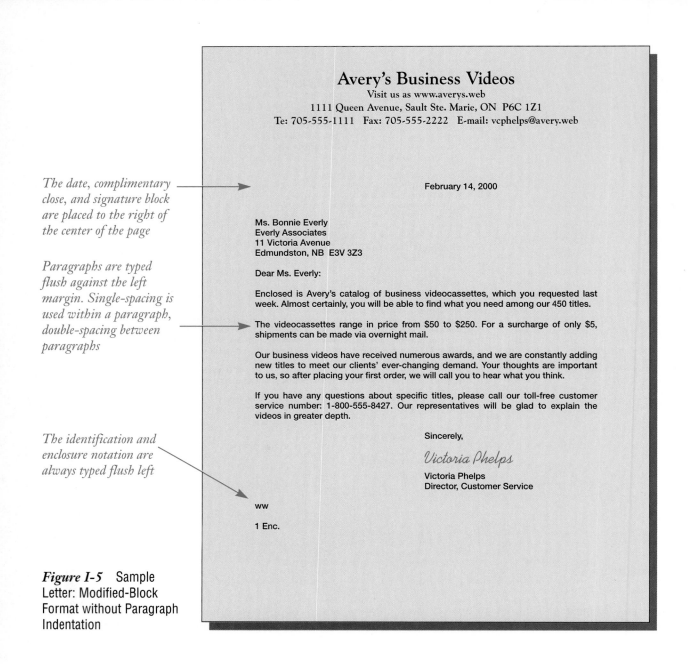

The date, complimentary close, and signature block are placed to the right of the center of the page

Paragraphs are typed flush against the left margin. Single-spacing is used within a paragraph, double-spacing between paragraphs

The identification and enclosure notation are always typed flush left

Avery's Business Videos
Visit us as www.averys.web
1111 Queen Avenue, Sault Ste. Marie, ON P6C 1Z1
Te: 705-555-1111 Fax: 705-555-2222 E-mail: vcphelps@avery.web

February 14, 2000

Ms. Bonnie Everly
Everly Associates
11 Victoria Avenue
Edmundston, NB E3V 3Z3

Dear Ms. Everly:

Enclosed is Avery's catalog of business videocassettes, which you requested last week. Almost certainly, you will be able to find what you need among our 450 titles.

The videocassettes range in price from $50 to $250. For a surcharge of only $5, shipments can be made via overnight mail.

Our business videos have received numerous awards, and we are constantly adding new titles to meet our clients' ever-changing demand. Your thoughts are important to us, so after placing your first order, we will call you to hear what you think.

If you have any questions about specific titles, please call our toll-free customer service number: 1-800-555-8427. Our representatives will be glad to explain the videos in greater depth.

Sincerely,

Victoria Phelps

Victoria Phelps
Director, Customer Service

ww

1 Enc.

Figure I-5 Sample Letter: Modified-Block Format without Paragraph Indentation

▼ the signature line appears approximately five lines below the body of the letter because there is no complimentary close; often, the writer's name and title are keyed in all capital letters

All lines in this format are keyed flush against the left margin; there are no paragraph indentations.

The simplified-letter format enables you to address the reader when you don't know who the reader is. For example, when writing to a company rather than a specific individual, eliminating the salutation enables you to avoid stilted openings like "Dear Customer Service Representative." The sample letter in Figure I-7 is constructed in a simplified format.

The dateline, complimentary close, and signature block appear to the right of the center of the page. Paragraphs are indented five to ten character spaces. Paragraphs are single-spaced with double-spacing between paragraphs.

Lark Corporation

www.lark.web
11 Fitzroy Avenue
Charlottetown, Prince Edward Island C1A 2Z2
Tel: 902-555-1111 Fax: 902-555-2222
E-mail: mwild@lark.web

April 11, 2000

Mr. Sven Seligson
Canadian Cancer Society
11 Atlantic Avenue
Charlottetown, PE C1A 1T1

Dear Mr. Seligson:

There is no more worthwhile charitable organization in our community than the Canadian Cancer Society. I am honoured by your invitation to speak at your annual banquet next month.

My membership on several corporate boards places a great many demands on my time, and next month is my busiest travel period. Regrettably, because of previous commitments, I will not be able to accept your invitation.

Is there another Canadian Cancer Society function at which I can speak? I have enclosed open dates in my schedule over the next three months.

Call me after you have looked at the schedule. I look forward to the opportunity to speak before an organization as worthwhile as your own.

Sincerely,

Martha Wilder

Martha Wilder
Chief Executive Officer

jr

Enclosure

Figure I-6 Sample Letter: Modified-Block Format with Paragraph Indentation

Documenting Sources

When your report or proposal relies on secondary sources for information, you must acknowledge these sources. You can make your acknowledgment either by inserting parenthetical references within your text or by footnoting or endnoting your reference material. Footnotes and endnotes can also add meaning by including additional commentary. Complete source lists should appear at the end of your document.

PARENTHETICAL REFERENCES

Parenthetical references specify for readers the points in a document at which material has been quoted, paraphrased, or summarized. They also give readers enough information to find specific, fully cited sources listed at the end of your document.

All elements appear flush against the left margin

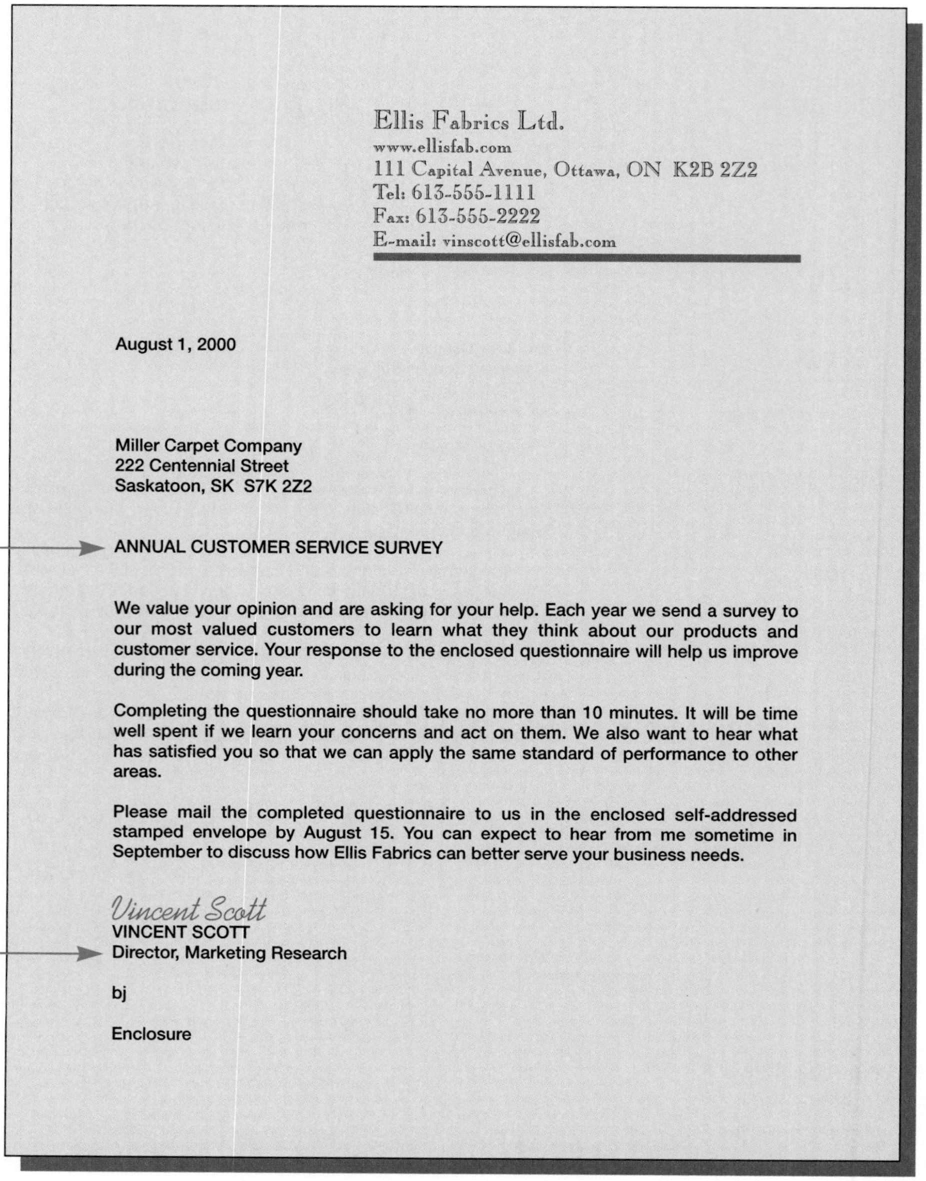

Ellis Fabrics Ltd.
www.ellisfab.com
111 Capital Avenue, Ottawa, ON K2B 2Z2
Tel: 613-555-1111
Fax: 613-555-2222
E-mail: vinscott@ellisfab.com

August 1, 2000

Miller Carpet Company
222 Centennial Street
Saskatoon, SK S7K 2Z2

Instead of a salutation, a subject line in all capital letters follows the inside address. Triple-space before and after the subject line

ANNUAL CUSTOMER SERVICE SURVEY

We value your opinion and are asking for your help. Each year we send a survey to our most valued customers to learn what they think about our products and customer service. Your response to the enclosed questionnaire will help us improve during the coming year.

Completing the questionnaire should take no more than 10 minutes. It will be time well spent if we learn your concerns and act on them. We also want to hear what has satisfied you so that we can apply the same standard of performance to other areas.

Please mail the completed questionnaire to us in the enclosed self-addressed stamped envelope by August 15. You can expect to hear from me sometime in September to discuss how Ellis Fabrics can better serve your business needs.

Vincent Scott
VINCENT SCOTT
Director, Marketing Research

The letter contains a signature block in all capital letters but no complimentary close

bj

Enclosure

Figure I-7 Sample Letter: Simplified Format

Both parenthetical references and concluding source lists are usually written in one of two documentation styles: the *MLA style*, developed by the Modern Language Association; and the *APA style*, developed by the American Psychological Association. In MLA style the end-of-document source list is called *Works Cited*; in APA style it is called *References*.

MLA STYLE   In MLA style parenthetical references include the author's name and the page number after the material requiring documentation. In its simplest form, the parenthetical reference looks like this:

Men and women often suffer from cross-cultural communication (Tannen 14).

Notice that the author's name and the page number are enclosed in parentheses and that the reference includes no internal punctuation. Note also that the reference appears before the punctuation that ends the sentence.

When the author's name is used in the documented sentence, you need not repeat it in the parenthetical reference, which will include only the page number. For example:

> According to Deborah Tannen, men and women often suffer from a form of cross-cultural communication (14).

References to works written by *two authors* cite both names (joined by *and*) and the page number. When the source has *two or three authors*, all the names are cited in the reference. When a work has *more than three authors*, use the first author's name plus the Latin abbreviation *et al.* For example:

> Cultural differences in the workplace must not be taken for granted; they must be managed (Harris and Moran 3).
>
> Adjustment letters should avoid emphasizing the negative situation described in the original complaint letter, but should focus on the actions being taken to correct the situation (Brusaw et al. 23).

If you must cite *two or more works by the same author*, your parenthetical references must differentiate between the works. Do this by providing the author's last name, a shortened title of the work, and page numbers. For example:

> (Tannen, *Understand* 111)
> (Tannen, Conversational Style 89)

Notice, by the way, that a comma separates the author's name and the title and that the title is either italicized or underlined.

If the author of the work is a corporation or other organization, and if no individual author is cited, use the organization's name in your parenthetical reference. For example:

> (Xerox Corp. 57)

When no author, individual or corporate, is cited, your parenthetical reference should use the title of the work itself or an abbreviated version of that title. The abbreviated title should start with the word by which the work is alphabetized in the Works Cited list at the end of your document. For example:

> (*Statistical*, 345)

Here the title is italicized (or underlined) because it is a book. When citing articles, use quotation marks.

There are times, of course, when more than one source will contribute to an idea cited in your document. In this case both sources (separated by a semicolon) should be included in your parenthetical reference:

> (Tannen 167; Baron 64)

When your source cites another source, the names of both authors should be mentioned in your parenthetical reference. For example:

> (Gilligan qtd. in Tannen 113)

In this citation, the abbreviation *qtd.* tells the reader that Deborah Tannen's book includes a *quote* by Carol Gilligan and that the source list at the back of the document includes an entry under Tannen's name.

Always place parenthetical references immediately after quoted material, even if the quote ends in the middle of a sentence. For example:

According to Deborah Tannen, "For most women, the language of conversation is primarily a language of rapport" (77), which establishes connections and forms relationships.

If the quote ends the sentence, place the parenthetical reference immediately after the quoted material, but before the closing period. For instance:

"For most women, the language of conversation is primarily a language of rapport" (Tannen 77).

This format gives the reader enough information to locate the source of the quote in your Works Cited list.

APA STYLE In APA style parenthetical references also point the reader to the full citation at the end of your document. The purpose, then, is the same as that of MLA style; it's the format that differs.

First, APA references distinguish between quoted material on the one hand and paraphrased or summarized material on the other. When citing *quoted material*, include the author's name, the year of the work's publication, and page number(s), which should be introduced with *p.* for one page and *pp.* for two or more pages. For example:

(Tannen, 1990, p. 101)

Notice that commas separate each element and that a period is used after *p*.

References to *paraphrased or summarized material* may or may not include page numbers; as a rule, the writer may decide whether or not the reader is likely to need the exact location of the cited material.

Although the same basic rules govern both MLA and APA citations, there are a few noteworthy requirements in APA style:

▼ If you mention a work more than once, the full parenthetical reference is used the first time; all subsequent references include only author and page number.

▼ When citing works written in the same year by the same author, alphabetize the works in your References list and then assign a letter to each work (*a, b, c,* and so on); these same letters should then appear in your parenthetical references as a means of distinguishing among the author's various works. For example:

(Tannen, 1990a, p. 39)

Whether you choose MLA or APA style, it is important to use your chosen style consistently, both in your parenthetical references and in the source list at the end of your document. Do not mix citation styles.

FOOTNOTE AND ENDNOTE REFERENCES

Footnotes and endnotes are alternatives to the parenthetical-reference method. In footnotes, complete sources appear at the bottom of the page on which cited material appears. A *superscript* in the form of a raised Arabic number coordinates the text reference to the footnote. Footnotes are numbered sequentially by page, chapter, or document. The same system is used in endnotes except that sources are listed at the end of each chapter or the end of the work as a whole. Endnotes are easier to format in a report and, therefore, tend to be much more popular than footnotes.

Both footnotes and endnotes may perform two different functions. *Explanatory notes* include commentary that supplements or explains the main point made in the text itself. Explanatory footnotes may also cross-reference other parts of the document or other sources. *Reference notes* establish the sources for quoted, paraphrased, or summarized material.

Use the following guidelines to include note numbers in your document:

1. The number should appear as superscript; that is, a little above the line of words and in a reduced font size.
2. The number should appear as close as possible to the text to which it refers, but after any accompanying punctuation.
3. One space should follow the number when it appears in the middle of a sentence; use two spaces when the number is followed by a new sentence.

Whether you use footnote numbers, endnote numbers, or parenthetical references, your citations must be coordinated with the *source list* in which you collect references to the material that you have used in your document. We will examine these source lists next.

SOURCE LISTS

Both parenthetical and endnote references are coordinated with a list of sources that appears at the end of your document; the sources for footnotes are found at the bottom of pages. As we noted earlier, MLA style refers to the source list as *Works Cited*; in APA style, it is called *References*. When you use endnotes, label your list *Notes*.

In each case your list should contain *all* the sources actually cited in your document. If you consult a source but do not actually cite it in a quotation, paraphrase, or summary, you need not include it in your source list.

Your source list should begin on a new page, with entries arranged alphabetically according to authors' names. When an author is not named on a work, alphabetize the entry by the first significant word of the title (*The*, *A*, and *An* are not considered significant words).

We will turn next to the basic citation styles used to create lists of *Works Cited*, *References*, and *Notes*.

MLA DOCUMENTATION STYLE: WORKS CITED LIST

Books   Citations for books include author, title, and publication information (place of publication, publisher, and date of publication). Each element is separated by a period and two spaces. All major words of the title are capitalized. When the source requires more than one line, the first line appears flush left and all following lines are indented five spaces. For example:

> Harris, Philip R., and Robert T. Moran. *Managing Cultural Differences*. Houston: Gulf Publishing, 1991.

Articles   Citations of articles from magazines, journals, and newspapers also contain three major parts: author, article title, and publication information. Publication information includes the title of the periodical, volume number, year of publication, and applicable page numbers. For example:

> Sadker, Myra, and David Sadker. "Sexism in the Classroom: From Grade School to Graduate School." *Phi Delta Kappa* 67 (1986): 7.

Note that MLA style reverses the order of the first and last names *for the first author only*. The title of the periodical is italicized (or underlined), and the publication date is enclosed in parentheses.

When citing an article in a popular periodical or a newspaper, use the full date rather than a volume number. For example:

Sadker, Myra, and David Sadker. "Sexism in the Schoolroom of the '80s." *Psychology Today*, March 1985: 54–57.

When the date includes a specific day, the day should be written first, as in *14 March 1985*.

Citing Online Databases   To cite information offered on online databases, such as the Internet, the MLA requires three elements that citations for printed information do not. The additional elements are the publication medium (Online), the name of the computer service or network through which you accessed the source (Internet, Nexis, CompuServe, and so on), and the date of retrieval. An optional element is the electronic address (or user resource locator, URL) you used to access the document, preceded by the word *Available*. Each new element is separated by a period and two spaces. The new elements follow the information about the original source. If you cannot find some of the information required, cite what is available. Some examples follow:

Angier, Natalie. "Chemists Learn Why Vegetables Are Good for You." *New York Times*, 13 Apr. 1993, late ed.: C1. *New York Times Online*. Online. Nexis. 10 Feb. 1996.

"Time Warner, Inc.: Sales Summary, 1988–1992." *Disclosure/Worldscope*. Online. Nexis. 4 Jan. 1996.

Wilke, Jennifer. "A History of Team Communication." *Psychology Today*, 62 (1996) 153–159. Online. Internet. 3 Apr. 1998. Available http://www.pt.org/journals/wilke.html

Note that a closing period is not used after an Internet address given in a source list.

For the correct MLA form for all possible citations, consult Joseph Gibaldi, *MLA Handbook for Writers of Research Papers*, 4th ed. (New York: MLA, 1995).

APA DOCUMENTATION STYLE: REFERENCES LIST

Books   In APA-style book citations, include four major parts: author, date, title, and publication information. For example:

Hall, E. T., and Hall, M. R. (1987). *Hidden differences: Doing business with the Japanese*. Garden City, NY: Doubleday.

In APA style the last name of each author always appears first. The date of publication appears next in parentheses, followed by the title, which is italicized (or underlined). Only the first word of the title is capitalized, as is any word following a colon. If the reader is likely to be unfamiliar with the city of publication (as with *Red Deer, Alberta*), the Canada Post provincial abbreviation can be added.

Articles   APA article citations also include four major parts: author, date, article title, and publication information. Publication information includes the publication title, volume number, and applicable pages. For example:

Cox, T., and Nkomo, S. M. (1990). Invisible men and women: A status report on race as a variable in organization behavior research. *Journal of Organizational Behavior, 11*, 1990. 238–256.

Note that quotation marks do *not* enclose the title of the article and that the inclusive page numbers are given in full. Page referencing contrasts with MLA style: MLA uses the full second number through 99 (for example, 26–37) but then only the last two digits (187–93) unless confusion could result (191–203).

In some journals page numbers run continuously throughout an annual volume; that is, if the first issue of a volume ends on page 125, the second issue starts on page 126. In most journals, however, pagination is separate for each issue. To cite articles from journals in the latter group, include both the *volume number* and the *issue number*.

In APA style the volume number is italicized (or underlined) and the issue number follows immediately after within parentheses. For example:

> Droge, C., and Germain, R. (1990). Note on marketing and the corporate annual report: 1930–1950. *Journal of the Academy of Marketing Science. 18*(4), 345–363.

Information Retrieved from the Internet   Many types of information can be retrieved electronically via the Internet. In citing these sources, begin with the same information that would be provided for a printed source (author, date, title, and publication information), or as much of that information as possible. Then add a description in brackets of the document type, a retrieval notice (where the information was obtained from), and the URL (Uniform Resource Locator, or Internet address). Again, do not use a closing period at the end of a URL, as the address does not have a final period. Here are some examples:

> Wilke, J. R. (1996). A history of team communication. *Pyschology Today, 62*, 153–159 [Journal, selected articles online]. Retrieved from World Wide Web: http://www.pt.org/journals/wilke.html
>
> Sleek, S. (1996, January). Psychologists build a culture of peace. *APA Monitor*, pp. 1, 33 [Newspaper, selected stories online]. Retrieved from World Wide Web: http://www.apa.org/journals/ab1.html

For further information about citations using APA style, contact the APA at its home page: http.//www.apa.org or consult American Psychological Association, *Publication Manual of the American Psychological Association*, 4th ed. (Washington, D.C.: APA, 1994).

FOOTNOTES AND ENDNOTES   When you use a note format, your source can appear either at the bottom of the page with the footnote or listed on separate pages at the end of the document. When you use endnotes, centre the word *Notes* (no underlining or quotation marks) at the top of a separate page. Then skip four lines before starting the first note. Indent the first line of each note five character spaces; all other lines start at the left margin. Each note number is raised slightly above the entry and is written without a period.

The MLA style is frequently used to format footnotes and endnotes. MLA style is slightly different from that used in the Works Cited list that is usually coordinated with parenthetical references. For example, there is no reversal in the order of authors' names, and the publication information (place of publication, publisher, and date) is enclosed in parentheses.

First References   Here are some first-reference note forms for common types of sources. As you will see, subsequent references use a shortened form.

> [1]Dennis Baron, *Grammar and Gender* (New Haven: Yale University Press, 1986) 134.
> [2]Philip R. Harris and Robert T. Moran, *Managing Cultural Differences*, 3rd ed. (Houston: Gulf Publishing, 1991) 256.
> [3]Dean Baquet and Martin Gottlieb, "Hospital Rewrote Reports in Failed Accreditation Bid," *New York Times* 11 March 1992: A1.
> [4]Kerry J. Rottenberger, "Can Anyone Become a More Effective Communicator?" *Sales & Marketing Management* August 1992: 60–63.
> [5]Blair Johnson, personal interview, 25 May 1993.

[6]Tharon Howard, "Wide-Area Computer-Mediated Communication in Business Writing," *Bulletin of the Association for Business Communication* 55.4 (1992) 10–12.

Subsequent References   To save time and avoid repetition, subsequent references appear in shortened form. Shortened source notes can use either a traditional style, which includes Latin abbreviations, or the MLA style, which does not.

In the traditional style, the following Latin abbreviations are commonly used:

▼   ibid. (Latin meaning "in the same place")   This abbreviation is used when an entry is the same as the one immediately preceding it; when page numbers follow the abbreviation, the entry is the same but the page number is different.

▼   op. cit. (Latin meaning "in the work cited")   This abbreviation is used when one or more references separate a reference from its original citation; to coordinate the reference with the original citation, include the last names of the authors as well as page numbers.

▼   loc. cit. (Latin meaning "in the place cited")   This abbreviation is used in the same way as op. cit., except that it refers to exactly the same page number as the previous citation.

The following examples show how these abbreviations apply to actual sources:

[1]Dennis Baron, *Grammar and Gender* (New Haven: Yale University Press, 1986) 134.
[2]Ibid., 47.
[3]Philip R. Harris and Robert T. Moran, *Managing Cultural Differences*, 3rd ed. (Houston: Gulf Publishing, 1991) 256.
[4]Baron, op. cit., 67.
[5]Dean Baquet and Martin Gottlieb, "Hospital Rewrote Reports in Failed Accreditation Bid," *New York Times* 11 March 1992: A1.
[6]Ibid.
[7]Harris and Moran, loc. cit.

MLA style does not use Latin expressions to indicate subsequent references. Rather, MLA relies on shortened references to original sources. When footnotes or endnotes include only one work by an author, subsequent references need include only the author's last name and the page reference:

[18]O'Neill, 199.

To avoid confusion when you must cite more than one work by the same author, use a shortened form of each title, along with the author's name and page numbers:

[19]Smythe, *Communication* 234.
[20]Smythe, *Corporate Culture* 49–54.

A formal report may also include a bibliography whose purpose is to guide readers to additional sources. We will examine bibliographies next.

BIBLIOGRAPHIES

A *bibliography* is an alphabetized list of the sources used to prepare a body of written material. A bibliography differs from lists of works cited, references, and notes in that it may include works not specifically referred to in the document. In addition, the bibliography uses inclusive page numbers for entire articles in periodicals, not just the pages specifically referred to as sources of cited information.

Each entry in the bibliography begins at the left margin, with the author's last name appearing first. Entries with no author are listed alphabetically by title (use the first significant word). All subsequent lines are indented five spaces. Entries are usually single-spaced, with a double line space between entries. As you can see from the following examples, the date in a bibliography appears later than it does in a source list:

Adler, Nancy J. "Cultural Synergy: Managing the Impact of Cultural Diversity." In *The 1986 Annual: Developing Human Resources.* San Diego: University Associates, 1986, 229–38.

Copeland, Lennie. "Valuing Diversity: Making the Most of Cultural Differences at the Workplace," *Personnel,* 42 (June 1988): 52–60.

Hymowitz, Carol. "One Firm's Bid to Keep Blacks, Women: Corning Battles to Overcome Ingrained Biases." *Wall Street Journal,* 16 February 1989, B1.

International Dimensions of Organizational Behavior. Boston: Kent Publishing, 1986.

Johnston, William B., and Arnold E. Packer. *Workforce 2000: Work and Workers for the Twenty-first Century.* Indianapolis: Hudson Institute, June 1987.

Leffler, Ann, Diane Gillespie, and Joan C. Conaty. "The Effects of Status Differentiation on Nonverbal Behavior," *Social Psychology Quarterly* 45:3 153–61.

Tannen, Deborah. *That's Not What I Meant! How Conversational Style Makes or Breaks Your Relations with Others.* New York: William Morrow, 1986.

When you cite several different sources by the same authors in a bibliography, you can eliminate the need to repeat authors' names by using a long dash instead of the same name each time.

To make an extensive bibliography more manageable, you can divide the entries into categories according to subject. For example, in a report on workforce diversity, the bibliography might be divided into the following headings: age, communication, cultural diversity, disability, gender, and race and ethnicity. It can also be divided by types of entries: books, journal articles, magazine and newspaper articles, and government publications.

To help readers evaluate the usefulness of sources, *annotated bibliographies* provide short comments on each entry. For example:

Hirsch, James S. "Older Workers Chafe under Young Managers." *Wall Street Journal,* 26 February 1990, B1. Discusses how the 3.4 million workers aged 65 and older create unique problems and opportunities for themselves and their corporations.

If you decide to annotate your bibliography, remember that all of the entries must be annotated.

II

Basics of Grammar and Usage

For written communication to be successful, it must follow established rules for grammar and usage.[1] These rules allow both writers and readers to operate according to practices that communicate shared meaning. Appendix II begins with a review of the basics of grammar and usage rules, starting with the parts of speech—nouns, pronouns, verbs, adjectives, adverbs, prepositions, and conjunctions. We then examine sentence formation, punctuation, mechanics, and word usage.

Parts of Speech

NOUNS

A **noun** is a part of speech that names a person, a place, a thing, or an idea. Only proper nouns require capitalization. **Proper nouns** include names (*Wayne Gretzky*), titles (*former Prime Minister Pierre Trudeau*), groups of people (*French Canadians*), organizations (*Wal-Mart Canada*), and places (*St. Lawrence River*). **Common nouns,** which refer to general classes of people, places, and things, are not capitalized. For example, although the company name *Avon* is capitalized, references to *the company* are not; although *Ottawa* is capitalized, *city* is not.

SINGULAR AND PLURAL NOUNS   When nouns refer to one person, place, thing, or idea, they are considered **singular;** when they refer to more than one person, place, thing, or idea, they are considered **plural.** To pluralize a regular noun, add an *s* to the end of the noun. An *es* is added to words that end in *ch, s, sh, x,* or *z* to make pronunciation possible. For example:

Singular	Plural
desk	desks
book	books
flower	flowers
cross	crosses
match	matches
sash	sashes
tax	taxes

Irregular nouns are nouns that are pluralized by making changes other than adding a final *s* or *es*. Here are some important rules that govern the spelling of irregular nouns:

1. In general, words ending in *f* or *fe* are pluralized by using a *v* in place of the *f* or *fe* and adding *es:*

leaf	leaves
wife	wives
life	lives

2. In general, words ending in *y* are pluralized by removing the *y* and adding *ies:*

party	parties
study	studies

3. Some nouns require internal changes to convert them from singular to plural. Here are just a few:

mouse	mice
man	men
woman	women
foot	feet
child	children

4. In a compound word, the noun is pluralized, not its modifier:

brother-in-law	brothers-in-law
kilometre per hour	kilometres per hour
editor in chief	editors in chief

   When two nouns make up the compound, the first acts as a modifier, and the *s* or *es* is placed at the end of the entire compound:

tractor-trailer	tractor-trailers
nurse-practitioner	nurse-practitioners

5. Some nouns are spelled the same in both singular and plural forms. Words in this category include *deer, elk, fish, trout, salmon, rice,* and *wheat.*

POSSESSIVE NOUNS **Possessive nouns** indicate ownership or a close relationship. Possession is generally shown by adding an *'s:*

the writer's papers
the manager's office
the executive assistant's computer
the report's illustrations

When a singular noun ends in an *s*, add an *'s* to show possession—for example:

Charles Dickens's novel *David Copperfield*
the business's assets were considerable

When a plural noun ends in an *s*, show possession by adding an apostrophe—for example:

Two years' neglect has left the building in disrepair.
Clients' problems must be dealt with before personnel problems.

PRONOUNS

A **pronoun** is a word that replaces or refers to a noun. The noun for which the pronoun stands is known as an **antecedent.** For example:

> The *CEO* wants an immediate *increase*.
> *He* wants *it* by the end of next week.

Here, the pronoun *he* replaces the noun *CEO* and the pronoun *it* replaces the noun *increase*.

MAKING PRONOUNS AND ANTECEDENTS AGREE   If different pronouns refer to different nouns in the same paragraph, clarity requires that the nouns sometimes be repeated. In the following paragraph, for example, the pronoun reference is unclear.

> Martha Feingold submitted the trip report three days after Elaine Wilky, her supervisor, asked for it. She analyzed her meetings in Montreal and discussed how her insistence on the highest standards of customer service was making a positive impression on clients.

Who analyzed the Montreal meetings? Who insisted on high standards of customer service? The following version clarifies the confusion:

> Martha Feingold submitted the trip report three days after Elaine Wilky asked for it. Feingold analyzed her meetings in Montreal and discussed how Wilky's insistence on the highest standards of customer service was making a positive impression on clients.

To avoid confusion, pronouns should be placed as close as possible to their antecedents. In addition, many writers prefer to use a noun rather than a pronoun at the start of a new paragraph when the noun was used in the prior paragraph. Repetition of this type often improves clarity.

Pronouns can be either singular or plural, and they must match their antecedents in number. The following guidelines will help ensure accurate usage:

1. When two or more nouns are joined by the word *and*, the pronoun that refers to the nouns should be plural.

    > Although Reebok and Nike are both in the athletic footwear business, they use different technology.

2. When singular nouns are preceded by *each* or *every* and are connected by the word *and*, use a singular pronoun:

    > Every elected mayor and deputy mayor takes an oath of office following the election.

3. **Indefinite pronouns** do not refer to any specific person, thing, or idea; rather, they depend on context for their meaning. Indefinite pronouns include such words as *anybody, anyone, each, every, everybody, nobody,* and *someone*. In most cases a singular pronoun is used to refer to an indefinite pronoun:

    > Anyone who has contributed to the project should submit his or her final draft by tomorrow.

CHOOSING GENDER-NEUTRAL PRONOUNS   Be sensitive to the gender implications of chosen pronouns. The conventions of grammar, like the conventions of society, have changed over the years. As a result, it is no longer proper to use masculine pronouns to refer to indefinite pronouns, to nouns, or to general categories that might include both men and women. This shift in acceptable form has occurred because it is now recognized that the pronouns *he, his, him,* and *himself* implicitly exclude women.

Sexist language can be avoided in three ways:

1. By using a pronoun pair (he and she, his or her);
2. By making the antecedent plural;
3. By rewriting the sentence to avoid the use of sexist language.

Thus, this sentence—

> Every participant at the meeting championed his own personal agenda.

can be recast as one of the following:

> Every participant at the meeting championed his or her own personal agenda.
>
> The nine participants at the meeting championed their own personal agendas.
>
> Everyone came to the meeting with a personal agenda in mind.

SELECTING THE PROPER PRONOUN CASE   The **case** of a pronoun refers to the relationship that word has to the other words in a sentence. Case shows changes in both person (first, second, and third person) and number (singular and plural). The **first person** refers to the speaker or writer; the **second person** to the person spoken or written to, and the **third person** to the person or thing that is spoken or written about.

Pronouns have three cases: subjective, objective, and possessive. Used in the **subjective case,** pronouns act as the subject of a sentence:

> We will review the report after lunch.
>
> You will be expected to complete the assignment by next week.

Used in the **objective case,** pronouns have three functions in the sentence: a **direct object,** an **indirect object,** or the **object of a preposition:**

> We watched *her* deliver the keynote speech. (*Her* is the direct object.)
>
> I gave *them* our estimate. (*Them* is the indirect object.)
>
> Please give the cheque to *him*. (*Him* is the object of the preposition *to*.)

Used in the **possessive case,** pronouns show possession or ownership:

> *Our* car was in an accident. Please bring the accident report to *her* office. (The possessive pronouns *our* and *her* show ownership.)

Although a compound construction should not affect the choice of pronoun, it often does when writers mistakenly use the wrong case for one or more of the pronouns. For example, if instead of correctly writing,

> *Bill and I* plan to attend the conference

you were to write,

> *Bill and me* plan to attend the conference

you would have chosen the objective case (*me*) instead of the subjective case (*I*) to refer to one of the subjects of your sentence. Similarly, look at the following pair of sentences:

> The manager told *Karen and me* to start the new project.
>
> The manager told *Karen and I* to start the new project.

The first sentence is correct because the pronoun (*me*) is a direct object and thus takes the objective case; the second sentence, therefore, is incorrect because the *I* is in the subjective case, not the objective.

Confusion also frequently occurs after the use of linking verbs. A **linking verb** connects the subject of a sentence to a word that renames it. This confusion occurs most often with linking verbs that indicate a state of being (*am, is, are, was, were*). The pronoun that follows the linking verb renames the subject of that verb and must therefore be in the subjective case. For example:

> Last year, the top salesperson in the country was *I*.

It would be incorrect to write,

> Last year, the top salesperson in the country was *me*.

The linking verb (*was*) connects its subject (*salesperson*) with a pronoun (*I*) that must be in the subjective case.

Quite often confusion also occurs over the correct form of the possessive personal pronouns *its* and *whose*. Although these pronouns express ownership, they do not require the use of an apostrophe. Thus, the second sentence in each of the following pairs is incorrect.

> The mailroom has to revise *its* delivery schedule.
> The mailroom has to revise *it's* delivery schedule.

> The investors, *whose* stock skyrocketed after the merger announcement, were happy.
> The investors, *who's* stock skyrocketed after the merger announcement, were happy.

Remember: *It's* is a contraction for *it is* or *it has*, and *who's* is a contraction for *who is* or *who has*.

VERBS

Verbs describe an action (*write, think, deliver, scratch*), a state of being (*be, seem, exist*), or an occurrence (*become, happen*).

VERB TENSES   The **tense** of a verb tells you when an action, a state of being, or an occurrence took place. Tense tells you whether the action is current, happened in the past, or will happen in the future.

There are six verb tenses in the English language—three simple tenses and three perfect tenses. Whereas both the simple and perfect tenses divide time into past, present, and future, the perfect tenses express more complex relationships.

The three **perfect tenses** show complex *time* relationships in the past, present, and future. These tenses combine an **auxiliary verb** (usually some form of the helping verb *have*) with the past participle form of the main verb.

It is extremely important to be able to recognize the **past participle** form of a verb. A typical dictionary, for example, shows the following forms of the verb *awake:*

> *awake; awoke* or *awaked; awaked* or *awoken; awaking*

This entry means that either of the two forms *awoke* or *awaked* may be used as the past tense of the verb; either of the two forms *awaked* or *awoken* may be used as the past participle. However, the two different forms of *awaked* are not the same form of the verb any more than *awoke* and *awoken* are the same form. *Awaking* is the present participle.

It may also help to remember that a participle always has some of the characteristics of an adjective. For example, the past participle of the verb *speak* is *spoken*; the present participle is *speaking*. Thus, you can refer to the "the *spoken* word" as opposed to "the *written* word" or to "a *speaking* part" in a play.

Remember: the perfect tenses of a verb are formed with the past participle, not the past tense.

With this principle in mind, we can examine the formation of perfect verb tenses in English. The **present perfect tense** shows that action which started in the past continues into the present. The auxiliary verb *have* indicates the continuing action:

> I *have behaved* with integrity throughout this affair.

The **past perfect tense** describes a situation in which an action started in the past, continued for a period of time, and was completed in the past. It is usually formed by combining *had* with the past participle:

> I *had behaved* with integrity until the rumours began.

The **future perfect tense** indicates that an action will have been completed in relation to some specific future time. The auxiliary *will have* generally signals the future perfect tense:

> By the turn of the century, I *will have completed* my graduate education.

REGULAR AND IRREGULAR VERBS Forming the simple and perfect tenses is straightforward for regular verbs. As a rule, add a *d* or an *ed* to form both the past tense and the past participle of regular verbs. In other words, the past participle is spelled and pronounced exactly like the past tense. However, anyone who has ever studied a foreign language knows that experience or memorization is required to use the principal parts of irregular verbs. A native speaker of English knows that the past tense of *take* is *took*, not *taked.* The non-native speaker must learn and remember that lesson.

THE VOICE OF VERBS Through its **voice,** a verb indicates whether the subject of a sentence is performing or receiving the action named by the verb. Verbs using the **active voice** indicate that the subject is performing an action; verbs using the **passive voice** indicate that the subject is receiving the action. For example:

> Active Voice: The manager *combined* two departments.
> Passive Voice: Two departments *were combined* by the manager.

Sentences using the passive voice may or may not indicate who performed the action—for example:

> Two departments *were combined.*

Sometimes the performers are unknown, and sometimes they are relatively unimportant to the message. Sometimes the writer chooses not to mention them. Chapter 6, for example, includes guidelines for when to choose the active and passive voices in business writing.

VERB MOOD Verbs also communicate a writer's attitude toward a statement. This attitude is known as **mood.** English verbs have three moods: the indicative mood, the imperative mood, and the subjunctive mood.

The most common mood, the **indicative,** makes statements or asks questions:

> The consultant *sat down* at the head of the table.
> *Do* you *need* help completing the project?

The **imperative mood** is used to issue commands and direct orders:

> *Distribute* these pamphlets now.
> Please *take* this suit to the cleaners.

The **subjunctive mood** expresses conditions, including wishes, indirect requests, and speculation, and is often preceded by words like *if, unless,* or *that.* As you can see in the following example, verbs in the subjunctive mood are used in special ways:

> If the division *were run* correctly, profits would be higher.
> Unless profits *soar*, we'll have to declare bankruptcy.
> I wish [that] he *were* ten years younger.

ADJECTIVES

Adjectives describe nouns and pronouns. For example:

> The *studious* boy walked to the library. (The adjective *studious* modifies the noun *boy*.)
> The *beautiful* vase graced the table. (The adjective *beautiful* modifies the noun *vase*.)

Adjectives can also communicate relative degrees of intensity by shifting from positive to comparative to superlative form. **Positive adjectives** are used in sentences that make no comparisons. **Comparative adjectives** compare two items; they usually end with an *er* or are accompanied by the word *more* or *less*. **Superlative adjectives** compare three or more things and usually end with an *est* or are accompanied by helping words such as *most* or *least*. For example:

Positive	Comparative	Superlative
smart	smarter	smartest
fast	faster	fastest
strong	stronger	strongest
successful	more successful	most successful
verbal	less verbal	least verbal
busy	busier	busiest

The proper form of comparatives and superlatives—using the *er* and *est* endings or the helping words—is largely determined by the number of syllables in the adjective. As a general rule, use the *er* and *est* endings when an adjective has one syllable. Use *more*, *most*, *less*, and *least* when the adjective has three or more syllables. Remember, however, that adjectives with two syllables are sometimes treated one way and sometimes the other. When a two-syllable adjective ends in *y*—for example, *busy*—the *y* changes to an *i* before the *er* or *est* is added.

The irregular adjectives in the following list do not follow these rules; comparative and superlative forms must simply be learned.

Positive	Comparative	Superlative
good	better	best
bad	worse	worst
many	more	most
some	more	most
little	less	least

ADVERBS

Adverbs modify verbs, adjectives, other adverbs, and entire sentences. For example:

> The artist *carefully* painted the portrait. (The adverb *carefully* modifies the verb *painted*.)

The manager made an *extremely* urgent phone call. (The adverb *extremely* modifies the adjective *urgent*.)

Tom is *so* highly qualified for the job that we can stop interviewing other candidates. (The adverb *so* modifies the adverb *highly*.)

Unfortunately, we cannot meet the production schedule. (The adverb *unfortunately* modifies the entire sentence.)

Many adverbs are formed by adding *ly* to adjectives—for example, *quick/quickly*, *slow/slowly*, *rapid/rapidly*.

Conjunctive adverbs are modifiers that logically connect ideas. They express addition (*also, furthermore, moreover, besides*), contrast (*still, nevertheless, conversely, however*), comparison (*similarly, likewise*), results (*therefore, consequently, thus*), time (*finally, next, then*), and emphasis (*indeed, certainly*).

PREPOSITIONS

Prepositions are part of **prepositional phrases,** which often describe relationships in time or space. Prepositional phrases are composed of a preposition and a noun or pronoun that acts as an object—that is, it is governed by the preposition. For example:

Please give the report *to Joan*. (*To* is a preposition, *Joan* its object.)

We will eat lunch *after the sales meeting*. (*After* is a preposition, and the noun phrase *the sales meeting* is its object.)

Some common prepositions are included in the following list. As you review them, keep in mind that some of these words may also function as other parts of speech.

about	as	concerning	in addition to	on	through
above	at	despite	into	out	till
across	because of	down	near	over	toward
after	before	except	next	past	under
along	between	for	of	regarding	upon
around	by	in	off	since	with

CONJUNCTIONS

Coordinating conjunctions connect two or more grammatically equivalent structures, including nouns, verbs, adjectives, and independent clauses. These common conjunctions include *and, but, nor, or, yet, for,* and *so*. In the following sentences, the conjunction *and* connects, respectively, two nouns, two verbs, two adjectives, and two independent clauses:

Please move the desk *and* chair.

We still have to type *and* collate the report.

The manuscript is correct *and* current.

He sent a copy to Smith, *and* he was sure to make four copies for Jones.

Correlative conjunctions also join equivalent grammatical structures, but they do so by functioning in pairs. Correlative conjunctions include:

both . . . and
either . . . or
neither . . . nor
not only . . . but also
whether . . . or

For example:

You can *either* have a draft now *or* a final report later.
Both Sam *and* I worked on it together.

Writing Correct Sentences _____

Sentences are formed when the parts of speech are combined in grammatically correct ways. This combination produces *simple sentences, compound sentences,* and *complex sentences.*

SIMPLE SENTENCES

A **simple sentence** contains a subject and a predicate. The **predicate** is the part of a sentence that contains the verb and its modifiers, as well as direct and indirect objects. A **direct object** receives the verb's action; an **indirect subject** refers to whom or for whom the action expressed by the verb was done. Consider the following examples of simple sentences:

> The boy ran.

The subject of the sentence is *boy,* the predicate *ran.* This sentence has a simple predicate because it contains only a verb.

> The boy ran quickly.

The predicate in this sentence is considered a complete predicate because it contains both the verb and its modifier (*quickly*).

> The customer bought the car.

The complete predicate in this sentence includes an object (*car*) as well as a verb.

> The recruiter gave the student an application.

This complete predicate includes a direct object (*application*) as well as an indirect object (*student*).

COMPOUND SENTENCES

A **compound sentence** contains two or more independent clauses and may be connected by a coordinating conjunction (*and, but, for, or, nor, yet,* or *so*). An **independent clause** is a clause that contains a subject and a predicate and which can function on its own as an independent grammatical unit:

> The recruiter liked the candidate, but she doubted that he would be willing to relocate to Whitehorse.

Here the two independent clauses are connected by a comma and the coordinating conjunction *but.*

COMPLEX SENTENCES

A **complex sentence** contains one independent clause and at least one dependent clause. A **dependent clause** cannot function as an independent sentence and must be joined to an independent clause.

> Although consumers reacted positively to the new product during market tests, first-year sales were poor.

In this case the dependent clause appears before the comma and is introduced by the subordinating conjunction *although.*

Constructing simple, compound, and complex sentences is not always straightforward. Consequently, writers sometimes make errors in sentence formation. In the next section, we will examine common types of errors by focusing on sentence fragments, comma splices and fused sentences, and sentences with internal flaws that affect communication.

SENTENCE FRAGMENTS

A **sentence fragment** is a part of a sentence that is treated as if it were a complete sentence. In most cases sentence fragments are phrases or dependent clauses. For example:

> Although the market improved.
> The office with the panoramic view.
> After the proposal was presented.
> When the administrative assistant learned the word processing program.

To determine whether a sentence is complete, check to see whether it contains a subject and a verb. If it does not contain both a subject and a verb, it is a **phrase** and cannot be a complete sentence. Does a subordinating word introduce the subject and verb and thus transform the clause into a dependent clause? For example:

> Wrote the report. (This fragment is a phrase that lacks a subject.)
> The report's cover. (This fragment is a phrase that lacks a verb.)
> Unless we receive a signed contract tomorrow. (This fragment is a dependent clause introduced by a subordinating conjunction.)

As in the last fragment above, a dependent clause often begins with a subordinating conjunction. Among the most common subordinating conjunctions are *after, although, as, because, before, even though, if, since, though, unless, until, when, whenever,* and *where*.

To correct sentence fragments that involve dependent clauses, you can either combine the dependent clause with an independent clause or drop the subordinating word that creates the dependent clause. For example, look at the following sentence fragment:

> The strike centred on wages and health-insurance benefits. Because these issues had the greatest economic impact on the average worker.

The fragment can be eliminated by combining the two sentences:

> The strike centred on wages and health-insurance benefits because these issues had the greatest economic impact on the average worker.

It can also be eliminated by dropping the subordinating conjunction (*because*) and creating an independent clause that functions as a complete sentence:

> The strike centred on wages and health-insurance benefits. These issues had the greatest economic impact on the average worker.

To correct sentence fragments that contain phrases, you can either rewrite the phrase so that it becomes an independent clause or combine the phrase with an adjoining independent clause to form a complex sentence. Here, for example, is a combination phrase and independent clause:

> Expecting a raise. He bought a new car.

This fragment can be transformed by creating an independent clause:

> He expected a raise. He bought a new car.

It can also be rewritten by combining the phrase and independent clause to form a complex sentence:

> Expecting a raise, he bought a new car.

COMMA SPLICES
AND FUSED SENTENCES

Although a comma is used to *separate* parts of a sentence, it cannot *join*—that is, *splice* together—independent clauses without a coordinating conjunction following (*and*, *but*, *for*, *or*, *nor*, *yet*, and *so*) to complete the connection. A **comma splice** (or **comma fault**) occurs when a writer tries to connect two independent clauses with nothing but a comma. For example:

> The auditor reviewed all the books, she focused on accounts receivable.

A **fused sentence** (also known as a **run-on sentence**) joins two independent clauses without the use of punctuation or coordinating conjunction. For example:

> The letter attempted to establish goodwill between the customer and the company the customer responded positively.

Both comma splices and fused sentences can be corrected with periods or semi-colons:

Comma splice	The writer compiled the research, the first part of the project was complete.
Fused sentence	The writer compiled the research the first part of the project was complete.
Correction with a period	The writer compiled the research. The first part of the project was complete.
Correction with a semicolon	The writer compiled the research; the first part of the project was complete.

Comma splices and fused sentences can also be corrected with coordinating conjunctions:

Correction with a coordinating conjunction	The writer compiled the research, and the first part of the project was complete.

Finally, comma splices and fused sentences can be corrected by turning one of the independent clauses into a dependent clause and, in the process, creating a complex sentence:

Correction by creating a complex sentence	Once the writer compiled the research, the first part of the project was complete.

INTERNAL SENTENCE FLAWS

Among the sentence flaws that can affect communication are *misplaced modifiers* and *dangling modifiers*.

MISPLACED MODIFIERS A **modifier** is a word or a group of words that describes other words, phrases, or clauses. The position of a modifier in a sentence can affect the meaning of that sentence, sometimes significantly. A **misplaced modifier** is wrongly or awkwardly placed in the sentence so that the writer's intended meaning is obscured. For example:

> Women began entering the labour force in record number, although their opportunities for advancement were limited beginning in the 1970s.

What began in the 1970s—the entry of women into the labour force or the limitation of advancement opportunities? This error can usually be avoided by placing the modifier as close as possible to what is being described. In this case because the modified event is the entry of women into the labour force, the meaning of the sentence is clarified when the modifier is placed at the beginning:

Beginning in the 1970s, women began entering the labour force in record number, although their opportunities for advancement were limited.

DANGLING MODIFIERS   A **dangling modifier** describes something that is implied but not stated in the sentence. When such sentences are read carefully, they simply do not make sense:

Hearing the whistle, the train pulled into the station.

The train, of course, cannot hear the whistle, and the reader must assume that appropriate listeners are implied—probably waiting passengers. With any luck, they will be waiting in the next sentence, where they can be brought into this sentence to eliminate the dangling modifier and clarify the subject of both sentences:

Hearing the whistle, the passengers lined up on the platform to board the train when it pulled into the station.

PUNCTUATION

Punctuation marks occur within sentences (**internal punctuation**) and at the end of sentences (**end punctuation**). They separate thoughts into recognizable, digestible units that enable the reader to understand what is being said. First, we will examine end punctuation—the period, the question mark, and the exclamation point. Then we will discuss internal punctuation—the comma, the semicolon, the colon, the apostrophe, quotation marks, the dash, parentheses, brackets, and the ellipsis.

PERIOD

A period is used to end sentences that are considered statements, mild commands, or indirect questions.

Statement	Here is the marketing plan for our new product line.
Mild command	Add more statistical data to the report.
Indirect question	The manager questioned why the department failed to meet its production schedule.

Periods are also used at the end of many abbreviations (*Dr.*, *Ph.D.*, *Ms.*, *Mrs.*, *Mr.*, *A.M.*) and to separate dollars and cents in numerical expressions of money.

QUESTION MARK

A question mark is used at the end of a direct question:

Will your report tell me where to place the new distribution centre?

In order to be polite, a request is sometimes phrased in the form of a question:

Would you please send me five copies of the completed report?

The question mark is optional in this request, which is actually a mild command:

Would you send me five copies of the completed report.

EXCLAMATION POINT

The exclamation point is used after a strong command or an emphatic declaration:

Don't touch that!
Watch out for the thin ice!

COMMA

The comma is used within sentences and is the most common internal punctuation mark. It is used to separate and group words and phrases in order to make sentences more readable. The following guidelines will help you decide when a comma is necessary and when it is not.

1. Place a comma before a coordinating conjunction that connects independent clauses. Coordinating conjunctions include *and, but, or, nor, yet, so,* and *for.* When a comma is used in this way, the end result is a compound sentence. For example:

> The budget figures are due today, and I have seven other things on my desk.
> She will take the job, but she can't start until next month.
> You can move directly into the new office, or movers can place your belongings in storage.

2. Use a comma after an introductory word, phrase, or clause at the beginning of a sentence. For example:

> First, I would like to discuss the economy.
> On the other hand, our salesforce is the best in the business.
> From its inception, the company has dominated the market.
> After obtaining a mortgage, she bought a house.
> Although I think we can get financing, I'm not sure.

3. Use a comma to separate items in a series. When items in a series, including words, phrases, and clauses, have the same grammatical form, commas are used to separate each item:

> The ideal candidate should have experience, creativity, and judgment.
> To move up the career ladder, you have to demonstrate a willingness to work, an ability to get the job done, and the common sense to take the advice of those who are willing to give it.

4. Use a comma to separate adjectives that equally modify the same noun. For example:

> The luxurious, spacious conference room was the site for the board meeting.

However, a comma is not used to separate **noncoordinate adjectives**—that is, adjectives that do not equally modify a noun. For example:

> Affluent Canadian teenagers make up a large part of the consumer electronics market.

5. Use commas to set off nonessential elements in a sentence—that is, elements that can be removed from the sentence without changing the basic meaning of the independent clause. For example:

> Caitlen Lau, who joined the company last year, is handling the production problem.
> An issue of concern to all employees, medical insurance benefits are being renegotiated this year.

By contrast, an essential element is *not* set off by commas because the basic meaning of the independent clause would change if the element were removed:

> Packages marked "Fragile" generally arrive in good shape.

Because the phrase *marked "Fragile"* is an essential element of the sentence, it is not set off by commas.

6. Use commas to set off words of direct address:

I want to thank you, David, for helping the department meet its production goals.

7. Use commas to set off quotations that appear in a sentence from short explanations that appear in the same sentence. These short explanations often take the form of **speaker tags**—explanatory clauses like *he said*, *they answered*, and *she explained*. For example:

> "Here are the disks with the final manuscript," said Peter, as he handed over the material.

However, a comma is not used when the word *that* separates the short explanation from the quoted material. For example:

> As Peter handed over the material, he said that "the disks are in final form."

8. Follow the accepted rules in using commas in dates, names, and addresses:

> May 21, 2000 *but* May 2000 *and* May 21
> Michael Armstrong, Ph.D. *and* Michelle Peller, M.D.
> McGrath, Angela (A comma is required when names are inverted.)
> Winnipeg, Manitoba

When a city and province/territory are used in a sentence, a comma is placed after the province/territory as well:

> Many people believe that the Canadian movie industry has been centred in Toronto, Ontario, since its inception.

If an address appears as part of a sentence, use commas to separate the elements of the address. However, no comma is used to separate the province/territory from the postal code:

> You can reach me in care of Mr. Arthur Pond, Pond and Pluck Inc., 1334 Main Street, Moncton, New Brunswick E1B 6Z6.

9. Unless using open punctuation in a letter, use commas after the complimentary close in a letter:

> Sincerely,
> Best wishes,
> Cordially,

SEMICOLON

Like a comma, the semicolon separates elements in a sentence, but it does so in a stronger way than the comma. Semicolons are used in three distinct ways.

1. Semicolons separate closely related independent clauses:

> The copy machine produces colour copies; it also collates.

You can also separate these clauses with a period, making each into a complete sentence. A semicolon, then, may be used where a period can be used; it signals less of a separation and indicates a closer connection between ideas.

2. Semicolons separate two independent clauses when the second clause begins with such words and phrases as *moreover, however, furthermore, nevertheless, consequently, on the one hand, as a result,* and *in short:*

> Every employee receives two months of training; however, many require additional on-the-job instruction.

Remember: these words are *conjunctive adverbs*, not conjunctions, and cannot be used to connect two independent clauses. Without the semicolon, the result is a comma splice (fused sentence).

3. Semicolons separate lengthy items in a series or series items that already contain commas:

> To prepare for this career, get a college degree; do extensive travelling in Germany, France, and Great Britain; and learn to speak German and French fluently.

COLON

The colon is used to introduce quotations:

> In the current annual report, the chairperson writes: "The company achieved its best earnings in more than a decade."

It is also used to introduce lists:

> When you start the job, bring three things: a willingness to work hard, the ability to work smart, and old-fashioned common sense.

A colon is also used after the salutation of a business letter.

APOSTROPHE

Use the apostrophe to indicate the possessive form of a noun or an indefinite pronoun. **Indefinite pronouns** refer to nonspecific persons or things and include such words as *all, anyone, each,* and *everyone*:

> The manager's style was direct and abrupt.
> Ann's comments were directed at everyone's work.

When a singular noun ends in *s*, show possession by adding *'s*. However, when a plural noun ends in *s*, show possession by adding only an apostrophe. For example:

> The cleaning business's employee turnover is high.
> The retailing and wholesaling businesses' sales are down.
> Chris's injury is covered by the workers' compensation law.

When a sentence contains two or more consecutive nouns and you want to indicate *individual* possession, end each noun with *'s*. The following sentence says that Anita and Ron contributed separate comments:

> Anita's and Ron's comments are contained in this memo.

To indicate *joint* possession, add *'s* only to the last noun. The following sentence says that Joy and Mike are joint owners of the house:

> Joy and Mike's house is selling for $200 000.

Apostrophes are also used when one or more letters have been intentionally omitted from a word to form a **contraction.** Although contractions are common in both speech and informal writing, they should not be used in reports and other formal documents. Here are some of the most common contractions:

aren't (are not)	I'm (I am)	let's (let us)
can't (cannot)	I've (I have)	there's (there is)
didn't (did not)	I'd (I would)	won't (will not)
he'll (he will)	isn't (is not)	you're (you are)
she's (she is)	it's (it is or it has)	

QUOTATION MARKS

Quotation marks tell the reader that you are citing the exact words spoken or written by someone else. For example:

> Page 12 of the report states that "no employee is entitled to more than four weeks' vacation a year."

Quotation marks always appear in pairs and are used to enclose short quotations of no more than four lines. Longer quoted passages are displayed on the page without quotation marks. A **displayed quotation** begins on a new line and uses a block-indentation format.

Quotation marks are also used to enclose titles of short published works, including magazine and journal articles, essays, brochures, and pamphlets. They may also enclose words that are being used in a slightly different way than the reader might expect and often indicate irony:

> The CEO keeps talking about the company's "new spirit" but acts like nothing has changed.

Commas and periods are placed inside closing quotation marks, and colons and semicolons are placed outside. Quotations within quotations are enclosed within single quotation marks.

DASH

Dashes interrupt sentences to add information and, in the process, emphasize that same information. Dashes are also used to define or restate key concepts and thereby emphasize explanations and descriptions:

> Diversity training—practical lessons that help improve the way diverse groups communicate—has improved the interpersonal environment in many companies.

Dashes can also be used to add and emphasize new information:

> Consumer confidence has increased dramatically—by more than 50 percent—since last year.

Finally, dashes may be used to add an aside:

> With sales up, bonuses are likely to be large, but—if you believe the latest rumour—we may not see any bonus money for another month.

Dashes are formed by combining two hyphens, with no spaces left before, between, or after the hyphens.

PARENTHESES

Like dashes, parentheses set off information that interrupts the flow of a sentence. Unlike dashes, however, parentheses minimize and de-emphasize the information they enclose. Parentheses are often used to enclose explanations, examples, and asides:

> Electronic mail (also known as e-mail) has revolutionized the way people communicate in business.

> By moving the distribution centre to another location (Regina, for example), we will save millions of dollars in transportation costs each year.

> Everyone is working twice as hard (and management would claim, twice as smart) as last year.

Parentheses also have some specialized uses. They are sometimes used to enclose the numbers in numbered lists:

> The meeting will cover three major issues: (1) current sales, (2) current expenses and ways to reduce them, and (3) projected profits for the next fiscal year.

Business and legal writing sometimes require that numbers be spelled out first and then restated in numerical form. The restated numeral is enclosed in parentheses:

> The yearly rent for the Grove Street retail location is forty thousand dollars ($40 000).

BRACKETS

Brackets allow you to add words to a quotation that were not part of the original quote. Generally, these added words—or interpolations—enable you either to fit quoted material into the structure of your sentence or to clarify the quoted material:

> Jones made it clear that "[the company] is stronger now than it was a year ago."

> At the last meeting, Billings stated that "the dramatic increase in [consumer product] sales is responsible for at least half of the year's total profit."

ELLIPSIS

An ellipsis is a series of three dots that indicates that material has been omitted from a quotation. Consider, for example, the following quotation:

> "Every company faces a different marketing environment, depending on its products, competitors, customers, technologies, government influences, and so on, that helps define its corporate culture."

Now consider the same quotation with selected material left out:

> "Every company faces a different marketing environment . . . that helps define its corporate culture."

If the omission occurs at the end of a sentence, add the three spaced periods of the ellipsis after the period to produce a series of four spaced dots.

Writing Mechanics _____

Writing mechanics refers to the correct use of capital letters, italics (sometimes displayed as underlining in a keyed manuscript), abbreviations, and numbers.

CAPITAL LETTERS

The following guidelines will help you decide whether or not to capitalize a letter.

1. Begin the first word of every sentence with a capital letter.
2. Capitalize proper nouns, including the names of people, places, and things, and proper adjectives. **Proper adjectives** are formed from proper nouns. For example, from the proper noun *Canada*, we form the proper adjective *Canadian*.
3. When an introduced quotation appears in the middle of a sentence, capitalize the first letter of the quoted words:

> According to Thomas E. Deal and Allan A. Kennedy, "Companies that have cultivated their individual identities by shaping values, making heroes, spelling out rites and rituals, and acknowledging the cultural network have an edge."

However, when the quote runs into the structure of your own sentence, the first word is *not* capitalized:

> Thomas E. Deal and Allan A. Kennedy believe that "companies that have cultivated their individual identities by shaping values, making heroes, spelling out rites and rituals, and acknowledging the cultural network have an edge."

4. Use capital letters at the start of complete sentences that are part of run-in lists. A **run-in list** is a list of items that appears in normal sentence format. For example:

> The poor selling season was caused by three factors: (1) The recession placed thousands of consumers out of work. (2) Consumer confidence is at a ten-year low. (3) Bad weather made it impossible for people to reach the stores.

ITALICS AND UNDERLINING

Use **italics** or **underlining** with titles of long written works such as books, reports, journals, magazines, and newspapers; the titles of television series; the titles of artworks and long musical compositions, such as operas; and the names of ships. Italics are also used to differentiate foreign words from words written in English:

> There were only 14 *summa cum laude* graduates in the entire university.

Finally, underlining can be used for special emphasis—that is, to focus the reader's attention on a key word or sentence:

> If we do not receive payment by January 30, your credit will be suspended.

ABBREVIATIONS

Abbreviations are commonly used in business writing. Although many abbreviations are unique to particular fields, others cut across different types of business disciplines. Here are some of the most common business abbreviations:

c. or ©	copyright	Inc.	incorporated
cf.	compare	Ltd.	limited
e.g.	for example	ms.	manuscript
et al.	and others	P&L or P/L	profit and loss
f., ff	and the following page, pages	sec.	section
fax	facsimile	v. or vs.	versus (legal case)
i.e.	that is	vol., vols.	volume, volumes
		whsle.	wholesale

Acronyms are also common in business. **Acronyms** are abbreviations formed by combining the first letter or letters of several words. They usually include no punctuation and are pronounced as words. For example:

> compact disk read-only memory (CD-ROM)
> local area network (LAN)
> random-access memory (RAM)

The first time that an acronym or abbreviation unfamiliar to the reader appears in a work, write the complete term, followed by the abbreviated form in parentheses. Then use the abbreviated form throughout the rest of the document.

NUMBERS

Numbers *zero* through *ten* should be spelled out, whereas numbers *11* and greater should be written as figures.

If a sentence starts with a number, the number should be written out no matter how large it is. For example:

> Five hundred and twelve people attended the stockholders' meeting.

To avoid this awkward construction, you can simply rewrite the sentence so that the number does not appear first:

> The stockholders' meeting was attended by 512 people.

Commonly Misused Words _____

Words are misused for two major reasons: They are confused with other words or their meanings are misunderstood. Words are also considered misused when they are spelled incorrectly.

HOMONYMS AND OTHER COMMONLY CONFUSED WORDS

Homonyms are words that sound exactly alike but are spelled differently and have different meanings—for example, *hear* and *here*. These words are often misused in business writing. Other words that sound similar to one another are also subject to confusion. The following list contains some of the most commonly confused words:

Word	Meaning	Example
accept	to receive, to agree	We *accept* this cheque as payment in full.
except	with the exclusion of	We received all merchandise *except* one carton of books.
advice	opinion, recommendation	My *advice* is to delay the shipment for two weeks.
advise	to counsel, recommend	I *advise* you to hire Kristie Paulichuk.
affect	to influence, change (verb); an emotional response (noun, rare)	Changing the price will *affect* consumer demand
effect	result (noun); to cause (verb)	The *effect* of the new computer system will be improved productivity.
		The creation of the European Union will *effect* a major change in the way business is conducted in Western Europe.
allot	to distribute	I plan to *allot* a new car to every district sales manager.
a lot	many, much	A 10-percent raise is *a lot* when inflation is only 4 percent.
allude	to refer to in an indirect way	He *alluded* to the merger during the meeting.
elude	to avoid	She *eluded* contact for over a week by having her administrative assistant screen all her calls.
already	by this time	The contract has *already* been sent to the lawyer.
all ready	all prepared	We are *all ready* for the meeting.
assistance	help	I need *assistance* to finish the assignment on time.
assistants	helpers	You'll have three *assistants* on this project.
canvas	heavy cloth	Have the painting crew cover the desk with a *canvas*.
canvass	to poll	The marketing department will *canvass* the neighbourhood for consumer response.
capital	wealth; seat of government	Our expansion plan depends on raising $100 000 in new *capital*.
		Ottawa, Ontario, is the capital of Canada.
capitol	government building	Let's meet at the *capitol* building.
cite	to refer to	She *cited* poor health as the reason for her resignation.

Word	Meaning	Example
sight	vision, scene	The store was quite a *sight* after the big sale.
site	location	The Jones Street *site* is likely to attract the greatest number of passersby.
complement	something that completes	Gracious remarks that build goodwill are the perfect *complement* to many business letters.
compliment	a flattering remark	Thank you for the *compliment*.
council	governing body	We need the approval of the city *council* before we can build.
counsel	to advise	*Counsel* Ellen on the details of the contract before she talks to the client.
consul	foreign embassy official	Bring your trade idea to the French *consul*.
defer	to postpone	I plan to *defer* my bonus until retirement.
differ	to be dissimilar	My plans *differ* from yours in three fundamental ways.
dissent	disagreement	He cast the single vote in *dissent* of the purchase.
descent	a decline or downward movement	The stock price's steep *descent* was shocking.
descend	to come down	Use the elevator to *descend* to the basement.
device	a mechanism	This *device* may make us all millionaires.
devise	to develop	I will *devise* a plan that can make us all rich.
elicit	to draw out	The survey questions will *elicit* the responses that we need.
illicit	illegal	*Illicit* merchandise was found on store shelves.
eminent	prominent, well-known	The research was conducted by Alexandra Jones, who is an *eminent* scholar in her field.
imminent	about to happen	Some major changes are *imminent*.
formally	officially, with tradition	The CEO *formally* welcomed the new chairperson.
formerly	previously	She was *formerly* an account executive at a major advertising agency.
incidence	frequency	The *incidence* of shoplifting has decreased since we installed the new security system.
incidents	events	Four shoplifting *incidents* were reported last month.
its	possessive form of *it*	The computer is in good shape except for *its* keyboard.
it's	contraction for *it is* or *it has*	*It's* been a long time since we talked business.
later	after a time	I will get back to you *later* with the details of the deal.
latter	the last-mentioned of two or more items	If there is a choice between an office with a northern or southern exposure, I prefer the *latter*.
lessen	to decrease	Adding another person to the department will *lessen* the load on everyone.
lesson	something learned	Ann Morgan will provide *lessons* on business writing.
loose	not tightly fastened	The plug at the back of the computer was *loose*.
lose	to misplace	Don't *lose* this file.

Word	Meaning	Example
moral	relating to the difference between right and wrong	The only *moral* decision is to tell the truth.
morale	attitude; state of mind	After the merger, employee *morale* was at an all-time low.
passed	past tense of *to pass*	Mike *passed* Mary in the hall.
past	at an earlier time	In the *past*, the company offered dental insurance to all employees.
patience	forbearance	After four postponements, my *patience* is wearing thin.
patients	people receiving medical care	On an average day, the doctor sees ten *patients*.
personal	private, intimate	Medical information is *personal* and confidential.
personnel	employees	All *personnel* files are kept in the human resources department.
precede	to come before	Research *precedes* writing.
proceed	to start, to continue	With the research complete, you can *proceed* to write a first draft.
presence	attendance at a place or event	Your *presence* is requested at the dinner honouring the chairperson.
presents	gifts	I will bring the *presents* with me when I come to the party.
principle	standard, moral conviction	Our company is built on the *principle* of treating the customer fairly.
principal	main, foremost (adjective); administrator of a school (noun)	One of the *principal* reasons for your promotion is your writing ability.
		The *principal* of the elementary school is active in community affairs.
respectfully	with respect	I *respectfully* request an appointment next Tuesday morning.
respectively	in that order	Third and fourth prizes went to John and Samantha, *respectively*.
stationary	not moving	We are ordering eight *stationary* bikes for the company exercise unit.
stationery	writing paper	Please write all letters on company *stationery*.
taught	past tense of *to teach*	I *taught* Kelly how to use the computer.
taut	tight	The wrapping is *taut*, and the box is ready to be mailed.
than	as compared to	Janet has a larger office *than* Roger.
then	at that time	Until *then*, I have nothing to say.
their	possessive form of *they*	Place *their* files over *there*.
there	in a certain place	
they're	contraction for *they are*	*They're* delivering the supplies tomorrow.
through	finished, done	When you are *through* with the memo, put it on my desk.
threw	past tense of *to throw*	The boy *threw* the ball to his father.
thorough	complete	The accounting department always does a *thorough* job.
to	toward	Give the original file *to* Mohamed and *two* copies to Trish, *too*.
too	also	
two	number following *one*	

Word	Meaning	Example
waive	forgo	I *waive* my right of first refusal.
wave	flutter, move back and forth	*Wave* to the mayor as he drives by.
weak	not strong	My *weak* back won't allow me to pick up the box.
week	seven days	You'll have the contract on your desk in a *week*.
weather	climatic conditions	Bad *weather* may require us to postpone the meeting.
whether	if it is the fact that; in case	Tell me *whether* or not you are interested in the job.
whose	possessive form of *who*	*Whose* property is this?
who's	contraction for *who is* or *who has*	*Who's* here for the meeting?
your	possessive form of *you*	Hang *your* coat in the closet.
you're	contraction for *you are*	*You're* welcome to join us for lunch.

WORDS WITH MISUNDERSTOOD MEANINGS

The following words are frequently used carelessly or incorrectly:

Word	Meaning	Example
among	refers to two or more things or people	Let's settle the matter *among* the three of us.
between	used when the referent is no more than two	This is *between* you and me and no one else.
continual	indicates a series of successive actions	*Continual* rain implies a series of rain showers interrupted by short spells of sunny weather.
continuous	implies unbroken, uninterrupted movement	*Continuous* rain means that the rain has not stopped.
disinterested	unbiased	Jose is a *disinterested* observer because he is not involved in the deal.
uninterested	without interest	Jose is *uninterested* in real estate law, and he is currently studying theatre.
imply	to suggest but not express	The manager *implied* that raises would be given in May.
infer	to deduce from the evidence at hand	The employees *inferred* that raises would be small.
loan	something lent (noun)	I need a $10 000 *loan*.
lend	to let another use (verb)	I'm willing to *lend* you $5000.
practical	useful, sensible, or worthwhile	Generally, she takes a realistic, *practical* approach.
practicable	capable of being put into practice and functioning	Using solar energy as a primary energy source is not *practicable* in many regions of the world.
regardless	Although many writers use the word *irregardless* instead of *regardless*, adding the prefix is incorrect	I want to buy the house *regardless* of the closing date.

Appendix

III

Internet Research

The Internet contains many research tools that speed the search for information and resources. One of those research tools, called a search engine, can aid your research efforts in the classroom and in business.

In this appendix we will discuss just a few of these search engines and a so-called *front-end* search engine which helps to speed your research. Each of these research tools can be found on the World Wide Web and can be used freely.

How Search Engines Work

Many different search engines are available. Although each search engine has different features and capabilities, the basic function of these tools is similar. Search engines receive information from and scan Internet sites for resources. The information is then reviewed and entered into the search engine's database of resources. When an Internet user requests information on a topic by entering in a descriptive word or phrase, the search engine scans its database for items that match the term, and returns a list of individual information sources (known as "hits").

The search engines described in this appendix include: Yahoo Canada; Excite; AltaVista Canada; and The Web Ferret.

YAHOO CANADA—http://www.yahoo.ca

Yahoo Canada, a **mirror site** of Yahoo, is among the more popular search tools available on the Internet. If you are new to these tools, Yahoo Canada is an excellent place to begin. While considered a search engine, Yahoo Canada is actually a **directory** of information assigned to appropriate categories.

Yahoo Canada allows researchers two basic options for finding information: search through the subject index, or use the built-in bilingual search engine, where searching and results are obtained in French or English.

YAHOO CANADA SUBJECT INDEX   When you connect to Yahoo Canada you will see a list of subjects, as shown in Figure III-1. Select the topic area that best fits your research needs. Follow the links until you find the information for which you are searching. The subject index is a good place to start business research.

YAHOO CANADA SEARCH ENGINE   Follow these steps to use the Yahoo search engine to look for information.

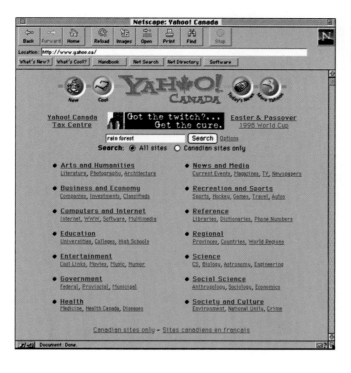

Figure III-1 Yahoo Canada keyword Window and subject index

1. Enter one or more descriptive words ("keywords") for your subject in the keyword window. Think of words that uniquely identify or describe what you are looking for. For example, if you were researching the environmental impact of deteriorating rain forests, you could enter "rain forest."

2. Determine if you want Yahoo to find keyword matches at any of the Yahoo sites, or at Canadian sites only, by selecting the appropriate box.

3. Determine how extensive you want your search to be. If you are using two keywords, do you want Yahoo to look for *either* word ("boolean *or*"), **both** keywords ("boolean *and*"), or *all* words as a single string?

   For example, in the search for "rain forest" you would select "boolean *and*" because you want to find resources that contain both of the words "rain" and "forest." You would not pick "boolean *or*" because the search would be too broad, finding all resources that contain the keyword "rain" and also all resources that contain the keyword "forests." You could also select all words in a single string because then the search would pick resources that contain only the phrase "rain forest," exactly as you entered it. A resource that has "forest rain" or "rain in the forest" would not be found.

   In our example, we selected the single string option.

4. Submit your query by clicking on the search button.

5. Review your return list of hits and adjust your search if necessary.

6. Submit the search again.

Search results will display both the categories and the Web sites that contains the keywords. The search results page can be seen in Figure III-2.

EXCITE—http://www.excite.com

Of all search engines, Excite provides the fullest range of services. It navigates the Web for keyword matches and creates summaries of each match. A comprehensive

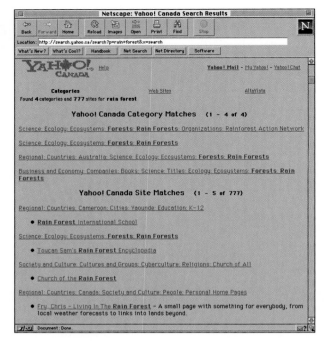

Figure III-2 Yahoo Canada results page from a keyword search on "rain" and "forest"

list of Excite's services can be found at http://corp.excite.com/company/what.html. Services include:

▼ **Excite Channels** Deliver information to the researcher in topic-based sections

▼ **Excite Search** Its patented search technology allows access to more than 50 million Web pages, more than 140 000 pre-selected Web site listings, and thousands of Usenet postings

▼ **Excite Boards and Chats** A form of bulletin board to express oneself, and a live chat facility to communicate with others in real-time mode

In addition to keyword searching, Excite provides *concept-based* searching. Concept-based searches are more advanced than keyword searches because they allow researchers to retrieve information on their topic, even though the source may not use the search term. For instance, if we wanted to conduct general research on rain forests, we would enter the search phrase "rain forest." A concept-based search will find not only all documents with the words "rain" and/or "forest" but will also solicit associated terms to add to your keyword search.

SEARCHING WITH EXCITE To conduct research using Excite, enter a descriptive search term that emphasizes critically important words, if needed, and select how you would like the search terms displayed.

1. *Search Term:* Use a search term that is as specific as possible. Try to avoid using general descriptive words. For example, if we want to search for information on the rain forest as an ideal ecosystem, we would add the words "ideal ecosystem" to specify our search options. The search term would read "rain forest ideal ecosystem," as in Figure III-3.

2. *Critically Important Words:* If certain words in your search phrase are critically important, you can add special emphasis by repeating them. For example, if we were especially interested in the vanishing rain forest, our search term could read "vanishing vanishing vanishing rain forests."

By repeating words that are critically important, you will be assured that the search results you get back are about vanishing rain forests and not simply rain forests.

3. *Spelling:* If you are not sure how to spell a word, type multiple spellings in your search phrase.

4. *Viewing Your Results:* Excite will display your results in the two following ways:

   ▼ **Grouped by confidence** Listed in order of most to least relevant

   ▼ **Listed by site** Listed according to the location for each source, such as a particular document origination address

The Excite results page (Figure III-4) provides researchers with another opportunity to add select words to the original search. By checking the appropriate associated-word box, their search can be enhanced.

ALTAVISTA CANADA—http://altavistacanada.com

AltaVista Canada provides researchers with access to the most comprehensive Canadian **index** on the Internet. More than 12 million pages of Canadian Web content are available as a result of AltaVisa Canada's unique country-specific search engine. The technology behind its immense capability is based on an automated **Web crawler** that searches for Canadian content within the borders of Canada.

AltaVista Canada also offers a fully bilingual search as an integral feature. A translation function allows researchers to translate Web-based text into English or French on demand.

AltaVista Canada's home page is shown in Figure III-5. Keyword searches are based on a boolean structure, but are further enhanced by a feature that automatically evaluates the researcher's keywords for others that *sound like* them. Figure III-6 shows a results page that includes both a results list and associated **hot link**

Figure III-4 Excite's initial search results page with options for selecting associated words to enhance the original search

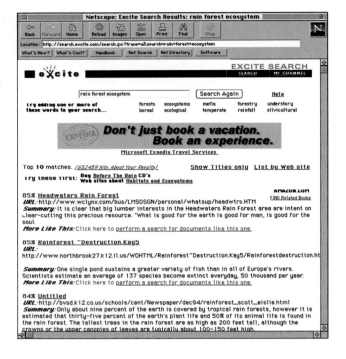

addresses. These addresses identify the source of the information and can be used by the researcher to link directly to the origin.

THE WEBFERRET—*http://www.ferretsoft.com*

The WebFerret is a cleverly designed directory that searches search engines. From the FerretSoft home page (Figure III-7), the researcher may download an executable file that, when evoked, presents a familiar keyword search window (Figure III-8). Again, using boolean logic for its search criteria, the WebFerret will scan its direc-

Figure III-5 AltaVista Canada's home page

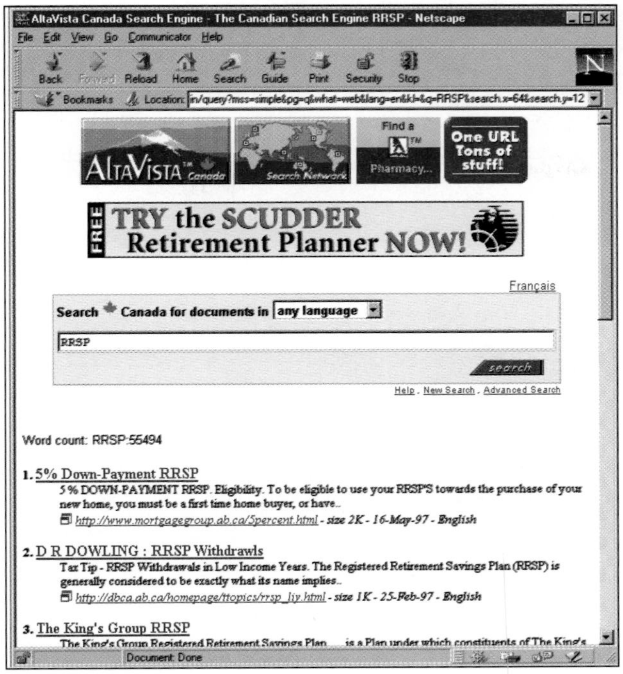

Figure III-6   AltaVista Canada's results page

tory of World Wide Web directories to provide the researcher with a results list of **hits** (Figure III-9). Dragging the mouse cursor over the individual results will bring up a dialogue box containing a preview of the information.

Each of the addresses returned as a result of your search may be used as a hot link to the originating site. The WebFerret is an excellent example of a front-end search engine that considerably reduces research time.

Figure III-7
FerretSoft's home page from which WebFerret software may be obtained

Figure III-8 WebFerret initial serach page soliciting "all" or "any" keyword search

Figure III-9 WebFerret's results page provides the researcher with a summary of addresses where keyword information may be found

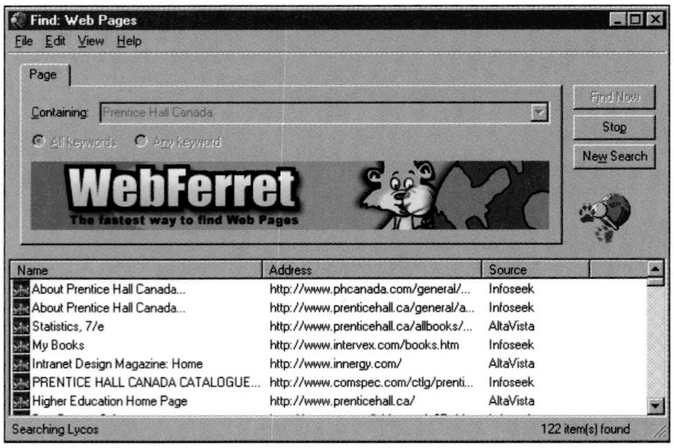

Some Final Search Tips

The Internet has a vast array of information that is difficult to harness without using search engines to guide your research. Experiment with the different search engines we've discussed and see which ones you find most useful. The following are some final tips to aid your Internet research:

▼ Avoid using commonly used words, such as articles and prepositions, in your searches. These words are usually ignored by search engines. Use specific, concrete search terms.

▼ Look for keywords that may be displayed with your search results. You may find keywords that better describe your topic. Resubmit your search using these new keywords.

▼ Keep a running list of information sites that may help with other research.

▼ Use more than one search engine for thorough research. Each search site has its own database resources, and some may have information that others do not have.

▼ Learn the strengths and weaknesses of each search engine's database. For instance, by learning which search engines have comprehensive information about current management and marketing business practice, you can better match your business research to the most appropriate search engine.

▼ Keep a running list of search engines that you find useful.

For further information about search engines and researching on the Internet, see Cynthia B. Leshin, *Netscape Adventures*, Prentice Hall, 1997; and Cynthia B. Leshin, *Internet Investigations in Business Communications*, Prentice Hall, 1997.

IV

Proofreader Marks

		DRAFT APPEARANCE	FINAL APPEARANCE
Close up	⌒	speakers ⌒ must remember	speakers must remember
Let it stand	*stet* or . . .	after delivering his speech	after delivering his speech
Delete	ℰ	prepare your resume and cover letter	prepare your cover letter
Paragraph	¶	¶ Persuasive writing tries to convince the reader of the	Persuasive writing tries to convince the reader of the
No paragraph	*No* ¶	*No* ¶ Persuasive writing tries to convince the reader of the	Persuasive writing tries to convince the reader of the
Move right	]	] 1. Letters, memos, graphs, spreadsheets	1. Letters, memos, graphs, spreadsheets
Move left	[	[1. Letters, memos, graphs, spreadsheets	1. Letters, memos, graphs, spreadsheets
Insert Space	#	staffroom	staff room
Insert comma	∧	However you	However, you
Insert apostrophe	∨	The nations	The nation's
Transpose	⎵	cente r	centre
Lower	⎵	H2O	H_2O
Raise	⎴	core idea."3	core idea."[3]
Set in lowercase	*lc* or /	the Sales Manager	the sales manager
Capitalize	*Cap* or ≡	mayor Smith	Mayor Smith
Align horizontally	═	Name: Benjamin Ross	Name: Benjamin Ross
Align vertically	‖	In addition to stating your point of view, your core idea should	In addition to stating your point of view, your core idea should
Spell out	◯	Stenberg Inc.	Stenberg Incorporated
Set in boldface	*bf*	Appendix IV	**Appendix IV**
Underline or italics	*ital*	Edmonton Journal	<u>Edmonton Journal</u>

Answer Key for ACT Questions

CHAPTER 1

1. The Mayor of Saskatoon **congratulated** the **Olympic** medalists upon their return from Nagano, Japan.
2. In the open office concept, employees' **desks** are often found grouped together and separated only by moveable **dividers**.
3. The **wives** of the **Canadian** bobsled team were **jubilant** when their husbands earned the gold medal.
4. At the **Calgary Zoo**, children enjoyed watching the games played by the **monkeys**.
5. On our adventure through the **Yukon**, we saw three **moose** and nine deer.
6. My two **brothers-in-law** are **entrepreneurs** working out of Chatham, Ontario.
7. Aurora **College** trained five **student teachers** in Dr. Waterton's **physics** class.
8. The result of ten **years'** work was stacked in piles on her desk.
9. The **children's** faces expressed surprise as the hologram figure appeared and began to **speak**.
10. Earl **Jones's** daughter was **successful** in **achieving** a place on the Canadian **women's** speed skating team.

CHAPTER 2

1. An employee of **West Edmonton Mall** wants **his or her** parking stall located outside the nearest entrance to **his or her** job location.
2. Although Russ and Karrie both used Burton snowboards, **they** used a different length.
3. Every figure skater and speed skater **has** suffered bruises from falling on the ice.
4. Every member of the sales team expressed **his or her** opinion regarding the quotas.
5. Stephan and **I** attended every meeting held for the volunteers in the Special Olympics.
6. The award for the volunteers **who** made the greatest contribution was given to Stephan and **me**.
7. The hockey coach asked Wayne and **me** to travel to **Victoria** to work with a Junior team.

8. At the 1998 Olympics, the winner of the **men's** figure skating was **I**.
9. The committee must review **its** policy regarding **foreign** languages.
10. The athletes **whose** performances were successful were rewarded with Olympic **medals**.

CHAPTER 3

1. I wish he **were** able to communicate in **French**.
2. Neither Yoshi nor Pierre **is** clear what the **English** speaker meant by the expression "break a leg."
3. Never assume that age **impairs** a person's ability to **understand** concepts.
4. Every culture in Canada **has** added value to this **country's** great diversity.
5. Each of the foreign students **is** requesting an **extension** of time in **Saskatchewan**.
6. Gender differences **affect** communication in the workplace just as **they do** at home.
7. The **physically** challenged student, along with his wife and daughter, **travels** to Kelowna every summer.
8. The **overwhelming** majority of victims of sexual **harassment are** women.
9. Stereotypes **are** responsible for a great deal of **miscommunication** that **occurs among** diverse groups of people.
10. The number of **immigrants** to Canada **is** increasing.

CHAPTER 4

1. To be effective, the writer should focus on the specific message and the **best** way to communicate that message to the audience.
2. Honda **decided** to construct an automobile assembly plant in Ontario so that **it** could become **more** competitive in the North American market.
3. Think of the specific purpose of a document as a **brief** summary of your reason for writing the message.
4. Attached are the regional **crime** reports for the six **largest** budget motels.
5. Readers of corporate **annual** reports include the general public and **interested** employees.
6. His message was softer than that of the speaker who lectured in the morning. (Note that the word **more** was removed.)
7. Primary sources of information contain **newer** information than do secondary sources.
8. Brainstorming is a planning **technique** where you list both the good and **poor** ideas.
9. When preparing the final report, take extra **precautions** with your **grammar** and **proofread carefully**.
10. Think **quickly** if you must analyze your audience during a **speech**.

CHAPTER 5

1. <u>In</u> crafting **an** effective business document, **it's** important <u>to</u> pay close attention <u>to</u> document organization <u>as</u> it **relates** <u>to</u> the placement <u>of</u> information.
2. Because reports must capture and hold attention <u>from</u> the **first** word, the opening is **an important** part.
3. Some issues lend themselves **naturally** <u>to</u> an **organization** that **focuses** <u>on</u> events or consequences <u>and</u> the reasons <u>for</u> them.

4. **Using** the deductive approach, **you** might propose that **a** new clothing shop would be **a** financial **success** in **West Edmonton Mall**.

5. Many reports **ask** the reader to take action by either adopting a **recommendation** or following a work plan.

6. Numbers often **mean** very little when presented out **of** context, but **they** are critical to the accuracy of the information.

7. Because design often **determines** whether a document will **actually** be read, **it's** crucial to the **document's** success.

8. Bullets are visual cues that indicate critical **information** by **highlighting** items contained in lists.

9. The organization patterns that shape a document determine how **directly its** message will be presented as well as the way in which **its** ideas are linked together.

10. **Important** document design **elements** include short paragraphs, **headings**, enhanced text, and bulleted lists.

CHAPTER 6

1. The writer liked his report, but he doubted that the committee would accept his ideas. **(CPS)**

2. Appearing at the end, the conclusion summarizes the report. **(CPX)**

3. Imprecise language can cause misinterpretation which may lead to costly errors. **(CPX)**

4. Reports give writers an opportunity to display their work. **(SS)**

5. In order to communicate a positive approach, avoid words that encourage negative responses. **(CPX)**

6. Effective writing reflects familiar patterns of speech, so try to vary the length of your sentences. **(CPX)**

7. By taking a positive approach, you can present information in a way that will encourage readers to respond. **(CPX)**

8. Too many short sentences can sound choppy. **(SS)**

9. Sentences can be either general or concrete. **(SS)**

10. There are some instances where the passive voice is acceptable, but we generally prefer to use the active voice. **(CPS)**

CHAPTER 7

1. Like all other human endeavours, **business** transactions are plagued by Murphy's Law.

2. Once a company receives a credit request, **it** tries to determine whether the applicant is creditworthy.

3. **Although** invitations are designed to communicate specific information, **they are** also intended to communicate goodwill.

4. When you need to ask a manager for information, **choose** a tone that acknowledges the power differences between you.

5. The complaint focused on wages and hours, **because** these issues had the greatest impact on the factory employees.

6. The writer should avoid being too direct, **since** directness is the fastest way to lose customers.

7. Some events require formal invitations; these invitations are written in the third person.

8. You may write a direct request; do this only when you are in a more powerful position than the recipient of your memo.

9. The writer from Victoria compiled the research; the first part of the project was complete.

10. The writer reviewed all the research; she focused on the qualitative answers.

CHAPTER 8

1. In painting four of her pictures, she used her boyfriend as her model.

2. To find the needed research, I had to search the entire library.

3. Because the leading actor was delayed by a car accident, his role was played by a local actor.

4. Because he moved from Ottawa at 12, his hometown no longer seemed familiar.

5. Tossing around in the heavy seas, our sailboat seemed like it would sink.

6. To avoid recognition, she wore sunglasses and a wide hat to cover her face.

7. Wagging his tail, the dog was fed by the man.

8. As I heard the horn, the car pulled into the garage.

9. Seeing the airplane plunge from the sky, the Toronto Air Show audience screamed with fear.

10. The store offered its customers a discount when the customers were shocked by the high prices.

CHAPTER 9

1. The manager asked why the bad news had to be shared with the employees.

2. Will the bad-news message destroy our employee **morale**?

3. The **Mayor** of Kelowna found it helpful to **acknowledge** the impact of his bad-news message by being sympathetic.

4. Stop wasting time now!

5. Naturally, most decisions begin with understanding the type of **message** to be sent.

6. A small company in Yellowknife could not fill the order immediately.

7. Be careful of the falling ice!

8. A **Scarborough** supplier refused to extend credit to a business client.

9. Why did the **Fredericton consumer** apply for credit in the **retail** store?

10. Would you please draft the bad-**news** memo before noon today. *(Could also end with a ?)*

CHAPTER 10

1. Effectively used, persuasive **techniques** work on three levels at once.

2. Reasoning involves presenting facts, statistics, examples and anecdotes, expert opinion, and analogies.

3. Wayne Gretsky, a famous **Canadian** hockey **star**, can send a persuasive message to youth.

4. Although the document may include photographs, your text must be **written** so that the reader can understand it without the pictures.

5. Sales letters are written by manufacturers, retailers, and **wholesalers**, as well as **government** agencies.

6. Purchasing a product involves a process of **problem** solving, and often includes the need to be **persuaded**.

7. While interest is largely an intellectual **response**, desire is basically **an** emotional reaction.

8. To interest the largest audience possible, you must provide both pleasure and logic.

9. "Here are the pages for the final report," said Amelia as she keyed the last line.

10. We left on our vacation to Halifax, Nova Scotia, on June 11, 1999.

CHAPTER 11

1. A well-written report requires planning; it also requires research.

2. When preparing a report, you must always take these three actions: research, research, and research.

3. The content of your report is very important; however, format is also important.

4. A chart will add to the appearance of a report; nevertheless, a chart that contains **inaccurate** information will detract from it.

5. In the annual report, the team leader wrote: "Our mission is to **exceed** the expectations of our clients."

6. A manager may send a short informal report to her staff; she may **send** a more formal report to her clients.

7. Table 11 shows a business report that falls into three major categories: information, study, and expert.

8. These three steps move writers from identifying the issue to finalizing the document: defining the audience; creating a work plan; and developing the outline.

9. The **collaborative** plan forms the basis of writing **an** extensive report; nevertheless, independent work is always essential for the completion of the project.

10. Evaluate your research; it must be valid, reliable, and current.

CHAPTER 12

1. The **chart's** vertical bars will be different heights.

2. **You're** invited to the boardroom to view our maps and line charts.

3. When the comparison involves two or more items, the chart is called a "grouped line chart."

4. **James's** statistical information was included in the pictorial chart.

5. Using a grouped line chart, we compared **children's** television programs with programs suitable for adults.

6. The team says they **aren't** planning to prepare visual aids for their presentation.

7. **It's** a surprise that the pictorial chart displays greater poverty in Toronto than in Vancouver.

8. Nova **Scotia's** and New **Brunswick's** populations were displayed separately on the colourful column chart.

9. Chapter 12 states that "manually prepared drawings won't have the same impact as those prepared electronically."

10. During his presentation, the prime minister asked, "Does this graph increase your understanding of the relationship between the budget and the population?"

CHAPTER 13

1. Student attendance at Aurora College has increased a significant amount—about 55 **percent**—since we hired Shawn O'Neil to teach communication courses.

2. It is important to consider the outline as merely a guide—your revision may require adding, deleting, or rearranging information.

3. With attendance up, marks are likely to increase, but—if you **believe** the statistics—we may not **see** these results until the end of the semester.

4. Formal reports are usually linked to major projects—the development of new products, a company-wide structural reorganization, or a study of competitive products.

5. An overview is provided in the executive summary—a **synopsis** that **condenses** the report into relatively few pages.

6. With company profits rising, our salaries should increase, but—if you follow the news from union negotiations—we will be lucky to keep the salaries we have.

7. Team-building workshops—seminars designed to teach groups to work collaboratively—are presented by a number of small **organizations** in St. Catharines.

8. The Canadian Postal Code Directory—a book listing all the postal codes in Canada—is an essential **reference** guide for every office.

9. Supplemental **information** is included in the back matter—the parts of the report that follow the report body.

10. The document was selected by **community** members—civic officials, parents, children, business people— who came together to work on the problem.

CHAPTER 14

1. **Winning** the sports championships (**soccer** and volleyball) bolstered the team's self-esteem.

2. A sample trip report will contain: (1) summary, (2) details, (3) conclusions and **recommendations**, and (4) closing.

3. **Informational** reports (also known as summary reports) present facts but not **interpretations**.

4. The bill listed the cost of preparing the report at three thousand dollars ($3000).

5. She originated from the West Coast (Whistler, British Columbia) and was proud to promote tourism in the region.

6. Effective proposals are **written** in clear, simple, nontechnical language (even when the subject matter is technical) that avoids jargon and explains **abbreviations**.

7. Will this project 1) reduce costs, 2) increase productivity, or 3) increase sales?

8. Many Total Quality Management (TQM) programs are intended to **improve** customer service and thereby improve profits.

9. As illustrated (Table III), the employees are **paid** on an hourly wage basis.

10. Canadians are required to **speak** one of our two official languages (English and/or French).

CHAPTER 15

1. Living near **Weyburn, Saskatchewan**, the children learned all about farming.

2. As a geologist, I've worked in the **Northwest Territories** as well as **Labrador** and **Southern Ontario**.

3. My subject today is the introduction of **Weight Watchers** meals to **Burger King** restaurants.

4. We met at **Lorne Akins Junior High School** in **St. Albert, Alberta**.

5. The book was titled <u>**You've Got What It Takes**</u>.

6. His consistently high marks qualified him to **receive** *summa cum laude* on his degree.

7. Premier Smith **gently** put his arm around me and said, "**Don't** let him upset you."

8. **Mark Twai**n said "**Eat** what you like and let the food fight it out inside."

9. The poor **presentation** was due to two reasons: (1) **She** lacked knowledge on the topic. (2) **The** technology was not operating properly.

10. All **Canadians** who earned gold medals at the **Olympics** were guests at the **Canada Day** parade.

CHAPTER 16

1. Eleven employees formed the audience for the manager's **20**-minute presentation.

2. An article about team **communications** was sent to us through the **fax** machine.

3. **Seventy-five** percent of the audience stood and cheered for an encore.

4. The company printed their **P & L** statements so the executive team could discuss the future direction for the company.

5. **Fifteen** participants is **too** large of a team for productive brainstorming to **occur**.

6. During the oral presentation, the group displayed a graph showing the **whsle.** operation.

7. The **ms.** (**c.** 1998) was accepted by the publisher.

8. Can **seven** people reach a **consensus**?

9. Why are there only ten people on this team and **12** people on the opposing team?

10. Glassmith **Inc.** is the finest stained-glass shop in Scarborough.

CHAPTER 17

1. I **accept** your offer for employment at the West Edmonton Mall security office.

2. After an employment interview, it's difficult to have the **patience** to wait for the results.

3. **Who's** been shortlisted for the interview for the Office Manager position?

4. Karen called the company to determine **whether** or not she was the successful applicant for the job.

5. Our organization was built on the **principle** of equal opportunity employment.

6. Applicants reported four **incidents** of unethical questioning.

7. The applicant **respectfully** requested an interview for the marketing position.

8. He printed his letter of application on personal **stationery**.

9. Don't **lose** your confidence when an employer asks behavioural questions on an interview.

10. The interviewer wrote comments about the applicant's lack of **presence**.

CHAPTER 18

1. The decision to advertise the position was made **among** the three managers.

2. The applicant faced **continual** questions interrupted only by his own short answers.

3. Catherine was released from her employment because the manager believed she was **uninterested** in her work.

4. During his presentation, the manager **implied** that **ten** percent of employees would be laid off.

5. Mitchell's father **lent** him an expensive suit for the interview.
6. Prior to an interview, you should do some research for **practical** information.
7. **Regardless** of the outcome, the interview will give you excellent experience.
8. The names of the job candidates are confidential and should be kept **between** the two of you.
9. From the lack of enthusiasm on the employer's face, the applicant **inferred** that the position was already filled.
10. Because the company was an equal opportunity employer, the interviewer was **disinterested** in the gender of the successful applicant.

Glossary

acknowledgment Informative letter telling the reader that information or materials have been received

acronyms Abbreviations formed by combining the first letters of several words

action Final step in the AIDA concept; implies that readers must be convinced to take specific steps to purchase a product

active listening Listening that requires involvement with the content of a message and empathy with its sender

active voice Writing style in which the subject of a sentence performs the action

adjectives Describe nouns and pronouns

adjustment Company's response to a claim

adjustment letter Good-news letter written in response to a claim letter to inform the customer how a company intends to handle a specific problem

adverbs Modify verbs, adjectives, other adverbs, and entire sentences

agenda Written document that defines a meeting by telling participants why it was called and what it should accomplish

aggressive collection notice Written correspondence in the form of a firm request that attempts to convince a debtor to pay a bill

AIDA concept Principle that an individual goes through four steps—attention, interest, desire, and action—before making a purchase decision

anecdote Short, entertaining account of some event

antecedent The noun for which a pronoun stands

appendix Back matter that supplements material presented in the text of a report or proposal

articulation Process of determining the clarity and distinctiveness of vocal sounds

attention In the AIDA concept, first step in capturing and holding an audience so it will continue to read a document or listen to an oral presentation

audience Receivers of verbal, nonverbal, and written messages

audience analysis Process by which business communicators analyze the needs and knowledge of their readers or listeners in order to communicate effectively

auxiliary verb Usually some form of the helping verb *have*

back matter Supplemental information included in the parts of the report that follow the report body

bar chart Diagram consisting of horizontal bars of varying lengths, each representing different items for comparison

bibliography Back-matter list identifying all references used in researching a report or proposal

bilateral bar chart Diagram starting from a central point to show positive or negative deviations from that point

blamers Meeting participants who focus on problems rather than solutions

boilers Meeting participants who typically respond with anger when they do not get their way

border Any line that surrounds a visual aid to separate it from surrounding text

brainstorming Creative problem-solving technique whereby ideas are listed as they come to mind and unrestrained participation in group discussion is encouraged

brainstorming session Group process of generating new ideas in an open, nonjudgmental, nonauthoritatian atmosphere

buffer Protective barrier that helps cushion the shock of bad news

bullets Visual cues such as asterisks and dashes that indicate critical information by highlighting items contained in lists

business communication Communication required of an organization in both its internal and external environments

business report Compilation of organized information gathered on a specific topic and delivered to specific users

campus recruiter Representative of an employer who visits campuses to interview students for jobs

CanCopy Non-profit organization that acts on behalf of publishers, writers, and artists, protecting their work from being copied without permission

caption Brief narrative that supports the title and focuses on the most important point of a visual aid

case A pronoun's case refers to the relationship that word has to the other words in a sentence

cause-and-effect diagrams Tool for identifying the possible causes of a problem; also referred to as a fish-bone diagram

cause-and-effect pattern Writing approach that focuses on events or consequences and the reasons for them

cellular phone Wireless telephone that transmits voice and data in the form of radio signals

channel Medium through which the message sender and audience communicate

chart (or graph) Diagram that presents numerical data in visual form to show trends, movements, distributions, and cycles

chronological pattern Writing approach used to describe a series of events chronologically, either in the order in which they occurred or in reverse sequence

chronological résumé Document in which the applicant's work experience, education, and personal history are arranged in a reverse time sequence; that is, with the most recent experience in each category listed first

claim Notice from a customer of a problem with a good or service

clicking The action of pressing one of the buttons on a mouse attached to a computer

climactic-order pattern Writing approach that presents first the material with which the reader is most likely to agree

cognitive dissonance State of conflict arising from exposure to messages that contradict one's value system

cold contacts Unsolicited letters in which job seekers introduce themselves and ask about job openings

collaboration Process in which two or more people work together in a team to produce and deliver a message

collaborative communication Team-based communication

collaborative meeting Formal meeting in which participants work together to prepare memos, letters, or reports, or to develop projects

collaborative writing Process of creating finished reports and proposals by groups or individuals working together

collection letter Written correspondence seeking to persuade a debtor to pay an outstanding debt while encouraging continued business

collection series Written correspondence categorized according to the four types of increasingly persuasive appeals used to collect outstanding debts: reminders, inquiries, aggressive notices, and last-resort letters

college placement advisor Job-search professional hired by colleges and universities to help students and alumni find jobs

column (or vertical-bar) chart Diagram consisting of vertical bars of different heights, each height representing a different quantity

comma splice (fault) Occurs when a writer tries to connect two independent clauses with nothing but a comma

common nouns Refer to general classes of people, places, and things.

communication Meaningful exchange of information through messages

communication barriers Problems that arise during the communication transaction and raise the potential of misunderstanding and confusion

communication channels Formal and informal pathways that define the manner in which messages are sent within an organization's communication networks

communication flow Direction taken by communication within a formal communication channel

communication network Interaction pattern involving upward, downward, and horizontal communication

comparative adjectives Compare two items

complex sentence Contains one independent clause and at least one dependent clause

component comparison Data representation technique in which the size of each item is shown as a percentage of the total

composition Process of planning, writing, illustrating, and structuring a document to make it inviting and easy to read

compound sentence Contains two or more independent clauses and may be connected by a coordinating conjunction

computer printer Computer hardware that moves words and images from the computer screen to the printed page

confirmation bias Specific examples of cultural behaviours that reinforce beliefs and attitudes about members of a culture

conjunctive adverbs Modifiers that logically connect ideas

connotation Implied meaning of a word or phrase

context Every factor surrounding and affecting the transmission of a message

contraction Formed when one or more letters of a word have been intentionally omitted

coordinating conjunctions Connect two or more grammatically equivalent structures

core idea One-sentence statement of the central message of a written or oral presentation; sometimes called the thesis statement

corporate culture Patterns, traditions, and values that make one organization distinctly different from another

correlation analysis Statistical technique used to measure the positive, negative, or nonexistent relationship between two or more variables

correlative conjunctions Join equivalent grammatical structures by functioning in pairs

cover letter Correspondence that accompanies a résumé in order to summarize an applicant's value to a prospective employer

credibility Degree to which a statement, a person, or a company is perceived to be ethical, believable, trustworthy, competent, responsible, and sincere

credit reference Good-news letter in which one company attests to the financial well-being of another

crossfunctional team Team in which each member has a unique expertise

culturally Deaf Term referring to individuals who are medically deaf and who identify with and participate in the culture, society, and language of Deaf people, which is based on sign language

culture Shared customs, beliefs, and social structures that make up a society, including languages, rules, myths, family patterns, and political systems

customer service Act of ensuring that customers feel valued and that their needs are met

dangling modifier Describes something that is implied but not stated in the sentence

database Set of logically related computer files that can be accessed for different purposes

decision-making meeting Formal meeting called to debate issues and make decisions

deductive organizational pattern Writing approach in which discussion moves from a general idea to a series of specific ideas

delegating meeting Formal meeting in which specific tasks are assigned to individuals or groups who are then responsible for their completion

delivery Method of giving any form of speech or oral presentation, including voice quality and body language

demography Statistical study of population size, density, and distribution that results in the collection of vital statistics

dependent clause Cannot function as an independent sentence and must be joined to an independent clause

descriptive summary Synopsis that acts as an expanded table of contents to tell the reader what to expect and that states the purpose and scope of a report

design Process of transforming a rough draft into a finished document by adding, deleting, replacing, and reorganizing words, sentences, and paragraphs

desire Third step in the AIDA concept; implies that a document can prompt an emotional reaction that propels people to action

dichotomous question Question whose answer is limited to one of only two possible responses, such as *yes* or *no*

digressing Not staying on topic

diplomacy Art of handling affairs in a tactful way to avoid arousing hostility

direct object Pronoun in the objective case that receives the verb's action

direct organizational pattern Writing approach that presents the main point in the beginning part of a message

direct request Straightforward written message that asks another individual for information, merchandise, or assistance

directories Lists of information developed by people who search the Internet for Web pages

discounting Showing lack of respect for others through criticism or lack of attention

displayed quotation Quotation that begins on a new line and uses a block-indentation format, used for quotations of more than four lines

diversity training Process of improving awareness of different attitudes, behaviours, and communication patterns and developing skills to deal with these differences

downward communication Message flowing from a superior to a subordinate level of an organization

drug testing Pre-employment screening for such illegal substances as cocaine and marijuana

editing Correcting mistakes in grammar, spelling, and punctuation and producing a document consistent in style for such elements as numbers, abbreviations, and capitalization

electronic assistant Telematic application that provides administrative services via computer, voice, and telecommunications

electronic bulletin board Public message centre that appears on computer networks

electronic mail (or e-mail) Computerized mail service enabling users to transmit messages and documents instantaneously over telephone and data lines from one computer to another

electronic whiteboard Writing board that combines the power of a computer, software, electronic pen, and an intelligent touch screen

empathy Ability to experience the world from another person's perspective

employee benefits Programs provided by employers for individual employees to cover costs for such services as medical insurance, parental and sick leave, vacations, and company savings plans

employment agency Organization that matches job candidates with specific jobs, often for a fee

employment-related letters Good-news letters presenting job offers, acknowledging candidates' applications, inviting applicants for interviews, or discussing additional details after an offer has been accepted

end punctuation Punctuation marks that occur at the end of sentences

ethics Standards of conduct and moral judgment accepted by society

ethnic identity Range of identifying characteristics that includes shared values, communication patterns, and behaviours

ethnocentrism Tendency to judge other cultures by the standards of one's own culture

evaluation Listening stage involving the decision to accept or reject, like or dislike, agree or disagree with a message

evidence Details that communicate information and support the core idea of a document

examples Descriptive stories and specific cases that make information real and memorable

executive search firm Specialized employment agency that represents employers rather than individual job applicants, usually to identify, evaluate, and select high-level personnel

executive summary Synopsis in the body of a report that condenses it into relatively few pages

extemporaneous speaking Delivery method in which the speaker relies on speaking notes rather than on a complete manuscript or memorization

external audience A company's customers and suppliers as well as the general public, other businesses, and government officials with whom it interacts

external communication Communication with the major audiences in a company's external environment

external data Data, primary or secondary, generated by sources outside an organization

external meeting Formal meeting that involves outsiders as well as company personnel

external proposal Proposal issued outside an organization to prospective clients in government or private industry

external report Report distributed to interested parties outside the writer's organization

facsimile machine (or fax machine) Electronic device that can copy and transmit original material, including text and graphics, to other machines in other locations

fax modem A device used with personal computers that has dual functionality as a modem and a facsimile

feedback Messages returned by the audience to the sender that may cause the sender to alter or cancel an original message

figure Any visual aid, other than tables, including charts, maps, drawings, photographs, and other illustrations

first person Refers to the speaker or writer

follow-up letter Informative letter that restates key points of a conversation

footnote Mechanism for explaining specific details in a visual aid or document

foreword Introductory statement written by a person who did not author the report to provide a context for the report by discussing its background information or broad, general applications

form report Document, such as an inventory-control report, following a specific format and focusing on specific information

formal agenda Agenda that schedules the order of meeting business and the approximate time allotted to each scheduled item

formal communication channel Communication sanctioned by company management

formal meeting Prearranged meeting with stated goals and involving a leader and participants

formal outline Organizational device that shows the precise relationship among ideas by following prescribed rules concerning content and format

formal report Relatively long document based on extensive research and organized according to a prescribed pattern

freewriting Unstructured writing process that allows writers to express their thoughts without worrying about spelling, grammatical mistakes, or organizational problems

frequency-distribution comparison Data-presentation technique showing how many items fall into defined, progressive numerical ranges

front-end search engine Searches directories and other search engines

front matter Parts of a formal report that are included before the body

functional résumé Résumé that highlights the applicant's accomplishments and abilities rather than his or her work history

future perfect tense Indicates that an action will have been completed in relation to some specific future time

fused (run-on) sentence Joins two independent clauses without the use of any punctuation or coordinating conjunction

general purpose Primary reason for which a document is written or an oral presentation is made; typically to inform, persuade, and/or initiate action

glossary Alphabetized back-matter list, accompanied by definitions, of words and phrases used in a report

goodwill message Message written to create a bond of friendship or understanding—personal, professional, or both—between writer and recipient

grapevine Internal information channel conducting information through unofficial, independent sources

greeting Goodwill message commemorating either holidays or special events

grid lines Series of horizontal and vertical lines crossing at 90-degree angles to establish specific values in an illustration

grouped bar chart Diagram comparing various parts of the same item

grouped column chart Diagram with grouped or overlapping columns that compare two different items at a given time and demonstrate how the relationship between those items changes over time

grouped line chart Line chart that makes comparisons between two or more items

headings Visual markers that indicate the parts of a document and give clues to its organization

high-context culture Culture in which communication depends not only on the message itself but also on the context surrounding the explicit message, including nonverbal language

hits Successful results from an Internet search

home page A screen of graphical information that provides information about a user or service on the Internet

homonyms Words that sound exactly alike but are spelled differently and have different meanings

horizontal communication (or lateral communication) Message flowing from sender to receiver within the same organizational level

hot link An embedded address link found in electronic documents

imperative mood Used to issue commands and direct orders

impromptu speaking Delivery method in which the speaker makes remarks without advance preparation

indefinite pronouns Pronouns that describe nonspecific persons or things and depend upon context for meaning

independent clause Contains a subject and a predicate and can function on its own as an independent grammatical unit

index Alphabetized back-matter list of report topics that includes references to the pages on which each topic appears

indicative Mood used to make statements or ask questions

indirect object Pronoun in the objective case

indirect organizational pattern Writing approach that presents the main point in the latter part of the message

indirect organizational plan Method of organizing documents by delaying bad news rather than announcing it immediately

indirect subject Refers to whom or for whom the action expressed by the verb was done

inducement Gifts or other consideration that encourages readers to take immediate action

inductive organizational pattern Writing approach in which discussion begins with a specific idea and moves step by step to a general topic

informal business conversation Unscheduled meeting between as few as two and as many as four people

informal communication channel Communication pattern independent of formal channels sanctioned by management

informal outline Organizational device that need not follow the strict structural rules of a formal outline

informal report Relatively short document typically written over a short period and based on a comparatively small research base

information overload Need to digest an expanding number of messages from a growing variety of sources

informational meeting Formal meeting in which information is delivered to participants by means of oral reports

informative summary Abbreviated version of a report that includes conclusions and recommendations as well as descriptions of purpose, scope, and methods

initial credibility Receiver's judgment of the sender prior to receiving the message

inquiry letter Written correspondence seeking to determine if a problem exists that is preventing a customer from making required payment; typically, the third step after a statement and reminder letter

inspirational meeting Formal meeting that attempts to build enthusiasm for the company and its products, encourage teamwork, or generally improve organizational morale or interaction

interest Second step in the AIDA concept; implies that the message has tapped a need in the reader, either to solve a problem or to satisfy a desire

internal audience A company's employees and owners

internal communication Communication through channels within an organization

internal data Data generated within an organization

internal meeting Formal meeting that involves only personnel within an organization

internal preview Sentences and paragraphs that appear at the beginning of text-discussion sections to introduce the material that will be covered in them; verbal signpost that tells listeners what the speaker intends to say before he or she says it

internal proposal Persuasive document that attempts to convince top management to spend money on specific projects intended to change or improve the organization

internal punctuation Punctuation marks that occur within sentences

internal report Report distributed to individuals within the writer's organization

internal summary In documents, sentences and paragraphs that appear at the close of text-discussion sections to restate key points and to link them both to other report sections and to the report's specific purpose; in oral communication, verbal signpost occurring at a key point within a speech, restating and emphasizing what was just stated, and connecting internal elements

Internet Global network of computer-based information and services

interpretation Listening stage during which the meaning of a message is construed

interview sequence Series of interviews, constituting a multistage approach for evaluating job applicants

Intranet Smaller, often corporate version of the Internet; Intranets often form part of the Internet

introduction Preamble in the body of a report intended to gain readers' attention by providing them with the information they need to evaluate the report itself

investigative report Short report that examines and analyzes details of a particular topic and presents conclusions and recommendations based on that analysis

invitation Request for business associates, potential customers, or personal acquaintances to attend a business or social event

irregular nouns Nouns that are pluralized by making changes other than adding a final *s* or *es*

italics Used for titles of long written works such as books, reports, journals, magazines, and newspapers; the titles of television series; the titles of artworks and long musical compositions; and the names of ships

item comparison Data-presentation technique in which relative rankings of individuals, geographic areas, products, production facilities, or other variables are examined to determine similarities or differences

jargon Vocabulary peculiar to a specific group, trade, or profession and used to describe its activities

job description Document specifying the objectives of a job, the work to be done, skill requirements, responsibilities involved, and working conditions

job interview Face-to-face encounter between a recruiter and a job candidate in which the recruiter assesses the candidate's background, skills, job objectives, interests, and attitudes; in turn, the candidate asks questions about the position and the organization

journalists' questions Six questions (who, when, where, what, why, and how) coined by journalists for use as guidelines to structure their thinking in interviewing and preparing stories

key words Descriptive words that are entered into search engine windows

know-it-alls Meeting participants who try to control meetings, often by leading participants in directions that they prefer regardless of group goals

labels Headings and subheadings that define the parts of a visual aid, including all identifications of items being compared

laliaphobia Fear of speaking to groups

last-resort letter Written correspondence expressing a reluctance to begin legal action but a determination to do so if a delinquent customer does not pay within a stated time limit

letter of condolence Goodwill message sent when a business associate or an associate's family member dies

letter of recommendation Good-news personnel letter that speaks positively about a candidate's background and performance and that may tie the candidate's knowledge, skills, and abilities to a specific job objective

letter of sympathy Goodwill message conveying personal concern on such occasions as illness, accident, or other misfortune

letter of transmittal (or cover letter) Front-matter page that officially conveys the report to the reader, identifying the specific report being sent, the person to whom it is directed, and the reason for sending it

line chart Diagram showing the relationship between numbers on the intersection of horizontal and vertical axes

linking verb Connects the subject of a sentence to a word that renames it

list of illustrations Front-matter list of the figures and tables included in a document

listening Act of sensing, interpreting, evaluating, and reacting to what is being said

low-context culture Culture in which communication depends on explicit written and verbal messages

management plan Component of a proposal that describes plans for managing a proposed change after it is approved

meeting minutes Written record of what occurred at a meeting

message Written, oral, or nonverbal communication transmitted by a sender to an audience

message of adoption Document that seeks to persuade readers to start doing something

message of continuance Persuasive message that urges the continuation of a behaviour

message of deterrence Persuasive message that attempts to prevent an action from taking place

message of discontinuance Persuasive message that asks for a behaviour change

mindmapping (or clustering) Visual technique for grouping information into categories

minutes See *meeting minutes*

mirror site Country-specific search engine that is referenced from a larger search engine

misplaced modifier Modifier that is wrongly or awkwardly placed in a sentence, obscuring the intended meaning

modem Special device used to convert computer signals to signals that can travel by telephone lines to another computer

modifier A word or group of words that describes other words, phrases, or clauses

mood The writer's attitude toward a statement

multinational corporation Firm that conducts significant business outside its home country and that views the world as its marketplace

multivote Where team members are given a limited number of votes to put against a list of issues

narrative report Report whose format is largely determined by what the writer decides to say and how he or she chooses to say it

negotiation Process of give and take in which both parties try to leave the bargaining table with what each perceives as a "good deal"

networking Process whereby a job seeker talks and writes to people for assistance in his or her job search

node Communications network routing or distribution hub; telecommunications signals are received and sent out from the node

noise Anything that interferes with a message by distorting its meaning

nominal group technique Well-structured method of group voting for narrowing down a list of issues

noncoordinate adjectives Adjectives that do not equally modify a noun

nonverbal communication Form of communication, including nonvocal and nonverbal vocal communication, taking place through such media as gestures, eye contact, clothing, and tone of voice

nonverbal vocal communication Form of nonverbal communication, including tone of voice and such voice qualities as loudness

nonvocal communication Form of nonverbal communication including gestures, eye contact, facial expressions, posture, touch, clothing, and the use of space

noun Person, place, thing, or idea

object of a preposition Pronoun in the objective case

objective case Pronouns that function as a direct object, an indirect object, or as the object of a preposition

observational study Method of collecting primary data by actually viewing the actions of respondents

obstructionist Meeting participant whose personality or hidden agenda threatens group success

on-campus recruiter Trained professionals in the company's human resources department who interview students for jobs

online database Computerized information-retrieval system operated by commercial suppliers and made available to business users for a service fee

oral presentation Extemporaneous speeches, frequently participative and delivered using only notes and visual aids to guide the speaker's performance

organization Process of arranging information and connecting different ideas to produce a unified, coherent message

pager Battery-powered device that signals telephone messages

paralanguage Nonverbal vocal messages embodied in tone, emphasis, volume, and pauses

passive voice Writing style in which the subject of a sentence is acted upon

past participle Verb form

past perfect tense Describes a situation in which an action started in the past, continued for a period of time, and was completed in the past

perfect tenses Show complex time relationships in the past, present, and future

periodic report Report distributed according to an established schedule, such as weekly, quarterly, or annually

personal communication services A digital wireless communication service that provides telephone, visual messages, and Internet access through one device

personal computer (PC) A computing device used for personal processing and connecting to a network

personal digital assistant (PDA) A pocket-sized, battery-powered device that provides similar but reduced functionality to that of a personal computer

personal space Physical space between people engaged in communication

persuasion Process of influencing or changing attitudes, beliefs, values, or behaviours

persuasive meeting Formal meeting involving presentations designed to achieve group consensus or support for a course of action

persuasive memo Document seeking to change the recipient's attitudes, beliefs, values, or behaviours

photocopier Machine that takes pictures of original documents to produce duplicates

phrase Words that do not form a complete sentence

pictorial chart Bar or column chart using graphic symbols instead of horizontal or vertical lines

pie chart Diagram presenting data as wedge-shaped sections of a circle; used for component comparisons, with the entire circle representing 100 percent of a given whole and each wedge a portion of the whole

plagiarism Act of using someone else's words or unique approach without crediting the source

planning Process by which document objectives are set, audience needs and responses assessed, and a course of action developed to accomplish established objectives

planning outline Full-content outline that includes every part of a speech or presentation

plural nouns Refer to more than one person, place, thing, or idea

polite listening Mechanical listening characterized by inattention

portable computer (PC) Lightweight computer powered either by batteries or AC adapters that can be used in remote locations.

positive adjectives Used in sentences that make no comparisons

possessive case Pronouns show possession or ownership

possessive nouns Indicate ownership or a close relationship

predicate Part of a sentence that contains the verb and its modifiers, as well as direct and indirect objects

pre-employment testing Process whereby employers evaluate job candidates through skills tests, physical examinations and drug tests, and reference checks

prepositions Part of prepositional phrases, which often state relationships in time or space

prepositional phrases Composed of a preposition and a noun or pronoun that acts as an object

presentation-graphics software Special computer programs used to create such visual aids as bar charts, line charts, pie charts, tables, drawings, and other graphics features by using data already in the computer

presentation visual Visual designed to support a message and requiring a directive title and interpretation by the writer or speaker

present perfect tense Shows that action which started in the past continues into the present

prewriting strategies Techniques for gathering and organizing ideas, including *brainstorming, mindmapping,* and *asking journalists' questions*

primary audience Reader for whom a document is directly intended and who will actually use its information

primary data Data collected specifically for use in preparing a report or proposal

primary headings Visual markers indicating major organizational sections in a document

primary source Person or organization supplying firsthand information on a subject

problem/solution pattern Writing approach that focuses first on a particular problem and then on possible solutions

progress report Short report providing status information on current work, including what has happened on a project since the previous report

pronoun Word that replaces or refers to a noun

pronunciation Formation of the proper sounds to create words

proofreading Process of checking for obvious errors or inconsistencies in a document's content, grammar, and spelling

proper adjectives Formed from proper nouns

proper nouns Names, titles, groups of people, organizations, and places

proposal In sales, written communication that tries to convince the reader that the writer or the writer's organization can solve a particular problem or meet a specific need; document presenting ideas and plans for consideration by others who may accept them and agree to invest funds in their development

public relations Communication conducted by an organization with, for example, stockholders or the general public

questionnaire Scientifically designed list of questions used to gather primary data

racial identity Identity attributed to a category of people who share similar physical characteristics

random sample (or probability sample) Sample chosen so that each member of a population has an equal chance of being selected

reaction Listening stage referring to the response generated by a message

reasoning Process of using available evidence to reach a conclusion

receiver Audience to whom a message is transmitted

reference check Effort made by an employer during the screening process to verify a candidate's educational claims and work history

reference table Table with a title and number that usually does not appear immediately following the text reference; ordinarily contains highlighted data

references In a report or proposal, the section in the document body that lists material from other sources actually cited in the text; in recruiting, a list of people that a prospective employer may contact to learn about a job applicant's abilities, character, and background

reliability Extent to which data collected in a research study is consistent, stable, and free from systematic sources of error

reminder letter Written correspondence informing a customer that payment has not been received

report visual Visual aid whose data is designed and presented to convey the necessary information

request for proposals (RFPs) Detailed, formal government documents requesting proposals and bids on specific projects

research Systematic investigation of a subject in order to discover facts, opinions, or beliefs

résumé Written document in which a job applicant relates his or her education, work experience, and personal accomplishments to the needs of prospective employers

revision Process of transforming a rough draft into a finished document by adding, deleting, replacing, and reorganizing words, sentences, and paragraphs

router Device that routes information from one network to another, allowing independent networks to function as a large virtual network

rule Internal line that separates the various elements of a chart or table

run-in list List of items that appears in normal sentence format

sales letter Letter that solicits prospective accounts or additional sales to current customers

sales proposal (or private-industry proposal) Persuasive document seeking to convince potential buyers to purchase a firm's goods or services

sample Group selected as a representative of a larger, statistically significant group

scanner Electronic device that scans and transforms all types of information into digitized data that can be read by computers

scope Any limitations, such as time and geography, that define a document's coverage

search engine Often called "crawlers," search engines crawl across the Internet and create catalogues of Web pages they visit

search strategy Systematic method for locating research sources

secondary audience Readers, other than the primary reader, who will use the document in a variety of ways or who may be asked to comment on its content

secondary data Data that has been previously analyzed, evaluated, organized, and published

secondary headings Visual markers indicating subsections within primary headings

secondary source Person or organization compiling data and ideas supplied by others

second person Refers to the person spoken or written to

self analysis Job-search process of defining your interests, skills, personal qualities, and accomplishments

sender credibility Extent to which a sender is perceived as believable, competent, authoritative, etc.

sender Participant in the transaction who communicates messages to an audience

sensation Physiological process whereby sound waves are transmitted from the ear to the brain

sentence fragment Part of a sentence that is treated as if it were a complete sentence

sexual harassment Illegal behaviours ranging from blatant physical contact to subtle sexually oriented hints, suggestions, and comments that contribute to a hostile working environment

simple agenda Agenda that outlines meeting goals without describing the sequence of meeting events

simple sentence Contains a subject and a predicate

singular nouns Refer to one person, place, thing, or idea

singular report One-time report designed to deal with specific issues and to aid in making specific decisions

skills tests Testing used by employers to measure the aptitudes and abilities of job applicants

solicited proposal Proposal submitted in response to a formal or informal request

speaker tags Explanatory clauses that clarify quoted material (e.g., he said, she said)

speaking notes Abbreviated keyword outline designed to guide a speaker's actual delivery

special-occasion speech Address of presentation, acceptance, or commemoration

specific purpose Brief summary of the reason for which a document is written or an oral presentation is made

speech Highly structured form of address in which a speaker addresses an audience gathered to hear a message

speech tension (or stage fright) The body's "fight-or-flight" reaction to the stress of delivering an oral presentation or otherwise performing before an audience

spot table Unnumbered, untitled table included in the text of a document; ordinarily contains incidental data

stereotype Distorting generalization based on the distinguishing characteristics of particular groups, including gender, race, physical appearance, occupation, and place of residence

strategic planning Process by which managers determine the major objectives of an organization and choose courses of action to achieve those objectives

structural guideposts Writing technique that helps the reader make connections between one point of a discussion and another

style Distinctive method of expressing thought in writing or speech; refers to the *way* something is said or written rather than *what* is said or written

subdivided bar chart Diagram dividing each bar of a figure or a chart into components of a single item

subdivided column chart Diagram showing how the individual parts of a whole change over time

subjective case Pronouns act as the subject of a sentence

subjunctive mood Expresses conditions, including wishes, indirect requests, and speculation

subtext Nonverbal cues with the power to communicate meaning

summary Closing section of a report that condenses its most important information

superlative adjectives Compare three or more things

surface chart Line chart that is shaded between the baseline and trend lines which add up to the uppermost line

table Systematic arrangement of data and/or words in rows and columns to provide readers with a fixed reference and a method of comparison

table of contents Front-matter list of a report's primary and secondary headings to provide readers with an overview of the material that follows

tactical planning Process by which objectives are translated into specific, achievable plans

targeted résumé Résumé that highlights abilities and achievements that relate to a specific job goal

team A group of two or more people working together on a common project.

technical plan (or work statement) Part of the body of the proposal that describes in detail the work that will be completed

telecommunications Process by which information is converted into electrical impulses transmitted through ordinary telephone or high-speed data lines and then reconverted by a receiver into usable information

telecommuter Worker who "travels" to and from a job by way of such communications technology as e-mail, voice mail, teleconferencing, answering machines, and telephone call-forwarding

teleconference (or conference call) Electronic meeting that uses ordinary telephone lines to bring together three or more people at various locations

telematics Set of applications that combines computer technology and telecommunications

tense Tells when an action, a state of being, or an occurrence took place

testimonial Words of praise for a firm, its products, or ideas generated by someone whose name or reputation the reader respects

third person Refers to the person or thing that is spoken or written about

time-series comparison Data-presentation technique that shows how items change over a specific time period, usually weeks, months, quarters, or years

title fly Optional opening page of a formal report that includes only the report title

title page Front-matter page of a formal report that usually includes the title, the name of the intended recipient, the author's name, and the submission date

topic sentence Sentence that states the purpose of a paragraph

transactional communication Communication involving two or more participants who react to one another in order to create meaning

transition Word, phrase, or sentence used to connect ideas and produce coherent paragraphs

transmittal letter (or cover letter) Informative letter accompanying materials sent from one person to another and providing written records that the materials have indeed been sent

trip report Short report that summarizes the events of a business trip

trouble report Short report that attempts to determine the cause of a problem and presents recommendations for solving it and preventing its recurrence

underlining Used in place of italics on a typewriter to indicate titles of long written works such as books, reports, journals, magazines, and newspapers; the titles of television series; the titles of artworks and long musical compositions; and the names of ships

unsolicited proposal Proposal that has not been invited by the potential customer who receives it

upward communication Message flowing from a subordinate to a superior level of an organization

validity Extent to which a research study accurately measures what it was intended to measure

verb Describes an action, a state of being, or an occurrence

verbal signpost Brief statement that gives listeners "clues" to the organization and structure of a speech

video conference Electronic meeting that allows participants in scattered geographic locations to hear and see one another on television monitors by way of images transmitted over telephone lines

virtual network A communications connection that may involve routing through several locations and devices; however, it has the appearance and functionality of two computers directly connected with wires

virtual office Collection of office equipment or communication devices that enables users to perform tasks away from their permanent offices

visual aids Tables, charts, and illustrations used to present data in visually appealing and understandable ways

voice Indicates whether the subject of a sentence is performing or receiving the action named by the verb

voice mail Computer-based call-processing system that handles both incoming and outgoing calls

voice quality (or paralanguage) Distinctive nature of a variety of voice elements, including loudness, pitch, rate, pauses, articulation, and pronunciation

Web crawler Automated search engine

Web site Addressable location on the World Wide Web, where information or links to other Web sites can be obtained

wireless phone A cellular phone (analogue) or personal communication service device (digital) that connects to the public telephone network via radio signals

word processing software General-purpose computer software that allows a variety of sophisticated typewriter-like functions to be used in document creation, data management, word processing, and telecommunications

work environment Physical, social, cultural, and economic conditions that define the work place and its surroundings

work plan Document specifying work to be accomplished, the individuals who will perform it, and completion deadlines for each phase of the project

"you" attitude Writing style that focuses on the reader rather than the writer

References

CHAPTER 1

1 Alan Deutschman, "The Trouble with MBAs," *Fortune*, 29 July 1991, 72.

2 Christopher Conte, "Labor Letter," *Wall Street Journal*, 3 September 1991, A1.

3 Ibid.

4 Stan Sutter, "The Cost of Advertising," *Marketing*, 17 October 1988, 14.

5 Quoted in Gabriella Stern, "Chief Executives Are Increasingly Chief Salesmen," *Wall Street Journal*, 6 August 1991, B1, B5.

6 This patterns of questioning is suggested in Phillip L. Hunsaker and Anthony J. Alessandra, "Giving—and Getting—Feedback," *Working Women*, April 1987, 35.

7 Christina Dugg, "'Tis the Season When No One Is Working," *Wall Street Journal*, 23 December 1994, B1.

8 Terrence E. Deal and Allen A. Kennedy, *Corporate Cultures: The Rites and Rituals of Corporate Life* (Reading, Mass.: Addison-Wesley, 1982), 3–28.

9 The concept of subtext is discussed and examined in Julius Fast, *Subtext: Making Body Language Work in the Workplace* (New York: Viking, 1991).

10 Albert Mehrabia, *Nonverbal Communication* (Chicago, Ill.: Aldine–Atherton, 1972).

11 "Updating the Hot Line to Moscow," *Newsweek*, 30 April 1984, 19.

12 See Albert Mehrabia, *Nonverbal Communication*.

13 K. L. Burns and E. G. Beier, "Significance of Vocal and Visual Channels for the Decoding of Emotional Meaning," *Journal of Communication*, vol. 23 (1973): 118–130; Albert Mehrabia and M. Weiner, "Decoding of Inconsistent Communications," *Journal of Personality and Social Psychology*, vol. 6 (1967): 109–114.

14 Daniel Goleman, "Non–verbal Cues Are Easy to Misinterpret," *New York Times*, 17 September 1991, C1, C9.

15 *Canada Year Book* (Statistics Canada, 1997), 136.

16 Peter Applebome, "Employers Wary of School System," *New York Times*, 20 February 1995, A1, A13.

17 Research reported in Philip R. Harris and Robert T. Moran, *Managing Cultural Differences: High Performance Strategies for a New World of Business*, 3rd ed. (Houston, Texas: Gulf Publishing Company, 1991), 36. For more information, see Lyman K. Steil, "Listen My Students...and You Shall Learn," *Toward Better Teaching* (Fall 1978).

18 Florence L. Wolff, Nadine C. Marsnik, William S. Tacey, and Ralph G. Nichols, *Perceptive Listening* (Englewood Cliffs, N.J.: Prentice Hall, 1983), 154.

19 Ralph G. Nichols, "Do We Know How to Listen? Practical Helps in a Modern Age," *Speech Teacher* (March 1961): 118–124; see also Lyman K. Steil, *Your Personal Listening Profile* (New York: Sperry Corp., 1980).

20 Lyman K. Steil, *Effective Listening: Key to Your Success* (New York: Random House, 1983).

21 Herman Moore's story is reported in Dana Milbank, "No Glamour, No Glory, Being a Manufacturer Today Can Take Guts," *Wall Street Journal*, 3 June 1991, A1, A7.

22 Leon Festinger, *A Theory of Cognitive Dissonance* (Stanford, Calif.: Stanford University Press, 1957).

23 Dana Milbank, "No Glamour, No Glory, Being a Manufacturer Today Can Take Guts," A7.

24 Daniel Pearl, "More Firms Pledge Guaranteed Service," *Wall Street Journal*, 17 July 1991, B1.

25 See Nichols, "Do We Know How to Listen? Practical Helps in a Modern Age," 118–124.

26 Ibid.

27 William Watson, "Quality Awareness," AT&T Quality Presentation (Toronto, 1997), 4.

28 Thomas J. Peters and Robert H. Waterman Jr., *In Search of Excellence: Lessons from America's Best–Run Companies* (New York: Harper & Row, 1982), 64–65.

29 Roberta Mamis, "Partner Wars: Six True Confessions," *Inc.*, June 1994, 38.

30 Faye Rice, "Champions of Communication," *Fortune*, 3 June 1991, 116.

31 Fred Luthans and J. K. Larsen, "How Managers Really Communicate," *Human Relations* 39 (1986): 181–188.

32 E. M. Rogers and A. Rogers, *Communicating in Organizations* (New York: Free Press, 1976).

33 Ford Motor Company press release, "1994 Mustang: Mustang Blazes Trail for Innovative Timing Process," Joseph B. White and Oscar Suris, "How a 'Skink Works' Kept the Mustang Alive—On a Tight Budget," *Wall Street Journal*, 21 September 1993, A1, 12.

34 Keith Davis, "Management Communication and the Grapevine," *Harvard Business Review* (September–October 1953): 43–49.

35 Studies cited in Terry R. Bacon, "Collaboration in a Pressure Cooker," *The Bulletin of the Association for Business Communication* 53:2 (June 1990): 4. See also Janis Forman, "Collaborative Business Writing: A Burkean Perspective for Future Research," *The Journal of Business Communication* 28:3 (Summer 1991): 236.

36 Hal Lancaster, "Managing Your Career: A New Social Contract to Benefit Employer and Employee," *Wall Street Journal*, 29 November 1994, B1.

37 George C. Dillon, "The Prospect of Competitive Ethics: Good Ethics Is Good Business," speech delivered at the Racing for a Competitive Edge Conference, 20 March 1991. Reprinted in *Vital Speeches of the Day*, 15 June 1991, 527.

38 Susan Kendal, "Manufacturing Excellence Earns Digital's Canadian Plant a Global Mandate," *Globe and Mail*, 13 December 1994, FS5.

39 *Canada Year Book*, 67.

40 Joshua Hyatt, "Reconcilable Differences," *Inc.*, April 1991, 78-87.

CHAPTER 2

1 Lourdes Lee Valeriano, "Executives Find They're Always on Call as Computer, Fax Supersede Time Zones, *Wall Street Journal*, 8 August 1991, B1.

2 Retrieved from World Wide Web: http://www.ebtmag.com/issue/9703

3 Retrieved from World Wide Web: http://www.apple.history.pair.com

4 U.S. Department of Commerce, Economics and Statistics Administration Bureau of the Census, *Statistical Abstract of the United States 1994*, 114th ed. (Washington D.C.: U.S. Government Printing Office, 1994), 771 (Table 1256).

5 Information based on W. E. Wang and Joe Kraynak, *The First Book of Personal Computing* (Carmel, Indiana: SAMS, 1990), 2–5, 155.

6 Sources for this section include Lynn Quitman Troyka, *Simon & Schuster Handbook for Writers*, 2nd ed. (Englewood Cliffs, N.J.: Prentice Hall, 1990), 763–768; W. E. Wang and Joe Kraynak, *The First Book of Personal Computing*, 57–71; Charles T. Brusaw, Gerald J. Alred, and Walter E. Oliu, *Handbook of Technical Writing*, 3rd ed. (New York: St. Martin's Press, 1987), 713–718.

7 Jennifer Senior, "V-Mail Trouble," *New York Times*, 9 January 1994, sec. 9, 1, 4.

8 These features are described in Cary Lu, "Hello? Hello?" *Inc.*, March 1989, 135–136. See also Claudia H. Deutsch, "Call It 'CEO Disease,' Then Listen," *New York Times*, 14 December 1991, F23.

9 Chip Johnson, "Telephone Companies Hope 'Voice Mail' Will Make Answering Machines Obsolete," *Wall Street Journal*, 23 July 1991, B1, B8.

10 Susan Greco, "Life After Voice-Mail Hell," *Inc.*, August 1994, 101.

11 Elizabeth Hunt, "Communicating Using the New Tools," *Engineering Dimensions*, November 1997, 20-24.

12 Randall Smith, "Conference Calls to Big Investors Often Leave Little Guys Hung Up," *Wall Street Journal*, 21 June 1995, C1.

13 Retrieved from World Wide Web: http://business.queensu.ca/execmba

14 Don L. Boroughs, "A High-Technology Meeting of Minds," *U.S. News & World Report*, 5 June 5 1995, 46–48.

15 Lauralee Kilgour, et al., *Administrative Procedures for the Canadian Office*, 4th ed., (Scarborough, Prentice Hall, 1997), 201.

16 Retrieved from World Wide Web: http://www.nordicity.com/communications/survey96

17 Retrieved from World Wide Web: http://citywideguide.com/InternetStatistics.html

18 Christopher B. Sullivan, "Preferences for Electronic Mail in Organizational Communication Tasks," *The Journal of Business Communication* (January 1995): 46–64.

19 G. Pascal Zachary, "It's a Mail Thing: Electronic Messaging Gets a Rating-Ex," *Wall Street Journal*, 22 June 1994, A8.

20 Annette Hamilton, "Beware The Coming Email Explosion," *ZDNet*, 16 June 1997, retrieved from World Wide Web: http://www.zdnet.com/anchordesk/story

21 Elizabeth Hunt, "The Downside to E-Mail: User Beware," *CGA Magazine*, May 1997, 20–24.

22 Seth Mydans, "High Ceilings and High Tech on the Triple 7," *New York Times*, 4 June 1995, 14.

23 U.S. Department of Commerce, Economics and Statistics Administration Bureau of the Census, *Statistical Abstract of the United States 1994*, 571 (Table 890).

24 Len Katz, "The Digital PCS Difference," from a presentation by Rogers Cantel, Inc., (Toronto, June 1997).

25 John Huey, "New Frontiers in Commuting," *Fortune*, 13 January 1992, 57.

26 Don Dunn, "Pagers That Do More Than Beep," *Business Week*, 4 February 1991, 101.

27 Ginger Trumfio, "For the Love of a Laptop," *Sales and Marketing Management*, Part 2, March 1995, 31–33.

28 Robert Lauriston, "Portable Computing," *Windows Magazine*, April 1994, 27.

29 Ross W. Manire, "Remote Access: The Drive to Work in the Information Age," *Telecommunications Magazine*, January 1997, 50-55.

30 Barbara Presley Noble, "Nudging Workers from Comfy Nests: AT&T Pushes for Telecommuting," *New York Times*, 30 July 1995, F10.

31 James E. Challenger, "The Potential Pitfalls of Telecommuting," *National Business Employment Weekly*, 18–24 October 1991, 13.

32 See Sue Shellenbarger, "Work & Family: Employers Set Rules for Doing Homework," *Wall Street Journal*, 16 August 1991, B1; "Doing their Home Work," *Monsanto Magazine*, October 1992, 7–13.

33 Edward Baig and Amy Dunkin, "Taking Care of Business—Without Leaving the House," *Business Week*, 17 April 1995, 106–107.

34 Susan Greco, "Companies Greet E-Mail Nation," *Inc.*, May 1995, 138.

35 Retrieved from World Wide Web: http://www.monsterboard.com

CHAPTER 3

1 *Canada Year Book*, 476.

2 Jack Linklater, "Six Keys to Successful Prison Management," May 1997.

3 *Canada Year Book*, 292.

4 Andrew Purvis, "Super Exporter," *Time Canadian Edition*, 28 April 1997.

5 Sondra Snowdon, *The Global Edge* (New York, NY: Simon & Schuster, 1986), 285.

6 Interview with Sana Reynolds, 6 November 1991.

7 Jonathan R. Moller, "Guidelines for International Protocol: Egypt, Hong Kong, and Brazil," *Federal Express International Newsletter*, June 1991, 2–3.

8 Discussion of cultural imperatives, adiaphora, and exclusives is based on Philip R. Cateora, *International Marketing* (Homewood, Ill.: Business One Irwin, 1990), 103–105, 108.

9 John O'Leary, "Prince Says Americans Are Ruining the Language," *London Times*, 24 March 1995, 2.

10 John Train, "English Spoken Here, Sort Of," *New York Times*, 30 October 1994, F9.

11 Copeland and Griggs, *Going International*, 100.

12 Elizabeth M. Fowler, "Career Managers Lack Fluency in Language," *New York Times*, 11 June 1991, D6. See also Harris Collingwood, "Ready to Travel?" *Business Week*, 2 March 1992, 46.

13 Andrew Pollack, "A Cyberspace Front in a Multicultural War," *New York Times*, 7 August 1995, D1, D4.

14 Mariah E. de Forest, "Manager's Journal: Insulation from Mexican Cultural Shock," *Wall Street Journal*, 17 October 1994, A14.

15 Edward T. Hall, *The Silent Language* (Garden City, NY: Doubleday, 1959), 209.

16 Edward T. Hall, *The Hidden Dimension* (Garden City, NY: Doubleday & Company, 1966), 149.

17 This section is based on information from Copeland and Griggs, *Going International*, 24–27. See also Ronald E. Dulek, John S. Fielden, and John S. Hill, "International Communication," *Business Horizons*, January–February 1991, 20–25; Harris and Moran, *Managing Cultural Differences*, 45–47, 397.

18 Sources for this section include Copeland and Griggs, *Going International*, 116–117; Dulek, Fielden, and Hill, "International Communication," 20–25; Hall, *The Hidden Dimension*, 131–132; and Frederick H. Katayama, "How to Act Once You Get There," *Fortune: Pacific Rim*, 1989, 88.

19 Adapted from Susan Crabtree and Marg Hile, "Cultural Diversity Challenges the Workplace," *Resource*, April 1990, 46–47.

20 The Canadian Hearing Society, "Statistics on Hearing Loss in the General Population," CHS Information Services, 1997.

21 Jennifer Senior, "Language of the Deaf Evolves to Reflect New Sensibilities," *New York Times*, 3 January 1994, A1, A12.

22 Michelle Falardeau-Ramsey, "Social Ethics and Equity," Keynote address to *The Interchange on Canadian Studies*, Prince Albert, SK (May 1997).

23 *Canada Year Book*, 67.

24 Statistics Canada Population Projections, CANSIM, Matrix 6900.

25 *Canada Year Book*, 70.

26 Peter T. Kilborn, "White Males and the Manager Class," *New York Times*, 17 March 1995, A14.

27 Deborah Tannen, "Gender Gap in Cyberspace," *Newsweek*, 16 May 1994, 52–53.

28 Barbara Carton, "At Jenny Craig, Men Are Ones Who Claim Sex Discrimination," *Wall Street Journal*, 29 November 1994, A1 and A11; Tamar Lewin, "Chevron Settles Sexual Harassment Charges," *New York Times*, 22 February 1995, A16.

29 Linda Greenhouse, "Court, 9–0, Makes Sex Harassment Easier to Prove," *New York Times*, 10 November 1993, A1, A22.

30 Human Resources Development Canada, "Information on Labour Standards: Sexual Harassment." Retrieved from World Wide Web: http://info.lead-etea.hrdc-drhc.gc.ca/~lsweb/harassen.html

31 These examples are patterned after Barbara Kantrowitz, "Striking a Nerve," *Newsweek*, 21 October 1991, 34–40.

32 *Canada Year Book*, 61.

33 *Canada Year Book*, 190.

34 Canadian Human Rights Commission, "Report on Employment Equity," (1997). Retrieved from: http://www.chrc.ca/ar/employ.html

35 Ibid.

36 Ibid.

37 Robert A. Mamis, "Word of Mouth (Literally)," *Inc.*, June 1994, 119.

38 Personal correspondence with Dianne LaMountain, LaMountain and Associates, 12 November 1991.

39 John Zubrezycki, "CNN Upsets Too Many Sacred Cows," *The Australian*, 7 July 1995, 23.

40 Christopher Chipello, "Small U.S. Companies Take the Plunge into Japan's Market," *Wall Street Journal*, 7 July 1992, B1, B2.

CHAPTER 4

1 Jim Carroll and Rick Broadhead, 1998 *Canadian Internet New User's Handbook* (Scarborough: Prentice Hall Canada, 1997), 129.

2 Information based on Donna Fenn, "Employee Freebies: All This Is Yours," *Inc.*, September 1995, 101.

3 Louis E. Boone, *Quotable Business* (New York: Random House, 1992), 155.

4 Cornelia Droge, Richard Germain, and Diane Halstead, "A Note on Marketing and the Corporate Annual Report: 1930–1950," *Journal of the Academy of Marketing Science* 18:4 (Fall 1990): 359.

5 This section is based on L. Sue Baugh, *Handbook for Memo Writing* (Lincolnwood, Ill.: NTC Business Books, 1990), 26–34; John Fielden, "What Do You Mean I Can't Write?" *Harvard Business Review*, May–June 1964. Reprinted in *Harvard Business Review*, September–October 1990, 238; Marya W. Holcombe and Judith K. Stein, *Writing for Decision Makers: Memos and Reports with a Competitive Edge* (Belmont, Calif.: Lifetime Learning Publications, 1981), 9–20; Thomas Leech, *How to Prepare, Stage, and Deliver Winning Presentations* (New York: AMACOM, 1982), 60–75; "Tax Report," *Wall Street Journal*, 29 January 1992, A1; Patricia H. Westheimer, *Power Writing for Executive Women* (Glenview, Ill.: Scott, Foresman, 1989), 45–58.

6 Fielden, "What Do You Mean I Can't Write?" 238.

7 "Tax Report," *Wall Street Journal*, A1.

8 Data on enrollments from Canada Yearbook (Statistcs Canada, 1997), 130.

9 Alex Osborn, *Applied Imagination* (New York: Charles Scribner's, 1958).

10 Information based on Joseph Pereira, "From Air to Pump to Puma's Disc System, Sneaker Gimmicks Bound to New Heights," *Wall Street Journal*, 31 October 1992, B1.

11 "Mindmapping: A New Way to Think on Paper," *Fortune*, 16 November 1992, 12.

12 Felicia R. Lee, "Publisher Sees Asian-American Identity as a Work in Progress," *New York Times*, 10 October 1993, E7; "Targeting the Asian-American Market in Direct Mail," *Mediaweek*, 17 April 1995, S3.

13 Alan Farnham, "State Your Values, Hold the Hot Air," *Fortune*, 19 April 1993, 117–124.

CHAPTER 5

1 William Strunk Jr., and E. B. White, *The Elements of Style*, 3rd ed. (New York: Macmillan, 1979), 15–71.

2 Telephone interview with Sana Reynolds, 1 September 1995.

3 Edward P. Bailey Jr., *The Plain English Approach to Business Writing* (New York: Oxford University Press, 1990), 26–27.

4 Charles T. Brusaw, Gerald J. Alred, and Walter E. Oliu, *Handbook of Technical Writing*, 3rd ed. (New York: St. Martin's Press, 1987), 469.

5 L. Sue Baugh, *Handbook for Memo Writing* (Lincolnwood, Ill.: NTC Business Books, 1990), 45.

6 Marya W. Holcombe, and Judith K. Stein, *Writing for Decision Makers: Memos and Reports with a Competitive Edge*, 61.

7 Information from Michael W. Miller, "AT&T Goes to Bat for Customers Against Credit Firms," *Wall Street Journal*, 12 June 1991, B1.

8 See Brusaw, Alred, and Oliu, *Handbook of Technical Writing*, 256–257.

9 Information for this section is from Bailey, *The Plain English Approach to Business Writing*, 37–46, 72–84; Baugh, *Handbook for Memo Writing*, 67–77; Holcombe and Stein, *Writing for Decision Makers*, 117–124; Roy W. Poe, *The McGraw-Hill Guide to Effective Business Reports* (New York: McGraw-Hill, 1982), 122–126; and John Tarrant, *Business Writing with Style: Strategies for Success* (New York: John Wiley, 1991), 41, 134–136, 168–169.

10 Information for memo draft based in part on Gabriella Stern, "As Old Cadillac Buyers Age, the GM Division Fights to Halt Slippage," *Wall Street Journal*, 24 August 1995, A1, A9.

11 Retrieved from World Wide Web: http://web20.mindlink.net/chrr/sexhar.htm

12 Retrieved from World Wide Web: http://aet.org/news/splash/nsapril19.html

13 Retrieved from World Wide Web: http://gurukul.ucc.american.edu/TED/CANCHOP.HTM

14 Ibid.

CHAPTER 6

1 Lynn Quitman Troyka, *Simon & Schuster Handbook for Writers*, 83.

2 William Zinsser, *Writing with a Word Processor* (New York: Harper & Row, 1983), 25.

3 The following section is based on suggestions made by Troyka, *Simon & Schuster Handbook for Writers*, 57–59.

4 Cited in Sherry Sweetnam, *The Executive Memo: A Guide to Perspective Business Communications* (New York: John Wiley, 1986), 155.

5 Sam Howe Verhovek, "Educators to Study Utilization (Use) of Plain English," *New York Times*, 4 October 1991, B1, B6.

6 Examples from William Lutz, *Doublespeak* (New York: Harper Perennial, 1989), 104–129.

7 John Tarrant, *Business Writing with Style: Strategies for Success*, 35.

8 Roy W. Poe, *The McGraw-Hill Guide to Effective Business Reports*, 48–49.

9 "Business Briefs," *Wall Street Journal*, 18 June 1991, A1.

10 Ibid.

11 Patricia H. Westheimer, *Power Writing for Executive Women* (Glenview, Ill.: Scott, Foresman, 1989), 18.

12 John S. Fielden, "What Do You Mean You Don't Like My Style?" *Harvard Business Review*, May–June 1982, 129.

13 See Sue A. Hershkowitz, "Improve Your Writing Skills: How to Write Material That Gets Results," *Business Credit*, December 1988, 33.

14 Sweetnam, *The Executive Memo*, 100.

15 These strategies are suggested by Fielden, "What Do You Mean?" 135–138.

16 Jeffrey L. Seglin, *The AMA Handbook of Business Letters* (New York: AMACOM, 1989), 11.

17 "How to Boost Sales: Pen a Better Letter," *Wall Street Journal*, 4 October 1991, B1.

18 Information for memo based in part on Gabriella Stern, "As Old Cadillac Buyers Age" A1, A9.

19 Interview with Sana Reynolds, 1 September 1995.

20 Quotations from David Wessel, "Small Victories," *The Wall Street Journal*, 23 June 1992, A1, A6.

21 Robert Frank, "Seeking a Pen Pal? Try Writing Reports on Matters at Coke," *Wall Street Journal*, 16 February 1996, A1, A4; Betsy Morris, "The Wealth Builders," *Fortune*, 11 December 1995, 80.

CHAPTER 7

1 John S. Fielden and Ronald E. Dulek, *Bottom-Line Business Writing* (Englewood Cliffs, N.J.: Prentice Hall, 1984), 17–18.

2 See Fielden and Dulek, *Bottom-Line Business Writing*, 28–46; Andrea B. Geffner, *How to Write Better Business Letters* (New York: Barron's Educational Series, 1982), 25–26; and Ellen Roddick, *Writing That Means Business: How to Get Your Message Across Simply and Effectively* (New York: Collier Books, 1986), 43–44.

3 Fielden and Dulek, *Bottom-Line Business Writing*, 31.

4 Geffner, *How To Write Better Business Letters*, 28.

5 Peter J. Leets, "Managing Your References," *National Business Employment Weekly*, 1–7 November 1991, 13.

6 Brenton Schlender, "China Really Is on the Move," *Fortune*, 5 October 1992, 114–123.

7 David Wessel, "Small Victories," *Wall Street Journal*, 23 June 1992, A1, A16.

CHAPTER 8

1 Robert L. Shurter and Donald J. Leonard, *Effective Letters in Business*, 3rd ed. (New York: McGraw-Hill, 1984), 89.

2 Ibid., 89–90.

3 Suggestions in this section are from John Tarrant, *Business Writing with Style*, 115–116; L. E. Frailey, *Handbook of Business Letters*, 3rd ed. (Englewood Cliffs, N.J.: Prentice Hall, 1989), 668–670; Charles T. Brusaw, Gerald J. Alred, and Walter E. Oliu, *Handbook of Technical Writing*, 23.

4 Frailey, *Handbook of Business Letters*, 681.

5 Ibid., 542.

6 Ibid., 562–563.

7 John S. Fielden, Jean D. Fielden, and Ronald E. Dulek, *The Business Writing Style Book* (Englewood Cliffs, N.J.: Prentice Hall, 1984), 62.

8 Thomas O'Boyle, "Working Together," *Wall Street Journal*, 5 June 1992, A1, A5.

9 "Gannett's $2 Billion Acquisition of Multimedia Last Year Allows Company to Develop Cable Presence and Expand Core News Products into Growth Areas," *Communications Daily*, 19 January 1996, 10; Patrick M. Reilly, "Keeping Low-Tech Profile, Gannett Co. Puts Its Faith in the Newspaper Business," *Wall Street Journal*, 3 October 1995, B1.

CHAPTER 9

1 Ray E. Barfield and Sylvia S. Titus, *Business Communications* (Hauppage, N.Y.: Baron's Business Library, 1992), 121.

2 Ibid., 122.

3 The following discussion is based on Robert L. Shurter and Donald J. Leonard, *Effective Letters in Business*, 131–140.

4 Barbara Kantrowitz, "The Net: An Apology From America Offline," *Newsweek*, 14 February 1994, 49.

5 The following discussion is based on John S. Fielden, Jean D. Fielden, and Ronald E. Dulek, *The Business Writing Style Book*, 45–61, 92–94.

6 Carol J. Loomis, "The Reed That Citicorp Leans On," *Fortune*, 12 July 1993, 92–93.

7 John D. Ong, "Meeting Communication Challenges at BF Goodrich," *The Bulletin of the Association for Business Communication* (December 1993): 5–6.

8 Michael Siconolfi, "Under Pressure," *Wall Street Journal*, 14 July 1992, A1, A4.

CHAPTER 10

1 Daniel S. Kennedy, *The Ultimate Sales Letter* (Holbrook, Mass.: Bob Adams, Inc., 1990), 30–31.

2 "The Sales Pyramid," *Success*, May 1992, 27.

3 "1990 Survey of Selling Costs," *Sales and Marketing Management*, 26 February 1990, 75.

4 Kennedy, *The Ultimate Sales Letter*, 56.

5 "The Ideal Collection Letter," *Inc.*, February 1991, 59.

6 Ibid.

7 Ibid.

8 G. Bruce Knecht, "Banks Profit by Sweet-Talking Overdue Payers," *Wall Street Journal*, 27 June 1994, B1, B3.

9 "The Ideal Collection Letter," 60.

10 The information on persuasive memos is based on a discussion in John S. Fielden, Ronald E. Dulek, and Jean D. Fielden, *Elements of Business Writing* (Englewood Cliffs, N.J.: Prentice Hall, 1984), 53–77.

11 Kevin C. Naff, "Teams Approach to Credit Management Gaining Popularity," *Business Credit*, April 1995, 35 (2).

12 "Sexual Harassment Should Not Be Tolerated," *American Medical News*, 28 December 1992, 25; Flora Johnson Skelly, "Poised for Flight: Women Are on the Threshold of Power in Medicine," *American Medical News*, 19 September 1994, 15; Meredith Wadman, "Often Belittled by Their Male Colleagues, Women Doctors Also Find Pay Disparity," *Wall Street Journal*, 25 November 1992, B1, B6.

CHAPTER 11

1 Ray E. Barfield and Sylvia S. Titus, *Business Communications*, 141–142.

2 Terese Brasen, "The Cancer Man," *Alberta Venture*, May 1997, 15.

3 John Markoff, "Britannica's 44 Million Words Are Going On Line," *New York Times*, 8 February 1994, D1–D2.

4 John R. Emshwiller, "Firms Find Profits Searching Databases," *Wall Street Journal*, 25 January 1993, B1.

5 Pamela Sebastian, "Business Bulletin," *Wall Street Journal*, 23 January 1992, A1.

6 Lauralee Kilgour et al., *Administrative Procedures for the Canadadian Office*, 270.

7 Ibid.

8 "On-Line: Quick Research," *Inc.*, June 1995,96.

9 National Library of Canada, Ottawa. Retrieved from World Wide Web: http://www.nlc-bnc.ca

10 Lourdes Lee Valeriano, "Western Firms Poll Eastern Europeans to Discern Tastes of Nascent Consumers," *Wall Street Journal*, 27 April 1992, B1, B2.

11 Susan Lawrence, "Reaching Out to Asia," *U.S. News & World Report*, 1 March 1993, 57–59.

CHAPTER 12

1 Statistics Canada. Catalogue No. 93-333.

2 Gene Zelazny, *Say It with Charts: The Executive's Guide to Successful Presentations* (Homewood, Ill.: Business One Irwin, 1991), 11.

3 Analysis suggested by Zelazny, *Say It with Charts*, 19.

4 This section is based on Zelazny, *Say It with Charts*, 21–24.

5 These guidelines are suggested by Charles T. Brusaw, Gerald J. Alred, and Walter E. Oliu, *Handbook of Technical Writing*, 207.

6 Michael Ornstein and Penni Stewart, "Gender and Faculty Pay in Canada," *Canadian Journal of Sociology* v.21 no.4 (Fall 1996), 461-481.

7 Ellen Shapiro, "Food Shoppers Warm to Toaster Cuisine," *Wall Street Journal*, 29 December 1992, B1.

CHAPTER 13

1 Ray E. Barfield and Sylvia S. Titus, *Business Communication*, 183.

2 John Schell and John Stratton, *Writing on the Job: A Handbook for Business & Government* (New York: New American Library, 1984), 208–219; Raymond V. Lesikar, *Report Writing for Business*, 6th ed. (Homewood, Ill.: Richard D. Irwin, 1981), 109–112.

3 These types of reports are discussed in Herman A. Estrin and Norbert Elliot, *Technical Writing in the Corporate World* (Los Altos, Calif.: Crisp Publications, 1990), 32–37; Charles T. Brusaw, Gerald J. Alred, and Walter E. Oliu, *Handbook of Technical Writing*, 346–347, 686–693; William C. Paxon, *Write It Now! A Timesaving Guide to Writing Better* (Reading, Mass.: Addison-Wesley, 1986), 27–46.

4 Lawrence D. Brennan, personal interview, 25 November 1992.

5 Information from Brusaw, Alred, and Oliu, *Handbook of Technical Writing*, 339–346; Paxson, *Write It Now!*, 52–53; Patricia C. Weaver and Robert G. Weaver, *Persuasive Writing: A Manager's Guide to Effective Letters and Reports* (New York: Free Press, 1977), 76–79.

6 This sample report is based on the "Report of the Bus Safety Committee," a document issued in Westport, Connecticut, 8 June 1992.

7 *Canada Year Book*, 474.

8 Richard Melcher, "Britain's Rather Good Show," *Business Week*, 13 July 1992, 50–52.

9 Timothy O'Brien, "Pride of Ownership," *Wall Street Journal*, 22 January 1993, A1, A5.

CHAPTER 14

1 William C. Paxson, *Write It Now!* 75.

2 John Schell and John Stratton, *Writing on the Job*, 148.

3 Information for this proposal is based on Edward O. Welles, "Show and Sell," *Inc.*, October 1995, 74–81.

4 Ron Tepper, *How to Write Winning Proposals for Your Company or Client* (New York: John Wiley, 1990), 135–136.

5 Proposal provided by Dr. Beatrice Harris, partner in Harris, Rothenberg International, 14 October 1992.

6 Jacob Rahul, "The Struggle to Create an Organization for the 21st Century," *Fortune*, 3 April 1995, 90+; Brian Dumaine, "The Trouble with Teams," *Fortune*, 5 September 1994, 86; Thomas Stewart, "The Search for the Organization of Tomorrow," *Fortune*, 18 May 1992, 92–98; Sami Abbasi and Kenneth Hollman, "Managing Cultural Diversity: The Challenge of the '90s," *Records Management Quarterly*, July 1991, 24–32.

CHAPTER 15

1 Interview with Jim Elms quoted in Thomas Leech, *How to Prepare, Stage, and Deliver Winning Presentations*, 48–49.

2 *Canada Year Book*, 136.

3 Ron Hoff, *I Can See You Naked: A Fearless Guide to Making Great Presentations* (Kansas City, Mo.: Andrews and McMeel, 1988), 9.

4 T. Boone Pickens, "Foreign Investment in Japan: Keiretsu Business Practices." Speech delivered to the Japan Society, Los Angeles and San Diego, 23 October 1990. Reprinted in *Vital Speeches of the Day*, 1 January 1991, 171.

5 Interview with Professor Melvin Heltzer cited in John J. Makay, *Public Speaking: Theory Into Practice* (Fort Worth, Tex.: Harcourt Brace College Publishers, 1992), 262.

6 Tracie Rozhon, "Day of the Doers: Success Stories on the Podium," *New York Times*, 4 June 1995, F10.

7 Ibid.

8 John Cady, "The Food Industry's Role in Advancing Public Confidence: Strategies for Regaining Public Confidence." Speech delivered before the Food and Drug Law Institute, Palm Beach, Florida, 24 April 1991. Reprinted in *Vital Speeches of the Day*, 1 July 1991, 567.

9 Leech, *How to Prepare, Stage, and Delivery Winning Presentations*, 96.

10 Linda Winikow, "How Women and Minorities are Reshaping Corporate America." Speech delivered to the Women's Bureau Conference, Washington, D.C., 23 October 1990. Reprinted in *Vital Speeches of the Day*, 1 February 1991, 244.

11 Harvey MacKay, "How to Get a Job: How to be Successful." Speech delivered as an MBA Commencement Address, Pennsylvania State University, University Park, Pennsylvania, 11 May 1991. Reprinted in *Vital Speeches of the Day*, 1 July 1991, 659.

12 George V. Grune, "Challenges to the Magazine Industry: Some Plain Talk." Speech delivered to the Magazine Publishing Congress, New York, 31 October 1989. Reprinted in *Vital Speeches of the Day*, 15 January 1990, 204.

13 Remarks by Keith L. Reinhard, GTE Directories Leadership Conference, Newport Beach, California, 25 January 1993.

14 Herman Holtz, *The Executive's Guide to Winning Presentations* (Toronto: John Wiley & Sons, Inc., 1991), 44.

15 Ibid., 44–50.

16 Interview with Sarah Weddington, 19 March 1990.

17 Hoff, *I Can See You Naked*, 216.

18 Herman Holtz, *The Executive's Guide to Winning Presentations*, 79.

19 Ibid., 65–85.

20 Jeremy Main, "How to Steal the Best Ideas Around," *Fortune*, 19 October 1992, 102–106.

CHAPTER 16

1 Nuala Beck, *Excelerate: Growing in the new Economy*, (Toronto: HarperCollins Publishers Ltd., 1995), 28.

2 Clyde W. Burleson, *Effective Meetings: The Complete Guide* (New York: John Wiley, 1990), 1.

3 Ibid., 32.

4 Mukul Pandya, "Little Time for Play at Conferences Today," *New York Times*, 11 December 1994, F23.

5 Terrence E. Deal and Allen A. Kennedy, *Corporate Cultures: The Rites and Rituals of Corporate Life* (Reading, Mass.: Addison-Wesley, 1982), 71.

6 George David Kieffer, *The Strategy of Meetings: How to Make Your Next Business Meeting a Win for Your Company and Your Career* (New York: Warner Books, 1988), 124.

7 Mary Kay Ash, *Mary Kay on People Management* (New York: Warner Books, 1984), 54.

8 Factual information about advance ticketing is from Thomas R. King, "Tired of Lines? Theaters Take Orders by Phone," *Wall Street Journal*, 11 October 1991, B1, B8.

9 Juliet Nierenberg and Irene S. Ross, *Women and the Art of Negotiating: Techniques for Achieving Success in Your Business and Personal Relationships* (New York: Simon & Schuster, 1985), 169.

10 Kilgour et al., *Administrative Procedures for the Canadian Office*, 16.

11 Ibid., 16.

12 Ibid., 16.

13 Ibid., 16.

14 Ibid., 16.

15 Outline suggested by Burleson, *Effective Meetings*, 85–86.

16 Peter R. Scholtes et al., *The Team Handbook*, 2nd ed. (Madison: Joiner Associates, 1996), 4–14.

17 Ibid., 4–18.

18 Ibid., 4–15.

19 Ibid., 4–19.

20 Ibid., 2–24.

21 Mary Beth Grover, "Letting Both Sides Win," *Forbes*, 30 September 1991, 178.

22 These negotiating steps can be found in Burleson, *Effective Meetings*, 46–49.

23 Mark H. McCormack, *What They Still Don't Teach You at the Harvard Business School* (New York: Bantam Books, 1989), 70.

24 Thomas J. Peters and Robert H. Waterman Jr., *In Search of Excellence: Lessons from America's Best-Run Companies* (New York: Harper & Row, 1982), 122.

25 Joan E. Rigdon, "Even When They Ask, Bosses Don't Want Your Complaints," *Wall Street Journal*, 10 August 1994, B1.

26 Ash, *Mary Kay on People Management*, 35–36.

27 Stephanie Strom, "At Neiman Marcus, Mail-Order Frenzy Nears Peak," *New York Times*, 25 November 1994, D1, D7.

28 Enid Nemy, "New Yorkers, Etc.," *New York Times*, 3 November 1991, 1: 50.

29 Peter Nulty, "I Have a Dream," *Fortune*, 16 November 1992, 142–144.

30 Joye Mercer, "A Gift Transforms a College," *The Chronicle of Higher Education* (December 8, 1995): A29, A31; Pamela Sebastian and Gary Putka, "Glassboro Gift: A Small Appeal Has Big Payoff," *Wall Street Journal*, 13 July 1992, B1, B10.

CHAPTER 17

1 The following approach to self-analysis was suggested by Tom Jackson, *The Perfect Résumé* (New York: Doubleday, 1990), 16–38.

2 Amy Saltzman, "The New Meaning of Success," *U.S. News & World Report*, 17 September 1990, 56.

3 Nuala Beck, *Shifting Gears: Thriving in the New Economy* (Toronto: Harper Collins, 1992), 172.

4 Nuala Beck, *Excelerate*, 16.

5 *Canada Year Book*, 200.

6 Nuala Beck, *Excelerate*, 52.

7 Trip Gabriel, "Peering Into the Murky Jobs Crystal Ball for 2015," *New York Times*, 3 September 1995, F9.

8 Albert R. Karr, "Labor Letter," *Wall Street Journal*, 5 May 1992, A1.

9 "Résumés: Read Between the Lines," *Inc*, June 1995, 90.

10 Hal Lancaster, "Stop Working Those Phones—Networking is Out of Order," *Wall Street Journal*, 22 November 1994, B1; Karr, "Labor Letter," A1.

11 Sandra McCance, "Preparing Your Résumé for Scanning and Internet Retrieval," *Career Options—Surf Your Way to Work* (Kingston: Queen's University Press, 1996/97), 20.

12 Kilgour et al., *Administrative Procedures for the Canadian Office*, 366.

13 Jeremy Shapiro, "Format Your Résumé to be Scanned by a Computer," Career Resource Centre. Retrieved from World Wide Web: http://www.careermosaic.com

14 Kilgour et al., *Administrative Procedures for the Canadian Office*, 366.

15 *Job Search—The Product Is You*, Alberta Advanced Education and Career Development, Edmonton, 1996, 60–61.

16 Elizabeth M. Fowler, "When You Can't Get in the Front Door," *New York Times*, 20 August 1991, D17.

17 Lancaster, "Stop Working Those Phones—Networking is Out of Order," B1.

18 Mary Rowland, "The Art of Trading Information," *New York Times*, 28 November 1993.

19 Robin Goldwyn Blumenthal, "Entrepreneurs Vying for Graduates the Giants Recruit," *Wall Street Journal*, 4 February 1994, B2, F15.

20 Wendy Bounds, "All Work and No Play," *Wall Street Journal*, 27 February 1995, R7; Stephen E. Frank, "Taking Out the Garbage, Walking the Boss's Dog and Other Intern's Tales," *Wall Street Journal*, 19 July 1994, B1.

21 Kilgour et al., *Administrative Procedures for the Canadian Office*, 347.

22 Ibid., 346–347.

23 Brenton Schlender, "How Sony Keeps the Magic Going," *Fortune*, 24 February 1992, 76–84.

24 Catherine Friedman, "Proofreader Wanted," quoted in "Other Comments," *Forbes*, 7 December 1992, 30. First appeared in *Working Women*, November 1992.

25 Stephen J. Kaplan, *Don't wait 'til you graduate—The Canadian job search guide for the real world*, (Toronto: CACEE, 1995), 69.

CHAPTER 18

1 Taken from Jeff B. Speck, *Hot Tips, Sneaky Tricks and Last-Ditch Tactics: An Insider's Guide to Getting Your First Corporate Job* (New York: John Wiley, 1989), 61.

2 Leonore Cervera, "First Impressions Count," *USA Today*, 19 September 1988, B1.

3 Lucinda Harper, "Actors Have One Motivation, to Win a Job," *Wall Street Journal*, 16 August 1994, B1, B4.

4 Rochelle Sharpe, "Work Week," *Wall Street Journal*, 31 October 1995, A1.

5 Timothy D. Schellhardt, "Managing Your Career: While the Recruiter Checks Your Résumé, Investigate the Firm's," *Wall Street Journal*, 23 February 1994, B1; Jolie Solomon, "CEOs: John Sculley's Management Minute," *Newsweek*, 21 February 1994, 72.

6 Kilgour, et al., *Administrative Procedures for the Canadian Office*, 358

7 Stephen J. Kaplan, *Don't wait 'til you graduate*, (Toronto: CACEE, 1995), 126.

8 Tom Washington, "Why It Pays to Master the Art of Story-Telling," *National Business Employment Weekly*, 18 August 1991, 9.

9 Stephen J. Kaplan, *Don't wait 'til you graduate*, 118.

10 Joan E. Rigdon, "Talk Isn't Cheap," *Wall Street Journal*, 27 February 1995, R13.

11 Jennifer Steinhauer, "It's 'The Gap' Once You're Hired, But Job Hunters Must Spiff It Up," *New York Times*, 2 April 1995, F13.

12 Stephen J. Kaplan, *Don't wait 'til you graduate*, 100.

13 Model interview described in Morin and Cabrera, *Parting Company*, 278–286; Information from Henry Morgan and John Cogger, *The Interviewer's Manual* (New York: Drake Beam Morin, 1980).

14 Stephen J. Kaplan, *Don't wait 'til you graduate*, 137.

15 Morin and Cabrera, *Parting Company*, 280.

16 Ibid., 284.

17 Kilgour, et al., *Administrative Procedures for the Canadian Office*, 362.

18 These suggestions are contained in Laine, "How to Respond to Negative Questions," *National Business Employment Weekly*, 1–8 November, 1991, 5–6.

19 Stephen J. Kaplan, *Don't wait 'til you graduate*, 100.

20 Sources for this section are Jeffrey G. Allen, *The Complete Q&A Job Interview Book* (New York: John Wiley, 1988), 38, 55, 84; and Morin and Cabrera, *Parting Company*, 292–306.

21 Stephen J. Kaplan, *Don't wait 'til you graduate*, 137.

22 "In Search of Equity," *Maclean's*, Volume 105, No. 21, 25 May 1992, 15

23 Joan E. Rigdon, "Talk Isn't Cheap," R13; Timothy D. Schellhardt and Tony Lee, "Hints for Hunters," *Wall Street Journal*, 27 February 1995, R6; Laurie P. Cohen, William Power, and Michael Siconolfi, "Financial Firms Act to Curb Office Sexism, with Mixed Results," *Wall Street Journal*, 5 November 1991, A1, A12.

24 Interviewee responses in this section suggested by Robert Half, *How to Get a Better Job in This Crazy World* (New York: Plume Books, 1990), 186–187.

25 Hal Lancaster, "Managing Your Career: Compromise Is Key to Successful Talks on Salary for New Job," *Wall Street Journal*, 22 August 1995, B1.

26 U.S. Equal Employment Opportunity Commision, *The Americans with Disabilities Act: Your Responsibilities as an Employer* (Washington, DC.: U.S. Government Printing Office, 1991), 6–7.

27 Canadian Human Rights Commision, *Drug Testing*, 1–3

28 "Doomed Days: The Worst Mistakes Recruiters Have Ever Seen," *Wall Street Journal*, February 1995, R4.

29 Stacey Slaughter Miller, "Employment Briefs: Reasons to Refuse an Offer," *National Business Employment Weekly*, 1–7 November 1991, 17.

30 Michael H. Cimini, "Drug Testing at Campbell Soup," *Monthly Labor Review* (May 1995): 61; Marci M. DeLancey, "Creating a Successful Drug-Free Workplace Program, *Employment Relations Today* (Summer 1995): 53+; Joseph B. Treaster, "Testing Workers for Drug Reduces Company Problems," *New York Times*, 10 October 1993, 1, 42.

31 Brian O'Reilly, "The Perils of Too Much Freedom," *Fortune*, 11 January 1993, 79.

APPENDIX II

1 This appendix is based on Lynn Quitman Troyka, *Simon & Schuster Handbook for Writers*, 4th ed. (Englewood Cliffs, NJ.: Prentice Hall, 1996).

Photo and Ad Credits

Name and Organization Index

Subject Index